THE [illegible] ONS

ROBERT HARRIS

FATHERLAND

AND

ENIGMA

ARROW

Other authors in the series

STEPHEN FRY
CHARLES HANDY
JAMES HAWES
TIM PARKS
ANNE TYLER

Further praise for
FATHERLAND

'Gripping in the way John Buchan, Len Deighton and John le Carré are. The writing is superb. This novel lifts its author into a new and superior class' WOODROW WYATT, *The Times*

'Tightly constructed . . . the story . . . grips as tightly as a Nazi's glove' *Independent on Sunday*

'A powerful and chilling story: the past rewritten. The plot is convincing in every detail, the characters are entirely believable' MARTHA GELLHORN, *Daily Telegraph*

'Not since *The Day of the Jackal* has a thriller captured the imagination of so many readers' SHERIDAN MORLEY, judge of the *Sunday Express* Book of the Year Award

'*Fatherland* works on all levels. It's a triumph' *Washington Times*

'Absorbing, expertly written' *New York Times*

'A singular achievement displaying original and carefully wrought suspense all its own . . . *Fatherland* easily transcends convention' *Washington Post*

'A fantastic thriller . . . The final solution is an utter surprise. Harris reaches it with speed, conveying a whole culture of grotesquery and kitsch' *Mail on Sunday*

'Terrifying . . . A wonderful new novel' *Newsday*

'*Fatherland* is based on a brilliant idea . . . Not only do the intricacies of the plot make for compelling reading but the accuracy and detail of what a victorious Germany might have been like are surprising coming from one who was not born when the War began' MILTON SHULMAN

'Ingenious . . . fast-paced and beautifully written' *Esquire*

'A sly and scary page turner' *Los Angeles Times*

'A world so chillingly realistic and controversial that *Fatherland* was initially turned down by every German publisher until even they could no longer ignore its commercial appeal' *Yorkshire Post*

'Truly captivating' ROBERT LUDLUM

'Powerful, tense, clever' *Sunday Express*

'Robert Harris's ingenious new thriller is a triumph . . . Suspenseful and elegant . . . a thoughtful, frightening story' *San Francisco Chronicle*

'*Fatherland* is being compared to Martin Cruz Smith's *Gorky Park*, but Harris's narrative is more unsettling . . . His brooding, brown-and-black setting of a victorious Nazi regime is believable and troubling, the stuff of long nights of little sleep' *Time*

'I picked it up at an airport bookstall the other day, and couldn't put it down. Its depth, invention and characterisation lift it well into the realm of literature' *Independent on Sunday*

'A formidable thriller . . . terse, involving and expertly-constructed . . . It is five days since I finished *Fatherland* and it is still rumbling around in my head' *London Review of Books*

'*Fatherland* is, thankfully, fiction . . . an intriguing way to look at Germany's never-buried past' *Newsweek*

By the same author

fiction

Enigma

non-fiction

Good and Faithful Servant

Selling Hitler

The Making of Neil Kinnock

Gotcha!

A Higher Form of Killing
(with Jeremy Paxman)

FATHERLAND

ROBERT HARRIS

ARROW

BY ROBERT HARRIS

fiction
Archangel
Fatherland
Enigma

non-fiction
Good and Faithful Servant
Selling Hitler
The Making of Neil Kinnock
Gotcha!
A Higher Form of Killing
(with Jeremy Paxman)

ACKNOWLEDGEMENTS

I thank the Librarian and staff of the Wiener Library in London for their help over several years.

I also wish to thank David Rosenthal and – especially – Robyn Sisman, without whom this book would never have been started, let alone finished.

Hitler's Berlin 1964

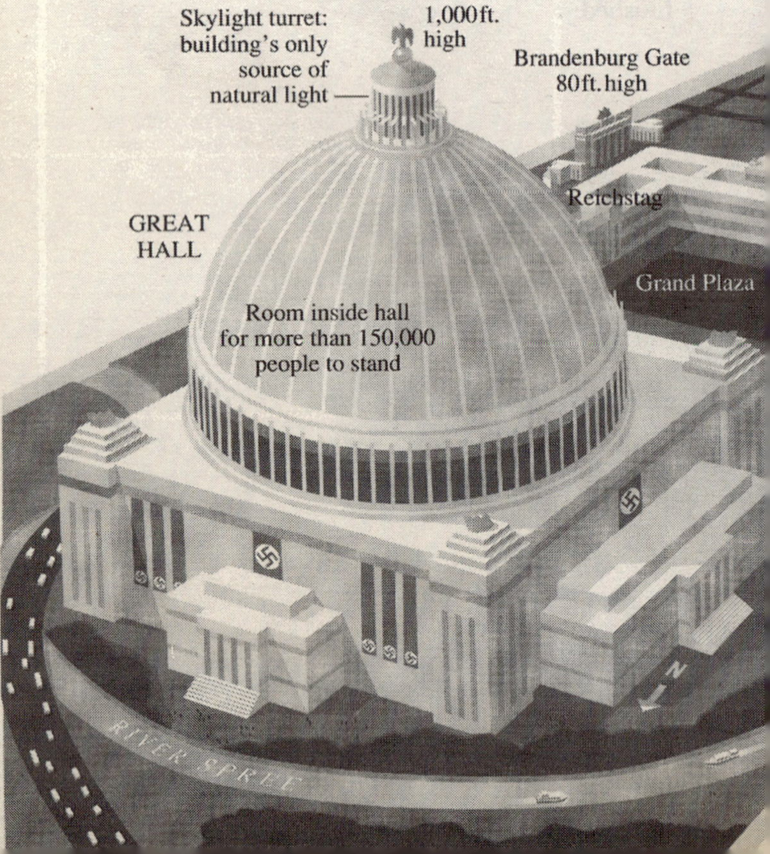

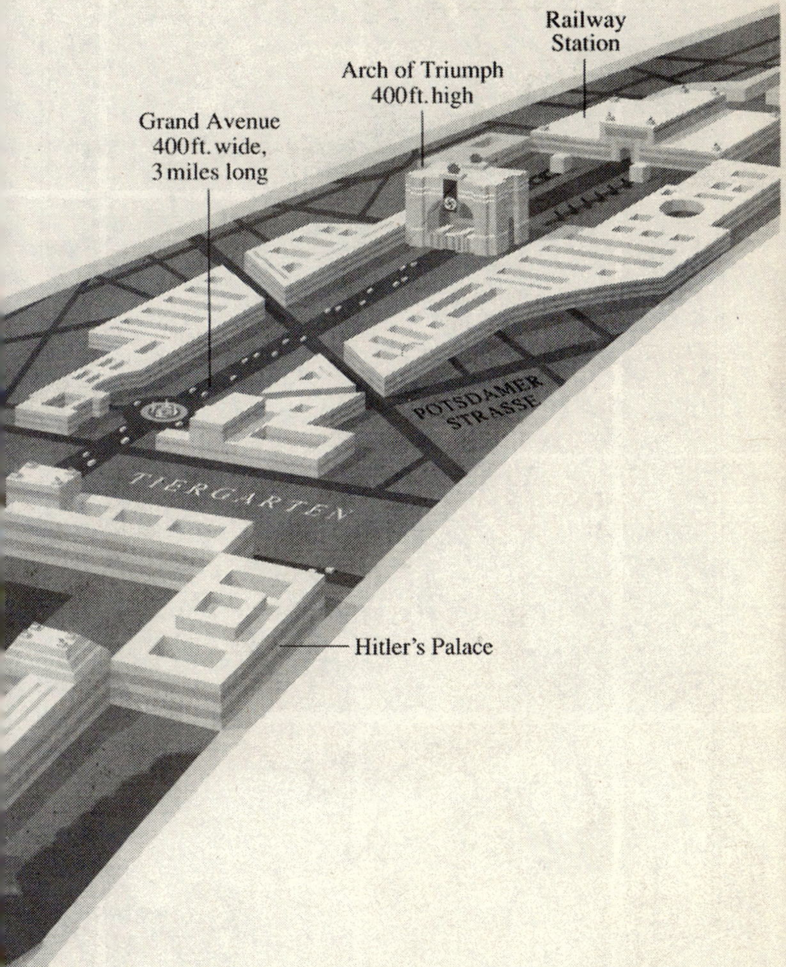

Railway
Station
Arch of Triumph
400ft. high
Grand Avenue
400ft. wide,
3 miles long
POTSDAMER
STRASSE
TIERGARTEN
Hitler's Palace

The Greater German
Reich, 1964
Atlantic Ocean
Hamburg
Berlin
Danzig
Königsberg
Riga
St. Petersburg
Moscow
Ufa
Rovno
Krakau
Melitopol
Gotenburg
Theoderichshafen
Tiflis
Caspian Sea
REICHSKOMMISSARIAT MUSCOVY
REICHSKOMMISSARIAT OSTLAND
REICHSKOMMISSARIAT UKRAINE
GENERALKOMMISSARIAT TAURIDA
REICHSKOMMISSARIAT CAUCASUS
GENERAL GOVERNMENT
MOSELLAND
WEST-MARK
PROTEKTORAT OF BOHEMIA AND MORAVIA
OSTMARK
Kilometers
0
400
800
1200

The hundred million self-confident German masters were to be brutally installed in Europe, and secured in power by a monopoly of technical civilisation and the slave-labour of a dwindling native population of neglected, diseased, illiterate cretins, in order that they might have leisure to buzz along infinite Autobahnen, admire the Strength-Through-Joy Hostel, the Party headquarters, the Military Museum and the Planetarium which their Führer would have built in Linz (his new Hitleropolis), trot round local picture-galleries, and listen over their cream buns to endless recordings of *The Merry Widow*. This was to be the German Millennium, from which even the imagination was to have no means of escape.

HUGH TREVOR-ROPER
The Mind of Adolf Hitler

People sometimes say to me: 'Be careful! You will have twenty years of guerilla warfare on your hands!' I am delighted at the prospect . . . Germany will remain in a state of perpetual alertness.

ADOLF HITLER
29 August 1942

PART ONE

TUESDAY 14 APRIL 1964

I swear to Thee, Adolf Hitler,
As Führer and Chancellor of the German Reich,
Loyalty and Bravery.
I vow to Thee and to the superiors
Whom Thou shalt appoint
Obedience unto Death,
So help me God.

SS OATH

ONE

Thick cloud had pressed down on Berlin all night, and now it was lingering into what passed for the morning. On the city's western outskirts, plumes of rain drifted across the surface of Lake Havel, like smoke.

Sky and water merged into a sheet of grey, broken only by the dark line of the opposite bank. Nothing stirred there. No lights showed.

Xavier March, homicide investigator with the Berlin Kriminalpolizei – the Kripo – climbed out of his Volkswagen and tilted his face to the rain. He was a connoisseur of this particular rain. He knew the taste of it, the smell of it. It was Baltic rain, from the north, cold and sea-scented, tangy with salt. For an instant he was back twenty years, in the conning tower of a U-boat, slipping out of Wilhelmshaven, lights doused, into the darkness.

He looked at his watch. It was just after seven in the morning.

Drawn up on the roadside before him were three other cars. The occupants of two were asleep in the drivers' seats. The third was a patrol car of the Ordnungspolizei – the Orpo, as every German called them. It was empty. Through its open window, sharp in the damp air, came the crackle of static, punctuated by jabbering bursts of speech. The revolving light on its roof lit up the forest beside the road: blue-black, blue-black, blue-black.

March looked around for the Orpo patrolmen, and saw them sheltering by the lake under a dripping birch tree. Something gleamed pale in the mud at their feet. On a nearby log sat a young man in a black tracksuit, SS insignia on his breast pocket. He was hunched forward, elbows resting on his knees, hands pressed against the sides of his head – the image of misery.

March took a last draw on his cigarette and flicked it away. It fizzed and died on the wet road.

As he approached, one of the policemen raised his arm.

'Heil Hitler!'

March ignored him and slithered down the muddy bank to inspect the corpse.

It was an old man's body – cold, fat, hairless and shockingly white. From a distance, it could have been an alabaster statue dumped in the mud. Smeared with dirt, the corpse sprawled on its back half out of the water, arms flung wide, head tilted back. One eye was screwed shut, the other squinted balefully at the filthy sky.

'Your name, Unterwachtmeister?' March had a soft voice. Without taking his eyes off the body, he addressed the Orpo man who had saluted.

'Ratka, Herr Sturmbannführer.'

Sturmbannführer was an SS title, equivalent in Wehrmacht rank to major, and Ratka – dog-tired and skin-soaked though he was –seemed eager to show respect. March knew his type without even looking round: three applications to transfer to the Kripo, all turned down; a dutiful wife who had produced a football team of children for the Führer; an income of 200 Reichsmarks a month. A life lived in hope.

'Well, Ratka,' said March, in that soft voice again. 'What time was he discovered?'

'Just over an hour ago, sir. We were at the end of our shift, patrolling in Nikolassee. We took the call. Priority One. We were here in five minutes.'

'Who found him?'

Ratka jerked his thumb over his shoulder.

The young man in the tracksuit rose to his feet. He could not have been more than eighteen. His hair was cropped so close the pink scalp showed through the dusting of light brown hair. March noticed how he avoided looking at the body.

'Your name?'

'SS-Schütze Hermann Jost, sir.' He spoke with a Saxon accent – nervous, uncertain, anxious to please. 'From the Sepp Dietrich training academy at Schlachtensee.' March knew it: a monstrosity of concrete and asphalt built in the 1950s, just south of the Havel. 'I run here most mornings. It was still dark. At first, I thought it was a swan,' he added, helplessly.

Ratka snorted, contempt on his face. An SS cadet scared of one dead old man! No wonder the war in the Urals was dragging on forever.

'Did you see anyone else, Jost?' March spoke in a kindly tone, like an uncle.

'Nobody, sir. There's a telephone box in the picnic area, half a kilometre back. I called, then came here and waited until the police arrived. There wasn't a soul on the road.'

March looked again at the body. It was very fat. Maybe 110 kilos.

'Let's get him out of the water.' He turned towards the road. 'Time to raise our sleeping beauties.' Ratka, shifting from foot to foot in the downpour, grinned.

It was raining harder now, and the Kladow side of the lake had virtually disappeared. Water pattered on the leaves of the trees and drummed on the car roofs. There was a heavy rain-smell of corruption: rich earth and rotting vegetation. March's hair was plastered to his scalp, water trickled down the back of his neck. He did not notice. For March, every case, however routine, held – at the start, at least – the promise of adventure.

He was forty-two years old – slim, with grey hair and cool grey eyes that matched the sky. During the war, the Propaganda Ministry had invented a nickname for the men of the U-boats – the 'grey wolves' – and it would have been a good name for March, in one sense, for he was a determined detective. But he was not by nature a wolf, did not run with the pack, was more reliant on brain than muscle, so his colleagues called him 'the fox' instead.

U-boat weather!

He flung open the door of the white Skoda, and was hit by a gust of hot, stale air from the car heater.

'Morning, Spiedel!' He shook the police photographer's bony shoulder. 'Time to get wet.' Spiedel jerked awake. He gave March a glare.

The driver's window of the other Skoda was already being wound down as March approached it. 'All right, March. All right.' It was SS-Surgeon August Eisler, a Kripo pathologist, his voice a squeak of affronted dignity. 'Save your barrack-room humour for those who appreciate it.'

THEY gathered at the water's edge, all except Doctor Eisler, who stood apart, sheltering under an ancient black umbrella he did not offer to share. Spiedel screwed a flash bulb on to his camera and carefully planted his right foot on a lump of clay. He swore as the lake lapped over his shoe.

'Shit!'

The flash popped, freezing the scene for an instant: the white faces, the silver threads of rain, the darkness of the woods. A swan came scudding out of some nearby reeds to see what was happening, and began circling a few metres away.

'Protecting her nest,' said the young SS man.

'I want another here.' March pointed. 'And one here.'

Spiedel cursed again and pulled his dripping foot out of the mud. The camera flashed twice more.

March bent down and grasped the body under the armpits. The flesh was hard, like cold rubber, and slippery.

'Help me.'

The Orpo men each took an arm and together, grunting with the effort, they heaved, sliding the corpse out of the water, over the muddy bank and on to the sodden grass. As March straightened, he caught the look on Jost's face.

The old man had been wearing a pair of blue swimming trunks which had worked their way down to his knees. In the freezing water, the genitals had shrivelled to a tiny clutch of white eggs in a nest of black pubic hair.

The left foot was missing.

It had to be, thought March. This was a day when nothing would be simple. An adventure, indeed.

'Herr Doctor. Your opinion, please.'

With a sigh of irritation, Eisler daintily stepped forward, removing the glove from one hand. The corpse's leg ended at the bottom of the calf. Still holding the umbrella, Eisler bent stiffly and ran his fingers around the stump.

'A propeller?' asked March. He had seen bodies dragged out of busy waterways – from the Tegler See and the Spree in Berlin, from the Alster in Hamburg – which looked as if butchers had been at them.

'No.' Eisler withdrew his hand. 'An old amputation. Rather well done in fact.' He pressed hard on the chest with his fist. Muddy water gushed from the mouth and bubbled out of the nostrils. 'Rigor mortis fairly advanced. Dead twelve hours. Maybe less.' He pulled his glove back on.

A diesel engine rattled somewhere through the trees behind them.

'The ambulance,' said Ratka. 'They take their time.'

March gestured to Spiedel. 'Take another picture.'

Looking down at the corpse, March lit a cigarette. Then he squatted on his haunches and stared into the single open eye. He stayed that way a long while. The camera flashed again. The swan reared up, flapped her wings, and turned towards the centre of the lake in search of food.

TWO

Kripo headquarters lie on the other side of Berlin, a twenty-five-minute drive from the Havel. March needed a statement from Jost, and offered to drop him back at his barracks to change, but Jost said no: he would sooner make his statement quickly. So once the body had been stowed aboard the ambulance and dispatched to the morgue, they set off in March's little four-door Volkswagen through the rush-hour traffic.

It was one of those dismal Berlin mornings, when the famous Berliner-luft seems not so much bracing as merely raw, the moisture stinging the face and hands like a thousand frozen needles. On the Potsdamer Chaussee, the spray from the wheels of the passing cars forced the few pedestrians close to the sides of the buildings. Watching them through the rain-flecked window, March imagined a city of blind men, feeling their way to work.

It was all so *normal*. Later, that was what would strike him most. It was like having an accident: before it, nothing out of the ordinary; then, the moment; and after it, a world that was changed forever. For there was nothing more routine than a body fished out of the Havel. It happened twice a month – derelicts and failed businessmen, reckless kids and lovelorn teenagers; accidents and suicides and murders; the desperate, the foolish, the sad.

The telephone had rung in his apartment in Ansbacher Strasse shortly after six-fifteen. The call had not woken him. He had been lying in the semi-darkness with his eyes open, listening to the rain. For the past few months he had slept badly.

'March? We've got a report of a body in the Havel.' It was Krause, the Kripo's Night Duty Officer. 'Go and take a look, there's a good fellow.'

March had said he was not interested.

'Your interest or lack of it is beside the point.'

'I am not interested,' said March, 'because I am not on duty. I was on duty last week, and the week before.' *And the week before that*, he might have added. 'This is my day off. Look again at your list.'

There had been a pause at the other end, then Krause had come back on the line, grudgingly apologetic. 'You are in luck, March. I was looking at last week's rota. You can go back to sleep. Or . . .' He had sniggered: 'Or whatever else it was you were doing.'

A gust of wind had slashed rain against the window, rattling the pane.

There was a standard procedure when a body was discovered: a pathologist, a police photographer and an investigator had to attend the scene at once. The investigators worked off a rota kept at Kripo headquarters in Werderscher Markt.

'Who is on today, as a matter of interest?'

'Max Jaeger.'

Jaeger. March shared an office with Jaeger. He had looked at his alarm clock and thought of the little house in Pankow where Max lived with his wife and four daughters: during the week, breakfast was just about the only time he saw them. March, on the other hand, was divorced and lived alone. He had set aside the afternoon to spend with his son. But the long hours of the morning stretched ahead, a blank. The way he felt it would be good to have something routine to distract him.

'Oh, leave him in peace,' he had said. 'I'm awake. I'll take it.'

That had been nearly two hours ago. March glanced at his passenger in the rear-view mirror. Jost had been silent ever since they left the Havel. He sat stiffly in the back seat, staring at the grey buildings slipping by.

At the Brandenburg Gate, a policeman on a motorcycle flagged them to a halt.

In the middle of Pariser Platz, an SA band in sodden brown uniforms wheeled and stamped in the puddles. Through the closed windows of the Volkswagen came the muffled thump of drums and trumpets, pounding out an old Party marching song. Several dozen people had gathered outside the Academy of Arts to watch them, shoulders hunched against the rain.

It was impossible to drive across Berlin at this time of year without encountering a similar rehearsal. In six days' time it would be Adolf Hitler's birthday – the Führertag, a public holiday – and every band in the Reich would be on parade. The windscreen wipers beat time like a metronome.

'Here we see the final proof,' murmured March, watching the crowd, 'that in the face of martial music, the German people are *mad*.'

He turned to Jost, who gave a thin smile.

A clash of cymbals ended the tune. There was a patter of damp applause. The bandmaster turned and bowed. Behind him, the SA men had already begun half-walking, half-running, back to their bus. The motorcycle cop waited until the Platz was clear, then blew a short blast on his whistle. With a white-gloved hand he waved them through the Gate.

The Unter den Linden gaped ahead of them. It had lost its lime trees in '36 – cut down in an act of official vandalism at the time of the Berlin Olympics. In their place, on either side of the boulevard, the city's Gauleiter, Josef Goebbels, had erected an avenue of ten-metre-high stone columns, on each of which perched a Party eagle, wings outstretched. Water dripped from their beaks and wingtips. It was like driving through a Red Indian burial ground.

March slowed for the lights at the Friedrich Strasse

intersection and turned right. Two minutes later they were parking in a space opposite the Kripo building in Werderscher Markt.

It was an ugly place – a heavy, soot-streaked, Wilhelmine monstrosity, six storeys high, on the south side of the Markt. March had been coming here, nearly seven days of the week, for ten years. As his ex-wife had frequently complained, it had become more familiar to him than home. Inside, beyond the SS sentries and the creaky revolving door, a board announced the current state of terrorist alert. There were four codes, in ascending order of seriousness: green, blue, black and red. Today, as always, the alert was red.

A pair of guards in a glass booth scrutinised them as they entered the foyer. March showed his identity card and signed in Jost.

The Markt was busier than usual. The workload always tripled in the week before the Führertag. Secretaries with boxes of files clattered on high heels across the marble floor. The air smelled thickly of wet overcoats and floor polish. Groups of officers in Orpo-green and Kripo-black stood whispering of crime. Above their heads, from opposite ends of the lobby, garlanded busts of the Führer and the Head of the Reich Main Security Office, Reinhard Heydrich, stared at one another with blank eyes.

March pulled back the metal grille of the elevator and ushered Jost inside.

The security forces which Heydrich controlled were divided into three. At the bottom of the pecking order were the Orpo, the ordinary cops. They picked up the drunks, cruised the Autobahnen, issued the speeding tickets, made the arrests, fought the fires, patrolled the railways and the airports, answered the emergency calls, fished the bodies out of the lakes.

At the top were the Sipo, the Security Police. The Sipo

embraced both the Gestapo and the Party's own security force, the SD. Their headquarters were in a grim complex around Prinz-Albrecht Strasse, a kilometre south-west of the Markt. They dealt with terrorism, subversion, counter-espionage and 'crimes against the state'. They had their ears in every factory and school, hospital and mess; in every town, in every village, in every street. A body in a lake would concern the Sipo only if it belonged to a terrorist or a traitor.

And somewhere between the other two, and blurring into both, came the Kripo – Department V of the Reich Main Security Office. They investigated straightforward crime, from burglary, through bank robbery, violent assault, rape and mixed marriage, all the way up to murder. Bodies in lakes – who they were and how they got there – they were Kripo business.

The elevator stopped at the second floor. The corridor was lit like an aquarium. Weak neon bounced off green linoleum and green-washed walls. There was the same smell of polish as in the lobby, but here it was spiced with lavatory disinfectant and stale cigarette smoke. Twenty doors of frosted glass lined the passage, some half open. These were the investigators' offices. From one came the sound of a solitary finger picking at a typewriter; in another, a telephone rang unanswered.

' "The nerve centre in the ceaseless war against the criminal enemies of National Socialism",' said March, quoting a recent headline in the Party newspaper, the *Völkischer Beobachter*. He paused, and when Jost continued to look blank he explained: 'A joke.'

'Sorry?'

'Forget it.'

He pushed open a door and switched on the light. His office was little more than a gloomy cupboard, a cell, its solitary window opening on to a courtyard of blackened brick. One wall was shelved: tattered, leather-bound volumes of statutes and decrees, a handbook on forensic science, a dictionary, an atlas, a Berlin street guide, telephone directories, box files with labels gummed to them – 'Braune', 'Hundt', 'Stark', 'Zadek' – every one a bureaucratic tombstone, memorialising some long-forgotten victim. Another side of the office was taken up by four filing cabinets. On top of one was a spider plant, placed there by a middle-aged secretary two years ago at the height of an unspoken and unrequited passion for Xavier March. It was now dead. That was all the furniture, apart from two wooden desks pushed together beneath the window. One was March's; the other belonged to Max Jaeger.

March hung his overcoat on a peg by the door. He preferred not to wear uniform when he could avoid it, and this morning he had used the rainstorm on the Havel as an excuse to dress in grey trousers and a thick blue sweater. He pushed Jaeger's chair towards Jost. 'Sit down. Coffee?'

'Please.'

There was a machine in the corridor. 'We've got fucking *photographs*. Can you believe it? Look at that.' Along the passage March could hear the voice of Fiebes of VB3 – the sexual crimes division – boasting of his latest success. 'Her maid took them. Look, you can see every *hair*. The girl should turn professional.'

What would this be? March thumped the side of the coffee machine and it ejected a plastic cup. Some officer's wife, he guessed, and a Polish labourer shipped in from the General Government to work in the garden. It was usually a Pole; a dreamy, soulful Pole, plucking at the heart of a wife whose husband was away at the front. It sounded as if they had been photographed *in flagrante* by some jealous girl from the Bund deutscher Mädel, anxious to please the authorities. This was a sexual crime, as defined in the 1935 Race Defilement Act.

He gave the machine another thump.

There would be a hearing in the People's Court, salaciously recorded in *Der Stürmer* as a warning to others. Two years in Ravensbrück for the wife. Demotion and disgrace for the husband. Twenty-five years for the Pole, if he was lucky; death if he was not.

'Fuck!' A male voice muttered something and Fiebes, a weaselly inspector in his mid-fifties whose wife had run off with an SS ski instructor ten years before, gave a shout of laughter. March, a cup of black coffee in either hand, retreated to his office and slammed the door behind him as loudly as he could with his foot.

Reichskriminalpolizei *Werderscher Markt 5/6*
Berlin

STATEMENT OF WITNESS

My name is Hermann Friedrich Jost. I was born on 23.2.45 in Dresden. I am a cadet at the Sepp Dietrich Academy, Berlin. At 05.30 this morning, I left for my regular training run. I prefer to run alone. My normal route takes me west through the Grunewald Forest to the Havel, north along the lakeshore to the Lindwerder Restaurant, then south to the barracks in Schlachtensee. Three hundred metres north of the Schwanenwerder causeway, I saw an object lying in the water at the edge of the lake. It was the body of a male. I ran to a telephone half a kilometre along the lake-path and informed the police. I returned to the body and waited for the arrival of the authorities. During all this time it was raining hard and I saw nobody.

I am making this statement of my own free will in the presence of Kripo investigator Xavier March.

SS-Schütze H. F. Jost.
08.24/14.4.64

March leaned back in his chair and studied the young man as he signed his statement. There were no hard lines to his face. It was as pink and soft as a baby's, with a clamour of acne around the mouth, a whisper of blond hair on the upper lip. March doubted if he shaved.

'Why do you run alone?'

Jost handed back his statement. 'It gives me a chance to think. It is good to be alone once in the day. One is not often alone in a barracks.'

'How long have you been a cadet?'

'Three months.'

'Do you enjoy it?'

'Enjoy it!' Jost turned his face to the window. 'I had just begun studying at the university at Göttingen when my call-up came through. Let us say, it was not the happiest day of my life.'

'What were you studying?'

'Literature.'

'German?'

'What other sort is there?' Jost gave one of his watery smiles. 'I hope to go back to the university when I have served my three years. I want to be a teacher; a writer. Not a soldier.'

March scanned his statement. 'If you are so anti-military, what are you doing in the SS?' He guessed the answer.

'My father. He was a founder member of the Leibstandarte Adolf Hitler. You know how it is: I am his only son; it was his dearest wish.'

'You must hate it.'

Jost shrugged. 'I survive. And I have been told – unofficially, naturally – that I will not have to go to the front. They need an assistant at the officer school in Bad Tolz to teach a course on the degeneracy of American literature. That sounds more my kind of thing: degeneracy.'

He risked another smile. 'Perhaps I shall become an expert in the field.'

March laughed and glanced again at the statement. Something was not right here, and now he saw it. 'No doubt you will.' He put the statement to one side and stood up. 'I wish you luck with your teaching.'

'Am I free to go?'

'Of course.'

With a look of relief, Jost got to his feet. March grasped the door handle. 'One thing.' He turned and stared into the SS cadet's eyes. 'Why are you lying to me?'

Jost jerked his head back. 'What. . . ?'

'You say you left the barracks at five-thirty. You call the cops at five past six. Schwanenwerder is three kilometres from the barracks. You are fit: you run every day. You do not dawdle: it is raining hard. Unless you suddenly developed a limp, you must have arrived at the lake quite some time before six. So there are – what? – twenty minutes out of thirty-five unaccounted for in your statement. What were you doing, Jost?'

The young man looked stricken. 'Maybe I left the barracks later. Or maybe I did a couple of circuits of the running track there first . . .'

' "Maybe, maybe . . ." ' March shook his head sadly. 'These are facts that can be checked, and I warn you: it will go hard for you if I have to find out the truth and bring it to you, rather than the other way round. You are a homosexual, yes?'

'Herr Sturmbannführer! For God's sake . . .'

March put his hands on Jost's shoulders. 'I don't care. Perhaps you run alone every morning so you can meet some fellow in the Grunewald for twenty minutes. That's your business. It's no crime in my book. All I'm interested in is the body. Did you see something? What did you really do?'

Jost shook his head. 'Nothing. I swear.' Tears were welling in his wide, pale eyes.

'Very well.' March released him. 'Wait downstairs. I'll arrange transport to take you back to Schlachtensee.' He opened the door. 'Remember what I said: better you tell me the truth now than I find it out for myself later.'

Jost hesitated, and for a moment March thought he might say something, but then he walked out into the corridor and was gone.

March rang down to the basement garage and ordered a car. He hung up and stared out of the grimy window at the wall opposite. The black brick glistened under the film of rainwater pouring down from the upper storeys. Had he been too hard on the boy? Probably. But sometimes the truth could only be ambushed, taken unguarded in a surprise attack. Was Jost lying? Certainly. But then if he was a homosexual, he could scarcely afford not to lie: anyone found guilty of 'anti-community acts' went straight to a labour camp. SS men arrested for homosexuality were attached to punishment battalions on the Eastern front; few returned.

March had seen a score of young men like Jost in the past year. There were more of them every day. Rebelling against their parents. Questioning the state. Listening to American radio stations. Circulating their crudely printed copies of proscribed books – Günter Grass and Graham Greene, George Orwell and J. D. Salinger. Chiefly, they protested against the war – the seemingly endless struggle against the American-backed Soviet guerillas, which had been grinding on east of the Urals for twenty years.

He felt suddenly ashamed of his treatment of Jost, and considered going down to apologise to him. But then he decided, as he always did, that his duty to the dead came first. His penance for his morning's bullying would be to put a name to the body in the lake.

*

THE Duty Room of the Berlin Kriminalpolizei occupies most of Werderscher Markt's third floor. March mounted the stairs two at a time. Outside the entrance, a guard armed with a machine gun demanded his pass. The door opened with a thud of electronic bolts.

An illuminated map of Berlin takes up half the far wall. A galaxy of stars, orange in the semi-darkness, marks the capital's one hundred and twenty-two police stations. To its left is a second map, even larger, depicting the entire Reich. Red lights pinpoint those towns big enough to warrant their own Kripo divisions. The centre of Europe glows crimson. Further east, the lights gradually thin until, beyond Moscow, there are only a few isolated sparks, winking like camp fires in the blackness. It is a planetarium of crime.

Krause, the Duty Officer for the Berlin Gau, sat on a raised platform beneath the display. He was on the telephone as March approached and raised his hand in greeting. Before him, a dozen women in starched white shirts sat in glass partitions, each wearing a headset with a microphone attached. What they must hear! A sergeant from a Panzer division comes home from a tour in the East. After a family supper, he takes out his pistol, shoots his wife and each of his three children in turn. Then he splatters his skull across the ceiling. An hysterical neighbour calls the cops. And the news comes here – is controlled, evaluated, reduced – before being passed downstairs to that corridor with cracked green linoleum, stale with cigarette smoke.

Behind the Duty Officer, a uniformed secretary with a sour face was making entries on the night incident board. There were four columns: crime (serious), crime (violent), incidents, fatalities. Each category was further quartered: time reported, source of information, detail of report, action taken. An average night of mayhem in the world's largest city, with its population of ten million, was reduced to hieroglyphics on a few square metres of white plastic.

There had been eighteen deaths since ten o'clock the previous night. The worst incident – *1H 2D 4K* – was three adults and four children killed in a car smash in Pankow just after 11. No action taken; that could be left to the Orpo. A family burned to death in a house-fire in Kreuzberg, a stabbing outside a bar in Wedding, a woman beaten to death in Spandau. The record of March's own disrupted morning was last on the list: *06:07 [O]* (that meant notification had come from the Orpo) *1H Havel/March*. The secretary stepped back and recapped her pen with a sharp click.

Krause had finished his telephone call and was looking defensive. 'I've already apologised, March.'

'Forget it. I want the missing list. Berlin area. Say: the last forty-eight hours.'

'No problem.' Krause looked relieved and swivelled round in his chair to the sour-faced woman. 'You heard the investigator, Helga. Check whether anything's come in in the last hour.' He spun back to face March, red-eyed with lack of sleep. 'I'd have left it an hour. But any trouble around that place – you know how it is.'

March looked up at the Berlin map. Most of it was a grey cobweb of streets. But over to the left were two splashes of colour: the green of the Grunewald Forest and, running alongside it, the blue ribbon of the Havel. Curling into the lake, in the shape of a foetus, was an island, linked to the shore by a thin umbilical causeway.

Schwanenwerder.

'Does Goebbels still have a place there?'

Krause nodded. 'And the rest.'

It was one of the most fashionable addresses in Berlin, practically a government compound. A few dozen large houses screened from the road. A sentry at the entrance to the causeway. A good place for privacy, for security, for forest views and private moorings; a bad place to discover a body. The corpse had been washed up fewer than three hundred metres away.

Krause said: 'The local Orpo call it "the pheasant run".'

March smiled: 'golden pheasants' was street slang for the Party leadership.

'It's not good to leave a mess for too long on *that* doorstep.'

Helga had returned. 'Persons reported missing since Sunday morning,' she announced, 'and still unaccounted for.' She gave a long roll of printed-out names to Krause, who glanced at it and passed it on to March. 'Plenty to keep you busy there.' He seemed to find this amusing. 'You should give it to that fat friend of yours, Jaeger. He's the one who should be looking after this business, remember?'

'Thanks. I'll make a start at least.'

Krause shook his head. 'You put in twice the hours of the others. You get no promotions. You're on shitty pay. Are you crazy or what?'

March had rolled the list of missing persons into a tube. He leaned forward and tapped Krause lightly on the chest with it. 'You forget yourself, comrade,' he said. 'Arbeit macht frei.' The slogan of the labour camps. Work Makes You Free.

He turned and made his way back through the ranks of telephonists. Behind him he could hear Krause appealing to Helga. 'See what I mean? What the hell kind of a joke is that?'

MARCH arrived back in his office just as Max Jaeger was hanging up his coat. 'Zavi!' Jaeger spread his arms wide. 'I got a message from the Duty Room. What can I say?' He wore the uniform of an SS Sturmbannführer. The black tunic still bore traces of his breakfast.

'Put it down to my soft old heart,' said March. 'And don't get too excited. There was nothing on the corpse to identify it and there are a hundred people missing in Berlin since Sunday. It'll take hours just to go through the list. And I've promised to take my boy out this afternoon, so you'll be on your own with it.'

He lit a cigarette and explained the details: the location, the missing foot, his suspicions about Jost. Jaeger took it in with a series of grunts. He was a shambling, untidy hulk of a man, two metres tall, with clumsy hands and feet. He was fifty, nearly ten years older than March, but they had shared an office since 1959 and sometimes worked as a team. Colleagues in Werderscher Markt joked about them behind their backs: the Fox and the Bear. And maybe there was something of the old married couple about them, in the way they bickered with and covered for each other.

'This is the "missing" list.' March sat down at his desk and unrolled the print-out: names, dates of birth, times of disappearance, addresses of informants. Jaeger leaned over his shoulder. He smoked stubby fat cigars and his uniform reeked of them. 'According to the good doctor Eisler, our man probably died some time after six last night, so the chances are nobody missed him until seven or eight at the earliest. They may even be waiting to see if he shows up this morning. So he may not be on the list. But we have to consider two other possibilities, do we not? One: he went missing some time *before* he died. Two – and we know from hard experience this is not impossible – Eisler has screwed up the time of death.'

'The guy isn't fit to be a vet,' said Jaeger.

March counted swiftly. 'One hundred and two names. I'd put the age of our man at sixty.'

'Better say fifty, to be safe. Twelve hours in the drink and nobody looks their best.'

'True. So we exclude everyone on the list born after 1914. That should bring it down to a dozen names. Identification couldn't be much easier: was grandpa missing a foot?' March folded the sheet, tore it in two, and handed one half to Jaeger. 'What are the Orpo stations around the Havel?'

'Nikolassee,' said Max. 'Wannsee. Kladow. Gatow. Pichelsdorf –but that's probably too far north.'

Over the next half hour, March called each of them in turn, including Pichelsdorf, to see if any clothing had been handed in, or if some local derelict matched the description of the man in the lake. Nothing. He turned his attention to his half of the list. By eleven-thirty he had exhausted every likely name. He stood up and stretched.

'Mister Nobody.'

Jaeger had finished calling ten minutes earlier and was staring out of the window, smoking. 'Popular fellow, isn't he? Makes even you looked loved.' He removed his cigar and picked some shreds of loose tobacco from his tongue. 'I'll see if the Duty Room have received any more names. Leave it to me. Have a good time with Pili.'

THE late morning service had just ended in the ugly church opposite Kripo headquarters. March stood on the other side of the street and watched the priest, a shabby raincoat over his vestments, locking the door. Religion was officially discouraged in Germany. How many worshippers, March wondered, had braved the Gestapo's spies to attend? Half-a-dozen? The priest slipped the heavy iron key into his pocket and turned round. He saw March looking at him, and immediately scuttled away, eyes cast down, like a man caught in the middle of an illegal transaction. March buttoned his trenchcoat and followed him into the filthy Berlin morning.

THREE

'Construction of the Arch of Triumph was commenced in 1946 and work was completed in time for the Day of National Reawakening in 1950. The inspiration for the design came from the Führer and is based upon original drawings made by him during the Years of Struggle.'

The passengers on the tour bus – at least those who could understand – digested this information. They raised themselves out of their seats or leaned into the aisle to get a better view. Xavier March, half-way down the bus, lifted his son on to his lap. Their guide, a middle-aged woman clad in the dark green of the Reich Tourist Ministry, stood at the front, feet planted wide apart, back to the windscreen. Her voice over the address system was thick with cold.

'The Arch is constructed of granite and has a capacity of two million, three hundred and sixty-five thousand, six hundred and eighty-five cubic metres.' She sneezed. 'The Arc de Triomphe in Paris will fit into it forty-nine times.'

For a moment, the Arch loomed over them. Then, suddenly, they were passing through it – an immense, stone-ribbed tunnel, longer than a football pitch, higher than a fifteen-storey building, with the vaulted, shadowed roof of a cathedral. The headlights and tail-lights of eight lanes of traffic danced in the afternoon gloom.

'The Arch has a height of one hundred and eighteen metres. It is one hundred and sixty-eight metres wide and has a depth of one hundred and nineteen metres. On the inner walls are carved the names of the three million soldiers who fell in defence of the Fatherland in the wars of 1914 to 1918 and 1939 to 1946.'

She sneezed again. The passengers dutifully craned their

necks to peer at the Roll of the Fallen. They were a mixed party. A group of Japanese, draped with cameras; an American couple with a little girl Pili's age; some German settlers, from Ostland or the Ukraine, in Berlin for the Führertag. March looked away as they passed the Roll of the Fallen. Somewhere on it were the names of his father and both his grandfathers. He kept his eyes on the guide. When she thought no one was looking, she turned away and quickly wiped her nose on her sleeve. The coach re-emerged into the drizzle.

'Leaving the Arch we enter the central section of the Avenue of Victory. The Avenue was designed by Reich Minister Albert Speer and was completed in 1957. It is one hundred and twenty-three metres wide and five-point-six kilometres in length. It is both wider, and two and a half times longer, than the Champs Elysées in Paris.'

Higher, longer, bigger, wider, more expensive . . . Even in victory, thought March, Germany has a parvenu's inferiority complex. Nothing stands on its own. Everything has to be compared with what the foreigners have . . .

'The view from this point northwards along the Avenue of Victory is considered one of the wonders of the world.'

'One of the wonders of the world,' repeated Pili in a whisper.

And it was, even on a day like this. Dense with traffic, the Avenue stretched before them, flanked on either side by the glass and granite walls of Speer's new buildings: ministries, offices, big stores, cinemas, apartment blocks. At the far end of this river of light, rising as grey as a battleship through the spray, was the Great Hall of the Reich, its dome half hidden in the low cloud.

There were appreciative murmurs from the settlers. 'It's like a mountain,' said the woman sitting behind March. She was with her husband and four boys. They had probably been planning this trip all winter. A Tourist

Ministry brochure and a dream of April in Berlin: comforts to warm them in the snowbound, moonless nights of Minsk or Kiev, a thousand kilometres from home. How had they got here? A package tour organised by Strength-Through-Joy, perhaps: two hours in a Junkers jet with a stop-off in Warsaw. Or a three-day drive in the family Volkswagen on the Berlin-Moscow Autobahn.

Pili wriggled out of his father's grasp and walked unsteadily to the front of the coach. March pinched the bridge of his nose between thumb and forefinger, a nervous habit he had picked up – when? – in the U-boat service, he supposed, when the screws of the British warships sounded so close the hull shook and you never knew if their next depth charge would be your last. He had been invalided out of the navy in 1948 with suspected TB and spent a year convalescing. Then, for want of anything better to do, he had joined the Marine-Küstenpolizei, the Coastal Police, in Wilhelmshaven as a lieutenant. That year he had married Klara Eckart, a nurse he had met at the TB clinic. In 1952, he had joined the Hamburg Kripo. In 1954, with Klara pregnant and the marriage already failing, he had been promoted to Berlin. Paul – Pili – had been born exactly ten years and one month ago.

What had gone wrong? He did not blame Klara. She had not changed. She had always been a strong woman who wanted certain simple things from life: home, family, friends, acceptance. But March: he *had* changed. After ten years in the navy and twelve months in virtual isolation, he had stepped ashore into a world he barely recognised. As he went to work, watched television, ate with friends, even – God help him – slept beside his wife, he sometimes imagined himself aboard a U-boat still: cruising beneath the surface of everyday life; solitary, watchful.

He had picked Pili up at noon from Klara's place – a bungalow on a dreary post-war housing estate in

Lichtenrade, in the southern suburbs. Park in the street, sound the horn twice, watch for the twitch in the parlour curtain. This was the routine which had evolved, unspoken, since their divorce five years ago – a means of avoiding embarrassing encounters; a ritual to be endured one Sunday in four, work permitting, under the strict provisions of the Reich Marriages Act. It was rare for him to see his son on a Tuesday, but this was a school vacation: since 1959, children had been given a week off for the Führer's birthday, rather than for Easter.

The door had opened and Pili had appeared, like a shy child-actor being pushed out on stage against his will. Wearing his new Pimpf uniform – crisp black shirt and dark blue shorts – he had climbed wordlessly into the car. March had given him an awkward hug.

'You look smart. How's school?'

'All right.'

'And your mother?'

The boy shrugged.

'What would you like to do?'

He shrugged again.

They had lunch in Budapester Strasse, opposite the Zoo, in a modern place with vinyl seats and a plastic-topped table: father and son, one with beer and sausages, the other with apple juice and a hamburger. They talked about the Pimpf and Pili brightened. Until you were a Pimpf you were nothing, 'a non-uniformed creature who has never participated in a group meeting or a route march'. You were allowed to join when you were ten, and stayed until you were fourteen, when you passed into the full Hitler Youth.

'I was top in the initiation test.'

'Good lad.'

'You have to run sixty metres in twelve seconds,' said Pili. 'Do the long jump and the shot-put. There's a route march – a day and a half. Written stuff. Party philosophy. And you have to recite the *Horst Wessel Lied.*'

For a moment, March thought he was about to break into song. He cut in hurriedly: 'And your dagger?'

Pili fumbled in his pocket, a crease of concentration on his forehead. How like his mother he is, thought March. The same wide cheekbones and full mouth, the same serious brown eyes, set far apart. Pili laid the dagger carefully on the table before him. He picked it up. It reminded him of the day he got his own – when was it? '34? The excitement of a boy who believes he's been admitted to the company of men. He turned it over and the swastika on the hilt glinted in the light. He felt the weight of it in his hand, then gave it back.

'I'm proud of you,' he lied. 'What do you want to do? We can go to the cinema. Or the zoo.'

'I want to go on the bus.'

'But we did that last time. And the time before.'

'Don't care. I want to go on the bus.'

'THE Great Hall of the Reich is the largest building in the world. It rises to a height of more than a quarter of a kilometre, and on certain days – observe today – the top of its dome is lost from view. The dome itself is one hundred and forty metres in diameter and St Peter's in Rome will fit into it sixteen times.'

They had reached the top of the Avenue of Victory, and were entering Adolf Hitler Platz. To the left, the square was bounded by the headquarters of the Wehrmacht High Command, to the right by the new Reich Chancellery and Palace of the Führer. Ahead was the hall. Its greyness had dissolved as their distance from it had diminished. Now they could see what the guide was telling them: that the pillars supporting the frontage were of red granite, mined in

Sweden, flanked at either end by golden statues of Atlas and Tellus, bearing on their shoulders spheres depicting the heavens and the earth.

The building was as crystal-white as a wedding cake, its dome of beaten copper a dull green. Pili was still at the front of the coach.

'The Great Hall is used only for the most solemn ceremonies of the German Reich and has a capacity of one hundred and eighty thousand people. One interesting and unforeseen phenomenon: the breath from this number of humans rises into the cupola and forms clouds, which condense and fall as light rain. The Great Hall is the only building in the world which generates its own climate . . .'

March had heard it all before. He looked out of the window and saw the body in the mud. Swimming trunks! What had the old man been thinking of, swimming on Monday night? Berlin had been blanketed by black clouds from late afternoon. When the storm finally broke the rain had descended in steel rods, drilling the streets and roofs, drowning the thunder. Suicide, perhaps? Think of it. Wade into the cold lake, strike out for the centre, tread water in the darkness, watch the lightning over the trees, wait for tiredness to do the rest . . .

Pili had returned to his seat and was bouncing up and down in excitement.

'Are we going to see the Führer, papa?'

The vision evaporated and March felt guilty. This daydreaming was what Klara used to complain of: *'Even when you're here, you're not really here . . .'*

He said: 'I don't think so.'

The guide again: 'On the right is the Reich Chancellery and Residence of the Führer. Its total façade measures exactly seven hundred metres, exceeding by one hundred metres the façade of Louis XIV's palace at Versailles.'

The Chancellery slowly uncoiled as the bus drove by:

marble pillars and red mosaics, bronze lions, gilded silhouettes, gothic script – a Chinese dragon of a building, asleep at the side of the square. A four-man SS honour guard stood at attention beneath a billowing swastika banner. There were no windows, but set into the wall, five storeys above the ground, was the balcony on which the Führer showed himself on those occasions when a million people gathered in the Platz. There were a few dozen sightseers even now, gazing up at the tightly drawn shutters, faces pale with expectation, hoping . . .

March glanced at his son. Pili was transfixed, his little dagger clutched tightly in his hand like a crucifix.

THE coach dropped them back at its pick-up point outside the Berlin-Gotenland railway station. It was after five as they descended from the bus, and the last vestiges of natural light were fading. The day was giving up on itself in disgust.

The entrance to the station was disgorging people – soldiers with kitbags walking with girlfriends and wives, foreign workers with cardboard suitcases and shabby bundles tied with string, settlers emerging after two days' travelling from the Steppes, staring in shock at the lights and the crowds. Uniforms were everywhere. Dark blue, green, brown, black, grey, khaki. It was like a factory at the end of a shift. There was a factory sound of shunting metal and shrill whistles, and a factory smell of heat and oil, stale air and steel-dust. Exclamation marks clamoured from the walls. 'Be vigilant at all times!' 'Attention! Report suspicious packages at once!' 'Terrorist alert!'

From here, trains as high as houses, with a gauge of four metres, left for the outposts of the German Empire – for Gotenland (formerly the Crimea) and Theoderichshafen (formerly Sevastopol); for the Generalkommissariat of Taurida and its capital, Melitopol; for Volhynia-Podolia,

Zhitomir, Kiev, Nikolaev, Dnepropetrovsk, Karkov, Rostov, Saratov . . . It was the terminus of a new world. Announcements of arrivals and departures punctuated the 'Coriolan Overture' on the public address system. March tried to take Pili's hand as they wove through the crowd, but the boy shook him away.

It took fifteen minutes to retrieve the car from the underground car park, and another fifteen to get clear of the clogged streets around the station. They drove in silence. It was not until they were almost back at Lichtenrade that Pili suddenly blurted out: 'You're an asocial, aren't you?'

It was such an odd word to hear on the lips of a ten-year-old, and so carefully pronounced, that March almost laughed out loud. An asocial: one step down from traitor in the Party's lexicon of crime. A non-contributor to Winter Relief. A non-joiner of the endless National Socialist associations. The NS Skiing Federation. The Association of NS Ramblers. The Greater German NS-Motoring Club. The NS Criminal Police Officers Society. He had even one afternoon come across a parade in the Lustgarten organised by the NS-League of Wearers of the Life-Saving Medal.

'That's nonsense.'

'Uncle Erich says it's true.'

Erich Helfferich. So he had become 'Uncle' Erich now, had he? A zealot of the worst sort, a full-time bureaucrat at the Party's Berlin headquarters. An officious, bespectacled scout master . . . March felt his hands tightening on the steering wheel. Helfferich had started seeing Klara a year ago.

'He says you don't give the Führer-salute and you make jokes about the Party.'

'And how does he know all this?'

'He says there's a file on you at Party Headquarters and it's only a matter of time before you're picked up.' The boy was almost in tears with the shame of it. 'I think he's right.'

'Pili!'

They were drawing up outside the house.

'I hate you.' This was delivered in a calm, flat voice. He got out of the car. March opened his door, ran round and followed him up the path. He could hear a dog barking inside the house.

'Pili!' he shouted once more.

The door opened. Klara stood there in the uniform of the NS-Frauenschaft. Lurking behind her, March glimpsed the brown-clad figure of Helfferich. The dog, a young German shepherd, came running out and leapt up at Pili, who pushed his way past his mother and disappeared into the house. March wanted to follow him, but Klara blocked his path.

'Leave the boy alone. Get out of here. Leave us all alone.'

She caught the dog and dragged it back by its collar. The door slammed on its yelping.

LATER, as he drove back towards the centre of Berlin, March kept thinking about that dog. It was the only living creature in the house, he realised, which was not wearing a uniform.

Had he not felt so miserable, he would have laughed.

FOUR

'What a pig of a day,' said Max Jaeger. It was seven-thirty in the evening and he was pulling on his coat in Werderscher Markt. 'No possessions handed in; no clothing. I've gone back on the missing list to Thursday. Nothing. So that's more than twenty-four hours since estimated time of death and not a soul has missed him. You sure he's not just some derelict?'

March gave a brief shake of the head. 'Too well-fed. And derelicts don't own swimming trunks. As a rule.'

'To cap it all,' Max took a last puff on his cigar and stubbed it out, 'I've got to go to a Party meeting tonight. "The German Mother: Warrior of the Volk on the Home Front".'

Like all Kripo investigators, including March, Jaeger had the SS rank of Sturmbannführer. Unlike March, he had joined the Party the previous year. Not that March blamed him. You had to be a Party member to gain promotion.

'Is Hannelore going?'

'Hannelore? Holder of the Honour Cross of the German Mother, Bronze Class? Naturally she's going.' Max looked at his watch. 'Just time for a beer. What do you say?'

'Not tonight, thanks. I'll walk down with you.'

They parted on the steps of the Kripo building. With a wave, Jaeger turned left towards the bar in Ob-wall Strasse, while March turned right, towards the river. He walked quickly. The rain had stopped, but the air was still damp and misty. The pre-war street lights gleamed on the black pavement. From the Spree came the low note of a foghorn, muffled by the buildings.

He turned a corner and walked alongside the river, enjoying the sensation of the cold night air against his face.

A barge was chugging upstream, a single light at its prow, a cauldron of dark water boiling at its stern. Apart from that, there was silence. There were no cars here; no people. The city might have vaporised in the darkness. He left the river with reluctance, crossing Spittel Markt to Seydel Strasse. A few minutes later he entered the Berlin city morgue.

Doctor Eisler had gone home. No surprise there. 'I love you,' breathed a woman's voice in the deserted reception, 'and I want to bear your children.' An attendant in a stained white tunic reluctantly turned away from his portable television and checked March's ID. He made a note in his register, picked up a bunch of keys, and gestured to the detective to follow him. Behind them, the theme tune of the Reichsrundfunk's nightly soap opera began to play.

Swing doors led on to a corridor identical to a dozen back in Werderscher Markt. Somewhere, thought March, there must be a Reichsdirektor for green linoleum. He followed the attendant into an elevator. The metal grille closed with a crash and they descended into the basement.

At the entrance to the storeroom, beneath a No Smoking sign, they both lit cigarettes – two professionals taking the same precaution, not against the smell of the bodies (the room was refrigerated: there was no stink of corruption) but to blot out the stinging fumes of the disinfectant.

'You want the old fellow? Came in just after eight?'

'Right,' said March.

The attendant pulled a large handle and swung open the heavy door. There was a whoosh of cold air as they stepped inside. Harsh neon strips lit a floor of white tiles, slightly sloping on either side down to a narrow gutter in the centre. Heavy metal drawers like filing cabinets were set into the walls. The attendant took a clipboard from a hook by the light-switch and walked along them, checking the numbers. 'This one.'

He tucked the clipboard under his arm and gave the

drawer a hard tug. It slid open. March stepped over and pulled back the white sheet.

'You can go now, if you like,' he said, without looking round. 'I'll call when I've finished.'

'Not allowed. Regulations.'

'In case I tamper with the evidence? Do me a favour.'

The body did not improve on second acquaintance. A hard, fleshy face, small eyes and a cruel mouth. The scalp was almost entirely bald, apart from the odd strand of white hair. The nose was sharp, with two deep indentations on either side of the bridge. He must have worn spectacles for years. The face itself was unmarked, but there were symmetrical bruises on either cheek. March inserted his fingers into the mouth and encountered only soft gum. At some point a complete set of false teeth must have been knocked loose.

March pulled the sheet right back. The shoulders were broad, the torso that of a powerful man, just beginning to run to fat. He folded the cloth neatly a few centimetres above the stump. He was always respectful of the dead. No society doctor on the Kurfürstendamm was more tender with his clients than Xavier March.

He breathed warmth on to his hands and reached into the inside pocket of his overcoat. He pulled out a small tin case, which he opened, and two white cards. The cigarette smoke tasted bitter in his mouth. He grasped the corpse's left wrist – so *cold*; it never ceased to shock him – and prised open the fingers. Carefully, he pressed each tip on to the pad of black ink in the tin. Then he put the tin down, picked up one of the cards, and pressed each finger on to that. When he was satisfied, he repeated the process on the old man's right hand. The attendant watched him, fascinated.

The smears of black on the white hands looked shocking; a desecration.

'Clean him up,' said March.

THE headquarters of the Reich Kripo are in Werderscher Markt, but the actual hardware of police business – the forensic laboratories, criminal records, armoury, workshops, detention cells – are in the Berlin Police Praesidium building in Alexander Platz. It was to this sprawling Prussian fortress, opposite the busiest U-bahn station in the city, that March went next. It took him fifteen minutes, walking briskly.

'You want *what*?'

The voice, edged high with incredulity, belonged to Otto Koth, deputy head of the fingerprint section.

'Priority,' repeated March. He took another draw on his cigarette. He knew Koth well. Two years ago they had trapped a gang of armed robbers who had killed a policeman in Lankwitz. Koth had got a promotion on the strength of it. 'I know you've got a backlog from here to the Führer's hundredth birthday. I know you've got the Sipo on your back for terrorists and God knows what. But do this for me.'

Koth leaned back in his chair. In the bookcase behind him, March could see Artur Nebe's book on criminology, published thirty years ago, but still the standard text. Nebe had been head of the Kripo since 1933.

'Let me see what you've got,' said Koth.

March handed over the cards. Koth glanced at them, nodding.

'Male,' said March. 'About sixty. Dead for a day.'

'I know how he feels.' Koth took off his glasses and rubbed his eyes. 'All right. They'll go to the top of the pile.'

'How long?'

'Should have an answer by morning.' Koth put his glasses back on. 'What I don't understand is how you know this man, whoever he was, had a criminal record.'

March did not know, but he was not going to hand Koth an excuse to wriggle out of his promise. 'Trust me,' he said.

MARCH arrived back at his flat at eleven. The ancient cage lift was out of order. The stairs, with their threadbare brown carpet, smelled of other people's old meals, of boiled cabbage and burned meat. As he passed the second floor he could hear the young couple who lived beneath him quarrelling.

'How can you say that?'

'You've done nothing! Nothing!'

A door slammed. A baby cried. Elsewhere, someone turned up the volume of their radio in response. The symphony of apartment life. This had been a fashionable block, once. Now, like many of its tenants, it had fallen on harder times. He continued on up to the next floor and let himself in.

The rooms were cold, the heating having failed to come on, as usual. He had five: a sitting room, with a good high ceiling, looking out on to Ansbacher Strasse; a bedroom with an iron bedstead; a small bathroom and an even smaller kitchen; a spare room was filled with salvage from his marriage, still packed in boxes five years later. Home. It was bigger than the forty-four square metres which was the standard size of a Volkswohnung – a People's Flat – but not much.

Before March had moved in it had been occupied by the widow of a Luftwaffe general. She had lived in it since the war and had let it go to ruin. On his second weekend, redecorating the bedroom, he had stripped off the mildewed wallpaper and found tucked behind it a photograph, folded up very small. A sepia portrait, all misty browns and creams, dated 1929, taken by a Berlin studio. A family stood before a painted backdrop of trees and fields. A dark-haired woman gazed at a baby in her arms. Her husband stood proud behind her, his hand resting on her shoulder. Next to him, a little boy. He had kept it on the mantelpiece ever since.

The boy was Pili's age, would be March's age today.

Who were these people? What had happened to the child? For years he had wondered, but hesitated – he always had plenty at the Markt to stretch his mind, without finding fresh mysteries to unravel. Then, just before last Christmas, for no reason he could properly define – a vague and growing uneasiness that happened to coincide with his birthday, no more than that – he had started to seek an answer.

The landlord's records showed that the apartment had been rented between 1928 and 1942 to one Weiss, Jakob. But there was no police file on any Jakob Weiss. He was not registered as having moved, or fallen sick, or died. Calls to the records bureaux of the Army, Navy and Luftwaffe confirmed he had not been conscripted to fight. The photographer's studio had become a television rental shop, its records lost. None of the young people in the landlord's office remembered the Weisses. They had vanished. *Weiss. White.* A *blank*. By now, in his heart, March knew the truth – perhaps had always known it – but he went round one evening with the photograph even so, like a policeman, seeking witnesses, and the other tenants in the house had looked at him as if he were crazy even for asking. Except one.

'They were Jews,' the crone in the attic had said as she closed the door in his face.

Of course. The Jews had all been evacuated to the east during the war. Everyone knew that. What had happened to them since was not a question anyone asked in public – or in private either, if they had any sense, not even an SS-Sturmbannführer.

And that, he could see now, was when his relationship with Pili had started to go bad; the time when he had started to wake up before it was light, and to volunteer for every case that came along.

MARCH stood for a few minutes without switching on the lights, looking down at the traffic heading south to Wittenberg Platz. Then he went into the kitchen and poured himself a large whisky. Monday's *Berliner Tageblatt* was lying by the sink. He carried it back with him into the sitting room.

March had a routine for reading the paper. He started at the back, with the truth. If Leipzig was said to have beaten Cologne four-nil at football, the chances were it was true: even the Party had yet to devise a means of rewriting the sports results. The sports news was a different matter. COUNTDOWN TO TOKYO OLYMPICS. US MAY COMPETE FOR FIRST TIME IN 28 YEARS. GERMAN ATHLETES STILL LEAD WORLD. Then the advertisements. GERMAN FAMILIES! PLEASURE BECKONS IN GOTENLAND, RIVIERA OF THE REICH! French perfume, Italian silks, Scandinavian furs, Dutch cigars, Belgian coffee, Russian caviar, British televisions – the cornucopia of Empire spilled across the pages. Births, marriages and deaths: TEBBE, Ernst and Ingrid; a son for the Führer. WENZEL, Hans, aged 71; a true National Socialist, sadly missed.

And the lonely hearts:

FIFTY years old. Pure Aryan doctor, veteran of the Battle of Moscow, who intends to settle on the land, desires male progeny through marriage with healthy, Aryan, virginal, young, unassuming, thrifty woman, adapted to hard work; broad-hipped, flat-heeled and earring-less essential.

WIDOWER aged sixty once again wishes to have Nordic

mate prepared to present him with children so that old family should not die out in male line.

Arts pages: Zarah Leander, still going strong, in *Woman of Odessa*, now showing at the Gloria-Palast: the epic story of the resettlement of the South Tyrolese. A piece by the music critic attacking the 'pernicious, Negroid wailings' of a group of young Englishmen from Liverpool, playing to packed audiences of German youth in Hamburg. Herbert von Karajan to conduct a special performance of Beethoven's Ninth Symphony – the European anthem – at the Royal Albert Hall in London on the Führer's birthday.

Editorial on the student anti-war demonstrations in Heidelberg: TRAITORS MUST BE SMASHED BY FORCE! The *Tageblatt* always took a firm line.

Obituary: some old Bonze from the Ministry of the Interior. 'A lifetime's service to the Reich . . .'

Reich news: SPRING THAW BRINGS FRESH FIGHTING ON SIBERIAN FRONT! GERMAN TROOPS SMASH IVAN TERROR GROUPS! In Rovno, capital of the Reichskommissariat Ukraine, five terrorist leaders had been executed for organising the massacre of a family of German settlers. There was a photograph of the Reich's latest nuclear submarine, the *Grossadmiral Dönitz*, at its new base in Trondheim.

World news: In London it had been announced that King Edward and Queen Wallis were to pay a state visit to the Reich in July 'further to strengthen the deep bonds of respect and affection between the peoples of Great Britain and the German Reich'. In Washington, it was believed that President Kennedy's latest victory in the US primaries had strengthened his chances of winning a second term . . .

The paper slipped from March's fingers and on to the floor.

Half an hour later, the telephone rang.

'*So* sorry to wake you.' Koth was sarcastic. 'I had the impression this was supposed to be priority. Shall I call back tomorrow?'

'No, no.' March was wide awake.

'This you will love. This is beautiful.' For the first time in his life, March heard Koth chuckle. 'Now, you are not playing a joke on me? This is not some little trick you and Jaeger have worked out between you?'

'Who is it?'

'The background first.' Koth was enjoying himself too much to be hurried. 'We had to go back a long way to get a match. A very long way. But we got one. Perfect. No mistake. Your man has a record all right. He was arrested just once in his life. By our colleagues in Munich, forty years ago. To be precise, on the ninth of November 1923.'

There was a silence. Five, six, seven seconds elapsed.

'Ah! I can tell that even you appreciate the significance of the date.'

'An alter Kämpfer.' March reached down beside his chair for his cigarettes. 'His name?'

'Indeed. An old comrade. Arrested with the Führer after the Bürgerbräukeller Putsch. You have fished out of the lake one of the glorious pioneers of the National Socialist Revolution.' Koth laughed again. 'A wiser man might have left him where he was.'

'*What is his name?*'

AFTER Koth had rung off, March paced around the apartment for five minutes, smoking furiously. Then he made three calls. The first was to Max Jaeger. The second was to the Duty Officer at Werderscher Markt. The third was to a Berlin number. A man's voice, slurred with sleep, answered just as March was about to give up.

'Rudi? It's Xavier March.'

'Zavi? Are you crazy? It's midnight.'

'Not quite.' March patrolled the faded carpet, the body of the telephone in one hand, the receiver tucked beneath his chin. 'I need your help.'

'For God's sake!'

'What can you tell me about a man named Josef Buhler?'

THAT night, March had a dream. He was at the lakeshore again in the rain and there was the body, face down in the mud. He pulled at the shoulder – pulled hard – but he could not move it. The body was grey-white lead. But when he turned to leave, it grabbed his leg, and began pulling him towards the surface of the lake. He scrabbled at the earth, trying to dig his fingers into the soft mud, but there was nothing to hold on to. The corpse's grip was immensely strong. And as they went under, its face became Pili's, contorted with rage, grotesque in its shame, screaming 'I hate you . . . I hate you . . . I hate you . . .'

PART TWO

WEDNESDAY 15 APRIL

détente, s.f. 1 (a) Relaxation, loosening, slackening (of something that is taut); relaxing (of muscles). (b) Easing (of political situation).

[illegible] and apartment [illegible]

[illegible] the [illegible] and [illegible] the shower dangled a thin [illegible] cold water [illegible] with his father's old cut-throat razor [illegible] through the open [illegible]

[illegible] of the [illegible] on [illegible] of the early [illegible] in the [illegible] the gates or [illegible] in the [illegible] the [illegible] with possibilities, the day had yet to fall.

[illegible] was laid out [illegible]

[illegible] with Black [illegible]

[illegible]

[illegible]

Black Sam Browne belt. Black cap with [illegible] and [illegible] eagle. Black leather gloves.

[illegible] at himself in the [illegible] He [illegible] stared back. He picked up his service pistol, a 9 mm Luger, from the dressing table, checked the action, and slotted it into his holster. Then he stepped out into the morning.

ONE

Yesterday's rain was a bad memory, already half-faded from the streets. The sun – the miraculous, impartial sun – bounced and glittered on the shopfronts and apartment windows.

In the bathroom, the rusted pipes clanked and groaned, the shower dangled a thread of cold water. March shaved with his father's old cut-throat razor. Through the open bathroom window, he could hear the sounds of the city waking up: the whine and clatter of the first tram; the distant hum of the traffic on Tauentzien Strasse; the footsteps of the early risers hurrying to the big Wittenberg Platz U-bahn station; the rattle of shutters going up in the bakery across the street. It was not quite seven and Berlin was alive with possibilities the day had yet to dull.

His uniform was laid out in the bedroom: the body-armour of authority.

Brown shirt, with black leather buttons. Black tie. Black breeches. Black jackboots (the rich smell of polished leather).

Black tunic: four silver buttons; three parallel silvered threads on the shoulder tabs; on the left sleeve, a red-white-and-black swastika armband; on the right, a diamond enclosing the gothic letter 'K', for Kriminalpolizei.

Black Sam Browne belt. Black cap with silver death's head and Party eagle. Black leather gloves.

March stared at himself in the mirror, and a Sturmbannführer of the Waffen-SS stared back. He picked up his service pistol, a 9 mm Luger, from the dressing table, checked the action, and slotted it into his holster. Then he stepped out into the morning.

*

'SURE you have enough?'

Rudolf Halder grinned at March's sarcasm and unloaded his tray: cheese, ham, salami, three hard-boiled eggs, a pile of black bread, milk, a cup of steaming coffee. He arranged the dishes in a neat row on the white linen tablecloth.

'I understand that breakfasts provided by the Reich Main Security Office are not normally so lavish.'

They were in the dining room of the Prinz Friedrich Karl Hotel in Dorotheen Strasse, midway between Kripo headquarters and Halder's office in the Reichsarchiv. March used it regularly. The Friedrich Karl was a cheap stopover for tourists and salesmen, but it did a good breakfast. Dangling limply from a pole over the entrance was a European flag – the twelve gold stars of the European Community nations, on a dark-blue background. March guessed that the manager, Herr Brecker, had bought it second-hand and hung it there in an effort to drum up some foreign custom. It did not appear to have worked. A glance around the restaurant's shabby clientele and bored staff suggested little danger of being overheard.

As usual, people gave March's uniform a wide berth. Every few minutes, the walls shook as a train pulled into the Friedrich Strasse station.

'Is that all you're having?' asked Halder. 'Coffee?' He shook his head. 'Black coffee, cigarettes and whisky. As a diet: not good. Now I think of it, I haven't seen you eat a decent meal since you and Klara split.' He cracked one of his eggs and began removing pieces of shell.

March thought: of all of us, Halder has changed the least. Beneath the layer of fat, behind the slackened muscle of incipient middle age, there lurked still the ghost of the gangling recruit, straight from university, who had joined the U-174 more than twenty years before. He had been a wireless operator – a bad one, rushed through training and into service at the start of 1942, when losses were at their height, and Dönitz was ransacking Germany for replacements. Then as now, he wore wire-framed glasses and had thin ginger hair which stuck out at the back in a duck's tail. During a voyage, while the rest of the men grew beards, Halder sprouted orange tufts on his cheeks and chin, like a moulting cat. The fact that he was in the U-boat service at all was a ghastly mistake, a joke. He was clumsy, barely capable of changing a fuse. He had been designed by nature to be an academic, not a submariner, and he passed each voyage in a sweat of fear and sea-sickness.

Yet he was popular. U-boat crews were superstitious, and somehow the word got around that Rudi Halder brought good luck. So they looked after him, covering his mistakes, letting him have an extra half-hour to groan and thrash around on his bunk. He became a sort of mascot. When peace came, astonished to find that he had survived, Halder resumed his studies at the history faculty of Berlin University. In 1958 he had joined the team of academics working at the Reichsarchiv on the official history of the war. He had come full circle, spending his days hunched in a subterranean chamber in Berlin, piecing together the same grand strategy of which he had once been a tiny, frightened component. *The U-boat Service: Operations and Tactics, 1939–46* had been published in 1963. Now Halder was helping compile the third volume of the history of the German Army on the Eastern Front.

'It's like working at the Volkswagen works in Fallersleben,' said Halder. He took a bite out of his egg and chewed for a while. 'I do the wheels, Jaeckel does the doors, Schmidt drops in the engine.'

'How long is it going to take?'

'Oh, forever, I should think. Resources no object. This is the Arch of Triumph in words, remember? Every shot, every skirmish, every snowflake, every sneeze. Someone is even going to write the Official History of the Official Histories. Me, I'll do another five years.'

'And then?'

Halder brushed egg crumbs from his tie. 'A chair in a small university somewhere in the south. A house in the country with Ilse and the kids. A couple of books, respectfully reviewed. My ambitions are modest. If nothing else, this kind of work gives you a sense of perspective about your own mortality. Talking of which . . .' From his inside pocket he pulled a sheet of paper. 'With the compliments of the Reichsarchiv.'

It was a photocopy of a page from an old Party directory. Four passport-sized portraits of uniformed officials, each accompanied by a brief biography, Brün, Brunner. Buch. And Buhler.

Halder said: '*Guide to the Personalities of the NSDAP*. 1951 edition.'

'I know it well.'

'A pretty bunch, you'll agree.'

The body in the Havel was Buhler's, no question of it. He stared up at March through his rimless spectacles, prim and humourless, his lips pursed. It was a bureaucrat's face, a lawyer's face; a face you might see a thousand times and never be able to describe; sharp in the flesh, fudged in memory; the face of a machine-man.

'As you will see,' resumed Halder, 'a pillar of National Socialist respectability. Joined the Party in '22 – that's as respectable as they come. Worked as a lawyer with Hans Frank, the Führer's own attorney. Deputy President of the Academy of German Law.'

' "State Secretary, General Government, 1939," ' read March. ' "SS-Brigadeführer." ' Brigadeführer, by God. He took out a notebook and began to write.

'Honorary rank,' said Halder, his mouth full of food. 'I doubt if he ever fired a shot in anger. He was strictly a desk man. When Frank was sent out as Governor in '39 to run what was left of Poland, he must have taken his old legal partner, Buhler, with him, to be chief bureaucrat. You should try some of this ham. Very good.'

March was scribbling quickly. 'How long was Buhler in the East?'

'Twelve years, I guess. I checked the *Guide* for 1952. There's no entry for Buhler. So '51 must have been his last year.'

March stopped writing and tapped his teeth with his pen. 'Will you excuse me for a couple of minutes?'

There was a telephone booth in the foyer. He rang the Kripo switchboard and asked for his own extension. A voice growled: 'Jaeger.'

'Listen, Max.' March repeated what Halder had told him. 'The *Guide* mentions a wife.' He held up the sheet of paper to the booth's dim electric light and squinted at it. 'Edith Tulard. Can you find her? To get the body positively identified.'

'She's dead.'

'What?'

'She died more than ten years ago. I checked with the SS records bureau – even honorary ranks have to give next of kin. Buhler had no kids, but I've traced his sister. She's a widow, seventy-two years old, named Elizabeth Trinkl. Lives in Fürstenwalde.' March knew it: a small town about forty-five minutes' drive south-east of Berlin. 'The local cops are bringing her straight to the morgue.'

'I'll meet you there.'

'Another thing. Buhler had a house on Schwanenwerder.'

So that explained the location of the body. 'Good work, Max.' March rang off and made his way back to the dining room.

Halder had finished his breakfast. He threw down his

napkin as March returned and leaned back in his chair. 'Excellent. Now I can almost tolerate the prospect of sorting through fifteen hundred signals from Kleist's First Panzer Army.' He began picking his teeth. 'We should meet up more often. Ilse is always saying: When are you going to bring Zavi round?' He leaned forward. 'Listen: there's a woman at the archives, working on the history of the Bund deutscher Mädel in Bavaria, 1935 to 1950. A stunner. Husband disappeared on the Eastern front last year, poor devil. Anyway: you and she. What about it? We could have you both round, say next week?'

March smiled. 'You're very kind.'

'That's not an answer.'

'True.' He tapped the photocopy. 'Can I keep this?'

Halder shrugged. 'Why not?'

'One last thing.'

'Go ahead.'

'State Secretary to the General Government. What would he have done, exactly?'

Halder spread his hands. The backs were thick with freckles, wisps of reddish-gold hair curled from his cuffs. 'He and Frank had absolute authority. They did whatever they liked. At that time, the main priority would have been resettlement.'

March wrote 'resettlement' in his notebook, and ringed it. 'How did that happen?'

'What is this? A seminar?' Halder arranged a triangle of plates in front of him – two smaller ones to the left, a larger one to the right. He pushed them together so they touched. 'All this is Poland before the war. After '39, the western provinces' – he tapped the small plates – 'were brought into Germany. Reichsgau Danzig-West Prussia and Reichsgau Wartheland.' He detached the large plate. 'And this became the General Government. The rump state. The two western provinces were Germanised. It's not my field, you understand, but I've seen some figures. In 1940, they set a target density of one hundred Germans per square kilometre. And they managed it in the first three years. An incredible operation, considering the war was still on.'

'How many people were involved?'

'One million. The SS eugenics bureau found Germans in places you'd never have dreamed of – Rumania, Bulgaria, Serbia, Croatia. If your skull had the proper measurements and you came from the right village – you were just given a ticket.'

'And Buhler?'

'Ah. Well. To make room for a million Germans in the new Reichsgaue, they had to move out a million Poles.'

'And they went to the General Government?'

Halder turned his head and glanced around furtively, to make sure he was not overheard – 'the German look', people called it. 'They also had to cope with the Jews being expelled from Germany and the western territories – France, Holland, Belgium.'

'Jews?'

'Yes, yes. Keep your voice down.' Halder was speaking so quietly, March had to lean across the table to hear. 'You can imagine – it was chaos. Overcrowding. Starvation. Disease. From what one can gather, the place is still a shit-hole, despite what they say.'

Every week the newspapers and television carried appeals from the East Ministry for settlers willing to move to the General Government. 'Germans! Claim your birthright! A farmstead – free! Income guaranteed for the first five years.' The advertisements showed happy colonists living in luxury. But word of the real story had filtered back – an existence conditioned by poor soil, back-breaking work, and drab satellite towns to which the Germans had to return at dusk for fear of attack from local partisans. The General Government was worse than the Ukraine; worse than Ostland; worse, even, than Muscovy.

A waiter came over to offer more coffee. March waved him away. When the man was out of earshot, Halder continued in the same low tone: 'Frank ran everything from Wawel Castle in Krakau. That would have been where Buhler was based. I have a friend who works in the official archives there. God, he has some stories . . . Apparently, the luxury was incredible. Like something out of the Roman Empire. Paintings, tapestries, looted treasures from the church, jewellery. Bribes in cash and bribes in kind, if you know what I mean.' Halder's blue eyes shone at the thought, his eyebrows danced.

'And Buhler was involved in this?'

'Who knows? If not, he must have been about the only one who wasn't.'

'That would explain why he had a house on Schwanenwerder.'

Halder whistled softly. 'There you are then. We had the wrong sort of war, my friend. Cooped up in a stinking metal coffin two hundred metres under the Atlantic, when we could have been in a Silesian castle, sleeping on silk with a couple of Polish girls for company.'

There was more March would have liked to ask him but he had no time. As they were leaving, Halder said: 'So you'll come round to dinner with my BdM woman?'

'I'll think about it.'

'Maybe we can persuade her to wear her uniform.' Standing outside the hotel, with his hands thrust deep in his pockets and his long scarf wrapped twice around his neck, Halder looked even more like a student. Suddenly he struck his forehead with the flat of his hand. 'I clean forgot! I meant to tell you. My memory . . . A couple of Sipo guys were round at the Archiv last week asking about you.'

March felt his smile shrink. 'The Gestapo? What did they want?' He managed to keep his tone light, off-hand.

'Oh, the usual sort of stuff. "What was he like during the

war? Does he have any strong political views? Who are his friends?" What's going on, Zavi? You up for promotion or something?'

'I must be.' He told himself to relax. It was probably only a routine check. He must remember to ask Max if he had heard anything about a new screening.

'Well, when they've made you head of the Kripo, don't forget your old friends.'

March laughed. 'I won't.' They shook hands. As they parted, March said: 'I wonder if Buhler had any enemies.'

'Oh yes,' said Halder, 'of course.'

'Who were they then?'

Halder shrugged. 'Thirty million Poles, for a start.'

THE only person on the second floor at Werderscher Markt was a Polish cleaning woman. Her back was to March as he came out of the lift. All he could see was a large rump resting on the soles of a pair of black rubber boots, and the red scarf tied round her hair bobbing as she scrubbed the floor. She was singing softly to herself in her native language. As she heard him approach she stopped and turned her head to the wall. He squeezed past her and went into his office. When the door had closed he heard her begin singing again.

It was not yet nine. He hung his cap by the door and unbuttoned his tunic. There was a large brown envelope on his desk. He opened it and shook out the contents, the scene-of-crime photographs. Glossy colour pictures of Buhler's body, sprawled like a sunbather's at the side of the lake.

He lifted the ancient typewriter from the top of the filing cabinet and carried it across to his desk. From a wire basket he took two pieces of much-used carbon paper, two flimsy sheets and one standard report form, arranged them in order, and wound them into the machine. Then he lit a cigarette and stared at the dead plant for a few minutes.

He began to type.

To: Chief, VB3(a)
Subject: Unidentified body (male)
From: X. March, SS-Sturmbannführer 15.4.64

I beg to report the following.

1. At 06.28 yesterday, I was ordered to attend the recovery of a body from the Havel. The body had been discovered by SS-Schütze Hermann Jost at 06.02 and reported to the Ordnungspolizei (statement attached).

2. No male of the correct description having been reported missing, I arranged for the fingerprints of the subject to be checked against records.

3. This has enabled the subject to be identified as Doctor Josef Buhler, a Party member with the honorary rank of SS-Brigadeführer. The subject served as State Secretary in the General Government, 1939–51.

4. A preliminary investigation at the scene by SS-Sturmbannführer Doctor August Eisler indicated the likely cause of death as drowning, and the likely time of death some time on the night of 13 April.

5. The subject lived on Schwanenwerder, close to where the body was found.

6. There were no obvious suspicious circumstances.

7. A full autopsy examination will be carried out following formal identification of the subject by next-of-kin.

March pulled the report out of the typewriter, signed it, and left it with a messenger in the foyer on his way out.

THE old woman was sitting erect on a hard wooden bench in the Seydel Strasse mortuary. She wore a brown tweed suit, brown hat with a drooping feather, sturdy brown shoes and grey woollen stockings. She was staring straight ahead, a handbag clasped in her lap, oblivious to the medical orderlies, the policemen, the grieving relatives passing in the corridor. Max Jaeger sat beside her, arms folded, legs outstretched, looking bored. As March arrived, he took him to one side.

'Been here ten minutes. Hardly spoken.'

'In shock?'

'I suppose.'

'Let's get it over with.'

The old woman did not look up as March sat on the bench beside her. He said softly: 'Frau Trinkl, my name is March. I am an investigator with the Berlin Kriminalpolizei. We have to complete a report on your brother's death, and we need you to identify his body. Then we'll take you home. Do you understand?'

Frau Trinkl turned to face him. She had a thin face, thin nose (her brother's nose), thin lips. A cameo brooch gathered a blouse of frilly purple at her bony throat.

'Do you understand?' he repeated.

She gazed at him with clear grey eyes, unreddened by crying. Her voice was clipped and dry: 'Perfectly.'

They moved across the corridor into a small, windowless reception room. The floor was made of wood blocks. The walls were lime green. In an effort to lighten the gloom, someone had stuck up tourist posters given away by the Deutsche Reichsbahn Gesellschaft: a night-time view of the Great Hall, the Führer Museum at Linz, the

Starnberger See in Bavaria. The poster which had hung on the fourth wall had been torn down, leaving pockmarks in the plaster, like bullet holes.

A clatter outside signalled the arrival of the body. It was wheeled in, covered by a sheet, on a metal trolley. Two attendants in white tunics parked it in the centre of the floor – a buffet lunch awaiting its guests. They left and Jaeger closed the door.

'Are you ready?' asked March. She nodded. He turned back the sheet and Frau Trinkl stationed herself at his shoulder. As she leaned forward, a strong smell – of peppermint lozenges, of perfume mingled with camphor, an old lady's smell – washed across his face. She stared at the corpse for a long time, then opened her mouth as if to say something, but all that emerged was a sigh. Her eyes closed. March caught her as she fell.

'IT'S him,' she said. 'I haven't set eyes on him for ten years, and he's fatter, and I've never seen him before without his spectacles, not since he was a child. But it's him.' She was on a chair under the poster of Linz, leaning forward with her head between her knees. Her hat had fallen off. Thin strands of white hair hung down over her face. The body had been wheeled away.

The door opened and Jaeger returned carrying a glass of water, which he pressed into her skinny hand. 'Drink this.' She held it for a moment, then raised it to her lips and took a sip. 'I never faint,' she said. 'Never.' Behind her, Jaeger made a face.

'Of course,' said March. 'I need to ask some questions. Are you well enough? Stop me if I tire you.' He took out his notebook. 'Why had you not seen your brother for ten years?'

'After Edith died – his wife – we had nothing in

common. We were never close in any case. Even as children. I was eight years older than him.'

'His wife died some time ago?'

She thought for a moment. 'In '53, I think. Winter. She had cancer.'

'And in all the time since then you never heard from him? Were there any other brothers and sisters?'

'No. Just the two of us. He did write occasionally. I had a letter from him on my birthday two weeks ago.' She fumbled in her handbag and produced a single sheet of notepaper – good quality, creamy and thick, with an engraving of the Schwanenwerder house as a letterhead. The writing was copperplate, the message as formal as an official receipt: 'My dear sister! Heil Hitler! I send you greetings on your birthday. I earnestly hope that you are in good health, as I am. Josef.' March refolded it and handed it back. No wonder nobody missed him.

'In his other letters, did he ever mention anything worrying him?'

'What had he to be worried about?' She spat out the words. 'Edith inherited a fortune in the war. They had money. He lived in fine style, I can tell you.'

'There were no children?'

'He was sterile.' She said this without emphasis, as if describing his hair colour. 'Edith was so unhappy. I think that was what killed her. She sat alone in that big house – it was cancer of the soul. She used to love music – she played the piano beautifully. A Bechstein, I remember. And he – he was such a cold man.'

Jaeger grunted from the other side of the room: 'So you didn't think much of him?'

'No, I did not. Not many people did.' She turned back to March. 'I have been a widow for twenty-four years. My husband was a navigator in the Luftwaffe, shot down over France. I was not left destitute – nothing like that. But the pension . . . *very* small for one who was used to something a little better. Not once in all that time did Josef offer to help me.'

'What about his leg?' It was Jaeger again, his tone antagonistic. He had clearly decided to take Buhler's side in this family dispute. 'What happened to that?' His manner suggested he thought she might have stolen it.

The old lady ignored him and gave her answer to March. 'He would never speak of it himself, but Edith told me the story. It happened in 1951, when he was still in the General Government. He was travelling with an escort on the road from Krakau to Kattowitz when his car was ambushed by Polish partisans. A landmine, she said. His driver was killed. Josef was lucky only to lose a foot. After that, he retired from government service.'

'And yet he still swam?' March looked up from his notebook. 'You know that we discovered him wearing swimming trunks?'

She gave a tight smile. 'My brother was a fanatic about everything, Herr March, whether it was politics or health. He did not smoke, he never touched alcohol, and he took exercise every day, despite his . . . disability. So, no: I am not in the least surprised that he should have been swimming.' She set down her glass and picked up her hat. 'I would like to go home now, if I may.'

March stood up and held out his hand, helping her to her feet. 'What did Doctor Buhler do after 1951? He was only – what? – in his early fifties?'

'That is the strange thing.' She opened her handbag and took out a small mirror. She checked her hat was on straight, tucking stray hairs out of sight with nervous, jerky movements of her fingers. 'Before the war, he was so ambitious. He would work eighteen hours a day, every day of the week. But when he left Krakau, he gave up. He never even returned to the law. For more than ten years after poor

Edith died, he just sat alone in that big house all day and did nothing.'

Two floors below, in the basement of the morgue, SS Surgeon August Eisler of Kriminalpolizei Department VD2 (Pathology) was going about his business with his customary clumsy relish. Buhler's chest had been opened in the standard fashion: a Y incision, a cut from each shoulder to the pit of the stomach, a straight line down to the pubic bone. Now Eisler had his hands deep inside the stomach, green gloves sheened with red, twisting, cutting, pulling. March and Jaeger leaned against the wall by the open doorway, smoking a couple of Jaeger's cigars.

'Have you seen what your man had for lunch?' said Eisler. 'Show them, Eck.'

Eisler's assistant wiped his hands on his apron and held up a transparent plastic bag. There was something small and green in the bottom.

'Lettuce. Digests slowly. Stays in the intestinal tract for hours.'

March had worked with Eisler before. Two winters ago, with snow blocking the Unter den Linden and ice skating competitions on the Tegeler See, a barge master named Kempf had been pulled out of the Spree, almost dead with cold. He had expired in the ambulance on the way to hospital. Accident or murder? The time at which he had fallen into the water was crucial. Looking at the ice extending two metres out from the banks, March had estimated fifteen minutes as the maximum time he could have survived in the water. Eisler had said forty-five and his view had prevailed with the prosecutor. It was enough to destroy the alibi of the barge's second mate, and hang him.

Afterwards, the prosecutor – a decent, old-fashioned sort – had called March into his office and locked the door.

Then he'd shown him Eisler's 'evidence': copies of documents stamped geheime Reichssache – Top Secret State Document – and dated Dachau, 1942. It was a report of freezing experiments carried out on condemned prisoners, restricted to the department of the SS Surgeon-General. The men had been handcuffed and dumped in tanks of icy water, retrieved at intervals to have their temperatures taken, right up to the point at which they died. There were photographs of heads bobbing between floating chunks of ice, and charts showing heat-loss, projected and actual. The experiments had lasted two years and been conducted, among others, by a young Untersturmführer, August Eisler. That night, March and the prosecutor had gone to a bar in Kreuzberg and got blind drunk. Next day, neither of them mentioned what had happened. They never spoke to one another again.

'If you expect me to come out with some fancy theory, March, forget it.'

'I'd never expect that.'

Jaeger laughed. 'Nor would I.'

Eisler ignored their mirth. 'It was a drowning, no question about it. Lungs full of water, so he must have been breathing when he went into the lake.'

'No cuts?' asked March. 'Bruises?'

'Do you want to come over here and do this job? No? Then believe me: he drowned. There are no contusions to the head to indicate he was hit or held under.'

'A heart attack? Some kind of seizure?'

'Possible,' admitted Eisler. Eck handed him a scalpel. 'I won't know until I've completed a full examination of the internal organs.'

'How long will that take?'

'As long as it takes.'

Eisler positioned himself behind Buhler's head. Tenderly, he stroked the hair towards him, off the corpse's forehead, as if soothing a fever. Then he hunched down low and jabbed the scalpel through the left temple. He drew it in an arc across the top of the face, just below the hairline. There was a scrape of metal and bone. Eck grinned at them. March sucked a lungful of smoke from his cigar.

Eisler put the scalpel into a metal dish. Then he bent down once more and worked his forefingers into the deep cut. Gradually, he began peeling back the scalp. March turned his head away and closed his eyes. He prayed that no one he loved, or liked, or even vaguely knew, ever had to be desecrated by the butcher's work of an autopsy.

Jaeger said: 'So what do you think?'

Eisler had picked up a small, hand-sized circular saw. He switched it on. It whined like a dentist's drill.

March took a final puff on his cigar. 'I think we should get out of here.'

They made their way down the corridor. Behind them, from the autopsy room, they heard the saw's note deepen as it bit into the bone.

TWO

Half an hour later, Xavier March was at the wheel of one of the Kripo's Volkswagens, following the curving path of the Havelchaussee, high above the lake. Sometimes the view was hidden by trees. Then he would round a bend, or the forest would thin, and he would see the water again, sparkling in the April sun like a tray of diamonds. Two yachts skimmed the surface – children's cut-outs, white triangles brilliant against the blue.

He had the window wound down, his arm resting on the sill, the breeze plucking at his sleeve. On either side, the bare branches of the trees were flecked with the green of late spring. In another month, the road would be nose-to-tail with cars: Berliners escaping from the city to sail or swim, or picnic, or simply to lie in the sun on one of the big public beaches. But today there was still enough of a chill in the air, and winter was still close enough, for March to have the road to himself. He passed the red-brick sentinel of the Kaiser Wilhelm Tower and the road began to drop to lake level.

Within ten minutes he was at the spot where the body had been discovered. In the fine weather it looked utterly different. This was a tourist spot, a vantage-point known as the Grosse Fenster: the Picture Window. What had been a mass of grey yesterday was now a gloriously clear view, across eight kilometres of water, right up to Spandau.

He parked, and retraced the route Jost had been running when he discovered the body – down the woodland track, a sharp right turn, and along the side of the lake. He did it a second time; and a third. Satisfied, he got back into the car and drove over the low bridge on to Schwanenwerder. A red and white pole blocked the road. A sentry emerged from a small hut, a clipboard in his hand, a rifle slung across his shoulder.

'Your identification, please.'

March handed his Kripo ID through the open window. The sentry studied it and returned it. He saluted. 'That's fine, Herr Sturmbannführer.'

'What's the procedure here?'

'Stop every car. Check the papers and ask where they're going. If they look suspicious, we ring the house, see if they're expected. Sometimes we search the car. It depends whether the Reichsminister is in residence.'

'Do you keep a record?'

'Yes, sir.'

'Do me a favour. Look and see if Doctor Josef Buhler had any visitors on Monday night.'

The sentry hitched his rifle and went back into his hut. March could see him turning the pages of a ledger. When he returned he shook his head. 'Nobody for Doctor Buhler all day.'

'Did he leave the island at all?'

'We don't keep a record of residents, sir, only visitors. And we don't check people going, only coming.'

'Right.' March looked past the guard, across the lake. A scattering of seagulls swooped low over the water, crying. Some yachts were moored to a jetty. He could hear the clink of their masts in the wind.

'What about the shore. Is that watched at all?'

The guard nodded. 'The river police have a patrol every couple of hours. But most of those houses have enough sirens and dogs to guard a KZ. We just keep the sightseers away.'

KZ: pronounced *kat-set*. Less of a mouthful than Konzentrationslager. Concentration camp.

There was a sound of powerful engines gunning in the distance. The guard turned to look up the road behind him, towards the island.

'One moment, sir.'

Round the bend, at high speed, came a grey BMW with its headlights on, followed by a long black Mercedes limousine, and then another BMW. The sentry stepped back, pressed a switch, the barrier rose, and he saluted. As the convoy swept by, March had a glimpse of the Mercedes's passengers – a young woman, beautiful, an actress perhaps, or a model, with short blonde hair; and, next to her, staring straight ahead, a wizened old man, his rodent-like profile instantly recognisable. The cars roared off towards the city.

'Does he always travel that quickly?' asked March.

The sentry gave him a knowing look. 'The Reichsminister has been screen-testing, sir. Frau Goebbels is due back at lunchtime.'

'Ah. All is clear.' March turned the key in the ignition and the Volkswagen came to life. 'Did you know that Doctor Buhler was dead?'

'No, sir.' The sentry gave no sign of interest. 'When did that happen?'

'Monday night. He was washed up a few hundred metres from here.'

'I heard they'd found a body.'

'What was he like?'

'I hardly noticed him, sir. He didn't go out much. No visitors. Never spoke. But then, a lot of them end up like that out here.'

'Which was his house?'

'You can't miss it. It's on the east side of the island. Two large towers. It's one of the biggest.'

'Thanks.'

As he drove down the causeway, March checked in his mirror. The sentry stood looking after him for a few seconds, then hitched his rifle again, turned and walked slowly back to his hut.

Schwanenwerder was small, less than a kilometre long and half a kilometre wide, with a single loop of road running one-way, clockwise. To reach Buhler's property, March had to travel three-quarters of the way round the island. He drove cautiously, slowing almost to a halt each time he glimpsed one of the houses off to his left.

The place had been named after the famous colonies of swans which lived at the southern end of the Havel. It had become fashionable towards the end of the last century. Most of its buildings dated from then: large villas, steep-roofed and stone-fronted in the French style, with long drives and lawns, protected from prying eyes by high walls and trees. A piece of the ruined Tuileries Palace stood incongruously by the roadside – a pillar and a section of arch carted back from Paris by some long-dead Wilhelmine businessman. No one stirred. Occasionally, through the bars of a gate, he saw a guard dog, and – once – a gardener raking leaves. The owners were either at work in the city, or away, or lying low.

March knew the identities of a few of them: Party bosses; a motor industry tycoon, grown fat on the profits of slave labour immediately after the war; the managing director of Wertheim's, the great department store on Potsdamer Platz that had been confiscated from its Jewish owners more than thirty years before; an armaments manufacturer; the head of an engineering conglomerate building the great Autobahnen into the eastern territories. He wondered how Buhler could have afforded to keep such wealthy company, then he remembered Halder's description: luxury like the Roman Empire . . .

'KP17, this is KHQ. KP17, answer please!' A woman's urgent voice filled the car. March picked up the radio handset concealed under the dashboard.

'This is KP17. Go ahead.'

'KP17, I have Sturmbannführer Jaeger for you.'

He had arrived outside the gates to Buhler's villa. Through the metalwork, March could see a yellow curve of drive and the towers, exactly as the sentry had described.

'You said trouble,' boomed Jaeger, 'and we've got it.'

'Now what?'

'I hadn't been back here ten minutes when two of our esteemed colleagues from the Gestapo arrived. "In view of Party Comrade Buhler's prominent position, blah blah blah, the case has been redesignated a security matter." '

March thumped his hand against the steering wheel. 'Shit!'

' "All documents to be handed over to the Security Police forthwith, reports required from investigating officers on current status of inquiry, Kripo inquiry to be closed, effective immediately." '

'When did this happen?'

'It's happening now. They're sitting in our office.'

'Did you tell them where I am?'

'Of course not. I just left them to it and said I'd try and find you. I've come straight to the control room.' Jaeger's voice dropped. March could imagine him turning his back on the woman operator. 'Listen, Zavi, I wouldn't recommend any heroics. They mean serious business, believe me. The Gestapo will be swarming over Schwanenwerder any minute.'

March stared at the house. It was utterly still, deserted. Damn the Gestapo.

He made up his mind at that moment. He said: 'I can't hear you, Max. I'm sorry. The line is breaking up. I haven't been able to understand anything you've said. Request you report radio fault. Out.' He switched off the receiver.

About fifty metres before the house, on the right side of the road, March had passed a gated track leading into the woods that covered the centre of the island. Now he put the Volkswagen into reverse gear, rapidly backed up to it, and parked. He trotted back to Buhler's gates. He did not have much time.

They were locked. That was to be expected. The lock itself was a solid metal block a metre and a half off the ground. He wedged the toe of his boot into it and stepped up. There was a row of iron spikes, thirty centimetres apart, running along the top of the gate, just above his head. Gripping one in either hand, he hauled himself up until he was in a position to swing his left leg over. A hazardous business. For a moment he sat astride the gate, recovering his breath. Then he dropped down to the gravel driveway on the other side.

The house was large and of a curious design. It had three storeys capped by a steep roof of blue slate. To the left were the two stone towers the sentry had described. These were attached to the main body of the house, which had a balcony with a stone balustrade running the entire length of the first floor. The balcony was supported by pillars. Behind these, half-hidden in the shadows, was the main entrance. March started towards it. Beech trees and firs grew in untended profusion along the sides of the drive. The borders were neglected. Dead leaves, unswept since the winter, blew across the lawn.

He stepped between the pillars. The first surprise. The front door was unlocked.

March stood in the hall and looked round. There was an oak staircase to the right, two doors to the left, a gloomy passage straight ahead which he guessed led to the kitchen.

He tried the first door. Behind it was a panelled dining room. A long table and twelve high-backed carved chairs. Cold and musty from disuse.

The next door led to the drawing room. He continued his mental inventory. Rugs on a polished wooden floor. Heavy furniture upholstered in rich brocade. Tapestries on the wall – good ones, too, if March was any judge, which he wasn't. By the window was a grand piano on which stood two large photographs. March tilted one towards the light, which shone weakly through the dusty leaded panes. The frame was heavy silver, with a swastika motif. The picture showed Buhler and his wife on their wedding day, coming down a flight of steps between an honour guard of SA men holding oak boughs over the happy couple. Buhler was also in SA uniform. His wife had flowers woven into her hair and was – to use a favourite expression of Max Jaeger – as ugly as a box of frogs. Neither was smiling.

March picked up the other photograph, and immediately felt his stomach lurch. There was Buhler again, slightly bowing this time, and shaking hands. The man who was the object of this obeisance had his face half-turned to the camera, as if distracted in mid-greeting by something behind the photographer's shoulder. There was an inscription. March smeared his finger through the grime on the glass to decipher the crabbed writing. 'To Party Comrade Buhler,' it read. 'From Adolf Hitler. 17 May 1945.'

Suddenly, March heard a noise. A sound like a door being kicked, followed by a whimper. He replaced the photograph and went back into the hall. The noise was coming from the end of the passage.

He drew his pistol and edged down the corridor. As he had suspected, it gave on to the kitchen. The noise came again. A cry of terror and a drumming of feet. There was a smell, too – of something filthy.

At the far end of the kitchen was a door. He reached out and grasped the handle and then, with a jerk, pulled the door open. Something huge leapt out of the darkness. A dog, muzzled, eyes wide in terror, went crashing across the floor, down the passage, into the hall and out through the open front door. The larder floor was stinking-thick with faeces and urine and food which the dog had pulled down from the shelves but been unable to eat.

After that, March would have liked to have stopped for a few minutes to steady himself. But he had no time. He put the Luger away and quickly examined the kitchen. A few greasy plates in the sink. On the table, a bottle of vodka, nearly empty, with a glass next to it. There was a door to a cellar, but it was locked; he decided not to break it down. He went upstairs. Bedrooms, bathrooms – everywhere had the same atmosphere of shabby luxury; of a grand lifestyle gone to seed. And everywhere, he noticed, there were paintings – landscapes, religious allegories, portraits – most of them thick with dust. The place had not been properly cleaned for months, maybe years.

The room which must have been Buhler's study was on the top floor of one of the towers. Shelves of legal text books, case studies, decrees. A big desk with a swivel chair next to a window overlooking the back lawn of the house. A long sofa with blankets draped beside it, which appeared to have been regularly slept on. And more photographs. Buhler in his lawyer's robes. Buhler in his SS uniform. Buhler with a group of Nazi big-wigs, one of whom March vaguely recognised as Hans Frank, in the front row of what might have been a concert. All the pictures seemed to be at least twenty years old.

March sat at the desk and looked out of the window. The lawn led down to the Havel's edge. There was a small jetty with a cabin cruiser moored to it and, beyond that, a clear view of the lake, right across to the opposite shore. Far in the distance, the Kladow–Wannsee ferry chugged by.

He turned his attention to the desk itself. A blotter. A heavy brass inkstand. A telephone. He stretched his hand towards it.

It began to ring.

His hand hung motionless. One ring. Two. Three. The stillness of the house magnified the sound; the dusty air vibrated. Four. Five. He flexed his fingers over the receiver. Six. Seven. He picked it up.

'Buhler?' The voice of an old man more dead than alive; a whisper from another world. 'Buhler? Speak to me. Who is that?'

March said: 'A friend.'

Pause. *Click.*

Whoever it was had hung up. March replaced the receiver. Quickly, he began opening the desk drawers at random. A few pencils, some notepaper, a dictionary. He pulled the bottom drawers right out, one after the other, and put his hand into the space.

There was nothing.

There was something.

At the very back, his fingers brushed against an object small and smooth. He pulled it out. A small notebook bound in black leather, an eagle and swastika in gold lettering on the cover. He flicked through it. The Party diary for 1964. He slipped it into his pocket and replaced the drawers.

Outside, Buhler's dog was going crazy, running from side to side along the water's edge, staring across the Havel, whinnying like a horse. Every few seconds it would get down on its hind legs, before resuming its desperate patrol. He could see now that almost the whole of its right side was matted with dried blood. It paid no attention to March as he walked down to the lake.

The heels of his boots rang on the planks of the wooden jetty. Through the gaps between the rickety boards he could see the muddy water a metre below, lapping in the shallows. At the end of the jetty he stepped down into the boat. It rocked with his weight. There were several centimetres of rainwater on the aft deck, clogged with dirt and leaves, a rainbow of oil on the surface. The whole boat stank of fuel. There must be a leak. He stooped and tried the small door to the cabin. It was locked. Cupping his hands, he peered through the window, but it was too dark to see.

He jumped out of the boat and began retracing his steps. The wood of the jetty was weathered grey, except in one place, along the edge opposite the boat. Here there were orange splinters; a scrape of white paint. March was bending to examine the marks when his eye was caught by something pale gleaming in the water, close to the place where the jetty left the shore. He walked back and knelt, and by holding on with his left hand and stretching down as far as he could with his right, he was just able to retrieve it. Pink and chipped, like an ancient china doll, with leather straps and steel buckles, it was an artificial foot.

THE dog heard them first. It cocked its head, turned, and trotted up the lawn towards the house. At once, March dropped his discovery back into the water and ran after the wounded animal. Cursing his stupidity, he worked his way round the side of the house until he stood in the shadow of the towers and could see the gate. The dog was leaping up at the iron work, grunting through its muzzle. On the other side, March could make out two figures standing looking at the house. Then a third appeared with a large pair of bolt-cutters which he clamped on to the lock. After ten seconds of pressure, it gave way with a loud crack.

The dog backed away as the three men filed into the grounds. Like March, they wore the black uniforms of the SS. One seemed to take something from his pocket and walked towards the dog, hand outstretched, as if offering it a treat. The animal cringed. A single shot exploded the silence, echoing round the grounds, sending a flock of rooks cawing into the air above the woods. The man holstered his revolver and gestured at the corpse to one of his companions, who seized it by the hind legs and dragged it into the bushes.

All three men strode towards the house. March stayed

behind the pillar, slowly edging round it as they came up the drive, keeping himself out of sight. It occurred to him that he had no reason to hide. He could tell the Gestapo men he had been searching the property, that he had not received Jaeger's message. But something in their manner, in the casual ruthlessness with which they had disposed of the dog, warned him against it. *They had been here before.*

As they came closer, he could make out their ranks. Two Sturmbannführer and an Obergruppenführer – a brace of majors and a general. What matter of state security could demand the personal attention of a full Gestapo general? The Obergruppenführer was in his late fifties, built like an ox, with the battered face of an ex-boxer. March recognised him from the television, from newspaper photographs.

Who was he?

Then he remembered. Odilo Globocnik. Familiarly known throughout the SS as Globus. Years ago he had been Gauleiter of Vienna. It was Globus who had shot the dog.

'You – ground floor,' said Globus. 'You – check the back.'

They drew their guns and disappeared into the house. March waited half a minute, then set off for the gate. He skirted the perimeter of the garden, avoiding the drive, picking his way instead, almost bent double, through the tangled shrubbery. Five metres from the gate, he paused for breath. Built into the right-hand gatepost, so discreet it was scarcely noticeable, was a rusty metal container – a mail box – in which rested a large brown package.

This is madness, he thought. Absolute madness.

He did not run to the gate: nothing, he knew, attracts the human eye like sudden movement. Instead he made himself stroll from the bushes as if it were the most natural thing in the world, tugged the package from the mail box, and sauntered out of the open gate.

He expected to hear a shout from behind him, or a shot. But the only sound was the rustle of the wind in the trees. When he reached his car, he found his hands were shaking.

THREE

'Why do we believe in Germany and the Führer?'

'Because we believe in God, we believe in Germany which He created in His world, and in the Führer, Adolf Hitler, whom He has sent us.'

'Whom must we primarily serve?'

'Our people and our Führer, Adolf Hitler.'

'Why do we obey?'

'From inner conviction, from belief in Germany, in the Führer, in the Movement and the SS, and from loyalty.'

'Good!' The instructor nodded. 'Good. Reassemble in thirty-five minutes on the south sports field. Jost: stay behind. The rest of you: dismissed!'

With their cropped hair and their loose-fitting light-grey drill uniforms, the class of SS cadets looked like convicts. They filed out noisily, with a scraping of chairs and a stamping of boots on the rough wooden floor. A large portrait of the late Heinrich Himmler smiled down on them, benevolently. Jost looked forlorn, standing to attention, alone in the centre of the classroom. Some of the other cadets gave him curious glances as they left. It had to be Jost, you could see them thinking. Jost: the queer, the loner, always the odd one out. He might well be due another beating in the barracks tonight.

The instructor nodded towards the back of the classroom. 'You have a visitor.'

March was leaning against a radiator, arms folded, watching. 'Hello again, Jost,' he said.

They walked across the vast parade ground. In one corner, a batch of new recruits was being harangued by an SS Hauptscharführer. In another, a hundred youths in black tracksuits stretched, twisted and touched their toes in perfect obedience to shouted commands. Meeting Jost here reminded March of visiting prisoners in jail. The same institutionalised smell, of polish and disinfectant and boiled food. The same ugly concrete blocks of buildings. The same high walls and patrols of guards. Like a KZ, the Sepp Dietrich Academy was both huge and claustrophobic; an entirely self-enclosed world.

'Can we go somewhere private?' asked March.

Jost gave him a contemptuous look. 'There is no privacy here. That's the point.' They took a few more paces. 'I suppose we could try the barracks. Everyone else is eating.'

They turned, and Jost led the way into a low, grey-painted building. Inside, it was gloomy, with a strong smell of male sweat. There must have been a hundred beds, laid out in four rows. Jost had guessed correctly: it was deserted. His bed was two-thirds of the way down, in the centre. March sat on the coarse brown blanket and offered Jost a cigarette.

'It's not allowed in here.'

March waved the packet at him. 'Go ahead. Say I ordered you.'

Jost took it, gratefully. He knelt, opened the metal locker beside the bed, and began searching for something to use as an ashtray. As the door hung open, March could see inside: a pile of paperbacks, magazines, a framed photograph.

'May I?'

Jost shrugged. 'Sure.'

March picked up the photograph. A family group, it reminded him of the picture of the Weisses. Father in an SS uniform. Shy-looking mother in a hat. Daughter: a pretty girl with blonde plaits; fourteen, maybe. And Jost himself: fat-cheeked and smiling, barely recognisable as the harrowed, cropped figure now kneeling on the stone barracks floor.

Jost said: 'Changed, haven't I?'

March was shocked, and tried to hide it. 'Your sister?' he asked.

'She's still at school.'

'And your father?'

'He runs an engineering business in Dresden now. He was one of the first into Russia in '41. Hence the uniform.'

March peered closely at the stern figure. 'Isn't he wearing the Knight's Cross?' It was the highest decoration for bravery.

'Oh yes,' said Jost. 'An authentic war hero.' He took the photograph and replaced it in the locker. 'What about your father?'

'He was in the Imperial Navy,' said March. 'He was wounded in the First War. Never properly recovered.'

'How old were you when he died?'

'Seven.'

'Do you still think about him?'

'Every day.'

'Did you go into the Navy?'

'Almost. I was in the U-boat service.'

Jost shook his head slowly. His pale face had flushed pink. 'We all follow our fathers, don't we?'

'Most of us, maybe. Not all.'

They smoked in silence for a while. Outside, March could hear the physical training session still in progress. 'One, two, three . . . One, two, three . . .'

'These people,' said Jost, and shook his head. 'There's a poem by Erich Kästner – "Marschliedchen".' He closed his eyes and recited:

'You love hatred and want to measure the world against it.
You throw food to the beast in man,
That it may grow, the beast deep within you!
Let the beast in man devour man.'

The young man's sudden passion made March uncomfortable. 'When was that written?'

'1932.'

'I don't know it.'

'You wouldn't. It's banned.'

There was a silence, then March said: 'We now know the identity of the body you discovered. Doctor Josef Buhler. An official of the General Government. An SS-Brigadeführer.'

'Oh God.' Jost rested his head in his hands.

'It has become a more serious matter, you see. Before coming to you, I checked with the sentries' office at the main gate. They have a record that you left the barracks at five-thirty yesterday morning, as usual. So the times in your statement make no sense.'

Jost kept his face covered. The cigarette was burning down between his fingers. March leaned forward, took it, and stubbed it out. He stood.

'Watch,' he said. Jost looked up and March began jogging on the spot.

'This is you, yesterday, right?' March made a show of exhaustion, puffing out his cheeks, wiping his brow with his forearms. Despite himself, Jost smiled. 'Good,' said March. He continued jogging. 'Now you're thinking about some book, or how awful your life is, when you come through the woods and on to the path by the lake. It's pissing with rain and the light's not good, but off to your left you see something . . .'

March turned his head. Jost was watching him intently.

'. . . Whatever it is, it's not the body . . .'

'But . . .'

March stopped and pointed at Jost. 'Don't dig yourself any deeper into the shit, is my advice. Two hours ago I went back and checked the place where the corpse was found – there's no way you could have seen it from the road.'

He resumed jogging. 'So: you see something, but you don't stop. You run past. But being a conscientious fellow, five minutes up the road you decide you had better go back for a second look. And then you discover the body. And only then do you call the cops.'

He grasped Jost's hands and pulled him to his feet. 'Run with me,' he commanded.

'I can't . . .'

'Run!'

Jost broke into an unwilling shuffle. Their feet clattered on the flagstones.

'Now describe what you can see. You're coming out of the woods and you're on the lake path . . .'

'Please . . .'

'Tell me!'

'I . . . I see . . . a car . . .' Jost's eyes were closed. '. . . Then three men . . . It's raining fast, they have coats, hoods – like monks . . . Their heads are down . . . Coming up the slope from the lake . . . I . . . I'm scared . . . I cross the road and run up into the trees so they don't see me . . .'

'Go on.'

'They get into the car and drive off . . . I wait, and then I come out of the woods and I find the body . . .'

'You've missed something.'

'No, I swear . . .'

'You see a face. When they get into the car, you see a face.'

'No . . .'

'Tell me whose face it is, Jost. You can see it. You know it. Tell me.'

'Globus!' shouted Jost. 'I see Globus.'

FOUR

The package he had taken from Buhler's mailbox lay unopened on the front seat next to him. Perhaps it was a bomb, thought March, as he started the Volkswagen. There had been a blitz of parcel bombs over the past few months, blowing off the hands and faces of half a dozen government officials. He might just make page three of the *Tageblatt*: 'Investigator Dies in Mysterious Blast Outside Barracks'.

He drove around Schlachtensee until he found a delicatessen, where he bought a loaf of black bread, some Westphalian ham and a quarter-bottle of Scotch whisky. The sun still shone; the air was fresh. He pointed the car westwards, back towards the lakes. He was going to do something he had not done for years. He was going to have a picnic.

After Göring had been made Chief Reich Huntsman in 1934, there had been some attempt to lighten the Grunewald. Chestnut and linden, beech, birch and oak had all been planted. But the heart of it – as it had been a thousand years ago, when the plains of northern Europe were still forest – the heart remained the hilly woods of melancholy pine. From these forests, five centuries before Christ, the warring German tribes had emerged; and to these forests, twenty-five centuries later, mostly at weekends, in their campers and their trailers, the victorious German tribes returned. The Germans were a race of forest-dwellers. Make a clearing in your mind, if you liked; the trees just waited to reclaim it.

March parked and took his provisions and Buhler's mail bomb, or whatever it was, and walked carefully up a steep path into the forest. Five minutes' climbing brought him to a spot which commanded a clear view of the Havel and of the smoky blue slopes of trees, receding into the distance. The pines smelled strong and sweet in the warmth. Above his head, a large jet rumbled across the sky, making its approach to Berlin Airport. As it disappeared, the noise died, until at last the only sound was birdsong.

March did not want to open the parcel yet. It made him uneasy. So he sat on a large stone – no doubt casually deposited here by the municipal authorities for this very purpose – took a swig of whisky, and began to eat.

Of Odilo Globocnik—Globus—March knew little, and that only by reputation. His fortunes had swung like a weathercock over the past thirty years. An Austrian by birth, a builder by profession, he had become Party leader in Carinthia in the mid-1930s, and ruler of Vienna. Then there had been a period of disgrace, connected with illegal currency speculation, followed by a restoration, as a police chief in the General Government when the war started – he must have known Buhler there, thought March. At the end of the war, there had been a second fall to – where was it? – Trieste, he seemed to remember. But with Himmler's death Globus had come back to Berlin, and now he held some unspecified position within the Gestapo, working directly for Heydrich.

That smashed and brutal face was unmistakable, and, despite the rain and the poor light, Jost had recognised it at once. A portrait of Globus hung in the Academy's Hall of Fame, and Globus himself had delivered a lecture to the awestruck cadets – on the police structures of the Reich – only a few weeks earlier. No wonder Jost had been so frightened. He should have called the Orpo anonymously, and cleared out before they arrived. Better still, from his point of view, he should not have called them at all.

March finished his ham. He took the remains of the bread, broke it into pieces, and scattered the crumbs across the forest floor. Two blackbirds, which had watched him eat, emerged cautiously from the undergrowth and began pecking at them.

He took out the pocket diary. Standard issue to Party members, available in any stationers. Useful information at the beginning. The names of the Party hierarchy: government ministers, kommissariat bosses, gauleiters.

Public holidays: Day of National Reawakening, 30 January; Potsdam Day, 21 March; Führer's birthday, 20 April; National Festival of the German People, 1 May . . .

Map of the Empire with railway journey times: Berlin–Rovno, sixteen hours; Berlin–Tiflis, twenty-seven hours; Berlin–Ufa, four days . . .

The diary itself was a week to two pages, the entries so sparse that at first March thought it was blank. He went through it carefully. There was a tiny cross against 7 March. For 1 April, Buhler had written 'My sister's birthday'. There was another cross against 9 April. On 11 April, he had noted 'Stuckart/Luther, morning – 10'. Finally, on 13 April, the day before his death, Buhler had drawn another small cross. That was all.

March wrote down the dates in his notebook. He began a new page. The death of Josef Buhler. Solutions. One: the death was accidental, the Gestapo had learned of it some hours before the Kripo were informed, and Globus was merely inspecting the body when Jost passed by. Absurd.

Very well. Two: Buhler had been murdered by the Gestapo, and Globus had carried out the execution. Absurd again. The 'Night and Fog' order of 1941 was still in force. Buhler could have been bundled away quite legally to some secret death in a Gestapo cell, his property confiscated by the state. Who would have mourned him? Or questioned his disappearance?

And so, three: Buhler had been murdered by Globus, who had covered his tracks by declaring the death a matter of state security, and by taking over the investigation himself. But why had the Kripo been allowed to get involved at all? What was Globus's motive? Why was Buhler's body left in a public place?

March leaned back against the stone and closed his eyes. The sun on his face made the darkness blood red. A warm haze of whisky enveloped him.

He could not have been asleep more than half an hour, when he heard a rustle in the undergrowth beside him and felt something touch his sleeve. He was awake in an instant, in time to see the white tail and the hindquarters of a deer darting into the trees. A rural idyll, ten kilometres from the heart of the Reich! Either that, or the whisky. He shook his head and picked up the package.

Thick brown paper, neatly wrapped and taped. Indeed, *professionally* wrapped and taped. Crisp lines and sharp creases, an economy of materials used and effort expended. A paradigm of a parcel. No man March had ever met could have produced such an object – it must have been wrapped by a woman. Next, the postmark. Three Swiss stamps, showing tiny yellow flowers on a green background. Posted in Zürich at 1600 hours on 13.4.64. That was the day before yesterday.

He felt his palms begin to sweat as he unwrapped it with exaggerated care, first peeling off the tape and then slowly, centimetre by centimetre, folding back the paper. He lifted it fractionally. Inside was a box of chocolates.

Its lid showed flaxen-haired girls in red check dresses dancing around a maypole in a flowery meadow. Behind them, white-peaked against a fluorescent blue sky, rose the Alps. Overprinted in black gothic script was the legend: 'Birthday Greetings to Our Beloved Führer, 1964'. But there was something odd about it. The box was too heavy just to contain chocolates.

He took out a penknife and cut round the cellophane

cover. He set the box gently on the log. With his face turned away and his arm fully extended, he lifted the lid with the point of the blade. Inside, a mechanism began to whirr. Then this:

Love unspoken
Faith unbroken
All life through
Strings are playing
Hear them saying
'I love you'
Now the echo answers
'Say you'll want me too'
All the world's in love with love
And I love you

Only the tune, of course, not the words; but he knew them well enough. Standing alone on a hill in the Grunewald Forest, March listened as the box played the waltz-duet from Act Three of *The Merry Widow*.

FIVE

The streets on the way back into central Berlin seemed unnaturally quiet and when March reached Werderscher Markt he discovered the reason. A large noticeboard in the foyer announced there would be a government statement at four-thirty. Personnel were to assemble in the staff canteen. Attendance: compulsory. He was just in time.

They had developed a new theory at the Propaganda Ministry, that the best time to make big announcements was at the end of the working day. News was thus received communally, in a comradely spirit: there was no opportunity for private scepticism or defeatism. Also, the broadcasts were always timed so that the workers went home slightly early – at four-fifty, say, rather than five – fostering a sense of contentment, subliminally associating the regime with good feelings. That was how it was these days. The snow-white Propaganda palace on Wilhelm Strasse employed more psychologists than journalists.

The Werderscher Markt staff were filing into the canteen: officers and clerks and typists and drivers, shoulder to shoulder in a living embodiment of the National Socialist ideal. The four television screens, one in each corner, were showing a map of the Reich with a swastika superimposed, accompanied by selections from Beethoven. Occasionally, a male announcer would break in excitedly: 'People of Germany, prepare yourselves for an important statement!' In the old days, on the radio, you got only the music. Progress again.

How many of these events could March remember? They stretched away behind him, islands in time. In '38, he had been called out of his classroom to hear that German troops were entering Vienna and that Austria had returned to the Fatherland. The headmaster, who had been gassed in the First War, had wept on the stage of the little gymnasium, watched by a gaggle of uncomprehending boys.

In '39, he had been at home with his mother in Hamburg. A Friday morning, 11 o'clock, the Führer's speech relayed live from the Reichstag: '*I am from now on just the first soldier of the German Reich. I have once more put on that uniform that was most sacred and dear to me. I will not take it off until victory is secured, or I will not survive the outcome.*' A thunder of applause. This time his mother had wept – a hum of misery as her body rocked backwards and forwards. March, seventeen, had looked away in shame, sought out the photograph of his father – splendid in the uniform of the Imperial German Navy – and he had thought: *Thank God. War at last. Maybe now I will be able to live up to what you wanted.*

He had been at sea for the next few broadcasts. Victory over Russia in the spring of '43 – a triumph for the Führer's strategic genius! The Wehrmacht summer offensive of the year before had cut Moscow off from the Caucasus, separating the Red armies from the Baku oilfields. Stalin's war machine had simply ground to a halt for want of fuel.

Peace with the British in '44 – a triumph for the Führer's counter-intelligence genius! March remembered how all U-boats had been recalled to their bases on the Atlantic coast to be equipped with a new cipher system: the treacherous British, they were told, had been reading the Fatherland's codes. Picking off merchant shipping had been easy after that. England was starved into submission. Churchill and his gang of war-mongers had fled to Canada.

Peace with the Americans in '46 – a triumph for the Führer's scientific genius! When America defeated Japan by detonating an atomic bomb, the Führer had sent a V-3 rocket to explode in the skies over New York to prove he could retaliate in kind if struck. After that, the war had dwindled to a series of bloody guerilla conflicts at the fringes of the new German Empire. A nuclear stalemate which the diplomats called the Cold War.

But still the broadcasts had gone on. When Goering had died in '51, there had been a whole day of solemn music before the announcement was made. Himmler had received similar treatment when he was killed in an aircraft explosion in '62. Deaths, victories, wars, exhortations for sacrifice and revenge, the dull struggle with the Reds on the Urals front with its unpronounceable battlefields and offensives – Oktyabr'skoye, Polunochnoye, Alapayevsk . . .

March looked at the faces around him. Forced humour, resignation, apprehension. People with brothers and sons and husbands in the East. They kept glancing at the screens.

'People of Germany, prepare yourselves for an important statement!'

What was coming now?

The canteen was almost full. March was pressed up against a pillar. He could see Max Jaeger a few metres away, joking with a bosomy secretary from VA(1), the legal department. Max spotted him over her shoulder and gave him a grin. There was a roll of drums. The room was still. A newsreader said: 'We are now going live to the Foreign Ministry in Berlin.'

A bronze relief glittered in the television lights. A Nazi eagle, clutching the globe, shot rays of illumination, like a child's drawing of a sunrise. Before it, with his thick black eyebrows and shaded jowls, stood the Foreign Ministry spokesman, Drexler. March suppressed a laugh: you would have thought that, in the whole of Germany, Goebbels could have found one spokesman who did not look like a convicted criminal.

'Ladies and gentlemen, I have a brief statement for you from the Reich Ministry for Foreign Affairs.' He was addressing an audience of journalists, who were off-camera. He put on a pair of glasses and began to read.

'In accordance with the long-standing and well-documented desire of the Führer and People of the Greater German Reich to live in peace and security with the countries of the world, and following extensive consultations with our allies in the European Community, the Reich Ministry for Foreign Affairs, on behalf of the Führer, has today issued an invitation to the President of the United States of America to visit the Greater German Reich for personal discussions aimed at promoting greater understanding between our two peoples. This invitation has been accepted. We understand that the American administration has indicated this morning that Herr Kennedy intends to meet the Führer in Berlin in September. Heil Hitler! Long live Germany!'

The picture faded to black and another drum roll signalled the start of the national anthem. The men and women in the canteen began to sing. March pictured them at that moment all over Germany – in shipyards and steelworks and offices and schools – the hard voices and the high merged together in one great bellow of acclamation rising to the heavens.

Deutschland, Deutschland über Alles!
Über Alles in der Welt!

His own lips moved in conformity with the rest, but no sound emerged.

'MORE fucking work for us,' said Jaeger. They were back in their office. He had his feet on the desk and was puffing at a cigar. 'If you think the Führertag is a security nightmare – forget it. Can you imagine what it will be like with Kennedy in town as well?'

March smiled. 'I think, Max, you are missing the historic dimension of the occasion.'

'Screw the historic dimension of the occasion. I'm thinking about my sleep. The bombs are already going off like fire crackers. Look at this.'

Jaeger swung his legs off the desk and rummaged through a pile of folders. 'While you were playing around by the Havel, some of us were having to do some work.'

He picked up an envelope and tipped out the contents. It was a PPD file. Personal Possessions of the Deceased. From a mound of papers he pulled out two passports and handed them to March. One belonged to an SS officer, Paul Hahn; the other to a young woman, Magda Voss.

Jaeger said: 'Pretty thing, isn't she? They'd just married. Were leaving the reception in Spandau. On their way to their honeymoon. He's driving. They turn into Nawener Strasse. A lorry pulls out in front of them. Guy jumps out the back with a gun. Our man panics. Goes into reverse. Wham! Up the kerb, straight into a lamp-post. While he's trying to get back into first gear – bang! – shot in the head. End of groom. Little Magda gets out of the car, tries to make a run for it. Bang! End of bride. End of honeymoon. End of every fucking thing. Except it isn't, because the families are still back at the reception toasting the newlyweds and nobody bothers to tell them what's happened for another two hours.'

Jaeger blew his nose on a grimy handkerchief. March looked again at the girl's passport. She was pretty: blonde and dark-eyed; now dead in the gutter at twenty-four.

'Who did it?' He handed the passports back.

Jaeger counted off on his fingers. 'Poles. Latvians. Estonians. Ukrainians. Czechs. Croats. Caucasians.

Georgians. Reds. Anarchists. Who knows? Nowadays it could be anybody. The poor idiot stuck up an open invitation to the reception on his barracks noticeboard. The Gestapo reckon a cleaner, a cook, someone like that, saw it and passed on the word. Most of these barracks ancillaries are foreigners. They were all taken away this afternoon, poor bastards.'

He put the passports and identity cards back into the envelope and tossed it into a desk drawer.

'How did it go with you?'

'Have a chocolate.' March handed the box to Jaeger, who opened it. The tinny music filled the office.

'Very tasteful.'

'What do you know about it?'

'What? *The Merry Widow*? The Führer's favourite operetta. My mother was mad about it.'

'So was mine.'

Every German mother was mad about it. *The Merry Widow* by Franz Lehar. First performed in Vienna in 1905: as sugary as one of the city's cream cakes. Lehar had died in 1948, and Hitler had sent a personal representative to his funeral.

'What else is there to say?' Jaeger took a chocolate in one of his great paws and popped it into his mouth. 'Who are these from? A secret admirer?'

'I took them from Buhler's mailbox.' March bit into a chocolate and winced at the sickly taste of liquid cherry. 'Consider: you have no friends, yet someone sends you an expensive box of chocolates from Switzerland. With no message. A box that plays the Führer's favourite tune. Who would do that?' He swallowed the other half of the chocolate. 'A poisoner, perhaps?'

'Oh Christ!' Jaeger spat the contents of his mouth into his hand, pulled out his handkerchief and began wiping the brown smears of saliva from his fingers and lips. 'Sometimes I have my doubts about your sanity.'

'I am systematically destroying state evidence,' said March. He forced himself to eat another chocolate. 'No, worse than that: I am *consuming* state evidence, thereby committing a double offence. Tampering with justice while enriching myself.'

'Take some leave, man. I'm serious. You need a rest. My advice is to go down and dump those fucking chocolates in the trash as fast as possible. Then come home and have supper with me and Hannelore. You look as if you haven't had a decent meal in weeks. The Gestapo have taken the file. The autopsy report is going straight to Prinz-Albrecht Strasse. It's over. Done. Forget it.'

'Listen, Max.' March told him about Jost's confession, about how Jost had seen Globus with the body. He pulled out Buhler's diary. 'These names written here. Who are Stuckart and Luther?'

'I don't know.' Jaeger's face was suddenly drawn and hard. 'What's more, I don't want to know.'

A STEEP flight of stone steps led down to the semi-darkness. At the bottom, March hesitated, the chocolates in his hand. A doorway to the left led out to the cobbled centre courtyard, where the rubbish was collected from large, rusty bins. To the right, a dimly lit passage led to the Registry.

He tucked the chocolates under his arm and turned right.

The Kripo Registry was housed in what had once been a warren of rooms next to the boilerhouse. The closeness of the boilers and the web of hot water pipes criss-crossing the ceiling kept the place permanently hot. There was a reassuring smell of warm dust and dry paper, and in the poor light, between the pillars, the wire racks of files and reports seemed to stretch to infinity.

The Registrar, a fat woman in a greasy tunic who had once been a wardress at the prison in Plötzensee, demanded his ID. He handed it to her, as he had done more than once a week for the past ten years. She looked at it, as she always did, as if she had never seen it before, then at his face, then back, then returned it, and gave an upward tilt of her chin, something between an acknowledgement and a sneer. She wagged her finger. 'And no smoking,' she said, for the five-hundredth time.

From the shelf of reference books next to her desk he selected *Wer Ist's?*, the German *Who's Who* – a red-bound directory a thousand pages thick. He also took down the smaller, Party publication, *Guide to the Personalities of the NSDAP*, which included passport-sized photographs of each entrant. This was the book Halder had used to identify Buhler that morning. He lugged both volumes across to a table, and switched on the reading light. In the distance the boilers hummed. The Registry was deserted.

Of the two books, March preferred the Party's *Guide*. This had been published more or less annually since the mid-1930s. Often, during the dark, quiet afternoons of the winter, he had come down to the warmth to browse through old editions. It intrigued him to trace how the faces had changed. The early volumes were dominated by the grizzled ex-Freikorps red-baiters, men with necks wider than their foreheads. They stared into the camera, scrubbed and ill at ease, like nineteenth-century farmhands in their Sunday best. But by the 1950s, the beer-hall brawlers had given way to the smooth technocrats of the Speer type – well-groomed university men with bland smiles and hard eyes.

There was one Luther. Christian name: Martin. Now here, comrades, is an historic name to play with. But this Luther looked nothing like his famous namesake. He was pudding-faced with black hair and thick horn-rimmed glasses. March took out his notebook.

> Born: 16 December 1895, Berlin. Served in the German Army transport division, 1914–18. Profession: furniture remover. Joined the NSDAP and the SA on 1 March 1933. Sat on the Berlin City Council for the Dahlem district. Entered the Foreign Office, 1936. Head of Abteilung Deutschland – the 'German Division' – of the Foreign Office until retirement in 1955. Promoted to Under State Secretary, July 1941.

The details were sparse, but clear enough for March to guess his type. Chippy and aggressive, a rough-and-tumble street politician. And an opportunist. Like thousands of others, Luther had rushed to join the Party a few weeks after Hitler had come to power.

He flicked through the pages to Stuckart, Wilhelm, Doctor of Law. The photograph was a professional studio portrait, the face cast in a film star's brooding half-shadow. A vain man, and a curious mixture: curly grey hair, intense eyes, straight jawline – yet a flabby, almost voluptuous mouth. He took more notes.

> Born 16 November 1902, Wiesbaden. Studied law and economics at Munich and Frankfurt-am-Main universities. Graduated Magna Cum Laude, June 1928. Joined the Party in Munich in 1922. Various SA and SS positions. Mayor of Stettin, 1933. State Secretary, Ministry of the Interior, 1935–53. Publication: *A Commentary on the German Racial Laws* (1936). Promoted honorary SS-Obergruppenführer, 1944. Returned to private legal practice, 1953.

Here was a character quite different from Luther. An intellectual; an alter Kämpfer, like Buhler; a high-flyer. To be Mayor of Stettin, a port city of nearly 300,000, at the age of thirty-one . . . Suddenly, March realised he had read all this before, very recently. But where? He could not remember. He closed his eyes. *Come on.*

Wer Ist's? added nothing new, except that Stuckart was unmarried whereas Luther was on his third wife. He found a clean double-page in his notebook and drew three columns; headed them Buhler, Luther and Stuckart; and began making lists of dates. Compiling a chronology was a favourite tool of his, a method of finding a pattern in what seemed otherwise to be a fog of random facts.

They had all been born in roughly the same period. Buhler was sixty-four; Luther, sixty-eight; Stuckart, sixty-one. They had all become civil servants in the 1930s – Buhler in 1939, Luther in 1936, Stuckart in 1935. They had all held roughly similar ranks – Buhler and Stuckart had been state secretaries; Luther, an under state secretary. They had all retired in the 1950s – Buhler in 1951, Luther in 1955, Stuckart in 1953. They must all have known one another. They had all met at 10 am the previous Friday. Where was the pattern?

March tilted back in his chair and stared up at the tangle of pipes chasing one another like snakes across the ceiling.

And then he remembered.

He pitched himself forward, on to his feet.

Next to the entrance were loosely bound volumes of the *Berliner Tageblatt*, the *Völkischer Beobachter* and the SS paper, *Das Schwarzes Korps*. He wrenched back the pages of the *Tageblatt*, back to yesterday's issue, back to the obituaries. There it was. He had seen it last night.

> Party Comrade Wilhelm Stuckart, formerly State Secretary of the Ministry of the Interior, who died suddenly of heart failure on Sunday, 13 April, will be remembered as a dedicated servant of the National Socialist cause . . .

The ground seemed to shift beneath his feet. He was aware of the Registrar staring at him.

'Are you ill, Herr Sturmbannführer?'

'No. I'm fine. Do me a favour, will you?' He picked up a file requisition slip and wrote out Stuckart's full name and date of birth. 'Will you see if there's a file on this person?'

She looked at the slip and held out a hand. 'ID.'

He gave her his identity card. She licked her pencil and entered the twelve digits of March's service number on to the requisition form. By this means a record was kept of which Kripo investigator had requested which file, and at what time. His interest would be there for the Gestapo to see, a full eight hours after he had been ordered off the Buhler case. Further evidence of his lack of National Socialist discipline. It could not be helped.

The Registrar had pulled out a long wooden drawer of index cards and was marching her square-tipped fingers along the tops of them. 'Stroop,' she murmured. 'Strunck. Struss. Stülpnagel . . .'

March said: 'You've gone past it.'

She grunted and pulled out a slip of pink paper. ' "Stuckart, Wilhelm." ' She looked at him. 'There is a file. It's out.'

'Who has it?'

'See for yourself.'

March leaned forwards. Stuckart's file was with Sturmbannführer Fiebes of Kripo Department VB3. The sexual crimes division.

THE whisky and the dry air had given him a thirst. In the corridor outside the Registry was a water-cooler. He poured himself a drink and considered what to do.

What would a sensible man have done? That was easy. A sensible man would have done what Max Jaeger did every day. He would have put on his hat and coat and gone home to his wife and children. But for March that was not an option. The empty apartment in Ansbacher Strasse, the quarrelling neighbours and yesterday's newspaper, these held no attractions for him. He had narrowed his life to such a point, the only thing left was his work. If he betrayed that, what else was there?

And there was something else, the instinct that propelled him out of bed every morning into each unwelcoming day, and that was the desire to *know*. In police work, there was always another junction to reach, another corner to peer around. Who were the Weiss family, and what had happened to them? Whose was the body in the lake? What linked the deaths of Buhler and Stuckart? It kept him going, his blessing or his curse, this compulsion to *know*. And so, in the end, there was no choice.

He tossed the paper cup into the waste bin, and went upstairs.

SIX

Walther Fiebes was in his office, drinking schnapps. Watching him from a table beneath the window was a row of five human heads – white plaster casts with hinged scalps, all raised like lavatory seats, displaying their brains in red and grey sections – the five strains which made up the German Empire.

Placards announced them from left to right, in descending order of acceptability to the authorities. Category One: Pure Nordic. Category Two: Predominantly Nordic or Phalic. Category Three: Harmonious Bastard with Slight Alpine Dinaric or Mediterranean Characteristics. These groups qualified for membership of the SS. The others could hold no public office and stared reproachfully at Fiebes. Category Four: Bastard of Predominantly East-Baltic or Alpine Origin. Category Five: Bastard of Extra-European Origin.

March was a One/Two; Fiebes, ironically, a borderline Three. But then, the racial fanatics were seldom the blue-eyed Aryan supermen – they, in the words of *Das Schwarzes Korps*, were 'too inclined to take their membership of the Volk for granted'. Instead, the swampy frontiers of the German race were patrolled by those less confident of their blood-worthiness. Insecurity breeds good border guards. The knock-kneed Franconian schoolmaster, ridiculous in his Lederhosen; the Bavarian shopkeeper with his pebble glasses; the red-haired Thuringian accountant with a nervous tic and a predilection for the younger members of the Hitler Youth; the lame and the ugly, the runts of the national litter – these were the loudest defenders of the Volk.

So it was with Fiebes – the myopic, stooping, buck-toothed, cuckolded Fiebes – whom the Reich had blessed with the one job he really wanted. Homosexuality and miscegenation had replaced rape and incest as capital offences. Abortion, 'an act of sabotage against Germany's racial future', was punishable by death. The permissive 1960s were showing a strong increase in such sex crimes. Fiebes, a sheet-sniffer by temperament, worked all the hours the Führer sent and was as happy, in Max Jaeger's words, as a pig in horseshit.

But not today. Now, he was drinking in the office, his eyes were moist, and his bat's-wing toupee hung slightly askew.

March said: 'According to the newspapers, Stuckart died of heart failure.'

Fiebes blinked.

'But according to the Registry, the file on Stuckart is out to you.'

'I cannot comment.'

'Of course you can. We are colleagues.' March sat down and lit a cigarette. 'I take it we are in the familiar business of "sparing the family embarrassment".'

Fiebes muttered: 'Not just the family.' He hesitated. 'Could I have one of those?'

'Sure.' March gave him a cigarette and flicked his lighter. Fiebes took an experimental draw, like a schoolboy.

'This affair has left me pretty well shaken, March, I don't mind admitting. The man was a hero to me.'

'You knew him?'

'By reputation, naturally. I never actually *met* him. Why? What is your interest?'

'State security. That is all I can say. You know how it is.'

'Ah. Now I understand.' Fiebes poured himself another large helping of schnapps. 'We're very much alike, March, you and I.'

'We are?'

'Sure. You're the only investigator who's in this place as often as I am. We've got rid of our wives, our children – all that shit. We live for the job. When it goes well, we're well. When it goes badly . . .' His head fell forward. Presently, he said: 'Do you know Stuckart's book?'

'Unfortunately, no.'

Fiebes opened a desk drawer and handed March a battered, leather-bound volume. A *Commentary on the German Racial Laws*. March leafed through it. There were chapters on each of the three Nuremberg Laws of 1935: the Reich Citizenship Law, the Law for the Protection of German Blood and German Honour, the Law for the Protection of the Genetic Health of the German People. Some passages were underlined in red ink, with exclamation marks beside them. 'For the avoidance of racial damage, it is necessary for couples to submit to medical examination before marriage.' 'Marriage between persons suffering from venereal disease, feeble-mindedness, epilepsy or "genetic infirmities" (see 1933 Sterilisation Law) will be permitted only after production of a sterilisation certificate.' There were charts: 'An Overview of the Admissibility of Marriage between Aryans and non-Aryans', 'The Prevalence of Mischling of the First Degree'.

It was all gobbledygook to Xavier March.

Fiebes said: 'Most of it is out of date now. A lot of it refers to Jews, and the Jews, as we know' – he gave a wink – 'have all gone east. But Stuckart is still the bible of my calling. This is the foundation stone.'

March handed him the book. Fiebes cradled it like a baby. 'Now what I really need to see', said March, 'is the file on Stuckart's death.'

He was braced for an argument. Instead, Fiebes merely made an expansive gesture with his bottle of schnapps. 'Go ahead.'

*

THE Kripo file was an ancient one. It went back more than a quarter of a century. In 1936, Stuckart had become a member of the Interior Ministry's 'Committee for the Protection of German Blood' – a tribunal of civil servants, lawyers and doctors who considered applications for marriage between Aryans and non-Aryans. Shortly afterwards, the police had started receiving anonymous allegations that Stuckart was providing marriage licences in exchange for cash bribes. He had also apparently demanded sexual favours from some of the women involved.

The first name complainant was a Dortmund tailor, a Herr Maser, who had protested to his local Party office that his fiancée had been assaulted. His statement had been passed to the Kripo. There was no record of any investigation. Instead, Maser and his girlfriend had been dispatched to concentration camps. Various other stories from informants, including one from Stuckart's wartime Blockwart, were included in the file. No action had ever been taken.

In 1953, Stuckart had begun a liaison with an eighteen-year-old Warsaw girl, Maria Dymarski. She had claimed German ancestry back to 1720 in order to marry a Wehrmacht captain. The conclusion of the Interior Ministry's experts was that the documents were forged. The following year, Dymarski had been given a permit to work as a domestic servant in Berlin. Her employer's name was listed as Wilhelm Stuckart.

March looked up. 'How did he get away with it for ten years?'

'He was an Obergruppenführer, March. You don't make complaints about a man like that. Remember what happened to Maser when he complained? Besides, nobody had any evidence – then.'

'And there is evidence now?'

'Look in the envelope.'

Inside the file, in a manila envelope, were a dozen colour photographs, of startlingly good quality, showing Stuckart and Dymarski in bed. White bodies against red satin sheets. The faces – contorted in some shots, relaxed in others – were easy to identify. They were all taken from the same position, alongside the bed. The girl's body, pale and undernourished, looked fragile beneath the man's. In one shot she sat astride him – thin white arms clasped behind her head, face tilted towards the camera. Her features were broad, Slavic. But with her shoulder-length hair dyed blonde she could have passed as a German.

'These weren't taken recently?'

'About ten years ago. He turned greyer. She put on a bit of weight. She looked more of a tart as she got older.'

'Do we have any idea where they are?' The background was a blur of colours. A brown wooden bedhead, red-and-white striped wallpaper, a lamp with a yellow shade; it could have been anywhere.

'It's not his apartment – at least, not the way it's decorated now. A hotel, maybe a whorehouse. The camera is behind a two-way mirror. See the way they sometimes seem to be staring into the camera? I've seen that look a hundred times. They're checking themselves in the mirror.'

March examined each of the pictures again. They were glossy and unscratched – new prints from old negatives. The sort of pictures a pimp might try and sell you in a back street in Kreuzberg.

'Where did you find them?'

'Next to the bodies.'

Stuckart had shot his mistress first. According to the autopsy report, she had lain, fully clothed, face down on the bed in Stuckart's apartment in Fritz Todt-Platz. He had put a bullet in the back of her head with his SS Luger (if that was so, thought March, it was probably the first time the old pen-pusher had ever used it). Traces of impacted cotton and down in the wound suggested he had fired the bullet through a pillow. Then he had sat on the edge of the bed and apparently shot himself through the roof of his mouth. In the scene-of-crime photographs neither body was recognisable. The pistol was still clutched in Stuckart's hand.

'He left a note,' said Fiebes, 'on the dining room table.'

'By this action I hope to spare embarrassment to my family, the Reich and the Führer. Heil Hitler! Long live Germany! Wilhelm Stuckart.'

'Blackmail?'

'Presumably.'

'Who found the bodies?'

'This is the best part.' Fiebes spat out each word as if it were poison: 'An American woman journalist.'

Her statement was in the file: Charlotte Maguire, aged 25, Berlin representative of an American news agency, World European Features.

'A real little bitch. Started shrieking about her rights the moment she was brought in. Rights!' Fiebes took another swig of schnapps. 'Shit, I suppose we have to be *nice* to the Americans now, do we?'

March made a note of her address. The only other witness questioned was the porter who worked in Stuckart's apartment block. The American woman claimed to have seen two men on the stairs immediately before the discovery of the bodies; but the porter insisted there had been no one.

March looked up suddenly. Fiebes jumped. 'What is it?'

'Nothing. A shadow at your door, perhaps.'

'My God, this place . . .' Fiebes flung open the frosted glass door and peered both ways along the corridor. While his back was turned, March detached the envelope pinned to the back of the file and slipped it into his pocket.

'Nobody.' He shut the door. 'You're losing your nerve, March.'

'An over-active imagination has always been my curse.' He closed the folder and stood up.

Fiebes swayed, squinting. 'Don't you want to take it with you? Aren't you working on this with the Gestapo?'

'No. A separate matter.'

'Oh.' He sat down heavily. 'When you said "state security", I assumed . . . Doesn't matter. Out of my hands. The Gestapo have taken it over, thank God. Obergruppenführer Globus has assumed responsibility. You must have heard of him? A thug, it is true, but he'll sort it out.'

THE information bureau at Alexander Platz had Luther's address. According to police records, he still lived in Dahlem. March lit another cigarette, then dialled the number. The telephone rang for a long time – a bleak, unfriendly echo, somewhere in the city. Just as he was about to hang up, a woman answered.

'Yes?'

'Frau Luther?'

'Yes.' She sounded younger than he had expected. Her voice was thick, as if she had been crying.

'My name is Xavier March. I am an investigator with the Berlin Kriminalpolizei. May I speak to your husband?'

'I'm sorry . . . I don't understand. If you're from the Polizei, surely you know . . .'

'Know? Know what?'

'That he is missing. He disappeared on Sunday.' She started to cry.

'I'm sorry to hear that.' March balanced his cigarette on the edge of the ashtray.

God in heaven, another one.

'He said he was going on a business trip to Munich and

would be back on Monday.' She blew her nose. 'But I have already explained all this. Surely you know that this matter is being dealt with at the *very highest* level. What. . . ?'

She broke off. March could hear a conversation at the other end. There was a man's voice in the background: harsh and questioning. She said something he could not hear, then came back on the line.

'Obergruppenführer Globocnik is with me now. He would like to talk to you. What did you say your name was?'

March replaced the receiver.

ON his way out, he thought of the call at Buhler's place that morning. An old man's voice:

'Buhler? Speak to me. Who is that?'

'A *friend*.'

Click.

SEVEN

Bülow Strasse runs west to east for about a kilometre, through one of the busiest quarters of Berlin, close to the Gotenland railway station. The American woman's address proved to be an apartment block midway down.

It was seedier than March had expected: five storeys high, black with a century of traffic fumes, streaked with bird shit. A drunk sat on the pavement next to the entrance, turning his head to follow each passer-by. On the opposite side of the street was an elevated section of the U-bahn. As he parked, a train was pulling out of the Bülow Strasse station, its red and yellow carriages riding blue-white flashes of electricity, vivid in the gathering dark.

Her apartment was on the fourth floor. She was not in. 'Henry,' read a note written in English and pinned to her door, 'I'm in the bar on Potsdamer Strasse. Love, Charlie.'

March knew only a few words of English – but enough to grasp the sense of the message. Wearily, he descended the stairs. Potsdamer Strasse was a long street, with many bars.

'I'm looking for Fräulein Maguire,' he said to the concierge in the hall. 'Any idea where I might find her?'

It was like throwing a switch: 'She went out an hour ago, Sturmbannführer. You're the second man to ask. Fifteen minutes after she went out, a young chap came looking for her. Another foreigner – smartly dressed, short hair. She won't be back until after midnight, that much I can promise you.'

March wondered how many of her other tenants the old lady had informed on to the Gestapo.

'Is there a bar she goes to regularly?'

'Heini's, round the corner. That's where all the damned foreigners go.'

'Your powers of observation do you credit, madam.'

By the time he left her to her knitting five minutes later, March was laden with information about 'Charlie' Maguire. He knew she had dark hair, cut short; that she was small and slim; that she was wearing a raincoat of shiny blue plastic 'and high heels, like a tart'; that she had lived here six months; that she stayed out all hours and often got up at noon; that she was behind with the rent; that he should see the bottles of liquor the hussy threw out . . . No, thank you, madam, he had no desire to inspect them, that would not be necessary, you have been most helpful . . .

He turned right along Bülow Strasse. Another right took him to Potsdamer Strasse. Heini's was fifty metres up on the left. A painted sign showed a landlord with an apron and a handlebar moustache, carrying a foaming stein of beer. Beneath it, part of the red neon lettering had burnt out: Hei s.

The bar was quiet, except for one corner, where a group of six sat around a table, talking loudly in English accents. She was the only woman. She was laughing and ruffling an older man's hair. He was laughing, too. Then he saw March and said something and the laughter stopped. They watched him as he approached. He was conscious of his uniform, of the noise of his jackboots on the polished wooden floor.

'Fräulein Maguire, my name is Xavier March of the Berlin Kriminalpolizei.' He showed her his ID. 'I would like to speak with you, please.'

She had large dark eyes, glittering in the bar lights.

'Go ahead.'

'In private, please.'

'I've nothing more to say.' She turned to the man whose hair she had ruffled and murmured something March did not understand. They all laughed. March did not move.

Eventually, a younger man in a sports jacket and a button-down shirt stood up. He pulled a card from his breast pocket and held it out.

'Henry Nightingale. Second Secretary at the United States Embassy. I'm sorry, Herr March, but Miss Maguire has said all she has to say to your colleagues.'

March ignored the card.

The woman said: 'If you're not going to go, why don't you join us? This is Howard Thompson of the *New York Times*.' The older man raised his glass. 'This is Bruce Fallon of United Press. Peter Kent, CBS. Arthur Haines, Reuters. Henry, you've met. Me, you know, apparently. We're just having a little drink to celebrate the *great news*. Come on. The Americans and the SS – we're all friends now.'

'Careful, Charlie,' said the young man from the Embassy.

'Shut up, Henry. Oh, Christ, if this man doesn't move soon, I'll go and talk to him out of sheer boredom. Look –' There was a crumpled sheet of paper on the table in front of her. She tossed it to March. 'That's what I got for getting mixed up in this. My visa's withdrawn for "fraternising with a German citizen without official permission". I was supposed to leave today, but my friends here had a word with the Propaganda Ministry and got me a week's extension. Wouldn't have looked good, would it? Throwing me out on the day of the *great news*.'

March said: 'It's important.'

She stared at him, a cool look. The Embassy man put his hand on her arm. 'You don't have to go.'

That seemed to make up her mind. 'Will you shut up, Henry?' She shook herself free and pulled her coat over her shoulders. 'He looks respectable enough. For a Nazi. Thanks for the drink.' She downed the contents of her glass – whisky and water, by the look of it – and stood up. 'Let's go.'

The man called Thompson said something in English.

'I will, Howard. Don't worry.'

Outside, she said: 'Where are we going?'

'My car.'

'Then where?'

'Doctor Stuckart's apartment.'

'What fun.'

She *was* small. Even clattering on her high heels, she was several centimetres short of March's shoulder. He opened the door of the Volkswagen for her and, as she bent to get in, he smelled the whisky on her breath, and also cigarettes – French, not German – and perfume: something expensive, he thought.

The Volkswagen's 1300 cc engine rattled behind them. March drove carefully: west along Bülow Strasse, around the Berlin-Gotenland station, north up the Avenue of Victory. The captured artillery from the Barbarossa campaign lined the boulevard, barrels tilted towards the stars. Normally this section of the capital was quiet at night, Berliners preferring the noisy cafés behind the K-damm, or the jumbled streets of Kreuzberg. But on this evening, people were everywhere – standing in groups, admiring the guns and the floodlit buildings, strolling and window shopping.

'What kind of person wants to go out at night and look at guns?' She shook her head in wonderment.

'Tourists,' said March. 'By the twentieth, there'll be more than three million of them.'

It was risky, taking the American woman back to Stuckart's place, especially now Globus knew someone from the Kripo was looking for Luther. But he needed to see the apartment, to hear the woman's story. He had no plan, no real idea of what he might find. He recalled the Führer's words – 'I go the way that Providence dictates with the assurance of a sleepwalker' – and he smiled.

Ahead of them, searchlights picked out the eagle on top of the Great Hall. It seemed to hang in the sky, a golden bird of prey hovering over the capital.

She noticed his grin. 'What's funny?'

'Nothing.' He turned right at the European Parliament. The flags of the twelve member nations were lit by spots. The swastika which flew above them was twice the size of the other standards. 'Tell me about Stuckart. How well did you know him?'

'Hardly at all. I met him through my parents. My father was at the Embassy here before the war. He married a German, an actress. She's my mother. Monika Koch, did you ever hear of her?'

'No. I don't believe so.' Her German was flawless. She must have spoken it since childhood; her mother's doing, no doubt.

'She'd be sorry to hear that. She seems to think she was a big star over here. Anyway, they both knew Stuckart slightly. When I arrived in Berlin last year, they gave me a list of people to go and talk to – contacts. Half of them turned out to be dead, one way or another. Most of the rest didn't want to meet me. American journalists don't make healthy company, if you know what I mean. Do you mind if I smoke?'

'Go ahead. What was Stuckart like?'

'Awful.' Her lighter flared in the darkness; she inhaled deeply. 'He made a grab at me, even though this woman of his was in the apartment at the same time. That was just before Christmas. I kept away from him after that. Then, last week, I got a message from my office in New York. They wanted a piece for Hitler's seventy-fifth birthday, talking to some of the people who knew him from the old days.'

'So you rang Stuckart?'

'Right.'

'And arranged to meet him on Sunday, and when you got there, he was dead?'

'If you know it all,' she said irritably, 'why do you need to talk to me again?'

'I don't know it all, Fräulein. That's the point.'

After that, they drove in silence.

Fritz Todt-Platz was a couple of blocks from the Avenue of Victory. Laid out in the mid-1950s as part of Speer's redevelopment of the city, it was a square of expensive-looking apartment buildings, erected around a small memorial garden. In the centre stood an absurdly heroic statue of Todt, the creator of the Autobahnen, by Professor Thorak.

'Which one was Stuckart's?'

She pointed to a block on the other side of the square. March drove round and parked outside it.

'Which floor?'

'Fourth.'

He looked up. The fourth floor was in darkness. Good.

Todt's statue was floodlit. In the reflected light, her face was white. She looked as if she was about to be sick. Then he remembered the photographs Fiebes had shown him of the corpses – Stuckart's skull had been a crater, like a guttered candle – and he understood.

She said: 'I don't have to do this, do I?'

'No. But you will.'

'Why?'

'Because you want to know what happened as much as I do. That's why you've come this far.'

She stared at him again, then stubbed out her cigarette, twisting it and breaking it in the ashtray. 'Let's do it quickly. I want to get back to my friends.'

The keys to the building were still in the envelope which March had removed from Stuckart's file. There were five in all. He found the one that fitted the front door and let them into the foyer. It was vulgarly luxurious, in the new imperial style – white marble floor, crystal chandeliers, nineteenth-century gilt chairs with red plush upholstery, the air scented with dried flowers. No porter, thankfully: he must have gone off duty. Indeed, the entire building seemed deserted. Perhaps the tenants had left for their second homes in the country. Berlin could be unbearably crowded in the week before the Führertag. The smart set always fled the capital.

'Now what?'

'Just tell me what happened.'

'The porter was at the desk, here,' she said. 'I asked for Stuckart. He directed me to the fourth floor. I couldn't take the elevator, it was being repaired. There was a man working on it. So I walked.'

'What time was this?'

'Noon. Exactly.'

They climbed the stairs.

She went on: 'I had just reached the second floor when two men came running towards me.'

'Describe them, please.'

'It all happened too quickly for me to get a very good look. Both in their thirties. One had a brown suit, the other had a green anorak. Short hair. That's about it.'

'What did they do when they saw you?'

'They just pushed past me. The one in the anorak said something to the other, but I couldn't hear what it was. There was a lot of drilling going on from the elevator shaft. After that, I carried on up to Stuckart's apartment and rang the bell. There was no reply.'

'So what did you do?'

'I walked down to the porter and asked him to open Stuckart's door, to check he was okay.'

'Why?'

She hesitated. 'There was something about those two

men. I had a hunch. You know: that feeling when you knock on a door and nobody answers but you're sure someone's in.'

'And you persuaded the porter to open the door?'

'I told him I'd call the police if he didn't. I said he would have to answer to the authorities if anything had happened to Doctor Stuckart.'

Shrewd psychology, thought March. After thirty years of being told what to do, the average German was careful not to take final responsibility for anything, even for not opening a door. 'And then you found the bodies?'

She nodded. 'The porter saw them first. He screamed and I came running.'

'Did you mention the two men you'd seen on the stairs? What did the porter say?'

'He was too busy throwing up to talk at first. Then he just insisted he'd seen nobody. He said I must have imagined it.'

'Do you think he was lying?'

She considered this. 'No, I don't. I think he genuinely didn't see them. On the other hand, I don't see how he could have missed them.'

They were still on the second floor landing, at the point at which she said the men had passed her. March walked back down the flight of stairs. She waited for a moment, then followed him. At the foot of the steps a door led off to the first floor corridor.

He said, half to himself: 'They could have hidden along here, I suppose. Where else?'

They continued down to the ground floor. Here there were two more doors. One led to the foyer. March tried the other. It was unlocked. 'Or they could have got out down here.'

Bare concrete steps, neon-lit, led down to the basement. At the bottom was a long passage, with doors off it. March opened each in turn. A lavatory. A store-room. A generator room. A bomb shelter.

Under the 1948 Reich Civil Defence Law, every new building had to be equipped with a bomb shelter; those beneath offices and apartment blocks were also required to have their own generators and air-filtration systems. This one was particularly well-appointed: bunk beds, a storage cupboard, a separate cubicle with toilet facilities. March carried a metal chair across to the air vent, set into the wall two and a half metres above the ground. He grasped the metal cover. It came away easily in his hands. All the screws had been removed.

'The Ministry of Construction specifies an aperture with a diameter of half a metre,' said March. He unbuckled his belt and hung it and his pistol over the back of the chair. 'If only they appreciated the difficulties that gives us. Would you mind?'

He took off his jacket and handed it to the woman, then mounted the chair. Reaching into the shaft, he found something hard to hold on to, and pulled himself in. The filters and the fan had both been removed. By working his shoulders against the metal casing he was able to move slowly forwards. The darkness was complete. He choked on the dust. His hands, stretched out in front of him, touched metal, and he pushed. The outside cover yielded and crashed to the ground. The night air rushed in. For a moment, he felt an almost overpowering urge to crawl out into it, but instead he wriggled backwards and lowered himself into the basement shelter. He landed, dusty and grease-smeared.

The woman was pointing his pistol at him.

'Bang, bang,' she said. 'You're dead.' She smiled at his alarm: 'American joke.'

'Not funny.' He took the Luger and put it back in his holster.

'Okay,' she said, 'here's a better one. Two murderers are seen by a witness leaving a building and it takes the police four days to work out how they did it. I'd say that was funny, wouldn't you?'

'It depends on the circumstances.' He brushed the dust off his shirt. 'If the police found a note beside one of the victims in his own handwriting, saying it was suicide, I could understand why they wouldn't bother looking any further.'

'But then you come along and you do look further.'

'I'm the curious type.'

'Clearly.' She smiled again. 'So Stuckart was shot and the murderers tried to make it look like suicide?'

He hesitated. 'It's a possibility.'

He regretted the words the moment he uttered them. She had led him into disclosing more than was wise about Stuckart's death. Now a faint light of mockery played in her eyes. He cursed himself for underrating her. She had the cunning of a professional criminal. He considered taking her back to the bar and going on alone, but dismissed the idea. It was no good. To know what had happened, he needed to see it through her eyes.

He buttoned his tunic. 'Now we must inspect Party Comrade Stuckart's apartment.'

That, he was pleased to see, knocked the smile off her face. But she did not refuse to go with him. They climbed the stairs, and it struck him again that she was almost as anxious to see Stuckart's flat as he was.

They took the elevator to the fourth floor. As they stepped out, he heard, along the corridor to their left, a door being opened. He grabbed the American's arm and steered her round the corner, out of sight. When he looked back, he could see a middle-aged woman in a fur coat heading for the elevator. She was carrying a small dog.

'You're hurting my arm.'

'Sorry.'

He was hiding from shadows. The woman talked quietly

to the dog and disappeared into the lift. March wondered whether Globus had retrieved the file from Fiebes yet, whether he had discovered that the keys were missing. They would have to hurry.

The door to Stuckart's apartment had been sealed that day, close to the handle, with red wax. A note informed the curious that these premises were now under the jurisdiction of the Geheime Staatspolizei, the Gestapo, and that entry was forbidden. March pulled on a pair of thin leather gloves and broke the seal. The key turned easily in the lock.

He said: 'Don't touch anything.'

More luxury, to match the building: elaborate gilt mirrors, antique tables and chairs with fluted legs and ivory damask upholstery, a carpet of royal blue with Persian rugs. The spoils of war, the fruits of Empire.

'Now tell me again what happened.'

'The porter opened the door. We came into the hall.' Her voice had risen. She was trembling. 'He shouted and there was no reply, so we both came right in. I opened that door first.'

It was the sort of bathroom March had seen only in glossy magazines. White marble and brown smoky mirrors, a sunken bathtub, twin basins with gold taps . . . Here, he thought, was the hand of Maria Dymarski, leafing through German *Vogue* at the Ku-damm hairdressers, while her Polish roots were bleached Aryan white.

'Then, I came into the sitting room . . .'

March switched on the light. One wall consisted of tall windows, looking out over the square. The other three had large mirrors. Wherever he turned, he could see images of himself and the girl: the black uniform and the shiny blue coat incongruous among the antiques. Nymphs were the decorative conceit. Fashioned in gilt, they draped themselves around the mirrors; cast in bronze, they supported table lamps and clocks. There were paintings of nymphs and statues of nymphs; wood nymphs and water nymphs; Amphitrite and Thetis.

'I heard him scream. I went to help . . .'

March opened the door of the bedroom. She turned away. Blood in half-light looks black. Dark shapes, twisted and grotesque, leapt up the walls and across the ceiling, like the shadows of trees.

'They were on the bed, yes?'

She nodded.

'What did you do?'

'Rang the police.'

'Where was the porter?'

'In the bathroom.'

'Did you look at them again?'

'What do you think?' She brushed her sleeve angrily across her eyes.

'All right, Fräulein. It's enough. Wait in the sitting room.'

The human body contains six litres of blood: sufficient to paint a large apartment. March tried to avoid looking at the bed and the walls as he worked – opening the cupboard doors, feeling the lining of every item of clothing, skimming every pocket with his gloved hands. He moved on to the bedside cabinets. These had been unlocked and searched before. The contents of the drawers had been emptied out for inspection, then stuffed back haphazardly – a typical, clumsy Orpo job, destroying more clues than it uncovered.

Nothing, nothing. Had he risked everything for this?

He was on his knees, with his arm stretched beneath the bed, when he heard it. It took a second for the sound to register.

Love unspoken
Faith unbroken
All life through . . .

'I'm sorry,' she said, when he rushed in. 'I shouldn't have touched it.'

He took the chocolate box from her, carefully, and closed the lid on its tune.

'Where was it?'

'On that table.'

Someone had collected Stuckart's mail for the past three days and had inspected it, neatly slicing open the envelopes, pulling out the letters. They were heaped up next to the telephone. He had not noticed them when he came in. How had he missed them? The chocolates, he could see, had been wrapped exactly as Buhler's had been, postmarked Zürich, 16.00 hours, Monday afternoon.

Then he saw she was holding a paper knife.

'I told you not to touch anything.'

'I said I'm sorry.'

'Do you think this is a game?' *She's crazier than I am.* 'You're going to have to leave.' He tried to grab her, but she twisted free.

'No way.' She backed away, pointing the knife at him. 'I reckon I have as much right to be here as you do. You try and throw me out and I'll scream so loudly I'll have every Gestapo man in Berlin hammering on that door.'

'You have a knife, but I have a gun.'

'Ah, but you daren't use it.'

March ran his hand through his hair. He thought: *You believed you were so clever, finding her, persuading her to come back. And all the time, she wanted to come. She's looking for something* . . . He had been an idiot.

He said: 'You've been lying to me.'

She said: 'You've been lying to me. That makes us even.'

'This is dangerous. I beg you, you have no idea . . .'

'What I do know is this: my career could have ended because of what happened in this apartment. I could be fired when I get back to New York. I'm being thrown out of this lousy country, and I want to find out why.'

'How do I know I can trust you?'

'How do I know I can trust *you*?'

They stood like that for perhaps half a minute: he with his hand to his hair, she with the silver paper knife still pointed at him. Outside, across the Platz, a clock began to chime. March looked at his watch. It was already ten.

'We have no time for this.' He spoke quickly. 'Here are the keys to the apartment. This one opens the door downstairs. This one is for the main door up here. This fits the bedside cabinet. That is a desk key. This one' – he held it up – 'this, I think, is the key to a safe. Where is it?'

'I don't know.' Seeing his look of disbelief, she added: 'I swear.'

They searched in silence for ten minutes, shifting furniture, pulling up rugs, looking behind paintings. Suddenly she said: 'This mirror is loose.'

It was a small antique looking glass, maybe thirty centimetres square, above the table on which she had opened the letters. March grasped the ormolu frame. It gave a little but would not come away from the wall.

'Try this.' She gave him the knife.

She was right. Two-thirds down the left-hand side, behind the lip of the frame, was a tiny lever. March pressed it with the tip of the paper knife, and felt something yield. The mirror was on a hinge. It swung open to reveal the safe.

He inspected it and swore. The key was not enough. There was also a combination lock.

'Too much for you?' she asked.

' "In adversity," ' quoted March, ' "the resourceful officer will always discover opportunity." ' He picked up the telephone.

EIGHT

Across a distance of five thousand kilometres, President Kennedy flashed his famous smile. He stood behind a cluster of microphones, addressing a crowd in a football stadium. Banners of red, white and blue streamed behind him – 'Re-elect Kennedy!' 'Four More in Sixty-Four!' He shouted something March did not understand and the crowd cheered back.

'What is he talking about?'

The television cast a blue glow in the darkness of Stuckart's apartment. The woman translated. ' "The Germans have their system and we have ours. But we are all citizens of one planet. And as long as our two nations remember that, I sincerely believe: we can have peace." Cue loud applause from dumb audience.'

She had kicked off her shoes and was lying full-length on her stomach in front of the set.

'Ah. Here's the serious bit.' She waited until he finished speaking, then translated again. 'He says he plans to raise human rights questions during his visit in the Fall.' She laughed and shook her head. 'God, Kennedy is so full of shit. The only thing he really wants to raise is his vote in November.'

' "Human rights"?'

'The thousands of dissidents you people lock up in camps. The millions of Jews who vanished in the war. The torture. The killing. Sorry to mention them, but we have this bourgeois notion that human beings have rights. Where have you been the last twenty years?'

The contempt in her voice jolted him. He had never properly spoken to an American before, had only encountered the occasional tourist – and those few had been chaperoned around the capital, shown only what the Propaganda Ministry wanted them to see, like Red Cross officials on a KZ inspection. Listening to her now it occurred to him she probably knew more about his country's recent history than he did. He felt he should make some sort of defence but did not know what to say.

'You talk like a politician,' was all he could manage. She did not even bother to reply.

He looked again at the figure on the screen. Kennedy projected an image of youthful vigour, despite his spectacles and balding head.

'Will he win?' he asked.

She was silent. For a moment, he thought she had decided not to speak to him. Then she said: 'He will now. He looks in good shape for a man of seventy-five, wouldn't you say?'

'Indeed.' March was standing a metre back from the window smoking a cigarette, alternately watching the television and watching the square. Traffic was sparse – mostly people returning from dinner or the cinema. A young couple held hands under the statue of Todt. They might be Gestapo; it was hard to tell.

The millions of Jews who vanished in the war . . . He was risking court martial simply by talking to her. Yet her mind must be a treasure house, full of ill-considered objects which meant nothing to her but would be gold to him. If he could somehow overcome her furious resentment, pick his way around the propaganda . . .

No. A ridiculous thought. He had problems enough as it was.

A solemn blonde newsreader filled the screen; behind her, a composite picture of Kennedy and the Führer and the single word 'Détente'.

Charlotte Maguire had helped herself to a glass of Scotch from Stuckart's drinks cabinet. Now she raised it to the television in mock salute. 'To Joseph P. Kennedy: President of the United States – appeaser, anti-Semite, gangster and sonofabitch. May you roast in hell.'

THE clock outside struck ten-thirty, ten forty-five, eleven.

She said: 'Maybe this friend of yours had second thoughts.'

March shook his head. 'He'll come.'

A few moments later, a battered blue Skoda entered the square. It made one slow circuit of the Platz, then came round again and parked opposite the apartment block. Max Jaeger emerged from the driver's side; from the other came a small man in a shabby sports jacket and trilby, carrying a doctor's bag. He squinted up at the fourth floor and backed away, but Jaeger took his arm and propelled him towards the entrance.

In the stillness of the apartment, a buzzer sounded.

'It would be best,' said March, 'if you didn't speak.'

She shrugged. 'As you like.'

He went into the hall and picked up the intercom.

'Hello, Max.'

He pressed a switch and unlocked the door. The corridor was empty. After a minute, a soft *ping* signalled the arrival of the elevator and the little man appeared. He scuttled down the passage and into Stuckart's hall without uttering a word. He was in his fifties and carried with him, like bad breath, the reek of the back-streets – of furtive deals and triple-entry accounting, of card-tables folded away at the sound of a tread on the stairs. Jaeger followed close behind.

When the man saw March was not alone, he shrank back into the corner.

'Who's the woman?' He appealed to Jaeger. 'You never said anything about a woman. Who's the woman?'

'Shut up, Willi,' said Max. He gave him a gentle push into the drawing room.

March said: 'Never mind her, Willi. Look at this.'

He switched on the lamp, angling it upwards.

Willi Stiefel took in the safe at a glance. 'English,' he said. 'Casing: one and a half centimetres, high-tensile steel. Fine mechanism. Eight-figure code. Six, if you're lucky.' He appealed to March: 'I beg you, Herr Sturmbannführer. It's the guillotine for me next time.'

'It'll be the guillotine for you this time,' said Jaeger, 'if you don't get on with it.'

'Fifteen minutes, Herr Sturmbannführer. Then I'm out of here. Agreed?'

March nodded. 'Agreed.'

Stiefel gave the woman a last, nervous look. Then he removed his hat and jacket, opened his case, and took out a pair of thin rubber gloves and a stethoscope.

March took Jaeger over to the window, and whispered: 'Did he take much persuading?'

'What do you think? But then I told him he was still covered by Forty-two. He saw the light.'

Paragraph Forty-two of the Reich Criminal Code stated that all 'habitual criminals and offenders against morality' could be arrested on suspicion that they *might* commit an offence. National Socialism taught that criminality was in the blood: something you were born with, like musical talent or blond hair. Thus the character of the criminal rather than his crime determined the sentence. A gangster stealing a few Marks after a fist-fight could be sentenced to death, on the grounds that he 'displayed an inclination towards criminality so deep-rooted that it precluded his ever becoming a useful member of the folk community'. But the next day, in the same court, a loyal Party member who had shot his wife for an insulting remark might merely be bound over to keep the peace.

Stiefel could not afford another arrest. He had recently served nine years in Spandau for a bank robbery. He had no choice but to co-operate with the Polizei, whatever they asked him to be – informant, *agent provocateur*, or safebreaker. These days, he ran a watch repair business in Wedding and swore he was going straight: a protestation of innocence it was hard to believe, watching him now. He had placed the stethoscope against the safe door and was twisting the dial a digit at a time. His eyes were closed as he listened for the click of the lock's tumblers falling into place.

Come on, Willi. March rubbed his hands. His fingers were numb with apprehension.

'Jesus Christ,' said Jaeger, under his breath. 'I hope you know what you're doing.'

'I'll explain later.'

'No thanks. I told you: I don't want to know.'

Stiefel straightened and let out a long sigh. 'One,' he said. One was the first digit of the combination.

Like Stiefel, Jaeger kept glancing at the woman. She was sitting demurely on one of the gilt chairs, her hands folded in her lap. 'A foreign *woman*, for God's sake!'

'Six.'

So it went on, one digit every few minutes, until, at 11.35, Stiefel said to March: 'The owner: when was he born?'

'Why?'

'It would save time. I think he's set this with the date of his birth. So far, I've got one-six-one-one-one-nine. The sixteenth of the eleventh, nineteen . . .'

March checked his notes from Stuckart's *Wer Ist's?* entry.

'Nineteen hundred and two.'

'Zero-two.' Stiefel tried the combination, then smiled. 'It's usually the owner's birthday,' he said, 'or the Führer's birthday, or the Day of National Reawakening.' He pulled open the door.

The safe was small: a fifteen-centimetre cube containing no bank notes or jewellery, just paper – old paper, most of it. March piled it on to the table and began rifling through it.

'I'd like to leave now, Herr Sturmbannführer.'

March ignored him. Tied up in red ribbon were the title deeds to a property in Wiesbaden – the family home, by the look of it. There were stock certificates. Hoesch, Siemens, Thyssen: the companies were standard, but the sums invested looked astronomical. Insurance papers. One human touch: a photograph of Maria Dymarski, in a 1950s cheesecake pose.

Suddenly, from the window, Jaeger gave a shout of warning: 'Here they come, you fucking, *fucking* fool!'

An unmarked grey BMW was driving round the square, fast, followed by an army truck. The vehicles swerved to a halt outside, blocking the street. A man in a belted leather coat leapt out of the car. The tailgate of the lorry was kicked down and SS troops carrying automatic rifles began jumping out.

'Move! Move!' yelled Jaeger. He began pushing Charlie and Stiefel towards the door.

With shaking fingers, March worked his way through the remaining papers. A blue envelope, unmarked. Something heavy in it. The flap of the envelope was open. He saw a letterhead in copperplate – Zaugg & Cie, Bankiers – and stuffed it into his pocket.

The buzzer from the door downstairs began sounding in long, urgent bursts.

'They must know we're up here!'

Jaeger said: 'Now what?' Stiefel had turned grey. The woman stood motionless. She did not seem to know what was going on.

'The basement,' shouted March. 'They might just miss us. Get the elevator.'

The other three ran out into the corridor. He began stuffing the papers back into the safe, slammed it shut, twirled the dial, pushed the mirror back into place. There was no time to do anything about the broken seal on the apartment door. They were holding the lift for him. He squeezed in and they began their descent.

Third floor, second floor . . .

March prayed it would not stop at the ground floor. It did not. It opened on to the empty basement. Above their heads they could hear the heels of the stormtroopers on the marble floor.

'This way!' He led them into the bomb shelter. The grating from the air vent was where he had left it, leaning against the wall.

Stiefel needed no telling. He ran to the air shaft, lifted his bag above his head and tossed it in. He grabbed at the brickwork, tried to haul himself after it, his feet scrabbling for a purchase on the smooth wall. He was yelling over his shoulder: 'Help me!' March and Jaeger seized his legs and heaved. The little man wriggled head first into the hole and was gone.

Coming closer – the ring and scrape of boots on concrete. The SS had found the entrance to the basement. A man was shouting.

March to Charlie: 'You next.'

'I'll tell you something,' she said, pointing at Jaeger. 'He'll never make it.'

Jaeger's hands went to his waist. It was true. He was too fat. 'I'll stay. I'll think of something. You two get out.'

'No.' This was turning into a farce. March took the envelope from his pocket and pressed it into Charlie's hand. 'Take this. We may be searched.'

'And you?' She had her stupid shoes in one hand, was

already mounting the chair.

'Wait until you hear from me. Tell nobody.' He grabbed her, locked his hands just below her knees, and threw. She was so light, he could have wept.

The SS were in the basement. Along the passage – the crash of doors flung open.

March swung the grating back into place and kicked away the chair.

PART THREE

THURSDAY 16 APRIL

When National Socialism has ruled long enough, it will no longer be possible to conceive of a form of life different from ours.

Adolf Hitler,
11 July 1941

ONE

The grey BMW drove south down Saarland Strasse, past the slumbering hotels and deserted shops of central Berlin. At the dark mass of the Museum für Völkerkunde it turned left, into Prinz-Albrecht Strasse, towards the headquarters of the Gestapo.

There was a hierarchy in cars, as in everything. The Orpo were stuck with tinny Opels. The Kripo had Volkswagens – four-door versions of the original KdF-wagen, the round-backed workers' car which had been stamped out by the million at the Fallersleben works. But the Gestapo were smarter. They drove BMW 1800s – sinister boxes with growling, souped-up engines and dull grey bodywork.

Sitting in the back seat next to Max Jaeger, March kept his eyes on the man who had arrested them, the commander of the raid on Stuckart's apartment. When they had been led up from the basement into the foyer he had given them an immaculate Führer-salute. 'Sturmbannführer Karl Krebs, Gestapo!' That had meant nothing to March. It was only now, in the BMW, in profile, that he recognised him. Krebs was one of the two SS officers who had been with Globus at Buhler's villa.

He was about thirty years old with an angular, intelligent face, and without the uniform he could have been anything – a lawyer, a banker, a eugenicist, an executioner. That was how it was with young men of his age. They had come off an assembly line of Pimpf, Hitler Youth, National Service and Strength-Through-Joy. They had heard the same speeches, read the same slogans, eaten the same one-pot meals in aid of Winter Relief. They were the regime's workhorses, had known no authority but the Party, and were as reliable and commonplace as the Kripo's Volkswagens.

The car drew up and almost at once Krebs was on the pavement, opening the door. 'This way, gentlemen. Please.'

March hauled himself out and looked down the street. Krebs might be as polite as a scoutmaster, but ten metres back, the doors of a second BMW were opening even before it stopped and armed plain-clothes men were emerging. That was how it had been since their discovery at Fritz-Todt Platz. No rifle-butts in the belly, no oaths, no handcuffs. Just a telephone call to headquarters, followed by a quiet request to 'discuss these matters further'. Krebs had also asked them to surrender their weapons. Polite, but behind the politeness, always, the threat.

Gestapo headquarters were in a grand, five-storey Wilhelmine construction that faced north and never saw the sun. Years ago, in the days of the Weimar Republic, the museum-like building had housed the Berlin School of Arts. When the secret police took over, the students had been forced to burn their modernist paintings in the courtyard. Tonight, the high windows were shielded by thick net curtains, a precaution against terrorist attack. Behind the gauze, as if in fog, chandeliers burned.

March had made it a policy in life never to cross the threshold, and until this night he had succeeded. Three stone steps ran up into an entrance hall. More steps, and then a large, vaulted foyer: a red carpet on a stone floor, the hollow resonance of a cathedral. It was busy. The early hours of the morning were always busy for the Gestapo. From the depths of the building came the muffled echo of bells ringing, footsteps, a whistle, a shout. A fat man in the uniform of an Obersturmführer picked his nose and regarded them without interest.

They walked on, down a corridor lined with swastikas

and marble busts of the Party leadership – Göring, Goebbels, Bormann, Frank, Ley and the rest – modelled after Roman senators. March could hear the plainclothes guards following. He glanced at Jaeger, but Max was staring fixedly ahead, jaw clenched.

More stairs, another passage. The carpet had given way to linoleum. The walls were dingy. March guessed they were somewhere near the back of the building, on the second floor.

'If you would wait here,' said Krebs. He opened a stout wooden door. Neon stuttered into life. He stood aside to allow them to file in. 'Coffee?'

'Thank you.'

And he was gone. As the door closed, March saw one of the guards, arms folded, take up station in the corridor outside. He half-expected to hear a key turn in the lock, but there was no sound.

They had been put in some sort of interview room. A rough wooden table stood in the centre of the floor, one chair either side of it, half a dozen others pushed up against the walls. There was a small window. Opposite it was a reproduction of Josef Vietze's portrait of Reinhard Heydrich in a cheap plastic frame. On the floor were small brown stains which looked to March like dried blood.

PRINZ-ALBRECHT STRASSE was Germany's black heart, as famous as the Avenue of Victory and the Great Hall, but without the tourist coaches. At number eight: the Gestapo. At number nine: Heydrich's personal headquarters. Around the corner: the Prinz-Albrecht Palace itself, headquarters of the SD, the Party's intelligence service. A complex of underground passages linked the three.

Jaeger muttered something and collapsed into a chair. March could think of nothing adequate to say so he looked out of the window. It commanded a clear view of the palace grounds running behind the Gestapo building – the dark clumps of the bushes, the ink-pool of the lawn, the skeletal branches of the limes raised in claws against the sky. Away to the right, lit up through the bare trees, was the concrete and glass cube of the Europa-Haus, built in the 1920s by the Jewish architect Mendelsohn. The Party had allowed it to stand as a monument to his 'pygmy imagination': dropped among Speer's granite monoliths, it was just a toy. March could remember a Sunday afternoon tea with Pili in its roof-garden restaurant. Ginger beer and Obsttorte mit Sahne, the little brass band playing – what else? –selections from *The Merry Widow*, the elderly women with their elaborate Sunday hats, their little fingers crooked over the bone china.

Most were careful not to look at the black buildings beyond the trees. For others, the proximity of Prinz-Albrecht Strasse seemed to provide a frisson of excitement, like picnicking next to a prison. Down in the cellar the Gestapo was licensed to practise what the Ministry of Justice called 'heightened interrogation'. The rules had been drawn up by civilised men in warm offices and they stipulated the presence of a doctor. There had been a conversation in Werderscher Markt a few weeks ago. Someone had heard a rumour about the torturers' latest trick: a thin glass catheter inserted into the suspect's penis, then snapped.

Strings are playing
Hear them saying
'I love you . . .'

He shook his head, pinched the bridge of his nose, tried to clear his mind.

Think.

He had left a paper-trail of clues, any one of which would

have been enough to lead the Gestapo to Stuckart's apartment. He had requested Stuckart's file. He had discussed the case with Fiebes. He had rung Luther's home. He had gone looking for Charlotte Maguire.

He worried about the American woman. Even if she had managed to get clear of Fritz-Todt Platz, the Gestapo could pull her in tomorrow. '*Routine questions, Fräulein . . . . What is this envelope, please? . . . How did you come by it? . . . Describe the man who opened the safe . . .*' She was tough, with an actressy self-confidence, but in their hands she would not last five minutes.

March rested his forehead against the cold pane of glass. The window was bolted shut. There was a sheer drop of fifteen metres to the ground.

Behind him, the door opened. A swarthy man in shirt sleeves, stinking of sweat, came in and set two mugs of coffee on the table.

Jaeger, who had been sitting with his arms folded, looking at his boots, asked: 'How much longer?'

The man shrugged – *an hour? a night? a week?* – and left. Jaeger tasted the coffee and pulled a face. 'Pig's piss.' He lit a cigar, swilling the smoke around his mouth, before sending it billowing across the room.

He and March stared at one another. After a while, Max said: 'You know, you could have got out.'

'And left you to it? Hardly fair.' March tried the coffee. It was lukewarm. The neon light was flickering, fizzing, making his head throb. This was what they did to you. Left you until two or three in the morning, until your body was at its weakest, your defences at their most vulnerable. He knew this part of the game as well as they did.

He swallowed the filthy coffee and lit a cigarette. Anything to keep awake. Guilt about the woman, guilt about his friend.

'I'm a fool. I shouldn't have involved you. I'm sorry.'

'Forget it.' Jaeger waved away the smoke. He leaned forward and spoke softly. 'You have to let me carry my share of the blame, Zavi. Good Party Comrade Jaeger, here. Brownshirt. Blackshirt. Every goddamn shirt. Twenty years dedicated to the sacred cause of keeping my arse clean.' He grasped March's knee. 'I have favours to call in. I'm owed.'

His head was bent. He was whispering. 'They have you marked down, my friend. A loner. Divorced. They'll flay you alive. Me, on the other hand? The great conformer Jaeger. Married to a holder of the Cross of German Motherhood. Bronze Class, no less. Not so good at the job, maybe – '

'That's not true.'

' – but *safe*. Suppose I didn't tell you yesterday morning the Gestapo had taken over the Buhler case. Then when you got back *I* said let's check out Stuckart. They look at my record. They might buy that, coming from me.'

'It's good of you.'

'Christ, man – forget that.'

'But it won't work.'

'Why not?'

'Because this is beyond favours and clean sheets, don't you see? What about Buhler and Stuckart? They were in the Party before we were even born. And where were the favours when they needed them?'

'You really think the Gestapo killed them?' Jaeger looked scared.

March put his fingers to his lips and gestured to the picture. 'Say nothing to me you wouldn't say to Heydrich,' he whispered.

THE night dragged by in silence. At about three o'clock, Jaeger pushed some of the chairs together, lay down awkwardly, and closed his eyes. Within minutes, he was snoring. March returned to his post at the window.

He could feel Heydrich's eyes drilling into his back. He tried to ignore it, failed, and turned to confront the picture. A black uniform, a gaunt white face, silver hair – not a human countenance at all but a photographic negative of a skull; an X-ray. The only colour was in the centre of that death-mask face: those tiny pale blue eyes, like splinters of winter sky. March had never met Heydrich, or seen him; had only heard the stories. The press portrayed him as Nietzsche's Superman sprung to life. Heydrich in his pilot's uniform (he had flown combat missions on the Eastern front). Heydrich in his fencing gear (he had fenced for Germany in the Olympics). Heydrich with his violin (he could reduce audiences to tears by the pathos of his playing). When the aircraft carrying Heinrich Himmler had blown up in mid-air two years ago, Heydrich had taken over as Reichsführer-SS. Now he was said to be in line to succeed the Führer. The whisper around the Kripo was that the Reich's chief policeman liked beating up prostitutes.

March sat down. A numbing tiredness was seeping through him, a paralysis: the legs first, then the body, at last the mind. Despite himself, he drifted into a shallow sleep. Once, far away, he thought he heard a cry – human and forlorn – but it might have been a dream. Footsteps echoed in his mind. Keys turned. Cell doors clanged.

HE was jerked awake by a rough hand.

'Good morning, gentlemen. I hope you had some rest?'

It was Krebs.

March felt raw. His eyes were gritty in the sickly neon. Through the window the sky was pearl-grey with the approaching morning.

Jaeger grunted and swung his legs to the floor. 'Now what?'

'Now we talk,' said Krebs. 'Come.'

'Who is this kid,' grumbled Jaeger to March under his breath, 'to push us about?' But he was wary enough to keep his voice low.

They filed into the corridor and March wondered again what game was being played. Interrogation is a night-time art. Why leave it until the morning? Why give them a chance to regain their strength, to concoct a story?

Krebs had recently shaved. His skin was studded with pinpricks of blood. He said: 'Washroom on the right. You will wish to clean yourselves.' It was an instruction rather than a question.

In the mirror, red-eyed and unshaven, March looked more convict than policeman. He filled the basin, rolled up his sleeves and loosened his tie, splashed icy water on his face, his forearms, the nape of his neck, let it trickle down his back. The cold sting brought him back to life.

Jaeger stood alongside him. 'Remember what I said.'

March quickly turned the taps back on. 'Be careful.'

'You think they wire the toilet?'

'They wire everything.'

Krebs conducted them downstairs. The guards fell in behind them. *To the cellar?* They clattered across the vestibule – quieter now than when they had arrived – and out into the grudging light.

Not the cellar.

Waiting in the BMW was the driver who had brought them from Stuckart's apartment. The convoy moved off, north into the rush-hour traffic which was already building up around Potsdamer Platz. In the big shops, the windows piously displayed large, gilt-framed photographs of the Führer – the official portrait from the mid-1950s, by the English photographer, Beaton. Twigs and flowers garlanded the frames, the traditional decoration heralding the Führer's birthday. Four days to go, each of which would see a fresh sprouting of swastika banners. Soon the city would be a forest of red, white and black.

Jaeger was gripping the arm rest, looking sick. 'Come on, Krebs,' he said, in a wheedling voice. 'We're all the same rank. You can tell us where we're going.'

Krebs made no reply. The dome of the Great Hall loomed ahead. Ten minutes later, when the BMW turned left on to the East-West Axis, March guessed their destination.

It was almost eight by the time they arrived. The iron gates of Buhler's villa had been swung wide open. The grounds were filled with vehicles, dotted with black uniforms. One SS trooper was sweeping the lawn with a proton-magnetometer. Behind him, jammed into the ground, was a trail of red flags. Three more soldiers were digging holes. Drawn up on the gravel were Gestapo BMWs, a lorry, and a large armoured security van of the sort used for transporting gold bullion.

March felt Jaeger nudge him. Parked in the shadows beside the house, its driver leaning against the bodywork, was a bulletproof Mercedes limousine. A metal pennant hung above the radiator grille: silver SS lightning flashes on a black background; in one corner, like a cabbalistic symbol, the gothic letter K.

TWO

The head of the Reich Kriminalpolizei was an old man. His name was Artur Nebe, and he was a legend.

Nebe had been head of the Berlin detective force even before the Party came to power. He had a small head and the sallow, scaly skin of a tortoise. In 1954, to mark his sixtieth birthday, the Reichstag had voted him a large estate, including four villages, near Minsk in the Ostland, but he had never even been to look at it. He lived alone with his bed-ridden wife in Charlottenburg, in a large house marked by the smell of disinfectant and the whisper of pure oxygen. It was sometimes said that Heydrich wanted to get rid of him, to put his own man in charge of the Kripo, but dared not. 'Onkel Artur' they called him in Werderscher Markt. Uncle Artur. He knew everything.

March had seen Nebe from a distance but never met him. Now he was sitting at Buhler's grand piano, picking out a high note with a single, yellowish claw. The instrument was untuned, the sound discordant in the dusty air.

At the window, his broad back to the room, stood Odilo Globus.

Krebs brought his heels together and saluted. 'Heil Hitler! Investigators March and Jaeger.'

Nebe continued to tap the piano key.

'Ah!' Globus turned round. 'The great detectives.'

Close up, he was a bull in uniform. His neck strained at his collar. His hands hung at his sides, bunched in angry red fists. There was a mass of scar tissue on his left cheek, mottled crimson. Violence crackled around him in the dry air, like static electricity. Every time Nebe struck a note, he winced. He wants to punch the old man, thought March, but he can't. Nebe outranked him.

'If the Herr Oberstgruppenführer has finished his recital,' said Globus, through his teeth, 'we can begin.'

Nebe's hand froze over the keyboard. 'Why would anyone have a Bechstein, and leave it untuned?' He looked at March. 'Why would he do that?'

'His wife was the musician, sir,' said March. 'She died eleven years ago.'

'And nobody played in all that time?' Nebe closed the lid quietly over the keys and drew his finger through the dust. 'Curious.'

Globus said: 'We have much to do. Early this morning I reported certain matters to the Reichsführer. As you know, Herr Oberstgruppenführer, it is on his orders that this meeting is taking place. Krebs will put the position of the Gestapo.'

March exchanged glances with Jaeger. It had gone up as far as Heydrich.

Krebs had a typed memorandum. In his precise, expressionless voice he began to read.

'Notification of Doctor Josef Buhler's death was received by teleprinter message at Gestapo Headquarters from the Night Duty Officer of the Berlin Kriminalpolizei at two-fifteen yesterday morning, April fifteenth.

'At eight-thirty, in view of Party Comrade Buhler's honorary SS rank of Brigadeführer, the Reichsführer was personally informed of his demise.'

March had his hands clasped behind his back, his nails digging into his palms. In Jaeger's cheek, a muscle fluttered.

'At the time of his death, the Gestapo was completing an investigation into the activities of Party Comrade Buhler. In view of this, and in view of the deceased's former position in the General Government, the case was redesignated a matter of state security, and operational control was passed to the Gestapo.

'However, due to an apparent breakdown in liaison procedures, this redesignation was not communicated to Kripo Investigator Xavier March, who effected an illegal entry to the deceased's home.'

The Gestapo was investigating Buhler? March struggled to keep his gaze fixed on Krebs, his expression impassive.

'Next: the death of Party Comrade Wilhelm Stuckart. Inquiries by the Gestapo indicated that the cases of Stuckart and Buhler were linked. Once again, the Reichsführer was informed. Once again, investigation of the matter was transferred to the Gestapo. And once again, Investigator March, this time accompanied by Investigator Max Jaeger, conducted his own inquiries at the home of the deceased.

'At zero-zero-twelve, sixteenth April, Investigators March and Jaeger were apprehended by myself at Party Comrade Stuckart's apartment block. They agreed to accompany me to Gestapo Headquarters, pending clarification of this matter at a higher level.

'Signed, Karl Krebs, Sturmbannführer.

'I have dated it and timed it at six this morning.'

Krebs folded the memorandum and handed it to the head of the Kripo. Outside, a spade rang on gravel.

Nebe slipped the paper into his inside pocket. 'So much for the record. Naturally, we shall prepare a minute of our own. Now, Globus: what is this really about? You are desperate to tell us, I know.'

'Heydrich wanted you to see for yourself.'

'See what?'

'What your man here missed on his little freelance excursion yesterday. Follow me, please.'

IT was in the cellar, although even if March had smashed

the padlock on the entrance and forced his way down, he doubted if he would have found it. Past the usual household rubbish – broken furniture, discarded tools, rolls of filthy carpet bound with rope – was a wood-panelled wall. One of the panels was false.

'We knew what we were looking for, you see.' Globus rubbed his hands. 'Gentlemen, I guarantee you will never have clapped eyes on the likes of this in your entire lives.'

Beyond the panel was a chamber. When Globus turned on the lights, it was indeed dazzling: a sacristy; a jewelbox. Angels and saints; clouds and temples; high-cheeked noblemen in white furs and red damask; sprawling pink flesh on perfumed yellow silk; flowers and sunrises and Venetian canals . . .

'Go in,' said Globus. 'The Reichsführer is anxious that you should see it properly.'

It was a small room – four metres square, March guessed – with a bank of spotlights built into the ceiling, directed on to the paintings which covered every wall. In the centre was an old-fashioned swivel chair, of the sort a nineteenth-century clerk might have had in a counting-house. Globus placed a gleaming jackboot on the arm and kicked, sending it spinning.

'Imagine him, sitting here. Door locked. Like a dirty old man in a brothel. We found it yesterday afternoon. Krebs?'

Krebs took the floor. 'An expert is on his way this morning from the Führermuseum in Linz. We had Professor Braun of the Kaiser Friedrich, here in Berlin, give us a preliminary assessment last night.'

He consulted his sheaf of notes.

'At the moment, we know we have *Portrait of a Young Man* by Raphael, *Portrait of a Young Man* by Rembrandt, *Christ Carrying the Cross* by Rubens, Guardi's *Venetian Palace, Krakau Suburbs* by Bellotto, eight Canalettos, at least thirty-five engravings by Dürer and Kulmbach, a

Gobelin. The rest he could only guess at.'

Krebs reeled them off as if they were dishes in a restaurant. He rested his pale fingers on an altar-piece of gorgeous colours, raised on planks at the end of the room.

'This is the work of the Nuremberg artist, Viet Stoss, commissioned by the King of Poland in 1477. It took ten years to complete. The centre of the triptych shows the Virgin asleep, surrounded by angels. The side panels show scenes from the lives of Jesus and Mary. The predella' – he pointed to the base of the altar-piece – 'shows the genealogy of Christ.'

Globus said: 'Sturmbannführer Krebs knows of these things. He is one of our brightest officers.'

'I'm sure,' said Nebe. 'Most interesting. And where did it all come from?'

Krebs began: 'The Viet Stoss was removed from the Church of Our Lady in Krakau in November 1939 – '

Globus interrupted: 'It came from the General Government. Warsaw, mainly, we think. Buhler recorded it as either lost or destroyed. God alone knows how much else the corrupt swine got away with. Think what he must have sold just to buy this place!'

Nebe reached out and touched one of the canvases: the martyred Saint Sebastian, bound to a Doric pillar, arrows jutting from his golden skin. The varnish was cracked, like a dried river bed, but the colours beneath – red, white, purple, blue – were bright still. The painting gave off a faint smell of must and incense – the scent of pre-war Poland, of a nation vanished from the map. Some of the panels, March saw, had powdery lumps of masonry attached to their edges – traces of the monastery and castle walls from which they had been wrenched.

Nebe was rapt before the saint. 'Something in his expression reminds me of you, March.' He traced the body's outline with his fingertips and gave a wheezing laugh. ' "The willing martyr." What do you say, Globus?'

Globus grunted. 'I don't believe in saints. Or martyrs.' He glared at March.

'Extraordinary,' murmured Nebe, 'to think of Buhler, of all people, with these . . .'

'You knew him?' March blurted out the question.

'Slightly, before the war. A committed National Socialist, and a dedicated lawyer. Quite a combination. A fanatic for detail. Like our Gestapo colleague here.'

Krebs gave a slight bow. 'The Herr Oberstgruppenführer is kind.'

'The point is this,' said Globus, irritably. 'We have known about Party Comrade Buhler for some time. Known about his activities in the General Government. Known about his associates. Unfortunately, at some point last week, the bastard found out we were on to him.'

'And killed himself?' Nebe asked. 'And Stuckart?'

'The same. Stuckart was a complete degenerate. He not only helped himself to beauty on canvas. He liked to taste it in the flesh. Buhler had the pick of what he wanted in the East. What were those figures, Krebs?'

'A secret inventory was compiled in 1940 by the Polish museum authorities. We now have it. Art treasures removed from Warsaw alone: two thousand seven hundred paintings of the European school; ten thousand seven hundred paintings by Polish artists; fourteen hundred sculptures.'

Globus again: 'We're digging up some of the sculptures in the garden right now. Most of this stuff went where it was intended: the Führermuseum, Reichsmarschall Göring's museum at Carinhall, galleries in Vienna, Berlin. But there's a big discrepancy between the Polish lists of what was taken and our lists of what we got. It worked like this. As State Secretary, Buhler had access to everything. He would ship the stuff under escort to Stuckart at the Interior

Ministry. Everything legal-looking. Stuckart would arrange for it to be stored, or smuggled out of the Reich to be exchanged for cash, jewels, gold – anything portable and non-traceable.'

March could see that Nebe was impressed, despite himself. His little eyes were drinking in the art. 'Was anyone else of high rank involved?'

'You are familiar with the former Under-Secretary of State at the Foreign Ministry, Martin Luther?'

'Of course.'

'He is the man we seek.'

'Seek? He is missing?'

'He failed to return from a business trip three days ago.'

'I take it you are certain of Luther's involvement in this affair?'

'During the war, Luther was head of the Foreign Ministry's German Department.'

'I remember. He was responsible for Foreign Ministry liaison with the SS, and with us at the Kripo.' Nebe turned to Krebs. 'Another fanatical National Socialist. You would have appreciated his – ah – enthusiasm. A rough fellow, though. Incidentally, at this point, I should like to state, for the record, my astonishment at his involvement in anything criminal.'

Krebs produced his pen. Globus went on: 'Buhler stole the art. Stuckart received it. Luther's position at the Foreign Ministry gave him the opportunity to travel freely abroad. We believe he smuggled certain items out of the Reich, and sold them.'

'Where?'

'Switzerland, mainly. Also Spain. Possibly Hungary.'

'And when Buhler came back from the General Government –when was that?'

He looked at March, and March said: 'In 1951.'

'In 1951, this became their treasure chamber.'

Nebe lowered himself into the swivel chair and spun round, slowly, inspecting each wall in turn. 'Extraordinary. This must have been one of the best collections of art in private hands anywhere in the world.'

'One of the best collections in *criminal* hands,' cut in Globus.

'Ach.' Nebe closed his eyes. 'So much perfection in one space deadens the senses. I need air. Give me your arm, March.'

As he stood, March could hear the ancient bones cracking. But the grip on his forearm was steel.

NEBE walked with a stick – *tap, tap, tap* – along the verandah at the back of the villa.

'Buhler drowned himself. Stuckart shot himself. Your case seems to be resolving itself rather conclusively, Globus, without requiring anything so embarrassing as a trial. Statistically, I should say Luther's chances of survival look rather poor.'

'As it happens, Herr Luther *does* have a heart condition. Brought on by nervous strain during the war, according to his wife.'

'You surprise me.'

'According to his wife, he needs rest, drugs, quiet – none of which will he be getting at the moment, wherever he is.'

'This business trip . . .'

'He was supposed to return from Munich on Monday. We've checked with Lufthansa. There was nobody called Luther on any Munich flights that day.'

'Maybe he's fled abroad.'

'Maybe. I doubt it. We'll hunt him down eventually, wherever he is.'

Tap, tap. March admired Nebe's nimbleness of mind. As Police Commissioner for Berlin in the 1930s, he had written a treatise on criminology. He remembered seeing it on Koth's shelves in the fingerprint section on Tuesday night. It was still a standard text.

'And you, March.' Nebe halted and swung round. 'What is your view of Buhler's death?'

Jaeger, who had been silent since their arrival at the villa, butted in anxiously: 'Sir, if I might say, we were merely collecting data – '

Nebe rapped the stone with his stick. 'The question was not addressed to you.'

March wanted a cigarette, badly. 'I have only preliminary observations,' he began. He ran his hand through his hair. He was out of his depth here; a long way out. It was not where to start, he thought, but where to end. Globus had folded his arms and was staring at him.

'Party Comrade Buhler,' he began, 'died some time between six o'clock on Monday evening and six o'clock the following morning. We await the autopsy report, but cause of death was almost certainly drowning – his lungs were full of fluid, indicating he was breathing when he entered the water. We also know, from the sentry on the causeway, that Buhler received no visitors during those crucial twelve hours.'

Globus nodded. 'Thus: suicide.'

'Not necessarily, Herr Obergruppenführer. Buhler received no visitors *by land*. But the woodwork on the jetty has been recently scraped, suggesting a boat may have moored there.'

'Buhler's boat,' said Globus.

'Buhler's boat has not been used for months; maybe, years.'

Now he held the attention of his small audience, March felt a rush of exhilaration; a sense of release. He was starting to talk quickly. Slow down, he told himself, be careful.

'When I inspected the villa yesterday morning, Buhler's

guard dog was locked in the pantry, muzzled. The whole of one side of its head was bleeding. I ask myself: why would a man intending to commit suicide do that to his dog?'

'Where is this animal now?' asked Nebe.

'My men had to shoot it,' said Globus. 'The creature was deranged.'

'Ah. Of course. Go on, March.'

'I think Buhler's assailants landed late at night, in darkness. If you recall, there was a storm on Monday night. The lake would have been choppy – that explains the damage to the jetty. I think the dog was alerted, and they clubbed it senseless, muzzled it, took Buhler unawares.'

'And threw him in the lake?'

'Not immediately. Despite his disability, according to his sister, Buhler was a strong swimmer. You could see that by the look of him: his shoulders were well-developed. But after he had been cleaned up, I inspected his body in the morgue. There was bruising here' – March touched his cheeks – 'and on the gums at the front of his mouth. On the kitchen table yesterday was a bottle of vodka, most of it gone. I think the autopsy report will show alcohol in Buhler's bloodstream. I think they forced him to drink, stripped him, took him out on their boat, and dumped him over the side.'

'Intellectual pigshit,' said Globus. 'Buhler probably drank the vodka to give him the guts to kill himself.'

'According to his sister, Party Comrade Buhler was a teetotaller.'

There was a long silence. March could hear Jaeger breathing heavily. Nebe was gazing out across the lake. Eventually, Globus muttered: 'What this fancy theory doesn't explain is why these mysterious killers didn't just put a bullet in Buhler's brain and have done with it.'

'I would have thought that was obvious,' said March. 'They wanted to make it look like suicide. But they bungled it.'

'Interesting,' murmured Nebe. 'If Buhler's suicide was faked, then it is logical to suppose that Stuckart's was, also.'

Because Nebe was still staring at the Havel, March did not realise at first that the remark was a question, addressed to him.

'That was my conclusion. That was why I visited Stuckart's apartment last night. Stuckart's murder, I think, was a three-man operation: two in the flat; one in the foyer, pretending to repair the elevator. The noise from his electric drill was supposed to mask the sound of the shot, giving the killers time to get away before the body was discovered.'

'And the suicide note?'

'Forged, perhaps. Or written under duress. Or . . .'

He stopped himself. He was thinking aloud, he realised – a potentially fatal activity. Krebs was staring at him.

'Is that it?' asked Globus. 'Are the Grimms' fairy stories over for the day? Excellent. Some of us have work to do. Luther is the key to this mystery, gentlemen. Once we have him, all will be explained.'

Nebe said: 'If his heart condition is as bad as you say, we need to move quickly. I shall arrange with the Propaganda Ministry for Luther's picture to be carried in the press and on television.'

'No, no. Absolutely not.' Globus sounded alarmed. 'The Reichsführer has expressly forbidden any publicity. The last thing we need is a scandal involving the Party leadership, especially now, with Kennedy coming. God in heaven, can you imagine what the foreign press would make of this? No. I assure you, we can catch him without alerting the media. What we need is a confidential flash to all Orpo patrols; a watch on the main railway stations, ports, airports, border crossings . . . Krebs can handle that.'

'Then I suggest he does so.'

'At once, Herr Oberstgruppenführer.' Krebs gave a slight

bow to Nebe and trotted off along the verandah, into the house.

'I have business to attend to in Berlin,' said Nebe. 'March here will act as Kripo liaison officer until Luther is caught.'

Globus sneered. 'That will not be necessary.'

'Oh, but it will. Use him wisely, Globus. He has a brain. Keep him informed. Jaeger: you can return to your normal duties.'

Jaeger looked relieved. Globus seemed about to say something, but thought better of it.

'Walk me to my car, March. Good day to you, Globus.'

WHEN they were round the corner, Nebe said: 'You are not telling the truth, are you? Or at least, not all of it. That is good. Get in the car. We need to talk.'

The driver saluted and opened the rear door. Nebe manoeuvred himself painfully into the back seat. March got in the other side.

'At six o'clock this morning, this arrived at my house by courier.' Nebe unlocked his briefcase and pulled out a file, a couple of centimetres thick. 'It's all about you, Sturmbannführer. Flattering, isn't it, to merit such attention?'

The windows of the Mercedes were tinted green. In the half-light, Nebe looked like a lizard in a reptile house.

'Born, Hamburg, 1922; father died of wounds, 1929; mother killed in a British air raid, 1942; joined the Navy, 1939; transferred to the U-boat service, 1940; decorated for bravery and promoted, 1943; given command of your own boat, 1946 – one of the youngest U-boat commanders in the Reich. A glittering career. And then it all starts going wrong.'

Nebe leafed through the file. March stared at the green lawn, the green sky.

'No police promotions for *ten years*. Divorced, 1957. And then the reports start. Blockwart: persistent refusal to contribute to Winter-Relief. Party officials at Werderscher Markt: persistent refusal to join the NSDAP. Overheard in the canteen making disparaging comments about Himmler. Overheard in bars, overheard in restaurants, overheard in corridors . . .'

Nebe was pulling pages out.

'Christmas 1963 – you start asking round about some Jews who used to live in your apartment. Jews! Are you mad? There is a complaint here from your ex-wife; one from your son . . .'

'My son? My son is ten years old . . .'

'Quite old enough to form a judgement, and be listened to – as you know.'

'May I ask what it is I am supposed to have done to him?'

' "Shown insufficient enthusiasm for his Party activities." The point is, Sturmbannführer, that this file has been ten years maturing in the Gestapo registry – a little here, a little there, year in, year out, growing like a tumour in the dark. And now you've made a powerful enemy, and he wants to use it.'

Nebe put the folder back in his briefcase.

'Globus?'

'Globus, yes. Who else? He asked to have you transferred to Colombia House last night, pending court martial from the SS.' Colombia House was the private SS prison in General-Pape Strasse. 'I have to tell you, March, there is easily enough here to send you to a KZ. After that, you're beyond help – from me or anybody else.'

'What stopped him?'

'To start court-martial proceedings against a serving Kripo officer, he first had to get permission from Heydrich. And Heydrich referred it to me. So what I said to our beloved Reichsführer was this. "This fellow Globus," I said, "is obviously terrified that March has got something on him, so he wants him done away with." "I see," says the Reichsführer, "so what do you suggest?" "Why not," say I, "give him until the Führertag to prove his case against Globus? That's four days." "All right," says Heydrich. "But if he's not come up with anything by then, Globus can have him." ' Nebe gave a smile of contentment. 'Thus are the affairs of the Reich arranged between colleagues of long standing.'

'I suppose I must thank the Herr Oberstgruppenführer.'

'Oh no, don't thank me.' Nebe was cheerful. 'Heydrich genuinely wonders if you do have something on Globus. He would like to know. So would I. Perhaps for a different reason.' He seized March's arm again – the same fierce grip – and hissed: 'These bastards are up to something, March. What is it? You find out. You tell me. Don't trust anyone. That's how your Uncle Artur has lasted as long as he has. Do you know why some of the old-timers call Globus "the submarine"?'

'No, sir.'

'Because he had a submarine engine hooked up to a Polish basement during the war, and used the exhaust fumes to kill people. Globus likes killing people. He'd like to kill you. You should remember that.' Nebe released March's arm. 'Now, we must say goodbye.'

He rapped on the glass partition with the top of his cane. The driver came round and opened March's door.

'I would offer you a lift into central Berlin, but I prefer travelling alone. Keep me informed. Find Luther, March. Find him before Globus gets to him.'

The door slammed. The engine whispered. As the limousine crunched across the gravel, March could barely make out Nebe – just a green silhouette behind the bullet-proof glass.

He turned to find Globus watching him.

The SS general started walking towards him, holding a Luger outstretched.

He is crazy, thought March. He is just about crazy enough to shoot me on the spot, like Buhler's dog.

But all Globus did was hand him the gun. 'Your pistol, Sturmbannführer. You will need it.' And then he came very close – close enough for March to smell the sour odour of garlic sausage on his hot breath. 'You have no witness,' was all he whispered. 'You have no witness. Not any more.'

MARCH ran.

He ran out of the grounds and across the causeway and off, up, into the woods – right the way through them, until he came to the autobahn which formed the Grunewald's eastern boundary.

There he stopped, his hands clutching his knees, his breath coming in sobs, as beneath him the traffic hurtled towards Berlin.

Then he was off again, despite the pain in his side, more of a trot now, over the bridge, past the Nikolassee S-bahn station, down Spanische Allee towards the barracks.

His Kripo ID got him past the sentries, his appearance – red-eyed, breathless, with more than a day's growth of beard – suggestive of some terrible emergency which brooked no discussion. He found the dormitory block. He found Jost's bed. The pillow was gone, the blankets had been stripped. All that remained was the ironwork and a hard, brown mattress. The locker was bare.

A solitary cadet, polishing his boots a few beds away, explained what had happened. They had come for Jost in the night. There were two of them. He was to be sent East, they said, for 'special training'. He had gone without a word – seemed to have been expecting it. The cadet shook his head in amazement: Jost of all people. The cadet was jealous. They all were. He would see some *real* fighting.

THREE

The telephone kiosk stank of urine and ancient cigarette smoke, a used condom had been trodden into the dirt.

'Come on, come on,' whispered March. He rapped a one-Reichsmark piece against the cloudy glass and listened to the electronic purr of her telephone ringing, unanswered. He let it ring for a long time before he hung up.

Across the street a grocery store was opening. He crossed and bought a bottle of milk and some warm bread which he gulped down beside the road, conscious all the time of the shop's owner watching him from the window. It occurred to him that he was living like a fugitive already – stopping to grab food only when he happened across it, devouring it in the open, always on the move. Milk trickled down his chin. He brushed it away with the back of his hand. His skin felt like sandpaper.

He checked again to see if he was being followed. On this side of the street, a uniformed nanny pushed a baby carriage. On the other, an old woman had gone into the telephone kiosk. A schoolboy hurried towards the Havel, clutching a toy yacht. Normal, normal . . .

March, the good citizen, dropped the milk bottle into a waste bin and set off down the suburban road.

'You have no witness. Not any more . . .'

He felt a great rage against Globus, the greater for being fuelled by guilt. The Gestapo must have seen Jost's statement in the file on Buhler's death. They would have checked with the SS academy and discovered that March had been back to re-interrogate him yesterday afternoon. That would have set them scurrying in Prinz-Albrecht Strasse. So his visit to the barracks had been Jost's death warrant. He had indulged his curiosity – and killed a man.

And now the American girl was not answering her telephone. What might they do to her? An army truck overtook him, the draught sucked at him, and a vision of Charlotte Maguire lying broken in the gutter bubbled in his mind. *'The Berlin authorities deeply regret this tragic accident . . . The driver of the vehicle concerned is still being sought . . .'* He felt like the carrier of a dangerous disease. He should carry a placard: keep clear of this man, he is contagious.

Circulating endlessly in his head, fragments of conversation –

Artur Nebe: *'Find Luther, March. Find him before Globus gets to him . . .'*

Rudi Halder: 'A *couple of Sipo guys were round at the Archiv last week asking about you . . .'*

Nebe again: *'There is a complaint here from your ex-wife; one from your son . . .'*

He walked for half an hour along the blossoming streets, past the high hedges and picket fences of prosperous, suburban Berlin. When he reached Dahlem, he stopped a student to ask directions. At the sight of March's uniform, the young man bowed his head. Dahlem was a student quarter. The male undergraduates, like this one, let their hair grow a few centimetres over their collars; some of the women wore jeans – God only knew where they got them. White Rose, the student resistance movement which had flowered briefly in the 1940s until its leaders were executed, was suddenly alive again. 'Ihr Geist lebt weiter' said the graffiti: their spirit lives on. Members of White Rose grumbled about conscription, listened to banned music, circulated seditious magazines, were harassed by the Gestapo.

The student gestured vaguely in response to March's

question, his arms laden with books, and was glad to be on his way.

LUTHER'S house was close to the Botanischer Garten, set back from the road – a nineteenth-century country mansion at the end of a sickle of white gravel. Two men sat in an unmarked grey BMW, parked opposite the drive. The car and its colour branded them at once. There would be two more watching the back, and at least one cruising the neighbourhood streets. March walked past and saw one of the Gestapo watchers turn to the other and speak.

Somewhere, a motor mower was whining; the smell of freshly cut grass hung over the drive. The house and grounds must have cost a fortune – not as much as Buhler's villa, perhaps, but not far off it. The red box of a newly installed burglar alarm jutted beneath the eaves.

He rang the bell and felt himself come under inspection through the spy hole in the centre of the heavy door. After half a minute the door opened to reveal an English maid in a black and white uniform. He gave her his ID and she disappeared to check with her mistress, her feet flapping on the polished wooden floor. She returned to show March into the darkened drawing room. A sweet-smelling smog of eau de cologne lay over the scene. Frau Marthe Luther sat on a sofa, clutching a handkerchief. She looked up at him – glassy blue eyes cracked by minute veins.

'What news?'

'None, madam. I'm sorry to say. But you may be sure that no effort is being spared to find your husband.' *Truer than you know*, he thought.

She was a woman fast losing her attractiveness but gamely staging a fighting retreat. Her tactics, though, were ill-advised: unnaturally blonde hair, a tight skirt, a silk blouse undone just a button too far, to display fat, milky-white cleavage. She looked every centimetre a third wife. A romantic novel lay open, face down, on the embroidered cushion next to her. *The Kaiser's Ball* by Barbara Cartland.

She returned his identity card and blew her nose. 'Will you sit down? You look exhausted. Not even time to shave! Some coffee? Sherry, perhaps? No? Rose, bring coffee for the Herr Sturmbannführer. And perhaps I might fortify myself with just the *smallest* sherry.'

Perched uneasily on the edge of a deep, chintz-covered armchair, his notebook open on his knee, March listened to Frau Luther's woeful tale. Her husband? A very good man, short-tempered – yes, maybe, but that was his nerves, poor thing. Poor, poor thing – he had weepy eyes, did March know that?

She showed him a photograph: Luther at some Mediterranean resort, absurd in a pair of shorts, scowling, his eyes swollen behind the thick glasses.

On she went: a man of that age – he would be sixty-nine in December, they were going to Spain for his birthday. Martin was a friend of General Franco – a dear little man, had March ever met him?

No: a pleasure denied.

Ah, well. She couldn't bear to think what might have happened, always so careful about telling her where he was going, he had never done anything like this. It was such a help to talk, so sympathetic . . .

There was a sigh of silk as she crossed her legs, the skirt rising provocatively above a plump knee. The maid reappeared and set down coffee cup, cream jug and sugar bowl in front of March. Her mistress was provided with a glass of sherry, and a crystal decanter, three-quarters empty.

'Did you ever hear him mention the names Josef Buhler or Wilhelm Stuckart?'

A little crack of concentration appeared in the cake of makeup: 'No, I don't recall . . . No, definitely not.'

'Did he go out at all last Friday?'

'Last Friday? I think – yes. He went out early in the morning.' She sipped her sherry. March made a note.

'And when did he tell you he had to go away?'

'That afternoon. He returned about two, said something had happened, that he had to spend Monday in Munich. He flew on Sunday afternoon, so he could stay overnight and be up early.'

'And he didn't tell you what it was about?'

'He was old-fashioned about that sort of thing. His business was his business, if you see what I mean.'

'Before the trip, how did he seem?'

'Oh, irritable, as usual.' She laughed – a girlish giggle. 'Yes, perhaps he *was* a little more preoccupied than normal. The television news always depressed him – the terrorism, the fighting in the East. I told him to pay no attention – no good will come of worrying, I said – but things . . . yes, they preyed on his mind.' She lowered her voice. 'He had a breakdown during the war, poor thing. The strain . . .'

She was about to cry again. March cut in: 'What year was his breakdown?'

'I believe it was in '43. That was before I knew him, of course.'

'Of course.' March smiled and bowed his head. 'You must have been at school.'

'Perhaps not quite at *school* . . .' The skirt rose a little higher.

'When did you start to become alarmed for his safety?'

'When he didn't come home on Monday. I was awake all night.'

'So you reported him missing on Tuesday morning?'

'I was about to, when Obergruppenführer Globocnik arrived.'

March tried to keep the surprise out of his voice: 'He

arrived *before* you even told the Polizei? What time was that?'

'Soon after nine. He said he needed to speak to my husband. I told him the situation. The Obergruppenführer took it very seriously.'

'I'm sure he did. Did he tell you why he needed to speak to Herr Luther?'

'No. I assumed it was a Party matter. Why?' Suddenly, her voice had a harder edge. 'Are you suggesting my husband had done something wrong?'

'No, no . . .'

She straightened her skirt over her knees, smoothed it out with ring-encrusted fingers. There was a pause and then she said: 'Herr Sturmbannführer, what is the purpose of this conversation?'

'Did your husband ever visit Switzerland?'

'He used to, occasionally, some years ago. He had business there. Why?'

'Where is his passport?'

'It is not in his study. I checked. But I have been over this with the Obergruppenführer. Martin always carried his passport with him. He said he never knew when he might need it. That was his Foreign Ministry training. Really, there is nothing unusual about that, really . . .'

'Forgive me, madam.' He pressed on. 'The burglar alarm. I noticed it on my way in. It looks new.'

She glanced down at her lap. 'Martin had it installed last year. We had intruders.'

'Two men?'

She looked up at him with surprise. 'How did you know?'

That was a mistake. He said: 'I must have read the report in your husband's file.'

'Impossible.' Surprise had been replaced in her voice by suspicion. 'He never reported it.'

'Why not?'

She was on the point of making a blustering reply – 'What business is it of yours?' or something of the sort – but then she saw the expression in March's eyes and changed her mind. She said, in a resigned voice: 'I pleaded with him, Herr Sturmbannführer. But he wouldn't. And he wouldn't tell me why.'

'What happened?'

'It was last winter. We were planning to stay in for the evening. Some friends called at the last minute and we went out to dinner, at Horcher's. When we got back, there were two men *in this room.*' She looked around as if they might still be hiding somewhere. 'Thank God our friends came in with us. If we'd been alone . . . When they saw there were four of us, they jumped out of that window.' She pointed behind March's shoulder.

'So he put in an alarm system. Did he take any other precautions?'

'He hired a security guard. Four of them, in fact. They worked shifts. He kept them on until after Christmas. Then he decided he didn't trust them any more. He was so *frightened*, Herr Sturmbannführer.'

'Of what?'

'He wouldn't tell me.'

Out came the handkerchief. Another helping of sherry was sloshed from the decanter. Her lipstick had left thick pink smears around the rim of her glass. She was sliding towards the edge of tears again. March had misjudged her. She was frightened for her husband, true. But she was more frightened now that he might have been deceiving her. The shadows were chasing one another across her mind, and in her eyes they left their trails. Was it another woman? A crime? A secret? Had he fled the country? Gone for good? He felt sorry for her, and for a moment considered warning her of the Gestapo's case against her husband. But why add to her misery? She would know soon enough. He hoped the state would not confiscate the house.

'Madam, I have intruded too long.' He closed his notebook and stood. She clutched his hand, peered up at him.

'I'm never going to see him again, am I?'

'Yes,' he said.

No, he thought.

It was a relief to leave the dark and sickly room and escape into the fresh air. The Gestapo men were still sitting in the BMW. They watched him leave. He hesitated for a second, and then turned right, towards the Botanischer Garten railway station.

Four security guards!

He could begin to see it now. A meeting at Buhler's villa on Friday morning, attended by Buhler, Stuckart and Luther. A panicky meeting, old men in a sweat of fear – and with good reason. Perhaps they had each been given a separate task. At any rate, on Sunday, Luther had flown to Zürich. March was sure it was he who must have sent the chocolates from Zürich airport on Monday afternoon, maybe just as he was about to board another aircraft. What were they? Not a present: a signal. Was their arrival meant to be taken as a sign that his task had been completed successfully? Or that he had failed?

March checked over his shoulder. Yes, now he was being followed, he was almost certain. They would have had time to organise while he was in Luther's house. Which were their agents? The woman in the green coat? The student on his bicycle? Hopeless. The Gestapo were too good for him to spot. There would be three or four of them, at least. He lengthened his stride. He was nearing the station.

Question: did Luther return to Berlin from Zürich on

Monday afternoon, or did he stay out of the country? On balance, March inclined to the view that he had returned. That call to Buhler's villa yesterday morning – *'Buhler? Speak to me. Who is that?'* – that had been Luther, he was sure. So: assume Luther posted the packages just before he boarded his flight, say around five o'clock. He would have landed in Berlin about seven that evening. And disappeared.

The Botanischer Garten station was on the suburban electric line. March bought a one-Mark ticket and lingered around the barrier until the train approached. He boarded it and then, just as the doors sighed shut, jumped off, and sprinted over the metal foot-bridge to the other platform. Two minutes later he got on to the south-bound train, only to leap out at Lichterfelde, and re-cross the tracks. The station was deserted. He let the first north-bound train go by, caught the second, and settled into his seat. The only other occupant of the carriage was a pregnant woman. He gave her a smile; she looked away. Good.

Luther, Luther. March lit a cigarette. Nearing seventy with a nervous heart and rheumy eyes. Too paranoid to trust even your wife. They came for you six months earlier, and by luck you escaped. Why did you make a run for it from Berlin airport? Did you come through customs and decide to call your confederates? In Stuckart's apartment, the telephone would have rung unanswered, next to the silent, blood-washed bedroom. In Schwanenwerder, if Eisler's estimate of the time of death was accurate, Buhler must already have been surprised by his killers. Had they let the telephone ring? Or had one of them answered it, while the others held Buhler down?

Luther, Luther: something happened to make you run for your life – out into the freezing rain of that Monday night.

He got out at Gotenland station. It was yet another piece

of architectural fantasy come true – mosaic floors, polished stone, stained glass windows thirty metres high. The regime closed churches and compensated by building railway termini to look like cathedrals.

Gazing down from the overhead walkway on to the thousands of hurrying passengers, March almost gave in to despair. Myriad lives – each with its own secrets and plans and dreams, its individual luggage of guilt – criss-crossed beneath him, not one touching the other, separate and distinct. To think that he, alone, could possibly track down one old man among so many – for the first time, the idea struck him as fantastic, absurd.

But Globus could do it. Already, March could see, the police patrols had been increased in strength. That must have happened in the last half-hour. The Orpo men were scrutinising every male over sixty. A derelict without papers was being led away, complaining.

Globus! March turned away from the handrail and stepped on to the descending escalator, in search of the one person in Berlin who might be able to save his life.

FOUR

To travel on the central U-bahn line is, in the words of the Reich Ministry for Propaganda and Cultural Enlightenment, to take a trip through German history. Berlin-Gotenland, Bülow Strasse, Nollendorf Platz, Wittenberg Platz, Nürnberger Platz, Hohenzollern Platz – the stations succeed one another like pearls on a string.

The carriages which work this line are pre-war. Red cars for smokers, yellow for non-smokers. Hard wooden seats have been rubbed shiny by three decades of Berlin backsides. Most passengers stand, holding on to the worn leather hand-grips, swaying with the rhythm of the train. Signs urge them to turn informer. 'The fare-dodger's profit is the Berliner's loss! Notify the authorities of all wrong-doing!' 'Has he given up his seat to a woman or veteran? Penalty for failure: 25 Reichsmarks!'

March had bought a copy of the *Berliner Tageblatt* from a platform kiosk and was leaning next to the doors, skimming through it. Kennedy and the Führer, the Führer and Kennedy – that was all there was to read. The regime was clearly investing heavily in the success of the talks. That could only mean that things in the East were even worse than everyone thought. 'A permanent state of war on the Eastern front will help to form a sound race of men,' the Führer had once said, 'and will prevent us relapsing into the softness of a Europe thrown back upon itself.' But people *had* grown soft. What else was the point of victory? They had Poles to dig their gardens and Ukrainians to sweep their streets, French chefs to cook their food and English maids to serve it. Having tasted the comforts of peace they had lost their appetite for war.

Way down on an inside page, in type so small it was barely readable, was Buhler's obituary. He was reported as having died in a 'bathing accident'.

March stuffed the paper into his pocket and got out at Bülow Strasse. From the open platform he could see across to Charlotte Maguire's apartment. A shape moved against the curtain. She was at home. Or, rather, someone was at home.

The concierge was not in her chair, and when he knocked on the apartment door there was no reply. He knocked again, more loudly.

Nothing.

He walked away from the door and clattered down the first flight of steps. Then he stopped, counted to ten, and crept back up again, sideways, with his back pressed to the wall – one step, pause; another step, pause – wincing whenever he made a noise, until he stood once more outside the door. He drew his pistol.

Minutes passed. Dogs barked, cars and trains and planes went by, babies cried, birds sang: the cacophony of silence. And at one point, inside the apartment, loud above it all, a floorboard creaked.

The door opened a fraction.

March spun, rammed into it with his shoulder. Whoever was on the other side was knocked back by the force of the blow. And then March was in and on him, pushing him through the tiny hall and into the sitting room. A lamp toppled to the floor. He tried to bring up the gun, but the man had grabbed his arms. And now it was he who was being pushed backwards. The back of his legs made contact with a low table and he toppled over, cracking his head on something, the Luger skittering across the floor.

Well, now, this was quite funny, and in other circumstances March might have laughed. He had never been very good at this sort of thing, and now – having started with the advantage of surprise – he was on his back, unarmed, with his head in the fireplace and his legs still resting on top of the coffee table, in the position of a pregnant woman undergoing an internal examination.

His assailant fell on top of him, winding him. One gloved hand clawed at his face, the other seized his throat. March could neither see nor breathe. He twisted his head from side to side, chewed on the leather hand. He flailed at the other man's head with his fists, but could put no force behind his blows. What was on him was not human. It had the remorseless power of machinery. It was grinding him. Steel fingers had found that artery – the one March could never remember, let alone locate – and he felt himself surrendering to the force, the rushing blackness obliterating the pain. *So,* he thought, *I have walked the earth and come to this.*

A crash. The hands slackened, withdrew. March came swimming back into the fight, at least as a spectator. The man had been knocked sideways, hit on the head by a chair of tubular steel. Blood masked his face, pulsing from a cut above his eye. Crash. The chair again. With one arm, the man tried to ward off the blows, with the other he wiped frantically at his blinded eyes. He began shuffling on his knees for the door, a devil on his back – a hissing, spitting fury, claws scrabbling to find his eyes. Slowly, as if carrying an immense weight, he raised himself on one leg, then the other. All he wanted now was to get away. He blundered into the door frame, turned and hammered his tormentor against it – once, twice.

Only then did Charlie Maguire let him go.

CLUSTERS of pain, bursting like fireworks: his head, the backs of his legs, his ribs, his throat.

'Where did you learn to fight?'

He was in the tiny kitchen, bent over the sink. She was mopping blood from the cut on the back of his head.

'Try growing up as the only girl in a family with three brothers. You learn to fight. Hold still.'

'I pity the brothers. Ah.' March's head hurt the most. The bloody water dripping into the greasy plates a few centimetres from his face made him feel sick. 'In Hollywood, I think, it is traditional for the man to rescue the girl.'

'Hollywood is full of shit.' She applied a fresh cloth. 'This is quite deep. Are you sure you don't want to go to the hospital?'

'No time.'

'Will that man come back?'

'No. At least, not for a while. Supposedly, this is still a clandestine operation. Thank you.'

He held the cloth to the back of his head and straightened. As he did so, he discovered a new pain, at the base of his spine.

' "A clandestine operation"?' she repeated. 'You don't think he could have been an ordinary thief?'

'No. He was a professional. An authentic, Gestapo-trained professional.'

'And I beat him!' The adrenalin had given lustre to her skin; her eyes sparkled. Her only injury was a bruise on her shoulder. She was more attractive than he remembered. Delicate cheek bones, a strong nose, full lips, large brown eyes. She had brown hair, cut to the nape of her neck, which she wore swept back behind her ears.

'If his orders had been to kill you, he would have done so.'

'Really? Then why didn't he?' Suddenly she sounded angry.

'You're an American. A protected species, especially at the moment.' He inspected the cloth. The flow of blood had stopped. 'Don't underrate the enemy, Fräulein.'

'Don't underrate *me*. If I hadn't come home, he'd have killed you.'

He decided to say nothing. She clearly kept her temper on a hair-trigger.

The apartment had been thoroughly ransacked. Her clothes hung out of their drawers, papers had been spilled across the desk and on to the floor, suitcases had been upended. Not, he thought, that it could have been very neat before: the dirty dishes in the sink, the profusion of bottles (most of them empty) in the bathroom, the yellowing copies of the *New York Times* and *Time*, their pages sliced to ribbons by the German censors, stacked haphazardly around the walls. Searching it must have been a nightmare. Weak light filtered in through dirty net curtains. Every few minutes the walls shook as the trains passed.

'This is yours, I take it?' She pulled out the Luger from beneath a chair and held it up between finger and thumb.

'Yes. Thank you.' He took it. She had a gift for making him feel stupid. 'Is anything missing?'

'I doubt it.' She glanced around. 'I'm not sure I'd know if there was.'

'The item I gave you last night. . . ?'

'Oh that? It was here on the mantelpiece.' She ran her hand along it, frowning. 'It *was* here . . .'

He closed his eyes. When he opened them, she was grinning.

'Don't worry, Sturmbannführer. It's stayed close to my heart. Like a love-letter.'

She turned her back on him, unbuttoning her shirt. When she turned round, she had the envelope in her hand. He took it over to the window. It was warm to his touch.

It was long and slim, made of thick paper – a rich creamy-blue with brown specks of age, like liver spots. It was luxurious, hand-made, redolent of another age. There was no name or address.

Inside the envelope was a small brass key and a letter, on matching blue paper, as thick as cardboard. Printed in the top right-hand corner, in flowery copperplate, was: Zaugg & Cie, Bankiers, Bahnhof Strasse 44, Zürich. A single sentence, typed beneath, identified the bearer as a joint holder of account number 2402. The letter was dated 8 July 1942. It was signed Hermann Zaugg, Director.

March read it through again. He was not surprised Stuckart had kept it locked in his safe: it was illegal for a German citizen to possess a foreign bank account without the permission of the Reichsbank. The penalty for non-compliance was death.

He said: 'I was worried about you. I tried to call you a couple of hours ago, but there was no answer.'

'I was out, doing research.'

'Research?'

She grinned again.

AT March's suggestion, they went for a walk in the Tiergarten, the traditional rendezvous for Berliners with secrets to discuss. Even the Gestapo had yet to devise a means of bugging a park. Daffodils poked through the rough grass at the foot of the trees. Children fed the ducks on the Neuer See.

Getting out of Stuckart's apartment block had been easy, she said. The air shaft had emerged into the alley almost at ground level. There were no SS men. They were all round the front. So she had simply walked down the side of the building, to the street at the rear, and caught a taxi home. She had stayed up half the night waiting for him to call, re-reading the letter until she knew it off by heart. When, by nine o'clock, she had still heard nothing, she decided not to wait.

She wanted to know what had happened to him and

Jaeger. He told her only that they had been taken to Gestapo headquarters and released that morning.

'Are you in trouble?'

'Yes. Now tell me what you discovered.'

She had gone first to the public library in Nollendorf Platz – she had nothing better to do now her press accreditation had been withdrawn. In the library was a directory of European banks. Zaugg & Cie still existed. The bank's premises remained in Bahnhof Strasse. From the library she had gone to the US Embassy to see Henry Nightingale.

'Nightingale?'

'You met him last night.'

March remembered: the young man in the sports jacket and the button-down shirt, with his hand on her arm. 'You didn't tell him anything?'

'Of course not. Anyway, he's discreet. We can trust him.'

'I prefer to make my own judgements about whom I can trust.' He felt disappointed in her. 'Is he your lover?'

She stopped in her tracks. 'What kind of a question is that?'

'I have more at stake in this than you have, Fräulein. Much more. I have a right to know.'

'You have no right to know *at all.*' She was furious.

'All right.' He held up his hands. The woman was impossible. 'Your business.'

They resumed walking.

Nightingale, she explained, was an expert in Swiss commercial matters, having dealt with the affairs of several German refugees in the United States trying to extract their money from banks in Zürich and Geneva.

It was almost impossible.

In 1934, a Gestapo agent named Georg Hannes Thomae had been sent to Switzerland by Reinhard Heydrich to find out the names of as many German account-holders as possible. Thomae set up house in Zürich, began affairs with several lonely female cashiers, befriended minor bank officials. When the Gestapo had suspicions that a certain individual had an illegal account, Thomae would visit the bank posing as an intermediary and try to deposit money. The moment any cash was accepted, Heydrich knew an account existed. Its holder was arrested, tortured into revealing the details, and soon the bank would receive a detailed cable requesting, in proper form, the repatriation of all assets.

The Gestapo's war against the Swiss banks became increasingly sophisticated and extensive. Telephone calls, cables and letters between Germany and Switzerland were intercepted as a matter of routine. Clients were executed or sent to concentration camps. In Switzerland, there was an outcry. Finally, the Swiss National Assembly rushed through a new Banking Code making it illegal for banks to disclose any details of their clients' holdings, on pain of imprisonment. Georg Thomae was exposed and expelled.

Swiss banks came to regard doing business with German citizens as too dangerous and time-consuming to countenance. Communication with clients was virtually impossible. Hundreds of accounts had simply been abandoned by their terrified owners. In any case, respectable bankers had no desire to become involved in these life-and-death transactions. The publicity was damaging. By 1939 the once-lucrative German numbered-account business had collapsed.

'Then came the war,' said Charlie. They had reached the end of the Neuer See and were walking back. From beyond the trees came the hum of the traffic on the East-West Axis. The dome of the Great Hall rose above the trees. Berliners joked that the only way to avoid seeing it was to live inside it.

'After 1939, the demand for Swiss accounts increased dramatically, for obvious reasons. People were desperate to get their property out of Germany. So banks like Zaugg devised a new kind of deposit account. For a fee of 200 Francs, you received a box and a number, a key and a letter of authorisation.'

'Exactly like Stuckart.'

'Right. You simply needed to show up with the letter and the key, and it was all yours. No questions. Each account could have as many keys and letters of authorisation as the holder was prepared to pay for. The beauty of it was – the banks were no longer involved. One day, if she could get the travel permit, some little old lady might turn up with her life savings. Ten years later, her son could turn up with a letter and a key and walk off with his inheritance.'

'Or the Gestapo might turn up . . .'

'. . . and if they had the letter and the key, the bank could give them everything. No embarrassments. No publicity. No breaking the Banking Code.'

'These accounts – they still exist?'

'The Swiss Government banned them at the end of the war, under pressure from Berlin, and no new ones have been allowed since. But the old ones – they still exist, because the terms of the original agreement have to be honoured. They've become valuable in their own right. People sell them on to one another. According to Henry, Zaugg developed quite a speciality in them. God knows what he's got locked in those boxes.'

'Did you mention Stuckart's name to this Nightingale?'

'Of course not. I told him I was writing a piece for *Fortune* about "the lost legacies of the war".'

'Just as you told me you were going to interview Stuckart for an article about "the Führer's early years"?'

She hesitated, and said quietly: 'What's that supposed to mean?'

His head was throbbing, his ribs still ached. *What did he mean?* He lit a cigarette to give himself time to think.

'People who encounter violent death – they try to forget it, run away. Not you. Last night: your eagerness to go back to Stuckart's apartment, the way you opened his letters. This morning: turning up information about Swiss banks . . .'

He stopped speaking. An elderly couple passed on the footpath, staring at them. He realised they must look an odd pair: an SS Sturmbannführer, unshaven and slightly bashed around, and a woman who was clearly a foreigner. Her accent might be perfect, but there was something about her, in her expression, her clothes, her stance – something which betrayed that she was not German.

'Let's walk this way.' He led her off the path, towards the trees.

'Can I have one of those?'

In the shadows, as he lit her a cigarette, she cupped the flame. Reflections of the fire danced in her eyes.

'All right.' She took a pace back, hugging herself as if she were cold. 'It's true my parents knew Stuckart before the war. It's true I went to see him before Christmas. But I didn't call him. He called me.'

'When?'

'On Saturday. Late.'

'What did he say?'

She laughed. 'Oh no, Sturmbannführer. In my business information is a commodity, exchangeable on the open market. But I'm willing to trade.'

'What do you want to know?'

'Everything. Why you had to break into that apartment last night. Why you are keeping secrets from your own people. Why the Gestapo almost killed you an hour ago.'

'Oh *that* . . .' He smiled. He felt weary. He leaned his back against the rough bark of the tree and stared across the park. It seemed to him he had nothing to lose.

'Two days ago,' he began, 'I fished a body out of the Havel.'

He told her everything. He told her about Buhler's death and Luther's disappearance. He told her what Jost had seen, and what had happened to him. He told her about Nebe and Globus, about the art treasures and the Gestapo file. He even told her about Pili's statement. And – something he had noticed about criminals confessing, even those who knew that their confessions would one day hang them – when he finished, he felt better.

She was silent a long time. 'That's fair,' she said. 'I don't know how this helps, but this is what happened to me.'

SHE had gone to bed early on Saturday night. The weather had been foul – the start of that great bank of rain that had washed over the city for three days. She was not feeling sociable, had not for weeks. You know how it is. Berlin can get to you like that. Make you feel small and hopeless in the shade of those vast grey buildings; the endless uniforms; the unsmiling bureaucrats.

The phone went about eleven-thirty, just as she was drifting off to sleep. A man's voice. Taut. Precise. 'There is a telephone booth opposite your apartment. Go to it. I shall call you there in five minutes. If the booth is occupied, please wait.'

She had not recognised who it was, but something in the man's tone had told her it was not a joke. She had dressed, grabbed her coat, hobbled down the stairs, into the street, trying to pull on her shoes and walk at the same time. The rain had hit her like a slap across the face. Across the street, outside the station, was an old wooden telephone kiosk – empty, thank God.

It was while she was waiting for the call that she remembered where she had first heard the voice.

'Go back a bit,' said March. 'Your first meeting with Stuckart. Describe it.'

That was before Christmas. She had called him cold. Explained who she was. He seemed reluctant, but she had persisted, so he had invited her over for tea. He had a shock of white curly hair and one of those orangey tans, as if he had spent a long time in the sun, or under an ultraviolet lamp. The woman, Maria, was also in the apartment, but behaved like a maid. She served some tea then left them to it. Usual chat: how is your mother? Very well, thank you.

Ha, that was a joke.

She flicked ash from the end of her cigarette.

'My mother's career died when she left Berlin. My arrival buried it. As you can imagine, there wasn't a great demand for German actresses in Hollywood during the war.'

And then he had asked about her father, in a gritted-teeth kind of a way. And she had been able to take great pleasure in saying: very well, thank you. He had retired in 'sixty-one, when Kennedy took over. Deputy Under-Secretary of State Michael Maguire. God bless the United States of America. Stuckart had met him through Mom, had known him when he was at the Embassy here.

March interrupted: 'When was that?'

''Thirty-seven to 'thirty-nine.'

'Go on.'

Well, then he had wanted to know about the job and she had told him. World European Features: he had never heard of them. Not surprising, she said: nobody had. That sort of thing. Polite interest, you know. So when she left she gave him her card, and he had bent to kiss her hand, had lingered over it, made a meal of it, made her feel sick. He had patted her bottom on the way out. And that had been that, she was glad to say. Five months: nothing.

'Until Saturday night?'

Until Saturday night. She had been in the telephone kiosk no more than thirty seconds when he rang. Now all the arrogance was gone from his voice.

'Charlotte?' He had placed heavy emphasis on the second syllable. Shar-*lott*-e. 'Forgive this melodrama. Your telephone is tapped.'

'They say every foreigner's line is tapped.'

'This is true. When I was in the Ministry, I used to see transcripts. But public boxes are safe. I am in a public box now. I came on Thursday and took the number of the one you are in. It is serious, you see. I need to contact the authorities in your country.'

'Why not talk to the Embassy?'

'The Embassy is not safe.'

He had sounded terrified. And tight. Definitely, he had been drinking.

'Are you saying you want to defect?'

A long silence. Then there had been a noise behind her. A sound of metal tapping on glass. She had turned to discover, in the rain and the dark, a man, with his hands cupped round his eyes, peering into the kiosk, looking like a deep-sea diver. She must have let out a cry or something because Stuckart had got very frightened.

'What was that? What is it?'

'Nothing. Just someone wanting to use the phone.'

'We must be quick. I deal only with your father, not the Embassy.'

'What do you want me to do?'

'Come to me tomorrow and I will tell you everything. Shar-*lott*-e, I will make you the most famous reporter in the world.'

'Where? What time?'

'My apartment. Noon.'

'Is that safe?'

'Nowhere is safe.'

And then he had rung off. Those were the last words she had heard Stuckart speak.

She finished her cigarette, ground it under her foot.

The rest he knew, more or less. She had found the bodies, called the police. They had taken her to the big city station in Alexander Platz, where she had sat in a blank-walled room for more than three hours, going crazy. Then she had been driven to another building, to give a statement to some creepy SS man in a cheap wig, whose office had been more like that of a pathologist than a detective.

March smiled at the description of Fiebes.

She had already made up her mind not to tell the Polizei about Stuckart's call on Saturday night, for an obvious reason. If she had hinted that she had been preparing to help Stuckart defect, she would have been accused of 'activities incompatible with her status as a journalist', and arrested. As it was, they had decided to deport her anyway. So it goes.

THE authorities were planning a fireworks display in the Tiergarten, to commemorate the Führer's birthday. An area of the park had been fenced off, and pyrotechnicians in blue overalls were laying their surprises, watched by a curious crowd. Mortar tubes, sandbagged emplacements, dug-outs, kilometres of cable: these looked more like the preparations for an artillery bombardment than for a celebration. Nobody paid any attention to the SS-Sturmbannführer and the woman in the blue plastic coat.

He scribbled on a page of his notebook.

'These are my telephone numbers – office and home. Also, here are the numbers of a friend of mine called Max Jaeger. If you can't get hold of me, call him.' He tore out the page and gave it to her. 'If anything suspicious happens, anything worries you – it doesn't matter what the time is – call.'

'What about you? What are you going to do?'

'I'm going to try to get to Zürich tonight. Check out this bank account first thing tomorrow.'

He knew what she would say even before she opened her mouth.

'I'll come with you.'

'You will be much safer here.'

'But it's my story, too.'

She sounded like a spoilt child. 'It's not a story, for God's sake.' He bit back his anger. 'Look. A deal. Whatever I find out, I swear I'll tell you. You can have it all.'

'It's not as good as being there.'

'It's better than being dead.'

'They wouldn't do anything like that abroad.'

'On the contrary, that is exactly where they would do it. If something happens here, they are responsible. If something happens abroad . . .' He shrugged. 'Prove it.'

THEY parted in the centre of the Tiergarten. He strode briskly across the grass, towards the humming city. As he walked, he took the envelope out of his pocket, squeezed it to check the key was still in it and – on impulse – raised it to his nose. Her scent. He looked over his shoulder. She was walking through the trees with her back to him. She disappeared for a moment, then reappeared; disappeared, reappeared – a tiny birdlike figure – bright blue plumage against the dreary wood.

FIVE

The door to March's apartment hung off its hinges like a broken jaw. He stood on the landing, listening, his pistol drawn. The place was silent, deserted.

Like Charlotte Maguire's, his apartment had been searched, but by hands of greater malevolence. Everything had been tipped into a heap in the centre of the sitting room – clothes and books, shoes and old letters, photographs and crockery and furniture – the detritus of a life. It was as if someone had intended to make a bonfire but had been distracted at the last minute, before they could apply the torch.

Wedged upright on top of the pyre was a wooden-framed photograph of March, aged twenty, shaking hands with the commander of the *U-Boot Waffe*, Admiral Dönitz. Why had it been left like that? What point was being made? He picked it up, carried it over to the window, blew dust off it. He had forgotten he even had it. Doenitz liked to come aboard every boat before it left Wilhelmshaven: an awesome figure, ramrod, iron-gripped, gruff. 'Good hunting,' he had barked at March. He growled the same to everyone. The picture showed five young crewmen lined up beneath the conning tower to meet him. Rudi Halder was to March's left. The other three had died later that year, trapped in the hull of U-175.

Good hunting.

He tossed the picture back on the pile.

It had taken time to do all this. Time, and anger, and the certainty of not being disturbed. It must have happened while he was under guard in Prinz-Albrecht Strasse. It could only have been the work of the Gestapo. He remembered a line of graffiti scrawled by White Rose on a wall near Werderscher Markt: 'A police state is a country run by criminals'.

They had opened his mail. A couple of bills, long overdue – they were welcome to *them* – and a letter from his ex-wife, dated Tuesday. He glanced through it. She had decided he was not to see Pili in future. It upset the boy too much. She hoped he would agree this was for the best. If necessary, she would be willing to swear a deposition before the Reich Family Court, giving her reasons. She trusted this would not be necessary, both for his sake and the boy's. It was signed 'Klara Eckart'. So she had gone back to her maiden name. He screwed it up and threw it next to the photograph, with the rest of the rubbish.

The bathroom at least had been left intact. He showered and shaved, inspecting himself in the mirror for damage. It felt worse than it looked: a large bruise developing nicely on his chest, more on the back of his legs and at the base of his spine; a livid mark at his throat. Nothing serious. What was it his father used to say – his paternal balm for all the batterings of childhood? 'You'll live, boy.' That was it. 'You'll live!'

Naked, he went back into the sitting room and searched through the wreckage, pulling out clean clothes, a pair of shoes, a suitcase, a leather hold-all. He feared they might have taken his passport but it was there, at the bottom of the mound. It had been issued in 1961, when March had gone to Italy to bring back a gangster being held in Milan. His younger self stared up at him, fatter-cheeked, half-smiling. *My God*, he thought, *I have aged ten years in three.*

He brushed down his uniform and put it back on, together with a clean shirt, and packed his suitcase. As he bent to snap it shut his eye was caught by something in the empty grate. The photograph of the Weiss family was lying face down. He hesitated, picked it up, folded it into a small square – exactly as he had found it five years earlier – and slipped it into his wallet. If he was stopped and searched, he would say they were his family.

Then he took a last look round and left, closing the broken door behind him as best he could.

AT the main branch of the Deutschebank, in Wittenberg Platz, he asked how much he held in his account.

'Four thousand two hundred and seventy-seven Reichsmarks and thirty-eight pfennigs.'

'I'll take it.'

'All of it, Herr Sturmbannführer?' The teller blinked at him through wire-framed spectacles. 'You are closing the account?'

'All of it.'

March watched him count out forty-two one-hundred Mark notes, then stuffed them into his wallet, next to the photograph. Not much in the way of life savings.

This is what no promotions and seven years of alimony do to you.

The teller was staring at him. 'Did the Herr Sturmbannführer say something?'

He had given voice to his thoughts. He must be going mad. 'No. Sorry. Thank you.'

March picked up his suitcase, went out into the square and caught a taxi to Werderscher Markt.

ALONE in his office, he did two things. He rang the headquarters of Lufthansa and asked the head of security – a former Kripo investigator he knew, called Friedman – to check if the airline had carried a passenger by the name of Martin Luther on any of its Berlin-Zürich flights on Sunday or Monday.

'Martin Luther, right?' Friedman was greatly amused. 'Anyone else you want, March? Emperor Charlemagne? Herr von Goethe?'

'It's important.'

'It's always important. Sure. I know.' Friedman promised to find out the information at once. 'Listen. When you get tired of chasing ambulances, there's always a job for you here if you want it.'

'Thanks. I may well.'

After he hung up, March took the dead plant down from the filing cabinet. He lifted the atrophied roots out of the pot, put in the brass key, replaced the plant, and returned the pot to its old position.

Five minutes later, Friedman called him back.

ARTUR NEBE'S suite of offices was on the fourth floor – all cream carpets and cream paintwork, recessed lighting and black leather sofas. On the walls were prints of Thorak's sculptures. Herculean figures with gargantuan torsos rolled boulders up steep hills, in celebration of the building of the Autobahnen; Valkyries fought the triple demons Ignorance, Bolshevism and Slav. The immensity of Thorak's statuary was a whispered joke. 'Thorax' they called him: 'The Herr Professor is not receiving visitors today – he is working in the left ear of the horse.'

Nebe's adjutant, Otto Beck, a smooth-faced graduate of Heidelberg and Oxford, looked up as March came into the outer office.

March said: 'I need to speak with the Oberstgruppenführer.'

'He is seeing nobody.'

'He will see me.'

'He will not.'

March leaned very close to Beck's face, his fists on his desk. 'Ask.'

Behind him, he heard Nebe's secretary say: 'Shall I call security?'

'One moment, Ingrid.' It was fashionable among the graduates of the SS academy in Oxford to affect an English coolness. Beck flicked an invisible speck from the sleeve of his tunic. 'And what name is it?'

'March.'

'Ah. The famous *March.*' Beck picked up the telephone. 'Sturmbannführer March is demanding to see you, Herr Oberstgruppenführer.' He looked at March and nodded. 'Very well.'

Beck pressed a button concealed beneath the desk, releasing the electronic bolts. 'Five minutes, March. He has an appointment with the Reichsführer.'

The door to the inner office was solid oak, six centimetres thick. Inside, the blinds were tightly drawn against the day. Nebe was curled over his desk in a puddle of yellow light, studying a typed list through a magnifying glass. He turned one vast and blurry fish eye upon his visitor.

'What have we here. . . ?' He lowered the glass. 'Sturmbannführer March. Empty-handed, I assume?'

'Unfortunately.'

Nebe nodded. 'I learn from the duty office that the police stations of the Reich are even now being filled to overflowing with elderly beggars, ancient drunkards who have lost their papers, absconding geriatrics . . . Enough to keep Globus busy until Christmas.' He leaned back in his chair. 'If I know Luther, he is far too cunning to show himself yet. He will wait a few days. That must be your hope.'

'I have a favour to ask.'

'Proceed.'

'I wish to leave the country.'

Nebe let out a shout of laughter. He pounded the desk

with both hands. 'Your file is compendious, March, but nowhere does it mention your sense of humour. Excellent! Who knows? You may yet survive. Some KZ commandant may adopt you as a pet.'

'I wish to go to Switzerland.'

'Of course. The scenery is spectacular.'

'I have had a call from Lufthansa. Luther flew to Zürich on Sunday afternoon, and returned to Berlin on the last flight on Monday night. I believe he had access to a numbered bank account.'

Nebe's laughter had dwindled to an occasional snort. 'On what evidence?'

March placed the envelope on Nebe's desk. 'I removed this from Stuckart's apartment last night.'

Nebe opened it and inspected the letter through the magnifying glass. He glanced up. 'Should there not be a key with this?'

March was staring at the paintings behind Nebe's head – Schmutzler's 'Farm Girls Returning From the Fields', Padua's 'The Führer Speaks' – ghastly, orthodox muck.

'Ah. I see.' Nebe sat back again, stroking his cheek with the glass. 'If I don't allow you to go, I don't get the key. I could of course turn you over to the Gestapo, and they could persuade you to disgorge the key – probably quite quickly. But then it would be Globus and Heydrich who would learn the contents of the deposit box, rather than me.'

He was silent for a while. Then he dragged himself to his feet and hobbled across to the blinds. He opened the slats a fraction and peered out. March could see his eyes moving slowly from side to side.

At last he said: 'A tempting bargain. But why is it that I have this vision of myself, waving you off with a white handkerchief from the tarmac of Hermann Göring Airport, and of you never coming back?'

'I suppose giving you my word that I would return would be of no use?'

'The suggestion demeans our intelligence.'

Nebe went back to his desk and read the letter again. He pressed a switch on his desk. 'Beck.'

The adjutant appeared. 'March – give him your passport. Now, Beck, get that to the Interior Ministry and have them issue an immediate twenty-four-hour exit visa, starting at six tonight and expiring at six tomorrow.'

Beck glanced at March, then slid out of the office.

Nebe said: 'This is my offer. The Head of the Swiss Criminal Police, Herr Streuli, is a good friend of mine. From the moment you step off the aircraft until the moment you reboard it, his people will be watching you. Do not attempt to evade them. If you fail to return tomorrow, you will be arrested and deported. If you try to make a run to Bern, to enter a foreign embassy, you will be stopped. In any case, there is nowhere for you to go. After yesterday's happy announcement, the Americans will simply toss you back over the border to us. The British, French and Italians will do what we tell them. Australia and Canada will obey the Americans. There are the Chinese, I suppose, but if I were you I'd sooner take my chances in a KZ. And the moment you return to Berlin, you will tell me everything you have discovered. Good?'

March nodded.

'Good. The Führer calls the Swiss "a nation of hotel-keepers". I recommend the Baur au Lac on Tal Strasse, overlooking the See. Most luxurious. A fine place for a condemned man to spend a night.'

BACK in his office, a parody of a tourist, March booked his hotel room and reserved a plane seat. Within the hour, he had his passport back. The visa had been stamped inside:

the ubiquitous eagle and garlanded swastika, the blank spaces for the dates filled in by a crabbed and bureaucratic hand.

The duration of an exit visa was in direct ratio to the applicant's political reliability. Party bosses got ten years; Party members, five; citizens with unblemished records, one; the dregs of the camps naturally got nothing at all. March had been given a day-pass to the outside world. He was down there among the Untouchables of society – the grumblers, the parasites, the work-shy, the crypto-criminal.

He rang the Kripo's economic investigation division and asked for the resident Swiss expert. When he mentioned Zaugg's name and asked if the division had any information, the man at the other end laughed. 'How long do you have?'

'Start at the beginning.'

'Hold, please.' The man put down the phone and went to fetch the file.

Zaugg & Cie had been founded in 1877 by a Franco-German financier, Louis Zaugg. Hermann Zaugg, the signatory of Stuckart's letter, was the founder's grandson. He was still listed as the bank's chief director. Berlin had followed his activities for more than two decades. During the 1940s, Zaugg had dealt extensively with German nationals of dubious reliability. He was currently suspected of harbouring millions of Reichsmarks in cash, art, bullion, jewellery and precious stones – all of which rightfully should have been confiscated, but to none of which could the Finance Ministry gain access. They had been trying for years.

'What do we have on Zaugg personally?'

'Only the bare details. He's fifty-four, married, with one son. Has a mansion on the Zürichsee. Very respectable. Very private. Plenty of powerful friends in the Swiss government.'

March lit a cigarette and grabbed a scrap of paper. 'Give me that address again.'

MAX JAEGER arrived as March was writing him a note. He pushed open the door with his backside, came in carrying a stack of files, looking sweaty. Nearly two days' growth of beard gave him a menacing air.

'Zavi, thank Christ.' He peered over the top of the paperwork. 'I've been trying to reach you all day. Where have you been?'

'Around. What's this? Your memoirs?'

'The Spandau shootings. You heard Uncle Artur this morning.' He mimicked Nebe's reedy voice. ' "Jaeger, you can return to normal duties." '

He dropped the files on his desk. The window rattled. Dust shot across the office. 'Statements of witnesses and wedding guests. Autopsy report – they dug fifteen bullets out of that poor bastard.' He stretched, rubbed his eyes with his fists. 'I could sleep for a week. I tell you: I'm too old for scares like last night. My heart won't stand it.' He broke off. 'Now what the hell are you doing?'

March had lifted the dead plant from its pot and was retrieving the key to the safety deposit box.

'I have a plane to catch in two hours.'

Jaeger looked at his suitcase. 'Don't tell me – a holiday! A little balalaika music on the shores of the Black Sea . . .' He folded his arms and kicked out his legs in a dance, Russian-style.

March shook his head, smiling. 'Do you feel like a beer?'

'Do I feel like a beer?' Jaeger had danced out of the door before March could turn round.

THE little bar in Ob-wall Strasse was run by a retired Orpo

man called Fischer. It smelled of smoke and sweat, stale beer and fried onions. Most of its clientele were policemen. Green and black uniforms clustered around the bar, or lurked in the dimness of the wood-panelled booths.

The Fox and the Bear were greeted warmly.

'Taking a vacation, March?'

'Hey Jaeger! Stand a little closer to the razor next time!'

Jaeger insisted on buying the drinks. March took a booth in the corner, stowed his suitcase under the table, lit a cigarette. There were men here he had known for a decade. The drivers from Rahnsdorf with their poker schools and dirty stories. The heavy drinkers from Serious Crimes in Worth Strasse. He would not miss them. Walther Fiebes sat alone at the bar, moping over a bottle of schnapps.

Jaeger returned and raised his glass. 'Prost!'

'Prost.'

Max wiped the foam from his lips. 'Good sausages, good engines, good beer – Germany's three gifts to the world.' He always said this when they had a drink, and March always lacked the heart to point it out. 'So. What's this about a *plane*?' For Jaeger, the word seemed to conjure images of all that was exotic in the world. The furthest he had ever travelled from Berlin was to a family camp on the Black Sea – a holiday last summer near Gotenburg, organised by Strength-Through-Joy.

March turned his head slightly, glanced from side to side. The German look. The booths on either side were unoccupied. Shouts of laughter came from the bar.

'I have to go to Switzerland. Nebe's given me a twenty-four-hour visa. That key you saw just now in the office – I took it from Stuckart's safe last night. It opens a safety deposit box in Zürich.'

Jaeger's eyes opened wide. 'That must be where they keep the art stuff. Remember what Globus said this morning: they smuggled it out and sold it in Switzerland.'

'There's more to it than that. I've been speaking to the American girl again. It seems that Stuckart called her at home on Saturday night, wanting to defect.'

Defect. The unmentionable act. It hung in the air between them.

Jaeger said: 'But the Gestapo must know that already, Zavi. Surely her phone is tapped?'

March shook his head. 'Stuckart was too clever for that. He used the call box opposite her apartment.' He sipped his beer. 'You see how it goes, Max? I feel like a man descending stairs in the dark. First, the body in the lake turns out to be an alter Kämpfer. Then, his death is linked to Stuckart's. Last night, my one witness to Globus's involvement – the cadet, Jost – was taken away by the SS, on Globus's orders. Now it turns out that Stuckart wanted to defect. What comes next?'

'You'll fall down those stairs and break your neck, my friend. That's what comes next.'

'A fair prediction. And you don't know the worst of it.'

March told him about the Gestapo dossier. Jaeger looked stricken. 'Jesus Christ. What are you going to do?'

'I thought of trying to stay out of the Reich. I even withdrew all my money from the bank. But Nebe's right: no other country would touch me.' March finished his drink. 'Would you do something for me?'

'Name it.'

'The American woman's apartment was broken in to this morning. Could you ask the Orpo in Schöneberg to take a look occasionally –I've left the address on my desk. Also, I've given her your telephone number, in case of trouble.'

'No problem.'

'And can you look after this for Pili?' He handed Jaeger an envelope containing half the cash he had withdrawn from the bank. 'It's not much, but I may need the rest.

Hang on to it until he's old enough to know what to do with it.'

'Oh come on, man!' Max leaned across and clapped him on the shoulder. 'It's not as bad as that? Is it? Surely?'

March stared at him. After a second or two, Jaeger grunted and looked away. 'Yes. Well . . .' He tucked the envelope into his pocket. 'My God,' he said with sudden vehemence, 'if a lad of mine denounced me to the Gestapo, I'd be giving him something all right – and it wouldn't be money.'

'It's not the boy's fault, Max.'

Fault, thought March. *How could you fault a ten-year-old?* The boy needed a father-figure. That was what the Party provided –stability, companionship, something to believe in – all the things March should have given him and hadn't. Besides, the Pimpf *expected* the young to transfer their allegiance from their family to the state. No, he would not – could not – blame his son.

Gloom had settled over Jaeger. 'Another beer?'

'Sorry.' March stood. 'I have to go. I owe you.'

Jaeger lurched to his feet as well. 'When you get back, Zavi, come and stay with us for a couple of days. The younger girls are at a Bund deutscher Mädel camp for the week – you can have their room. We can work something out for the court martial.'

'Harbouring an asocial – that won't go down well with your local Party.'

'Fuck my local Party.'

This was said with feeling. Jaeger stuck out his hand, and March shook it – a great, calloused paw.

'Look after yourself, Zavi.'

'Look after yourself, Max.'

SIX

Drawn up on the runways of the Flughafen Hermann Göring, shimmering through the haze of fuel, was the new generation of passenger jets: the blue and white Boeings of Pan-American, the red, white and black swastika-decked Junkers of Lufthansa.

Berlin has two airports. The old Tempelhof aerodrome near the city centre handles short-haul, internal flights. International traffic passes through Hermann Göring in the north-western suburbs. The new terminal buildings are long, low edifices of marble and glass, designed – of course – by Speer. Outside the arrivals hall stands a statue of Hanna Reitsch, Germany's leading aviatrix, made of melted-down Spitfires and Lancasters. She scans the sky for intruders. A sign behind her says WELCOME TO BERLIN, CAPITAL OF THE GREATER GERMAN REICH, in five languages.

March paid the taxi driver, tipped him, and walked up the ramp towards the automatic doors. The air here was cold and man-made: drenched with aviation fuel, torn by the screams of throttling engines. Then the doors opened, hissed shut behind him, and suddenly he was in the sound-proofed bubble of the departure terminal.

'Lufthansa flight 401 to New York. Passengers are requested to make their way to gate number eight for boarding . . .'

'Final call for Lufthansa flight 014 to Theoderichshafen. Passengers . . .'

March went first to the Lufthansa sales desk to pick up his ticket, then to the check-in where his passport was scrutinised carefully by a blonde with 'Gina' pinned to her left breast, a swastika badge in her lapel.

'Does the Herr Sturmbannführer wish to check in any luggage?'

'No thank you. I have only this.' He patted his small suitcase.

She returned his passport with his boarding card folded inside it. Accompanying this act was a smile as bright and cheerless as neon.

'Boarding in thirty minutes. Have a good flight, Herr Sturmbannführer.'

'Thank you, Gina.'

'You are welcome.'

'Thank you.'

They were bowing like a pair of Japanese businessmen. Air travel was a new world to March, a strange land with its own impenetrable rituals.

He followed the signs to the lavatory, selected the cubicle furthest from the wash-basins, locked the door, opened the suitcase, took out the leather hold-all. Then he sat down and tugged off his boots. White light gleamed on chrome and tile.

When he had stripped to his shorts, he put the boots and his uniform into the hold-all, stuffed his Luger into the middle of the bag, zipped it up and locked it.

Five minutes later he emerged from the cubicle transformed. In a light grey suit, white shirt, pale blue tie and soft brown shoes, the Aryan Superman had turned back into a normal citizen. He could see the transformation reflected in people's eyes. No more frightened glances. The attendant at the left-luggage area where he deposited the hold-all was surly. He handed March the ticket.

'Don't lose it. If you do, don't bother coming back.' He jerked his head to the sign behind him: 'Warning! Items returned on production of ticket only!'

At the passport control zone March lingered, noting the security. Barrier one: checking of boarding cards, unobtainable without the proper visa. Barrier two: re-checking of the visas themselves. Three members of the Zollgrenzschutz, the border protection police, were stationed on either side of the entrance, carrying sub-machine guns. The elderly man in front of March was scrutinised with particular care, the customs officer speaking to someone on the telephone before waving him through. They were still looking for Luther.

When March's turn came, he saw how his passport baffled the customs man. An SS-Sturmbannführer with only a twenty-four-hour visa? The normal signals of rank and privilege, usually so clear, were too confused to read. Curiosity and servility warred in the customs man's face. Servility, as usual, won.

'Enjoy your journey, Herr Sturmbannführer.'

On the other side of the barrier, March resumed his study of airport security. All luggage was scanned by X-ray. He was frisked, then asked to open his case. Each item was inspected – the sponge bag unzipped, the shaving foam uncapped and sniffed. The guards worked with the care of men who knew that, if an aircraft was lost to hijackers or to a terrorist bomb during their watch, they would spend the next five years in a KZ.

Finally he was clear of the checks. He patted his inside pocket to make sure Stuckart's letter was still there, turned the little brass key over in his other hand. Then he went to the bar and had a large whisky and a cigarette.

HE boarded the Junkers ten minutes before take-off.

It was the day's last flight from Berlin to Zürich and the cabin was full of businessmen and bankers in dark three-piece suits reading pink financial newspapers. March had a seat next to the window. The place beside his was empty. He stowed his suitcase in a compartment above his head, settled back and closed his eyes. Inside the plane, a Bach cantata was playing. Outside, the engines started. They climbed the scale, from hum to brittle whine, one coming in after another like a chorus. The aircraft jolted slightly and began to move.

For thirty-three hours out of the past thirty-six March had been awake. Now the music bathed him, the vibrations lulled him. He slept.

He missed the safety demonstration. The take-off barely penetrated his dreams. Nor did he notice the person slip into the seat beside him.

Not until they were cruising at 10,000 metres and the pilot was informing them that they were passing over Leipzig did he open his eyes. The stewardess was leaning towards him, asking him if he wanted a drink. He started to say 'A whisky', but was too distracted to finish his reply. Sitting next to him, pretending to read a magazine, was Charlotte Maguire.

THE Rhine slid beneath them, a wide curve of molten metal in the dying sun. March had never see it from the air. 'Dear Fatherland, no danger thine:/Firm stands thy watch along the Rhine.' Lines from his childhood, hammered out on an untuned piano in a draughty gymnasium. Who had written them? He could not remember.

Crossing the river was a signal that they had passed out of the Reich and into Switzerland. In the distance: mountains, grey-blue and misty; below: neat rectangular fields and dark clumps of pine forests; steep red roofs and little white churches.

When he woke she had laughed at the surprise on his face. You may be used to dealing with hardened criminals, she had said, and with the Gestapo and the SS. But you've never come up against the good old American press.

He had sworn, to which she had responded with a wide-eyed look, mock-innocent, like one of Max Jaeger's daughters. An act, deliberately done badly, which made it naturally an even better act, turning his anger against him, making him part of the play.

She had then insisted on explaining everything, whether he wanted to listen or not, gesturing with a plastic tumbler of whisky. It had been easy, she said. He had told her he was flying to Zürich that night. There was only one flight. At the airport she had informed the Lufthansa desk that she was supposed to be with Sturmbannführer March. She was late: could she please have the seat next to him? When they agreed, she knew he must be on board.

'And there you were, asleep,' she concluded, 'like a babe.'

'And if they had said they had no passenger called March?'

'I would have come anyway.' She was impatient with his anger. 'Listen, I already have most of the story. An art fraud. Two senior officials dead. A third on the run. An attempted defection. A secret Swiss bank account. At worst, alone, I'd have picked up some extra colour in Zürich. At best I might have charmed Herr Zaugg into giving me an interview.'

'I don't doubt it.'

'Don't look so worried, Sturmbannführer – I'll keep your name out of it.'

Zürich is only twenty kilometres south of the Rhine. They were descending quickly. March finished his Scotch and set the empty container on the stewardess's outstretched tray.

Charlotte Maguire drained her own glass in one and placed it next to his. 'We have whisky in common, Herr March, at least.' She smiled.

He turned to the window. This was her skill, he thought:

to make him look stupid, a Teutonic flat-foot. First, she had failed to tell him about Stuckart's telephone call. Then she had manoeuvred him into letting her join in his search of Stuckart's apartment. This morning, instead of waiting for him to contact her, she had talked to the American diplomat, Nightingale, about Swiss banks. Now this. It was like having a child forever at your heels – a persistent, intelligent, embarrassing, deceitful, dangerous child. Surreptitiously he felt his pockets again, to check he still had the letter and key. She was not beyond stealing them while he was asleep.

The Junkers was coming in to land. Like a film gradually speeding up, the Swiss countryside began rushing past: a tractor in a field, a road with a few headlights in the smoky dusk, and then – one bounce, two – they were touching down.

Zürich airport was not how he had imagined it. Beyond the aircraft and hangars were wooded hillsides, with no evidence of a city. For a moment, he wondered if Globus had discovered his mission and had arranged for the plane to be diverted. Perhaps they had been set down in some remote airbase in southern Germany? But then he saw ZÜRICH on the terminal building.

The instant the plane had taxied to a halt, the passengers – professional commuters, most of them – rose as one. She was on her feet, too, pulling down her case and that ridiculous blue coat. He reached past her.

'Excuse me.'

She shrugged on the coat. 'Where now?'

'I am going to my hotel, Fräulein. What you do is your concern.'

He managed to squeeze in front of a fat Swiss who was cramming documents into a leather attaché case. The manoeuvre left her trapped some way behind him. He did not look back as they shuffled down the aisle and off the aircraft.

He walked briskly through the arrivals hall to passport control, overtaking most of the other passengers to station himself near the head of the queue. Behind him, he heard a commotion as she tried to catch up.

The Swiss border official, a serious young man with a drooping moustache, leafed through his passport.

'Business or pleasure, Herr March?'

'Business.' Definitely business.

'One moment.'

The young man picked up the telephone, dialled three digits, turned away from March and whispered something into the receiver. He said: 'Yes. Yes. Of course.' Then he hung up and returned the passport to March.

THERE were two of them waiting for him by the baggage carousel. He spotted them from fifty metres away: bulky figures with close-cropped hair, wearing stout black shoes and belted fawn raincoats. Policemen – they were the same the world over. He walked past them without a glance and sensed rather than saw them falling in behind him.

He went unchallenged through the green customs channel and out into the main concourse. Taxis. Where were taxis?

Clip-clop, clip-clop. Coming up behind him.

The air outside was several degrees colder than in Berlin. *Clip-clop, clip-clop*. He wheeled round. There she was, in her coat, clutching her case, balanced on her high heels.

'Go away, Fräulein. Do you understand me? Do you need it in writing? Go back to America and publish your stupid story. I have business to attend to.'

Without waiting for her reply, he opened the rear door of the waiting taxi, threw in his case, climbed in after it. 'Baur au Lac,' he said to the driver.

They pulled out of the airport and on to the highway,

heading south towards the city. The day had almost gone. Craning his neck to look out of the back window, March could see a taxi tucked in ten metres behind them, with an unmarked white Mercedes following it. Christ, what a comedy this was turning into. Globus was chasing Luther, he was chasing Globus, Charlie Maguire was chasing him, and now the Swiss police were on the tails of both of them. He lit a cigarette.

'Can't you read?' said the driver. He pointed to a sign: THANK YOU FOR NOT SMOKING.

'Welcome to Switzerland,' muttered March. He wound down the window a few centimetres, and the cloud of blue smoke was plucked into the chilly air.

Zürich was more beautiful than he had expected. Its centre reminded him of Hamburg. Old buildings clustered around the edge of the wide lake. Trams in a livery of green and white rattled along the front, past well-lit shops and cafés. The driver was listening to the Voice of America. In Berlin it was a blur of static; here, it was clear. 'I wanna hold your hand,' sang a youthful English voice. 'I wanna hold your ha-a-and!' A thousand teenage girls screamed.

The Baur au Lac was a street's-width from the lake. March paid the taxi driver in Reichsmarks – every country on the continent accepted Reichsmarks, it was Europe's common currency – and went inside. It was as luxurious as Nebe had promised. His room cost him half a month's salary. 'A *fine place for a condemned man to spend a night*. . .' As he signed the register he glimpsed a flash of blue at the door, swiftly followed by the fawn raincoats. I am like a movie star, thought March, as he caught the elevator. Everywhere I go, I have two detectives and a brunette in tow.

HE spread a map of the city on the bed and sat down beside

it, sinking into the spongy mattress. He had so little time. The broad expanse of the Zürich See thrust up into the complex of streets, like a blue blade. According to his Kripo file, Hermann Zaugg had a place on See Strasse. March found it. See Strasse ran alongside the eastern shore of the lake, about four kilometres south of the hotel.

Someone tapped softly on the door. A man's voice called his name.

Now what? He strode across the room, flung open the door. A waiter was in the corridor, holding a tray. He looked startled.

'Sorry, sir. With the compliments of the lady in room 277, sir.'

'Yes. Of course.' March stood aside to let him through. The waiter came in hesitantly, as if he thought March might hit him. He set down the tray, lingered fractionally for a tip and then, when none was forthcoming, left. March locked the door behind him.

On the table was a bottle of Glenfiddich, with a one-word note. 'Détente?'

HE stood at the window, his tie loosened, sipping the malt whisky, looking out across the Zürich See. Traceries of yellow lanterns were strung around the black water; on the surface, pinpricks of red, green and white bobbed and winked. He lit yet another cigarette, his millionth of the week.

People were laughing in the drive beneath his window. A light moved across the lake. No Great Hall, no marching bands, no uniforms. For the first time in – what was it? – a year, at least – he was away from the iron and granite of Berlin. So. He held up his glass and studied the pale liquid. There *were* other lives, other cities.

He noticed, along with the bottle, that she had ordered two glasses.

He sat down on the edge of the bed and looked at the telephone. He drummed his fingers on the little table.

Madness.

She had a habit of thrusting her hands deep into her pockets and standing with her head on one side, half-smiling. On the plane, he remembered, she had been wearing a red wool dress with a leather belt. She had good legs, in black stockings. And when she was angry or amused, which was most of the time, she would flick at the hair behind her ear.

The laughter outside drifted away.

'Where have you been the past twenty years?' Her contemptuous question to him in Stuckart's apartment.

She knew so much. She danced around him.

'The millions of Jews who vanished in the war . . .'

He turned her note over in his fingers, poured himself another drink and lay back on the bed. Ten minutes later he lifted the receiver and spoke to the operator.

'Room 277.'

Madness, *madness*.

THEY met in the lobby, beneath the fronds of a luxuriant palm. In the opposite corner a string quartet scraped its way through a selection from *Die Fledermaus*.

March said: 'The Scotch is very good.'

'A peace offering.'

'Accepted. Thank you.' He glanced across at the elderly cellist. Her stout legs were held wide apart, as if she were milking a cow. 'God knows why I should trust you.'

'God knows why I should trust *you*.'

'Ground rules,' he said firmly. 'One: no more lies. Two: we do what I say, whether you want to or not. Three: you show me what you plan to print, and if I ask you not to write something, you take it out. Agreed?'

'It's a deal.' She smiled and offered him her hand. He took it. She had a cool, firm grip. For the first time he noticed she had a man's watch around her wrist.

'What changed your mind?' she asked.

He released her hand. 'Are you ready to go out?' She was still wearing the red dress.

'Yes.'

'Do you have a notebook?'

She tapped her coat pocket. 'Never travel without one.'

'Nor do I. Good. Let's go.'

SWITZERLAND was a cluster of lights in a great darkness, enemies all around it: Italy to the south, France to the west, Germany north and east. Its survival was a source of wonder: 'the Swiss miracle', they called it.

Luxembourg had become Moselland, Alsace-Lorraine was Westmark; Austria was Ostmark. As for Czechoslovakia – that bastard child of Versailles had dwindled to the Protectorate of Bohemia and Moravia. Poland, Latvia, Lithuania, Estonia – vanished from the map. In the East, the German Empire was carved four ways into the Reichskommissariats Ostland, Ukraine, Caucasus, Muscovy.

In the West, twelve nations – Portugal, Spain, France, Ireland, Great Britain, Belgium, Holland, Italy, Denmark, Norway, Sweden and Finland – had been corralled by Germany, under the Treaty of Rome, into a European trading bloc. German was the official second language in all schools. People drove German cars, listened to German radios, watched German televisions, worked in German-owned factories, moaned about the behaviour of German tourists in German-dominated holiday resorts, while

German teams won every international sporting competition except cricket, which only the English played.

In all this, Switzerland alone was neutral. That had not been the Führer's intention. But by the time the Wehrmacht's planners had designed a strategy to subdue the Swiss state the stalemate of the Cold War had begun. It remained a patch of no man's land, increasingly useful to both sides as the years went by, a place to meet and deal in secret.

'There are only three classes of citizen in Switzerland,' the Kripo's expert had told March. 'American spies, German spies, and Swiss bankers trying to get hold of their money.'

Over the past century those bankers had settled around the northern rim of the Zürich See like a rich crust; a tide-mark of money. As on Schwanenwerder, their villas presented to the world a blank face of high walls and stout gates, backed by dense screens of trees.

March leaned forward and spoke to the driver. 'Slow down here.'

They were quite a cavalcade by now: March and Charlie in a taxi, followed by two cars, each occupied by a Swiss policeman. Bellerive Strasse turned into See Strasse. March counted off the numbers.

'Pull over here.'

The taxi swerved up on to the kerb. The police cars overtook them; a hundred metres down the road, their brake lights glowed.

Charlie looked around. 'Now what?'

'Now we take a look at the home of Doctor Hermann Zaugg.'

March paid the taxi driver, who promptly turned and set off back towards the city centre. The road was quiet.

All the villas were well-protected, but Zaugg's – the third they came to – was a fortress. The gates were solid metal, three metres high, flanked on either side by a stone wall. A security camera scanned the entrance. March took Charlie's arm and they strolled past, like lovers taking the air. They crossed the road and waited in a driveway on the other side. March looked at his watch. It was just after nine o'clock. Five minutes passed. He was about to suggest they leave when, with a clank and a hum of machinery, the gates began to swing open.

Charlie whispered: 'Someone's coming out.'

'No.' He nodded up the road. 'Coming in.'

The limousine was big and powerful: a British car, a Bentley, finished in black. It came from the direction of the city, travelling rapidly, swerved, and swung into the drive. A chauffeur and another man in the front; in the back, a flash of silver hair – Zaugg's, presumably. March just had time to notice how low the bodywork hung to the ground. Then, one after another, the tyres were absorbing the impact as the Bentley bounced over the kerb – *whump, whump, whump, whump* – and it was gone.

The gates started to close, then stopped halfway. Two men appeared from the direction of the house, walking fast.

'You!' one of them shouted. 'Both of you! Stay where you are!' He strode into the road. March seized Charlie by the elbow. At that instant, one of the police cars began reversing towards them, gearbox howling. The man glanced to his right, hesitated, and retreated.

The car skidded to a halt. The window was wound down. A weary voice said: 'For fuck's sake, get in.'

March opened the back door and ushered in Charlie, then slipped in after her. The Swiss policeman executed a rapid three-point turn, and accelerated away towards the city. Zaugg's bodyguards had already disappeared; the gates were banging shut behind them.

March twisted round to stare out of the rear window. 'Are all your bankers as well-protected as that?'

'Depends who they do business with.' The policeman adjusted his mirror to look at them. He was in his late forties, with bloodshot eyes. 'Are you planning any further adventures, Herr March? A brawl somewhere, perhaps? It would help if we had a little warning next time.'

'I thought you were supposed to be following us, not guarding us.'

' "Follow and protect as necessary": those are our orders. That's my partner in the car behind, by the way. It's been a fucking long day. Excuse my language, Fräulein – they never said there'd be a woman involved.'

'Can you drop us back at the hotel?' asked March.

The policeman grumbled. 'So now I am to add chauffeur to my list of duties?' He switched on his radio and spoke to his partner. 'Panic over. We're going back to the Baur au Lac.'

Charlie had her notebook open on her lap and was writing. 'Who are these people?'

March hesitated but then thought: what does it matter? 'This officer and his partner are members of the Swiss Polizei, here to ensure I don't attempt to defect while outside the borders of the Reich. And also to ensure I return in one piece.'

'Always a pleasure, assisting our German colleagues,' grunted a voice from the front.

Charlie said: 'There's a danger you might not?'

'Apparently.'

'Jesus.' She wrote something down. He looked away. Off to their left, a couple of kilometres across the See, the lights of Zürich formed a yellow ribbon on the dark water. His breath misted the window.

Zaugg must have been returning from his office. It was late, but the burghers of Zürich worked hard for their money – twelve or fourteen hours a day was common. The banker's house could only be reached by travelling this road, which ruled out the most effective security precaution: varying his route each night. And See Strasse, bounded on one side by the lake, and with several dozen streets leading off the other, was a security man's nightmare. That explained something.

'Did you notice his car?' he said to Charlie. 'How heavy it was, the noise its tyres made? You see those often in Berlin. That Bentley was armour-plated.' He ran his hand through his hair. 'Two bodyguards, a pair of prison gates, remote cameras and a bomb-proof car. What kind of banker is that?'

He could not see her face properly in the shadows, but he could feel her excitement beside him. She said: 'We've got the letter of authorisation, remember? Whatever kind of banker he is – he's *our* banker now.'

SEVEN

They ate at a restaurant in the old town – a place with thick linen napkins and heavy silver cutlery, where the waiters lined up behind them and whipped the covers from their plates like a troupe of conjurers performing a trick. If the hotel had cost him half a month's salary, this meal would cost him the other half, but March didn't care.

She was unlike any other woman he had met. She was not one of the homebodies of the Party's Women's League, all 'Kinder, Kirche und Kuche' – her husband's supper always ready on the table, his uniform freshly pressed, five children asleep upstairs. And while a good National Socialist girl abhorred cosmetics, nicotine and alcohol, Charlie Maguire made liberal use of all three. Her dark eyes soft in the candle-light, she talked almost without pause of New York, foreign reporting, her father's days in Berlin, the wickedness of Joseph Kennedy, politics, money, men, herself.

She had been born in Washington DC in the spring of 1939. ('The last spring of peace, my parents called it – in all senses.') Her father had recently returned from Berlin to work at the State Department. Her mother was trying to make a success as an actress, but after 1941 was lucky simply to escape internment. In the 1950s, after the war, Michael Maguire had gone to Omsk, capital of what was left of Russia, to serve in the US Embassy. It was considered too dangerous a place to take four children. *Charlotte* had been left behind to be educated at expensive schools in Virginia; *Charlie* had dropped out at seventeen – spitting and swearing and rebelling against everything in sight.

'I went to New York. Tried to be an actress. That didn't work. Tried to be a journalist. That suited me better. Enrolled at Columbia – to my father's great relief. And then – what do you know? – I start an affair with Teacher.' She shook her head. 'How stupid can you get?' She blew out a jet of cigarette smoke. 'Is there any more wine in there?'

He poured out the last of the bottle, ordered another. It seemed to be his turn to say something. 'Why Berlin?'

'A chance to get away from New York. My mother being German made it easier to get a visa. I have to admit: World European Features is not quite as grand as it sounds. Two men in an office on the wrong side of town with a telex machine. To be honest, they were happy to take anyone who could get a visa out of Berlin. Even me.' She looked at him with shining eyes. 'I didn't know he was married, you see. The teacher.' She snapped her fingers. 'Basic failure of research there, wouldn't you say?'

'When did it end?'

'Last year. I came to Europe to show them all I could do it. Him especially. That's why I felt so sick about being expelled. God, the thought of facing them all again . . .' She sipped her wine. 'Perhaps I've got a father-fixation. How old are you?'

'Forty-two.'

'Bang in my age range.' She smiled at him over the rim of her glass. 'You'd better watch out. Are you married?'

'Divorced.'

'Divorced! That's promising. Tell me about her.'

Her frankness kept catching him off-guard. 'She was,' he began, and corrected himself. 'She is . . .' He stopped. How did you summarise someone you were married to for nine years, divorced from for seven, who had just denounced you to the authorities? 'She is not like you,' was all he could think to say.

'Meaning?'

'She does not have ideas of her own. She is concerned about what people think. She has no curiosity. She is bitter.'

'About you?'

'Naturally.'

'Is she seeing anyone else?'

'Yes. A Party bureaucrat. Much more suitable than me.'

'And you? Do you have anyone?'

A klaxon sounded in March's mind. *Dive, dive, dive.* He had had two affairs since his divorce. A teacher who had lived in the apartment beneath his, and a young widow who taught history at the university – another friend of Rudi Halder's: he sometimes suspected Rudi had made it his mission in life to find him a new wife. The liaisons had drifted on for a few months, until both women had tired of the last-minute calls from Werderscher Markt: 'Something's come up, I'm sorry . . .'

Instead of answering her, March said: 'So many questions. You should have been a detective.'

She made a face at him. 'So few answers. *You* should have been a reporter.'

THE waiter poured more wine. After he had moved away, she said: 'You know, when I met you, I hated you on sight.'

'Ah. The uniform. It blots out the man.'

'That uniform does. When I looked for you on the plane this afternoon I barely recognised you.'

It occurred to March that here was another reason for his good mood: he had not caught a glimpse of his black silhouette in a mirror, had not seen people shrinking away at his approach.

'Tell me,' he said, 'what do they say of the SS in America?'

She rolled her eyes. 'Oh come on, March. Please. Don't let's ruin a good evening.'

'I mean it. I'd like to know.' He had to coax her into answering.

'Well, murderers,' she said eventually. 'Sadists. Evil personified. All that. You asked for it. Nothing personal intended, you understand? Any other questions?'

'A million. A lifetime's worth.'

'A lifetime! Well go ahead. I have nothing planned.'

He was momentarily dumbfounded, paralysed by choice. Where to start?

'The war in the East,' he said. 'In Berlin we hear only of victories. Yet the Wehrmacht has to ship the coffins home from the Urals front at night, on special trains, so nobody sees how many dead there are.'

'I read somewhere that the Pentagon estimates a hundred thousand Germans killed since 1960. The Luftwaffe is bombing the Russian towns flat day after day and still they keep coming back at you. You can't win because they've nowhere else to go. And you daren't use nuclear weapons in case we retaliate and the world blows up.'

'What else?' He tried to think of recent headlines. 'Goebbels says German space technology beats the Americans every time.'

'Actually, I think that's true. Peenemünde had satellites in orbit years ahead of ours.'

'Is Winston Churchill still alive?'

'Yes. He's an old man now. In Canada. He lives there. So does the Queen.' She noticed his puzzlement. 'Elizabeth claims the English throne from her uncle.'

'And the Jews?' said March. 'What do the Americans say we did to them?'

She was shaking her head. 'Why are you doing this?'

'Please. The truth.'

'The truth? How do I know what the truth is?' Suddenly she had raised her voice, was almost shouting. People at the next table were turning round. 'We're brought up to think of Germans as something from outer space. Truth doesn't enter into it.'

'Very well then. Give me the propaganda.'

She glanced away, exasperated, but then looked back with an intensity that made it difficult for him to meet her eyes. 'All right. They say you scoured Europe for every living Jew – men, women, children, babies. They say you shipped them to ghettos in the East where thousands died of malnutrition and disease. Then you forced the survivors farther East, and nobody knows what happened after that. A handful escaped over the Urals into Russia. I've seen them on TV. Funny old men, most of them; a bit crazy. They talk about execution pits, medical experiments, camps that people went into but never came out of. They talk about millions of dead. But then the German ambassador comes along in his smart suit and tells everyone it's all just communist propaganda. So nobody knows what's true and what isn't. And I'll tell you something else – most people don't care.' She sat back in her chair. 'Satisfied?'

'I'm sorry.'

'So am I.' She reached for her cigarettes, then stopped and looked at him again. 'That's why you changed your mind at the hotel about bringing me along, isn't it? Nothing to do with whisky. You wanted to pick my brains.' She started to laugh. 'And I thought *I* was using *you*.'

AFTER that, they got on better. Whatever poison there was between them had been drawn. He told her about his father and how he had followed him into the Navy, about how he had drifted into police work and found a taste for it – a vocation, even.

She said: 'I still don't understand how you can wear it.'

'What?'

'That uniform.'

He poured himself another glass of wine. 'Oh, there's a simple answer to that. In 1936, the Kriminalpolizei was merged into the SS; all officers had to accept honorary SS rank. So I have a choice: either I am an investigator in that uniform, and try to do a little good; or I am something else without that uniform, and do no good at all.'

And the way things are going, I shall soon not have that choice, he thought.

She tilted her head to one side and nodded. 'I can see that. That seems fair.'

He felt impatient, sick of himself. 'No it's not. It's bullshit, Charlie.' It was the first time he had called her that since she had insisted on it at the beginning of the dinner; using it sounded like a declaration. He hurried on: 'That's the answer I've given everybody, including myself, for the past ten years. Unfortunately, even I have stopped believing it.'

'But what happened – the worst of what happened – was during the war, and you weren't around. You told me: you were at sea.'

He looked down at his plate, silent. She went on: 'And anyway, wartime is different. All countries do wicked things in wartime. My country dropped an atom bomb on Japanese civilians – killed a quarter of a million people in an instant. And the Americans have been allies of the Russians for the past twenty years. Remember what the Russians did?'

There was truth in what she said. One by one, as they advanced eastwards, beginning with the bodies of 10,000 Polish officers in the Katyn forest, the Germans had discovered the mass graves of Stalin's victims. Millions had died in the famines, purges, deportations of the 1930s. Nobody knew the exact figure. The execution pits, the torture chambers, the gulags inside the Arctic Circle – all were now preserved by the Germans as memorials to the dead, museums of Bolshevik evil. Children were taken round them; ex-prisoners acted as guides. There was a whole school of historical studies devoted to investigating the crimes of communism. Television showed documentaries on Stalin's holocaust – bleached skulls and walking skeletons, bulldozed corpses and the earth-caked rags of women and children bound with wire and shot in the back of the neck.

She put her hand on his. 'The world is as it is. Even I see that.'

He spoke without looking at her. 'Yes. Fine. But everything you've said, I've already heard. "It was a long time ago." "That was war." "The Ivans were worst of all." "What can one man do?" I've listened to people whisper that for ten years. That's all they ever do, by the way. Whisper.'

She withdrew her hand and lit another cigarette, turning the little gold lighter over and over in her fingers. 'When I first came to Berlin, and my parents gave me that list of people they knew in the old days, there were lots of theatre people on it, artists – friends of my mother. I suppose quite of few them, in the way of things, must have been Jews, or homosexuals. And I went looking for them. All of them had gone, of course. That didn't surprise me. But they hadn't just vanished. *It was as if they'd never existed.*'

She tapped the lighter gently against the tablecloth. He noticed her fingers – slim, unmanicured, unadorned.

'Of course, there were people living in the places my mother's friends used to live in. Old people, often. They must have known, mustn't they? But they just looked blank. They were watching television, having tea, listening to music. There was nothing left *at all*.'

March said: 'Look at this.'

He pulled out his wallet, took out the photograph. It looked incongruous amid the plushness of the restaurant – a relic from someone's attic, rubbish from a flea market stall.

He gave it to her. She studied it. A strand of hair fell over her face and she brushed it away. 'Who are they?'

'When I moved into my apartment after Klara and I split, it hadn't been decorated for years. I found that tucked behind the wallpaper in the bedroom. I tell you, I took that place to pieces, but that was all there was. Their surname was Weiss. But who are they? Where are they now? What happened to them?'

He took the photograph, folded it into quarters, put it back in his wallet.

'What do you do,' he said, 'if you devote your life to discovering criminals, and it gradually occurs to you that the real criminals are the people you work for? What do you do when everyone tells you not to worry, you can't do anything about it, it was a long time ago?'

She was looking at him in a different way. 'I suppose you go crazy.'

'Or worse. Sane.'

SHE insisted, despite his protests, on paying half the bill. It was almost midnight by the time they left the restaurant. They walked in silence towards the hotel. Stars arched across the sky; at the bottom of the steep cobbled street, the lake waited.

She took his arm. 'You asked me if that man at the Embassy –Nightingale – if he was my lover.'

'That was rude of me. I'm sorry.'

'Would you have been disappointed if I'd said he was?'

He hesitated.

She went on: 'Well he isn't. He'd like to be. Sorry. That sounds like boasting.'

'It doesn't at all. I'm sure many would like to be.'

'I hadn't met anyone . . .'

Hadn't . . .

She stopped. 'I'm twenty-five. I go where I like. I do what I like. I choose whom I like.' She turned to him, touched him lightly on the cheek with a warm hand. 'God, I hate getting this sort of thing out of the way, don't you?'

She drew his head to hers.

*

How odd it is, thought March afterwards, *to live your life in ignorance of the past, of your world, yourself. Yet how easy to do it! You went along from day to day, down paths other people had prepared for you, never raising your head – enfolded in their logic, from swaddling clothes to shroud. It was a kind of fear.*

Well, goodbye to that. And good to leave it behind – whatever happened now.

His feet danced on the cobblestones. He slipped his arm around her. He had so many questions.

'Wait, wait,' she was laughing, holding on to him. 'Enough. Stop. I'm starting to worry you only want me for my *mind.*'

IN his hotel room, she unknotted his tie and reined him to her once more, her mouth soft on his. Still kissing him, she smoothed the jacket from his shoulders, unbuttoned his shirt, parted it. Her hands skimmed over his chest, around his back, across his stomach.

She knelt and tugged at his belt.

He closed his eyes and coiled his fingers in her hair.

After a few moments he pulled away gently, and knelt to face her, lifted her dress. Freed from it, she threw back her head and shook her hair. He wanted to know her completely. He kissed her throat, her breasts, her stomach; inhaled her scent, felt the firm flesh stretching smooth and taut beneath his hands, her soft skin on his tongue.

Later she guided him on to the bed and settled herself above him. The only light was cast by the lake. Rippling shadows all around them. When he opened his mouth to say something, she put a finger to his lips.

PART FOUR

FRIDAY 17 APRIL

The Gestapo, the Kriminalpolizei and the security services are enveloped in the mysterious aura of the political detective story.

REINHARD HEYDRICH

[illegible] taking [illegible] of [illegible].

A smart and [illegible] dressed [illegible] been [illegible] anxio[illegible] [illegible] company [illegible]. And, with [illegible] of the [illegible] really [illegible] on the [illegible] had been taking [illegible] sent a [illegible] close [illegible] had seized [illegible] would [illegible] always [illegible] or [illegible] matters [illegible] be made [illegible] on [illegible], [illegible] stopped [illegible]. Everyone [illegible] paid [illegible] alarm [illegible]. But [illegible]

[illegible]

This is where you found the [illegible] but you [illegible]. The Swiss [illegible] the place the money [illegible] in Zurich, the money [illegible] old, [illegible].

[illegible] the paving stones and [illegible] Bahnhof [illegible] the [illegible] of which [illegible] great [illegible] of Europe's rich [illegible] their wealth. [illegible] the shoppers and [illegible] along the [illegible]

ONE

The Berlin Börse had opened for trading thirty minutes earlier. In the window display of the Union des Banques Suisses on Zürich's Bahnhof Strasse, the numbers clicked like knitting needles. Bayer, Siemens, Thyssen, Daimler –up, up, up, up. The only stock falling on news of détente was Krupp.

A smart and well-dressed crowd had gathered anxiously, as they did every morning, to watch this monitor of the Reich's economic health. Prices on the Börse had been falling for six months and a mood close to panic had seized investors. But this week, thanks to old Joe Kennedy – he always knew a thing or two about markets, old Joe: made half a billion dollars on Wall Street in his day – yes, thanks to Joe, the slide had stopped. Berlin was happy. Everyone was happy. Nobody paid attention to the couple walking up the street from the lake, not holding hands but close enough for their bodies to touch occasionally, followed by a weary-looking pair of gentlemen in fawn raincoats.

March had been given a short briefing on the customs and practices of Swiss banking the afternoon he left Berlin.

'Bahnhof Strasse is the financial centre. It looks like the main shopping street, which it is. But it's the courtyards behind the shops and the offices above them that matter. That's where you'll find the banks. But you'll have to keep your eyes open. The Swiss say: the older the money, the harder to see it. In Zürich, the money's so old, it's invisible.'

Beneath the paving stones and tramlines of Bahnhof Strasse ran the catacomb of vaults in which three generations of Europe's rich had buried their wealth. March looked at the shoppers and tourists pouring along the street and wondered upon what ancient dreams and secrets, upon what bones they were treading.

These banks were small, family-run concerns: a dozen or two employees, a suite of offices, a small brass plate. Zaugg & Cie was typical. The entrance was in a side-street, behind a jewellers, scanned by a remote camera identical to the one outside Zaugg's villa. As March rang the bell beside the discreet door he felt Charlie brush his hand.

A woman's voice over the intercom demanded his name and business. He looked up at the camera.

'My name is March. This is Fräulein Maguire. We wish to see Herr Zaugg.'

'Do you have an appointment?'

'No.'

'The Herr Direktor sees no one without an appointment.'

'Tell him we have a letter of authorisation for account number 2402.'

'One moment, please.'

The policemen were lounging at the entrance to the side-street. March glanced at Charlie. It seemed to him her eyes were brighter, her skin more lustrous. He supposed he flattered himself. Everything looked heightened today – the trees greener, the blossom whiter, the sky bluer, as if washed with gloss.

She was carrying a leather shoulder bag, from which she now produced a camera, a Leica. 'I think a shot for the family album.'

'As you like. But leave me out of it.'

'Such modesty.'

She took a photograph of Zaugg's door and nameplate. The receptionist's voice snapped over the intercom. 'Please come to the second floor.' There was a buzz of bolts being released, and March pushed at the heavy door.

The building was an optical illusion. Small and

nondescript from the outside, inside a staircase of glass and tubular chrome led to a wide reception area, decorated with modern art. Hermann Zaugg was waiting to meet them. Behind him stood one of the bodyguards from last night.

'Herr March, is it?' Zaugg extended his hand. 'And Fräulein Maguire?' He shook her hand, too, and gave a slight bow. 'English?'

'American.'

'Ah. Good. Always a pleasure to meet our American friends.' He was like a little doll: silver hair, shiny pink face, tiny hands and feet. He wore a suit of immaculate black, a white shirt, a pearl-grey tie. 'I understand you have the necessary authorisation?'

March produced the letter. Zaugg held the paper swiftly to the light and studied the signature. 'Yes indeed. The hand of my youth. I fear my script has deteriorated since those years. Come.'

In his office, he directed them to a low sofa of white leather. He sat behind his desk. Now the advantage of height lay with him: the oldest trick.

March had decided to be frank. 'We passed your home last night. Your privacy is well protected.'

Zaugg had his hands folded on his desk. He made a non-committal gesture with his tiny thumbs, as if to say: *You know how it is.* 'I gather from my associates that you had protection of your own. Do I take it this visit is official, or private?'

'Both. That is to say, neither.'

'I am familiar with the situation. Next you will tell me it is "a delicate matter".'

'It is a delicate matter.'

'My speciality.' He adjusted his cuffs. 'Sometimes, it seems to me that the whole history of twentieth-century Europe has flowed through this office. In the 1930s, it was Jewish refugees who sat where you now sit – often pathetic creatures, clutching whatever they had managed to salvage. They were usually followed closely by gentlemen from the Gestapo. In the 1940s, it was German officials of – how shall we say? – recently-acquired wealth. Sometimes the very men who had once come to close the accounts of others now returned to open new ones on their own behalf. In the 1950s, we dealt with the descendants of those who had vanished during the 1940s. Now, in the 1960s, I anticipate an increase in American custom, as your two great countries come together once more. The 1970s I shall leave to my son.'

'This letter of authorisation,' said March, 'how much access does it give us?'

'You have the key?'

March nodded.

'Then you have total access.'

'We would like to begin with the account records.'

'Very well.' Zaugg studied the letter, then picked up his telephone. 'Fräulein Graf, bring in the file for 2402.'

She appeared a minute later, a middle-aged woman carrying a thin sheaf of papers in a manila binding. Zaugg took it. 'What do you wish to know?'

'When was the account opened?'

He looked through the papers. 'July 1942. The eighth day of that month.'

'And who opened it?'

Zaugg hesitated. He was like a miser with his store of precious information: parting with each fact was agony. But under the terms of his own rules he had no choice.

He said at last: 'Herr Martin Luther.'

March was making notes. 'And what were the arrangements for the account?'

'One box. Four keys.'

'*Four* keys?' March's eyebrows rose in surprise. That was Luther himself, and Buhler and Stuckart, presumably. But who held the fourth key? 'How were they distributed?'

'They were all issued to Herr Luther, along with four letters of authorisation. Naturally, what he chose to do with them is not our concern. You appreciate that this was a special form of account – an emergency, wartime account – designed to protect anonymity, and also to allow ease of access for any heirs or beneficiaries, should anything happen to the original account-holder.'

'How did he pay for the account.'

'In cash. Swiss francs. Thirty years' rental. In advance. Don't worry, Herr March – there is nothing to pay until 1972.'

Charlie said: 'Do you have a record of transactions relating to the account?'

Zaugg turned to her. 'Only the dates on which the box was opened.'

'What are they?'

'The eighth of July 1942. The seventeenth of December 1942. The ninth of August 1943. The thirteenth of April 1964.'

April the thirteenth! March barely suppressed a cry of triumph. His guess had been right. Luther *had* flown to Zürich at the start of the week. He scribbled the dates in his notebook. 'Only four times?' he asked.

'Correct.'

'And until last Monday, the box had not been opened for nearly twenty-one years?'

'That is what the dates indicate.' Zaugg closed the file with a flick of annoyance. 'I might add, there is nothing especially unusual about that. We have boxes here which have lain untouched for fifty years or more.'

'You set up the account originally?'

'I did.'

'Did Herr Luther say why he wanted to open it, or why he needed these particular arrangements?'

'Client privilege.'

'I'm sorry?'

'That is privileged information between client and banker.'

Charlie interrupted. 'But we are your clients.'

'No, Fräulein Maguire. You are beneficiaries of my client. An important distinction.'

'Did Herr Luther open the box personally on each occasion?' asked March.

'Client privilege.'

'Was it Luther who opened the box on Monday? What sort of mood was he in?'

'Client privilege, client privilege.' Zaugg held up his hands. 'We can go on all day, Herr March. Not only am I under no obligation to give you that information, it would be illegal under the Swiss Banking Code for me to do so. I have passed on all you are entitled to know. Is there anything else?'

'Yes.' March closed his notebook and looked at Charlie. 'We would like to inspect the box for ourselves.'

A SMALL elevator led down to the vault. There was just enough room for four passengers. March and Charlie, Zaugg and his bodyguard stood awkwardly pressed together. Close to, the banker reeked of eau de Cologne; his hair glistened beneath an oily pomade.

The vault was like a prison, or a mortuary: a white-tiled corridor which stretched ahead of them for thirty metres, with bars on either side. At the far end, next to the gate, a security guard sat at a desk. Zaugg pulled a heavy bunch of keys from his pocket, attached by a chain to his belt. He hummed as he searched for the right one.

The ceiling vibrated slightly as a tram passed overhead.

He let them into the cage. Steel walls gleamed in the neon light: banks of doors, each half a metre square. Zaugg moved in front of them, unlocked one at waist height and stood back. The security guard pulled out a long box, the size of a metal footlocker, and carried it over to a table.

Zaugg said: 'Your key fits the lock on that box. I shall wait outside.'

'There's no need.'

'Thank you, but I prefer to wait.'

Zaugg left the cage and stood outside, with his back to the bars. March looked at Charlie, and gave her the key.

'You do it.'

'I'm shaking . . .'

She inserted the key. It turned easily. The end of the box opened. She reached inside. There was a look of puzzlement on her face, then disappointment.

'It's empty, I think.' Her expression changed. 'No . . .'

She smiled and pulled out a flat cardboard box, about fifty centimetres square, five centimetres deep. The lid was sealed with red wax, with a typewritten label gummed on top: 'Property of the Reich Foreign Ministry Treaty Archive, Berlin.' And underneath, in Gothic lettering: 'Geheime Reichssache'. Top Secret State Document.

A *treaty?*

March broke the seal, using the key. He lifted the lid. The interior released a scent of mingled must and incense.

Another tram passed. Zaugg was still humming, jingling his keys.

Inside the cardboard box was an object wrapped in an oilcloth. March lifted it out and laid it flat on the desk. He drew back the cloth: a panel of wood, scratched and ancient; one of the corners was broken off. He turned it over.

Charlie was next to him. She murmured: 'It's beautiful.'

The edges of the panel were splintered, as if it had been wrenched from its setting. But the portrait itself was perfectly preserved. A young woman, exquisite, with pale brown eyes, was glancing to the right, a string of black beads looped twice around her neck. In her lap, in long, aristocratic fingers, she held a small animal with white fur. Not a dog, exactly; more like a weasel.

Charlie was right. It *was* beautiful. It seemed to suck in the light from the vault and radiate it back. The girl's pale skin glowed –luminous, like an angel's.

'What does it mean?' whispered Charlie.

'God knows.' March felt vaguely cheated. Was the deposit box no more than an extension of Buhler's treasure chamber? 'How much do you know about art?'

'Not much. But there is something familiar about it. May I?' She took it, held it at arm's length. 'It's Italian, I think. You see her costume – the way the neckline of her dress is cut square, the sleeves. I'd say Renaissance. Very old, and very genuine.'

'And very stolen. Put it back.'

'Do we have to?'

'Of course. Unless you can think of a good story for the Zollgrenzschutz at Berlin Airport.'

Another painting: that was all! Cursing under his breath, March ran the oilcloth through his hands, checked the cardboard container. He turned the safety deposit box on its end and shook it. Nothing. The empty metal mocked him. What had he hoped for? He did not know. But something to give him a better clue than this.

'We must leave,' he said.

'One minute.'

Charlie propped the panel up against the box. She crouched and took half-a-dozen photographs. Then she rewrapped the picture, replaced it in its container, and locked the box.

March called: 'We've finished here, Herr Zaugg. Thank you.'

Zaugg reappeared with the security guard – a fraction too

quickly, March thought. He guessed the banker had been straining to overhear them.

Zaugg rubbed his hands. 'All is to your satisfaction, I trust?'

'Perfectly.'

The guard slid the box back into the cavity, Zaugg locked the door, and the girl with the weasel was re-interred in darkness. '*We have boxes here which have lain untouched for fifty years or more . . .*' Was that how long it would be before she saw the light again?

They rode the elevator in silence. Zaugg shepherded them out at street-level. 'And so we say goodbye.' He shook hands with each of them in turn.

March felt he had to say something more, should try one final tactic. 'I feel I must warn you, Herr Zaugg, that two of the joint holders of this account have been murdered in the past week, and that Martin Luther himself has disappeared.'

Zaugg did not even blink. 'Dear me, dear me. Old clients pass away and new ones' – he gestured to them – 'take their place. And so the world turns. The only thing you can be sure of, Herr March, is that – whoever wins – still standing when the smoke of battle clears will be the banks of the cantons of Switzerland. Good day to you.'

They were out on the street and the door was closing when Charlie shouted: 'Herr Zaugg!'

His face appeared and before he could withdraw it, the camera clicked. His eyes were wide, his little mouth popped into a perfect O of outrage.

ZÜRICH'S lake was misty-blue, like a picture from a fairy-story – a landscape fit for sea-monsters and heroes to do battle in. If only the world had been as we were promised, thought March. Then castles with pointed turrets would have risen through that haze.

He was leaning against the damp stone balustrade outside the hotel, his suitcase at his feet, waiting for Charlie to settle her bill.

He wished he could have stayed longer – taken her out on the water, explored the city, the hills; had dinner in the old town; returned to his room each night, to make love, to the sound of the lake . . . A dream. Fifty metres to his left, sitting in their cars, his guardians from the Swiss Polizei yawned.

Many years ago, when March was a young detective in the Hamburg Kripo, he had been ordered to escort a prisoner serving a life-sentence for robbery, who had been given a special day-pass. The man's trial had been in the papers; his childhood sweetheart had seen the publicity and written to him; had visited him in gaol; agreed to marry him. The affair had touched that streak of sentimentality that runs so strong in the German psyche. There had been a public campaign to let the ceremony go ahead. The authorities had relented. So March took him to his wedding, stood handcuffed beside him throughout the service and even during the wedding pictures, like an unusually attentive best man.

The reception had been in a grim hall next to the church. Towards the end, the groom had whispered that there was a storeroom with a rug in it, that the priest had no objections . . . And March – young husband that he was – had checked the storeroom and seen there were no windows and had left the man and his wife alone for twenty minutes. The priest – who had worked as a chaplain in Hamburg's docks for thirty years, and seen most things – had given March a grave wink.

On the way back to prison, as the high walls came into view, March had expected the man to be depressed, to plead for extra time, maybe even dive for the door. Not at all. He had sat smiling, finishing his cigar. Standing by the

Zürich See, March realised how he had felt. It had been sufficient to know that the possibility of another life existed; one day of it had been enough.

He felt Charlie come up beside him. She kissed him lightly on the cheek.

A SHOP at Zürich airport was piled high with brightly coloured gifts – cuckoo clocks, toy skis, ashtrays glazed with pictures of the Matterhorn, and chocolates. March picked out one of the musical boxes with 'Birthday Greetings to Our Beloved Führer, 1964' written on the lid and took it to the counter where a plump middle-aged woman was waiting.

'Could you wrap this and send it for me?'

'No problem, sir. Write down where you want it to go.'

She gave him a form and a pencil and March wrote Hannelore Jaeger's name and address. Hannelore was even fatter than her husband, a lover of chocolates. He hoped Max would see the joke.

The assistant wrapped the box swiftly in brown paper, with skilled fingers.

'Do you sell many of these?'

'Hundreds. You Germans certainly love your Führer.'

'We do, it is true.' He was looking at the parcel. It was wrapped exactly like the one he had taken from Buhler's mailbox. 'You don't, I suppose, keep a record of the places to which you send these packages?'

'That would be impossible.' She addressed it, stuck on a stamp, and added it to the pile behind her.

'Of course. And you wouldn't remember serving an elderly German here, about four o'clock on Monday afternoon? He had thick glasses and runny eyes.'

Her face was suddenly hard with suspicion. 'What are you? A policeman?'

'It's of no importance.' He paid for the chocolates, and also for a mug with 'I LOVE ZÜRICH' printed on the side.

Luther would not have come all the way to Switzerland to *put* that painting in the bank vault, thought March. Even as a retired Foreign Ministry official, he could never have smuggled a package that size, stamped top secret, past the Zollgrenzschutz. He must have come here to *retrieve* something, to take it back to Germany. And as it was the first time he had visited the vault for twenty-one years, and as there were three other keys, and as he trusted nobody, he must have had doubts about whether *that other thing* would still be here.

He stood looking at the departure lounge and tried to imagine the elderly man hurrying into the terminal building, clutching his precious cargo, his weak heart beating sharply against his ribs. The chocolates must have been a message of success: so far, my old comrades, so good. What could he have been carrying? Not paintings or money, surely; they had plenty of both in Germany.

'*Paper.*'

'What?' Charlie, who had been waiting for him in the concourse, turned round in surprise.

'That must have been the link. Paper. They were all civil servants. They lived their lives by paper, on paper.'

He pictured them in wartime Berlin – sitting in their offices at night, circulating memos and minutes in a perpetual bureaucratic paper chase, building themselves a paper fortress. Millions of Germans had fought in the war: in the freezing mud of the Steppes, or in the Libyan desert, or in the clear skies over southern England, or – like March – at sea. But these old men had fought their war – had bled and expended their middle age – *on paper*.

Charlie was shaking her head. 'You're making no sense.'

'I know. To myself, perhaps. I bought you this.'

She unwrapped the mug and laughed, clasped it to her heart.

'I shall treasure it.'

THEY walked quickly through passport control. Beyond the barrier, March turned for a final look. The two Swiss policemen were watching from the ticket desk. One of them – the one who had rescued them outside Zaugg's villa – raised his hand. March waved in return.

Their flight number was being called for the last time: *'Passengers for Lufthansa flight 227 to Berlin must report immediately . . .'*

He let his arm fall back and turned towards the departure gate.

TWO

No whisky on this flight, but coffee – plenty of it, strong and black. Charlie tried to read a newspaper but fell asleep. March was too excited to rest.

He had torn a dozen blank pages from his notebook, had ripped them in half and half again. Now he had them spread out on the plastic table in front of him. On each he had written a name, a date, an incident. He reshuffled them endlessly – the front to the back, the back to the middle, the middle to the beginning – a cigarette dangling from his lips, smoke billowing, his head in the clouds. To the other passengers, a few of whom stole curious glances, he must have looked like a man playing a particularly demented form of patience.

July 1942. On the Eastern Front, the Wehrmacht has launched Operation 'Blue': the offensive which will eventually win Germany the war. America is taking a hammering from the Japanese. The British are bombing the Ruhr, fighting in North Africa. In Prague, Reinhard Heydrich is recovering from an assassination attempt.

So: good days for the Germans, especially those in the conquered territories. Elegant apartments, girlfriends, bribes – packing cases of plunder to send back home. Corruption from high to low; from corporal to Kommissar; from alcohol to altar-pieces. Buhler, Stuckart and Luther have an especially good racket in play. Buhler requisitions art treasures in the General Government, sends them under cover to Stuckart at the Interior Ministry – quite safe, for who would dare tamper with the mail of such powerful servants of the Reich? Luther smuggles the objects abroad to sell – safe again, for who would dare order the head of the Foreign Ministry's German Division to open his bags? All three retire in the 1950s, rich and honoured men.

And then, in 1964: catastrophe.

March shuffled his bits of paper, shuffled them again.

On Friday, 11 April, the three conspirators gather at Buhler's villa: the first piece of evidence which suggests a panic . . .

No. That was not right. He leafed back through his notes, to Charlie's account of her conversation with Stuckart. Of course.

On Thursday, 10 April, the day before the meeting, Stuckart stands in Bülow Strasse and notes the number of the telephone in the booth opposite Charlotte Maguire's apartment. Armed with that, he goes to Buhler's villa on Friday. Something so terrible threatens to overwhelm them that the three men contemplate the unthinkable: defection to the United States of America. Stuckart lays out the procedure. They cannot trust the Embassy, because Kennedy has stuffed it with appeasers. They need a direct link with Washington. Stuckart has it: Michael Maguire's daughter. It is agreed. On Saturday, Stuckart telephones the girl to arrange a meeting. On Sunday, Luther flies to Switzerland: not to fetch pictures or money, which they have in abundance in Berlin, but to collect something put there in the course of three visits, between the summer of 1942 and the spring of 1943.

But already it is too late. By the time Luther has made the withdrawal, sent the signal from Zürich, landed in Berlin, Buhler and Stuckart are dead. And so he decides to disappear, taking with him whatever he removed from the vault in Zürich.

March sat back and contemplated his half-finished puzzle. It was a version of events, as valid as any other.

Charlie sighed and stirred in her sleep, twisted to rest her head on his shoulder. He kissed her hair. Today was Friday. The Führertag was Monday. He had only the weekend left. 'Oh, my dear Fräulein Maguire,' he murmured. 'I fear we have been looking in the wrong place.'

'LADIES *and gentlemen, we shall shortly be beginning our descent to Flughafen Hermann Goering. Please return your seats to the upright position and fold away the tables in front of you . . .*'

Carefully, so as not to wake her, March withdrew his shoulder from beneath Charlie's head, gathered up his pieces of paper, and made his way, unsteadily, towards the back of the aircraft. A boy in the uniform of the Hitler Youth emerged from the lavatory and held the door open, politely. March nodded, went inside and locked it behind him. A dim light flickered.

The tiny compartment stank of stale air, endlessly recycled; of cheap soap; of faeces. He lifted the lid of the metal lavatory basin and dropped in the paper. The aircraft pitched and shook. A warning light pinged. ATTENTION! RETURN TO YOUR SEAT! The turbulence made his stomach lurch. Was this how Luther had felt, as the aircraft dropped towards Berlin? The metal was clammy to the touch. He pulled a lever and the lavatory flushed, his notes sucked from sight in a whirlpool of blue water.

Lufthansa had stocked the toilet not with towels but with moist little paper handkerchiefs, impregnated with some sickly liquid. March wiped his face. He could feel the heat of his skin through the slippery fabric. Another vibration, like a U-boat being depth-charged. They were falling fast. He pressed his burning forehead to the cool mirror. *Dive, dive, dive . . .*

*

SHE was awake, dragging a comb through her thick hair. 'I was beginning to think you had jumped.'

'It's true, the thought did enter my mind.' He fastened his seatbelt. 'But you may be my salvation.'

'You say the nicest things.'

'I said "may be".' He took her hand. 'Listen. Are you sure Stuckart told you he came on *Thursday* to check out that telephone opposite your apartment?'

She thought for a moment. 'Yes, I'm sure. I remember it made me realise: this man is serious, he's done his homework.'

'That's what I think. The question is, was Stuckart acting on his own – trying to set up his own private escape route – or was ringing you a course of action he had discussed with the others?'

'Does it matter?'

'Very much. Think about it. If he agreed it with the others on Friday, it means Luther may know who you are, and know the procedure for contacting you.'

She pulled her hand back in surprise. 'But that's crazy. He'd never trust me.'

'You're right, it's crazy.' They had dropped through one layer of cloud; beneath them was another. March could see the tip of the Great Hall poking through it, like the top of a helmet. 'But suppose Luther is still alive down there, what are his options? The airport is being watched. So are the docks, the railway stations, the border. He can't risk going direct to the American Embassy, not after what's happened about Kennedy's visit. He can't go home. What can he do?'

'I don't believe it. He could have called me Tuesday or Wednesday. Or Thursday morning. Why would he wait?'

But he could hear the doubt in her voice. He thought: You don't *want* to believe it. You thought you were clever, looking for your story in Zürich, but all the time your story might actually have been looking for you, in Berlin.

She had turned away from him, to stare through the window.

March felt suddenly deflated. In truth, he hardly knew her, despite everything. He said: 'The reason he would have waited is to try and find something better to do, something safer. Who knows? Maybe he's found it.'

She did not answer.

THEY landed in Berlin, in a thin drizzle, just before two o'clock. At the end of the runway, as the Junkers turned, the moisture scudded across the window, leaving threads of droplets. The swastika above the terminal building hung limp in the wet.

There were two queues at passport control: one for German and European Community nationals, one for the rest of the world.

'This is where we part,' said March. He had persuaded her, with some difficulty, to let him carry her case. Now he handed it back. 'What are you going to do?'

'Go back to my apartment, I guess, and wait for the telephone to ring. What about you?'

'I thought I would arrange myself a history lesson.' She looked at him, uncomprehending. He said: 'I'll call you later.'

'Be sure you do.'

A vestige of the old mistrust had returned. He could see it in her eyes, felt her searching it out in his. He wanted to say something, to reassure her. 'Don't worry. A deal is a deal.'

She nodded. An awkward silence. Then abruptly she stood on tiptoe and brushed her cheek against his. She was gone before he could think of a response.

*

THE line of returning Germans shuffled one at a time, in silence, into the Reich. March waited patiently with his hands clasped behind his back while his passport was scrutinised. In these last few days before the Führer's birthday, the border checks were always more stringent, the guards more jittery.

The eyes of the Zollgrenzschutz officer were hidden in the shade of his visor. 'The Herr Sturmbannführer is back with three hours to spare.' He drew a thick black line through the visa, scrawled 'void' across it, and handed the passport back. 'Welcome home.'

In the crowded customs hall March kept a look out for Charlie, but could not see her. Perhaps they had refused to let her back into the country. He almost hoped they had: it would be safer for her.

The Zollgrenzschutz were opening every bag. Never had he seen such security. It was chaos. The passengers milling and arguing around the mounds of clothes made the hall look like an Indian bazaar. He waited his turn.

It was after three by the time March reached the left-luggage area and retrieved his case. In the toilets he changed back into his uniform, folded his civilian clothes and packed them away. He checked his Luger and slipped it into his holster. As he left, he glanced at himself in the mirror. A familiar black figure.

Welcome home.

THREE

When the sun shone the Party called it 'Führer weather'. They had no name for rain.

Nevertheless, it had been decreed, drizzle or not, that this afternoon was to be the start of the three-day holiday. And so, with dogged National Socialist determination, the people set about their celebrations.

March was in a taxi heading south through Wedding. This was workers' Berlin, a communist stronghold of the 1920s. The factory whistles, in a festive gesture, had sounded an hour earlier than usual. Now the streets were dense with damp revellers. The Blockwarts had been active. From every second or third building, a banner hung –mostly swastikas, but also the occasional slogan, strung between the iron balconies of the fortress-tenements. WORKERS OF BERLIN SALUTE THE FÜHRER ON HIS 75TH BIRTHDAY! LONG LIVE THE GLORIOUS NATIONAL SOCIALIST REVOLUTION! LONG LIVE OUR GUIDE AND FIRST COMRADE ADOLF HITLER! The back streets were in a delirium of colour, throbbing to the oohm-pah! of the local SA bands. And this was only Friday. March wondered what the Wedding authorities had planned for the day itself.

During the night, on the corner of Wolff Strasse, some rebellious spirit had added a piece of graffiti, in white paint: ANYONE FOUND NOT ENJOYING THEMSELVES WILL BE SHOT. A couple of anxious-looking brownshirts were trying to clean it off.

March took the taxi as far as Fritz-Todt Platz. His Volkswagen was still outside Stuckart's apartment, where he had parked it the night before last. He looked up at the fourth floor. Someone had drawn all the curtains.

At Werderscher Markt, he stowed his suitcase in his

office and rang the Duty Officer. Martin Luther had not been located.

Krause said: 'Between you and me, March, Globus is driving us all fucking mad. In here every half-hour, ranting and raving that someone will go to a KZ unless he gets results.'

'The Herr Obergruppenführer is a very dedicated officer.'

'Oh, he is, he is.' Krause's voice was suddenly panicky. 'I didn't mean to suggest – '

March hung up. That would give whoever was listening to his calls something to think about.

He lugged the typewriter across to his desk and inserted a single sheet of paper. He lit a cigarette.

> TO: Artur Nebe, SS-Oberstgruppenführer, Reich Kriminalpolizei
> FROM: X. March, SS-Sturmbannführer 17.4.64
>
> 1. I have the honour to inform you that at 10.00 this morning I attended the premises of Zaugg & Cie, Bankiers, Bahnhof Strasse, Zürich.
>
> 2. The numbered account, whose existence we discussed yesterday, was opened by Foreign Ministry Under State Secretary Martin Luther on 8.7.42. Four keys were issued.
>
> 3. The box was subsequently opened on three occasions: 17.12.42, 9.8.43, 13.4.64.
>
> 4. On inspection by myself, the box was found to contain

March leaned back in his seat and blew a pair of neat smoke rings towards the ceiling. The thought of that painting in the hands of Nebe – dumped into his collection of bombastic, syrupy Schmutzlers and Kirchners – was repugnant, even sacrilegious. Better to leave her at peace in the darkness. He let his fingers rest on the typewriter keys for a moment, then tapped:

nothing.

He wound the paper out of the typewriter, signed it, and sealed it in an envelope. He called Nebe's office and was ordered to bring it up at once, personally. He hung up and stared out the window at the brickwork view.

Why not?

He stood and checked along the bookshelves until he found the Berlin area telephone directory. He took it down and looked up a number, which he dialled from the office next door, so as not to be overheard.

A man's voice answered: 'Reichsarchiv.'

TEN minutes later his boots were sinking into the soft mire of Artur Nebe's office carpet.

'Do you believe in coincidences, March?'

'No, sir.'

'No,' said Nebe. 'Good. Neither do I.' He put down his magnifying glass and pushed away March's report. 'I don't believe two retired public servants of the same age and rank *just happen* to choose to commit suicide rather than be exposed as corrupt. My God' – he gave a harsh little laugh – 'if every government official in Berlin took that approach, the streets would be piled high with the dead. Nor do they *just happen* to be murdered in the week an American president announces he will grace us with a visit.'

He pushed back his chair and hobbled across to a small bookcase lined with the sacred texts of National Socialism: *Mein Kampf*, Rosenberg's *Mythus der XX. Jahrhunderts*, Goebbels's *Tagebücher* . . . He pressed a switch and the front of the bookcase swung open to reveal a cocktail cabinet. The tomes, March saw now, were merely the spines of books, pasted on to the wood.

Nebe helped himself to a large vodka and returned to his desk. March continued to stand before him, neither fully at attention nor fully at ease.

'Globus works for Heydrich,' said Nebe. 'That's simple. Globus wouldn't wipe his own arse unless Heydrich told him it was time to do it.'

March said nothing.

'And Heydrich works for the Führer most of the time, and all of the time he works for himself . . .'

Nebe held the heavy tumbler to his lips. His lizard's tongue darted into the vodka, playing with it. He was silent for a while. Then he said: 'Do you know why we're greasing up to the Americans, March?'

'No, sir.'

'Because we're in the shit. Here is something you won't read in the little Doctor's newspapers. Twenty million settlers in the East by 1960, that was Himmler's plan. Ninety million by the end of the century. Fine. Well, we shipped them out all right. Trouble is, half of them want to come back. Consider that cosmic piece of irony, March: living space that no one wants to live in. Terrorism' – he gestured with his glass, the ice clinked – 'I don't need to tell an officer of the Kripo how serious terrorism has become. The Americans supply money, weapons, training. They've kept the Reds going for twenty years. As for us: the young don't want to fight and the old don't want to work.'

He shook his grey head at such follies, fished an ice cube out of his drink and sucked it noisily.

'Heydrich's mad for this American deal. He'd kill to keep it sweet. Is that what's happening here, March? Buhler, Stuckart, Luther – were they a threat to it somehow?'

Nebe's eyes searched his face. March stared straight ahead.

'You're an irony yourself, March, in a way. Did you ever consider that?'

'No, sir.'

' "No, sir." ' Nebe mimicked him. 'Well consider it now. We set out to breed a generation of supermen to rule an empire, yes? We trained them to apply hard logic – pitilessly, even cruelly. Remember what the Führer once said? "My greatest gift to the Germans is that I have taught them to think clearly." And what happens? A few of you – perhaps the best of you – begin to turn this pitiless clear thinking on to *us*. I tell you, I'm glad I'm an old man. I fear the future.' He was quiet for a minute, lost in his own thoughts.

At length, disappointed, the old man picked up the magnifying glass. 'Corruption it is, then.' He read through March's report once more, then tore it up and dropped it into his waste bin.

CLIO, the Muse of History, guarded the Reichsarchiv: an Amazonian nude designed by Adolf Ziegler, the 'Reich Master of the Pubic Hair'. She frowned across the Avenue of Victory towards the Soldiers' Hall, where a long queue of tourists waited to file past Frederick the Great's bones. Pigeons perched on the slopes of her immense bosom, like mountaineers on the face of a glacier. Behind her, a sign had been carved above the entrance to the archive, gold leaf inlaid on polished granite. A quotation from the Führer: FOR ANY NATION, THE RIGHT HISTORY IS WORTH 100 DIVISIONS.

Rudolf Halder led March inside, and up to the third floor. He pushed at the double-doors and stood aside to let him walk through. A corridor with stone walls and a stone floor seemed to stretch for ever.

'Impressive, yes?' In his place of work, Halder spoke in

the tone of a professional historian, conveying pride and sarcasm simultaneously. 'We call the style mock-Teutonic. This, you will not be surprised to hear, is the largest archive building in the world. Above us: two floors of administration. On this floor: researchers' offices and reading rooms. Beneath us: *six floors* of documents. You are treading, my friend, on the history of the Fatherland. For my part, I tend Clio's lamp in here.'

It was a monkish cell: small, windowless, the walls made of blocks of granite. Papers were stacked in piles half a metre high on the table; they spilled over on to the floor. Books were everywhere – several hundred of them – each sprouting a thicket of markers: multi-coloured bits of paper, tram tickets, pieces of cigarette carton, spent matches.

'The historian's mission. To bring out of chaos – more chaos.' Halder lifted a stack of old army signals off the solitary chair, knocked the dust off it, and gestured to March to sit.

'I need your help, Rudi – again.'

Halder perched on the edge of his desk. 'I don't hear from you for months, then suddenly it's twice in a week. I presume this also has to do with the Buhler business? I saw the obituary.'

March nodded. 'I should say now that you are talking to a pariah. You may be endangering yourself merely by meeting me.'

'That only makes it sound more fascinating.' Halder put his long fingers together and cracked the joints. 'Go on.'

'This is a real challenge for you.' March paused, took a breath. 'Three men: Buhler, Wilhelm Stuckart and Martin Luther. The first two dead; the last, a fugitive. All three senior civil servants, as you know. In the summer of 1942, they opened a bank account in Zürich. At first I assumed they put away a hoard of money or art treasures – as you suspected, Buhler was up to his armpits in corruption – but now I think it is more likely to have been documents.'

'What sort of documents?'

'Not sure.'

'Sensitive?'

'Presumably.'

'You've got one problem straight away. You're talking about three different ministries – Foreign, Interior and General Government, which isn't really a ministry at all. That's tons of documents. I mean it, Zavi, literally – tons.'

'Do you have their records here?'

'Foreign and Interior, yes. General Government is in Krakau.'

'Do you have access to them?'

'Officially – no. Unofficially . . .' He wobbled a bony hand. '. . . Perhaps, if I'm lucky. But, Zavi, it would take a lifetime simply to look through them. What are you suggesting we do?'

'There must be some clue in there. Perhaps there are papers missing.'

'But this is an impossible task.'

'I told you it was a challenge.'

'And how soon does this "clue" need to be discovered?'

'I need to find it tonight.'

Halder made an explosive sound, of mingled incredulity, anger, scorn. March said quietly: 'Rudi, in three days' time, they're threatening to put me in front of an SS Honour Court. You know what that means. *I have to find it now*.'

Halder looked at him for a moment, unwilling to believe what he was hearing, then turned away, muttering: 'Let me think . . .'

March said: 'Can I have a cigarette?'

'In the corridor. Not in here – this stuff is irreplaceable.'

As March smoked he could hear Halder, in his office,

pacing up and down. He looked at his watch. Six o'clock. The long corridor was deserted. Most of the staff must have gone home, to begin the holiday weekend. March tried a couple of office doors, but both were locked. The third was open. He picked up the telephone, listened to the tone, and dialled nine. The tone changed: an outside line. He rang Charlie's number. She answered at once.

'It's me. Are you all right?'

She said: 'I'm fine. I've discovered something – just a tiny thing.'

'Don't tell me over an open line. I'll talk to you later.' He tried to think of something else to say, but she had replaced the receiver.

Now Halder was on the telephone, his cheerful voice echoing down the flagstone corridor. 'Eberhard? Good evening to you . . . Indeed, no rest for some of us. A quick question, if I may. The Interior Ministry series . . . Oh, they have been? Good. On an office basis? . . . I see. Excellent. And all that is done? . . .'

March leaned against the wall with his eyes closed, trying not to think of the ocean of paper beneath his feet. Come on, Rudi. *Come on*.

He heard a bell tinkle as Halder hung up. A few seconds later Rudi appeared in the corridor, pulling on his jacket. A bunch of pen-tops jutted from his breast pocket. 'One small piece of luck. According to my colleague, the Interior Ministry files at least have been catalogued.' He set off down the passage at a rapid pace. March strode beside him.

'What does that mean?'

'It means there should be a central index, showing us which papers actually crossed Stuckart's desk, and when.' He hammered at the buttons beside the elevator. Nothing happened. 'Looks as if they've turned this thing off for the night. We'll have to walk.'

As they clattered down the wide spiral staircase, Halder

shouted: 'You appreciate this is completely against the rules? I'm cleared for Military, Eastern Front, not Administration, Internal. If we're stopped, you'll have to spin Security some yarn about Polizei business – something that'll take them a couple of hours to check. As for me, I'm just a poor sucker, doing you a favour, right?'

'I appreciate it. How much further?'

'All the way to the bottom.' Halder was shaking his head. 'An Honour Court! Dear God, Zavi, what's happened to you?'

Sixty metres beneath the ground the air circulated cool and dry, the lights were dimmed, to protect the archives. 'They say this place was built to withstand a direct hit from an American missile,' said Halder.

'What's behind there?'

March pointed to a steel door, covered with warning signs: 'ATTENTION! NO ADMITTANCE TO UNAUTHORISED PERSONS!' 'ENTRY FORBIDDEN!' 'PASSES MUST BE SHOWN'.

' "The right history is worth a hundred divisions", remember? That's the place where the wrong history goes. Shit. Look out.'

Halder pulled March into a doorway. A security guard was coming towards them, bent like a miner in an underground shaft, pushing a metal cart. March thought he was certain to see them, but he went straight past, grunting with effort. He stopped at the metal barrier and unlocked it. There was a glimpse of a furnace, a roar of flame, before the door clanged shut behind him.

'Let's go.'

As they walked, Halder explained the procedure. The archive worked on warehouse principles. Requisitions for files came down to a central handling area on each floor. Here, in ledgers a metre high and twenty centimetres thick, was kept the main index. Entered next to each file was a stack number. The stacks themselves were in fire-proof storerooms leading off from the handling area. The secret, said Halder, was to know your way round the index. He paraded in front of the crimson leather spines, tapping each with his finger until he found the one he wanted, then lugged it over to the floor manager's desk.

March had once been below-decks on the aircraft carrier, *Grossadmiral Raeder*. The depths of the Reichsarchiv reminded him of that: low ceilings strung with lights, the sense of something vast pressing down from above. Next to the desk: a photocopier – a rare sight in Germany, where their distribution was strictly controlled, to stop subversives producing illegal literature. A dozen empty carts were drawn up by the lift-shaft. He could see fifty metres in either direction. The place was deserted.

Halder gave a cry of triumph. 'State Secretary: Office Files, 1939 to 1950. Oh Christ: four hundred boxes. What years do you want to look at?'

'The Swiss bank account was opened in July '42, so let's say the first seven months of that year.'

Halder turned the page, talking to himself. 'Yes. I see what they've done. They've arranged the papers in four series: office correspondence, minutes and memoranda, statutes and decrees, ministry personnel . . .'

'What I'm looking for is something that connects Stuckart with Buhler and Luther.'

'In that case, we'd better start with office correspondence. That should give us a feel for what was going on at the time.' Halder was scribbling notes. 'D/15/M/28–34. Okay. Here we go.'

Storeroom D was twenty metres down on the left. Stack fifteen, section M was in the dead centre of the room. Halder said: 'Only six boxes, thank God. You take January to April, I'll do May to August.'

The boxes were made of cardboard, each the size of a large desk drawer. There was no table, so they sat on the floor. With his back pressed against the metal shelving, March opened the first box, pulled out a handful of papers, and began to read.

YOU need a little luck in this life.

The first document was a letter dated 2 January, from the under state secretary at the Air Ministry, regarding the distribution of gas masks to the Reichsluftschutzbund, the Air Raid Protection organisation. The second, dated 4 January, was from the Office of the Four-Year Plan and concerned the alleged unauthorised use of gasoline by senior government officials.

The third was from Reinhard Heydrich.

March saw the signature first – an angular, spidery scrawl. Then his eyes travelled to the letterhead – the Reich Main Security Office, Berlin SW 11, Prinz-Albrecht Strasse 8 – then to the date: 6 January 1942. And only then to the text:

> This is to confirm that the inter-agency discussion followed by luncheon originally scheduled for 9 December 1941 has now been postponed to 20 January 1942 in the office of the International Criminal Police Commission, Berlin, Am grossen Wannsee, Nr. 56/58.

March leafed through the other letters in the box: carbon flimsies and creamy originals; imposing letterheads – Reichschancellery, Economics Ministry, Organisation-Todt; invitations to luncheons and meetings; pleas, demands, circulars. But there was nothing else from Heydrich.

March passed the letter to Halder. 'What do you make of this?'

Halder frowned. 'Unusual, I would say, for the Main

Security Office to convene a meeting of government agencies.'

'Can we find out what they discussed?'

'Should be able to. We can cross-reference it to the minutes and memoranda series. Let's see: 20 January . . .'

Halder looked at his notes, pulled himself to his feet and walked along the stack. He dragged out another box, returned with it and sat, cross-legged. March watched him flick through the contents. Suddenly, he stopped. He said slowly: 'My God . . .'

'What is it?'

Halder handed him a single sheet of paper, on which was typed: 'In the interests of state security, the minutes of the inter-agency meeting of 20 January 1942 have been removed at the request of the Reichsführer-SS.'

Halder said: 'Look at the date.'

March looked. It was 6 April 1964. The minutes had been extracted by Heydrich eleven days earlier.

'Can he do that – legally, I mean?'

'The Gestapo can weed out whatever it wants on the grounds of security. They usually transfer the papers to the vaults in Prinz-Albrecht Strasse.'

There was a noise in the corridor outside. Halder held up a warning finger. Both men were silent, motionless, as the guard clattered past, wheeling the empty cart back from the furnace room. They listened as the sounds faded towards the other end of the building.

March whispered: 'Now what do we do?'

Halder scratched his head. 'An inter-agency meeting at the level of state-secretary . . .'

March saw what he was thinking. 'Buhler and Luther would have been invited, as well?'

'It would seem logical. At that rank, they get fussy about protocol. You wouldn't have a state secretary from one ministry attending, and only a junior civil servant from another. What time is it?'

'Eight o'clock.'

'They're an hour ahead in Krakau.' Halder chewed his lip for a moment, then reached a decision. He stood. 'I'll telephone my friend who works at the archives in the General Government and ask if the SS have been sniffing around there in the past couple of weeks. If they haven't, maybe I can persuade him to go in tomorrow and see if the minutes are still in Buhler's papers.'

'Couldn't we just check here, in the Foreign Ministry archives? In Luther's papers?'

'No. Too vast. It could take us weeks. This is the best way, believe me.'

'Be careful what you say to him, Rudi.'

'Don't worry. I'm aware of the dangers.' Halder paused at the door. 'And no smoking while I'm gone, for Christ's sake. This is the most inflammable building in the Reich.'

True enough, thought March. He waited until Halder had gone and then began walking up and down between the stacks of boxes. He wanted a cigarette, badly. His hands were trembling. He thrust them into his pockets.

What a monument to German bureaucracy this place was. Herr A, wishing to do something, asked permission of Doctor B. Doctor B covered himself by referring it upwards to Ministerialdirektor C. Ministerialdirektor C shuffled it to Reichsminister D, who said he would leave it to the judgement of Herr A, who naturally went back to Doctor B . . . The alliances and rivalries, traps and intrigues of three decades of Party rule wove in and out of these metal stacks; ten thousand webs, spun from paper threads, suspended in the cool air.

Halder was back within ten minutes. 'The SS were in Krakau two weeks ago all right.' He was rubbing his hands uneasily. 'Their memory is still vivid. A distinguished visitor. Obergruppenführer Globocnik himself.'

'Everywhere I turn,' said March. 'Globocnik!'

'He flew in on a Gestapo jet from Berlin, with special authorisation from Heydrich, personally signed. He gave them all the shits, apparently. Shouting and swearing. Knew exactly what he was looking for: one file removed. He was out of there by lunchtime.'

Globus, Heydrich, Nebe. March put his hand to his head. It was dizzying. 'So here it ends?'

'Here it ends. Unless you think there might be something else in Stuckart's papers.'

March looked down at the boxes. The contents seemed to him as dead as dust; dead men's bones. The thought of sifting through them any more was repugnant to him. He needed to breathe some fresh air. 'Forget it, Rudi. Thanks.'

Halder stooped to pick up Heydrich's note. 'Interesting that the conference was postponed, from December the ninth to January the twentieth.'

'What's the significance of that?'

Halder gave him a pitying look. 'Were you really so completely cooped-up in that fucking tin can we had to live in? Did the outside world never penetrate? On December the seventh, 1941, you blockhead, the forces of His Imperial Majesty, Emperor Hirohito of Japan, attacked the US Pacific fleet at Pearl Harbor. On December the eleventh, Germany declared war on the United States. Good reasons to postpone a conference, wouldn't you say?' Halder was grinning, but slowly the grin faded, to be replaced by a more thoughtful expression. 'I wonder . . .'

'What?'

He tapped the paper. 'There must have been an original invitation, before this one.'

'So what?'

'It depends. Sometimes our friends from the Gestapo are not quite as efficient at weeding out embarrassing details as they like to think, especially if they're in a hurry . . .'

March was already standing in front of the stack of boxes, glancing up and down, his depression lifted. 'Which one? Where do we start?'

'For a conference at that level, Heydrich would have had to have given the participants at least two weeks' notice.' Halder looked at his notes. 'That would mean Stuckart's office correspondence file for November 1941. Let me see. That should be box twenty-six, I think.'

He joined March in front of the shelves and counted off the boxes until he found the one he wanted. He pulled it down, cradled it. 'Don't snatch, Zavi. All in good time. History teaches us patience.'

He knelt, placed the box in front of him, opened it, pulled out an armful of papers. He glanced at each in turn, placing them in a pile to his left. 'Invitation to a reception given by the Italian ambassador: boring. Conference organised by Walther Darre at the Agriculture Ministry: *very* boring . . .'

He went on like that for perhaps two minutes, with March standing, watching, nervously grinding his fist into his palm. Then suddenly Halder froze. 'Oh shit.' He read it through again and looked up. 'Invitation from Heydrich. Not boring at all, I'm afraid. Not boring at all.'

FOUR

The heavens were in chaos. Nebulae exploded. Comets and meteors rushed across the sky, disappeared for an instant, then detonated against green oceans of cloud.

Above the Tiergarten, the firework display was nearing its climax. Parachute flares lit up Berlin like an air raid.

As March waited in his car to turn left on to Unter den Linden, a gang of SA men lurched out in front of him. Two of them, their arms draped around one another, performed a drunken can-can in the beam of the headlights. The others banged on the Volkswagen's body work, or pressed their faces against the windows – eyes bulging, tongues lolling; grotesque apes. March put the engine into first gear and skidded away. There was a thud as one of the dancers was sent spinning.

He drove back to Werderscher Markt. All police leave had been cancelled. Every window was ablaze with electric light. In the foyer, someone hailed him, but March ignored them. He clattered down the stairs to the basement.

Bank vaults and basements and underground store rooms . . . I am turning into a troglodyte, thought March; a cave-dweller, a recluse; a robber of paper tombs.

The Gorgon of the Registry was still sitting in her lair. Did she never sleep? He showed her his ID. There were a couple of other detectives at the central desk, leafing in a languid manner through the ubiquitous manila files. March took a seat in the farthest corner of the room. He switched on an angle-poise lamp, bent its shade low over the table. From inside his tunic he drew the three sheets of paper he had taken from the Reichsarchiv.

They were poor-quality photostats. The machine had been set too faint, the originals had been thrust into it, hastily and skewed. He did not blame Rudi for that. Rudi had not wanted to make the copies at all. Rudi had been terrified. All his schoolboy bravado had vanished when he read Heydrich's invitation. March had been obliged virtually to drag him to the photocopier. The moment the historian had finished, he had darted back into the storeroom, shovelled the papers back into the boxes, put the boxes back on to the shelves. At his insistence, they had left the archive building by a rear entrance.

'I think, Zavi, we should not see one another for a long time now.'

'Of course.'

'You know how it is . . .'

Halder had stood, miserable and helpless, while above their heads the fireworks had whooshed and banged. March had embraced him –'Don't feel bad; I know: your family come first' – and quickly walked away.

Document One. Heydrich's original invitation, dated 19 November 1941:

> On 31.7.1941, the Reichsmarschall of the Greater German Reich charged me, in co-operation with all the other relevant central agencies, to make all the necessary preparations with regard to organisational, technical and material measures for a complete solution of the Jewish question in Europe and to present him shortly with a complete draft proposal on this matter. I enclose a photocopy of this commission.
>
> In view of the extraordinary importance which must be accorded to these questions, and in the interest of securing a uniform view among the relevant central agencies of the further tasks concerned with the remaining work on this final solution, I propose to make these problems the subject of a general discussion. This is particularly necessary since from 10 October onwards the Jews have been evacuated

> from Reich territory, including the Protectorate, to the East in a continuous series of transports.
>
> I therefore invite you to join me and others, whose names I enclose, at a discussion followed by luncheon on 9 December 1941 at 12.00 in the office of the International Criminal Police Commission, Berlin, Am grossen Wannsee, Nr. 56/58.

Document Two. A photostat of a photostat, almost illegible in places, the words rubbed away like an ancient inscription on a tomb. Hermann Goering's directive to Heydrich, dated 31 July 1941:

> To supplement the task that was assigned to you on 24 January 1939, which dealt with the solution of the Jewish problem by emigration and evacuation in the most suitable way, I hereby charge you with making all necessary preparations with regard to organisational, technical and material matters for bringing about a complete solution of the Jewish question within the German sphere of influence in Europe.
>
> Wherever other governmental agencies are involved, these are to co-operate with you.
>
> I request you further to send me, in the near future, an overall plan covering the organisational, technical and material measures necessary for the accomplishment of the final solution of the Jewish question which we desire.

Document Three. A list of the fourteen people Heydrich had invited to the conference. Stuckart was third on the list; Buhler, sixth; Luther, seventh. March recognised a couple of the others.

He ripped a sheet from his notebook, wrote down eleven names and took it to the issuing desk. The two detectives had gone. The Registrar was nowhere to be seen. He rapped on the counter and shouted: 'Shop!' From behind a row of filing cabinets came a guilty clink of glass on bottle. So that was her secret. She must have forgotten he was there. A moment later, she waddled into view.

'What do we have on these eleven men?'

He tried to hand her the list. She folded a pair of plump arms across a greasy tunic. 'No more than three files at any one time, without special authorisation.'

'Never mind that.'

'It is not permitted.'

'It is not permitted to drink alcohol on duty, either, yet you stink of it. Now get me these files.'

TO every man and woman, a number; to every number, a file. Not all files were held at Werderscher Markt. Only those whose lives had come into contact with the Reich Kriminalpolizei, for whatever reason, had left their spoor here. But by using the information bureau at Alexander Platz, and the obituaries of the *Völkischer Beobachter* (published annually as *The Roll Call of the Fallen*) March was able to fill in the gaps. He tracked down every name. It took him two hours.

The first man on the list was Doctor Alfred Meyer of the East Ministry. According to his Kripo file, Meyer had committed suicide in 1960 after undergoing treatment for various mental illnesses.

The second name: Doctor Georg Leibrandt, also of the East Ministry. He had died in an automobile accident in 1959, his car crushed by a truck on the autobahn between Stuttgart and Augsburg. The driver of the truck had never been found.

Erich Neumann, State Secretary in the Office of the Four Year Plan, had shot himself in 1957.

Doctor Roland Freisler, State Secretary from the Justice Ministry: hacked to death by a maniac with a knife on the steps of the Berlin People's Court in the winter of 1954. An investigation into how his security guards had managed to let a criminal lunatic come so close had concluded that nobody was to blame. The assassin had been shot seconds after the attack on Freisler.

At this point, March had gone into the corridor for a cigarette. He drew the smoke deep into his lungs, tilted back his head and let it out slowly, as if taking a cure.

He returned to find a fresh heap of files on his desk.

SS-Oberführer Gerhard Klopfer, deputy head of the Party Chancellery, had been reported missing by his wife in May 1963; his body had been found by building-site workers in southern Berlin, stuffed into a cement mixer.

Friedrich Kritzinger. That name was familiar. Of course. March remembered the scenes from the television news: the familiar taped-off street, the wrecked car, the widow supported by her sons. Kritzinger, the former Ministerialdirektor from the Reich Chancellery, had been blown up outside his home in Munich just over a month ago, on 7 March. No terrorist group had yet claimed responsibility.

Two men were recorded by the *Völkischer Beobachter* as having died of natural causes. SS-Standartenführer Adolf Eichmann of the Reich Main Security Office had succumbed to a heart attack in 1961. SS-Sturmbannführer Doctor Rudolf Lange of KdS Latvia had died of a brain tumour in 1955.

Heinrich Müller. Here was another name March knew. The Bavarian policeman Müller, the former head of the Gestapo, had been on board Himmler's plane when it crashed in 1962, killing everyone on board.

SS-Oberführer Doctor Karl Schöngarth, representing the security services of the General Government, had fallen beneath the wheels of a U-bahn train pulling into Zoo Station on 9 April 1964 – barely more than a week ago. There were no witnesses.

SS-Obergruppenführer Otto Hoffmann of the Reich Security Office had been found hanging from a length of clothesline in his Spandau apartment on Boxing Day 1963.

That was all. Of the fourteen men who had attended the conference at Heydrich's invitation, thirteen were dead. The fourteenth – Luther – was missing.

As part of its campaign to raise public awareness about terrorism, the Propaganda Ministry had produced a series of children's cartoons. Someone had pinned one up on the noticeboard on the second floor. A little girl receives a parcel and begins opening it. In each succeeding picture she removes more layers of wrapping paper, until she is left holding an alarm clock with two sticks of dynamite attached to it. The last picture is an explosion, with the caption: 'Warning! Do not open a parcel unless you know its contents!'

A good joke. A maxim for every German policeman. Do not open a parcel unless you know its contents. Do not ask a question unless you know the answer.

Endlösung: final solution. *Endlösung*. *Endlösung*. The word tolled in March's head as he half-walked, half-ran along the corridor and into his office.

Endlösung.

He wrenched open the drawers of Max Jaeger's desk and searched through the clutter. Max was notoriously inefficient about administrative matters, had often been reprimanded for his laxity. March prayed he had not taken the warnings to heart.

He had not.

Bless you, Max, you dumbhead.

He slammed the drawers shut.

Only then did he notice it. Someone had attached a

yellow message slip to March's telephone: 'Urgent. Contact the Duty Office immediately.'

FIVE

In the marshalling yards of the Gotenland railway station, they had set up arc lights around the body. From a distance the scene looked oddly glamorous, like a film set.

March stumbled towards it, up and down, across the wooden sleepers and metal tracks, over the diesel-soaked stone.

Before it had been renamed Gotenland, this had been the Anhalter Bahnhof: the Reich's main eastern railway terminus. It was from here that the Führer had set out in his armoured train, *Amerika*, for his wartime headquarters in East Prussia; from here, too, that Berlin's Jews – the Weisses among them – must have embarked on their journey east.

'. . . *from 10 October onwards the Jews have been evacuated from Reich territory to the East in a continuous series of transports* . . .'

In the air behind him, growing fainter: the platform announcements; somewhere ahead, the clank of wheels and couplings, a bleak whistle. The yard was vast – a dreamscape in the orange sodium lighting – at its centre, the one patch of brilliant white. As March neared it, he could make out a dozen figures standing in front of a high-sided goods train: a couple of Orpo men, Krebs, Doctor Eisler, a photographer, a group of anxious officials of the Deutsche Reichsbahn, and Globus.

Globus saw him first, and slowly clapped his gloved hands in muffled and mocking applause. 'Gentlemen, we can relax. The heroic forces of the Kriminalpolizei have arrived to give us their theories.'

One of the Orpo men sniggered.

The body, or what was left of it, was under a rough woollen blanket spread across the tracks, and also in a green plastic sack.

'May I see the corpse?'

'Of course. We haven't touched him yet. We've been waiting for you, the great detective.' Globus nodded to Krebs, who pulled away the blanket.

A man's torso, neatly cropped at either end, along the lines of the rails. He was belly down, slanted across the tracks. One hand had been severed, the head was crushed. Both legs had also been run over, but the bloodied shards of clothing made it difficult to gauge the precise point of amputation. There was a strong smell of alcohol.

'And now you must look in here.' Globus was holding the plastic sack up to the light. He opened it and brought it close to March's face. 'The Gestapo does not wish to be accused of concealing evidence.'

The stumps of feet, one of them still shod; a hand ending in ragged white bone and the gold band of a wristwatch. March did not close his eyes, which seemed to disappoint Globus. 'Ach, well.' He dropped the sack. 'They're worse when they stink, when the rats have been at them. Check his pockets, Krebs.'

In his flapping leather coat, Krebs squatted over the body like carrion. He reached beneath the corpse, feeling for the inside of the jacket. Over his shoulder, Krebs said: 'We were informed two hours ago by the Reichsbahn Polizei that a man answering Luther's description had been seen here. But by the time we got here . . .'

'He had already suffered a fatal accident.' March smiled bitterly. 'How unexpected.'

'Here we are, Herr Obergruppenführer.' Krebs had retrieved a passport and wallet. He straightened, and handed them to Globus.

'This is his passport, no question,' said Globus, flicking

through it. 'And here are several thousand Reichsmarks in cash. Money enough for silk sheets at the Hotel Adlon. But, of course, the bastard couldn't show his face in civilised company. He had no choice but to sleep rough out here.'

This thought appeared to give him satisfaction. He showed March the passport: Luther's ponderous face peered out from above his calloused thumb. 'Look at it, Sturmbannführer, then run along and tell Nebe it is all over. The Gestapo will handle everything from now on. You can clear off and get some rest.' *And enjoy it*, his eyes said, *while you can*.

'The Herr Obergruppenführer is kind.'

'You'll discover how kind I am, March, that much I promise you.' He turned to Eisler. 'Where's that fucking ambulance?'

The pathologist stood to attention. 'On its way, Herr Obergruppenführer. Most definitely.'

March gathered he had been dismissed. He moved towards the railway workers, standing in a forlorn group about ten metres away. 'Which of you discovered the body?'

'I did, Herr Sturmbannführer.' The man who stepped forward wore the dark blue tunic and soft cap of a locomotive driver. His eyes were red, his voice raw. Was that because of the body, wondered March, or was it fear at the unexpected presence of an SS general?

'Cigarette?'

'God, yes, sir. Thanks.'

The driver took one, giving a furtive glance towards Globus, who was now talking to Krebs.

March offered him a light. 'Relax. Take your time. Has this happened to you before?'

'Once.' The man exhaled and looked gratefully at the cigarette. 'It happens here every three or four months. The derelicts sleep under the wagons, to keep out of the rain, poor devils. Then, when the engines start, instead of staying where they are, they try to get out of the way.' He put his hand to his eyes. 'I must have reversed over him, but I never heard a thing. When I looked back up the track, there he was – just a heap of rags.'

'Do you get many derelicts in this yard?'

'Always a couple of dozen. The Reichsbahn Polizei try to keep them away, but the place is too big to patrol properly. Look over there. Some of them are making a run for it.'

He pointed across the tracks. At first, March could make out nothing, except a line of cattle-trucks. Then, almost invisible in the shadow of the train, he spotted a movement – a shape, running jerkily, like a marionette; then another; then more. They ran along the sides of the wagons, darted into the gaps between the trucks, waited, then scampered out again towards the next patch of cover.

Globus had his back to them. Oblivious to their presence, he was still talking to Krebs, smacking his right fist into the palm of his left hand.

March watched as the stick-figures worked their way to safety –then suddenly the rails were vibrating, there was a rush of wind, and the view was cut off by the sleeper train to Rovno, accelerating out of Berlin. The wall of double-decker dining cars and sleeping compartments took half a minute to pass and by the time it had cleared the little colony of drifters had vanished into the orangey dark.

PART FIVE

SATURDAY 18 APRIL

Most of you know what it means when one hundred corpses are lying side by side. Or five hundred. Or one thousand. To have stuck it out and at the same time – apart from some exceptions caused by human weakness – to have remained decent fellows, that is what has made us hard. This is a page of glory in our history which has never to be written and is never to be written.

Heinrich Himmler
secret speech to senior SS officers,
Poznan, 4 October 1943

ONE

A crack of light showed beneath her door. Inside her apartment a radio was playing. Lovers' music – soft strings and low crooning, appropriate for the night. A party? Was this how Americans behaved in the presence of danger? He stood alone on the tiny landing and looked at his watch. It was almost two. He knocked and after a few moments the volume was turned down. He heard her voice.

'Who is it?'

'The police.'

A second or two elapsed, then there was a clatter of bolts and chains, and the door opened. She said: 'You're very funny,' but her smile was a false one, pasted on for his benefit. In her dark eyes exhaustion showed, and also – was it? – fear? He bent to kiss her, his hands resting lightly on her waist, and immediately felt a pricking of desire. *My God*, he thought, *she's turning me into a sixteen-year-old . . .*

Somewhere in the apartment: a footstep. He looked up. Over her shoulder, a man loomed in the doorway of the bathroom. He was a couple of years younger than March: brown brogues, sports jacket, a bow tie, a white jersey pulled on casually over a business shirt. Charlie stiffened in March's embrace and gently broke free of him. 'You remember Henry Nightingale?'

He straightened, feeling awkward. 'Of course. The bar in Potsdamer Strasse.'

Neither man made a move towards the other. The American's face was a mask.

March stared at Nightingale and said softly: 'What's going on here, Charlie?'

She stood on tiptoe and whispered in his ear. 'Don't say anything. Not here. Something's happened.' Then, loudly: 'Isn't this interesting, the three of us?' She took March's arm and guided him towards the bathroom. 'I think you should come into my parlour.'

In the bathroom, Nightingale assumed a proprietorial air. He turned on the cold water taps above the basin and the bath, increased the volume of the radio. The programme had changed. Now the clapboard walls vibrated to the strains of 'German jazz' – a watery syncopation, officially approved, from which all traces of 'Negroid influences' had been erased. When he had arranged everything to his satisfaction, Nightingale perched on the edge of the bath. March sat next to him. Charlie squatted on the floor.

She opened the meeting: 'I told Henry about my visitor the other morning. The one you had the fight with. He thinks the Gestapo may have planted a bug.'

Nightingale gave an amiable grin. 'Afraid that's the way your country works, Herr Sturmbannführer.'

Your country . . .

'I'm sure – a wise precaution.'

Perhaps he isn't younger than me, thought March. The American had thick blond hair, blond eyelashes, a ski-tan. His teeth were absurdly regular – strips of enamel, gleaming white. Not many one-pot meals in *his* childhood, no watery potato soups or sawdust sausages in *that* complexion. His boyish looks embraced all ages from twenty-five to fifty.

For a few moments nobody spoke. Euro-pap filled the silence. Charlie said to March: 'I know you told me not to speak to anyone. But I had to. Now you have to trust Henry and Henry has to trust you. Believe me, there's no other way.'

'And, naturally, we *both* have to trust you.'

'Oh come on . . .'

'All right.' He held up his hands in a gesture of surrender.

Next to her, balanced on top of the lavatory, was the latest in American portable tape recorders. Trailing from one of its sockets was a cable, at the end of which, instead of a microphone, was a small suction cup.

'Listen,' she said. 'You'll understand.' She leaned across and pressed a switch. The spools of tape began to revolve.

'Fräulein Maguire?'

'Yes?'

'The same procedure as before, Fräulein, if you please.'

There was a click, followed by a buzz.

She pressed another switch, stopping the tape. 'That was the first call. You said he'd ring. I was waiting for him.' She was triumphant. 'It's Martin Luther.'

THIS was a crazy business, the craziest he had ever known, like picking your way through a haunted house in the Tiergarten fun fair. No sooner did you plant your feet on solid ground than the floorboards gave way beneath you. You rounded a corner and a madman rushed out. Then you stepped back and found that all the time you had been looking at yourself in a distorting mirror.

Luther.

March said: 'What time was that?'

'Eleven forty-five.'

Eleven forty-five: forty minutes after the discovery of the body on the railway tracks. He thought of the exultant look on Globus's face, and he smiled.

Nightingale said: 'What's so funny?'

'Nothing. I'll explain. What happened next?'

'Exactly as before. I went over to the telephone box and five minutes later he rang again.'

March raised his hand to his brow. 'Don't tell me you dragged that machine all the way across the street?'

'Damn it, I needed some proof!' She glared at him. 'I knew what I was doing. Look.' She stood to demonstrate. 'The deck hangs from this shoulder strap. The whole thing fits under my coat. The wire runs down my sleeve. I attach the suction cup to the receiver, like this. Easy. It was dark. Nobody could have seen a thing.'

Nightingale, the professional diplomat, cut in smoothly: 'Never mind how you got the tape, Charlie, or whether you should have got it.' He said to March: 'May I suggest we simply let her play it?'

Charlie pushed a button. There was a fumbling noise, greatly magnified – the sound of her attaching the microphone to the telephone – and then:

'We have not much time. I am a friend of Stuckart.'

An elderly voice, but not frail. A voice with the sarcastic, sing-song quality of the native Berliner. He spoke exactly as March had expected. Then Charlie's voice, in her good German:

'Tell me what you want.'

'Stuckart is dead.'

'I know. I found him.'

A long pause. On the tape, in the background, March could hear a station announcement. Luther must have used the distraction caused by the discovery of the body to make a phone call from the Gotenland platform.

Charlie whispered: 'He went so quiet, I thought I'd frightened him away.'

March shook his head. 'I told you. You're his only hope.'

The conversation on the tape resumed.

'You know who I am?'

'Yes.'

Wearily: *'You say: What do I want? What do you think I want? Asylum in your country.'*

'Tell me where you are.'

'I can pay.'

'That won't – '

'I have information. Certain facts.'

'Tell me where you are. I'll come and fetch you. We'll go to the Embassy.'

'Too soon. Not yet.'

'When?'

'Tomorrow morning. Listen to me. Nine o'clock. The Great Hall. Central steps. Have you got that?'

'Right.'

'Bring someone from the Embassy. But you must be there as well.'

'How do we recognise you?'

A laugh. *'No. I shall recognise* you, *show myself when* I *am satisfied.'* Pause. *'Stuckart said you were young and pretty.'* Pause. *'That was Stuckart all over.'* Pause. *'Wear something that stands out.'*

'I have a coat. Bright blue.'

'Pretty girl in blue. It is good. Until the morning, Fräulein.'

Click.

Purr.

The clatter of the tape machine being switched off.

'Play it again,' said March.

She rewound the tape, stopped it, pressed PLAY. March looked away, watched the rusty water swirling down the plughole, as Luther's voice mingled with the reedy sound of a single clarinet. *'Pretty girl in blue . . .'* When they had heard it through for the second time, Charlie reached over and turned off the machine.

'After he hung up, I came over here and dropped off the tape. Then I went back to the telephone box and tried to call you. You weren't there. So I called Henry. What else could I do? He says he wants someone from the Embassy.'

'Got me out of bed,' said Nightingale. He yawned and stretched, revealing an expanse of pale, hairless leg. 'What I don't understand is why he didn't just let Charlie pick him up and bring him straight to the Embassy tonight.'

'You heard him,' said March. 'Tonight is too soon. He daren't show himself. He has to wait until the morning. By then the Gestapo's search for him will probably have been called off.'

Charlie frowned. 'I don't understand . . .'

'The reason you couldn't reach me two hours ago was because I was on my way to the Gotenland marshalling yards, where the Gestapo were hugging themselves with joy that they had finally discovered Luther's body.'

'That can't be.'

'No. It can't.' March pinched the bridge of his nose and shook his head. It was hard to keep his mind clear. 'My guess is Luther's been hiding in the rail yard for the past four days, ever since he got back from Switzerland, trying to work out some way of contacting you.'

'But how did he survive all that time?'

March shrugged. 'He had money, remember. Perhaps he picked out some drifter he thought he could trust, paid him to bring him food and drink; warm clothes, maybe. Until he had his plan.'

Nightingale said: 'And what was his plan, Sturmbannführer?'

'He needed someone to take his place, to convince the Gestapo he was dead.' Was he talking too loudly? The Americans' paranoia was contagious. He leaned forward and said softly: 'Yesterday, when it was dark, he must have killed a man. A man of roughly his age and build. Got him drunk, knocked him out – I don't know how he did it – dressed him in his clothes, gave him his wallet, his passport, his watch. Then he put him under a goods train, with his hands and head on the rails. Stayed with him to make sure he didn't move until the wheels went over him. He's trying to buy himself some time. He's gambling that by nine o'clock this morning, the Berlin Polizei will have stopped looking for him. A fair bet, I would say.'

'Jesus Christ.' Nightingale looked from March to Charlie and back again. 'And this is the man I'm supposed to take in to the Embassy?'

'Oh, it gets better than that.' From the inside pocket of his tunic, March produced the documents from the archive. 'On the twentieth of January 1942, Martin Luther was one of fourteen men summoned to attend a special conference at the headquarters of Interpol in Wannsee. Since the end of the war, six of those men have been murdered, four have committed suicide, one has died in an accident, two have supposedly died of natural causes. Today only Luther is left alive. A freak of statistics, you would agree?' He handed Nightingale the papers. 'As you will see, the conference was called by Reinhard Heydrich to discuss the final solution of the Jewish question in Europe. My guess is Luther wants to make you an offer: a new life in America in exchange for documentary proof of what happened to the Jews.'

The water ran. The music ended. An announcer's silky voice whispered in the bathroom: 'And now, for you night-lovers everywhere, Peter Kreuder and his orchestra with their version of *I'm in Heaven . . .*'

Without looking at him, Charlie held out her hand. March took it. She laced her fingers into his and squeezed, hard. Good, he thought, she should be afraid. Her grip tightened. Their hands were linked like parachutists in free fall. Nightingale had his head hunched over the documents and was murmuring 'Jesus Christ, Jesus Christ' over and over again.

*

'WE have a problem here,' said Nightingale. 'I'll be frank with you both. Charlie, this is off the record.' He was talking so quietly they had to strain to hear. 'Three days ago, the President of the United States, for whatever reason, announced he was going to visit this Godforsaken country. At which point, twenty years of American foreign policy was turned upside down. Now this guy Luther, in theory – if what you say is true – could turn it upside down again, all in the space of seventy-two hours.'

Charlie said: 'Then at least it would end the week the right way up.'

'That's a cheap crack.'

He said this in English. March stared at him. 'What are you saying, Mister Nightingale?'

'I'm saying, Sturmbannführer, that I'm going to have to talk to Ambassador Lindbergh and Ambassador Lindbergh is going to have to talk to Washington. And my hunch is they're both going to want a lot more proof than this – ' he tossed the photocopies on to the floor ' – before they open the Embassy gates to a man you say is probably a common murderer.'

'But Luther is offering you the proof.'

'So *you* say. But I don't think Washington will want to risk all the progress that's been made on détente this week just because of your . . . theories.'

Now Charlie was on her feet. 'This is insane. If Luther doesn't go straight with you to the Embassy, he'll be captured and killed.'

'Sorry, Charlie. I can't do that.' He appealed to her. 'Come on! I can't take in every old Nazi who wants to defect. Not without authorisation. Especially not with things as they are.'

'I don't believe what I'm hearing.' She had her hands on her hips and was staring at the floor, shaking her head.

'Just think it through for a minute.' He was almost

pleading. 'This Luther character seeks asylum. The Germans say: hand him over, he's just killed a man. We say: no, because he's going to tell us what you bastards did to the Jews in the war. What will that do for the summit? No – Charlie – don't just look away. *Think*. Kennedy put on ten points in the polls *overnight* on Wednesday. How's the White House going to react if we drop this on them?' For a second time, Nightingale glimpsed the implications; for a second time he shuddered. 'Jesus Christ, Charlie, what have you got yourself mixed up in here?'

THE Americans argued back and forth for another ten minutes, then March said quietly: 'Aren't you overlooking something, Mister Nightingale?'

Nightingale switched his attention reluctantly from Charlie. 'Probably. You're the policeman. You tell me.'

'It seems to me that all of us – you, me, the Gestapo – we all keep underestimating good Party Comrade Luther. Remember what he said to Charlie about the nine o'clock meeting: "*you must be there as well*".'

'So what?'

'He knew this would be your reaction. Don't forget he had worked at the Foreign Ministry. With a summit coming, he guessed the Americans might want to throw him straight back to the Gestapo. Otherwise, why did he not simply take a taxi from the airport to the Embassy on Monday night? That's why he wanted to involve a journalist. As a witness.' March stooped and picked up the documents. 'Forgive me, as a mere *policeman* I do not understand the workings of the American press. But Charlie has her story now, does she not? She has Stuckart's death, the Swiss bank account, these papers, her tape-recording of Luther . . .' He turned to her. 'The fact that the American government chooses not to give Luther asylum, but abandons him to the Gestapo – won't that just make it even more attractive to the degenerate US media?'

Charlie said: 'You bet.'

Nightingale had started to look desperate again. 'Hey. Come on, Charlie. All that was off the record. I never said I agreed with any of it. There are plenty of us at the Embassy who don't think Kennedy should come here. At all. Period.' He fiddled with his bow-tie. 'But this situation – it's as tricky as hell.'

EVENTUALLY they reached an agreement. Nightingale would meet Charlie on the steps of the Great Hall at five minutes to nine. Assuming Luther turned up, they would hustle him quickly into a car which March would drive. Nightingale would listen to Luther's story and decide on the basis of what he heard whether to take him to the Embassy. He would not tell the Ambassador, Washington, or anyone else what he was planning to do. Once they were inside the Embassy compound, it would be up to what he called 'higher authorities' to decide Luther's fate – but they would have to act in the knowledge that Charlie had the whole story, and would print it. Charlie was confident the State Department would not dare turn Luther away.

Exactly how they would smuggle him out of Germany was another matter.

'We have methods,' said Nightingale. 'We *have* handled defectors before. But I'm not discussing it. Not in front of an SS officer. However trustworthy.' It was Charlie, he said, whom he was most worried about. 'You're going to come under a lot of pressure to keep your mouth shut.'

'I can handle it.'

'Don't be so sure. Kennedy's people – they fight dirty. All right. Let's suppose Luther *has* got something. Let's say it stirs everybody up – speeches in Congress, demonstrations, editorials – this is election year, remember? So suddenly the White House is in trouble over the summit. What do you think they're going to do?'

'I can handle it.'

'They're going to tip a truckful of shit over your head, Charlie, and over this old Nazi of yours. They'll say: what's he got that's new? The same old story we've heard for twenty years, plus a few documents, probably forged by the communists. Kennedy'll go on TV and he'll say: "My fellow Americans, ask yourselves: why has all this come up now? In whose interest is it to disrupt the summit?" ' Nightingale leaned close to her, his face a few centimetres from hers. 'First off, they'll put Hoover and the FBI on to it. Know any left-wingers, Charlie? Any Jewish militants? Slept with any? Because, sure as hell, they'll find a few who say you have, whether you've ever met them or not.'

'Screw you, Nightingale.' She shoved him away with her fist. 'Screw *you*.'

NIGHTINGALE really was in love with her, thought March. Lost in love, hopeless in love. And she knew it, and she played on it. He remembered that first night he saw them together in the bar: how she had shrugged off his restraining hand. Tonight: how he had looked at March when he saw him kissing her; how he had absorbed her temper, watching her with his moony eyes. In Zürich, her whisper: '*You asked if he was my lover . . . He'd like to be . . .*'

And now, on her doorstep, in his raincoat: hovering, uncertain, reluctant to leave them behind together, then finally disappearing into the night.

He would be there to meet Luther tomorrow, thought March, if only to make sure she was safe.

*

AFTER the American had gone they lay side by side on her narrow bed. For a long time neither spoke. The street lights cast long shadows, the window frame slanted across the ceiling like cell bars. In the slight breeze the curtains trembled. Once, there were the sounds of shouts and car doors slamming – revellers returning from watching the fireworks.

They listened to the voices fade along the street, then March whispered: 'Last night on the telephone – you said you had found something.'

She touched his hand, climbed off the bed. In the sitting room he could hear her rummaging among the heaps of paper. She returned half a minute later carrying a large coffee-table book. 'I bought this on the way back from the airport.' She sat on the edge of the bed, switched on the lamp, turned the pages. 'There.' She handed March the open book.

It was a reproduction, in black and white, of the painting in the Swiss bank vault. The monochrome did not do it justice. He marked the page with his finger and closed the book to read its title. *The Art of Leonardo da Vinci*, by Professor Arno Braun of the Kaiser Friedrich Museum, Berlin.

'My God.'

'I know. I thought I recognised it. Read it.'

The Lady with the Ermine, the scholars called it. 'One of the most mysterious of all Leonardo's works.' It was believed to have been painted *circa* 1483–6, and 'believed to show Cecilia Gallerani, the young mistress of Lodovico Sforza, ruler of Milan'. There were two published references to it: one in a poem by Bernardino Bellincioni (died 1492); the other, an ambiguous remark about an 'immature' portrait, written by Cecilia Gallerani herself in a letter dated 1498. 'But sadly for the student of Leonardo, the real mystery today is the painting's whereabouts. It is known to have entered the collection of the Polish Prince Adam Czartoryski in the late eighteenth century, and was photographed in Krakau in 1932. Since then it has disappeared into what Karl von Clausewitz so eloquently called "the fog of war". All efforts by the Reich authorities to locate it have so far failed, and it must now be feared that this priceless flowering of the Italian Renaissance is lost to mankind forever.'

He closed the book. 'I think, another story for you.'

'And a good one. There are only nine undisputed Leonardos in the world.' She smiled. 'If I ever get out of here to write it.'

'Don't worry. We'll get you out.' He lay back and closed his eyes. After a few moments he heard her put down the book, then she joined him on the bed, wriggling close to him.

'And you?' she breathed in his ear. 'Will you come out with me?'

'We can't talk now. Not here.'

'Sorry. I forgot.' Her tongue tip touched his ear.

A jolt, like electricity.

Her hand rested lightly on his leg. With her fingers, she traced the inside of his thigh. He started to murmur something, but again, as in Zürich, she placed a finger to his lips.

'The object of the game is: not to make a sound.'

LATER, unable to sleep himself, he listened to her: the sigh of her breath, the occasional mutter – far away and indistinct. In her dreams, she turned towards him, groaning. Her arm was flung across the pillow, shielding her face. She seemed to be fighting some private battle. He stroked the tangle of her hair, waiting until whatever demon it was had released her, then he slipped out from beneath the sheets.

The kitchen floor was cold to his naked feet. He opened a couple of cupboards. Dusty crockery and a few half-empty packets of food. The refrigerator was ancient, might have been borrowed from some institute of biology, its contents blue-furred and mottled with exotic moulds. Self-catering, it was clear, was not a priority around here. He boiled a kettle, rinsed a mug and heaped in three spoonfuls of instant coffee.

He wandered through the apartment sipping the bitter drink. In the sitting room he stood beside the window and pulled back the curtain a fraction. Bülow Strasse was deserted. He could see the telephone box, dimly illuminated, and the shadows of the station entrance behind it. He let the curtain fall back.

America. The prospect had never occurred to him before. When he thought of it, his brain reached automatically for the images Doctor Goebbels had thoughtfully planted there. Jews and Negroes. Top-hatted capitalists and smokestack factories. Beggars on the streets. Striptease bars. Gangsters shooting at one another from vast automobiles. Smouldering tenements and modern jazz bands, wailing across the ghettos like police sirens. Kennedy's toothy smile. Charlie's dark eyes and white limbs. *America*.

He went into the bathroom. The walls were stained by steam clouds and splashes of soap. Bottles everywhere, and tubes, and small pots. Mysterious feminine objects of glass and plastic. It was a long time since he had seen a woman's bathroom. It made him feel clumsy and foreign – the heavy-footed ambassador of some other species. He picked up a few things and sniffed at them, squeezed a drop of white cream on to his finger and rubbed at it with his thumb. This smell of her mingled with the others already on his hands.

He wrapped himself in a large towel and sat down on the floor to think. Three or four times before dawn he heard her shout out in her sleep – cries of real fear. Memory or prophecy? He wished he knew.

TWO

Just before seven he went down into Bülow Strasse. His Volkswagen was parked a hundred metres up the street, on the left, outside a butcher's shop. The owner was hanging plump carcasses in the window. A heaped tray of blood-red sausages at his feet reminded March of something.

Globus's fingers, that's what it was – those immense raw fists.

He bent over the back seat of the Volkswagen, tugging his suitcase towards him. As he straightened, he glanced quickly in either direction. There was nothing special to see – just the usual signs of an early Saturday morning. Most shops would open as normal but then close at lunchtime in honour of the holiday.

Back in the apartment he made more coffee, set a mug on the bedside table beside Charlie, and went into the bathroom to shave. After a couple of minutes he heard her come in behind him. She clasped her arms around his chest and squeezed, her breasts pressing into his bare back. Without turning round he kissed her hand and wrote in the steam on the mirror: PACK. NO RETURN. As he wiped away the message, he saw her clearly for the first time – hair tangled, eyes half-closed, the lines of her face still soft with sleep. She nodded and ambled back into the bedroom.

He dressed in his civilian clothes as he had for Zürich, but with one difference. He slipped his Luger into the right-hand pocket of his trench coat. The coat – old surplus Wehrmacht-issue, picked up cheaply long ago – was baggy enough for the weapon not to show. He could even hold the pistol and aim it surreptitiously through the material of the pocket, gangster-style: 'Okay, buddy, let's go.' He smiled to himself. America, again.

The possible presence of a microphone cast a shadow over their preparations. They moved quietly around the apartment without speaking. At ten past eight she was ready. March collected the radio from the bathroom, placed it on the table in the sitting room, and turned up the volume. *'From the pictures sent in for exhibition it is clear that the eye of some men shows them things other than as they are – that there really are men who on principle feel meadows to be blue, the heavens green, the clouds sulphur-yellow . . .'* It was the custom at this time to rebroadcast the Führer's most historic speeches. They replayed this one every year – the attack on modern painters, delivered at the inauguration of the House of German Art in 1937.

Ignoring her silent protests, March picked up her suitcase as well as his own. She donned her blue coat. From one shoulder she hung a leather bag. Her camera dangled from the other. On the threshold, she turned for a final look.

'Either these "artists" do really see things in this way and believe in that which they represent – then one has but to ask how the defect in vision arose, and if it is hereditary the Minister of the Interior will have to see to it that so ghastly a defect shall not be allowed to perpetuate itself – or, if they do not *believe in the reality of such impressions but seek on other grounds to impose them upon the nation, then it is a matter for a criminal court.'*

They closed the door on a storm of laughter and applause.

As they went downstairs, Charlie whispered: 'How long does this go on?'

'All weekend.'

'That will please the neighbours.'

'Ah, but will anyone dare ask you to turn it down?'

At the foot of the stairs, as still as a sentry, stood the concierge – a bottle of milk in one hand, a copy of the *Völkischer Beobachter* tucked under her arm. She spoke to Charlie but stared at March: 'Good morning, Fräulein.'

'Good morning, Frau Schustermann. This is my cousin, from Aachen. We are going to record the images of spontaneous celebration on the streets.' She patted her camera. 'Come on, Harald, or we'll miss the start.'

The old woman continued to scowl at March and he wondered if she recognised him from the other night. He doubted it: she would only remember the uniform. After a few moments she grunted and waddled back into her apartment.

'You lie very plausibly,' said March, when they were out on the street.

'A journalist's training.' They walked quickly towards the Volkswagen. 'It was lucky you weren't wearing your uniform. Then she really would have had some questions.'

'There is no possibility of Luther getting into a car driven by a man in the uniform of an SS-Sturmbannführer. Tell me: do I look like an Embassy chauffeur?'

'Only a very distinguished one.'

He stowed the suitcases in the trunk of the car. When he was settled in the front seat, before he switched on the engine, he said: 'You can never go back, you realise that? Whether this works or not. Assisting a defector – they'll think you're a spy. It won't be a question of deporting you. It's much more serious than that.'

She waved her hand dismissively. 'I never cared for that place anyway.'

He turned the key in the ignition and they pulled out into the morning traffic.

DRIVING carefully, checking every thirty seconds to make

sure they were not being followed, they reached Adolf Hitler Platz at twenty to nine. March executed one circuit of the square. Reich Chancellery, Great Hall, Wehrmacht High Command building – all seemed as it should be: masonry gleamed, guards marched; everything was as crazily out of scale as ever.

A dozen tour buses were already disgorging their awed cargoes. A crocodile file of children made its way up the snowy steps of the Great Hall, towards the red granite pillars, like a line of ants. In the centre of the Platz, beneath the great fountains, were piles of crush barriers, ready to be put into position on Monday morning, when the Führer was due to drive from the Chancellery to the Hall for the annual ceremony of thanksgiving. Afterwards he would return to his residence to appear on the balcony. German television had erected a scaffolding tower directly opposite. Live broadcast vans clustered around its base.

March pulled into a parking space close to the tourist coaches. From here he had a clear view across the lanes of traffic to the centre of the Hall.

'Walk up the steps,' he said, 'go inside, buy a guide book, look as natural as you can. When Nightingale appears, bump into him: you're old friends, isn't it marvellous, you stop and talk for a while.'

'What about you?'

'When I see you've made contact with Luther, I'll drive across and pick you up. The rear doors are unlocked. Keep to the lower steps, close to the road. And don't let him drag you into a long conversation – we need to get out of here fast.'

She was gone before he could wish her luck.

Luther had chosen his ground well. There were vantage points all around the Platz: the old man would be able to watch the steps without showing himself. Nobody would pay any attention to three strangers meeting. And if something did go wrong, the throngs of visitors offered the ideal cover for escape.

March lit a cigarette. Twelve minutes to go. He watched as Charlie climbed the long flight of steps. She paused at the top for breath, then turned and disappeared inside.

Everywhere: activity. White taxis and the long, green Mercedes of the Wehrmacht High Command circled the Platz. The television technicians checked their camera angles and shouted instructions at one another. Stall-holders arranged their wares – coffee, sausages, postcards, newspapers, ice cream. A squadron of pigeons wheeled overhead in tight formation and fluttered in to land beside one of the fountains. A couple of young boys in Pimpf uniforms ran towards them, flapping their arms, and March thought of Pili – a stab – and closed his eyes for an instant, confining his guilt to the dark.

At five to nine exactly she came out of the shadows and began descending the steps. A man in a fawn raincoat strode towards her. Nightingale.

Don't make it too obvious, idiot . . .

She stopped and threw her arms wide – a perfect mime of surprise. They began talking.

Two minutes to nine.

Would Luther come? If so, from which direction? From the Chancellery to the east? The High Command building to the west? Or directly north, from the centre of the Platz?

Suddenly, at the window beside him, a gloved hand appeared. Attached to it: the body of an Orpo traffic cop in leather uniform.

March wound down the window.

The cop said: 'Parking here suspended.'

'Understood. Two minutes and I'm out of here.'

'Not two minutes. Now.' The man was a gorilla, escaped from Berlin Zoo.

March tried to keep his eyes on the steps, maintain a

conversation with the Orpo man, while pulling his Kripo ID out of his inside pocket.

'You are screwing up badly, friend,' he hissed. 'You are in the middle of a Sipo surveillance operation and, I have to tell you, you are blending into the background as well as a prick in a nunnery.'

The cop grabbed the ID and held it close to his eyes. 'Nobody told me about any operation, Sturmbannführer. What operation? Who's being watched?'

'Communists. Freemasons. Students. Slavs.'

'Nobody told me about it. I'll have to check.'

March clutched the steering wheel to steady his shaking hands. 'We are observing radio silence. You break it and Heydrich personally will have your balls for cufflinks, I guarantee you. Now: my ID.'

Doubt clouded the Orpo man's face. For an instant he almost looked ready to drag March out of the car, but then he slowly returned the ID. 'I don't know . . .'

'Thank you for your co-operation, Unterwachtmeister.' March wound up his window, ending the discussion.

One minute past nine. Charlie and Nightingale were still talking. He glanced in his mirror. The cop had walked a few paces, had stopped, and was staring back at the car. He looked thoughtful, then made up his mind, went over to his bike and picked up his radio.

March swore. He had two minutes, at the outside.

Of Luther: no sign.

AND then he saw him.

A man with thick-framed glasses, wearing a shabby overcoat, had emerged from the Great Hall. He stood, peering around him, his hand touching one of the granite pillars as if afraid to let go. Then, hesitantly, he began to make his way down the steps.

March switched on the engine.

Charlie and Nightingale still had their backs to him. He was heading towards them.

Come on. Come on. Look round at him, for God's sake.

At that moment Charlie did turn. She saw the old man and recognised him. Luther's arm came up, like an exhausted swimmer reaching for the shore.

Something is going to go wrong, thought March suddenly. *Something is not right. Something I haven't thought of . . .*

Luther had barely five metres to go when his head disappeared. It vanished in a puff of moist red sawdust and then his body was pitching forward, rolling down the steps, and Charlie was putting up her hand to shield her face from the sunburst of blood and brain.

A beat. A beat and a half. Then the crack of a high-velocity rifle howled around the Platz, scooping up the pigeons, scattering them like grey litter across the square.

PEOPLE started to scream.

March threw the car into gear, flashed his indicator and cut sharply into the traffic, ignoring the outraged hooting – across one lane, and then another. He drove like a man who believed himself invulnerable, as if faith and willpower alone would protect him from collision. He could see a little group had formed around the body which was leaking blood and tissue down the steps. He could hear police whistles. Figures in black uniforms were converging from all directions – Globus and Krebs among them.

Nightingale had Charlie by the arm and was propelling her away from the scene, towards the road, where March was braking to a halt. The diplomat wrenched open the door and threw her into the back seat, crammed himself in after her. The door slammed. The Volkswagen accelerated away.

We were betrayed.

Fourteen men summoned; now fourteen dead.

He saw Luther's hand outstretched, the fountain bursting from his neck, his trunk exploded toppling forwards. Globus and Krebs running. Secrets scattered in that shower of tissue; salvation gone . . .

Betrayed . . .

He drove to an underground parking lot just off Rosen Strasse, close to the Börse, where the Synagogue used to stand – a favourite spot of his for meeting informers. Was there anywhere more lonely? He took a ticket from the machine and pointed the car down the steep ramp. The tyres cried against the concrete; the headlights picked out ancient stains of oil and carbon on the floors and walls, like cave paintings.

Level two was empty – on Saturdays, the financial sector of Berlin was a desert. March parked in a central bay. When the engine died the silence was complete.

Nobody said anything. Charlie was dabbing at her coat with a paper handkerchief. Nightingale was leaning back with his eyes closed. Suddenly, March slammed his fists down on the top of the steering wheel.

'Whom did you tell?'

Nightingale opened his eyes. 'Nobody.'

'The Ambassador? Washington? The resident spy-master?'

'I told you: nobody.' There was anger in his voice.

'This is no help,' said Charlie.

'It's also insulting and absurd. Christ, you two . . .'

'Consider the possibilities.' March counted them off on his fingers. 'Luther betrayed *himself* to somebody – ridiculous. The telephone box in Bülow Strasse was tapped – impossible: even the Gestapo does not have the resources to bug every public telephone in Berlin. Very well. So was our discussion last night overheard? Unlikely, as we could hardly hear it ourselves!'

'Why does it have to be this big conspiracy? Maybe Luther was just followed.'

'Then why not pick him up? Why shoot him in public, at the very moment of contact?'

'He was looking straight at me . . .' Charlie covered her face with her hands.

'It needn't have been me,' said Nightingale. 'The leak could have come from one of you two.'

'How? We were together all night.'

'I'm sure you were.' He spat out the words and fumbled for the door. 'I don't have to take this sort of shit from you. Charlie – you'd better come back to the Embassy with me. Now. We'll get you on a flight out of Berlin tonight and just hope to Christ no one connects you with any of this.' He waited. 'Come on.'

She shook her head.

'If not for your sake, then think of your father.'

She was incredulous. 'What's my father got to do with it?'

Nightingale hauled himself out of the Volkswagen. 'I should never have let myself be talked into this insanity. You're a fool. As for him' – he nodded towards March – 'he's a dead man.'

He walked away from the car, his footsteps ricocheting around the deserted lot – loud at first, but fast becoming fainter. There was the clang of a metal door banging shut, and he was gone.

March looked at Charlie in the mirror. She seemed very small, huddled up in the back seat.

Far away: another noise. The barrier at the top of the ramp was being raised. A car was coming. March felt suddenly panicky, claustrophic. Their refuge could serve equally well as a trap.

'We can't stay here,' he said. He switched on the engine. 'We have to keep moving.'

'In that case I want to take more pictures.'

'Do you have to?'

'You assemble your evidence, Sturmbannführer, and I'll assemble mine.'

He glanced at her again. She had put aside her handkerchief and was staring at him with a fragile defiance. He took his foot off the brake. Crossing the city was risky, no question, but what else were they to do? Lie behind a locked door waiting to be caught?

He swung the car round in a circle and headed towards the exit as headlights flashed in the gloom behind them.

THREE

They parked beside the Havel and walked to the shore. March pointed to the spot where Buhler's body had been found. Her camera clicked as Spiedel's had four days before, but there was little left to record. A few footprints were just visible in the mud. The grass was flattened slightly where the corpse had been dragged from the water. But in a day or two these signs would disappear. She turned away from the water and drew her coat around her, shivering.

It was too dangerous to drive to Buhler's villa so he stopped at the end of the causeway with the engine running. She leaned out to take a picture of the road leading to the island. The red and white pole was down. No sign of the sentry.

'Is that it?' she asked. '*Life* won't pay much for these.'

He thought for a moment. 'Perhaps there is another place.'

NUMBERS fifty-six to fifty-eight Am grossen Wannsee turned out to be a large nineteenth-century mansion with a pillared façade. It no longer housed the German headquarters of Interpol. At some point in the years since the war it had become a girls' school. March looked this way and that, up and down the leafy street where the blossom was in full pink bloom, and tried the gate. It was unlocked. He gestured to Charlie to join him.

'We are Herr and Frau March,' he said, as he pushed open the gate. 'We have a daughter . . .'

Charlie nodded. 'Yes, of course, Heidi. She is seven. With plaits . . .'

'She is unhappy at her present school. This one was recommended. We wanted to look around . . .' They stepped into the grounds. March closed the gates behind them.

She said: 'Naturally, if we are trespassing, we apologise . . .'

'But surely Frau March does not look old enough to have a sevenyear-old daughter?'

'She was seduced at an impressionable age by a handsome investigator . . .'

'A likely story.'

The gravel drive looped around a circular flower bed. March tried to picture it as it might have looked in January 1942. A dusting of snow on the ground, perhaps, or frost. Bare trees. A couple of guards shivering by the entrance. The government cars, one after the other, crunching over the icy gravel. An adjutant saluting and stepping forward to open the doors. Stuckart: handsome and elegant. Buhler: his lawyer's notes carefully arranged in his briefcase. Luther: blinking behind his thick spectacles. Did their breath hang in the air after them? And Heydrich. Would he have arrived first, as host? Or last, to demonstrate his power? Did the cold impart colour even to those pale cheeks?

The house was barred and deserted. While Charlie took a picture of the entrance, March picked his way through a small shrubbery to peer through a window. Rows of dwarf-sized desks with dwarf-sized chairs up-ended and stacked on top. A pair of blackboards from which the pupils were being taught the Party's special grace. On one:

> Before meals –
> Führer, my Führer, bequeathed to me by the Lord,
> Protect and preserve me as long as I live!
> Thou hast rescued Germany from deepest distress,

I thank thee today for my daily bread.
Abideth thou long with me, forsaketh me not,
Führer, my Führer, my faith and my light!
Heil, mein Führer!

On the other:

AFTER MEALS –
Thank thee for this bountiful meal,
Protector of youth and friend of the aged!
I know thou hast cares, but worry not,
I am with thee by day and by night.
Lie thy head in my lap,
Be assured, my Führer, that thou art great.
Heil, mein Führer!

Childish paintings decorated the walls – blue meadows, green skies, clouds of sulphur-yellow. Children's art was perilously close to degenerate art; such perversity would have to be knocked out of them . . . March could smell the school-smell even from here: the familiar compound of chalk dust, wooden floors and stale, institutional food. He turned away.

Someone in a neighbouring garden had lit a bonfire. Pungent white smoke – wet wood and dead leaves – drifted across the lawn at the back of the house. A wide flight of steps flanked by stone lions with frozen snarls led down to the lawn. Beyond the grass, through the trees, lay the dull, glassy surface of the Havel. They were facing south. Schwanenwerder, less than half a kilometre away, would be just visible from the upstairs windows. When Buhler bought his villa in the early 1950s, had the proximity of the two sites been a motive –was he the villain being drawn back to the scene of his crime? If so, what crime was it exactly?

March bent and dug up a handful of soil, sniffed at it, let it run through his fingers. The trail had gone cold years ago.

At the bottom of the garden were a couple of wooden barrels, green with age, used by the gardener to collect rainwater. March and Charlie sat on them side by side, legs dangling, looking across the lake. He was in no hurry to move on. Nobody would look for them here. There was something indescribably melancholy about it all – the silence, the dead leaves blowing across the lawn, the smell of the smoke – something that was the opposite of spring. It spoke of autumn, of the end of things.

He said: 'Did I tell you that before I went away to sea, there were Jews in our town? When I got back, they were all gone. I asked about it. People said they had been evacuated to the East. For resettlement.'

'Did they believe that?'

'In public, of course. Even in private it was wiser not to speculate. And easier. To pretend it was true.'

'Did *you* believe it?'

'I didn't think about it.

'Who cares?' he said suddenly. 'Suppose everyone knew all the details. Who would care? Would it really make any difference?'

'Someone thinks so,' she reminded him. 'That's why everyone who attended Heydrich's conference is dead. Except Heydrich.'

He looked back at the house. His mother, a firm believer in ghosts, used to tell him that brickwork and plaster soaked up history, stored what they had witnessed, like a sponge. Since then March had seen his share of places in which evil had been done and he did not believe it. There was nothing especially wicked about Am grossen Wannsee 56/58. It was just a large, businessman's mansion, now converted into a girls' school. So what were the walls absorbing now? Teenage crushes? Geometry lessons? Exam nerves?

He pulled out Heydrich's invitation. 'A discussion followed by luncheon.' Starting at noon. Ending at – what? – three or four in the afternoon. It would have been growing dark by the time they left. Yellow lamps in the windows; mist from the lake. Fourteen men. Well-fed; maybe some of them tipsy on the Gestapo's wine. Cars to take them back to central Berlin. Chauffeurs who had waited a long time outside, with cold feet and noses like icicles . . .

And then, less than five months later, in Zürich in the heat of midsummer, Martin Luther had marched into the offices of Hermann Zaugg, banker to the rich and frightened, and opened an account with four keys.

'I wonder why he was empty-handed.'

'What?' She was distracted. He had interrupted her thoughts.

'I always imagined Luther carrying a small suitcase of some sort. Yet when he came down the steps to meet you, he was empty-handed.'

'Perhaps he had stuffed everything into his pockets.'

'Perhaps.' The Havel looked solid; a lake of mercury. 'But he must have landed from Zürich with luggage of some sort. He had spent the night out of the country. And he had collected something from the bank.'

The wind stirred in the trees. March looked round. 'He was a suspicious old bastard after all. It would have been in his character to have kept back the really valuable material. He wouldn't have risked giving the Americans everything at once – otherwise how could he have bargained?'

A jet passed low overhead, dropping towards the airport, the pitch of its engines descending with it. Now *that* was a sound which did not exist in 1942 . . .

Suddenly he was on his feet, lifting her down to join him, and then he was striding up the lawn towards the house and she was following – stumbling, laughing, shouting at him to slow down.

HE parked the Volkswagen beside the road in Schlachtensee and sprinted into the telephone kiosk. Max Jaeger was not replying, neither at Werderscher Markt nor at his home. The lonely purr of the unanswered phone made March want to reach someone, anyone.

He tried Rudi Halder's number. Perhaps he could apologise, somehow hint it had been worth the risk. Nobody was in. He looked at the receiver. What about Pili? Even the boy's hostility would be contact of a sort. But in the bungalow in Lichtenrade there was no response either.

The city had shut down on him.

He was halfway out of the kiosk when, on impulse, he turned back and dialled the number of his own apartment. On the second ring, a man answered.

'Yes?' It was the Gestapo: Krebs's voice. 'March? I know it's you! Don't hang up!'

He dropped the receiver as if it had bitten him.

HALF an hour later he was pushing through the scuffed wooden doors into the Berlin city morgue. Without his uniform he felt naked. A woman cried softly in one corner, a female police auxiliary sitting stiffly beside her, embarrassed at this display of emotion in an official place. He showed the attendant his ID and asked after Martin Luther. The man consulted a set of dog-eared notes.

'Male, mid-sixties, identified as Luther, Martin. Brought in just after midnight. Railway accident.'

'What about the shooting this morning, the one in the Platz?'

The attendant sighed, licked a nicotined forefinger and

turned a page. 'Male, mid-sixties, identified as Stark, Alfred. Came in an hour ago.'

'That's the one. How was he identified?'

'ID in his pocket.'

'Right.' March moved decisively towards the elevator, forestalling any objection. 'I'll make my own way down.'

It was his misfortune, when the elevator doors opened, to find himself confronted by Doctor August Eisler.

'March!' Eisler looked shocked and took a pace backwards. 'The word is, you've been arrested.'

'The word is wrong. I'm working under cover.'

Eisler was staring at his civilian suit. 'What as? A pimp?' This amused the SS surgeon so much he had to take off his spectacles and wipe his eyes. March joined in his laughter.

'No, as a pathologist. I'm told the pay is good and the hours are non-existent.'

Eisler stopped smiling. '*You* can say that. *I've* been here since midnight.' He dropped his voice. 'A very senior man. Gestapo operation. Hush hush.' He tapped the side of his long nose. 'I can say nothing.'

'Relax, Eisler. I am aware of the case. Did Frau Luther identify the remains?'

Eisler looked disappointed. 'No,' he muttered. 'We spared her that.'

'And Stark?'

'My, my, March – you are well-informed. I'm on my way to deal with him now. Would you care to join me?'

In his mind March saw again the exploding head, the thick spurt of blood and brain. 'No. Thank you.'

'I thought not. What was he shot with? A Panzerfaust?'

'Have they caught the killer?'

'You're the investigator. You tell me. "Don't probe too deeply" was what I heard.'

'Stark's effects. Where are they?'

'Bagged and ready to go. In the property room.'

'Where's that?'

'Follow the corridor. Fourth door on the left.'

March set off. Eisler shouted after him: 'Hey March! Save me a couple of your best whores!' The pathologist's high-pitched laughter pursued him down the passage.

The fourth door on the left was unlocked. He checked to make sure he was unobserved, then let himself in.

It was a small storeroom, three metres wide, with just enough room for one person to walk down the centre. On either side of the gangway were racks of dusty metal shelving heaped with bundles of clothing wrapped in thick polythene. There were suitcases, handbags, umbrellas, artificial legs, a pushchair – grotesquely twisted – hats . . . From the morgue the deceased's belongings were usually collected by the next-of-kin. If the circumstances were suspicious, they would be taken away by the investigators, or sent direct to the forensic laboratories in Schönweld. March began inspecting the plastic tags, each of which recorded the time and place of death and the name of the victim. Some of the stuff here went back years – pathetic bundles of rags and trinkets, the final bequests of corpses nobody cared about, not even the police.

How typical of Globus not to admit to his mistake. The infallibility of the Gestapo must be preserved at all costs! Thus Stark's body continued to be treated as Luther's, while Luther would go to a pauper's grave as the drifter, Stark.

March tugged at the bundle closest to the door, turned the label to the light. *18.4.64. Adolf Hitler Pl. Stark, Alfred.*

So Luther had left the world like the lowest inmate of a KZ – violently, half-starved, in someone else's filthy clothes, his body unhonoured, with a stranger picking over his belongings after his death. Poetic justice – about the only sort of justice to be found.

He pulled out his pocket knife and slit the bulging plastic. The contents spilled over the floor like guts.

He did not care about Luther. All he cared about was how, in the hours between midnight and nine that morning, Globus had discovered Luther was still alive.

Americans!

He tore away the last of the polythene.

The clothes stank of shit and piss, of vomit and sweat – of every odour the human body nurtures. God only knew what parasites the fabric harboured. He went through the pockets. They were empty. His hands itched. *Don't give up hope. A left-luggage ticket is a small thing – tightly rolled, no bigger than a matchstick; an incision in a coat collar would conceal it.* With his knife he hacked at the lining of the long brown overcoat, matted with congealing blood, his fingers turning brown and slippery . . .

Nothing. All the usual scraps that in his experience tramps will carry – the bits of string and paper, the buttons, the cigarette-ends –had been removed already. The Gestapo had searched Luther's clothes with care. Naturally they had. He had been a fool to think they wouldn't. Furious, he slashed at the material – right to left, left to right, right to left . . .

He stood back from the heap of rags panting like an assassin. Then he picked up a piece of rag and wiped his knife and hands.

'YOU know what I think?' said Charlie when he returned to the car empty-handed. 'I think he never brought anything here from Zürich at all.'

She was still in the back seat of the Volkswagen. March turned to look at her. 'Yes he did. Of course he did.' He tried to hide his impatience; it was not her fault. 'But he was too scared to keep it with him. So he stored it, received a ticket for it – either at the airport or the station – and planned on collecting it later. I'm sure that's it. Now Globus has it, or it's lost for good.'

'No. Listen. I was thinking. Yesterday, when I was coming through the airport, I thanked God you stopped me trying to bring the painting back with us to Berlin. Remember the queues? They searched every bag. How could Luther have got *anything* past the Zollgrenzschutz?'

March considered this, massaging his temples. 'A good question,' he said eventually. 'Maybe,' he added a minute later, 'the best question I ever heard.'

AT the Flughafen Hermann Göring the statue of Hanna Reitsch was steadily oxidising in the rain. She stared across the concourse outside the departure terminal with rust-pitted eyes.

'You'd better stay with the car,' said March. 'Do you drive?'

She nodded. He dropped the keys in her lap. 'If the Flughafen Polizei try to move you on, don't argue with them. Drive off and come round again. Keep circling. Give me twenty minutes.'

'Then what?'

'I don't know.' His hand fluttered in the air. 'Improvise.'

He strode into the airport terminal. The big digital clock above the passport control zone flicked over: 13:22. He glanced behind him. He could measure his freedom probably in minutes. Less than that, if Globus had issued a general alert, for nowhere in the Reich was more heavily patrolled than the airport.

He kept thinking of Krebs in his apartment, and Eisler: '*The word is, you've been arrested.*'

A man with a souvenir bag from the Soldiers' Hall looked familiar. A Gestapo watcher? March abruptly changed direction and headed into the toilets. He stood at the urinal, pissing air, his eyes fixed on the entrance. Nobody came in. When he emerged, the man had gone.

'Last call for Lufthansa flight two-zero-seven to Tiflis . . .'

He went to the central Lufthansa desk and showed his ID to one of the guards. 'I need to speak to your head of security. Urgently.'

'He may not be here, Sturmbannführer.'

'Look for him.'

The guard was gone a long time. 13:27 said the clock. 13:28. Perhaps he was calling the Gestapo. 13:29. March put his hand in his pocket and felt the cold metal of the Luger. Better to make a stand here than crawl around the stone floor in Prinz-Albrecht Strasse spitting teeth into your hand.

13:30.

The guard returned. 'This way, Herr Sturmbannführer. If you please.'

FRIEDMAN had joined the Berlin Kripo at the same time as March. He had left it five years later, one step ahead of a corruption investigation. Now he wore hand-made English suits, smoked duty-free Swiss cigars, and made five times his official salary by methods long suspected but never proved. He was a merchant prince, the airport his corrupt little kingdom.

When he realised March had come not to investigate him but to beg a favour he was almost ecstatic. His excellent mood persisted as he led March along a passage away from the terminal building. 'And how is Jaeger? Spreading chaos I suppose? And Fiebes? Still jerking-off over pictures of Aryan maidens and Ukrainian window-cleaners? Oh, how

I miss you all, I don't think! Here we are.' Friedman transferred his cigar from his hand to his mouth and tugged at a large door. 'Behold the cave of Aladdin!'

The metal slid open with a crash to reveal a small hangar stuffed with lost and abandoned property. 'The things people leave behind,' said Friedman. 'You would not believe it. We even had a leopard once.'

'A leopard? A cat?'

'It died. Some idle bastard forgot to feed it. It made a good coat.' He laughed and snapped his fingers and from the shadows an elderly, stoop-shouldered man appeared – a Slav, with wide-set, fearful eyes.

'Stand up straight, man. Show respect.' Friedman gave him a shove that sent him staggering backwards. 'The Sturmbannführer here is a good friend of mine. He's looking for something. Tell him, March.'

'A case, perhaps a bag,' said March. 'The last flight from Zürich on Monday night, the thirteenth. Either left on the aircraft, or in the baggage reclaim area.'

'Got that? Right?' The Slav nodded. 'Well go on then!' He shuffled away and Friedman gestured to his mouth. 'Dumb. Had his tongue cut out in the war. The ideal worker!' He laughed and clapped March on the shoulder. 'So. How goes it?'

'Well enough.'

'Civilian clothes. Working the weekend. Must be something big.'

'It may be.'

'This is the Martin Luther character, right?' March made no reply. 'So you're dumb, too. I see.' Friedman flicked cigar ash on the clean floor. 'Fair enough by me. A brown-pants job. Possibly?'

'A what?'

'Zollgrenzschutz expression. Someone plans to bring in something they shouldn't. They get to the customs shed, see the security, start shitting themselves. Drop whatever it is and run.'

'But this is special, yes? You don't open every case every day?'

'Just in the week before the Führertag.'

'What about the lost property, do you open that?'

'Only if it looks valuable!' Friedman laughed again. 'No. A jest. We haven't the manpower. Anyway, it's been X-rayed, remember –no guns, no explosives. So we just leave it here, wait for someone to claim it. If no one's turned up in a year, then we open it, see what we've got.'

'Pays for a few suits, I suppose.'

'What?' Friedman plucked at his immaculate sleeve. 'These poor rags?' There was a sound and he turned round. 'Looks like you're in luck, March.'

The Slav was returning, carrying something. Friedman took it from him and weighed it in his hand. 'Quite light. Can't be gold. What do you think it is, March? Drugs? Dollars? Contraband silk from the East? A treasure map?'

'Are you going to open it?' March touched the gun in his pocket. He would use it if he had to.

Friedman appeared shocked. 'This is a favour. One friend to another. Your business.' He handed the case to March. 'You'll remember that, Sturmbannführer, won't you? A favour? One day you'll do the same for me, comrade to comrade?'

THE case was of the sort that doctors carry, with brass-reinforced corners and a stout brass lock, dull with age. The brown leather was scratched and faded, the heavy stitching dark, the hand-grip worn smooth like a brown pebble by years of carrying, until it felt like an extension of the hand. It proclaimed reliability and reassurance; professionalism; quiet wealth. It was certainly pre-war, maybe even pre-

Great War – built to last a generation or two. Solid. Worth a lot.

All this March absorbed on the walk back to the Volkswagen. The route avoided the Zollgrenzschutz – another favour from Friedman.

Charlie fell upon it like a child upon a birthday present and swore with disappointment when she found it locked. As March drove out of the airport perimeter she fished in her own bag and retrieved a pair of nail scissors. She picked desperately at the lock, the blades making ineffective scrabblings on the brass.

March said: 'You're wasting your time. I'll have to break it open. Wait till we get there.'

She shook the bag with frustration. 'Get where?'

He ran a hand through his hair.

A good question.

EVERY room in the city was booked. The Eden with its roof-garden café, the Bristol on Unter den Linden, the Kaiserhof in Mohren Strasse – all had stopped taking reservations months ago. The monster hotels with a thousand bedrooms and the little rooming houses dotted around the railway termini were filled with uniforms. Not just the SA and the SS, the Luftwaffe and the Wehrmacht, the Hitler Youth and the League of German Girls, but all the others besides: the National Socialist Empire War Association, the German Falconry Order, the National Socialist Leadership Schools . . .

Outside the most famous and luxurious of all Berlin's hotels – the Adlon, on the corner of Pariser Platz and Wilhelm Strasse – the crowds were straining at the metal barriers for a glimpse of celebrity: a film star, a footballer, a Party satrap in town for the Führertag. As March and Charlie passed it, a Mercedes was drawing up, its black-uniformed passengers bathed in the light of a score of flashguns.

March drove straight over the Platz into Unter den Linden, turned left and then right into Dorotheen Strasse. He parked among the dustbins at the back of the Prinz Friedrich Karl Hotel. It was here, over breakfast with Rudi Halder, that this business had really begun. When was that? He could not remember.

The manager of the Friedrich Karl was habitually clad in an old-fashioned black jacket and a pair of striped pants and he bore a striking resemblance to the late President Hindenburg. He came bustling out to the front desk, smoothing a large pair of white whiskers as if they were pets.

'Sturmbannführer March, what a pleasure! What a pleasure indeed! And dressed for relaxation!'

'Good afternoon, Herr Brecker. A difficult request. I must have a room.'

Brecker threw up his hands in distress. 'It is impossible! Even for as distinguished a customer as yourself.'

'Come, Herr Brecker. You must have something. An attic would do, a broom cupboard. You would be rendering the Reichskriminalpolizei the greatest assistance . . .'

Brecker's elderly eye travelled over the luggage and came to rest on Charlie, at which point a gleam entered it. 'And this is Frau March?'

'Unfortunately, no.' March put his hand on Brecker's sleeve and guided him into a corner, where they were watched with suspicion by the elderly receptionist. 'This young lady has information of a crucial character, but we wish to interrogate her . . . how shall I put it?'

'In an informal setting?' suggested the old man.

'Precisely!' March pulled out what was left of his life savings and began peeling off notes. 'For this "informal setting" the Kriminalpolizei naturally would wish to reimburse you handsomely.'

'I see.' Brecker looked at the money and licked his lips. 'And since this is a matter of security, no doubt you would prefer it if certain formalities – registration, for example – were dispensed with?'

March stopped counting, pressed the entire roll of notes into the manager's moist hands and closed his fingers around it.

In return for bankrupting himself March was given a kitchen maid's room in the roof, reached from the third floor by a rickety back staircase. They had to wait in the reception for five minutes while the girl was turned out of her home and fresh linen was put on the bed. Herr Brecker's repeated offers to help with their luggage were turned down by March, who also ignored the lascivious looks which the old man kept giving Charlie. He did, however, ask for some food – some bread, cheese, ham, fruit, a flask of black coffee – which the manager promised to bring up personally. March told him to leave it in the corridor.

'It's not the Adlon,' said March when he and Charlie were alone. The little room was stifling. All the heat in the hotel seemed to have risen and become trapped beneath the tiles. He climbed on a chair to tug open the attic window and jumped down in a shower of dust.

'Who cares about the Adlon?' She flung her arms around him, kissed him hard on the mouth.

The manager set down the tray of food as instructed outside the door. Climbing the stairs had almost done for him. Through three centimetres of wood, March listened to his ragged breathing, and then to his footsteps retreating along the passage. He waited until he was sure the old man had gone before retrieving the tray and setting it on the flimsy dressing table. There was no lock on the bedroom door, so he wedged a chair under the handle.

MARCH laid Luther's case on the hard wooden bed and took out his pocket knife.

The lock had been fashioned to withstand exactly this sort of assault. It took five minutes of hacking and twisting, during which he snapped one short blade, before the fastener broke free. He pulled the bag open.

That papery smell again – the odour of a long-sealed filing cabinet or desk drawer, a whiff of typewriter oil. And behind that, something else: something antiseptic, medicinal . . .

Charlie was at his shoulder. He could feel her warm breath on his cheek. 'Don't tell me. It's empty.'

'No. It's not empty. It's full.'

He pulled out his handkerchief and wiped the sweat from his hands. Then he turned the case upside down and shook the contents out on to the counterpane.

FOUR

AFFIDAVIT SWORN BY WILHELM STUCKART,
STATE SECRETARY, INTERIOR MINISTRY:

[4 pages; typewritten]

On Sunday 21 December 1941, the Interior Ministry's Adviser on Jewish Affairs, Dr Bernhard Losener, made an urgent request to see me in private. Dr Losener arrived at my home in a state of extreme agitation. He informed me that his subordinate, the Assistant Adviser on Racial Affairs, Dr Werner Feldscher, had heard 'from a fully reliable source, a friend' that the one thousand Jews recently evacuated from Berlin had been massacred in the Rumbuli Forest in Poland. He further informed me that his feelings of outrage were sufficient to prevent him from continuing his present employment in the Ministry, and he therefore requested to be transferred to other duties. I replied that I would seek clarification on this matter.

The following day, at my request, I visited Obergruppenführer Reinhard Heydrich in his office in Prinz-Albrecht Strasse. The Obergruppenführer confirmed that Dr Feldscher's information was correct, and pressed me to discover its source, as such breaches of security could not be tolerated. He then dismissed his adjutant from the room and said that he wished to speak to me on a private basis.

He informed me that in July he had been summoned to the Führer's headquarters in East Prussia. The Führer had spoken to him frankly in the following terms: He had decided to resolve the Jewish Question once and for all. The hour had arrived. He could not rely upon his successors having the necessary will or the military power which he now commanded. He was not afraid of the consequences. People presently revered the French Revolution, but who now remembered the thousands of innocents who died? Revolutionary times were governed by their own laws. When Germany had won the war, nobody would ask afterwards how we did it. Should Germany lose the mortal struggle, at least those who had hoped to profit from the defeat of National Socialism would be wiped out. It was necessary to remove the biological bases of Judaism once and for all. Otherwise the problem would erupt to plague future generations. That was the lesson of history.

Obergruppenführer Heydrich stated further that the necessary powers to enable him to implement this Führer Order had been granted to him by Reichsmarschall Goering on 31.7.41. These matters would be discussed at the forthcoming inter-departmental conference. In the meantime, he urged me to use whatever means I considered necessary to discover the identity of Dr Feldscher's source. This was a matter of the highest security classification.

I thereupon suggested that, in view of the grave issues involved, it would be appropriate, from a legal point of view, to have the Führer Order placed in writing. Obergruppenführer Heydrich stated that such a course was impossible, due to political considerations, but that if I had any reservations I should take them up with the Führer personally. Obergruppenführer Heydrich concluded our meeting by remarking in a jocular manner that we should have no cause for concern on legalistic grounds, considering that I was the Reich's chief legal draftsman and he was the Reich's chief policeman.

I hereby swear that this is a true record of our conversation, based upon notes taken by myself that same evening.

SIGNED, Wilhelm Stuckart (attorney)
DATED 4 June 1942, Berlin
WITNESSED, Josef Buhler (attorney)

FIVE

Across the city the day died. The sun dropped behind the dome of the Great Hall, gilding it like the cupola of a giant mosque. With a hum, the floodlights cut in along the Avenue of Victory and the East-West Axis. The afternoon crowds melted, dissolved, re-formed as night-time queues outside the cinemas and restaurants, while above the Tiergarten, lost in the gloom, an airship droned.

REICH MINISTRY FOR FOREIGN AFFAIRS SECRET STATE DOCUMENT

DISPATCH FROM GERMAN AMBASSADOR IN LONDON,
HERBERT VON DIRKSEN

Account of conversations with Ambassador Joseph P. Kennedy, United States Ambassador to Great Britain

[Extracts; two pages, printed]

Received Berlin, 13 June 1938

Although he did not know Germany, [Ambassador Kennedy] had learned from the most varied sources that the present Government had done great things for Germany and that the Germans were satisfied and enjoyed good living conditions.

The Ambassador then touched upon the Jewish question and stated that it was naturally of great importance to German–American relations. In this connection it was not so much the fact that we wanted to get rid of the Jews that was harmful to us, but rather the loud clamour with which we accompanied this purpose. He himself understood our Jewish policy completely; he was from Boston and there, in one golf club, and in other clubs, no Jews had been admitted for the past fifty years.

Received Berlin, 18 October 1938
Today, too, as during former conversations, Kennedy mentioned that very strong anti-Semitic tendencies existed in the United States and that a large portion of the population had an understanding of the German attitude toward the Jews . . . From his whole personality I believe he would get on very well with the Führer.

'WE can't do this alone.'

'We must.'

'Please. Let me take them to the Embassy. They could smuggle them out through the diplomatic bag.'

'No!'

'You can't be certain he betrayed us . . .'

'Who else could it be? And look at this. Do you really think American diplomats would want to touch it?'

'But if we're caught with it . . . It's a death warrant.'

'I have a plan.'

'A good one?'

'It had better be.'

CENTRAL CONSTRUCTION OFFICE, AUSCHWITZ, TO GERMAN EQUIPMENT WORKS, AUSCHWITZ, 31 MARCH 1943

Your letter of 24 March 1943

[Excerpt]

In reply to your letter, the three airtight towers are to be built in accordance with the order of 18 January 1943, for Bw 30B and 3c, in the same dimensions and in the same manner as the towers already delivered.

We take this occasion to refer to another order of 6 March 1943, for the delivery of a gas door 100/192 for

> corpse cellar I of crematory III, Bw 30a, which is to be built in the manner and according to the same measure as the cellar door of the opposite crematory II, with peep-hole of double 8 millimetre glass encased in rubber. This order is to be viewed as especially urgent . . .

NOT far from the hotel, north of Unter den Linden, was an all-night pharmacy. It was owned, as all businesses were, by Germans, but it was run by Rumanians – the only people poor enough and willing enough to work such hours. It was stocked like a bazaar with cooking pans, paraffin heaters, stockings, baby food, greeting cards, stationery, toys, film . . . Among Berlin's swollen population of guest workers it did a brisk trade.

They entered separately. At one counter, Charlie spoke to the elderly woman assistant who promptly disappeared into a back room and returned with an assortment of bottles. At another, March bought a school exercise book, two sheets of thick brown paper, two sheets of gift wrap paper and a roll of clear tape.

They left and walked two blocks to the Friedrich Strasse station where they caught the south-bound U-bahn train. The carriage was packed with the usual Saturday night crowd – lovers holding hands, families off to the illuminations, young men on a drinking spree – and nobody, as far as March could tell, paid them the slightest attention. Nevertheless, he waited until the doors were about to slide shut before he dragged her out on to the platform of the Tempelhof station. A ten-minute journey on a number thirty-five tram brought them to the airport.

Throughout all this they sat in silence.

KRAKAU

18.7.43

[Handwritten]

My dear Kritzinger,
Here is the list.

Auschwitz	50.02N	19.11E
Kulmhof	53.20N	18.25E
Blezec	50.12N	23.28E
Treblinka	52.48N	22.20E
Majdanek	51.18N	22.31E
Sobibor	51.33N	23.31E

Heil Hitler!

[Signed]

Buhler [?]

TEMPELHOF was older than the Flughafen Hermann Goering – shabbier, more primitive. The departures terminal had been built before the war and was decorated with pictures of the pioneering days of passenger flight – old Lufthansa Junkers with corrugated fuselages, dashing pilots with goggles and scarves, intrepid women travellers with stout ankles and cloche hats. Innocent days! March took up a position by the entrance to the terminal and pretended to study the photographs as Charlie approached the car rentals desk.

Suddenly, she was smiling, making apologetic gestures with her hands – playing to perfection the lady in distress. She had missed the flight, her family was waiting . . . The rental agent was charmed, and consulted a typed sheet. For a moment, the issue hung in the balance – and then, yes, as it happened, Fräulein, he *did* have something. Something for someone with eyes as pretty as yours, of course . . . Your driving licence, please . . .

She handed it over. It had been issued the previous year in the name of Voss, Magda, aged twenty-four, of Mariendorf, Berlin. It was the licence of the girl murdered on her wedding day five days ago – the licence Max Jaeger had left in his desk, along with all the other papers from the Spandau shootings.

March looked away, forcing himself to study an old aerial photograph of the Tempelhof airfield. BERLIN was painted in huge white letters along the runway. When he glanced back, the agent was entering details of the licence on the rental form, laughing at some witticism of his own.

As a strategy it was not without risk. In the morning, a copy of the rental agreement would be forwarded automatically to the Polizei, and even the Orpo would wonder why a murdered woman was hiring a car. But tomorrow was Sunday, Monday was the Führertag, and by Tuesday – the earliest the Orpo were likely to pull their fingers out of their backsides – March reckoned he and Charlie would either be safe or arrested, or dead.

Ten minutes later, with a final exchange of smiles, she was given the keys to a four-door black Opel, with ten thousand kilometres on the clock. Five minutes after that, March joined her in the parking lot. He navigated while she drove. It was the first time he had seen her behind the wheel: another side of her. In the busy traffic she displayed an exaggerated caution which he felt did not come naturally.

Sketch of Installation by Martin Luther

[*Dated 15 July 1943; handwritten; 1 page*]

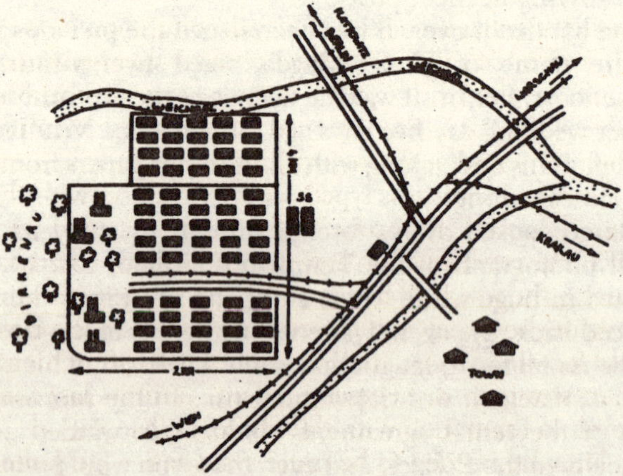

THE lobby of the Prince Friedrich Karl was deserted: the guests were out for the night. As they passed through it towards the stairs the receptionist kept her head down. They were just another of Herr Brecker's little scams – best not to know too much.

Their room had not been searched. The cotton threads hung where March had wedged them, between door and frame. Inside, when he pulled Luther's case out from beneath the bed, the single strand of hair was still laced through the lock.

CHARLIE stepped out of her dress and wrapped a towel around her shoulders.

In the bathroom at the end of the passage, a naked

bulb lit a grimy sink. A bath stood on tiptoe, on iron claws.

MARCH walked back to the bedroom, shut himself in, and once more propped the chair up against the door. He piled the contents of the case on the dressing table – the map, the various envelopes, the minutes and memoranda, the reports, including the one with the rows of statistics, typed on the machine with the extra-large letters. Some of the paper crackled with age. He remembered how he and Charlie had sat during the sunlit afternoon, with the rumble of traffic outside; how they had passed the evidence backwards and forwards to one another – at first with excitement, then stunned, disbelieving, silent, until at last they came to the pouch with the photographs.

Now he needed to be more systematic. He pulled up a chair, cleared a space, and opened the exercise book. He tore out thirty pages. At the top of each sheet he wrote the year and the month, beginning with July 1941 and ending in January 1944. He took off his jacket and draped it over the back of the chair. Then he began to work his way through the heap of papers, making notes in his clear script.

A RAILWAY timetable – badly printed on yellowing wartime paper:

Date	*Train no*	*From*	*Departs*	*To*	*Arrives*
26.1	Da 105	Theresienstadt		Auschwitz	
27.1	Lp 106	Auschwitz		Theresienstadt	
29.1	Da 13	Berlin	17.20	Auschwitz	10.48
	Da 107	Theresienstadt		Auschwitz	
30.1	Lp 108	Auschwitz		Theresienstadt	

31.1	Lp 14	Auschwitz		Zamocz	
1.2	Da 109	Theresienstadt		Auschwitz	
2.2	Da 15	Berlin	17.20	Auschwitz	10.48
	Lp 110	Auschwitz		Myslowitz	
3.2	Po 65	Zamocz	11.00	Auschwitz	
4.2	Lp 16	Auschwitz		Litzmannstadt	

. . . and so on, until, in the second week of February, a new destination appeared. Now almost all the times had been worked out to the minute:

11.2	Pj 131	Bialystok	9.00	Treblinka	12.10
	Lp 132	Treblinka	21.18	Bialystok	1.30
12.2	Pj 133	Bialystok	9.00	Treblinka	12.10
	Lp 134	Treblinka	21.18	Grodno	
13.2	Pj 135	Bialystok	9.00	Treblinka	12.10
	Lp 136	Treblinka	21.18	Bialystok	1.30
14.2	Pj 163	Grodno	5.40	Treblinka	12.10
	Lp 164	Treblinka		Scharfenwiese	

. . . and so on again, until the end of the month.

A rusty paper clip had mottled the edge of the timetable. Attached to it was a telegraphic letter from the General Management, Directorate East, of the German Reich Railways, dated Berlin, 13 January 1943. First, a list of recipients:

Reich Railway Directorates
Berlin, Breslau, Dresden, Erfurt, Frankfurt, Halle (S), Karlsruhe, Königsberg (Pr), Linz, Mainz, Oppeln, East in Frankfurt (O), Posen, Vienna
General Directorate of East Railway in Krakau
Reichsprotektor, Group Railways in Prague
General Traffic Directorate Warsaw
Reich Traffic Directorate Minsk

Then, the main text:

Subject: Special trains for resettlers during the period from 20 January to 28 February 1943.
We enclose a compilation of the special trains (Vd, Rm, Po, Pj and Da) agreed upon in Berlin on 15 January 1943 for the period from 20 January 1943 to 28 February 1943 and a circulatory plan for cars to be used in these trains.

Train formation is noted for each recirculation and attention is to be paid to these instructions. After each full trip cars are to be well cleaned, if necessary fumigated, and upon completion of the programme prepared for further use. Number and kinds of cars are to be determined upon dispatch of the last train and are to be reported to me by telephone with confirmation on service cards.

[Signed] Dr Jacobi

33 Bfp 5 Bfsv Minsk 9 Feb. 1943

March flicked back to the timetable and read it through again. Theresienstadt/Auschwitz, Auschwitz/Theresienstadt, Bialystok/ Treblinka, Treblinka/Bialystok: the syllables drummed in his tired brain like the rhythm of wheels on a railway track.

He ran his finger down the columns of figures, trying to decipher the message behind them. So: a train would be loaded in the Polish town of Bialystok at breakfast time. By lunchtime, it would be at this hell, Treblinka. (Not all the journeys were so brief – he shuddered at the thought of the *seventeen hours* from Berlin to Auschwitz.) In the afternoon, the cars would be unloaded at Treblinka and fumigated. At nine o'clock that evening they would return to Bialystok, arriving in the early hours, ready to be loaded up again at breakfast.

On 12 February, the pattern breaks. Instead of going back to Bialystok, the empty train is sent to Grodno. Two days in the sidings there, and then – in the dark, long before dawn – the train is once more heading back, fully laden, to Treblinka. It arrives at lunchtime. Is unloaded. And that night begins rattling back westwards again, this time to Scharfenweise.

What else could an investigator of the Berlin Kriminalpolizei deduce from this document?

Well, he could deduce numbers. Say: sixty persons per car, an average of sixty cars per train. Deduction: three thousand six hundred persons per transport.

By February, the transports were running at the rate of one per day. Deduction: twenty-five thousand persons per week; one hundred thousand persons per month; one and a quarter million persons per year. And this was the average achieved in the depths of the Central European winter, when the points froze and drifts of snow blocked the tracks and the partisans materialised from the woods like ghosts to plant their bombs.

Deduction: the numbers would be even greater in the spring and summer.

HE stood at the bathroom door. Charlie, in a black slip, had her back to him and was bending over the wash basin. With her hair wet she looked smaller; almost fragile. The muscles in her pale shoulders flexed as she massaged her scalp. She rinsed her hair a final time and stretched a hand out blindly behind her. He gave her a towel.

Along the edge of the bath she had set out various objects – a pair of green rubber gloves, a brush, a dish, a spoon, two bottles. March picked up the bottles and studied their labels. One contained a mixture of magnesium carbonate and sodium acetate, the other a twenty-volume solution of hydrogen peroxide. Next to the mirror above the basin she had propped open the girl's passport. Magda Voss regarded March with wide and untroubled eyes.

'Are you sure this is going to work?'

Charlie wound the towel around her head into a turban.

'First I go red. Then orange. Then white-blonde.' She took the bottles from him. 'I was a fifteen-year-old schoolgirl with a crush on Jean Harlow. My mother went crazy. Trust me.'

She squeezed her hands into the rubber gloves and measured the chemicals into the dish. With the spoon she began to mix them into a thick blue paste.

SECRET REICH MATTER. CONFERENCE MINUTES. 30 COPIES. COPY NUMBER . . .

(The figure had been scratched out.)

The following participated in the conference of 20 January 1942, in Berlin, Am grossen Wannsee 56/58, on the final solution of the Jewish question . . .

March had read the minutes twice that afternoon. Nevertheless, he forced himself to wade through the pages again. 'Around 11 million Jews are involved in this final solution of the Jewish problem . . .' Not just German Jews. The minutes listed more than thirty European nationalities, including French Jews (865,000), Dutch Jews (160,000), Polish Jews (2,284,000), Ukrainian Jews (2,994,684); there were English, Spanish, Irish, Swedish and Finnish Jews; the conference even found room for the Albanian Jews (all 200 of them).

In the course of the final solution, the Jews should be brought under appropriate direction in a suitable manner to the east for labour utilisation. Separated by sex, the Jews capable of work will be led into these areas in large labour columns to build roads, whereby doubtless a large part will fall away through natural reduction.

The inevitable final remainder which doubtless constitutes the toughest element will have to be dealt with

> appropriately, since it represents a natural selection which upon liberation is to be regarded as a germ cell of a new Jewish development. (See the lesson of history.)
>
> In the course of the practical implementation of the final solution, Europe will be combed from west to east.

'Brought under appropriate direction in a suitable manner . . . the toughest element will have to be dealt with appropriately . . .' 'Appropriate, appropriately'. The favourite words in the bureaucrat's lexicon – the grease for sliding round unpleasantness, the funk-hole for avoiding specifics.

March unfolded a set of rough photostats. These appeared to be copies of the original draft minutes of the Wannsee conference, compiled by SS-Standartenführer Eichmann of the Reich Main Security Office. It was a typewritten document, full of amendments and angry crossings-out in a neat hand which March had come to recognise as belonging to Reinhard Heydrich.

For example, Eichmann had written:

> Finally, Obergruppenführer Heydrich was asked about the practical difficulties involved in the processing of such large numbers. The Obergruppenführer stated that various methods had been employed. Shooting was to be regarded as an inadequate solution for various reasons. The work was slow. Security was poor, with the consequent risk of panic among those awaiting special treatment. Also, this method had been observed to have a deleterious effect upon our men. He invited Sturmbannführer Dr Rudolf Lange (KdS Latvia) to give an eyewitness report.
>
> Sturmbannführer Lange stated that three methods had been undertaken recently, providing an opportunity for comparison. On 30 November, one thousand Berlin Jews had been shot in the forest near Riga. On 8 December, his

> men had organised a special treatment at Kulmhof with gas lorries. In the meantime, commencing in October, experiments had been conducted at the Auschwitz camp on Russian prisoners and Polish Jews using Zyklon B. Results here were especially promising from the point of view of both capacity and security.

Against this, in the margin, Heyrich had written 'No!' March checked in the final version of the minutes. This entire section of the conference had been reduced to a single phrase:

> Finally, there was a discussion of the various types of solution possibilities.

Thus sanitised, the minutes were fit for the archives.

March scribbled more notes: October, November, December 1941. Slowly the blank sheets were being filled. In the dim light of the attic room, a picture was developing: connections, strategies, causes and effects . . . He looked up the contributions of Luther, Stuckart and Buhler to the Wannsee conference. Luther foresaw problems in 'the nordic states' but 'no major difficulties in south-eastern and western Europe'. Stuckart, when asked about persons with one Jewish grandparent, 'proposed to proceed with compulsory sterilisation'. Buhler, characteristically, toadied to Heydrich: 'He had only one favour to ask – that the Jewish question in the General Government be solved as rapidly as possible.'

HE broke off for five minutes to smoke a cigarette, pacing the corridor, shuffling his papers, an actor learning his lines. From the bathroom: the sound of running water. From the rest of the hotel: nothing except creaks in the darkness, like a galleon at anchor.

SIX

Notes on a visit to Auschwitz-Birkenau by Martin Luther, Under State Secretary, Reichs Ministry for Foreign Affairs

[Handwritten; 11 pages]

14 July 1943

At last, after almost a year of repeated requests, I am given permission to undertake a full tour of inspection of the Auschwitz-Birkenau camp, on behalf of the Foreign Ministry.

I land at Krakau airfield from Berlin shortly before sunset and spend the night with Governor-General Hans Frank, State Secretary Josef Buhler and their staff at Wawel Castle. Tomorrow morning at dawn I am to be picked up from the castle and driven to the camp (journey time: approximately one hour) where I am to be received by the Commandant, Rudolf Hoess.

15 July 1943

The camp. My first impression is of the sheer scale of the installation, which measures, according to Hoess, almost 2 km. × 4 km. The earth is of yellowish clay, similar to that of Eastern Silesia – a desert-like landscape broken occasionally by green thickets of trees. Inside the camp, stretching far beyond the limits of my vision, are hundreds of wooden barracks, their roofs covered with green tar-paper. In the distance, moving between them, I see small groups of prisoners in blue-and-white striped clothing – some carrying planks, others shovels and picks; a few are loading large crates on to the backs of trucks. A smell hangs over the place.

I thank Hoess for receiving me. He explains the administrative set-up. This camp is under the jurisdiction of the SS Economic Administration Main Office. The others, in the Lublin district, fall under the control of SS-Obergruppenführer Odilo Globocnik. Unfortunately, the pressure of his work prevents Hoess from conducting me around the camp personally, and he therefore entrusts me into the care of a young Untersturmführer, Weidemann. He orders Weidemann to ensure I am shown everything, and that all my questions are answered fully. We begin with breakfast in the SS barracks.

After breakfast: we drive into the southern sector of the camp. Here: a railway siding, approx 1.5 km. in length. On either side: wire fencing supported from concrete pylons, and also wooden observation towers with machine-gun nests. It is already hot. The smell is bad here, a million flies buzz. To the west, rising above trees: a square, red-brick factory chimney, belching smoke.

7.40 am: the area around the railway track begins to fill with SS troops, some with dogs, and also with special prisoners delegated to assist them. In the distance we hear the whistle of a train. A few minutes later: the locomotive pulls slowly through the entrance, its exhalations of steam throw up clouds of yellow dust. It draws to a halt in front of us. The gates close behind it. Weidemann: 'This is a transport of Jews from France.'

I reckon the length of the train to be some 60 freight cars, with high wooden sides. The troops and special prisoners crowd round. The doors are unbolted and slid open. All along the train the same words are shouted: 'Everyone get out! Bring your hand-baggage with you! Leave all heavy baggage in the cars!' The men come out first, dazed by the light, and jump to the ground – 1.5 metres – then turn to help their women and children and the elderly, and to receive their luggage.

The deportees' state: pitiful – filthy, dusty, holding out bowls and cups, gesturing to their mouths, crying with thirst. Behind them in the trucks lie the dead and those too sick to move – Weidemann says their journey began four nights ago. SS guards force those able to walk into two lines. As families separate, they shout to one another. With many gestures and calls the columns march off in different directions. The able-bodied men go towards the work camp. The rest head towards the screen of trees, with Weidemann and myself following. As I look back, I see the prisoners in their striped clothing clambering into the freight cars, dragging out the baggage and the bodies.

8.30 am: Weidemann puts the size of the column at nearly 2,000: women carrying babies, children at their skirts; old men and women; adolescents; sick people; mad people. They walk five abreast down a cinder path for 300 metres, through a courtyard, along another path, at the end of which twelve concrete steps lead down to an immense underground chamber, 100 metres long. A sign proclaims in several languages (German, French, Greek, Hungarian): 'Baths and Disinfecting Room'. It is well-lit, with scores of benches, hundreds of numbered pegs.

The guards shout: 'Everyone undress! You have 10 minutes!' People hesitate, look at one another. The order is repeated, more harshly, & this time, hesitantly but calmly, they comply. 'Remember your peg number, so you can recover your clothes!' The camp trusties move among them, whispering encouragement, helping the feeble-bodied and the feeble-minded to strip. Some mothers try to hide their babies in the piles of discarded clothing, but the infants are quickly discovered.

9.05 am: Naked, the crowd shuffles through large oak doors flanked by troops into a second room, as large as the first, but utterly bare, apart from four thick, square columns supporting the ceiling at twenty-metre intervals. At the bottom of each column is a metal grille. The chamber fills, the doors swing shut. Weidemann gestures. I follow him out through the empty changing room, up the concrete steps, into the air. I can hear the sound of an automobile engine.

Across the grass which covers the roof of the installation bounces a small van with Red Cross markings. It stops. An SS officer & a doctor emerge wearing gas masks & carrying four metal canisters. Four squat concrete pipes jut from the grass, twenty metres apart. The doctor & SS man lift the lids of the pipes & pour in a mauve granulated substance. They remove the masks, light cigarettes in sunshine.

9.09 am: Weidemann conducts me back downstairs. Only sound is a muffled drumming coming from the far end of the room, from beyond the suitcases & the piles of still-warm clothes. A small glass panel is set into the oak doors. I put my eye to it. A man's palm beats against the aperture & I jerk my head away.

Says one guard: 'The water in the shower rooms must be very hot today, since they shout so loudly.'

Outside, Weidemann says: now we must wait twenty minutes. Would I care to visit Canada? I say: What? He laughs: 'Canada' – a section of the camp. Why Canada? He shrugs: nobody knows.

Canada. 1 km. north of gas chamber. Huge rectangular yard, watchtower in each corner & surrounded by barbed wire. Mountains of belongings – trunks, rucksacks, cases, kitbags, parcels; blankets; prams, wheelchairs, false limbs; brushes, combs. Weidemann: figures prepared for RF-SS on property recently sent to Reich – men's shirts: 132,000, women's coats: 155,000, women's hair: 3,000 kg. ('a freight car'), boys' jackets: 15,000, girls' dresses: 9,000, handkerchiefs: 135,000. I get doctor's bag, beautifully made, as souvenir – Weidemann insists.

9.31 am: Return underground installation. Loud electric humming fills the air – the patented 'Exhator' system, for evacuation of gas. Doors open. The bodies are piled up at one end *[Illegible]* legs smeared excrement, menstrual blood; bite & claw marks. Jewish *Sonderkommando* detachment enters to hose down corpses, wearing rubber boots, aprons, gas masks (according to W., pockets of gas remain trapped at floor level for up to 2 hours). Corpses slippery. Straps around wrists used to haul them to four double-doored elevators. Capacity of each: 25 *[Illegible]* bell rings, ascend one floor to . . .

10.02 am: Incineration room. Stifling heat: 15 ovens

operating full-blast. Loud noise: diesel motors ventilating flames. Corpses from elevator loaded on to conveyor belt (metal rollers). Blood etc into concrete gutter. Barbers either side shave heads. Hair collected in sacks. Rings, necklaces, bracelets, etc dropped into metal box. Last: dental team – 8 men with crowbars & pliers – removal gold (teeth, bridgework, fillings). W. gives me tin of gold to test weight: very heavy. Corpses tipped into furnaces from metal pushcarts.

Weidemann: four such gas chamber/crematorium installations in camp. Total capacity of each: 2,000 bodies per day = 8,000 overall. Operated by Jewish labour, changed every 2–3 months. The operation thus self-supporting; the secret self-sealing. Biggest security headache – stink from chimneys & flames at night, visible over many kilometres, especially to troop trains heading east on main line.

MARCH checked dates. Luther had visited Auschwitz on 15 July. On 17 July Buhler had forwarded the map locations of the six camps to Kritzinger of the Reich Chancellery. On 9 August the last deposit had been made in Switzerland. That same year, according to his wife, Luther had suffered a breakdown.

He made a note. Kritzinger was the fourth man. His name was everywhere. He checked with Buhler's pocket diary. Those dates tallied also. Another mystery solved.

His pen moved across the paper. He was almost finished.

A SMALL thing, it had passed unnoticed during the afternoon; one of a dozen or so scraps of paper stuffed at random into a torn folder. It was a circular from SS-Gruppenführer Richard Glücks, Chief of *Amtsgruppe* D in the SS Economic Administration Main Office. It was dated 6 August 1942.

> Re: the utilisation of cut hair.
>
> In response to a report, the Chief of the SS Economic Administration Main Office, SS-Obergruppenführer Pohl, has ordered that all human hair cut off in concentration camps should be utilised. Human hair will be processed for industrial felt and spun into thread. Female hair which has been cut and combed out will be used as thread to make socks for U-boat crews and felt stockings for the railways.
>
> You are instructed, therefore, to store the hair of female prisoners after it has been disinfected. Cut hair from male prisoners can only be utilised if it is at least 20 mm. in length.
>
> The amounts of hair collected each month, separated into female and male hair, must be reported on the 5th of each month to this office, beginning with the 5th September 1942.

He read it again: '*U-boat crews . . .*'

'ONE. Two. Three. Four. Five . . .' March was underwater, holding his breath, counting. He listened to the muffled noises, saw patterns like strings of algae float past him in the dark. 'Fourteen. Fifteen. Sixteen . . .' With a roar he rose above the surface, sucking in air, streaming water. He filled his lungs a few more times, took an immense gulp of oxygen, then went down again. This time he made it to twenty-five before his breath exploded and he burst upwards, slopping water on to the bathroom floor.

Would he ever be clean again?

Afterwards, he lay with his arms dangling over the sides of the tub, his head tilted back, staring at the ceiling, like a drowned man.

PART SIX

SUNDAY 19 APRIL

However this war may end, we have won the war against you; none of you will be left to bear witness, but even if someone were to survive, the world would not believe him. There will perhaps be suspicions, discussions, research by historians, but there will be no certainties, because we will destroy the evidence together with you. And even if some proof should remain and some of you survive, people will say that the events you describe are too monstrous to be believed: they will say that they are the exaggerations of Allied propaganda and will believe us, who will deny everything, and not you. We will be the ones to dictate the history of the Lagers.

SS officer, quoted in *The Drowned and the Saved*
by Primo Levi

ONE

In July 1953, when Xavier March had not long turned thirty and his work as yet consisted of little more than the arresting of whores and pimps around the docks of Hamburg, he and Klara had taken a holiday. They had started in Freiburg, in the foothills of the Black Forest, had driven south to the Rhine, then eastwards in his battered KdF-wagen towards the Bodensee, and in one of the little riverside hotels, during a showery afternoon, with a rainbow cast across the sky, they had planted the seed that grew into Pili.

He could see the place still: the wrought-iron balcony, the Rhine valley beyond, the barges moving lazily in the wide water; the stone walls of the old town, the cool church; Klara's skirt, waist to ankle, sunflower yellow.

And there was something else he could still see: a kilometre down-river, spanning the gulf between Germany and Switzerland – the glint of a steel bridge.

Forget about trying to escape through the main air or sea ports: they were watched and guarded as tightly as the Reich Chancellery. Forget about crossing the border to France, Belgium, Holland, Denmark, Hungary, Yugoslavia, Italy – that was to scale the wall of one prison merely to drop into the exercise yard of another. Forget about mailing the documents out of the Reich: too many packages were routinely opened by the postal service for that to be safe. Forget about giving the material to any of the other correspondents in Berlin: they would only face the same obstacles and were, in any case, according to Charlie, as trustworthy as rattlesnakes.

The Swiss border offered the best hope; the bridge beckoned.

*

Now hide it. Hide it all.

He knelt on the threadbare carpet and spread out a single sheet of brown paper. He made a neat stack of the documents, squaring off the edges. From his wallet he took the photograph of the Weiss family. He stared at it for a moment, then added it to the pile. He wrapped the entire collection tightly in the paper, binding the clear sticky tape around and around it until the package felt as solid as a block of wood.

He was left with an oblong parcel, ten centimetres thick, unyielding to the touch, anonymous to the eye.

He let out a breath. That was better.

He added another layer, this time of gift paper. Golden letters spelled GOOD LUCK! and HAPPINESS!, the words curling like streamers amid balloons and champagne corks behind a smiling bride and groom.

By autobahn from Berlin to Nuremberg: five hundred kilometres. By autobahn from Nuremberg to Stuttgart: one hundred and fifty kilometres. From Stuttgart the road then wound through the valleys and forests of Wurttemberg to Waldshut on the Rhine: a hundred and fifty kilometres again. Eight hundred kilometres in all.

'What's that in miles?'

'Five hundred. Do you think you can manage it?'

'Of course. Twelve hours, maybe less.' She was perched on the edge of the bed, leaning forward, attentive. She wore two towels –one wrapped around her body, the other in a turban around her head.

'No need to rush it – you've got twenty-four. When you reckon you've put a safe distance between yourself and Berlin, telephone the Hotel Bellevue in Waldshut and reserve a room – it's out of season, there should be no difficulty.'

'Hotel Bellevue. Waldshut.' She nodded slowly as she memorised it. 'And you?'

'I'll be following a couple of hours behind. I'll aim to join you at the hotel around midnight.'

He could see she did not believe him. He hurried on: 'If you're willing to take the risk, I think you should carry the papers, and also this . . .' From his pocket he drew out the other stolen passport. Paul Hahn, SS-Sturmbannführer, born Cologne, 16 August 1925. Three years younger than March, and looked it.

'She said: Why don't you keep it?'

'If I'm arrested and searched, they'll find it. Then they'll know whose identity you're using.'

'You've no intention of coming.'

'I've every intention of coming.'

'You think you're finished.'

'Not true. But my chances of travelling eight hundred kilometres without being stopped are less than yours. You must see that. That's why we go separately.'

She was shaking her head. He came and sat beside her, stroked her cheek, turned her face to his, her eyes to his. 'Listen. You're to wait for me – listen! – wait for me at the hotel until eight-thirty tomorrow morning. If I haven't arrived, you drive across without me. Don't wait any longer, because it won't be safe.'

'Why eight-thirty?'

'You should aim to cross the border as close to nine as you can.' Her cheeks were wet. He kissed them. He kept on talking. She had to understand. 'Nine is the hour when the beloved Father of the German People leaves the Reich Chancellery to travel to the Great Hall. It's months since he's been seen – their way of building excitement. You may be sure the guards will have a radio in the customs post, and be listening to it. If ever there's a time when they're more likely just to wave you through, that's it.'

SHE stood and unwrapped the turban. In the weak light of the attic room, her hair gleamed white.

She let the second towel drop.

Pale skin, white hair, dark eyes. A ghost. He needed to know that she was real, that they were both alive. He stretched out a hand and touched her.

THEY lay entwined on the little wooden cot and she whispered their future to him. Their flight would land at New York's Idlewild airport early tomorrow evening. They would go straight to the *New York Times* building. There was an editor there she knew. The first thing was to make a copy – a dozen copies – and then to get as much printed as possible, as soon as possible. The *Times* was ideal for that.

'What if they won't print it?' This idea of people printing whatever they wanted was hard for him to grasp.

'They'll print it. God, if they won't, I'll stand on Fifth Avenue like one of those mad people who can't get their novels published and hand out copies to passers-by. But don't worry – they'll print it, and we'll change history.'

'But will anyone believe it?' That doubt had grown within him ever since the suitcase had been opened. 'Isn't it unbelievable?'

No, she said, with great certainty, because now they had facts, and facts changed everything. Without them, you had nothing, a void. But produce facts – provide names, dates, orders, numbers, times, locations, map references, schedules, photographs, diagrams, descriptions – and suddenly that void had geometry, was susceptible to measurement, had become a solid thing. Of course, this solid thing could be denied, or challenged, or simply ignored. But each of these reactions was, by definition, a *reaction*, a response to some thing which existed.

'Some people won't believe it – they wouldn't believe it no matter how much evidence we had. But there's enough here, I think, to stop Kennedy in his tracks. No summit. No re-election. No détente. And five years from now, or fifty years, this society will fall apart. You can't build on a mass grave. Human beings are better than that – they have to be better than that – I do believe it – don't you?'

He did not reply.

HE was awake to see another dawn in the Berlin sky. A familiar grey face at the attic window, an old opponent.

'Your name is?'

'Magda Voss.'

'Born?'

'Twenty-fifth October 1939.'

'Where?'

'Berlin.'

'Your occupation?'

'I live at home with my parents, in Berlin.'

'Where are you going?'

'To Waldshut, on the Rhine. To meet my fiancé.'

'Name?'

'Paul Hahn.'

'What is the purpose of your visit to Switzerland?'

'A friend's wedding.'

'Where?'

'In Zürich.'

'What is this?'

'A wedding present. A photograph album. Or a Bible? Or a book? Or a chopping board?' She was testing the answers on him.

'Chopping board – very good. Exactly the sort of gift a girl like Magda *would* drive eight hundred kilometres to give.' March had been pacing the room. Now he stopped and pointed at the package in Charlie's lap. 'Open it, please, Fräulein.'

She thought for a moment. 'What do I say to that?'

'There's nothing you can say.'

'Terrific.' She took out a cigarette and lit it. 'Well, would you look at that? My hands are trembling.'

It was almost seven. 'Time to go.'

THE hotel was beginning to wake. As they passed the lines of flimsy doors they heard water splashing, a radio, children laughing. Somewhere on the second floor, a man snored on regardless.

They had handled the package with care, at arm's length, as if it were uranium. She had hidden it in the centre of her suitcase, buried in her clothes. March carried it down the stairs, across the empty lobby and out the narrow fire exit at the rear of the hotel. She was wearing a dark blue suit, her hair hidden by a scarf. The hired Opel stood next to his Volkswagen. From the kitchens came shouts, the smell of fresh coffee, the hiss of frying food.

'When you leave the Bellevue, turn right. The road follows the line of the valley. You can't miss the bridge.'

'You've told me this already.'

'Try and see what level of security they're operating, before you commit yourself. If it looks as if they're searching everything, turn round and try and hide it somewhere. Woods, ditch, barn – somewhere you can remember, a place where someone can go back and retrieve it. Then get out. Promise me.'

'I promise you.'

'There's a daily Swissair flight from Zürich to New York. It leaves at two.'

'At two. I know. You've told me twice.'

He took a step towards her, to hold her, but she fended him away. 'I'm not saying goodbye. Not here. I shall see you tonight. *I shall see you.*'

There was a moment of anti-climax when the Opel refused to start. She pulled out the choke and tried again, and this time the engine fired. She reversed out of the parking space, still refusing to look at him. He had one last glimpse of her profile – and then she was gone, leaving a trail of blue-white vapour hanging in the chilly morning air.

MARCH sat alone in the empty room, on the edge of the bed, holding her pillow. He waited until an hour had passed before putting on his uniform. He stood in front of the dressing-table mirror, buttoning his black tunic. It would be the last time he wore it, one way or the other.

'*We'll change history . . .*'

He donned his cap, adjusted it. Then he took his thirty sheets of paper, his notebook and Buhler's pocket diary, folded them together, wrapped them in the remaining sheet of brown paper, and slipped them into his inside pocket.

Was history changed so easily? he wondered. Certainly, it was his experience that secrets were an acid – once spilled, they could eat their way through anything: if a marriage, why not a presidency, why not a state? But talk of history – he shook his head at his own reflection – history was beyond him. Investigators turned suspicion into evidence. He had done that. History he would leave to her.

HE carried Luther's bag into the bathroom and shovelled

into it all the rubbish that Charlie had left behind – the discarded bottles, the rubber gloves, the dish and spoon, the brushes. He did the same in the bedroom. It was strange how much she had filled these places, how empty they seemed without her. He looked at his watch. It was eight-thirty. She should be well clear of Berlin by now, perhaps as far south as Wittenberg.

In the reception, the manager hovered.

'Good day, Herr Sturmbannführer. Is the interrogation finished?'

'It is indeed, Herr Brecker. Thank you for your patriotic assistance.'

'A pleasure.' Brecker gave a short bow. He was twisting his fat white hands together as if rubbing in oil. 'And if ever the Sturmbannführer feels the desire to do a little more interrogation . . .' His bushy eyebrows danced. 'Perhaps I might even be able to supply him with a suspect or two. . . ?'

March smiled. 'Good day to you, Herr Brecker.'

'Good day to *you*, Herr Sturmbannführer.'

HE sat in the front passenger seat of the Volkswagen and thought for a moment. Inside the spare tyre would be the ideal place, but he had no time for that. The plastic door panels were securely fastened. He reached under the dashboard until his fingers encountered a smooth surface. It would serve his purpose. He tore off two lengths of sticky tape and attached the package to the cold metal.

Then he dropped the roll of tape into Luther's case and dumped the bag in one of the rubbish bins outside the kitchens. The brown leather looked too incongruous lying on the surface. He found a broken length of broom-handle and dug a grave for it, burying it at last beneath the coffee dregs, the stinking fish-heads, the lumps of grease and maggoty pork.

TWO

Yellow signs bearing the single word *Fernverkehr* – long-distance traffic – pointed the way out of Berlin, towards the race-track autobahn that girdled the city. March had the southbound carriageway almost to himself – the few cars and buses about this early on a Sunday morning were heading the other way. He passed the perimeter wire of the Tempelhof aerodrome and abruptly he was into the suburbs, the wide road pushing through dreary streets of red-brick shops and houses, lined by sickly trees with blackened trunks.

To his left, a hospital; to his right, a disused church, shuttered and daubed with Party slogans. 'Marienfelde,' said the signs. 'Bückow.' 'Lichtenrade.'

At a set of traffic lights he stopped. The road to the south lay open – to the Rhine, to Zürich, to America . . . Behind him someone hooted. The lights had changed. He flicked the indicator, turned off the main road and was quickly lost in the gridiron streets of the housing estate.

IN the early 'fifties, in the glow of victory, the roads had been named for generals: Student Strasse, Reichenau Strasse, Manteuffel Allee. March was always confused. Was it right off Model into Dietrich? Or was it left into Paulus, and *then* Dietrich? He drove slowly along the rows of identical bungalows until at last he recognised it.

He pulled over in the familiar place and almost sounded the horn until he remembered that this was the third Sunday in the month, not the first – and therefore not his – and that in any case his access had been revoked. A frontal assault would be needed, an action in the spirit of Hasso Manteuffel himself.

There was no litter of toys along the concrete drive and when he rang the bell, no dog barked. He cursed silently. It seemed to be his fate this week to stand outside deserted houses. He backed away from the porch, his eyes fixed on the window beside it. The net curtain flickered.

'Pili! Are you there?'

The corner of the curtain was abruptly parted, as if some hidden dignitary had pulled a cord unveiling a portrait, and there it was – his son's white face staring at him.

'Can I come in? I want to talk!'

The face was expressionless. The curtain dropped back.

A good sign or bad? March was uncertain. He waved to the blank window and pointed to the garden. 'I'll wait for you here!'

He walked back to the little wooden gate and checked the street. Bungalows on either side, bungalows opposite. They extended in every direction, like the huts of an army camp. Old folks lived in most of them: veterans of the First War, survivors of all that followed – inflation, unemployment, the Party, the Second War. Even ten years ago, they were grey and bowed. They had seen enough, endured enough. Now they stayed at home, and shouted at Pili for making too much noise, and watched television all day.

March prowled around the tiny handkerchief of lawn. Not much of a life for the boy. Cars passed. Two doors down an old man was repairing a bicycle, inflating the tyres with a squeaky pump. Elsewhere, the noise of a lawnmower . . . No sign of Pili. He was wondering if he would have to get down on his hands and knees and shout his message through the letter box when he heard the door being opened.

'Good lad. How are you? Where's your mother? Where's Helfferich?' He could not bring himself to say 'Uncle Erich'.

Pili had opened the door just enough to enable him to peer around it. 'They're out. I'm finishing my picture.'

'Out where?'

'Rehearsing for the parade. I'm in charge. They said so.'

'I bet. Can I come in and talk to you?'

He had expected resistance. Instead, the boy stood aside without a word and March found himself crossing the threshold of his ex-wife's house for the first time since their divorce. He took in the furniture –cheap, but good-looking; the bunch of fresh daffodils on the mantelpiece; the neatness; the spotless surfaces. She had done it as well as she could, without much to spend. He would have expected that. Even the picture of the Führer above the telephone – a photograph of the old man hugging a child – was tasteful: Klara's deity always was a benign god, New Testament rather than Old. He took off his cap. He felt like a burglar.

He stood on the nylon rug and began his speech. 'I have to go away, Pili. Maybe for a long time. And people, perhaps, are going to say some things to you about me. Horrible things, that aren't true. And I wanted to tell you . . .' His words petered out. *Tell you what?* He ran his hand through his hair. Pili was standing with his arms folded, gazing at him. He tried again. 'It's hard not having a father around. My father died when I was very little – younger even than you are now. And sometimes, I hated him for that . . .'

Those cool eyes . . .

'. . . But that passed, and then – I missed him. And if I could talk to him now – ask him . . . I'd give anything . . .'

'. . . *all human hair cut off in concentration camps should be utilised. Human hair will be processed for industrial felt and spun into thread* . . .'

He was not sure how long he stood there, not speaking, his head bowed. Eventually he said: 'I have to go now.'

And then Pili was coming towards him and tugging at his

hand. 'It's all right, papa. Please don't go yet. Please. Come and look at my picture.'

THE boy's bedroom was like a command centre. Model Luftwaffe jets assembled from plastic kits swooped and fought, suspended from the ceiling by invisible lengths of fishing-line. On one wall, a map of the Eastern front, with coloured pins to show the positions of the armies. On another, a group photograph of Pili's Pimpf unit – bare knees and solemn faces, photographed against a concrete wall.

As he drew, Pili kept up a running commentary, with sound effects. 'These are our jets – rrroowww! – and these are the Reds' AA-guns. Pow! Pow!' Lines of yellow crayon streaked skywards. 'Now we let them have it. Fire!' Little black ants' eggs rained down, creating jagged red crowns of fire. 'The commies call up their own fighters, but they're no match for ours . . .' It went on for another five minutes, action piled on action.

Abruptly, bored by his own creation, Pili dropped the crayons and dived under the bed. He pulled out a stack of wartime picture magazines.

'Where did you get those?'

'Uncle Erich gave them to me. He collected them.'

Pili flung himself on the bed and began to turn the pages. 'What do the captions say, papa?' He gave March the magazine and sat close to him, holding on to his arm.

' "The sapper has worked his way right up to the wire obstacles protecting the machine gun position," ' read March. ' "A few spurts of flame and the deadly stream of burning oil has put the enemy out of action. The flame throwers must be fearless men with nerves of steel." '

'And that one?'

This was not the farewell March had envisaged, but if it

was what the boy wanted . . . He ploughed on: ' "I want to fight for the new Europe: so say three brothers from Copenhagen with their company leader in the SS training camp in Upper Alsace. They have fulfilled all the conditions relating to questions of race and health and are now enjoying the manly open-air life in the camp in the woods." '

'What about these?'

He was smiling. 'Come on, Pili. You're ten years old. You can read these easily.'

'But I want you to read them. Here's a picture of a U-boat, like yours. What does it say?'

He stopped smiling and put down the magazine. There was something wrong here. What was it? He realised: the silence. For several minutes now, nothing had happened in the street outside –not a car, not a footstep, not a voice. Even the lawnmower had stopped. He saw Pili's eyes flick to the window, and he understood.

Somewhere in the house: a tinkle of glass. March scrambled for the door, but the boy was too quick for him – rolling off the bed, grabbing his legs, curling himself around his father's feet in a foetal ball, a parody of childish entreaty. *'Please don't go, papa,'* he was saying, '*please* . . .' March's fingers grasped the door-handle but he couldn't move. He was anchored, mired. *I have dreamed this before,* he thought. The window imploded behind them, showering their backs with glass – now real uniforms with real guns were filling the bedroom – and suddenly March was on his back gazing up at the little plastic warplanes bobbing and spinning crazily at the ends of their invisible wires.

He could hear Pili's voice: 'It's going to be all right, papa. They're going to help you. They'll make you better. Then you can come and live with us. They promised . . .'

THREE

His hands were cuffed tight behind his back, wrists outwards. Two SS men propped him against the wall, against the map of the Eastern front, and Globus stood before him. Pili had been hustled away, thank God. 'I have waited for this moment,' said Globus, 'as a bridegroom waits for his bride', and he punched March in the stomach, hard. March folded, dropped to his knees, dragging the map and all its little pins down with him, thinking he would never breathe again. Then Globus had him by the hair and was pulling him up, and his body was trying to retch and suck in oxygen at the same time and Globus hit him again and he went down again. This process was repeated several times. Finally, while he was lying on the carpet with his knees drawn up, Globus planted his boot on the side of his head and ground his toe into his ear. 'Look,' he said, 'I've put my foot on shit' and from a long way away, March heard the sound of men laughing.

'WHERE's the girl?'

'What girl?'

Globus slowly extended his stubby fingers in front of March's face, then brought his hand arcing down in a karate blow to the kidneys.

This was much worse than anything else – a blinding white flash of pain that shot straight through him and put him on the floor again, retching bile. And the worst was to know that he was merely in the foothills of a long climb. The stages of torture stretched before him, ascending as notes on a scale, from the dull bass of a blow in the belly, through the middle register of kidney-punches, onwards and upwards to some pitch beyond the range of the human ear, a pinnacle of crystal.

'Where's the girl?'

'What . . . girl. . . ?'

THEY disarmed him, searched him, then they half-pushed, half-dragged him out of the bungalow. A little crowd had gathered in the road. Klara's elderly neighbours watched as he was bundled, head bowed, into the back of the BMW. He glimpsed briefly along the street four or five cars with revolving lights, a lorry, troops. What had they been expecting? A small war? Still no sign of Pili. The handcuffs forced him to sit hunched forward. Two Gestapo men were jammed on the back seat, one on either side of him. As the car pulled away, he could see some of the old folks already shuffling back into their houses, back to the reassuring glow of their television sets.

HE was driven north through the holiday traffic, up into Saarland Strasse, east into Prinz-Albrecht Strasse. Fifty metres past the main entrance to Gestapo headquarters, the convoy swung right, through a pair of high prison gates, into a brick courtyard at the back of the building.

He was pulled out of the car and through a low entrance, down steep concrete steps. Then his heels were scraping along the floor of an arched passage. A door, a cell, and silence.

THEY left him alone, to allow his imagination to go to work – standard procedure. Very well. He crawled into a corner and rested his head against the damp brick. Every minute which passed was another minute's travelling time for her. He thought of Pili, of all the lies, and clenched his fists.

The cell was lit by a weak bulb above the door, imprisoned in its own rusty metal cage. He glanced at his wrist, a useless reflex, for they had taken away his watch. Surely she could not be far from Nuremberg by now? He tried to fill his mind with images of the Gothic spires – St Lorenz, St Sebaldus, St Jakob . . .

Every limb – every part of him to which he could put a name – ached, yet they could not have worked him over for more than five minutes, and still they had managed not to leave a mark on his face. Truly, he had fallen into the hands of experts. He almost laughed, but that hurt his ribs, so he stopped.

HE was taken along the passage to an interview room: whitewashed walls, a heavy oak table with a chair on each side; in the corner, an iron stove. Globus had disappeared, Krebs was in command. The handcuffs were removed. Standard procedure again – first the hard cop, then the soft. Krebs even attempted a joke: 'Normally, we would arrest your son and threaten him as well, to encourage your co-operation. But in your case, we know that such a course would be counter-productive.' Secret policeman's humour! He leaned back in his chair, smiling, and pointed his pencil. 'Nevertheless. A remarkable boy.'

' "Remarkable" – your word.' At some point during his beating, March had bitten his tongue. He talked now as if he had spent a week in a dentist's chair.

'Your ex-wife was given a telephone number last night,' said Krebs, 'in case you attempted contact. The boy memorised it. The instant he saw you, he called. He's inherited your brains, March. Your initiative. You should feel some pride.'

'At this moment, my feelings towards my son are indeed strong.'

Good, he thought, *let's keep this up. Another minute, another kilometre.*

But Krebs was already down to business, turning the pages of a thick folder. 'There are two issues here, March. One: your general political reliability, going back over many years. That does not concern us today – at least, not directly. Two: your conduct over the past week – specifically, your involvement in the attempts of the late Party Comrade Luther to defect to the United States.'

'I have no such involvement.'

'You were questioned by an officer of the Ordnungspolizei in Adolf Hitler Platz yesterday morning – at the exact time the traitor Luther was planning to meet the American journalist, Maguire, together with an official of the United States Embassy.'

How did they know that? 'Absurd.'

'Do you deny you were in the Platz?'

'No. Of course not.'

'Then why were you there?'

'I was following the American woman.'

Krebs was making notes. 'Why?'

'She was the person who discovered the body of Party Comrade Stuckart. I was also naturally suspicious of her, in her role as an agent of the bourgeois democratic press.'

'Don't piss me about, March.'

'All right. I had insinuated myself into her company. I thought: if she can stumble across the corpse of one retired state secretary, she might stumble across another.'

'A fair point.' Krebs rubbed his chin and thought for a moment, then opened a fresh pack of cigarettes and gave one to March, lighting it for him from an unused box of matches. March filled his lungs with smoke. Krebs had not taken one for himself, he noticed – they were merely a part of his act, an interrogator's props.

The Gestapo man was leafing through his notes again, frowning. 'We believe that the traitor Luther was planning to disclose certain information to the journalist Maguire. What was the nature of this information?'

'I have no idea. The art fraud, perhaps?'

'On Thursday, you visited Zürich. Why?'

'It was the place Luther went before he vanished. I wanted to see if there was any clue there which might explain why he disappeared.'

'And was there?'

'No. But my visit was authorised. I submitted a full report to Oberstgruppenführer Nebe. Have you not seen it?'

'Of course not.' Krebs made a note. 'The Oberstgruppenführer shows his hand to no one, not even us. Where is Maguire?'

'How should I know?'

'You should know because you picked her up from Adolf Hitler Platz after the shooting yesterday.'

'Not me, Krebs.'

'Yes you, March. Afterwards, you went to the morgue and searched through the traitor Luther's personal effects – this we know absolutely from Doctor Eisler.'

'I was not aware that the effects *were* Luther's,' said March. 'I understood they belonged to a man named Stark who was three metres away from Maguire when he was shot. Naturally, I was interested to see what he was carrying, because I was interested in Maguire. Besides, if you recall, *you* showed me what you said was Luther's body on Friday night. Who did shoot Luther, as a matter of interest?'

'Never mind that. What did you expect to pick up at the morgue?'

'Plenty.'

'What? Be exact!'

'Fleas. Lice. A skin rash from his shitty clothes.'

Krebs threw down his pencil. He folded his arms. 'You're a brainy fellow, March. Take comfort from the fact we credit you with that, at least. Do you think we'd give a shit if you were just some dumb fat fuck, like your friend Max Jaeger? I bet you could keep this up for hours. But we don't have hours, and we're less stupid than you think.' He shuffled through his papers, smirked, and then he played his ace.

'What was in the suitcase you took from the airport?'

March looked straight back at him. *They had known all along*. 'What suitcase?'

'The suitcase that looks like a doctor's bag. The suitcase that doesn't weigh very much, but might contain paper. The suitcase Friedman gave you thirty minutes before he called us. He got back to find a telex, you see, March, from Prinz-Albrecht Strasse – an alert to stop you leaving the country. When he saw that, he decided – as a patriotic citizen – he'd better inform us of your visit.'

'Friedman!' said March. 'A "patriotic citizen"? He's fooling you, Krebs. He's hiding some scheme of his own.'

Krebs sighed. He got to his feet and came round to stand behind March, his hands resting on the back of March's chair. 'When this is over, I'd like to get to know you. Really. Assuming there's anything left of you to get to know. Why did someone like you go bad? I'm interested. From a technical point of view. To try to stop it happening in the future.'

'Your passion for self-improvement is laudable.'

'There you go again, you see? A problem of attitude. Things are changing in Germany, March – from within – and you could have been a part of it. The Reichsführer himself takes a personal interest in the new generation – listens to us, promotes us. He believes in restructuring, greater openness, talking to the Americans. The day of men like Odilo Globocnik is passing.' He stooped and whispered in March's ear: 'Do you know why Globus doesn't like you?'

'Enlighten me.'

'Because you make him feel stupid. In Globus's book, that's a capital offence. Help me, and I can shield you from him.' Krebs straightened and resumed, in his normal voice: 'Where is the woman? What was the information Luther wanted to give her? Where is Luther's suitcase?'

Those three questions, again and again.

INTERROGATIONS have this irony, at least: they can enlighten those being questioned as much – or more – than those who are doing the questioning.

From what Krebs asked, March could measure the extent of his knowledge. This was, on certain matters, very good: he knew March had visited the morgue, for example, and that he had retrieved the suitcase from the airport. But there was a significant gap. Unless Krebs was playing a fiendishly devious game, it seemed he had no idea of the *nature* of the information Luther was promising the Americans. Upon this one, narrow ground rested March's only hope.

After an inconclusive half-hour, the door opened and Globus appeared, swinging a long truncheon of polished wood. Behind him stood two thick-set men in black uniforms.

Krebs leapt to attention.

Globus said: 'Has he made a full confession?'

'No, Herr Obergruppenführer.'

'What a surprise. My turn then, I think.'

'Of course.' Krebs stooped and collected his papers.

Was it March's imagination, or did he see on that long, impassive face a flicker of regret, even of distaste?

*

After Krebs had gone, Globus prowled around, humming an old Party marching song, dragging the length of wood over the stone floor.

'Do you know what this is, March?' He waited. 'No? No answer? It's an American invention. A baseball bat. A pal of mine at the Washington Embassy brought it back for me.' He swung it around his head a couple of times. 'I'm thinking of raising an SS team. We could play the US Army. What do you think? Goebbels is keen. He thinks the American masses would respond well to the pictures.'

He leant the bat against the heavy wooden table and began unbuttoning his tunic.

'If you want my opinion, the original mistake was in 'thirty-six, when Himmler said every Kripo flat-foot in the Reich had to wear SS uniform. That's when we were landed with scum like you, and shrivelled-up old cunts like Artur Nebe.'

He handed his jacket to one of the two guards and began rolling up his sleeves. Suddenly he was shouting.

'My God, we used to know how to deal with people like you. But we've gone soft. It's not "Has he got guts?" any more, it's "Has he got a doctorate?" We didn't need doctorates in the East, in 'forty-one, when there was fifty degrees of frost and your piss froze in mid-air. You should have heard Krebs, March. You'd've loved it. Fuck it, I think he's one of your lot.' He adopted a mincing voice. ' "With permission, Herr Obergruppenführer, I would like to question the suspect first. I feel he may respond to a more subtle approach." Subtle, my arse. What's the point of you? If you were my dog, I'd feed you poison.'

'If I were your dog, I'd eat it.'

Globus grinned at one of the guards. 'Listen to the big man!' He spat on his hands and picked up the baseball bat. He turned to March. 'I've been looking at your file. I see you're a great one for writing. Forever taking notes, compiling lists. Quite the frustrated author. Tell me: are you left-handed or right-handed?'

'Left-handed.'

'Another lie. Put your right arm on the table.'

March felt as if iron bands had been fastened around his chest. He could barely breathe. 'Go screw yourself.'

Globus glanced at the guards and powerful hands seized March from behind. The chair toppled and he was being bent head first over the table. One of the SS men twisted his left arm high up his back, wrenched it, and March was roaring with the pain of that as the other man grabbed his free hand. The man half-climbed on to the table and planted his knee just below March's right elbow, pinning his forearm, palm down, to the wooden planks.

In seconds, everything was locked in place except his fingers, which were just able to flutter slightly, like a trapped bird.

Globus stood a metre from the table, brushing the tip of the bat lightly across March's knuckles. Then he lifted it, swung it in a great arc, like an axe, through three hundred degrees, and with all his force brought it smashing down.

HE did not faint, not at first. The guards let him go and he slid to his knees, a thread of spit dribbling from the corner of his mouth, leaving a snail's trail across the table. His arm was still stretched out. He stayed like that for a while, until he raised his head and saw the remains of his hand – some alien pile of blood and gristle on a butcher's slab – and then he fainted.

FOOTSTEPS in the darkness. Voices.

'Where is the woman?'

Kick.

'What was the information?'

Kick.

'What did you steal?'

Kick. Kick.

A jackboot stamped on his fingers, twisted, ground them into the stone.

WHEN he came to again he was lying in the corner, his broken hand resting on the floor next to him, like a still-born baby left beside its mother. A man – Krebs perhaps – was squatting in front of him, saying something. He tried to focus.

'What is this?' Krebs's mouth was saying. 'What does it mean?'

The Gestapo man was breathless, as if he had been running up and down stairs. With one hand he grasped March's chin, twisting his face to the light. In the other he held a sheaf of papers.

'What does it mean, March? They were hidden in the front of your car. Taped underneath the dashboard. What does it mean?'

March pulled his head away and turned his face to the darkening wall.

Tap, tap, tap. In his dreams. *Tap, tap, tap.*

SOME time later – he could not be more accurate than that, for time was beyond measurement, now speeding, now slowing to an infinitesimal crawl – a white jacket appeared above him. A flash of steel. A thin blade poised vertically before his eyes. March tried to back away but fingers locked around his wrist, the needle was jabbed into a vein. At first, when his hand was touched, he howled, but then he felt the fluid spreading through his veins and the agony subsided.

THE torture doctor was old and hunch-backed and it seemed to March, who brimmed with gratitude towards him, that he must have lived in the basement for many years. The grime had settled in his pores, the darkness hung in pouches beneath his eyes. He did not speak. He cleaned the wound, painted it with a clear liquid that smelled of hospitals and morgues, and bound it tightly in a white crepe bandage. Then, still without speaking, he and Krebs helped March to his feet. They put him back in his chair. An enamel mug of sweet, milky coffee was set on the table before him. A cigarette was slipped into his good hand.

FOUR

In his mind March had built a wall. Behind it he placed Charlie in her speeding car. It was a high wall, made of everything his imagination could collect – boulders, concrete blocks, burnt-out iron bedsteads, overturned tramcars, suitcases, prams – and it stretched in either direction across the sunlit German countryside like a postcard of the Great Wall of China. In front of it, he patrolled the ground. *He would not let them beyond the wall.* Everything else, they could have.

Krebs was reading March's notes. He sat with both elbows on the table, his chin resting on his knuckles. Occasionally he removed a hand to turn a page, replaced it, went on reading. March watched him. After his coffee and his cigarette and with the pain dulled he felt almost euphoric.

Krebs finished and momentarily closed his eyes. His complexion was white, as always. Then he straightened the pages and laid them in front of him, alongside March's notebook and Buhler's diary. He adjusted them by millimetres, into a line of parade-ground precision. Perhaps it was the effect of the drug, but suddenly March was seeing everything so clearly – how the ink on the cheap fibre pages had spread slightly, each letter sprouting minute hairs; how badly Krebs had shaved: that clump of black stubble in the fold of skin below his nose. In the silence he actually believed he could hear the dust falling, pattering across the table.

'Have you killed me, March?'

'Killed you?'

'With these.' Krebs's hand hovered a centimetre above the notes.

'It depends who knows you have them.'

'Only some cretin of an Unterscharführer who works in the garage. He found them when we brought in your car. He gave them directly to me. Globus doesn't know a thing – yet.'

'Then that is your answer.'

Krebs started rubbing his face vigorously, as if drying himself. He stopped, his hands pressed to his cheeks, and stared at March through his spread fingers. 'What is happening here?'

'You can read.'

'I can read, but I don't understand.' Krebs snatched up the pages and leafed through them. 'Here, for example – what is "Zyklon B"?'

'Crystallised hydrogen cyanide. Before that, they used carbon monoxide. Before that, bullets.'

'And here – "Auschwitz/Birkenau". "Kulmhof". "Belzec". "Treblinka". "Majdanek". "Sobibor".'

'The killing grounds.'

'These figures: eight thousand a day . . .'

'That's the total they could destroy at Auschwitz/Birkenau using the four gas chambers and crematoria.'

'And this "eleven million"?'

'Eleven million is the total number of European Jews they were after. Maybe they succeeded. Who knows? I don't see many around, do you?'

'Here: the name "Globocnik" . . .'

'Globus was SS and Police Leader in Lublin. He built the killing centres.'

'I didn't know.' Krebs dropped the notes on the table as if they were contagious. 'I didn't know any of this.'

'Of course you knew! You knew every time someone made a joke about "going East", every time you heard a mother tell her child to behave or they'd go up the chimney. We knew when we moved into their houses, when we took over their property, their jobs. We knew but we didn't have the facts.' He pointed to the notes with his left hand. 'Those put flesh on the bones. Put bones where there was just clear air.'

'I meant: I didn't know that Buhler, Stuckart and Luther were involved in this. I didn't know about Globus . . .'

'Sure. You just thought you were investigating an art robbery.'

'It's true! It's true,' repeated Krebs. 'Wednesday morning – can you remember back that far? – I was investigating corruption at the Deutsche Arbeitsfront: the sale of labour permits. Then, out of the blue, I am summoned to see the Reichsführer, one-to-one. He tells me retired civil servants have been discovered in a colossal art fraud. The potential embarrassment for the Party is huge. Obergruppenführer Globocnik is in charge. I am to go at once to Schwanenwerder and take my orders from him.'

'Why you?'

'Why not? The Reichsführer knows of my interest in art. We have spoken of these matters. My job was simply to catalogue the treasures.'

'But you must have realised that Globus killed Buhler and Stuckart?'

'Of course. I'm not an idiot. I know Globus's reputation as well as you. But Globus was acting on Heydrich's orders, and if Heydrich had decided to let him loose, to spare the Party a public scandal – who was I to object?'

'Who were you to object?' repeated March.

'Let's be clear, March. Are you saying their deaths had nothing to do with the fraud?'

'Nothing. The fraud was a coincidence that became a useful cover story, that's all.'

'But it made sense. It explained why Globus was acting as state executioner, and why he was desperate to head off an investigation by the Kripo. On Wednesday night I was still cataloguing the pictures on Schwanenwerder when he called in a rage – about you. Said you'd been officially taken off the case, but you'd broken in to Stuckart's apartment. I was to go and bring you in, which I did. And I tell you: if Globus had had his way, that would have been the end of you right there, but Nebe wouldn't have it. Then, on Friday night, we found what we thought was Luther's body in the railway yard, and that seemed to be the end of it.'

'When did you discover the corpse wasn't Luther's?'

'Around six on Saturday morning. Globus telephoned me at home. He said he had information Luther was still alive and was planning to meet the American journalist at nine.'

'He knew this,' asserted March, 'because of a tip-off from the American Embassy.'

Krebs snorted. 'What sort of crap is that? He knew because of a wire-tap.'

'That cannot be . . .'

'Why can't it be? See for yourself.' Krebs opened one of his folders and extracted a single sheet of flimsy brown paper. 'It was rushed over from the wire-tappers in Charlottenburg in the middle of the night.'

March read:

Forschungsamt *Geheime Reichssache*
G745,275
23:51

MALE:	You say: What do I want? What do you think I want? Asylum in your country.
FEMALE:	Tell me where you are.
MALE:	I can pay.
FEMALE:	[Interrupts]
MALE:	I have information. Certain facts.
FEMALE:	Tell me where you are. I'll come and fetch you. We'll go to the Embassy.
MALE:	Too soon. Not yet.

FEMALE: When?
MALE: Tomorrow morning. Listen to me. Nine o'clock. The Great Hall. Central Steps. Have you got that?

Once more he could hear her voice; smell her; touch her.

In a recess of his mind, something stirred.

He slid the paper back across the table to Krebs, who returned it to the folder and resumed: 'What happened next, you know. Globus had Luther shot the instant he appeared – and, let me be honest, that shocked me. To do such a thing in a public place . . . I thought: this man is mad. Of course, I didn't know then quite why he was so anxious Luther shouldn't be taken alive.' He stopped abruptly, as if he had forgotten where he was, the role he was supposed to be playing. He finished quickly: 'We searched the body and found nothing. Then we came after you.'

March's hand had started to throb again. He looked down and saw crimson spots soaking through the white bandage.

'What time is it?'

'Five forty-seven.'

She had been gone almost eleven hours.

God, his hand . . . The specks of red were spreading, touching; forming archipelagos of blood.

'THERE were four of them in it altogether,' said March. 'Buhler, Stuckart, Luther and Kritzinger.'

'Kritzinger?' Krebs made a note.

'Friedrich Kritzinger, Ministerialdirektor of the Reich Chancellery. I wouldn't write any of this down if I were you.'

Krebs laid aside his pencil.

'What concerned them wasn't the extermination programme itself – these were senior Party men, remember – it was the lack of a proper Führer Order. Nothing was written down. All they had were verbal assurances from Heydrich and Himmler that this was what the Führer wanted. Could I have another cigarette?'

After Krebs had given him one, and he had taken a few sweet draughts, he went on: 'This is conjecture, you understand?' His interrogator nodded. 'I assume they asked themselves: why is there no direct written link between the Führer and this policy? And I assume their answer was: because it is so monstrous, the Head of State cannot be seen to be involved. So where did this leave them? It left them in the shit. Because if Germany lost the war, they could be tried as war criminals, and if Germany won it, they might one day be made the scapegoats for the greatest act of mass-murder in history.'

Krebs murmured: 'I am not sure I want to know this.'

'So they took out an insurance policy. They swore affidavits – that was easy: three of them were lawyers – and they removed documents whenever they could. And gradually they put together a documentary record. Either outcome was covered. If Germany won and action was taken against them, they could threaten to expose what they knew. If the Allies won, they could say: look, we opposed this policy and even risked our lives to collect information about it. Luther also added a touch of blackmail – embarrassing documents about the American Ambassador to London, Kennedy. Give me those.'

He nodded to his notebook and to Buhler's diary. Krebs hesitated, then slid them across the table.

It was difficult to open the notebook with only one hand. The bandage was sodden. He was smearing the pages.

'The camps were organised to make sure there were no witnesses. Special prisoners ran the gas chambers, the crematoria. Eventually, those special prisoners were themselves destroyed, replaced by others, who were also destroyed. And so on. If that could happen at the lowest level, why not the highest? Look. Fourteen people at the Wannsee conference. The first one dies in 'fifty-four. Another in 'fifty-five. Then one a year in 'fifty-seven, 'fifty-nine, 'sixty, 'sixty-one, 'sixty-two. Intruders probably planned to kill Luther in 'sixty-three, and he hired security guards. But time passed and nothing happened, so he assumed it was just a coincidence.'

'That's enough, March.'

'By 'sixty-three, it had started to accelerate. In May, Klopfer dies. In December, Hoffmann hangs himself. In March this year, Kritzinger is blown up by a car bomb. Now, Buhler is really frightened. Kritzinger is the trigger. He's the first of the group to die.'

March picked up the pocket diary.

'Here – you see – he marks the date of Kritzinger's death with a cross. But after that the days go by; nothing happens; perhaps they are safe. Then, on April the ninth – another cross! Buhler's old colleague from the General Government, Schöngarth, has slipped beneath the wheels of a U-bahn train in Zoo Station. Panic on Schwanenwerder! But by then it's too late . . .'

'I said: that's enough!'

'One question puzzled me: why were there eight deaths in the first nine years, followed by six deaths in just the last six months? Why the rush? Why this terrible risk, after the exercise of so much patience? But then, we policemen seldom lift our eyes from the mud to look at the broader picture, do we? Everything was supposed to be completed by last Tuesday, ready for the visit of our good new friends, the Americans. And that raises a further question – '

'Give me those!' Krebs pulled the diary and the notebook from March's grasp. Outside in the passage: Globus's voice . . .

' – Would Heydrich have done all this on his own initiative, or was he acting on orders from a higher level? Orders, perhaps, from the same person who would not put his signature to any document. . . ?'

Krebs had the stove open and was stuffing in the papers. For a moment they lay smouldering on the coals, then ignited into yellow flame as the key turned in the cell door.

FIVE

'Kulmhof!' he shouted at Globus when the pain became too bad. 'Belzec! Treblinka!'

'Now we're getting somewhere.' Globus grinned at his two assistants.

'Majdanek! Sobibor! Auschwitz/Birkenau!' He held up the names like a shield to ward off the blows.

'What am I supposed to do? Shrivel up and die?' Globus squatted on his haunches and grabbed March by the ears, twisting his face towards him. 'They're just names, March. There's nothing there any more, not even a brick. Nobody will ever believe it. And shall I tell you something? *Part of you can't believe it either.*' Globus spat in his face – a gobbet of greyish-yellow phlegm. 'That's how much the world will care.' He thrust him away, bouncing his head against the stone floor.

'Now. Again. Where's the girl?'

SIX

Time crawled on all fours, broken-backed. He was shivering. His teeth chattered like a clockwork toy.

Other prisoners had been here years before him. In lieu of tombstones they had scratched on the cell's walls with splintered fingernails. 'J.F.G. 22.2.57'. 'Katja'. 'H.K. May 44'. Someone had got no further than half the letter 'E' before strength or time or will had run out on them. Yet still this urge to write . . .

None of the marks, he noticed, was more than a metre above the floor.

The pain in his hand was making him feverish. He had hallucinations. A dog ground his fingers between its jaws. He closed his eyes and wondered what time was doing now. When he had last asked Krebs it had been – what? – almost six. Then they had talked for perhaps another half-hour. After that there had been his second session with Globus – infinite. Now this stretch alone in his cell, slithering in and out of the light, tugged one way by exhaustion, the other by the dog.

The floor was warm to his cheek, the smooth stone dissolved.

HE dreamed of his father – his childhood dream – the stiff figure in the photograph come to life, waving from the deck of the ship as it pulled out of harbour, waving until he had dwindled to a stick-figure, until he disappeared. He dreamed of Jost, running on the spot, intoning his poetry in his solemn voice: 'You throw food to the beast in man/That it may grow . . .' He dreamed of Charlie.

But most often he dreamed he was back in Pili's bedroom

at that dreadful instant when he understood what the boy had done out of kindness – *kindness!* – when his arms were reaching for the door but his legs were trapped – and the window was exploding and rough hands were dragging at his shoulders . . .

THE jailer shook him awake.

'On your feet!'

He was curled up tight on his left side, foetus-like – his body raw, his joints welded. The guard's push awoke the dog and he was sick. There was nothing in him to bring up, but his stomach convulsed anyway, for old time's sake. The cell retreated a long way and came rushing back. He was pulled upright. The jailer swung a pair of handcuffs. Next to him stood Krebs, thank God, not Globus.

Krebs looked at him with distaste and said to the guard: 'You'd better put them on at the front.'

His wrists were locked before him, his cap was stuffed on his head, and he was marched, hunched forward, along the passage, up the steps, into the fresh air.

A cold night, and clear. The stars sprayed across the sky above the courtyard. The buildings and the cars were silver-edged in the moonlight. Krebs pushed him into the back seat of a Mercedes and climbed in after him. He nodded to the driver: 'Columbia House. Lock the doors.'

As the bolts slid home in the door beside him, March felt a flicker of relief.

'Don't raise your hopes,' said Krebs. 'The Obergruppenführer is still waiting for you. We have more modern technology at Columbia, that's all.'

They pulled out through the gates, looking to any who saw them like two SS officers and their chauffeur. A guard saluted.

Columbia House was three kilometres south of Prinz-

Albrecht Strasse. The darkened government buildings quickly yielded to shabby office blocks and boarded-up warehouses. The area close to the prison had been scheduled for redevelopment in the nineteen-fifties, and here and there Speer's bulldozers had made destructive forays. But the money had run out before anything could be built to replace what they had knocked down. Now, overgrown patches of derelict land gleamed in the bluish light like the corners of old battlefields. In the dark side-streets between them dwelt the teeming colonies of East European gastarbeiter.

March was sitting stretched out, his head resting on the back of the leather seat, when Krebs suddenly leaned towards him and shouted: 'Oh, for fuck's sake!' He turned to the driver: 'He's pissing himself. Pull over here.'

The driver swore, and braked hard.

'Open the doors!'

Krebs got out, came round to March's side, and yanked him out. 'Quickly! We haven't got all night!' To the driver: 'One minute. Keep the engine running.'

Then March was being pushed – stumbling across rough stones, down an alley, into the doorway of a disused church, and Krebs was unlocking the handcuffs.

'You're a lucky man, March.'

'I don't understand . . .'

Krebs said: 'You've got a favourite uncle.'

Tap, tap, tap. From the darkness of the church. *Tap, tap, tap.*

'YOU should have come to me at once, my boy,' said Artur Nebe. 'You would have spared yourself such agony.' He brushed March's cheek with his fingertips. In the heavy shadows, March could not make out the detail of his face, only a pale blur.

'Take my pistol.' Krebs pressed the Luger into March's left hand. 'Take it! You tricked me. Got hold of my gun. Understand?'

He was dreaming, surely? But the pistol felt solid enough . . .

Nebe was still talking – a low, urgent voice. 'Oh March, March. Krebs came to me this evening – shocked! so shocked! – told me what you had. We all suspected it, of course, but never had the proof. Now you've got to get it out. For all our sakes. You've got to stop these bastards . . .'

Krebs interrupted: 'Forgive me, sir, our time is almost gone.' He pointed. 'Down there, March. Can you see? A car.'

Parked under a broken street lamp at the far end of the alley March could just see a low shape, could hear a motor running.

'What is this?' He looked from one man to the other.

'Walk to the car and get in. We've no more time. I count to ten, then I yell.'

'Don't fail us, March.' Nebe squeezed his cheek. 'Your uncle is an old man, but he hopes to live long enough to see those bastards hang. Go on. Get the papers out. Get them published. We're risking everything, giving you a chance. Take it. Go.'

Krebs said: 'I'm counting: one, two, three . . .'

March hesitated, started to walk, then broke into a loping run. The car door was opening. He looked back. Nebe had already disappeared into the dark. Krebs had cupped his hands to his mouth and was starting to shout.

March turned and struggled towards the waiting car where a familiar voice was calling: 'Zavi! Zavi!'

PART SEVEN

FÜHRERTAG

The railway to Krakau continues north-east past Auschwitz (348 kilometres from Vienna), an industrial town of 12,000 inhabitants, the former capital of the Piast Duchies of Auschwitz and Zator (Hotel Zator 20 bedrooms), whence a secondary railway runs via Skawina to Krakau (69 kilometres in three hours) . . .

Baedeker's *General Government*, 1943

ONE

Midnight peals of bells rang out to welcome the day. Drivers whipped past, flashing their headlights, hammering their horns, leaving a smear of sound hanging over the road behind them. Factory hooters called to one another across Berlin, like stationary trains.

'My dear old friend, what have they done to you?'

Max Jaeger was trying to concentrate on driving, but every few seconds his head would swivel to the right, in horrified fascination, to the passenger seat beside him.

He kept repeating it: 'What have they done to you?'

March was in a daze, uncertain what was dream and what reality. He had his back half-turned and was staring out of the rear window. 'Where are we going, Max?'

'God alone knows. Where do you want to go?'

The road behind was clear. March carefully pulled himself round to look at Jaeger. 'Didn't Nebe tell you?'

'Nebe said *you'd* tell me.'

March looked away, at the buildings sliding by. He did not see them. He was thinking of Charlie in the hotel room in Waldshut. Awake, alone, waiting for him. There were still more than eight hours to go. He and Max would have the Autobahnen almost to themselves. They could probably make it.

'I was at the Markt,' Jaeger was saying. 'This was about nine. The telephone rings. It's Uncle Artur. "Sturmbannführer! How good a friend is Xavier March?" "There's nothing I wouldn't do," I said – by this time, the word was out about where you were. He said, very quietly: "All right, Sturmbannführer, we'll see how good a friend you are. Kreuzberg. Corner of Axmann-weg, north of the abandoned church. Wait from quarter to midnight to quarter past. And not a word to anyone or you'll be in a KZ by morning." That was it. He hung up.'

There was a sheen of sweat on Jaeger's forehead. He glanced from the road to March and back again. 'Fuck it, Zavi. I don't know what I'm doing. I'm scared. I'm heading south. Is that okay?'

'You're doing fine.'

'Aren't you glad to see me?' asked Jaeger.

'Very glad.'

March felt faint again. He twisted his body and wound down the window with his left hand. Above the sound of the wind and the tyres: a noise. What was it? He put his head out and looked up. He could not see it, but he could hear it overhead. The clatter of a helicopter. He closed the window.

He remembered the telephone transcript. '*What do I want? What do you think I want? Asylum in your country . . .*'

The car's dials and gauges shone a soft green in the darkness. The upholstery smelled of fresh leather.

He said: 'Where did you get the car, Max?' It was a Mercedes he saw: the latest model.

'From the pool at Werderscher Markt. A beauty, yes? She's got a full tank. We can go anywhere you want. Anywhere at all.'

March began to laugh then. Not very hard and not for very long because his aching ribs soon forced him to stop. 'Oh Max, Max,' he said, 'Nebe and Krebs are such good liars, and you're so lousy, I almost feel sorry for them, having to have you on their team.'

Jaeger stared ahead. 'They've pumped you full of drugs, Zavi. They've hurt you. You're confused, believe me.'

'If they'd picked any other driver but you, I might almost have fallen for it. But you . . . Tell me, Max: why is the road behind so empty? I suppose, if you're following a shiny new car that's packed with electronics and transmitting a signal, you needn't come closer than a kilometre. Especially if you can use a helicopter.'

'I risk my life,' whined Jaeger, 'and this is my reward.'

March had Krebs's Luger in his hand – his left hand, it was awkward to hold. Nevertheless he managed a convincing enough show of digging the barrel into the thick folds of Jaeger's neck. 'Krebs gave me his gun. To add that essential touch of authenticity. Not loaded, I'm sure. But do you want to take that risk? I think not. Keep your left hand on the wheel, Max, and your eyes on the road, and with your right hand give me your Luger. Very slowly.'

'You've gone mad.'

March increased the pressure. The barrel slid up the sweaty skin and came to rest just behind Jaeger's ear.

'All right, all right . . .'

Jaeger gave him the gun.

'Excellent. Now, I'm going to sit with this pointed at your fat belly, and if you try anything, Max – anything – I'll put a bullet in it. And if you have any doubts about that, just sit there and work it out. And you'll conclude I've got nothing to lose.'

'Zavi . . .'

'Shut up. Just keep driving on this road until we reach the outer Autobahn.'

He hoped Max could not see his hand trembling. He rested the gun in his lap. It was good, he reassured himself. Really good. It proved they had not picked her up. Nor had they discovered where she was. Because if they had managed either, they would never have resorted to this.

TWENTY-FIVE kilometres south of the city, the lights of the Autobahn looped across the darkness like a necklace.

Great slabs of yellow thrust out of the ground bearing in black the names of the Imperial cities: clockwise from Stettin, through Danzig, Königsberg, Minsk, Posen, Krakau, Kiev, Rostov, Odessa, Vienna; then up through Munich, Nuremberg, Stuttgart, Strasbourg, Frankfurt and Hanover to Hamburg.

At March's direction, they turned anti-clockwise. Twenty kilometres later, at the Friedersdorf intersection, they forked right.

Another sign: Liegnitz, Breslau, Kattowitz . . .

The stars arched. Little flecks of luminous cloud shone above the trees.

THE Mercedes flew down the slip road and joined the moonlit Autobahn. The road gleamed like a wide river. Behind them, sweeping round to follow, he pictured a dragon's tail of lights and guns.

He was the head. He was pulling them after him – away from her, along the empty highway towards the east.

TWO

Pain and exhaustion stalked him. To keep awake he talked.

'I suppose,' he said, 'we have Krause to thank for this.'

Neither of them had spoken for almost an hour. The only sounds were the hum of the engine and the drumming of the wheels on the concrete road. Jaeger jumped at March's voice. 'Krause?'

'Krause mixed up the rotas, ordered me to Schwanenwerder instead of you.'

'Krause!' Jaeger scowled. His face was a stage demon's, painted green by the glow of the instrument panel. All the troubles in his life could be traced back to Krause!

'The Gestapo fixed it so you'd be on duty on Monday night, didn't they? What did they tell you? "There'll be a body in the Havel, Sturmbannführer. No hurry about identifying it. Lose the file for a few days . . ." '

Jaeger muttered: 'Something like that.'

'And then you overslept, and by the time you got to the Markt on Tuesday I'd taken over the case. Poor Max. Never could get up in the mornings. The Gestapo must have loved you. Whom were you dealing with?'

'Globocnik.'

'Globus himself!' March whistled. 'I bet you thought it was Christmas! What did he promise you, Max? Promotion? Transfer to the Sipo?'

'Fuck you, March.'

'So then you kept him informed of everything I was doing. When I told you Jost had seen Globus with the body at the lakeside, you passed it along and Jost disappeared. When I called you from Stuckart's apartment, you warned them where we were and we were arrested. They searched the woman's apartment the next morning because you told them she had something from Stuckart's safe. They left us together in Prinz-Albrecht Strasse so you could do their interrogation for them – '

Jaeger's right hand flashed across from the steering wheel and grabbed the gun barrel, twisting it up and away, but March's fingers were caught around the trigger and squeezed it.

The explosion in the enclosed space tore their eardrums. The car swerved across the Autobahn and up on to the grass strip separating the two carriageways and they were bouncing along the rough track. For an instant, March thought he had been hit, then he thought that Jaeger had been hit. But Jaeger had both hands on the wheel and was fighting to control the Mercedes and March still had the gun. Cold air was rushing into the car through a jagged hole in the roof.

Jaeger was laughing like a madman and saying something but March was still deaf from the shot. The car skidded off the grass and rejoined the Autobahn.

IN the shock of the blast, March had been thrown against his shattered hand and had almost blacked-out, but the stream of freezing air pummelled him back into consciousness. He had a frantic desire to finish his story – *I only knew for certain you'd betrayed me when Krebs showed me the wire-tap: I knew because you were the only person I'd told about the telephone kiosk in Bülow Strasse, how Stuckart called the girl* – but the wind whipped away his words. In any case, what did it matter?

In all this, the irony was Nightingale. The American had been an honest man; his closest friend, the traitor.

Jaeger was still grinning like a lunatic, talking to himself as he drove, the tears glistening on his plump cheeks.

*

JUST after five they pulled off the autobahn into an all-night filling station. Jaeger stayed in the car and told the attendant through the open window to fill the tank. March kept the Luger pressed to Jaeger's ribs, but the fight seemed to have gone out of him. He had dwindled. He was just a sack of flesh in a uniform.

The young man who operated the pumps looked at the hole in the roof and looked at them – two SS-Sturmbannführer in a brand-new Mercedes – bit his lip, and said nothing.

Through the line of trees separating the service area from the autobahn, March could see the occasional passing headlight. But of the cavalcade he knew was following them: no sign. He guessed they must have halted a kilometre back, to wait and see what he planned to do next.

WHEN they were back on the road, Jaeger said: 'I never meant any harm to come to you, Zavi.'

March, who had been thinking of Charlie, grunted.

'Globocnik is a police general, for God's sake. If he tells you: "Jaeger! Look the other way!" – you look the other way, right? I mean, that's the law, isn't it? We're policemen. We have to obey the law!'

Jaeger took his eyes off the road long enough to glance at March, who said nothing. He returned his attention to the Autobahn.

'Then, when he ordered me to tell him what you'd found out – what was I supposed to do?'

'You could have warned me.'

'Yes? And what would you have done? I know you: you'd have carried on anyway. And where would that have left me – me, and Hannelore and the kids? We're not all made to be heroes, Zavi. There have to be people like me, so people like you can look so clever.'

They were driving towards the dawn. Over the low wooded hills ahead of them was a pale glow, as if a distant city was on fire.

'Now I suppose they'll kill me, for allowing you to pull the gun on me. They'll say I let you do it. They'll shoot me. Jesus, it's a joke, isn't it?' He looked at March with wet eyes. 'It's a joke!'

'It's a joke,' said March.

IT was light by the time they crossed the Oder. The grey river stretched either side of the high steel bridge. A pair of barges crossed in the centre of the slow-moving water, and hooted a loud good morning to one another.

The Oder: Germany's natural frontier with Poland. Except there was no longer any frontier; there was no Poland.

March stared straight ahead. This was the road down which the Wehrmacht's Tenth Army had rolled in September 1939. In his mind, he saw again the old newsreels: the horse-drawn artillery, the Panzers, the marching troops . . . Victory had seemed so easy. How they had cheered!

There was an exit sign to Gleiwitz, the town where the war had started.

Jaeger was moaning. 'I'm shattered, Zavi. I can't drive much longer.'

March said, 'Not far now.'

HE thought of Globus. *'There's nothing there any more, not even a brick. Nobody will ever believe it. And shall I tell you something? Part of you can't believe it either.'* That had been his worst moment, because it was true.

A TOTENBURG – a Citadel of the Dead – stood on a bare hilltop not far from the road: four granite towers, fifty metres high, set in a square, enclosing a bronze obelisk. For a moment as they passed, the weak sun glinted on the metal, like a reflecting mirror. There were dozens of such tumuli between here and the Urals – imperishable memorials to the Germans who had died – were dying, would die – for the conquest of the East. Beyond Silesia, across the Steppes, the Autobahnen were built on ridges to keep them clear of the winter's snows – deserted highways ceaselessly swept by the wind . . .

THEY drove for another twenty kilometres, past the belching factory chimneys of Kattowitz, and then March told Jaeger to leave the Autobahn.

HE can see her in his mind.

She is checking out of the hotel. She says to the receptionist: 'You're sure there've been no messages?' The receptionist smiles. 'None, Fräulein.' She has asked a dozen times. A porter offers to help her with her luggage, but she refuses. She sits in the car overlooking the river, reading again the letter she found hidden in her case. 'Here is the key to the vault, my darling. Make sure she sees the light one day . . .' A minute passes. Another. Another. She keeps looking north, towards the direction from which he should come.

At last she checks her watch. Then she nods slowly, switches on the engine and turns right into the quiet road.

*

Now they were passing through industrialised countryside: brown fields bordered by straggling hedgerows; whitish grass; black slopes of coal waste; the wooden towers of old mineshafts with ghostly spinning wheels, like the skeletons of windmills.

'What a shit-hole,' said Jaeger. 'What happens here?'

The road ran beside a railway track, then crossed a river. Rafts of rubbery scum drifted along the banks. They were directly downwind of Kattowitz. The air stank of chemicals and coaldust. The sky here really was a sulphur-yellow, the sun an orange disc in the smog.

They dipped, went through a blackened railway bridge, then over a rail crossing. Close, now . . . March tried to remember Luther's crude sketch map.

They reached a junction. He hesitated.

'Turn right.'

Past corrugated iron sheds, scraps of trees, rattling over more steel tracks . . .

He recognised a disused rail line. 'Stop!'

Jaeger braked.

'This is it. You can turn off the engine.'

Such silence. Not even a birdcall.

Jaeger looked around with distaste at the narrow road, the barren fields, the distant trees. A wasteland. 'But we're in the middle of nowhere!'

'What time is it?'

'Just after nine.'

'Turn on the radio.'

'What is this? You want a little music? *The Merry Widow?*'

'Just turn it on.'

'Which channel?'

'The channel doesn't matter. If it's nine they'll all sound the same.'

Jaeger pressed a switch, turned a dial. A noise like an ocean breaking on a rocky shore. As he scanned the frequencies the noise was lost, came back, was lost and then came back at full strength: not the ocean, but a million human voices raised in acclamation.

'Take out your handcuffs, Max. That's it. Give me the key. Now attach yourself to the wheel. I'm sorry, Max.'

'Oh, Zavi . . .'

'Here he comes!' shouted the commentator. *'I can see him! Here he comes!'*

HE had been walking for a little over five minutes and had almost reached the birch woods when he heard the helicopter. He looked back a kilometre, past the waving grass, along the overgrown tracks. The Mercedes had been joined on the road by a dozen other cars. A line of black figures was starting towards him.

He turned and carried on walking.

SHE is pulling up at the border crossing – now. The swastika flag flaps over the customs post. The guard takes her passport. 'For what purpose are you leaving Germany, Fräulein?' 'To attend a friend's wedding. In Zürich.' He looks from the passport photograph to her face and back again, checks the dates on the visa. 'You are travelling alone?' 'My fiancé was supposed to be with me, but he's been delayed in Berlin. Doing his duty, officer. You know how it is.' Smiling, natural . . . That's it, my darling. Nobody can do this better than you.

HE had his eyes on the ground. There must be something.

*

One guard questions her, another circles the car. 'What luggage are you carrying, please?' 'Just overnight clothes. And a wedding present.' She puts on a puzzled expression: 'Why? Is there a problem? Would you like me to unpack?' She starts to open the door . . . Oh, Charlie, don't overplay it. The guards exchange looks . . .

And then he saw it. Almost buried at the base of a sapling: a streak of red. He bent and picked it up, turned it over in his hand. The brick was pitted with yellow lichen, scorched by explosive, crumbling at the corners. But it was solid enough. It existed. He scraped at the lichen with his thumb and the carmine dust crusted beneath his fingernail like dried blood. As he stooped to replace it, he saw others, half-hidden in the pale grass – ten, twenty, a hundred . . .

A pretty girl, a blonde, a fine day, a holiday . . . The guard checks the sheet again. It says here only that Berlin is anxious to trace an American, a brunette. 'No, Fräulein –' he gives her back her passport and winks at the other guard ' – a search will not be necessary.' The barrier lifts. 'Heil Hitler!' he says. 'Heil Hitler,' she replies.

Go on, Charlie. Go on . . .

It is as if she hears him. She turns her head towards the East, towards him, to where the sun is fresh in the sky, and as the car moves forward she seems to dip her head in acknowledgement. Across the bridge: the white cross of Switzerland. The morning light glints on the Rhine . . .

She had got away. He looked up at the sun and he knew it – knew it for an absolute, certain fact.

'Stay where you are!'

The black shape of the helicopter flapped above him. Behind him, shouts – much closer now – metallic, robot-like commands: 'Drop your weapon!'

'Stay where you are!'

'Stay where you are!'

He took off his cap and threw it, sent it skimming across the grass the way his father used to skim flat stones across the sea. Then he tugged the gun from his waistband, checked to make sure it was loaded, and moved towards the silent trees.

AUTHOR'S NOTE

Many of the characters whose names are used in this novel actually existed. Their biographical details are correct up to 1942. Their subsequent fates, of course, were different.

Josef Buhler, State Secretary in the General Government, was condemned to death in Poland and executed in 1948.

Wilhelm Stuckart was arrested at the end of the war and spent four years in detention. He was released in 1949 and lived in West Berlin. In December 1953 he was killed in a car 'accident' near Hanover: the 'accident' was probably arranged by a vengeance squad hunting down those Nazi war criminals still at large.

Martin Luther attempted to oust the German Foreign Minister, Joachim von Ribbentrop, in a power struggle in 1943. He failed and was sent to Sachsenhausen concentration camp where he attempted suicide. He was released in 1945, shortly before the end of the war, and died in a local hospital of heart failure in May 1945.

Odilo Globocnik was captured by a British patrol at Weissensee, Carinthia, on 31 May 1945. He committed suicide by swallowing a cyanide capsule.

Reinhard Heydrich was assassinated in Prague by Czech agents in the summer of 1942.

Artur Nebe's fate, typically, is more mysterious. He is believed to have been involved in the July 1944 plot against Hitler, to have gone into hiding on an island in the Wannsee, and to have been betrayed by a rejected mistress. Officially, he was executed in Berlin on 21 March 1945. However, he is said subsequently to have been sighted in Italy and Ireland.

Those named as having attended the Wannsee Conference all did so. Alfred Meyer committed suicide in 1945. Roland Freisler was killed in an air raid in 1945. Friedrich Kritzinger died at liberty after a severe illness. Adolf Eichmann was executed by the Israelis in 1962. Karl Schöngarth was condemned to death by a British court in 1946. Otto Hoffmann was sentenced to 15 years' imprisonment by a US military court. Heinrich Müller went missing at the end of the war. The others continued to live, either in Germany or South America.

The following documents quoted in the text are authentic: Heydrich's invitation to the Wannsee Conference; Goering's order to Heydrich of 31 July 1941; the dispatches of the German Ambassador describing the comments of Joseph P. Kennedy; the order from the Auschwitz Central Construction Office; the railway timetable (abridged); the extracts from the Wannsee Conference Minutes; the memorandum on the use of prisoners' hair.

Where I have created documents, I have tried to do so on the basis of fact – for example, the Wannsee Conference *was* postponed, its minutes *were* written up in a much fuller form by Eichmann and subsequently edited by Heydrich; Hitler did – notoriously – avoid putting his name to anything like a direct order for the Final Solution, but almost certainly issued a verbal instruction in the summer of 1941.

The Berlin of this book is the Berlin that Albert Speer planned to build.

Leonardo da Vinci's portrait of Cecilia Gallerani was recovered from Germany at the end of the war and returned to Poland.

Further praise for ENIGMA

'The brilliance of *Enigma* is that it gives the readers the sense of being contemporary with its characters and then leads them on a dark journey of discovery to arrive at another of the Second World War's blackest horror stories, one not fully admitted until half a century later . . . Altogether top-class stuff.'
Peter Millar, *The Times*

'Sometimes when a reviewer enjoys a novel he can simply summarise the contents, describe the flavour, add his comments, and pass on. Sometimes, as with *Enigma,* the success goes so deep that he has to pause and dig, so that he can explain to himself, as well as others, the different elements of that success.'
Douglas Hurd, *Daily Telegraph*

'Robert Harris is a superb writer of thrillers . . . He expertly recreates the past with a sense of admiration, anger and pity, from the unswallowable wartime food to the sounds a U-boat registers when a convoy passes overhead.'
Penelope Fitzgerald, *Independent*

'Robert Harris succeeds brilliantly in breaking the mould. He has written a novel about the arcane world of signals intelligence which is as gripping as a good spy thriller.'
Christopher Andrews, *Sunday Telegraph*

'Robert Harris must surely have had a previous life as a scientist at Bletchley Park to have been able to produce *Enigma* . . . it kept me happily awake for two nights.'
Gitta Sereny, 'Books of the Year', *Observer*

'A well-conceived, intelligent and rewarding book that is certain to enhance Harris's reputation as a novelist'
Literary Review

'From this group portrait of men and women under terrifying pressure Harris has fashioned as story that is as humane, intelligent and gripping as documentary fiction can get'
Anthony Quinn, *Financial Times*

‘What really sets this book apart is Harris’s extraordinary ability to conjure up the feeling of actually being there, waiting for reports from doomed convoys, or simply trying to keep warm during an English winter. So buy the book, snuggle into the sofa – and prepare to be there next morning.’
New Scientist

‘A complicated but brilliantly-paced account of an ace cryptographer working against time . . . I rate Robert Harris very highly indeed.’
Tablet

‘Harris is a supreme storyteller, and this tale of love and betrayal, codes and secrets, is a worthy successor to *Fatherland*’
Yorkshire Post

Robert Harris

ENIGMA

ARROW

Published in the United Kingdom in 1996 by
Arrow Books

11 13 15 17 19 20 18 16 14 12 10

First published in the United Kingdom in 1995 by Hutchinson

Arrow Books Limited
Random House UK Ltd
20 Vauxhall Bridge Road, London SW1V 2SA

Random House Australia (Pty) Limited
20 Alfred Street, Milsons Point, Sydney
New South Wales 2061, Australia

Random House New Zealand Limited
18 Poland Road, Glenfield, Auckland 10, New Zealand

Random House South Africa (Pty) Limited
Endulini, 5a Jubilee Road, Parktown 2193, South Africa

Random House UK Limited Reg. No. 954009

A CIP catalogue record for this book
is available from the British Library

Papers used by Random House UK Limited are natural, recyclable products made from wood grown in sustainable forests. The manufacturing processes conform to the environmental regulations of the country of origin

Printed and bound in the Great Britain by
Mackays of Chatham PLC, Chatham, Kent

ISBN 0 09 999200 0

For Gill,
and for Holly and Charlie
QXQF VFLR TXLG VLWD PRUA

Author's Note

This novel is set against the background of an actual historical event. The German naval signals quoted in the text are all authentic. The characters, however, are entirely fictional.

'It looks as if Bletchley Park is the single greatest achievement of Britain during 1939–45, perhaps during this century as a whole.'

George Steiner

'A mathematical proof should resemble a simple and clear-cut constellation, not a scattered cluster in the Milky Way. A chess problem also has unexpectedness, and a certain economy; it is essential that the moves should be surprising, and that every piece on the board should play its part.'

G. H. Hardy, *A Mathematician's Apology*

ONE

WHISPERS

WHISPERS: the sounds made by an enemy wireless transmitter immediately before it begins to broadcast a coded message.

A Lexicon of Cryptography
('Most Secret', Bletchley Park, 1943)

1

Cambridge in the fourth winter of the war: a ghost town.

A ceaseless Siberian wind with nothing to blunt its edge for a thousand miles whipped off the North Sea and swept low across the Fens. It rattled the signs to the air-raid shelters in Trinity New Court and battered on the boarded-up windows of King's College Chapel. It prowled through the quadrangles and staircases, confining the few dons and students still in residence to their rooms. By mid-afternoon the narrow cobbled streets were deserted. By nightfall, with not a light to be seen, the university was returned to a darkness it hadn't known since the Middle Ages. A procession of monks shuffling over Magdalene Bridge on their way to Vespers would scarcely have seemed out of place.

In the wartime blackout the centuries had dissolved.

It was to this bleak spot in the flatlands of eastern England that there came, in the middle of February 1943, a young mathematician named Thomas Jericho. The authorities of his college, King's, were given less than a day's notice of his arrival – scarcely enough time to reopen his rooms, put sheets on his bed, and have more than three years' worth of dust swept from his shelves and carpets. And they would not have gone to even that much trouble – it being wartime and servants so scarce – had not the Provost himself been telephoned at the Master's Lodge by an obscure but very senior official of His Majesty's Foreign Office, with a request that 'Mr Jericho be looked after until he is well enough to return to his duties'.

'Of course,' replied the Provost, who couldn't for the life of him put a face to the name of Jericho. 'Of course. A pleasure to welcome him back.'

As he spoke, he opened the college register and flicked through it until he came to: Jericho, T. R. G.; matriculated, 1935; Senior Wrangler, Mathematics Tripos, 1938; Junior Research Fellow at two hundred pounds a year; not seen in the university since the outbreak of war.

Jericho? Jericho? To the Provost he was at best a dim memory, a fuzzy adolescent blob on a college photograph. Once, perhaps, he would have remembered the name, but the war had shattered the sonorous rhythm of intake and graduation and all was chaos – the Pitt Club was a British Restaurant, potatoes and onions were growing in the gardens of St John's ...

'He has recently been engaged upon work of the gravest national importance,' continued the caller. 'We would appreciate it if he were not disturbed.'

'Understood,' said the Provost. 'Understood. I shall see to it he is left alone.'

'We are obliged to you.'

The official rang off. '*Work of the gravest national importance*', by God ... The old man knew what that meant. He hung up and looked thoughtfully at the receiver for a few moments, then went in search of the domestic bursar.

*

A Cambridge college is a village, with a village's appetite for gossip – all the keener when that village is nine-tenths empty – and the return of Jericho provoked hours of analysis among the college staff.

There was, for a start, the manner of his arrival – a few hours after the call to the Provost, late on a snowy night, swaddled in a travelling rug, in the back of a cavernous official Rover driven by a young chauffeuse in the dark blue uniform of the Women's Royal Navy. Kite, the porter, who offered to carry the visitor's bags to his rooms, reported that Jericho clung to his pair of battered leather suitcases and refused to let go of either, even though he looked so pale and worn out that Kite doubted he would make it up the spiral staircase unaided.

Dorothy Saxmundham, the bedder, saw him next, when she went in the following day to tidy up. He was propped on his pillows staring out at the sleet pattering across the river, and he never turned his head, never even looked at her, didn't seem to know she was there, poor lamb. Then she went to move one of his cases and he was up in a flash – 'Please don't touch that, thank you so much, Mrs Sax, thank you' – and she was out on the landing in a quarter of a minute.

He had only one visitor: the college doctor, who saw him twice, stayed for about fifteen minutes on each occasion, and left without saying a word.

He took all his meals in his room for the first week – not that he ate very much, according to Oliver Bickerdyke, who worked in the kitchens: he took up a tray three times a day, only to take it away again an hour later, barely touched. Bickerdyke's great coup, which led to at least an hour of speculation around the coke stove in the Porter's Lodge, was to come upon the young man working at his desk, wearing a coat over his pyjamas, a scarf and a pair of mittens. Normally, Jericho 'sported his oak' – that is to say, he kept the heavy outer door to his study firmly shut – and called politely for his tray to be left outside. But on this particular morning, six days after his dramatic arrival, he had left it slightly ajar. Bickerdyke deliberately brushed the wood lightly with his knuckles, so quietly as to be inaudible to any living creature, save possibly a grazing gazelle, and then he was across the threshold and within a yard of his quarry before Jericho turned round. Bickerdyke just had time to register piles of papers ('covered in figures and circuits and Greek and suchlike') before the work was hastily covered up and he was sent on his way. Thereafter the door remained locked.

Listening to Bickerdyke's tale the next afternoon, and not wishing to be outdone, Dorothy Saxmundham added a detail of her own. Mr Jericho had a small gas fire in his sitting room and a grate in his bedroom. In the grate, which she had cleaned that morning, he had obviously burned a quantity of paper.

There was silence while this intelligence was digested.

'Could be *The Times*,' said Kite eventually. 'I puts a copy of *The Times* under his door every morning.'

No, declared Mrs Sax. It was not *The Times*. They were still in a pile by the bed. 'He doesn't seem to read them, not as I've noticed. He just does the crosswords.'

Bickerdyke suggested he was burning letters. 'Maybe love letters,' he added, with a leer.

'Love letters? Him? Get away.' Kite took off his antique bowler hat, inspected its frayed brim, then replaced it carefully on his bald head. 'Besides, he ain't had any letters, not a single one, not since he's been here.'

And so they were forced to the conclusion that what Jericho was burning in his grate was his work – work so secret, nobody could be allowed to see even a fragment of the waste. In the absence of hard fact, fantasy was piled upon fantasy. He was a government scientist, they decided. No, he worked in Intelligence. No, no – he was a genius. He had had a nervous breakdown. His presence in Cambridge was an official secret. He had friends in high places. He had met Mr Churchill. He had met the King ...

In all of which speculation, they would have been gratified to learn, they were absolutely and precisely correct.

*

Three days later, early on the morning of Friday 26 February, the mystery was given a fresh twist.

Kite was sorting the first delivery of mail, stuffing a small sackful of letters into the few pigeon holes whose owners were still in college, when he came across not one but three envelopes addressed to T. R. G. Jericho Esq, originally sent care of the White Hart Inn, Shenley Church End, Buckinghamshire, and subsequently forwarded to King's. For a moment, Kite was taken aback. Did the strange young man, for whom they had constructed such an exotic identity, in reality manage a *pub*? He pushed his spectacles up on to his forehead, held the envelope at arm's length, and squinted at the postmarks.

Bletchley.

There was an old Ordnance Survey map hanging at the back of the lodge, showing the dense triangle of southern England enclosed by Cambridge, Oxford and London. Bletchley sat astride a big railway junction exactly midway between the two university towns. Shenley Church End was a tiny hamlet about four miles north-west of it.

Kite studied the more interesting of the three envelopes. He raised it to his bulbous, blue-veined nose. He sniffed it. He had been sorting mail for more than forty years and he knew a woman's handwriting when he saw it: clearer and neater, more looped and less angular than a man's. A kettle was boiling on the gas ring at the back of the stove. He glanced around. It was not yet eight, and barely light outside. Within seconds he had stepped into the alcove and was holding the flap of the envelope to the steam. It was made of thin, shoddy wartime paper, sealed with cheap glue. The flap quickly moistened, curled, opened, and Kite extracted a card.

He had just about read through to the end when he heard the lodge door open. A blast of wind shook the windows. He stuffed the card back into the envelope, dipped his little finger into the glue pot kept ready by the stove, stuck down the flap, then casually poked his head round the corner to see who had come in. He almost had a stroke.

'Good heavens – morning – Mr Jericho – sir ...'

'Are there any letters for me, Mr Kite?' Jericho's voice was firm enough, but he seemed to sway slightly and held on to the counter like a sailor who had just stepped ashore after a long voyage. He was a pale young man, quite short, with dark hair and dark eyes – twin darknesses that served to emphasise the pallor of his skin.

'Not as I've noticed, sir. I'll look again.'

Kite retreated with dignity to the alcove and tried to iron out the damp envelope with his sleeve. It was only slightly crumpled. He slipped it into the middle of a handful of letters, came out to the front, and performed – even if he said so himself – a virtuoso pantomime of searching through them.

'No, no, nothing, no. Ah, yes, here's something. Gracious. And two more.' Kite proffered them across the counter. 'Your birthday, sir?'

'Yesterday.' Jericho stuffed the envelopes into the inside pocket of his overcoat without glancing at them.

'Many happy returns, sir.' Kite watched the letters disappear and gave a silent sigh of relief. He folded his arms and leaned forward on the counter. 'Might I hazard a guess at your age, sir? Came up in 'thirty-five, as I recall. Would that make you, perhaps, twenty-six?'

'I say, is that my newspaper, Mr Kite? Perhaps I might take it. Save you the trouble.'

Kite grunted, pushed himself back up on his feet and fetched it.

He made one last attempt at conversation as he handed it over, remarking on the satisfactory progress of the war in Russia since Stalingrad and Hitler being finished if you asked him – but, of course, that he, Jericho, would surely be more up to date about such matters than he, Kite ...? The younger man merely smiled.

'I doubt if my knowledge about anything is as up to date as yours, Mr Kite, not even about myself. Knowing your methods.'

For a moment, Kite was not sure he had heard correctly. He stared sharply at Jericho, who met his gaze and held it with his dark brown eyes, which seemed suddenly to have acquired a glint of life. Then, still smiling, Jericho nodded 'Good morning', tucked his paper under his arm and was gone. Kite watched him through the lodge's mullioned window – a slender figure in a college scarf of purple and white, unsteady on his feet, head bowed into the wind. 'My methods,' he repeated to himself. 'My *methods*?'

That afternoon, when the trio gathered for tea as usual around the coke stove, he was able to advance a whole new explanation for Jericho's presence in their midst. Naturally, he could not disclose how he came by his information, only that it was especially reliable (he hinted at a man-to-man chat). Forgetting his earlier scorn about love letters, Kite now asserted with confidence that the young fellow was obviously suffering from a broken heart.

2

Jericho did not open his letters immediately. Instead he squared his shoulders and tilted forwards into the wind. After a week in his room, the richness of the oxygen pummelling his face made him feel light-headed. He turned right at the Junior Combination Room and followed the flagstone path that led through the college and over the little hump-back bridge to the water meadow beyond. To his left was the college hall, to his right, across a great expanse of lawn, the massive cliff-face of the chapel. A tiny column of choirboys was bobbing through its grey lee, gowns flapping in the gale.

He stopped, and a gust of wind rocked him on his heels, forcing him half a step backwards. A stone passageway led off from one side of the path, its arch grown over with untended ivy. He glanced, by force of habit, at the set of windows on the second floor. They were dark and shuttered. Here, too, the ivy had been allowed to grow unchecked, so that several of the small, diamond-shaped panes were lost behind thick foliage.

He hesitated, then stepped off the path, under the keystone, into the shadows.

The staircase was just as he remembered it, except that now this wing of the college was closed and the wind had blown dead leaves into the well of the steps. An old newspaper curled itself around his legs like a hungry cat. He tried the light switch. It clicked uselessly. There was no bulb. But he could still make out the name, one of three painted on a wooden board in elegant white capitals, now cracked and faded.

TURING, A.M.

How nervously he had climbed these stairs for the first time – when? in the summer of 1938? a world ago – to find a man barely five years older than himself, as shy as a freshman, with a hank of dark hair falling across his eyes: the great Alan Turing, the author of *On Computable Numbers*, the progenitor of the Universal Computing Machine ...

Turing had asked him what he proposed to take as his subject for his first year's research.

'Riemann's theory of prime numbers.'

'But I am researching Riemann myself.'

'I know,' Jericho had blurted out, 'that's why I chose it.'

And Turing had laughed at this outrageous display of hero worship, and had agreed to supervise Jericho's research, even though he hated teaching.

Now Jericho stood on the landing and tried Turing's door. Locked, of course. The dust smeared his hand. He tried to remember how the room had looked. Squalor had been the overwhelming impression. Books, notes, letters, dirty clothes, empty bottles and tins of food had been strewn across the floor. There had been a teddy bear called Porgy on the mantelpiece above the gas fire, and a battered violin leaning in the corner, which Turing had picked up in a junk shop.

Turing had been too shy a man to get to know well. In any case, from the Christmas of 1938 he was hardly ever to be seen. He would cancel supervisions at the last minute saying he had to be in London. Or Jericho would climb these stairs and knock and there would be no reply, even though Jericho could sense he was behind the door. When, at last, around Easter 1939, not long after the Nazis had marched into Prague, the two men had finally met, Jericho had nerved himself to say: 'Look, sir, if you don't want to supervise me ...'

'It's not that.'

'Or if you're making progress on the Riemann Hypothesis and you don't want to share it ...'

Turing had smiled. 'Tom, I can assure you I am making no progress on Riemann whatsoever.'

'Then what ...?'

'It's not Riemann.' And then he had added, very quietly: 'There are other things now happening in the world, you know, apart from mathematics ...'

Two days later Jericho had found a note in his pigeonhole.

'Please join me for a glass of sherry in my rooms this evening. F.J. Atwood.'

Jericho turned from Turing's room. He felt faint. He gripped the worn handrail, taking each step carefully, like an old man.

Atwood. Nobody refused an invitation from Atwood, professor of ancient history, dean of the college before Jericho was even born, a man with a spider's web of connections in Whitehall. It was tantamount to a summons from God.

'Speak any languages?' had been Atwood's opening question as he poured the drinks. He was in his fifties, a bachelor, married to the college. His books were arranged prominently on the shelf behind him. *The Greek and Macedonian Art of War*. *Caesar as Man of Letters*. *Thucydides and His History*.

'Only German.' Jericho had learned it in adolescence to read the great nineteenth-century mathematicians – Gauss, Kummer, Hilbert.

Atwood had nodded and handed over a tiny measure of very dry sherry in a crystal glass. He followed Jericho's gaze to the books. 'Do you know Herodotus, by any chance? Do you know the story of Histiaeus?'

It was a rhetorical question; Atwood's questions mostly were.

'Histiaeus wished to send a message from the Persian court to his son-in-law, the tyrant Aristagoras, at Miletus, urging him to rise in revolt. However, he feared any such communication would be intercepted. His solution was to shave the head of his most trusted slave, tattoo the message onto his naked scalp, wait for his hair to grow, then send him to Aristagoras with a request that he be given a haircut. Unreliable but, in his case, effective. Your health.'

Jericho learned later that Atwood told the same stories to all his recruits. Histiaeus and his bald slave gave way to Polybius and his cipher square, then came Caesar's letter to Cicero using an alphabet in which *a* was enciphered as *d*, *b* as *e*, *c* as *f*, and so forth.

Finally, still circling the subject, but closer now, had come the lesson in etymology.

'The Latin *crypta*, from the Greek root κρῦπτη meaning "hidden, concealed". Hence *crypt*, burial place of the dead, and *crypto*, secret. Crypto-communist, crypto-fascist ... By the way, you're not either, are you?'

'I'm not a burial place of the dead, no.'

'*Cryptogram* ...' Atwood had raised his sherry to the light and squinted at the pale liquid. '*Cryptanalysis* ... Turing tells me he thinks you might be rather good ...'

*

Jericho was running a fever by the time he reached his rooms. He locked the door and flopped face down on his unmade bed, still wearing his coat and scarf. Presently he heard footsteps and someone knocked.

'Breakfast, sir.'

'Just leave it outside. Thank you.'

'Are you all right, sir?'

'I'm fine.'

He heard the clatter of the tray being set down, and steps retreating. The room seemed to be lurching and swelling out of all proportion, a corner of the ceiling was suddenly huge and close enough to touch. He closed his eyes and the visions came up at him through the darkness –

– Turing, smiling his shy half smile: 'Tom, I can assure you, I am making no progress on Riemann whatsoever ...'

– Logie, pumping his hand in the Bombe Hut, shouting above the noise of the machinery, 'The Prime Minister has just been on the telephone with his congratulations ...'

– Claire, touching his cheek, whispering, 'Poor you, I've really got under your skin, haven't I, poor you ...'

– 'Stand back' – a man's voice, Logie's voice – 'Stand back, give him air ...'

And then there was nothing.

*

When he woke, the first thing he did was look at his watch. He'd been unconscious for about an hour. He sat up and patted his overcoat pockets. Somewhere he had a notebook in which he recorded the duration of each attack, and the symptoms. It was a distressingly long list. He found instead the three envelopes.

He laid them out on the bed and considered them for a while. Then he opened two of them. One was a card from his mother, the other from his aunt, both wishing him a happy birthday. Neither woman had any idea what he was doing and both, he knew, were guiltily disappointed he wasn't in uniform and being shot at, like the sons of most of their friends.

'But what do I tell people?' his mother had asked him in despair during one of his brief visits home, after he had refused yet again to tell her what he did.

'Tell them I'm in government communications,' he had replied, using the formula they had been instructed to deploy in the face of persistent enquiries.

'But perhaps they'd like to know a little more than that.'

'Then they're acting suspiciously and you should call the police.'

His mother had contemplated the social catastrophe of her bridge four being interviewed by the local inspector, and had fallen silent.

And the third letter? Like Kite before him, he turned it over and sniffed it. Was it his imagination or was there a trace of scent? Ashes of Roses by Bourjois, a minuscule bottle of which had practically bankrupted him just a month earlier. He used his slide rule as a paperknife and slit the envelope open. Inside was a cheap card, carelessly chosen – it showed a bowl of fruit, of all things – and a standard message for the circumstances, or so he guessed, never having been in this situation before. 'Dearest T ... always see you as a friend ... perhaps in the future ... sorry to hear about ... in haste ... much love ...' He closed his eyes.

*

Later, after he had filled in the crossword, after Mrs Sax had finished the cleaning, after Bickerdyke had deposited another tray of food and taken it away again untouched, Jericho got down on his hands and knees and tugged a suitcase from beneath his bed and unlocked it. Folded into the middle of his 1930 Doubleday first edition of *The Complete Sherlock Holmes* were six sheets of foolscap covered in his tiny writing. He took them over to the rickety desk beside the window and smoothed them out.

'The cipher machine converts the input (plain language, P) into cipher (Z) by means of a function f. Thus $Z = f(P,K)$ *where K denotes the key ...'*

He sharpened his pencil, blew away the shavings and bent over the sheets.

'Suppose K has N possible values. For each of the N assumptions we must see if $f^{-1}(Z,K)$ *produces plain language, where* f^{-1} *is the deciphering function which produces P if K is correct ...'*

The wind ruffled the surface of the Cam. A flotilla of ducks rode the waves, without moving, like ships at anchor. He put down his pencil and read her card again, trying to measure the emotion, the meaning behind the flat phrases. Could one, he wondered, construct a similar formula for letters – for love letters or for letters signalling the end of love?

'The input (sentiment, S) is converted into a message (M) by the

woman, by means of the function w. Thus M = w(S,V) where V denotes the vocabulary. Suppose V has N possible values ...'

The mathematical symbols blurred before his eyes. He took the card into the bedroom, to the grate, knelt and struck a match. The paper flared briefly and twisted in his hand, then swiftly turned to ash.

*

Gradually his days acquired a shape.

He would rise early and work for two or three hours. Not at cryptanalysis – he burned all that on the day he burned her card – but at pure mathematics. Then he would take a nap. He would fill in *The Times* crossword before lunch, timing himself on his father's old pocket watch – it never took him more than five minutes to complete it, and once he finished it in three minutes forty. He managed to solve a series of complex chess problems – 'the hymn tunes of mathematics', as G.H. Hardy called them – without using pieces or a board. All this reassured him his brain had not been permanently impaired.

After the crossword and the chess he would skim through the war news while trying to eat something at his desk. He tried to avoid the Battle of the Atlantic (DEAD MEN AT THE OARS: U-BOAT VICTIMS FROZEN IN LIFEBOATS) and concentrated instead on the Russian Front: Pavlograd, Demiansk, Rzhev ... the Soviets seemed to recapture a new town every few hours and he was amused to find *The Times* reporting Red Army Day as respectfully as if it were the King's Birthday.

In the afternoon he would walk, a little further on each occasion – at first confining himself to the college grounds, then strolling through the empty town, and finally venturing into the frozen countryside – before returning as the light faded to sit by the gas fire and read his Sherlock Holmes. He began to go into

Hall for dinner, although he declined politely the Provost's offer of a place at High Table. The food was as bad as at Bletchley, but the surroundings were better, the candlelight flickering on the heavy-framed portraits and gleaming on the long tables of polished oak. He learned to ignore the frankly curious stares of the college staff. Attempts at conversation he cut off with a nod. He didn't mind being solitary. Solitude had been his life. An only child, a stepchild, a 'gifted' child – always there had been something to set him apart. At one time he couldn't speak about his work because hardly anyone would understand him. Now he couldn't speak of it because it was classified. It was all the same.

By the end of his second week he had actually started to sleep through the night, a feat he hadn't managed for more than two years.

Shark, Enigma, kiss, bombe, break, pinch, drop, crib – all the weird vocabulary of his secret life he slowly succeeded in erasing from his conscious mind. To his astonishment, even Claire's image became diffuse. There were still vivid flashes of memory, especially at night – the lemony smell of newly washed hair, the wide grey eyes as pale as water, the soft voice half amused, half bored – but increasingly the parts failed to cohere. The whole was vanishing.

He wrote to his mother and persuaded her not to visit him.

'Nurse Time,' the doctor had said, snapping shut his bag of tricks, 'that's who'll cure you, Mr Jericho. Nurse Time.'

Rather to Jericho's surprise it seemed that the old boy was right. He was going to be well again. 'Nervous exhaustion' or whatever they called it was not the same as madness after all.

And then, without warning, on Friday 12 March, they came for him.

*

The night before it happened he had overheard an elderly don complaining about a new air base the Americans were building to the east of the city.

'I said to them, you do realise you're standing on a fossil site of the Pleistocene era? That I myself have removed from here the horncores of *Bos primigenius*? D'you know, the fellow merely *laughed* ...'

Good for the Yanks, thought Jericho, and he decided there and then it would make a suitable destination for his afternoon walk. Because it would take him at least three miles further than he had attempted so far, he left earlier than usual, straight after lunch.

He strode briskly along the Backs, past the Wren Library and the icing sugar towers of St John's, past the sports field in which two dozen little boys in purple shirts were playing football, and then turned left, trudging beside the Madingley Road. After ten minutes he was in open country.

Kite had gloomily predicted snow, but although it was still cold it was sunny and the sky was a glory – a pure blue dome above the flat landscape of East Anglia, filled for miles with the silver specks of aircraft and the white scratches of contrails. Before the war he had cycled through this quiet countryside almost every week and had barely seen a car. Now an endless succession of big American trucks lumbered past him, forcing him on to the verge – brasher, faster, more modern than British Army lorries, covered over at the back with camouflaged tarpaulins. The white faces of the US airmen peered out of the shadows. Sometimes the men shouted and waved and he waved back, feeling absurdly English and self-conscious.

Eventually he came within sight of the new base and stood beside the road watching three Flying Fortresses take off in the distance, one after the other – vast aircraft, almost too heavy, or so it seemed to Jericho, to escape the ground. They lumbered along the fresh concrete runway, roaring with frustration, clawing at the air for liberation until suddenly a crack of daylight appeared beneath them, and the crack widened, and they were aloft.

He stood there for almost half an hour, feeling the air pulse with the vibrations of their engines, smelling the faint scent of aviation spirit carried on the cold air. He had never seen such a demonstration of power. The fossils of the Pleistocene era, he reflected with grim delight, must now be so much dust. What was that line of Cicero that Atwood was so fond of quoting? '*Nervos belli, pecuniam infinitam.*' The sinews of war, unlimited money.

He looked at his watch and realised he had better turn back if he was going to reach the college before dark.

He had gone about a mile when he heard an engine behind him. A jeep overtook him, swerved and stopped. The driver, wrapped in a heavy overcoat, stood up and beckoned to him.

'Hey, fella! Wanna lift?'

'That would be kind. Thank you.'

'Jump in.'

The American didn't want to talk, which suited Jericho. He gripped the edges of his seat and stared ahead as they bounced and rattled at speed down the darkening lanes and into the town. The driver dropped him at the back of the college, waved, gunned the engine, and was gone. Jericho watched him disappear, then turned and walked through the gate.

Before the war, this three-hundred-yard walk, at this time of day, at this time of year, had been Jericho's favourite: the footpath running across a carpet of mauve and yellow crocuses, the worn stones lit by ornate Victorian lamps, the spires of the chapel to the left, the lights of the college to the right. But the crocuses were late, the lanterns had not been switched on since 1939, and a static water tank disfigured the famous aspect of the chapel. Only one light gleamed faintly in the college and as he walked towards it he gradually realised it was *his* window.

He stopped, frowning. Had he left his desk light on? He was sure he hadn't. As he watched, he saw a shadow, a movement, a figure in the pale yellow square. Two seconds later the light went on in his bedroom.

It wasn't possible, was it?

He started to run. He covered the distance to his staircase in thirty seconds and took the steps like an athlete. His boots clattered on the worn stone. 'Claire?' he shouted. 'Claire?' On the landing his door stood open.

'Steady on, old thing,' said a male voice from within, 'you'll do yourself a mischief.'

3

Guy Logie was a tall, cadaverous man, ten years older than Jericho. He lay on his back on the sofa facing the door, his neck on one armrest, his bony ankles dangling over the other, long hands folded neatly on his stomach. A pipe was clamped between his teeth and he was blowing smoke rings at the ceiling. Distended haloes drifted upwards, twisted, broke and melted into haze. He took his pipe from his mouth and gave an elaborate yawn which seemed to take him by surprise.

'Oh, God. Sorry.' He opened his eyes and swung himself into a sitting position. 'Hello, Tom.'

'Oh please. Please, don't get up,' said Jericho. 'Please, I insist, make yourself at home. Perhaps I could get you some tea?'

'Tea. What a grand idea.' Before the war Logie had been head of mathematics at a vast and ancient public school. He had a

Blue in rugger and another in hockey and irony bounced off him like pebbles off an advancing rhinoceros. He crossed the room and grasped Jericho by the shoulders. 'Come here. Let me look at you, old thing,' he said, turning him this way and that towards the light. 'Oh dear oh dear, you do look bloody terrible.'

Jericho shrugged himself free. 'I *was* fine.'

'Sorry. We did knock. Your porter chap let us in.'

'Us?'

There was a noise from the bedroom.

'We came in the car with the flag on it. Greatly impressed your Mr Kite.' Logie followed Jericho's gaze to the bedroom door. 'Oh, that? That's Leveret. Don't mind him.' He took out his pipe and called: 'Mr Leveret! Come and meet Mr Jericho. The *famous* Mr Jericho.'

A small man with a thin face appeared at the entrance to the bedroom.

'Good afternoon, sir.' Leveret wore a raincoat and trilby. His voice had a slight northern accent.

'What the hell are you doing in there?'

'He's just checking you're alone,' said Logie sweetly.

'Of course I'm bloody well alone!'

'And is the whole staircase empty, sir?' enquired Leveret. 'Nobody in the rooms above or below?'

Jericho threw up his hands in exasperation. 'Guy, for God's sake!'

'I think it's all clear,' said Leveret to Logie. 'I've already closed the blackout curtains in there.' He turned to Jericho. 'Mind if I do the same here, sir?' He didn't wait for permission. He crossed to the small leaded window, opened it, took off his hat and thrust his head out, peering up and down, left and right. A freezing mist was rising off the river and a blast of chill air filled the room. Satisfied,

Leveret ducked back inside, closed the window and drew the curtains.

There was a quarter of a minute's silence. Logie broke it by rubbing his hands and saying: 'Any chance of a fire, Tom? I'd forgotten what this place was like in winter. Worse than school. And tea? You mentioned tea? Would you like some tea, Mr Leveret?'

'I would indeed, sir.'

'And what about some toast? I noticed you had some bread, Tom, in the kitchen over there. Toast in front of a college fire? Wouldn't that take us back?'

Jericho looked at him for a moment. He opened his mouth to protest then changed his mind. He took a box of matches from the mantelpiece, struck a light and held it to the gas fire. As usual the pressure was low and the match went out. He lit another and this time it caught. A worm of flame glowed blue and began to spread. He went across the landing to the little kitchen, filled the kettle and lit the gas ring. In the bread bin there was indeed a loaf – Mrs Saxmundham must have put it there earlier in the week – and he sawed off three grey slices. In the cupboard he found a pre-war pot of jam, surprisingly presentable after he had scraped the white fur of mould from its surface, and a smear of margarine on a chipped plate. He arranged his delicacies on a tray and stared at the kettle.

Perhaps he *was* having a dream? But when he looked back into his sitting room, there was Logie stretched out again on the sofa, and Leveret perched uneasily on the edge of one of the chairs, his hat in his hands, like an unreliable witness waiting to go into court with an under-rehearsed story.

Of course they had brought bad news. What else could it be but bad news? The acting head of Hut 8 wouldn't travel fifty miles across country in the deputy director's precious bloody car just to pay a social call. They were going to sack him. '*Sorry, old thing, but we can't carry passengers ...*' Jericho felt suddenly very tired. He massaged his forehead with the heel of his hand. The familiar headache was beginning to return, spreading up from his sinuses to the back of his eyes.

He had thought it was her. That was the joke. For about half a minute, running towards the lighted window, he had been happy. It was pitiful.

The kettle was beginning to boil. He prised open the tea caddy to find age had reduced the tea leaves to dust. Nevertheless he spooned them into the pot and tipped in the hot water.

Logie pronounced it nectar.

*

Afterwards they sat in silence in the semi-darkness. The only illumination was provided by the faint gleam of the desk lamp behind them and the blue glow of the fire at their feet. The gas jet hissed. From beyond the blackout curtains came a faint flurry of splashes and the mournful quacking of a duck. Logie sat on the floor, his long legs outstretched, fiddling with his pipe. Jericho slouched in one of the two easy chairs, prodding the carpet absent-mindedly with the toasting fork. Leveret had been told to stand guard outside: 'Would you mind closing both doors, old thing? The inner door and the outer door, if you'd be so kind?'

The warm aroma of toast hung over the room. Their plates had been pushed to one side.

'This really is most companionable,' murmured Logie. He struck a match and the objects on the mantelpiece threw brief shadows on the damp wall. 'Although one appreciates that one is, in a sense, *fortunate* to be in a place like Bletchley, given where else one might be, one does start to get rather *down* with the sheer *drabness* of it all. Don't you find?'

'I suppose so.' Oh, do get on with it, thought Jericho, stabbing at a couple of crumbs. Just sack me and leave.

Logie made a contented sucking noise through his pipe, then said quietly: 'You know, we've all been terribly worried about you, Tom. I do hope you haven't felt abandoned.'

At this unexpected display of concern, Jericho was surprised and humiliated to find tears pricking at his eyes. He kept looking down at the carpet. 'I'm afraid I made the most frightful ass of myself, Guy. The worst of it is, I can't really remember much of what happened. There's almost a week that's pretty well a blank.'

Logie gave a dismissive wave of his pipe. 'You're not the first to bust his health in that place, old thing. Did you see in *The Times* poor Dilly Knox died last week? They gave him a gong at the end. Nothing too fancy – CMG, I think. Insisted on receiving it at home, personally, propped up in his chair. Dead two days later. Cancer. Ghastly. And then there was Jeffreys. Remember him?'

'He was sent back to Cambridge to recover as well.'

'That's the man. Whatever happened to Jeffreys?'

'He died.'

'Ah. Shame.' Logie performed a bit more pipe smoker's business, tamping down the tobacco and striking another match.

Just don't let them put me in admin, prayed Jericho. Or Welfare. There was a man in Welfare, Claire had told him, in charge of billeting, who made the girls sit on his knee if they wanted digs with a bathroom.

'It was Shark, wasn't it,' said Logie, giving him a shrewd look through a cloud of smoke, 'that did for you?'

'Yes. Perhaps. You could say that.'

Shark nearly did for all of us, thought Jericho.

'But you broke it,' pursued Logie. 'You broke Shark.'

'I wouldn't put it quite like that. *We* broke it.'

'No. *You* broke it.' Logie twirled the spent match in his long fingers. 'You broke it. And then it broke you.'

Jericho had a sudden memory-flash of himself on a bicycle, under a starlit sky. A cold night and the cracking of ice.

'Look,' he said, suddenly irritated, 'd'you think we could get to the point here, Guy? I mean, tea in front of the college fire talking about old times? It's all very pleasant, but come on –'

'This *is* the point, old thing.' Logie drew his knees up under his chin and wrapped his hands around his shins. 'Shark, Limpet, Dolphin, Oyster, Porpoise, Winkle. The six little fishes in our aquarium, the six German naval Enigmas. And the greatest of these is Shark.' He stared into the fire and for the first time Jericho was able to have a good look at his face, ghostly in the blue light, like a skull. The eye sockets were hollows of darkness. He looked like a man who hadn't slept for a week. He yawned again. 'You know, I was trying to remember, in the car coming over, who decided to call it Shark in the first place.'

'I can't recall,' said Jericho. 'I've an idea it was Alan. Or maybe it was me. Anyway, what the devil does it matter? It just emerged. Nobody argued. Shark was the perfect name for it. We could tell at once it was going to be a monster.'

'And it was.' Logie puffed on his pipe. He was starting to disappear in a bank of fumes. The cheap wartime tobacco smelled like burning hay. 'And it is.'

Something in the way he delivered that last word – some slight hesitation – made Jericho look up sharply.

*

The Germans called it Triton, after the son of Poseidon, the demigod of the ocean who blew through a twisted seashell to raise the furies of the deep. 'German humour,' Puck had groaned when they discovered the code name, 'German fucking humour ...' But at Bletchley they stuck to Shark. It was a tradition, and they were British and they liked their traditions. They named all the enemy's ciphers after sea creatures. The main German naval cipher they called Dolphin. Porpoise was the Enigma key for Mediterranean surface vessels and shipping in the Black Sea. Oyster was an 'officer only' variation on Dolphin. Winkle was the 'officer only' variant of Porpoise.

And Shark? Shark was the operational cipher of the U-boats.

Shark was unique. Every other cipher was produced on a standard three-rotor Enigma machine. But Shark came out of an Enigma with a specially adapted fourth rotor which made it twenty-six times more difficult to break. Only U-boats were allowed to carry it.

It came into service on 1 February 1942 and it blacked out Bletchley almost completely.

Jericho remembered the months that followed as a prolonged nightmare. Before the advent of Shark, the cryptanalysts in Hut 8 had been able to break most U-boat transmissions within a day of interception, allowing ample time to re-route convoys around the wolf packs of German submarines. But in the ten months after the introduction of Shark they read the traffic on just three occasions, and even then it took them seventeen days each time, so that the intelligence, when it did arrive, was virtually useless, was ancient history.

To encourage them in their labours a graph was posted in the code-breakers' hut, showing the monthly tonnages of shipping sunk by the U-boats in the North Atlantic. In January, before the blackout, the Germans destroyed forty-eight Allied ships. In February they sank seventy-three. In March, ninety-five. In May, one hundred and twenty ...

'The weight of our failure,' said Skynner, the head of the Naval

Section, in one of his portentous weekly addresses, 'is measured in the bodies of drowned men.'

In September, ninety-five ships were sunk. In November, ninety-three ...

And then came Fasson and Grazier.

*

Somewhere in the distance the college clock began to toll. Jericho found himself counting the chimes.

'Are you all right, old thing? You've gone terribly silent.'

'Sorry. I was just thinking. Do you remember Fasson and Grazier?'

'Fasson and who? Sorry, I don't think I ever met them.'

'No. Nor did I. None of us did.'

*

Fasson and Grazier. He never knew their Christian names. A first lieutenant and an able-bodied seaman. Their destroyer had helped trap a U-boat, the *U-459*, in the eastern Mediterranean. They had depth-charged her and forced her to the surface. It was about ten o'clock at night. A rough sea, a wind blowing up. After the surviving Germans had abandoned the submarine, the two British sailors had stripped off and swum out to her, lit by searchlights. The U-boat was already low in the waves, holed in the conning tower by cannon fire, shipping water fast. They'd brought off a bundle of secret papers from the radio room, handing them to a boarding party in a boat alongside, and had just gone back for the Enigma machine itself when the U-boat suddenly went bows up and sank. They went down with her – half a mile down, the Navy man had said when he told them the story in Hut 8. *'Let's just hope they were dead before they hit the bottom.'*

And then he'd produced the code books. This was on 24

November 1942. More than nine and a half months into the blackout.

At first glance they scarcely looked worth the cost of two men's lives: two little pamphlets, the Short Signal Book and the Short Weather Cipher, printed in soluble ink on pink blotting paper, designed to be dropped into water by the wireless operator at the first sign of trouble. But to Bletchley they were beyond price, worth more than all the sunken treasure ever raised in history. Jericho knew them by heart even now. He closed his eyes and the symbols were still there, burned into the back of his retina.

T = Lufttemperatur in ganzen Celsius-Graden. –28C = a. –27C = b. –26C = c ...

U-boats made daily weather reports: air temperature, barometric pressure, wind-speed, cloud-cover ... The Short Weather Cipher book reduced that data to a half-dozen letters. Those half-dozen letters were enciphered on the Enigma. The message was then broadcast from the submarine in Morse code and picked up by the German Navy's coastal weather stations. The weather stations used the U-boats' data to compile meteorological reports of their own. These reports were then re-broadcast, an hour or two later, in a standard three-rotor Enigma weather cipher – *a cipher Bletchley could break* – for the use of every German vessel.

It was the back door into Shark.

First, you read the weather report. Then you put the weather report back into the short weather cipher. And what you were left with, by a process of logical deduction, was the text that had been fed into the four-rotor Enigma a few hours earlier. It was a perfect crib. A cryptanalyst's dream.

But still they couldn't break it.

Every day the code-breakers, Jericho among them, fed their possible solutions into the bombes – immense electro-mechanical computers, each the size of a walk-in wardrobe, which made a noise like a knitting machine – and waited to be told which guess was correct. And every day they received no answer. The task was simply too great. Even a message enciphered on a three-rotor Enigma might take twenty-four hours to decode, as the bombes clattered their way through the billions of permutations. A four-rotor Enigma, multiplying the numbers by a factor of twenty-six, would theoretically take the best part of a month.

For three weeks Jericho worked round the clock, and when he did grab an hour or two's sleep it was only to dream fitfully of drowning men. '*Let's just hope they were dead before they hit the bottom* ...' His brain was beyond tiredness. It ached physically, like an overworked muscle. He began to suffer blackouts. These only lasted a matter of seconds but they were frightening enough. One moment he might be working in the Hut, bent over his slide-rule, and the next everything around him had blurred and jumped on, as if a film had slipped its sprockets in a projector. He managed to beg some Benzedrine off the camp doctor but that only made his mood swings worse, his frenzied highs followed by increasingly protracted lows.

Curiously enough, the solution, when it came, had nothing to do with mathematics, and afterwards he was to reproach himself furiously for becoming too immersed in detail. If he had not been so tired, he might have stepped back and seen it earlier.

It was a Saturday night, the second Saturday in December. At about nine o'clock Logie had sent him home. Jericho had tried to argue, but Logie had said: 'No, you're going to kill yourself if you go on at this rate, and that won't be any use to anyone, old love, especially you.' So Jericho had cycled wearily back to his digs above the pub in Shenley Church End and had crawled beneath the bedclothes. He heard last orders called downstairs, listened as the final few regulars departed and the bar was closed up. In the dead hours after midnight he lay looking at the ceiling wondering if he would ever sleep again, his mind churning like a piece of machinery he couldn't switch off.

It had been obvious from the moment Shark had first surfaced that the only acceptable, long-term solution was to redesign the bombes to take account of the fourth rotor. But that was proving a nightmarishly slow process. If only they could somehow complete the mission Fasson and Grazier had begun so heroically and steal a Shark Enigma. That would make the redesign easier. But Shark Enigmas were the crown jewels of the German Navy. Only the U-boats had them. Only the U-boats and, of course, U-boat communication headquarters in Sainte-Assise, southeast of Paris.

A commando raid on Sainte-Assise, perhaps? A parachute drop? He played with the image for a moment and then dismissed it. Impossible. And, in any case, useless. Even if, by some miracle, they got away with a machine, the Germans would know about it, and switch to a different system of communications. Bletchley's future rested on the Germans continuing to believe that Enigma was impregnable. Nothing could ever be done which might jeopardise that confidence.

Wait a minute.

Jericho sat upright.

Wait a bloody minute.

If only the U-boats and their controllers in Sainte-Assise were allowed to have four-rotor Enigmas – and Bletchley knew for a fact that that was the case – how the hell were the coastal weather stations deciphering the U-boats' transmissions?

It was a question no one had bothered to stop and ask, yet it was fundamental.

To read a message enciphered on a four-rotor machine you had to have a four-rotor machine.

Or did you?

If it is true, as someone once said, that genius is 'a zigzag of lightning across the brain', then, in that instant, Jericho knew what genius was. He saw the solution lit up like a landscape before him.

He seized his dressing gown and pulled it over his pyjamas. He grabbed his overcoat, his scarf, his socks and his boots and in less than a minute he was on his bike, wobbling down the moonlit country lane towards the Park. The stars were bright, the ground was iron-hard with frost. He felt absurdly euphoric, laughing like a madman, steering directly into the frozen puddles along the edge of the road, the ice crusts rupturing under his tyres like drum skins. Down the hill he freewheeled into Bletchley. The countryside fell away and the town spread out beneath him in the moonlight, familiarly drab and ugly but on this night beautiful, as beautiful as Prague or Paris, perched on either bank of a gleaming river of railway tracks. In the still air he could hear a train half a mile away being shunted in the sidings – the sudden, frantic chugging of a locomotive followed by a series of clanks, then a long exhalation of steam. A dog barked and set off another. He passed the church and the war memorial, braked to avoid skidding on the ice, and turned left into Wilton Avenue.

He was panting with exertion by the time he reached the Hut, fifteen minutes later, so much so he could barely blurt out his discovery and catch his breath and stop himself from laughing at the same time: 'They're – using – it – as – a – three-rotor – machine – they're – leaving – the – fourth – rotor – in – neutral – when – they – do – the – weather – stuff – the – silly – bloody – buggers –'

His arrival caused a commotion. The night shift all stopped working and gathered in a concerned half-circle round him – he remembered Logie, Kingcome, Puck and Proudfoot – and it was clear from their expressions they thought he really had gone mad. They sat him down and gave him a mug of tea and told him to take it again, slowly, from the beginning.

He went through it once more, step by step, suddenly anxious there might be a flaw in his logic. Four-rotor Enigmas were restricted to U-boats and Sainte-Assise: correct? Correct. Therefore coastal stations could only decipher three-rotor Enigma messages: correct? Pause. Correct. Therefore, when the U-boats sent their weather reports, the wireless operators must logically disengage the fourth rotor, probably by setting it at zero.

After that, everything happened quickly. Puck ran along the corridor to the Big Room and laid out the best of the weather cribs on one of the trestle tables. By 4 A.M. they had a menu for the bombes. By breakfast one of the bombe bays was reporting a drop and Puck ran through the canteen like a schoolboy shouting: 'It's out! It's out!'

It was the stuff of legend.

At midday Logie telephoned the Admiralty and told the Submarine Tracking Room to stand by. Two hours later, they broke the Shark traffic for the previous Monday and the Teleprincesses, the gorgeous girls in the Teleprinter Room, began sending the translated decrypts down the line to London. They were indeed the crown jewels. Messages to raise the hairs on the back of your neck.

FROM: U-BOAT CAPTAIN SCHRÖDER
FORCED TO SUBMERGE BY DESTROYERS. NO CONTACT. LAST POSITION OF ENEMY AT 0815 NAVAL GRID SQUARE 1849. COURSE 45 DEGREES, SPEED 9 KNOTS.

FROM: GILADORNE
HAVE ATTACKED. CORRECT POSITION OF CONVOY IS AK1984. 050 DEGREES. AM RELOADING AND KEEPING CONTACT.

FROM: HAUSE
AT 0115 IN SQUARE 3969 ATTACKED, FLARES AND GUNFIRE,

DIVED, DEPTH CHARGES. NO DAMAGE. AM IN NAVAL GRID SQUARE AJ3996. ALL TIN FISH, 70 CBM.

FROM: FLAG OFFICER, U-BOATS
TO: 'DRAUFGÄNGER' WOLF PACK
TOMORROW AT 1700 BE IN NEW PATROL LINE FROM NAVAL GRID SQUARE AK2564 TO 2994. OPERATIONS AGAINST EASTBOUND CONVOY WHICH AT 1200/7/12 WAS IN NAVAL GRID SQUARE AK4189. COURSE 050 TO 070 DEGREES. SPEED APPROX 8 KNOTS.

By midnight they had broken, translated and teleprintered to London ninety-two Shark signals giving the Admiralty the approximate whereabouts and tactics of half the Germans' U-boat fleet.

Jericho was in the Bombe Hut when Logie found him. He had been chasing about for the best part of nine hours and now he was supervising a changeover on one of the machines, still wearing his pyjamas under his overcoat, to the great amusement of the Wrens who tended the bombe. Logie clasped Jericho's hand in both of his and shook it vigorously.

'The Prime Minister!' he shouted in Jericho's ear, above the clattering of the bombes.

'What?'

'The Prime Minister has just been on the telephone with his congratulations!'

Logie's voice seemed a long way away. Jericho bent forward to hear better what Churchill had said and then the concrete floor melted beneath his feet and he was pitching forwards into darkness.

*

'Is,' said Jericho.

'What, old thing?'

'Just now, you said Shark *was* a monster and then you said it *is* a monster.' He pointed the toasting fork at Logie. 'I know why you've come. You've lost it, haven't you?'

Logie grunted and stared into the fire and Jericho felt as though someone had laid a stone on his heart. He sat back in his chair, shaking his head, then gave a snort of laughter.

'Thank you, Tom,' said Logie, quietly. 'I'm glad you find it funny.'

'And all the time I thought you'd come here to give me the push. That's funny. That's pretty funny, isn't it, *old thing*?'

*

'What day is it today?' asked Logie.

'Friday.'

'Right, right.' Logie extinguished his pipe with his thumb and stuffed it into his pocket. He sighed. 'Let me see. That means it must have happened on Monday. No, Tuesday. Sorry. We haven't had a lot of sleep lately.'

He passed a hand through his thinning hair and Jericho noticed for the first time that he'd turned quite grey. So it's not just me, he thought, it's all of us, we're all falling to pieces. No fresh air. No sleep. Not enough fresh food. Six-day weeks and twelve-hour days ...

'We were still just about ahead of the game when you left,' said Logie. 'You know the drill. Of course you do. You wrote the bloody book. We'd wait for Hut 10 to break the main naval weather cipher, then, by lunchtime, with a bit of luck we'd have enough cribs to tackle the day's short weather codes. That would give us three of the four rotor settings and then we'd get stuck into

Shark. The time-lag varied. Sometimes we'd break it in one day, sometimes three or four. Anyway, the stuff was gold-dust and we were Whitehall's blue-eyed boys.'

'Until Tuesday.'

'Until Tuesday.' Logie glanced at the door and dropped his voice. 'It's an absolute tragedy, Tom. We'd cut losses in the North Atlantic by 75 per cent. That's about three hundred thousand tons of shipping a month. The intelligence was amazing. We knew where the U-boats were almost as precisely as the Germans did. Of course, looking back, it was too good to last. The Nazis aren't fools. I always said: "Success in this game breeds failure, and the bigger the success, the bigger the failure's likely to be." You'll remember me saying it. The other side gets suspicious, you see. I said –'

'What happened on Tuesday, Guy?'

'Right-ho. Sorry. Tuesday. It was about eight in the evening. We got a call from one of the intercept stations. Flowerdown, I think, but Scarborough heard it too. I was in the canteen. Puck came and fetched me out. They'd started picking up something in the early afternoon. A single word, broadcast on the hour, every hour. It was coming out of Sainte-Assise on both main U-boat radio nets.'

'This word was enciphered in Shark I take it?'

'No, that's just it. That's what they were so excited about. It wasn't in cipher. It wasn't even in Morse. It was a human voice. A man. Repeating this one word: *Akelei*.'

'*Akelei*,' murmured Jericho. '*Akelei* ... That's a flower, isn't it?'

'Ha!' Logie clapped his hands. 'You are a bloody marvel, Tom. See how much we miss you? We had to go and ask one of the German swots on Z-watch what it meant. *Akelei*: a five-petalled flower of the buttercup family, from the Latin *Aquilegia*. We vulgarians call it columbine.'

'*Akelei*,' repeated Jericho. 'This is a prearranged signal of some sort, presumably?'

'It is.'

'And it means?'

'It means trouble, is what it means, old love. We found out just how much trouble at midnight yesterday.' Logie leaned forwards. The humour had left his voice. His face was lined and grave. '*Akelei* means: "Change the Short Weather Code Book." They've gone over to a new one and we haven't a bloody clue what to do about it. They've closed off our way into Shark, Tom. They've blacked us out again.'

*

It didn't take Jericho long to pack. He'd bought nothing since he arrived in Cambridge except a daily newspaper, so he took out exactly what he'd carried in three weeks earlier: a pair of suitcases filled with clothes, a few books, a fountain pen, a slide rule and pencils, a portable chess set and a pair of walking boots. He laid his cases on the bed and moved slowly about the room collecting his possessions while Logie watched him from the doorway.

Running round and round in his head, unbidden from some hidden depth in his subconscious, was a nursery rhyme: 'For want of a nail, the horse was lost; for want of a horse, the rider was lost; for want of a rider, the battle was lost; for want of a battle, the kingdom was lost; and all for the want of a horseshoe nail ...'

He folded a shirt and laid it on top of his books.

For want of a Short Weather Code Book they might lose the Battle of the Atlantic. So many men, so much material, threatened by so small a thing as a change in weather codes. It was absurd.

'You can always tell a boarding-school boy,' said Logie, 'they travel light. All those endless train journeys, I suppose.'

'I prefer it.'

He stuffed a pair of socks down the side of the case. He was going back. They wanted him back. He couldn't decide whether he was elated or terrified.

'You don't have much stuff in Bletchley, either, do you?'

Jericho swung round to look at him. 'How do you know that?'

'Ah.' Logie winced with embarrassment. 'I'm afraid we had to pack up your room, and, ah, give it to someone else. Pressure of space and all that.'

'You didn't think I'd be coming back?'

'Well, let's say we didn't know we'd need you back so soon. Anyway, there's fresh digs for you in town, so at least it'll be more convenient. No more long cycle rides late at night.'

'I rather like long cycle rides late at night. They clear the mind.' Jericho closed the lids on the suitcases and snapped the locks.

'I say, you are up to this, old love? Nobody wants to force you into anything.'

'I'm a damn sight fitter than you are, by the look of you.'

'Only I'd hate you to feel pressured ...'

'Oh do shut up, Guy.'

'Right-ho. I suppose we haven't left you with much choice, have we? Can I help you with those?'

'If I'm well enough to go back to Bletchley, I'm well enough to manage a couple of suitcases.'

He carried them to the door and turned off the light. In the sitting room he extinguished the gas fire and took a last look around. The overstuffed sofa. The scratched chairs. The bare mantelpiece. This was his life, he thought, a succession of cheaply furnished rooms provided by English institutions: school, college, government. He wondered what the next room would be like. Logie opened the doors and Jericho turned off the desk light.

The staircase was in darkness. The bulb had long since died. Logie got them down the stone steps by striking a series of matches. At the bottom, they could just make out the shape of Leveret, standing guard, his silhouette framed against the black mass of the chapel. He turned round. His hand went to his pocket.

'All right, Mr Leveret,' said Logie. 'It's only me. Mr Jericho's coming with us.'

Leveret had a blackout torch, a cheap thing swathed in tissue paper. By its pale beam, and by the faint residue of light still left in the sky, they made their way through the college. As they walked alongside the Hall they could hear the clatter of cutlery and the sound of the diners' voices, and Jericho felt a pang of regret. They passed the Porter's Lodge and stepped through the man-sized gate cut in the big oak door. A crack of light appeared in one of the lodge's windows as someone inside pulled back the curtain a fraction. With Leveret in front of him and Logie behind, Jericho had a curious sensation of being under arrest.

The deputy director's Rover was pulled up on the cobbled pavement. Leveret carefully unlocked it and ushered them into the back seat. The interior was cold and smelled of old leather and cigarette ash. As Leveret was stowing the suitcases in the boot Logie said suddenly: 'Who's Claire, by the way?'

'Claire?' Jericho heard his voice in the darkness, guilty and defensive.

'When you came up the staircase I thought I heard you shouting "Claire". Claire?' Logie gave a low whistle. 'I say, she's not the arctic blonde in Hut 3, is she? I bet she is. You lucky bugger ...'

Leveret started the engine. It stuttered and backfired. He let out the brake and the big car rocked over the cobbles on to King's Parade. The long street was deserted in both directions. A wisp of mist shone in the shaded headlamps. Logie was still chuckling to himself as they swung left.

'I bet she jolly well is. You lucky, lucky bugger ...'

*

Kite stayed at his post by the window, watching the red tail-lights until they vanished past the corner of Gonville and Caius. He let the curtain drop.

Well, well ...

This would give them something to talk about the next morning. Listen to this, Dottie. Mr Jericho was taken away at dead of night – oh, all right then, eight o'clock – by two men, one a tall fellow and the other very obviously a plain clothes copper. Escorted from the premises and not a word to anyone. The tall chap and the copper had arrived about five o'clock while the young master was still out walking and the big one – the detective, presumably – had asked Kite all sorts of questions: 'Has he seen anyone since he's been here? Has he written to anyone? Has anyone written to him? What's he been doing?' Then they'd taken his keys and searched Jericho's room before Jericho got back.

It was murky. Very murky.

A spy, a genius, a broken heart – and now what? A criminal of some sort? Quite possibly. A malingerer? A runaway? A deserter! Yes, that was it: a deserter!

Kite went back to his seat by the stove and opened his evening paper.

NAZI SUB TORPEDOES PASSENGER LINER, he read. WOMEN AND CHILDREN LOST.

Kite shook his head at the wickedness of the world. It was disgusting, a young man of that age, not wearing uniform, hiding away in the middle of England while mothers and kiddies were being killed.

TWO

CRYPTOGRAM

CRYPTOGRAM: message written in cipher or in some other secret form which requires a key qv for its meaning to be discovered.

A Lexicon of Cryptography
('Most Secret', Bletchley Park, 1943)

1

The night was impenetrable, the cold irresistible. Huddled in his overcoat inside the icy Rover, Tom Jericho could barely see the flickering of his breath or the mist it formed on the window beside him. He reached across and rubbed a porthole in the condensation, smearing his fingers with cold, wet grime. Occasionally their headlamps flashed on whitewashed cottages and darkened inns, and once they passed a convoy of lorries heading in the opposite direction. But mostly they seemed to travel in a void. There were no street lights or signposts to guide them, no lit windows; not even a match glimmered in the blackness. They might have been the last three people alive.

Logie had started to snore within fifteen minutes of leaving King's, his head dropping further forwards onto his chest each time the Rover hit a bump, a motion which caused him to mumble and nod, as if in profound agreement with himself. Once, when they turned a corner sharply, his long body toppled sideways and Jericho had to fend him off gently with his forearm.

In the front seat Leveret hadn't uttered a word, except to say, when Jericho asked him to turn it on, that the heater was broken. He was driving with exaggerated care, his face hunched inches from the windscreen, his right foot alternating cautiously between the brake pedal and the accelerator. At times they seemed to be travelling scarcely faster than walking-pace, so that although in daylight the journey to Bletchley might take little more than an hour and an half, Jericho calculated that tonight they would be lucky to reach their destination before midnight.

'I should get some sleep if I were you, old thing,' Logie had said, making a pillow of his overcoat. 'Long night ahead.'

But Jericho couldn't sleep. He stuffed his hands deep into his pockets and stared uselessly into the night.

Bletchley, he thought with disgust. Even the sensation of the name in the mouth was unpleasant, stranded somewhere between blanching and retching. Of all the towns in England, why did they have to choose *Bletchley*? Four years ago he'd never even heard of the place. And he might have lived the rest of his life in happy ignorance had it not been for that glass of sherry in Atwood's rooms in the spring of 1939.

How odd it was, how absurd to trace one's destiny and to find that it revolved around a couple of fluid ounces of pale manzanilla.

It was immediately after that first approach that Atwood had arranged for him to meet some 'friends' in London. Thereafter, every Friday morning for four months, Jericho would catch an early train and make his way to a dusty office block near St James's tube station. Here, in a shabby room furnished by a blackboard and a clerk's desk, he was initiated into the secrets of cryptography. And it was just as Turing had predicted: he loved it.

He loved the history, all of it, from the ancient runic systems and the Irish codes of the Book of Ballymote with their exotic names ('Serpent through the heather', 'Vexation of a poet's heart'), through the codes of Pope Sylvester II and Hildegard von Bingen, through the invention of Alberti's cipher disk – the first polyalphabetic cipher – and Cardinal Richelieu's grilles, all the way down to the machine-generated mysteries of the German Enigma, which were gloomily held to be unbreakable.

And he loved the secret vocabulary of cryptanalysis, with its homophones and polyphones, its digraphs and bigraphs and nulls. He studied frequency analysis. He was taught the intricacies of superencipherment, of placode and enicode. At the beginning of August 1939 he was formally offered a post at the Government Code and Cipher School at a salary of three hundred pounds a year and was told to go back to Cambridge and await developments. On 1 September he woke to hear on the wireless that the Germans had invaded Poland. On 3 September, the day Britain declared war, a telegram arrived at the Porter's Lodge ordering him to report the following morning to a place called Bletchley Park.

He left King's as instructed, as soon as it was light, wedged into the passenger seat of Atwood's antiquated sports car. Bletchley turned out to be a small Victorian railway town about fifty miles west of Cambridge. Atwood, who liked to cut a dash, insisted on driving with the roof off, and as they rattled down the narrow streets Jericho had an impression of smoke and soot, of little, ugly terraced houses and the tall, black chimneys of brick kilns. They passed under a railway bridge, along a lane, and were waved through a pair of high gates by armed sentries. To their right, a lawn sloped down to a lake fringed by large trees. To their left was a mansion – a long, low, late-Victorian monstrosity of red brick and sand-coloured stone that reminded Jericho of the veterans' hospital his father had died in. He looked around, half expecting to see wimpled nurses wheeling broken men in Bath chairs.

'Isn't it perfectly hideous?' squeaked Atwood with delight. 'Built by a Jew. A stockbroker. *A friend of Lloyd George*.' His voice rose with each statement, suggesting an ascending scale of social horror. He parked abruptly at a crazy angle, with a spurt of gravel, narrowly missing a sapper unrolling a large drum of electrical cable.

Inside, in a panelled drawing room overlooking the lake,

sixteen men stood around drinking coffee. Jericho was surprised at how many he recognised. They glanced at one another, embarrassed and amused. *So*, their faces said, *they got you too*. Atwood moved serenely among them, shaking hands and making sharp remarks they all felt obliged to smile at.

'It's not fighting the Germans I object to. It's going to war on behalf of these beastly Poles.' He turned to a handsome, intense-looking young man with a broad, high forehead and thick hair. 'And what's your name?'

'Pukowski,' said the young man, in perfect English. 'I'm a beastly Pole.'

Turing caught Jericho's eye and winked.

In the afternoon the cryptanalysts were split into teams. Turing was assigned to work with Pukowski, redesigning the 'bombe', the giant decryptor which the great Marian Rejewski of the Polish Cipher Bureau had built in 1938 to attack Enigma. Jericho was sent to the stable block behind the mansion to analyse encrypted German radio traffic.

How odd they were, those first nine months of the war, how unreal, how – it seemed absurd to say it now – *peaceful*. They cycled in each day from their digs in various country pubs and guest-houses around the town. They lunched and dined together in the mansion. In the evenings they played chess and strolled through the grounds before cycling home to bed. There was even a Victorian maze of yew hedges to get lost in. Every ten days or so, someone new would join the party – a classicist, a mathematician, a museum curator, a dealer in rare books – each recruited because he was a friend of someone already resident in Bletchley.

A dry and smoky autumn of golds and browns, the rooks whirling in the sky like cinders, gave way to a winter off a Christmas card. The lake froze. The elms drooped under the weight of snow. A robin pecked at breadcrumbs outside the stable window.

Jericho's work was pleasantly academic. Three or four times a day, a motorcycle dispatch-rider would clatter into the courtyard at the back of the big house bearing a pouch of intercepted German cryptograms. Jericho sorted them by frequency and call sign and marked them up on charts in coloured crayons – red for the Luftwaffe, green for the German Army – until gradually, from the unintelligible babble, shapes emerged. Stations in a radio net allowed to talk freely to one another made, when plotted on the stable wall, a crisscross pattern within a circle. Nets in which the only line of communication was two-way, between a headquarters and its out-stations, resembled stars. Circle-nets and star-nets. *Kreis und Stern*.

This idyll lasted eight months, until the German offensive in May 1940. Up to then, there had been scarcely enough material for the cryptanalysts to make a serious attack on Enigma. But as the Wehrmacht swept through Holland, Belgium, France, the babble of wireless traffic became a roar. From three or four motorcycle pouches of material, the volume increased to thirty or forty; to a hundred; to two hundred.

It was late one morning about a week after this had started that Jericho felt a touch on his elbow and turned to find Turing, smiling.

'There's someone I want you to meet, Tom.'

'I'm rather busy at present, Alan, to be honest.'

'Her name's Agnes. I really think you ought to see her.'

Jericho almost argued. A year later he would have argued, but at that time he was still too much in awe of Turing not to do as he was told. He tugged his jacket off the back of his chair and walked out, shrugging it on, into the May sunshine.

By this time the Park had already started to be transformed.

Most of the trees at the side of the lake had been chopped down to make way for a series of large wooden huts. The maze had been uprooted and replaced by a low brick building, outside which a small crowd of cryptanalysts had gathered. There was a sound coming from within it, of a sort Jericho had never heard before, a humming and a clattering, something between a loom and a printing press. He followed Turing through the door. Inside, the noise was deafening, reverberating off the whitewashed walls and the corrugated iron ceiling. A brigadier, an air commodore, two men in overalls and a frightened-looking Wren with her fingers in her ears were standing round the edge of the room staring at a large machine full of revolving drums. A blue flash of electricity arced across the top. There was a fizz and a crackle, a smell of hot oil and overheated metal.

'It's the redesigned Polish bombe,' said Turing. 'I thought I'd call her Agnes.' He rested his long, pale fingers tenderly on the metal frame. There was a bang and he snatched them away again. 'I do hope she works all right ...'

Oh yes, thought Jericho, rubbing another window into the condensation, oh yes, she worked all right.

The moon slid from beneath a cloud, briefly lighting the Great North Road. He closed his eyes.

She worked all right, and after that the world was different.

*

Despite his earlier wakefulness Jericho must have fallen asleep, for when he next opened his eyes Logie was sitting up and the Rover was passing through a small town. It was still dark and at first he couldn't get his bearings. But then they passed a row of shops, and when the headlights flickered briefly on the billboard of the County Cinema (NOW SHOWING: 'THE NAVY COMES THROUGH', 'SOMEWHERE I'LL FIND YOU'), he muttered to himself, and heard the weariness already creeping back into his voice: 'Bletchley.'

'Too bloody right,' said Logie.

Down Victoria Road, past the council offices, past a school ... The road curved and suddenly, in the distance, above the pavements, a myriad of fireflies were swarming towards them. Jericho passed his hands across his face and found that his fingers were numb. He felt mildly sick.

'What time is it?'

'Midnight,' said Logie. 'Shift change.'

The specks of light were blackout torches.

Jericho guessed the Park's workforce must now be about five or six thousand, toiling round the clock in eight-hour shifts – midnight till eight, eight till four, four till midnight. That meant maybe four thousand people were now on the move, half coming off shift, half going on, and by the time the Rover had turned into the road leading to the main gate it was barely possible to advance a yard without hitting someone. Leveret was alternately leaning out of the window, shouting and hammering on the horn. Crowds of people had spilled out into the road, most on foot, some on bicycles. A convoy of buses was struggling to get past. Jericho thought: the odds are two to one that Claire's among them. He had a sudden desire to shrink down in his seat, to cover his head, to get away.

Logie was looking at him curiously. 'Are you *sure* you're up to this, old thing?'

'I'm fine. It's just – it's hard to think it started with sixteen of us.'

'Wonderful, isn't it? And it'll be twice the size next year.' The pride in Logie's voice abruptly gave way to alarm. 'For God's sake Leveret, look out man, you nearly ran that lady over!'

In the headlights a blonde head spun angrily and Jericho felt a rush of nausea. But it wasn't her. It was a woman he didn't recognise, a woman in an army uniform, a slash of scarlet lipstick like a wound across her face. She looked as if she was tarted up and on her way to meet a man. She shook her fist and mouthed 'Bugger off' at them.

'Well,' said Logie, primly, 'I *thought* she was a lady.'

When they reached the guard post they had to dig out their identity cards. Leveret collected them and passed them on through the window to an RAF corporal. The sentry hitched his rifle and studied the cards by torchlight, then ducked down and directed the beam in turn on to each of their faces. The brilliance struck Jericho like a blow. Behind them he could hear a second sentry rummaging through the boot.

He flinched from the light and turned to Logie. 'When did all this start?' He could remember a time when they weren't even asked for passes.

'Not sure now you mention it.' Logie shrugged. 'They seem to have tightened up in the last week or two.'

Their cards were returned. The barrier rose. The sentry waved them through. Beside the road was a freshly painted sign. They had been given a new name some time around Christmas and Jericho could just about read the white lettering in the darkness: 'Government Communication Headquarters'.

The metal barrier came down after them with a crash.

2

Even in the blackout you could sense the size of the place. The mansion was still the same, and so were the huts, but these were now just a fraction of the overall site. Stretching away beyond them was a great factory of intelligence: low, brick-built offices and bombproof bunkers of concrete and steel, A-Blocks and B-Blocks and C-Blocks, tunnels and shelters and guard posts and garages ... There was a big military camp just beyond the wire. The barrels of anti-aircraft batteries poked through camouflaged netting in the nearby woods. And more buildings were under construction. There had never been a day when Jericho hadn't heard the racket of mechanical diggers and cement mixers, the ringing of pickaxes and the splintering of falling trees. Once, just before he left, he had paced out the distance from the new assembly hall to the far perimeter fence and had reckoned it at half a mile. What was it all for? He had no idea. Sometimes he thought they must be monitoring every radio transmission on the planet.

Leveret drove the Rover slowly past the darkened mansion, past the tennis court and the generators, and drew up a short distance from the huts.

Jericho clambered stiffly from the back seat. His legs had gone to sleep and the sensation of the blood returning made his knees buckle. He leaned against the side of the car. His right shoulder was rigid with cold. A duck splashed somewhere on the lake and its cry made him think of Cambridge – of his warm bed and his crosswords – and he had to shake his head to clear the memory.

Logie was explaining to him that he had a choice: Leveret could take him over to his new digs and he could have a decent night's kip, or he could come in straight away and take a look at things immediately.

'Why don't we start now?' said Jericho. His re-entry into the hut would be an ordeal. He'd prefer to get it over with.

'That's the spirit, old love. Leveret will look after your cases, won't you Leveret? And take them to Mr Jericho's room?'

'Yes, sir.' Leveret looked at Jericho for a moment, then stuck out his hand. 'Good luck, sir.'

Jericho took it. The solemnity surprised him. Anyone would think he was about to make a parachute jump into hostile territory. He tried to think of something to say. 'Thank you very much for driving us.'

Logie was fiddling with Leveret's blackout torch. 'What the hell's wrong with this thing?' He knocked it against his palm. 'Bloody thing. Oh, sod it. Come on.'

He strode away on his long legs and after a moment's hesitation Jericho wrapped his scarf tight around his neck and followed. In the darkness they had to feel their way along the blastproof wall surrounding Hut 8. Logie banged into what sounded like a bicycle and Jericho heard him swear. He dropped the torch. The impact made it come on. A trickle of light revealed the entrance to the hut. There was a smell of lime and damp here – lime and damp and creosote: the odours of Jericho's war. Logie rattled the handle, the door opened and they stepped into the dim glow.

Because he had changed so much in the month he had been away, somehow – illogically – he had expected that the hut would have changed as well. Instead, the instant he crossed the threshold, the familiarity of it almost overwhelmed him. It was like a recurrent dream in which the horror lay in knowing precisely what would happen next – the certainty that it always had been, and always would be, exactly like this.

A narrow, ill-lit corridor, perhaps twenty yards long, stretched in front of him, with a dozen doors leading off it. The wooden partitions were flimsy and the noise of a hundred people working at full stretch leaked from room to room – the clump and thud of boots and shoes on the bare boards, the hum of conversation, the occasional shout, the scrape of chair legs, the ringing of telephones, the *clack clack clack* of the Type-X machines in the Decoding Room.

The only tiny difference was that the walk-in cupboard on the right, immediately next to the entrance, now had a nameplate on it: 'Lt. Kramer US Navy Liaison Officer'.

Familiar faces loomed towards him. Kingcome and Proudfoot were whispering together outside the Catalogue Room and drew back to let him pass. He nodded to them. They nodded in return but didn't speak. Atwood hurried out of the Crib Room, saw Jericho, gawped, then put his head down. He muttered, 'Hello, Tom,' then almost ran towards Research.

Clearly, nobody had ever expected to see him again. He was an embarrassment. A dead man. A ghost.

Logie was oblivious, both to the general astonishment and to Jericho's discomfort. 'Hello, everybody.' He waved to Atwood. 'Hello, Frank. Look who's back! The prodigal returns! Give them a smile, Tom, old thing, it's not a ruddy funeral. Not yet, anyway.' He stopped outside his office and fiddled with his key for half a minute, then discovered the door was unlocked. 'Come in, come in.'

The room was scarcely bigger than a broom store. It had been Turing's cubbyhole until just before the break into Shark, when Turing had been sent to America. Now Logie had it – his tiny perquisite of rank – and he looked absurdly huge as he bent over his desk, like an adult poking around in a child's den. There was a fireproof safe in one corner, leaking intercepts, and a rubbish bin labelled CONFIDENTIAL WASTE. There was a telephone with a red handset. Paper was everywhere – on the floor, on the table, on the top of the radiator where it had baked crisp and yellow, in wire baskets and in box files, in tall stacks and in piles that had subsided into fans.

'Bugger, bugger, bugger.' Logie had a message slip in his hands and was frowning at it. He took his pipe out of his pocket and chewed on the stem. He seemed to have forgotten Jericho's presence until Jericho coughed to remind him.

'What? Oh. Sorry, old love.' He traced the words of the message with his pipe. 'The Admiralty's a bit exercised, apparently. Conference in A-Block at eight o'clock with Navy brass up from Whitehall. Want to know the score. Skynner's in a spin and demands to see me forthwith. Bugger, bugger.'

'Does Skynner know I'm back?' Skynner was the head of Bletchley's Naval Section. He'd never cared for Jericho, probably because Jericho had never concealed his opinion of him: that he was a bombast and a bully whose chief war aim was to greet the peace as Sir Leonard Skynner, OBE, with a seat on the Security Executive and a lease on an Oxford mastership. Jericho had a vague memory of actually telling Skynner some of this, or all of it, or possibly more, shortly before he was sent back to Cambridge to recover his senses.

'Of course he knows you're back, old thing. I had to clear it with him first.'

'And he doesn't mind?'

'Mind? No. The man's desperate. He'd do anything to get back into Shark.' Logie added quickly: 'Sorry, I don't mean ... that's not to say that bringing you back is an act of desperation. Only, well, you know ...' He sat down heavily and looked again at the message. He rattled his pipe against his worn yellow teeth. 'Bugger, bugger, bugger ...'

Looking at him then it occurred to Jericho that he knew almost nothing about Logie. They had worked together for two years, would regard themselves as friends, yet they'd never had a proper conversation. He didn't know if Logie was married, or if he had a girl.

'I'd better go and see him, I suppose. Excuse me, old love.'

Logie squeezed past his desk and shouted down the corridor:

'Puck!' Jericho could hear the cry being taken up somewhere in the recesses of the hut by another voice. 'Puck!' And then another: 'Puck! Puck!'

Logie ducked his head back into the office. 'One analyst per shift co-ordinates the Shark attack. Puck this shift, Baxter next, then Pettifer.' His head disappeared again. 'Ah-ha, here he comes. Come on, old thing. Look alive. I've a surprise for you. See who's in here.'

'So there you are, my dear Guy,' came a familiar voice from the corridor. 'Nobody knew where to find you.'

Adam Pukowski slid his lithe frame past Logie, saw Jericho and stopped dead. He was genuinely shocked. Jericho could almost see his mind struggling to regain control of his features, forcing his famous smile back on to his face. At last he managed it. He even threw his arms round Jericho and hugged him. 'Tom, it's ... I had begun to think you were never returning. It's marvellous.'

'It's good to see you again, Puck.' Jericho patted him politely on the back.

Puck was their mascot, their touch of glamour, their link with the adventure of war. He had arrived in the first week to brief them on the Polish bombe, then flown back to Poland. When Poland fell he had fled to France, and when France collapsed he had escaped across the Pyrenees. Romantic stories clustered around him: that he had hidden from the Germans in a goatherd's cottage, that he had smuggled himself aboard a Portuguese steamer and ordered the captain to sail to England at pistol-point. When he had popped up again in Bletchley in the winter of 1940 it was Pinker, the Shakespearian, who had shortened his name to Puck ('that merry wanderer of the night'). His mother was British, which explained his almost perfect English, distinctive only because he pronounced it so carefully.

'You have come to give us assistance?'

'So it seems.' He shyly disengaged himself from Puck's embrace. 'For what it's worth.'

'Splendid, splendid.' Logie regarded them fondly for a moment, then began rummaging among the litter on his desk. 'Now where is that thing? It was here this morning ...'

Puck nodded at Logie's back and whispered: 'Do you see, Tom? As organised as ever.'

'Now, now, Puck, I heard that. Let me see. Is this it? No. Yes. Yes!'

He turned and handed Jericho a typewritten document, officially stamped and headed 'By Order of the War Office'. It was a billeting notice, served on a Mrs Ethel Armstrong, entitling Jericho to lodgings in the Commercial Guesthouse, Albion Street, Bletchley.

'I'm afraid I don't know what it's like, old thing. Best I could do.'

'I'm sure it's fine.' Jericho folded the chit and stuffed it into his pocket. Actually, he was quite sure it *wasn't* fine – the last decent rooms in Bletchley had disappeared three years ago, and people now had to travel in from as far away as Bedford, twenty miles distant – but what was the point in complaining? On past experience he wouldn't be using the room much anyway, except to sleep in.

'Now don't you go exhausting yourself, my boy,' said Logie. 'We don't expect you to work a full shift. Nothing like that. You just come and go as you please. What we want from you is what you gave us last time. Insight. Inspiration. Spotting that something we've all missed. Isn't that so, Puck?'

'Absolutely.' His handsome face was more haggard than Jericho had ever seen it, more tired even than Logie's. 'God knows, Tom, we are certainly up against it.'

'I take it then we're no further forward?' said Logie. 'No good news I can give our lord and master?'

Puck shook his head.

'Not even a glimmer?'

'Not even that.'

'No. Well, why should there be? Damn bloody *admirals*.' Logie screwed up the message slip, aimed it at his rubbish bin and missed. 'I'd show you round myself, Tom, but the Skynner waits for no man, as you'll recall. All right with you, Puck? Give him the grand tour?'

'Of course, Guy. As you wish.'

Logie ushered them out into the passage and tried to lock the door, then gave up on it. As he turned he opened his mouth and Jericho nerved himself for one of Logie's excruciating housemaster's pep talks – something about innocent lives depending on them, and the need for them to do their best, and the race being not to the swift nor the battle to the strong (he had actually said this once) – but instead his mouth just widened into a yawn.

'Oh, dear. Sorry, old thing. Sorry.'

He shuffled off down the corridor, patting his pockets to make sure he had his pipe and tobacco pouch. They heard him mutter again, something about 'bloody admirals', and he was gone.

*

Hut 8 was thirty-five yards long by ten wide and Jericho could have toured it in his sleep, probably *had* toured it in his sleep, for all he knew. The outside walls were thin and the damp from the lake seemed to rise through the floorboards so that at night the rooms were chilly, cast in a sepia glow by bare, low-wattage bulbs. The furniture was mostly trestle tables and folding wooden chairs. It reminded Jericho of a church hall on a winter's night. All that was missing was a badly tuned piano and somebody thumping out 'Land of Hope and Glory'.

It was laid out like an assembly line, the main stage in a process that originated somewhere far out in the darkness, maybe two thousand miles away, when the grey hull of a U-boat rose close to the surface and squirted off a radio message to its controllers. The signals were intercepted at various listening-posts and teleprintered to Bletchley and within ten minutes of transmission, even as the U-boats were preparing to dive, they were emerging via a tunnel into Hut 8's Registration Room. Jericho helped himself to the contents of a wire basket labelled 'Shark' and carried them to the nearest light. The hours immediately after midnight were usually the busiest time. Sure enough, six messages had been intercepted in the last eighteen minutes. Three consisted of just eight letters: he guessed they were weather reports. Even the longest of the other cryptograms was no more than a couple of dozen four-letter groups:

JRLO GOPL DNRZ LQBT ...

Puck made a weary face at him, as if to say: What can you do?

Jericho said: 'What's the volume?'

'It varies. One hundred and fifty, perhaps two hundred messages a day. And rising.'

The Registration Room didn't just handle Shark. There was Porpoise and Dolphin and all the other different Enigma keys to log and then pass across the corridor to the Crib Room. Here, the cribsters sifted them for clues – radio station call signs they recognised (Kiel was JDU, for example, Wilhelmshaven KYU), messages whose contents they could guess at, or cryptograms that had already been enciphered in one key and then retransmitted in another (they marked these 'XX' and called them 'kisses'). Atwood was the champion cribster and the Wrens said cattily behind his back that these were the only kisses he had ever had.

It was in the big room next door – which they called, with their solemn humour, the Big Room – that the cryptanalysts used the cribs to construct possible solutions that could be tested on the bombes. Jericho took in the rickety tables, the hard chairs, the weak lighting, the fug of tobacco, the college-library atmosphere, the night chill (most of the cryptanalysts were wearing coats and mittens) and he wondered why – *why?* – he had been so ready to come back. Kingcome and Proudfoot were there, and Upjohn and Pinker and de Brooke, and maybe half a dozen newcomers whose faces he didn't recognise, including one young man sitting bold as you please in the seat which had once been reserved for Jericho. The tables were stacked with cryptograms, like ballot papers at an election count.

Puck was muttering something about back-breaks but Jericho, fascinated by the sight of someone else in his place, lost track and had to interrupt him. 'I'm sorry, Puck. What was that?'

'I was saying that from twenty minutes ago we are up to date. Shark is now fully read to the point of the code change. So that there is nothing left to us. Except history.' He gave a weak smile and patted Jericho's shoulder. 'Come. I'll show you.'

When a cryptanalyst believed he'd glimpsed a possible break into a message, his guess was sent out of the hut to be tested on a bombe. And if he'd been skilful enough, or lucky enough, then in an hour, or a day, the bombe would churn through a million permutations and reveal how the Enigma machine had been set up. That information was relayed back from the bombe bays to the Decoding Room.

Because of its noise, the Decoding Room was tucked away at the far end of the hut. Personally, Jericho liked the clatter. It was the sound of success. His worst memories were of the nights when the building was silent. A dozen British Type-X enciphering machines had been modified to mimic the actions of the German Enigma. They were big, cumbersome devices – typewriters with rotors, a plugboard and a cylinder – at which sat young and well-groomed debutantes.

Baxter, who was the hut's resident Marxist, had a theory that Bletchley's workforce (which was mainly female) was arranged in what he called 'a paradigm of the English class system'. The wireless interceptors, shivering in their coastal radio stations, were generally working-class and laboured in ignorance of the Enigma secret. The bombe operators, who worked in the grounds of some nearby country houses and in a big new installation just outside London, were petit-bourgeois and had a vague idea. And the Decoding Room girls, in the heart of the Park, were mostly upper-middle-class, even aristocratic, and they saw it all – the secrets literally passed through their fingers. They typed out the letters of the original cryptogram, and from the cylinder on the right of the Type-X a strip of sticky-backed paper, the sort you saw gummed down on telegram forms, slowly emerged, bearing the decrypted plaintext.

'Those three are doing Dolphin,' said Puck, pointing across the room, 'and the two by the door are just starting on Porpoise. And this charming young lady here, I believe' – he bowed to her – 'has Shark. May we?'

She was young, about eighteen, with curly red hair and wide hazel eyes. She looked up and smiled at him, a dazzling *Tatler* smile, and he leaned across her and began uncoiling the strip of tape from the cylinder. Jericho noticed as he did so that he left one hand resting casually on her shoulder, just as simply as that, and he thought how much he envied Puck the ease of that gesture. It would have taken him a week to pluck up the nerve. Puck beckoned him down to read the decrypt:

VONSCHULZEQU88521DAMPFER1TANKERWAHRSCHEINLICHAM63
TANKERFACKEL ...

Jericho ran his finger along it, separating the words and translating it in his mind: U-boat commander von Schulze was in grid square 8852 and had sunk one steamship (for certain) and one tanker (probably) and had set one other tanker on fire ...

'What date is this?'

'You can see it there,' said Puck. '*Sechs drei.* The sixth of March. We've broken everything from this week up to the code change on Wednesday night, so now we go back and pick up the intercepts we missed earlier in the month. This is – what? – six days old. Herr Kapitän von Schulz may be five hundred miles away by now. It is of academic interest only, I fear.'

'Poor devils,' said Jericho, passing his finger along the tape for a second time. *1DAMPFER1TANKER* ... What freezing and drowning and burning were concentrated in that one line! What were the ships called, he wondered, and had the families of the crews been told?

'We have approximately a further eighty messages from the sixth still to run through the Type-Xs. I shall put two more operators on to it. A couple of hours and we should be finished.'

'And then what?'

'Then, my dear Tom? Then I suppose we shall make a start on back-breaks from February. But that barely qualifies even as history. February? February in the Atlantic? Archaeology!'

'Any progress on the four-wheel bombe?'

Puck shook his head. 'First, it is impossible. It is out of the question. Then there is a design, but the design is theoretical nonsense. Then there is a design that should work, but doesn't. Then there is a shortage of materials. Then there is a shortage of engineers ...' He made a weary gesture with his hand, as if he were pushing it all out of the way.

'Has anything else changed?'

'Nothing that affects us. According to the direction finders, U-boat HQ has moved from Paris to Berlin. They have some wonderful new transmitter at Magdeburg they say will reach a U-boat forty-five feet under water at a range of two thousand miles.'

Jericho murmured: 'How very ingenious of them.'

The red-headed girl had finished deciphering the message. She tore off the tape, stuck it on the back of the cryptogram and handed it to another girl, who rushed out of the room. Now it would be turned into recognisable English and teleprintered to the Admiralty.

Puck touched Jericho's arm. 'You must be tired. Why don't you go now and rest?'

But Jericho didn't feel like sleeping. 'I'd like to see all the Shark traffic we haven't been able to break. Everything since midnight on Wednesday.'

Puck gave a puzzled smile. 'Why? There's nothing you can do with it.'

'Maybe so. But I'd like to see it.'

'Why?'

'I don't know.' Jericho shrugged. 'Just to handle it. To get a feel of it. I've been out of the game for a month.'

'You think we may have missed something, perhaps?'

'Not at all. But Logie has asked me.'

'Ah yes. The celebrated Jericho "inspiration" and "intuition".' Puck couldn't conceal his irritation. 'And so from science and logic we descend to superstition and "feelings".'

'For heaven's sake, Puck!' Jericho was starting to become annoyed himself. 'Just humour me, if that's how you prefer to look at it.'

Puck glared at him for a moment, and then, as quickly as they had arisen, the clouds seemed to pass. 'Of course.' He held up his hands in a gesture of surrender. 'You must see it all. Forgive me. I'm tired. We're all tired.'

Five minutes later, when Jericho walked into the Big Room carrying the folder of Shark cryptograms, he found his old seat had been vacated. Someone had also laid out in his place a new pile of jotting paper and three freshly sharpened pencils. He looked around, but nobody seemed to be paying him any attention.

He laid the intercepts out on the table. He loosened his scarf. He felt the radiator – as ever, it was lukewarm. He blew some warmth on to his hands and sat down.

He was back.

3

Whenever anyone asked Jericho why he was a mathematician – some friend of his mother, perhaps, or an inquisitive colleague with no interest in science – he would shake his head and smile and claim he had no idea. If they persisted, he might, with some diffidence, direct them to the definition offered by G. H. Hardy in his famous *Apology*: 'a mathematician, like a painter or a poet, is a *maker* of patterns'. If that didn't satisfy them, he would try to explain by quoting the most basic illustration he could think of: pi – 3.14 – the ratio of a circle's circumference to its diameter. Calculate pi to a thousand decimal places, he would say, or a million or more, and you will discover no pattern to its unending sequence of digits. It appears random, chaotic, ugly. Yet Leibnitz and Gregory can take the same number and tease from it a pattern of crystalline elegance:

$$\frac{pi}{4} = 1 - \frac{1}{3} + \frac{1}{5} - \frac{1}{7} + \frac{1}{9} - \ldots$$

and so on to infinity. Such a pattern had no practical usefulness, it was merely beautiful – as sublime, to Jericho, as a line in a fugue by Bach – and if his questioner still couldn't see what he was driving at, then, sadly, he would give up on them as a waste of time.

On the same principle, Jericho thought the Enigma machine was beautiful – a masterpiece of human ingenuity that created both chaos and a tiny ribbon of meaning. In the early days at Bletchley he used to fantasise that some day, when the war was over, he would track down its German inventor, Herr Arthur Scherbius, and buy him a glass of beer. But then he'd heard that Scherbius had died in 1929, killed – of all ludicrously illogical things – by a runaway horse, and hadn't lived to see the success of his patent.

If he had, he would have been a rich man. By the end of 1942 Bletchley estimated that the Germans had manufactured at least a hundred thousand Enigmas. Every Army headquarters had one, every Luftwaffe base, every warship, every submarine, every port, every big railway station, every SS brigade and Gestapo HQ. Never before had a nation entrusted so much of its secret communications to a single device.

In the mansion at Bletchley the cryptanalysts had a roomful of captured Enigmas and Jericho had played with them for hours. They were small (little more than a foot square by six inches deep), portable (they weighed just twenty-six pounds) and simple to operate. You set up your machine, typed in your message, and the ciphertext was spelled out, letter by letter, on a panel of small electric bulbs. Whoever received the enciphered message merely had to set up his machine in exactly the same way, type in the cryptogram, and there, spelled out on the bulbs, would be the original plaintext.

The genius lay in the vast number of different permutations the Enigma could generate. Electric current on a standard Enigma flowed from keyboard to lamps via a set of three wired rotors (at least one of which turned a notch every time a key was struck) and a plugboard with twenty-six jacks. The circuits changed constantly; their potential number was astronomical, but calculable. There were five different rotors to choose from (two were kept spare) which meant they could be arranged in any one of sixty possible orders. Each rotor was slotted on to a spindle and had twenty-six possible starting positions. Twenty-six to the power three was 17,576. Multiply that by the sixty potential rotor-orders and you got 1,054,560. Multiply *that* by the possible number of plugboard connections – about 150 million million – and you were looking at a machine that had around 150 million million *million* different starting positions. It didn't matter how many Enigma machines you captured or how long you played with them. They were useless unless you knew the rotor order, the rotor starting positions and the plugboard connections. And the Germans changed these daily, sometimes twice a day.

The machine had only one tiny – but, as it turned out, crucial – flaw. It could never encipher a letter as itself: an *A* would never emerge from it as an *A*, or a *B* as a *B*, or a *C* as a *C* ... *Nothing is ever itself*: that was the great guiding principle in the breaking of Enigma, the infinitesimal weakness that the bombes exploited.

Suppose one had a cryptogram that began:

IGWH BSTU XNTX EYLK PEAZ ZNSK UFJR CADV ...

And suppose one knew that this message originated from the Kriegsmarine's weather station in the Bay of Biscay, a particular friend of the Hut 8 cribsters, which always began its reports in the same way:

WEUBYYNULLSEQSNULLNULL

('Weather survey 0600', WEUB being an abbreviation for WETTERÜBERSICHT and SEQS for SECHS; YY and NULL being inserted to baffle eavesdroppers).

The cryptanalyst would lay out the ciphertext and slide the crib beneath it and on the principle that *nothing is ever itself* he would keep sliding it until he found a position in which there were no matching letters between the top and bottom lines. The result in this case would be:

BSTUXNTXEYLKPEAZZNSKUF
WEUBYYNULLSEQSNULLNULL

And at this point it became theoretically possible to calculate the original Enigma settings that alone could have produced this precise sequence of letter pairings. It was still an immense calculation, one which would have taken a team of human beings several weeks. The Germans assumed, rightly, that whatever intelligence might be gained would be too old to be of use. But Bletchley – and this was what the Germans had never reckoned on – *Bletchley didn't use human beings*. It used bombes. For the first time in history, a cipher mass-manufactured by machine was being broken by machine.

Who needed spies now? What need now of secret inks and dead-letter drops and midnight assignations in curtained *wagons-lits*? Now you needed mathematicians and engineers with oilcans and fifteen hundred filing clerks to process five thousand secret messages a day. They had taken espionage into the machine age.

But none of this was of much help to Jericho in breaking Shark.

Shark defied every tool he could bring to bear on it. For a start, there were almost no cribs. In the case of a surface Enigma key, if

Hut 8 ran out of cribs, they had tricks to get round it – 'gardening', for example. 'Gardening' was arranging for the RAF to lay mines in a particular naval grid square outside a German harbour. An hour later, you could guarantee, the harbour master, with Teutonic efficiency, would send a message using that day's Enigma settings, warning ships to beware of mines in naval grid square such-and-such. The signal would be intercepted, flashed to Hut 8, and give them their missing crib.

But you couldn't do that with Shark and Jericho could make only the vaguest guesses at the contents of the cryptograms. There were eight long messages originating from Berlin. They would be orders, he supposed, probably directing the U-boats into 'wolf packs' and stationing them in front of the oncoming convoys. The shorter signals – there were a hundred and twenty-two, which Jericho sorted into a separate pile – had been sent by the submarines themselves. These could contain anything: reports of ships sunk and of engine trouble; details of survivors floating in the water and of crewmen washed overboard; requests for spare parts and fresh orders. Shortest of all were the U-boats' weather messages or, very occasionally, contact reports: 'Convoy in naval grid square BE9533 course 70 degrees speed 9 knots ...' But these were encoded, like the weather bulletins, with one letter of the alphabet substituting for each piece of information. And then they were enciphered in Shark.

He tapped his pencil against the desk. Puck was quite right. There was not enough material to work with.

And even if there had been, there was still the wretched fourth rotor on the Shark Enigma, the innovation that made U-boat messages twenty-six times more difficult to break than those of surface ships. One hundred and fifty million million million multiplied by twenty-six. A phenomenal number. The engineers had been struggling for a year to develop a four-rotor bombe – but still, apparently, without success. It seemed to be just that one step beyond their technical ability.

No cribs, no bombes. Hopeless.

Hours passed during which Jericho tried every trick he could think of to prompt some fresh inspiration. He arranged the cryptograms chronologically. Then he arranged them by length. Then he sorted them by frequency. He doodled on the pile of paper. He prowled around the hut, oblivious now to who was looking at him and who wasn't. This was what it had been like for ten interminable months last year. No wonder he had gone mad. The chorus-lines of meaningless letters danced before his eyes. But they were not meaningless. They were loaded with the most vital meaning imaginable, if only he could find it. But where was the pattern? Where was the pattern? Where was the *pattern*?

*

It was the practice on the night shift at about four o'clock in the morning for everyone to take a meal-break. The cryptanalysts went off when they liked, depending on the stage they'd reached in their work. The Decoding Room girls and the clerks in the Registration and Catalogue rooms had to leave according to a rota so that the hut was never caught short-staffed.

Jericho didn't notice the drift of people towards the door. He had both elbows on the table and was leaning over the cryptograms, his knuckles pressed to his temples. His mind was eidetic – that is to say, it could hold and retrieve images with photographic accuracy, be they mid-game positions in chess, crossword puzzles or enciphered German naval signals – and he was working with his eyes closed.

'"Below the thunders of the upper deep,"' intoned a muffled voice behind him, '"Far, far beneath in the abysmal sea,/His ancient, dreamless, uninvaded sleep ..."'

'"... The Kraken sleepeth."' Jericho finished the quotation and turned to find Atwood pulling on a purple balaclava. 'Coleridge?'

'Coleridge?' Atwood's face abruptly emerged wearing an expression of outrage. '*Coleridge*? It's Tennyson, you barbarian. We wondered whether you'd care to join us for refreshment.'

Jericho was about to refuse, but decided that would be rude. In any case, he was hungry. He'd eaten nothing except toast and jam for twelve hours.

'That's kind. Thank you.'

He followed Atwood, Pinker and a couple of the others along the length of the hut and out into the night. At some stage while he'd been lost in the cryptograms it must have rained and the air was still moist. Along the road to the right he could hear people moving in the shadows. The beams of torches glistened on the wet tarmac. Atwood conducted them past the mansion and the arboretum and through the main gate. Discussing work outside the hut was forbidden and Atwood, purely to annoy Pinker, was declaiming on the suicide of Virginia Woolf, which he held to be the greatest day for English letters since the invention of the printing press.

'I c-c-can't believe you mmm-mmm-mmm ...' When Pinker snagged himself on a word, his whole body seemed to shake with the effort of trying to get himself free. Above his bow-tie, his face bloomed scarlet in the torchlight. They stopped and waited patiently for him. 'Mmm-mmm ...'

'Mean that?' suggested Atwood.

'Mean that, Frank,' gasped Pinker with relief. 'Thank you.'

Someone came to Atwood's support, and then Pinker's shrill voice started to argue again. They moved off. Jericho lagged behind.

The canteen, which lay just beyond the perimeter fence, was as big as an aircraft hangar, brightly lit and thunderously noisy, with perhaps five or six hundred people sitting down to eat or queuing for food.

One of the new cryptanalysts shouted to Jericho: 'I bet you've missed this!' Jericho smiled and was about to say something in return but the young man went off to collect a tray. The din was dreadful, and so was the smell – a blended steam of institutional food, of cabbage and boiled fish and custard, laced with cigarette smoke and damp clothes. Jericho felt simultaneously intimidated by it and detached from it, like a prisoner returning from solitary confinement, or a patient from an isolation ward released on to the street after a long illness.

He queued and didn't pay much attention to the food being slopped on his plate. It was only after he had handed over his two shillings and sat down that he took a good look at it – boiled potatoes in a curdled yellow grease and a slab of something ribbed and grey. He stabbed at the lump with his fork, then lifted a fragment cautiously to his mouth. It tasted like fishy liver, like congealed cod liver oil. He winced.

'This is perfectly vile.'

Atwood said, through a full mouth: 'It's whale meat.'

'Good heavens.' Jericho put his fork down hurriedly.

'Don't waste it, dear boy. Don't you know there's a war on? Pass it over.'

Jericho pushed the plate across the table and tried to swill the taste away with the milk-water coffee.

The pudding was some kind of fruit tart, and that was better, or, rather, it tasted of nothing more noxious than cardboard, but halfway through it, Jericho's wavering appetite finally died. Atwood was now giving them his opinion of Gielgud's interpretation of Hamlet, spraying the table in the process with particles of whale, and at that point Jericho decided he'd had enough. He took the leftovers that Atwood didn't want and scraped them into a milk churn labelled 'PIG SWILL'.

When he was halfway to the door he was suddenly overcome with remorse at his rudeness. Was this the behaviour of a good colleague, what Skynner would call 'a team player'? But then, when he turned and looked back, he saw that nobody had missed him. Atwood was still talking, waving his fork in mid-air, Pinker was shaking his head, the others were listening. Jericho turned once more for the door and the salvation of the fresh air.

*

Thirty seconds later he was out on the pavement, picking his way carefully in the darkness towards the guard post, thinking about Shark.

He could hear the *click click* of a woman's heels hurrying about twenty paces in front of him. There was no one else around. It was between sittings: everyone was either working or eating. The rapid footsteps stopped at the barrier and a moment later the sentry shone his torch directly in the woman's face. She glanced away with a murmur of annoyance, and Jericho saw her then, for an instant, spot-lit in the blackout, looking straight in his direction.

It was Claire.

For a fraction of a second, he thought she must have seen him. But he was in the shadows and reeling backwards in panic, four or five steps backwards, and she was dazzled by the light. With what seemed like infinite slowness she brought her hand up to shield her eyes. Her blonde hair gleamed white.

He couldn't hear what was said but very quickly the torch was quenched and everything was dark again. And then he heard her moving off down the path on the other side of the barrier, *click click click*, obviously in a rush about something, fading into the night.

He had to catch her up. He stumbled quickly to the guard post, searching for his wallet, searching for his pass, nearly tripping off the kerbstone, but he couldn't find the damned thing. The torch came on, blinding him – '*evening sir*', '*evening corporal*' – and his fingers were useless, he couldn't make them work, and the pass wasn't in his wallet, wasn't in his overcoat pockets, wasn't in his jacket pockets, breast pocket – he couldn't hear her footsteps now, just the sentry's boot tapping impatiently – and, yes, it *was* in his breast pocket, '*here you are*', '*thank you sir*', '*thank you corporal*', '*night sir*', '*night corporal*', night, night, night ...

She was gone.

The sentry's light had robbed him of what little vision he had. When he closed his eyes there was only the imprint of the torch and when he opened them the darkness was absolute. He found the edge of the road with his foot and followed its curve. It took him once again past the mansion and brought him out close to the huts. Far away, on the opposite bank of the lake, someone – perhaps another sentry – started to whistle 'We'll Gather Lilacs in the Spring Again', then stopped.

It was so quiet, he could hear the wind moving in the trees.

While he was hesitating, wondering what to do, a dot of light appeared along the footpath to his right, and then another. For some reason Jericho drew back into the shadows of Hut 8 as the torches bobbed towards him. He heard voices he didn't recognise – a man's and a woman's – whispered but emphatic. When they were almost level with him, the man threw his cigarette into the water. A cascade of red points ended in a hiss. The woman said: 'It's just a week, darling,' and went to embrace him. The fireflies danced and separated and moved on.

He stepped out onto the path again. His night vision was coming back. He looked at his watch. It was 4.30. Another ninety minutes and it would start to get light.

On impulse he walked down the side of Hut 8, keeping close to the blastproof wall. This brought him to the edge of Hut 6, where the ciphers of the German Army and Luftwaffe were broken. Straight ahead was a narrow alleyway of rough grass separating Hut 6 from the end wall of the Naval Section. And at the end of that, crouched low in the darkness, just about visible, was the side of another hut – Hut 3 – to which the decrypted ciphers from Hut 6 were sent for translation and dispatch.

Hut 3 was where Claire worked.

He glanced around. There was no one in sight.

He left the path and started to stumble down the passage. The ground was slippery and uneven and several times something grabbed at his ankle – ivy, maybe, or a tendril of discarded cable – and almost sent him sprawling. It took him about a minute to reach Hut 3.

Here, too, was a concrete wall, designed, optimistically, to shield the flimsy wooden structure from an exploding bomb. It was neck-high, but although he was short he was just about able to peer over the top.

A row of windows was set into the side of the building. Over these, from the outside, blackout shutters were fastened every day at dusk. All that was visible was the ghosts of squares, where the light seeped around the edges of the frames. The floor of Hut 3, like Hut 8's, was made of wood, suspended above a concrete base, and he could hear the muffled clumps and thuds of people moving about.

She must be on duty. She must be working the midnight shift. She might be three feet from where he stood.

He was on tiptoe.

He had never been inside Hut 3. For reasons of security, workers in one section of the Park were not encouraged to stray into another, not unless they had good reason. From time to time his work had taken him over the threshold of Hut 6, but Hut 3 was a mystery to him. He had no idea of what she did. She'd tried to tell him once, but he'd said gently that it was best he didn't know. From odd remarks he gathered it was something to do with filing and was 'deadly dull, darling'.

He stretched out as far as he could, until his fingertips were brushing the asbestos cladding of the hut.

What are you doing, darling Claire? Are you busy with your boring filing, or are you flirting with one of the night-duty officers, or gossiping with the other girls, or puzzling over that crossword you can never do?

Suddenly, about fifteen yards to his left, a door opened. From the oblong of dim light a uniformed man emerged, yawning. Jericho slid silently to the ground until he was kneeling in the wet earth and pressed his chest against the wall. The door closed and the man began to walk towards him. He stopped about ten feet away, breathing hard. He seemed to be listening. Jericho closed his eyes and shortly afterwards he heard a pattering and then a drilling noise and when he opened them he saw the faint silhouette of the man pissing against the wall, very hard. It went on for a wondrously long time and Jericho was close enough to get a whiff of pungent, beery urine. A fine spray was being borne downwind on the breeze. He had to put his hand to his nose and mouth to stop himself gagging. Eventually, the man gave a deep sigh – a groan, almost – of satisfaction, and fumbled with the buttons of his fly. He moved away. The door opened and closed again and Jericho was alone.

There was a certain humour in the situation, and later even he was to see it. But at the time he was on the edge of panic. What, in the name of reason, did he think he was doing? If he were to be caught, kneeling in the darkness, with his ear pressed to a hut in which he had no business, he would have – to put it mildly – a hard time explaining himself. For a moment he considered simply marching inside and demanding to see her. But his imagination recoiled at the prospect. He might be thrown out. Or she might appear in a fury and create a scene. Or she might appear and be the soul of sweetness, in which case what did he say? *'Oh, hello, darling. I just happened to be passing. You look in good form. By the way, I've been meaning to ask you, why did you wreck my life?'*

He used the wall to help him scramble to his feet. The quickest way back to the road was straight ahead, but that would take him past the door to the hut. He decided that the safest course would be to go back the way he had come.

He was more cautious after his scare. Each time he took a step he planted his foot carefully and on every fifth pace he paused to make sure that no one else was moving around in the blackout. Two minutes later he was back outside the entrance to Hut 8.

He felt as if he had been on a cross-country run. He was out of breath. There was a small hole in his left shoe and his sock was wet. Bits of damp grass were sticking to the bottoms of his trouser legs. His knees were sodden. And where he had rubbed against the concrete wall the front of his overcoat was streaked luminously white. He took out his handkerchief and tried to clean himself up. He had just about finished when he heard the others coming back from the canteen. Atwood's voice carried in the night: 'A dark horse, that one. Very dark. I recruited him, you know,' to which someone else chimed in: 'Yes, but he was once very good, wasn't he?'

Jericho didn't stop to hear the rest. He pushed open the door and almost ran down the passage, so that by the time the cryptanalysts appeared in the Big Room he was already seated at his desk, bent over the intercepts, knuckles to his temples, eyes closed.

*

He stayed like that for three hours.

At about six o'clock, Puck stopped by to drop on the table another forty encrypted signals, the latest batch of Shark traffic, and to enquire – not without a degree of sarcasm – if Jericho had 'solved it yet?' At seven, there was a rattle of step ladders against the outside wall and the blackout shutters were unfastened. A pale grey light filtered into the hut.

What was she doing, hurrying into the Park at that time of night? That was what he did not understand. Of course, the mere fact of seeing her again after a month spent trying to forget her was disturbing. But it was the circumstances, in retrospect, that troubled him more. She had not been in the canteen, he was sure of that. He had scrutinised every table, every face – had been so distracted he had barely even looked at what he was being given to eat. But if she had not been in the canteen, where had she been? Had she been with someone? Who? Who? And the way she was walking so hurriedly. Was there not something furtive, even panicky about it?

His memory replayed the scene frame by frame: the footsteps, the flash of light, the turn of her head, her cry, the halo of her hair, the way she had vanished ... That was something else. Could she really have walked the entire distance to the hut in the time it took him to fumble for his pass?

Just before eight o'clock he gathered the cryptograms together and slipped them into the folder. All around him, the cryptanalysts were preparing to go off shift – stretching and yawning and rubbing at tired eyes, pulling together their work, briefing their replacements. Nobody noticed Jericho walk quickly down the corridor to Logie's office. He knocked once. There was no reply. He tried the door. As he remembered: unlocked.

He closed it behind him and picked up the telephone. If he delayed for a second his nerve would fail him. He dialled '0' and on the seventh ring, just as he was about to give up, a sleepy operator answered.

His mouth was almost too dry to get the words out. 'Duty Officer, Hut 3, please.'

Almost immediately a man's voice said, irritably: 'Colonel Coker.'

Jericho nearly dropped the receiver.

'Do you have a Miss Romilly there?' He didn't need to disguise his voice: it was so strained and quavering it was unrecognisable. 'A Miss Claire Romilly?'

'You've come through to *completely* the wrong office. Who is this?'

'Welfare.'

'Oh, bloody *hell*!' There was a deafening bang, as if the colonel had thrown the telephone across the room, but the connection held. Jericho could hear the clatter of a teleprinter and a man's voice, very cultured, saying somewhere in the background: 'Yes, yes, I've got that. Right-oh. Cheerio.' The man ended one conversation and started another. 'Army Index here ...' Jericho glanced at the clock above the window. Now it was past eight. Come on, come on ... Suddenly there was more loud banging, much closer, and a woman said softly in Jericho's ear: 'Yes?'

He tried to sound casual but it came out as a croak. 'Claire?'

'No, I'm afraid it's Claire's day off. She won't be back on duty until eight tomorrow morning. Can I help?'

Jericho gently replaced the receiver in its cradle, just as the door was thrown open behind him.

'Oh, *there* you are, old thing ...'

4

Daylight diminished the huts.

The blackout had touched them with a certain mystery but the morning showed them up for what they were: squat and ugly, with brown walls and tarred roofs and a premature air of dereliction. Above the mansion, the sky was glossy white with streaks of grey, a dome of polished marble. A duck in drab winter plumage waddled across the path from the lake looking for food, and Logie almost kicked it as he strode past, sending it protesting back to the water.

He had not been in the least perturbed to find Jericho in his office and Jericho's carefully prepared excuse – that he was returning the Shark intercepts – had been waved away.

'Just dump 'em in the Crib Room and come with me.'

Drawn across the northern edge of the lake, next to the huts, was A-Block, a long, two-storey affair with brick walls and a flat top. Logie led the way up a flight of concrete steps and turned right. At the far end of the corridor a door opened and Jericho heard a familiar voice booming: '... all our resources, human and material, into this problem ...' and then the door closed again and Baxter peered down the passage towards them.

'So there you are. I was just coming to find you. Hello, Guy. Hello, Tom. How are you? Hardly recognised you. Upright.' Baxter had a cigarette in his mouth and didn't bother to remove it, so it bobbed as he spoke and sprayed ash down the front of his pullover. Before the war he had been a lecturer at the London School of Economics.

'What have we got?' said Logie, nodding towards the closed door.

'Our American "lee-ay-son officer", plus another American – some big shot from the Navy. A man in a suit – a lounge lizard from Intelligence by the look of him. Three from our Navy, of course, one of them an admiral. All up from London specially.'

'An admiral?' Logie's hand went automatically to his tie and Jericho noticed he had changed into a pre-war double-breasted suit. He licked his fingers and tried to plaster down his hair. 'I don't like the sound of an admiral. And how's Skynner?'

'At the moment? I'd say heavily out-gunned.' Baxter was staring at Jericho. The corners of his mouth twitched down briefly, the nearest Jericho had seen him come to a smile. 'Well, well, I suppose you don't look too bad, Tom.'

'Now, Alec, don't you go upsetting him.'

'I'm fine, Alec, thank you. How's the revolution?'

'Coming along, comrade. Coming along.'

Logie patted Jericho on the arm. 'Don't say anything when we get inside, Tom. You're only here for show, old love.'

Only here for show, thought Jericho, what the hell does that mean? But before he could ask, Logie had opened the door and all he could hear was Skynner – 'we must expect these setbacks from time to time' – and they were on.

*

There were eight men in the room. Leonard Skynner, the head of the Naval Section, sat at one end of the table, with Atwood to his right and an empty chair to his left, which Baxter promptly reclaimed. Gathered around the other end were five officers in dark blue naval uniform, two of them American and three British. One of the British officers, a lieutenant, had an eye-patch. They looked grim.

The eighth man had his back to Jericho. He turned as they came in and Jericho briefly registered a lean face with fair hair.

Skynner stopped speaking. He stood and held out a meaty hand. 'Come in Guy, come in Tom.' He was a big, square-faced man with thick black hair and wide bushy eyebrows that almost met above the bridge of his nose and reminded Jericho of the Morse code symbol for M. He beckoned to the newcomers eagerly, obviously thankful to see Allied reinforcements. 'This is Guy Logie,' he said to the admiral, 'our chief cryptanalyst, and Tom Jericho, of whom you may have heard. Tom was instrumental in getting us into Shark just before Christmas.'

The admiral's leathery old face was immobile. He was smoking a cigarette – they were all smoking cigarettes except for Skynner – and he regarded Jericho, as did the Americans, blankly, through a fog of tobacco, without the slightest interest. Skynner rattled off the introductions, his arm sweeping round the table like the hand of a clock. 'This is Admiral Trowbridge. Lieutenant Cave. Lieutenant Villiers. Commander Hammerbeck –' the older of the two Americans nodded '– Lieutenant Kramer, US Navy Liaison. Mr Wigram is observing for the Cabinet Office.' Skynner gave a little bow to everybody and sat down again. He was sweating.

Jericho and Logie each collected a folding chair from a stack beside the table and took up positions next to Baxter.

Almost the whole of the wall behind the admiral was taken up by a map of the North Atlantic. Clusters of coloured discs showed the positions of Allied convoys and their escorts: yellow for the merchantmen, green for the warships. Black triangles marked the suspected whereabouts of German U-boats. Beneath the chart was a red telephone, a direct link to the Submarine Tracking Room in the basement of the Admiralty. The only other decoration on the whitewashed walls was a pair of framed photographs. One was of the King, signed, looking nervous, presented after a recent visit. The other was of Grand Admiral Karl Dönitz, commander in chief of the German Navy: Skynner liked to think of himself as locked in a personal battle with the wily Hun.

Now, though, he seemed to have lost the thread of what he was saying. He sorted through his notes and in the time it took Logie and Jericho to take their places, one of the Royal Navy men – Cave, the one with the eye-patch – received a nod from the admiral and started speaking.

'Perhaps, if you've finished outlining your problems, it might be helpful for us now to set out the operational situation.' His chair scraped on the bare floor as he rose to his feet. His tone was insultingly polite. 'The position at twenty-one hundred ...'

Jericho passed his hand over his unshaven chin. He couldn't make up his mind whether to keep his overcoat on or take it off. On, he decided – the room was cold, despite the number of people in it. He undid the buttons and loosened his scarf. As he did so, he noticed the admiral watching him. They couldn't believe it, these senior officers, whenever they came up to visit – the lack of discipline, the scarves and cardigans, the first-name terms. There was a story about Churchill, who'd visited the Park in 1941 and given a speech to the cryptanalysts on the lawn. Afterwards, as he was being driven away, he'd said to the director: 'When I told you to leave no stone unturned recruiting for this place, I didn't expect you to take me literally.' Jericho smiled at the memory. The admiral glowered and flicked cigarette ash on the floor.

The one-eyed naval officer had picked up a pointer and was standing in front of the Atlantic chart, holding a sheaf of notes.

'It must be said, unfortunately, that the news you've given us couldn't have come at a worse moment. No fewer than three convoys have left the United States in the past week and are presently at sea. Convoy SC-122.' He rapped it once with the pointer, hard, as if he had a grudge against it, and read out his notes. 'Departed New York last Friday. Carrying fuel oil, iron ore, steel, wheat, bauxite, sugar, refrigerated meat, zinc, tobacco and tanks. Fifty merchant ships.'

Cave spoke in a clipped, metallic voice, without looking at his audience. His one good eye was fixed on the map.

'Convoy HX-229.' He tapped it. 'Departed New York Monday. Forty merchant vessels. Carrying meat, explosives, lubricating oil, refrigerated dairy produce, manganese, lead, timber, phosphate, diesel oil, aviation spirit, sugar and powdered milk.' He turned to them for the first time. The whole of the left side of his face was a mass of purple scar tissue. 'That, I might say, is two weeks' supply of powdered milk for the entire British Isles.'

There was some nervous laughter. 'Better not lose that,' joked Skynner. The laughter stopped at once. He looked so forlorn in the silence Jericho almost felt sorry for him.

Again, the pointer crashed down.

'And Convoy HX-229A. Left New York Tuesday. Twenty-seven ships. Similar cargoes to the others. Fuel oil, aviation spirit, timber, steel, naval diesel, meat, sugar, wheat, explosives. Three convoys. A total of one hundred and seventeen merchant ships, with a gross registered tonnage of just under one million tons, plus cargo of another million.'

One of the Americans – it was the senior one, Hammerbeck – raised his hand. 'How many men involved?'

'Nine thousand merchant seamen. One thousand passengers.'

'Who are the passengers?'

'Mainly servicemen. Some ladies from the American Red Cross. Quite a lot of children. A party of Catholic missionaries, curiously enough.'

'Jesus Christ.'

Cave permitted himself a crimped smile. 'Quite.'

'And whereabouts are the U-boats?'

'Perhaps I might let my colleague answer that.'

Cave sat down and the other British officer, Villiers, took the floor. He flourished the pointer.

'Submarine Tracking Room had three U-boat packs operational as of zero-zero-hundred Thursday – heah, heah and heah.' His accent barely qualified as recognisable English, it was the sort that pronounced 'cloth' as 'clawth' and 'really' as 'rarely', and when he spoke his lips hardly moved, as if it were somehow ungentlemanly – a betrayal of the amateur ethos – to put too much effort into talking. 'Gruppe Raubgraf heah, two hundred miles off the coast of Greenland. Gruppe Neuland heah, almost precisely mid-ocean. And Gruppe Westmark heah, due south of Iceland.'

'Zero-zero *Thursday*? You mean more than thirty hours ago?' Hammerbeck's hair was the colour and thickness of steel wool, close-cropped to his scalp. It glinted in the fluorescent light as he leaned forwards. 'Where the hell are they now?'

'I'm afraid I've no ideah. I thought that was why we were heah. They've blipped awf the screen.'

Admiral Trowbridge lit another cigarette from the tip of his old one. He had transferred his attention from Jericho and now he was staring at Hammerbeck through small, rheumy eyes.

Again, the American raised his hand. 'How many subs are we talking about in these three wolf packs?'

'I'm sorry to say, ah, they're quite large, ah, we estimate forty-six.'

Skynner squirmed in his chair. Atwood made a great show of rummaging through his papers.

'Let me get this straight,' said Hammerbeck. (He was certainly persistent – Jericho was beginning to admire him.) 'You're telling us one million tons of shipping –'

'Merchant shipping,' interrupted Cave.

'– merchant shipping, pardon me, one million tons of *merchant* shipping, with ten thousand people on board, including various ladies of the American Red Cross and assorted Catholic Bible-bashers, is steaming towards forty-six U-boats, and you have no idea where those U-boats are?'

'I'm rather afraid I am, yes.'

'Well, I'll be fucked,' said Hammerbeck, sitting back in his chair. 'And how long before they get there?'

'That's hard to say.' It was Cave again. He had an odd habit of turning his face away when he talked, and Jericho realised he was trying not to show his shattered cheekbone. 'The SC is the slower convoy. She's making about seven knots. The HXs are both faster, one ten knots, one eleven. I'd say we've got three days, at the maximum. After that, they'll be within operational range of the enemy.'

Hammerbeck had begun whispering to the other American. He was shaking his head and making short chopping motions with his hand. The admiral leaned over and muttered something to Cave, who said quietly: 'I'm afraid so, sir.'

Jericho looked up at the Atlantic, at the yellow discs of the convoys and the black triangles of the U-boats, sewn like shark's teeth across the sea lanes. The distance between the ships and the wolf packs was roughly eight hundred miles. The merchantmen were making maybe two hundred and forty miles every twenty-four hours. Three days was about right. My God, he thought, no wonder Logie was so desperate to get me back.

'Gentlemen, please, if I may?' said Skynner loudly, bringing the meeting back to order. Jericho saw he'd plastered on his 'come let us smile in the face of disaster' expression – invariably a sign of incipient panic. 'I think we should guard against too much pessimism. The Atlantic does cover thirty-two million square miles, you know.' He risked another laugh. 'That's an awful lot of ocean.'

'Yes,' said Hammerbeck, 'and forty-six is one hell of a lot of U-boats.'

'I agree. It's probably the largest concentration of hearses we've faced,' said Cave. 'I'm afraid we must assume the enemy will make contact. Unless, of course, we can find out where they are.'

He gave Skynner a significant look, but Skynner ignored it and pressed on. 'And let's not forget – these convoys are not unprotected?' He glanced around the table for support. 'They do have an escort?'

'Indeed.' Cave again. 'They have an escort of –' he consulted his notes ' – seven destroyers, nine corvettes and three frigates. Plus various other vessels.'

'Under an experienced commander ...'

The British officers glanced at one another, and then at the admiral.

'Actually, it's his first command.'

'Jesus Christ!' Hammerbeck rocked forwards in his chair and brought his fists down on the table.

'If I might step in heah. Obviously, we didn't know last Friday when the escorts were forming up that our intelligence was going to be shut awf.'

'How long will this blackout last?' This was the first time the admiral had spoken and everyone turned to look at him. He gave a sharp, explosive cough, which sounded as if small pieces of machinery were flying around loose in his chest, then sucked in another lungful of smoke and gestured with his cigarette. 'Will it be over in four days, d'you think?'

The question was addressed directly to Skynner and they all turned to look at him. He was an administrator, not a cryptanalyst – he'd been vice-chancellor of some northern university before the war – and Jericho knew he hadn't a clue. He didn't know whether the blackout would last four days, four months or four years.

Skynner said carefully: 'It's possible.'

'Yes, well, all things are possible.' Trowbridge gave an unpleasant rasping laugh that turned into another cough. 'Is it likely? Is it likely you can break this, whatever you call it – this Shark – before our convoys come within range of the U-boats?'

'We'll give it every priority.'

'I know damn well you'll give it every priority, Leonard. You keep saying you'll give it every priority. That's not the question.'

'Well, sir, as you press me, sir, yes.' Skynner stuck his big jaw out heroically. In his mind's eye he was steering his ship manfully into the face of the typhoon. 'Yes, I think we may be able to do it.'

You're mad, thought Jericho.

'And you all believe that?' The admiral stared hard in their direction. He had eyes like a bloodhound's, red-lidded and watery.

Logie was the first to break the silence. He looked at Skynner and winced and scratched the back of his head with the stem of his pipe. 'I suppose we do have the advantage of knowing more about Shark than we did before.'

Atwood jumped in: 'If Guy thinks we can do it, I certainly respect his opinion. I'd go along with whatever he estimates.' Baxter nodded judiciously. Jericho inspected his watch.

'And you?' said the admiral. 'What do you think?'

In Cambridge, they would just about be finishing breakfast. Kite would be steaming open the mail. Mrs Sax would be rattling round with her brushes and pails. In Hall on Saturdays they served vegetable pie with potatoes for lunch ...

He was aware that the room had gone quiet and he looked up to find all eyes were on him. The fair-haired man in the suit was staring at him with particular curiosity. He felt his face begin to colour.

And then he felt a spasm of irritation.

Afterwards Jericho was to think about this moment many

times. What made him act as he did? Was it tiredness? Was he simply disoriented, plucked out of Cambridge and set down in the middle of this nightmare? Was he still ill? Illness would certainly help explain what happened later. Or was he so distracted by the thought of Claire that he wasn't thinking straight? All he remembered for certain was an overwhelming feeling of annoyance. '*You're only here for show, old love.*' You're only here to make up the numbers, so Skynner can put on a good act for the Yanks. You're only here to do as you're told, so keep your views to yourself, and don't ask questions. He was suddenly sick of it all, sick of everything – sick of the blackout, sick of the cold, sick of the chummy first-name terms and the lime smell and the damp and the whale meat – *whale meat* – at four o'clock in the morning ...

'Actually, I'm not sure I am as optimistic as my colleagues.'

Skynner interrupted him at once. You could almost hear the klaxons going off in his mind, see the airmen sprinting across the deck and the big guns swivelling skywards as HMS *Skynner* came under threat. 'Tom's been ill, sir, I'm afraid. He's been away from us for the best part of a month ...'

'Why not?' The admiral's tone was dangerously friendly. 'Why aren't you optimistic?'

'... so I'm not sure he's altogether fully *au fait* with the situation. Wouldn't you admit that, Tom?'

'Well, I'm certainly *au fait* with Enigma, ah, Leonard.' Jericho could hardly believe his own words. He plunged on. 'Enigma is a very sophisticated cipher system. And Shark is its ultimate refinement. I've spent the past eight hours reviewing the Shark material and, ah, forgive me if I'm speaking out of turn, but it seems to me we are in a very serious situation.'

'But you *were* breaking it sucessfully?'

'Yes, but we'd been given a key. The weather code was the key that unlocked the door. The Germans have now changed the weather code. That means we've lost our key. Unless there's been some development I'm not aware of, I don't understand how we're going to ...' Jericho searched for a metaphor. '... pick the lock.'

The other American naval officer, the one who hadn't spoken so far – Jericho had momentarily forgotten his name – said: 'And you still haven't gotten those four-wheel bombes you promised us, Frank.'

'That's a separate issue,' muttered Skynner. He gave Jericho a murderous look.

'Is it?' Kramer – that was it. He was called Kramer. 'Surely if we had a few four-wheel bombes right now we wouldn't need the weather cribs?'

'Just stop there for a moment,' said the admiral, who had been following this conversation with increasing impatience. 'I'm a sailor, and an old sailor at that. I don't understand all this – *talk* – about keys and cribs and bombs with wheels. We're trying to keep the sea-lanes open from America and if we can't do that we're going to lose this war.'

'Hear, hear,' said Hammerbeck. 'Well said, Jack.'

'Now will somebody please give me a straight answer to a straight question? Will this blackout definitely be over in four days' time or won't it? Yes or no?'

Skynner's shoulders sagged. 'No,' he said wearily. 'If you put it like that, sir, I can't say *definitely* it will be over, no.'

'Thank you. So, if it isn't over in four days, when will it be over? You. You're the pessimist. What do you think?'

Once again Jericho was conscious of everyone watching him.

He spoke carefully. Poor Logie was peering inside his tobacco pouch as if he wished he could climb in and never come out. 'It's very hard to say. All we have to measure it by is the last blackout.'

'And how long did that go on?'

'Ten months.'

It was as if he had detonated a bomb. Everybody made a noise. The Navy men shouted. The admiral started coughing. Baxter and Atwood said 'No!' simultaneously. Logie groaned. Skynner, shaking his head, said: 'That really is defeatist of you, Tom.' Even Wigram, the fair-headed man, gave a snort and stared at the rafters, smiling at some private joke.

'I'm not saying it will definitely take us ten months,' Jericho resumed when he could make himself heard. 'But that's the measure of what we're up against and I think that four days is unrealistic. I'm sorry. I do.'

There was a pause, and then Wigram said, softly: '*Why*, I wonder ...'

'Mr Wigram?'

'Sorry, Leonard.' Wigram bestowed his smile around the table, and Jericho's immediate thought was how *expensive* he looked – blue suit, silk tie, Jermyn Street shirt, pomaded hair swept back and scented with some masculine cologne – he might have stepped out of the lobby of the Ritz. *A lounge lizard*, Baxter had called him, which was Bletchley code for *spy*.

'Sorry,' Wigram said again. 'Thinking aloud. I was just wondering *why* Dönitz should have decided to change this *particular* bit of code and *why* he should have chosen to do so *now*.' He stared at Jericho. 'From what you were saying, it sounds as though he couldn't have chosen any one thing more damaging to us.'

Jericho didn't have to reply; Logie did it for him. 'Routine. Almost certainly. They change their code books from time to time. Just our bad luck they did it now.'

'Routine,' repeated Wigram. 'Right.' He smiled once more. 'Tell me, Leonard, how many people know about this weather code and how important it is to us?'

'Really, Douglas,' laughed Skynner, 'whatever are you suggesting?'

'How many?'

'Guy?'

'A dozen, perhaps.'

'Couldn't make me a little list, could you?'

Logie looked to Skynner for approval. 'I, ah, well, I, ah ...'

'Thanks.'

Wigram resumed his examination of the ceiling.

The silence that followed was broken by a long sigh from the admiral. 'I think I gather the sense of the meeting.' He stubbed out his cigarette and reached down beside his chair for his briefcase. He began stuffing his papers into it and his lieutenants followed suit. 'I can't pretend it's the happiest of messages to take back to the First Sea Lord.'

Hammerbeck said: 'I guess I'd better signal Washington.'

The admiral stood and immediately they all pushed back their chairs and got to their feet.

'Lieutenant Cave will act as Admiralty liaison.' He turned to Cave: 'I'd like a daily report. On second thoughts, perhaps better make that twice a day.'

'Yes, sir.'

'Lieutenant Kramer: you'll carry on here and keep Commander Hammerbeck informed?'

'I sure will, sir. Yes, sir.'

'So.' He pulled on his gloves. 'I suggest we reconvene this meeting as and when there are developments to report. Which hopefully will be within four days.'

At the door, the old man turned. 'It's not just one million tons of shipping and ten thousand men, you know. It's one million tons of shipping and ten thousand men *every two weeks*. And it's not just the convoys. It's our obligation to send supplies to Russia. It's our chances of invading Europe and driving the Nazis out. It's everything. It's the whole war.' He gave another of his wheezing laughs. 'Not that I want to put any pressure on you, Leonard.' He nodded. 'Good morning, gentlemen.'

As they mumbled their 'good morning sirs', Jericho heard Wigram say quietly to Skynner: 'I'll talk to you later, Leonard.'

They listened to the visitors clatter down the concrete stairs, and then to the crunch of their feet on the path outside, and suddenly the room was quiet. A mist of blue tobacco hung over the table like smoke rising after a battle.

Skynner's lips were compressed. He was humming to himself. He gathered his papers into a pile and squared off the edges with exaggerated care. For what seemed a long time, nobody spoke.

'Well,' said Skynner eventually, 'that was a triumph. Thank you, Tom. Thank you very much indeed. I'd forgotten what a tower of strength you could be. We've missed you.'

'It's my fault, Leonard,' said Logie. 'Bad briefing. Should have put him in the picture better. Sorry. Bit of a rush first thing.'

'Why don't you just get back to the Hut, Guy? In fact, why don't you all go back, and then Tom and I can have a little chat.'

'Bloody fool,' said Baxter to Jericho.

Atwood took his arm. 'Come on, Alec.'

'Well, he is. Bloody fool.'

They left.

The moment the door closed Skynner said: 'I never wanted you back.'

'Logie didn't mention that.' Jericho folded his arms to stop his hands shaking. 'He said I was needed here.'

'I never wanted you back, not because I think you're a fool – Alec's wrong about that. You're not a fool. But you're a wreck. You're ruined. You've cracked once before under pressure and you'll do it again, as your little performance just now showed. You've outlived your usefulness to us.'

Skynner was leaning his large bottom casually against the edge of the table. He was speaking in a friendly tone and if you had seen him from a distance you would have thought he was exchanging pleasantries with an old acquaintance.

'Then why am I here? I never asked to come back.'

'Logie thinks highly of you. He's the acting head of the Hut and I listen to him. And, I'll be honest, after Turing, you probably have – or, rather, *had* – the best reputation of any cryptanalyst on the Park. You're a little bit of history, Tom. A little bit of a legend. Bringing you back, letting you attend this morning, was a way of showing our masters how seriously we take this, ah, temporary crisis. It was a risk. But obviously I was wrong. You've lost it.'

Jericho was not a violent man. He had never hit another person, not even as a boy, and he knew it was a mercy he had avoided military service: given a rifle he would have been a menace to no one except his own side. But there was a heavy brass ashtray on the table – the sawn-off end of a six-inch shell-case, brimful of cigarette stubs – and Jericho was seriously tempted to ram it into Skynner's smug face. Skynner seemed to sense this. At any rate, he pulled his bottom off the table and began to pace the floor. This must be one of the benefits of being a madman, thought Jericho, people can never take you entirely for granted.

'It was so much simpler in the old days, wasn't it?' said Skynner. 'A country house. A handful of eccentrics. Nobody expecting very much. You potter along. And then suddenly you're sitting on the greatest secret of the war.'

'And then people like you arrive.'

'That's right, people like myself are needed, to make sure this remarkable weapon is used properly.'

'Oh is that what you do, Leonard? You make sure the weapon is used properly. I've often wondered.'

Skynner stopped smiling. He was a big man, nearly a foot taller than Jericho. He came up very close, and Jericho could smell the stale cigarette smoke and the sweat on his clothes.

'You've no conception of this place any more. No idea of the problems. The Americans, for instance. In front of whom you've just humiliated me. Us. We're negotiating a deal with the Americans that –' He stopped himself. 'Never mind. Let's just say that when you – when you *indulge* yourself as you just did, you can't even conceive of the seriousness of what's at stake.'

Skynner had a briefcase with a royal crest stamped on it and 'G VI R' in faded gold lettering. He slipped his papers into it and locked it with a key attached to his belt by a long chain.

'I'm going to arrange for you to be taken off cryptanalytical work and put somewhere you can't do any damage. In fact, I'm going to have you transferred out of Bletchley altogether.' He pocketed the key and patted it. 'You can't return to civilian life, of course, not until the war's over, not knowing what you know. Still, I hear the Admiralty's on the lookout for an extra brain to work in statistics. Dull stuff, but cushy enough for a man of your ... delicacy. Who knows? Perhaps you'll meet a nice girl. Someone more – how shall we say? – more *suitable* for you than the person I gather you *were* seeing.'

Jericho did try to hit him then, but not with the ashtray, only with his fist, which in retrospect was a mistake. Skynner stepped to one side with surprising grace and the blow missed and then his right hand shot out and grabbed Jericho's forearm. Skynner dug his fingers very hard into the soft muscle.

'You are an ill man, Tom. And I am stronger than you, in every way.' He increased the pressure for a second or two, then abruptly let go of the arm. 'Now get out of my sight.'

5

God, but he was tired. Exhaustion stalked him like a living thing, clutching at his legs, squatting on his sagging shoulders. Jericho leaned against the outside wall of A-Block, rested his cheek against the smooth, damp concrete, and waited for his pulse to return to normal.

What had he done?

He needed to lie down. He needed to find some hole to crawl into and get some rest. Like a drunk searching for his keys, he felt first in one pocket and then another and finally pulled out the billeting chit and squinted at it. Albion Street? Where was that? He had a vague memory. He would know it when he saw it.

He pushed himself away from the wall and began to make his way, carefully, away from the lake towards the road that led to the main gate. A small, black car was parked about ten yards ahead and as he came closer the driver's door opened and a figure in a blue uniform appeared.

'Mr Jericho!'

Jericho stared with surprise. It was one of the Americans. 'Lieutenant Kramer?'

'Hi. Going home? Can I give you a ride?'

'Thank you. No. Really, it's only a short walk.'

'Aw, come on.' Kramer patted the roof of the car. 'I just got her. It'd be my pleasure. Come on.'

Jericho was about to decline again, but then he felt his legs begin to crumple.

'Whoa there, feller.' Kramer sprang forward and took his arm. 'You're all in. Long night, I guess?'

Jericho allowed himself to be guided to the passenger door and pushed into the front seat. The interior of the little car was cold and smelled as if it hadn't been used in a long while. Jericho guessed it must have been someone's pride and joy until petrol rationing forced it off the road. The chassis rocked as Kramer clambered in the other side and slammed the door.

'Not many people around here run their own cars.' Jericho's voice sounded oddly in his ears, as if from a distance. 'You have trouble getting fuel?'

'No, sir.' Kramer pressed the starter button and the engine rattled into life. 'You know us. We can get as much as we want.'

The car was carefully inspected at the main gate. The barrier rose and they headed out, past the canteen and the assembly hall, towards the end of Wilton Avenue.

'Which way?'

'Left, I think.'

Kramer flicked out one of the little amber indicators and they turned into the lane that led down to the town. His face was handsome – boyish and square-cut, with a faded tan that suggested service overseas. He was about twenty-five and looked formidably fit.

'I guess I'd like to thank you for that.'

'Thank me?'

'At the conference. You told the truth when the others all talked bullshit. "Four days" – Jesus!'

'They were just being loyal.'

'Loyal? Come on, Tom. D'you mind if I call you Tom? I'm Jimmy, by the way. They'd been fixed.'

'I don't think this is a conversation we should be having ...' The dizziness had passed and in the clarity that always followed it occurred to Jericho that the American must have been waiting for him to emerge from the meeting. 'This will do fine, thank you.'

'Really? But we've hardly gone any distance.'

'Please, just pull over.'

Kramer swerved into the kerb beside a row of small cottages, braked and turned off the engine.

'Listen, will you, Tom, just a minute? The Germans brought in Shark three months after Pearl Harbor –'

'Look –'

'Relax. Nobody's listening.' This was true. The lane was deserted. 'Three months after Pearl Harbor, and suddenly we're losing ships like we're going out of business. But nobody tells us why. After all, we're the new boys around here – we just route the convoys the way London tells us. Finally, it's getting so bad, we ask you guys what's happened to all this great intelligence you used to have.' He jabbed his finger at Jericho. 'Only *then* are we told about Shark.'

'I can't listen to this,' said Jericho. He tried to open the door but Kramer leaned across and seized the handle.

'I'm not trying to poison your mind against your own people. I'm just trying to tell you what's going on here. After we were told about Shark last year, we started to do some checking. Fast. And eventually, after one hell of a fight, we began to get some figures. D'you know how many bombes you guys had by the end of last summer? This is after two years of manufacture?'

Jericho was staring straight ahead. 'I wouldn't be privy to information like that.'

'Fifty! And d'you know how many our people in Washington said they could build within *four months*? Three hundred and sixty!'

'Well, build them, then,' said Jericho, irritably, 'if you're so bloody marvellous.'

'Oh no,' said Kramer. 'You don't understand. That's not allowed. Enigma is a British baby. Official. Any change in status has to be negotiated.'

'Is it being negotiated?'

'In Washington. Right now. That's where your Mr Turing is. In the meantime, we just have to take whatever you give us.'

'But that's absurd. Why not just build the bombes anyway?'

'Come on, Tom. Think about it for a minute. You have all the intercept stations over here. You have all the raw material. We're three thousand miles away. Damn hard to pick up Magdeburg from Florida. And what's the point in having three hundred and sixty bombes if there's nothing to put in them?'

Jericho shut his eyes and saw Skynner's flushed face, heard his rumbling voice: '*You've no conception of this place any more ... We're negotiating a deal with the Americans ... You can't even conceive of the seriousness* ...' Now, at least, he understood the reason for Skynner's anger. His little empire, so painfully put together, brick by bureaucratic brick, was mortally threatened by Shark. But the threat came not from Berlin. It came from Washington.

'Don't get me wrong,' Kramer was saying, 'I've been here a month and I think what you've all achieved is astounding. Brilliant. And nobody on our side is talking about a takeover. But it can't go on like this. Not enough bombes. Not enough typewriters. Those huts. Christ! "Was it dangerous in the war, Daddy?" "Sure was, I damned near froze to death." Did you know the whole operation almost stopped one time because you ran out of coloured pencils? I mean, what are we saying here? That men have to die because you don't have enough *pencils*?'

Jericho felt too tired to argue. Besides, he knew enough to know it was true: all true. He remembered a night, eighteen months ago, when he'd been asked to keep an eye open for strangers at the Shoulder of Mutton, standing near the door in the blackout, sipping halves of shandy, while Turing, Welchman and a couple of the other big chiefs met in a room upstairs and wrote a joint letter to Churchill. Exactly the same story: not enough clerks, not enough typists, the factory at Letchworth that made the bombes – it used to make cash registers, of all things – short of parts, short of manpower ... There'd been one hell of a row when Churchill got the letter – a tantrum in Downing Street, careers broken, machinery shaken up – and things had improved, for a while. But Bletchley was a greedy child. Its appetite grew with the feeding. '*Nervos belli, pecuniam infinitam.*' Or, as Baxter had put it, more prosaically, it all comes down to money in the end. The Poles had had to give Enigma to the British. Now the Brits would have to share it with the Yanks.

'I can't have anything to do with this. I've got to get some sleep. Thanks for the lift.'

He reached for the handle and this time Kramer made no attempt to stop him. He was halfway out of the door when Kramer said: 'I heard you lost your old man in the last war.'

Jericho froze. 'Who told you that?'

'I forget. Does it matter?'

'No. It's not a secret.' Jericho massaged his forehead. He had a filthy headache coming on. 'It happened before I was born. He was wounded by a shell at Ypres. He lived on for a bit but he wasn't much use after that. He never came out of hospital. He died when I was six.'

'What did he do? Before he got hit?'

'He was a mathematician.'

There was a moment's silence.

'I'll see you around,' said Jericho. He got out of the car.

'My brother died,' said Kramer suddenly. 'One of the first. He was in the Merchant Marine. Liberty ships.'

Of course, thought Jericho.

'This was during the Shark blackout, I suppose?'

'You got it.' Kramer looked bleak, then forced a smile. 'Let's keep in touch, Tom. Anything I can do for you – just ask.'

He reached over and pulled the door shut with a bang. Jericho stood alone on the roadside and watched as Kramer executed a rapid U-turn. The car backfired, then headed at speed up the hill towards the Park, leaving a little puff of dirty smoke hanging in the morning air.

THREE

PINCH

PINCH: (1) vb., to steal enemy cryptographic material; (2) n., any object stolen from the enemy that enhances the chances of breaking his codes or ciphers.

A Lexicon of Cryptography

('Most Secret', Bletchley Park, 1943)

1

Bletchley was a railway town. The great main line from London to Scotland split it down the middle, and then the smaller branch line from Oxford to Cambridge sliced it into quarters, so that wherever you stood there was no escaping the trains: the noise of them, the smell of their soot, the sight of their brown smoke rising above the clustered roofs. Even the terraced houses were mostly railway-built, cut from the same red brick as the station and the engine sheds, constructed in the same dour, industrial style.

The Commercial Guesthouse, Albion Street, was about five minutes' walk from Bletchley Park and backed on to the main line. Its owner, Mrs Ethel Armstrong, was, like her establishment, a little over fifty years old, solidly built, with a forbidding, late-Victorian aspect. Her husband had died of a heart attack a month after the outbreak of war, whereupon she had converted their four-storey property into a small hotel. Like the other townspeople – and there were about seven thousand of them – she had no idea of what went on in the grounds of the mansion up the road, and even less interest. It was profitable, that was all that mattered to her. She charged thirty-eight shillings a week and expected her five residents, in return for meals, to hand over all their food-rationing coupons. As a result, by the spring of 1943, she had a thousand pounds in War Savings Bonds and enough edible goods hoarded in her cellar to open a medium-sized grocery store.

It was on the Wednesday that one of her rooms had become vacant, and on the Friday that she had been served a billeting notice requiring her to provide accommodation to a Mr Thomas Jericho. His possessions from his previous address had been delivered to her door that same morning: two boxes of personal effects and an ancient iron bicycle. The bicycle she wheeled into the back yard. The boxes she carried upstairs.

One carton was full of books. A couple of Agatha Christies. *A Synopsis of Elementary Results in Pure and Applied Mathematics*, two volumes, by a fellow named George Shoobridge Garr. *Principia Mathematica*, whatever that was. A pamphlet with a suspiciously Germanic ring to it – *On Computable Numbers, with an Application to the Entscheidungsproblem* – inscribed 'To Tom, with fond respect, Alan'. More books full of mathematics, one so repeatedly read it was almost falling to pieces and stuffed full of markers – bus and tram tickets, a beer mat, even a blade of grass. It fell open at a heavily underlined passage:

> there is one purpose at any rate which the real mathematics may serve in war. When the world is mad, a mathematician may find in mathematics an incomparable anodyne. For mathematics is, of all the arts and sciences, the most remote.

Well, the last line's true enough, she thought. She closed the book, turned it around and squinted at the spine: *A Mathematician's Apology* by G. H. Hardy, Cambridge University Press.

The other box also yielded little of interest. A Victorian etching of King's College Chapel. A cheap Waralarm clock, set to go off at eleven, in a black fibre case. A wireless. An academic mortarboard and a dusty gown. A bottle of ink. A telescope. A copy of *The Times* dated 23 December 1942, folded to the crossword, which had been filled in by two different hands, one very small and precise, the other rounder, probably feminine. Written above it was 2712815. And, finally, at the bottom of the carton, a map, which, when she unfolded it, proved not to be of England, or even (as she had suspected and secretly hoped) of Germany, but of the night sky.

She was so put off by this dreary collection that when, at half past midnight that night, there was a knock on the door and another two suitcases were delivered by a small man with a northern accent, she didn't even bother to open them but dumped them straight in the empty room.

Their owner arrived at nine o'clock on Saturday morning. She was sure of the time, she explained later to her next-door neighbour, Mrs Scratchwood, because the religious service was just ending on the wireless and the news was about to start. And he was exactly as she'd suspected he would be. He wasn't very tall. He was thin. Bookish. Ill-looking, and nursing his arm, as if he'd just injured it. He hadn't shaved, was as white as – well, she was going to say 'as a sheet', but she hadn't seen sheets that white since before the war, certainly not in her house. His clothes were of good quality, but in a mess: she noticed there was a button missing on his overcoat. He was pleasant enough, though. Nicely spoken. Very good manners. A quiet voice. She'd never had any children herself, never had a son, but if she had, he would have been about the same age. Well, let's just say he needed feeding up, anyone could see that.

She was strict about the rent. She always demanded a month in advance – the request was made down in the hall, before she took them up to see the room – and there was usually an argument, at the end of which she grumpily agreed to settle for two weeks. But he paid up without a murmur. She asked for seven pounds six shillings and he gave her eight pounds, and when she pretended she hadn't any change, he said: 'Fine, give it me later.' When she mentioned his ration book he looked at her for a moment, very puzzled, and then he said (and she would remember it for the rest of her life): 'Do you mean this?'

'*Do you mean this?*' She repeated it in wonderment. As if he'd never seen one before! He gave her the little brown booklet – the precious weekly passport to four ounces of butter, eight ounces of bacon, twelve ounces of sugar – and told her she could do what she liked with it. 'I've never had any use for it.'

By this time she was so flustered she hardly knew what she was doing. She tucked the money and the ration book into her apron before he could change his mind and led him upstairs.

Now Ethel Armstrong was the first to admit that the fifth bedroom of the Commercial Guest House was not up to much. It was at the end of the passage, up a little twist of stairs, and the only furniture in it was a single bed and a wardrobe. It was so small the door wouldn't open properly because the bed got in the way. It had a tiny window flecked with soot which looked out over the wide expanse of railway tracks. In two and a half years it must have had thirty different occupants. None had stayed more than a couple of months and some had refused to sleep in it at all. But this one just sat on the edge of the bed, squeezed in between his boxes and his cases, and said wearily, 'Very pleasant, Mrs Armstrong.'

She quickly explained the rules of the house. Breakfast was at seven in the morning, dinner at six thirty in the evening, 'cold collations' would be left in the kitchen for those working irregular shifts. There was one bathroom at the far end of the passage, shared between the five guests. They were permitted one bath a week each, the depth of water not to exceed five inches (a line was marked on the enamel) and he would have to arrange his turn with the others. He would be given four lumps of coal per evening to heat his room. The fire in the parlour downstairs was extinguished at 9 p.m., sharp. Anyone caught cooking, drinking alcohol or entertaining visitors in their room, especially of the opposite sex – he'd smiled faintly at that – would be evicted, balance of rent to be paid as a forfeit.

She'd asked if he had any questions, to which he made no reply, which was a mercy, because at that moment a nonstop express shrieked past at sixty miles an hour no more than a hundred feet from the bedroom window, shaking the little room so violently that Mrs Armstrong had a brief and horrifying vision of the floor giving way and them both plummeting downwards, down through her own bedroom, down through the scullery, crashing down to land amid the waxy legs of ham and tinned peaches so carefully stacked and hidden in her Aladdin's cave of a cellar.

'Well, then,' she said, when the noise (if not yet the house) had finally subsided, 'I'll leave you to get some peace and quiet.'

*

Tom Jericho sat on the edge of the bed for a couple of minutes after listening to her footsteps descending the stairs. Then he took off his jacket and shirt and examined his throbbing forearm. He had a pair of bruises just below the elbow as neat and black as damsons, and he remembered now whom Skynner had always reminded him of: a prefect at school called Fane, the son of a bishop, who liked to cane the new boys in his study at teatime, and make them all say 'thank you, Fane' afterwards.

It was cold in the room and he started to shiver, his skin puckering into rashes of gooseflesh. He felt desperately tired. He opened one of his suitcases and took out a pair of pyjamas and changed into them quickly. He hung up his jacket and thought about unpacking the rest of his clothes, but decided against it. He might be out of Bletchley by the next morning. That was a point – he passed his hand across his face – he'd just given away eight pounds, more than a week's salary, for a room he might not need.

The wardrobe vibrated as he opened it and the wire coat hangers sounded a melancholy chime. Inside it stank of mothballs. He quickly shoved the carboard boxes into it and pushed the cases under the bed. Then he drew the curtains, lay down on the lumpy mattress, and pulled the blankets up under his chin.

For three years Jericho had led a nocturnal life, rising with the darkness, going to bed with the light, but he'd never got used to it. Lying there listening to the distant sounds of a Saturday morning made him feel like an invalid. Downstairs someone was running a bath. The water tank was in the attic directly above his head, and the noise of it emptying and refilling was deafening. He closed his eyes and all he could see was the chart of the North Atlantic. He opened them and the bed shook slightly as a train went by and that reminded him of Claire. The 15.06 out of London Euston – '*calling at Willesden, Watford, Apsley, Berkhamstead, Tring, Cheddington and Leighton Buzzard, arriving Bletchley four-nineteen*' – he could recite the station announcement even now, and see her now as well. It had been his first glimpse of her.

This must have been – what? – a week after the break into Shark? A couple of days before Christmas, anyway. He and Logie, Puck and Atwood had been ordered to present themselves at the office block in Broadway, near St James's tube station, from which Bletchley Park was run. 'C' himself had made a little speech about the value of their work. In recognition of their 'vital breakthrough', and on the orders of the Prime Minister, they had each received an iron handshake and an envelope containing a cheque for a hundred pounds, drawn on an ancient and obscure City bank. Afterwards, slightly embarrassed, they'd said goodbye to one another on the pavement and gone their various ways – Logie to lunch at the Admiralty, Puck to meet a girl, Atwood to a concert at the National Portrait Gallery – and Jericho back to Euston to catch the train to Bletchley, '*calling at Willesden, Watford, Apsley* ...'

There would be no more cheques now, he thought. Perhaps Churchill would ask for his money back.

A million tons of shipping. Ten thousand people. Forty-six U-boats. And that was just the beginning of it.

'*It's everything. It's the whole war.*'

He turned his face to the wall.

Another train went by, and then another. Someone else began to run a bath. In the back yard, directly beneath his window, Mrs Armstrong hung the parlour carpet over the washing line and began to beat it, hard and rhythmically, as if it were a tenant behind with his rent or some prying inspector from the Ministry of Food.

Darkness closed around him.

*

The dream is a memory, the memory a dream.

A teeming station platform – iron girders and pigeons fluttering against a filthy glass cupola. Tinny carols playing over the public address system. Steel light and splashes of khaki.

A line of soldiers bent sideways by the weight of kitbags runs towards the guard's van. A sailor kisses a pregnant woman in a red hat and pats her bottom. School children going home for Christmas, salesmen in threadbare overcoats, a pair of thin and anxious mothers in tatty furs, a tall, blonde woman in a well-cut, ankle-length grey coat, trimmed with black velvet at the collar and cuffs. A pre-war coat, *he thinks,* nothing so fine is made nowadays ...

She walks past the window and he realises with a jolt that she's noticed he is staring at her. He glances at his watch, snaps the lid shut with his thumb and when he looks up again she's actually stepping into his compartment. Every seat is taken. She hesitates. He stands to offer her his place. She smiles her thanks and gestures to show there's just sufficient room for her to squeeze between him and the window. He nods and sits again with difficulty.

Doors slam along the length of the train, a whistle blows, they shudder forwards. The platform is a blur of waving people.

He's wedged so tightly he can barely move. Such intimacy would never have been tolerated before the war, but nowadays, on these endless, uncomfortable journeys, men and women are always being thrown together, often literally so. Her thigh is pressed to his, so hard he can feel the firmness of muscle and bone beneath the padding of her flesh. Her shoulder is to his. Their legs touch. Her stocking rustles against his calf. He can feel the warmth of her, and smell her scent.

He looks past her and pretends to stare out of the window at the ugly houses sliding by. She's much younger than he thought at first. Her face in profile is not conventionally pretty, but striking – angular, strong – he supposes 'handsome' is the word for it. She has very blonde hair, tied back. When he tries to move, his elbow brushes the side of her breast and he thinks he might die of embarrassment. He apologises profusely but she doesn't seem to notice. She has a copy of The Times, *folded up very small so that she can hold it in one hand.*

The compartment is packed. Servicemen lie on the floor and jam the corridor outside. An RAF corporal has fallen asleep in the luggage rack and cradles his kit bag like a lover. Someone begins to snore. The air smells strongly of cheap cigarettes and unwashed bodies. But gradually, for Jericho, all this begins to disappear. There are just the two of them, rocking with the train. Where they touch his skin is burning. His calf muscles ache with the strain of neither moving too close nor drawing apart.

He wonders how far she's going. Each time they stop at one of the little stations he fears she might get off. But no: she continues to stare down at her square of newsprint. The dreary hinterland of northern London gives way to a dreary countryside, monochrome in the darkening December afternoon – frosted fields barren of livestock, bare trees and the straggling dark lines of hedgerows, empty lanes, little villages with smoking chimneys that stand out like smudges of soot in the white landscape.

An hour passes. They're clear of Leighton Buzzard and within five minutes of Bletchley when she suddenly says: 'German town partly in French disagreement with Hamelin.'

He isn't sure he's heard her properly, or even if the remark is addressed to him.

'I'm sorry?'

'German town partly in French disagreement with Hamelin.' She repeats it, as if he's stupid. 'Seven down. Eight letters.'

'Ah yes,' he says. 'Ratisbon.'

'How do you get that? I don't think I've even heard of it.' She turns her face to him. He has an impression of large features – a sharp nose, a wide mouth – but it is the eyes that hold him. Grey eyes – a cold grey, with no hint of blue. They're not dove-grey, he decides later, or pearl-grey. They're the grey of snow clouds waiting to break.

'It's a cathedral city. On the Danube, I believe. Partly in French – well, bon, obviously. Disagreement with Hamelin. That's easy. Hamelin – Pied Piper – rats. Rat is bon. Rat is good. Not the view in Hamelin.'

He starts to laugh then stops himself. Just hark at yourself, he thinks, you're babbling like an idiot.

'Fill up ten. Nine letters.'

'That's an anagram,' he says immediately. 'Plentiful.'

'Morning snack as far as it goes. Five letters.'

'Ambit.'

She shakes her head, smiling, filling in the answers. 'How do you get it so quickly?'

'It's not hard. You learn to know the way they think. Morning – that's a.m., obviously. Snack as far as it goes – bite with the e missing. As far as it goes – well, within one's ambit. One's limits. May I?'

He reaches over and takes the paper and pencil. Half his brain studies the puzzle, the other half studies her – how she takes a cigarette from her handbag and lights it, how she watches him, her head resting slightly to one side. Aster, tasso, lovage, landau ... It's the first and only time in *their relationship he's ever fully in control, and by the time he's completed the thirty clues and given her back the paper they're pulling through the outskirts of a small town, crawling past narrow gardens and tall chimneys. Behind her head he sees the familiar lines of washing, the air raid shelters, the vegetable plots, the little red-brick houses coated black by the passing trains. The compartment darkens as they pass beneath the iron canopy of the station. 'Bletchley,' calls the guard. 'Bletchley station!'*

He says, 'I'm afraid this is my stop.'

'Yes.' She looks thoughtfully at the finished crossword, then turns and smiles at him. 'Yes. D'you know, I rather guessed it might be.'

'Mr Jericho!' someone calls. 'Mr Jericho!'

*

'Mr Jericho!'

He opened his eyes. For a moment he was disoriented. The wardrobe loomed over him like a thief in the dim light.

'Yes.' He sat up in the strange bed. 'I'm sorry. Mrs Armstrong?'

'It's a quarter past six, Mr Jericho.' She was shouting to him from halfway up the stairs. 'Will you be wanting supper?'

A quarter past six? The room was almost dark. He pulled his watch out from beneath his pillow and flicked it open. To his astonishment he found he had slept through the entire day.

'That would be very kind, Mrs Armstrong. Thank you.'

The dream had been disturbingly vivid – more substantial, certainly, than this shadowy room – and as he threw off the blankets and swung his bare feet on to the cold floor, he felt himself to be in a no-man's-land between two worlds. He had a peculiar conviction that Claire had been thinking of him, that his subconscious had somehow acted like a radio receiver and had picked up a message from her. It was an absurd thought for a mathematician, a rationalist, to entertain, but he couldn't rid himself of it. He found his sponge-bag and slipped his overcoat over his pyjamas.

On the first floor a figure in a blue flannel dressing gown and white paper curlers hurried out of the bathroom. He nodded politely but the woman gave a squeak of embarrassment and scuttled down the passage. Standing at the basin, he laid out his toiletries: a sliver of carbolic soap, a safety razor with a six-month-old blade, a wooden toothbrush worn down to a fuzz of bristles, an almost empty tin of pink tooth powder. The taps clanked. There was no hot water. He scraped at his chin for ten minutes until it was red and pricked with blood. This was where the devil of the war resided, he thought, as he dabbed at his skin with the hard towel: in the details, in the thousand petty humiliations of never having enough toilet paper or soap or matches or baths or clean clothes. Civilians had been pauperised. They smelled, that was the truth of it. Body odour lay over the British Isles like a great sour fog.

There were two other guests downstairs in the dining room, a Miss Jobey and a Mr Bonnyman, and the three of them made discreet conversation while they waited for their food. Miss Jobey was dressed in black with a cameo brooch at her throat. Bonnyman wore mildew-coloured tweeds with a set of pens in his breast pocket and Jericho guessed he might be an engineer on the bombes. The door to the kitchen swung open as Mrs Armstrong brought in their plates.

'Here we go,' whispered Bonnyman. 'Brace yourself, old boy.'

'Now, don't you go getting her worked up again, Arthur,' said Miss Jobey. She gave his arm a playful pinch, at which Bonnyman's hand slid beneath the table and squeezed her knee. Jericho poured them all a glass of water and pretended not to notice.

'It's potato pie,' announced Mrs Armstrong, defiantly. 'With gravy. And potatoes.'

They contemplated their steaming plates.

'How very, ah, substantial,' said Jericho, eventually.

The meal passed in silence. Pudding was some kind of stewed apple with powdered custard. Once that had been cleared away Bonnyman lit his pipe and announced that, as it was a Saturday night, he and Miss Jobey would be going to the Eight Bells Inn on the Buckingham Road.

'Naturally, you're very welcome to join us,' he said, in a tone which implied that Jericho, naturally, wouldn't be welcome at all. 'Do you have any plans?'

'It's kind of you, but as a matter of fact I do have plans. Or, rather, *a* plan.'

After the others had gone, he helped Mrs Armstrong clear away the dishes, then went out into the back yard to check his bicycle. It was almost dark and there was a sharpness in the air that promised frost. The lights still worked. He cleaned the dirt off the regulation white patch on the mudguard and pumped some air into the tyres.

By eight o'clock he was back up in his room. At half past ten, Mrs Armstrong was on the point of laying aside her knitting to go up to bed when she heard him coming downstairs. She opened the door a crack, just in time to see Jericho hurrying along the passage and out into the night.

2

The moon defied the blackout, shining a blue torch over the frozen fields, quite bright enough for a man to cycle by. Jericho lifted himself out of the saddle and trod hard on the pedals, rocking from side to side as he toiled up the hill out of Bletchley, pursuing his own shadow, cast sharp on the road before him. From far in the distance came the drone of a returning bomber.

The road began to level out and he sat back on the saddle. For all his efforts with the pump, the tyres remained half-flat, the wheels and chain were stiff for want of oil. It was hard going, but Jericho didn't mind. He was taking action, that was the point. It was the same as code-breaking. However hopeless the situation, the rule was always to do *something*. No cryptogram, Alan Turing used to say, was ever solved by simply staring at it.

He cycled on for about two miles, following the lane as it continued to rise gently towards Shenley Brook End. This was hardly a village, more a tiny hamlet of perhaps a dozen houses, mostly farmworkers' cottages. He couldn't see the buildings, which sheltered in a slight hollow, but when he rounded a bend and caught the scent of woodsmoke he knew he must be close.

Just before the hamlet, on the left, there was a gap in the hawthorn hedge where a rutted track led to a little cottage that stood alone. He turned into it and skittered to a halt, his feet slipping on the frozen mud. A white owl, improbably huge, rose from a nearby branch and flapped soundlessly across the field. Jericho squinted at the cottage. Was it his imagination, or was there a hint of light in the downstairs window? He dismounted and began to wheel his bike towards it.

He felt wonderfully calm. Above the thatched roof the constellations spread out like the lights of a city – Ursa Minor and Polaris, Pegasus and Cepheus, the flattened M of Cassiopeia with the Milky Way flowing through it. No glow from earth obscured their brilliance. *You can at least say this for the blackout*, he thought, *it has given us back the stars*.

The door was stout and iron-studded. It was like knocking on stone. After half a minute he tried again.

'Claire?' he called. 'Claire?'

There was a pause, and then: 'Who is it?'

'It's Tom.'

He took a breath and braced himself, as if for a blow. The handle turned and the door opened slightly, just enough to reveal a dark-haired woman, thirtyish, about Jericho's height. She was wearing round spectacles and a thick overcoat and was holding a prayer book.

'Yes?'

For a moment he was speechless. 'I'm sorry,' he said, 'I was looking for Claire.'

'She's not in.'

'Not in?' he repeated, hopelessly. He remembered now that Claire shared the cottage with a woman called Hester Wallace (*'she works in Hut 6, she's a sweetie'*) but for some reason he had forgotten all about her. She did not look very sweet to Jericho. She had a thin face, split like a knife by a long, sharp nose. Her hair was wrenched back off a frowning forehead. 'I'm Tom Jericho.' She made no response. 'Perhaps Claire's mentioned me?'

'I'll tell her you called.'

'Will she be back soon?'

'I've no idea, I'm sorry.'

She began to close the door. Jericho pressed his foot against it. 'I say, I know this is awfully rude of me, but I couldn't possibly come in and wait, could I?'

The woman glanced at his foot, and then at his face. 'I'm afraid that's impossible. Good evening, Mr Jericho.' She pushed the door closed with surprising force.

Jericho took a step backwards on to the track. This was not a contingency envisaged in his plan. He looked at his watch. It was just after eleven. He picked up his bicycle and wheeled it back towards the lane, but at the last moment, instead of going out on to the road, he turned left and followed the line of the hedge. He laid the bicycle flat and drew into the shadows to wait.

After about ten minutes, the cottage door opened and closed

and he heard the rattle of a bicycle being wheeled over stone. It was as he thought: Miss Wallace had been dressed to go out because she was working the midnight shift. A pinprick of yellow light apeared, wobbled briefly from side to side, and then began to bob towards him. Hester Wallace passed within twenty feet in the moonlight, knees pumping, elbows stuck out, as angular as an old umbrella. She stopped at the entrance to the lane and slipped on a luminous armlet. Jericho edged further into the hawthorn. Half a minute later she was gone. He waited a full quarter of an hour in case she'd forgotten something, then headed back to the cottage.

There was only one key – ornate and iron and big enough to fit a cathedral. It was kept, he recalled, under a piece of slate beneath a flowerpot. Damp had warped the door and he had to push hard to open it, scraping an arc on the flagstone floor. He replaced the key and closed the door behind him before turning on the light.

He had only been inside once before, but there wasn't much to remember. Two rooms on the ground floor: a sitting room with low beams and a kitchen straight ahead. To his left, a narrow staircase led up to a little landing. Claire's bedroom was at the front, looking towards the lane. Hester's was at the rear. The lavatory was a chemical toilet just outside the back door, reached via the kitchen. There was no bathroom. A galvanised metal tub was kept in the shed next to the kitchen. Baths were taken in front of the stove. The whole place was cold and cramped and smelled of mildew. He wondered how Claire stuck it.

'Oh, but darling, it's so much better than having some ghastly landlady telling one what to do ...'

Jericho took a couple of steps across the worn rug and stopped. For the first time he began to feel uneasy. Everywhere he looked he saw evidence of a life being lived quite contentedly without him – the ill-assorted blue-and-white china in the dresser, the vase full of daffodils, the stack of pre-war *Vogues*, even the arrangement of the furniture (the two armchairs and the sofa drawn up cosily around the hearth). Every tiny domestic detail seemed significant and premeditated.

He had no business here.

He very nearly left at that moment. All that stopped him was the faintly pathetic realisation that he had nowhere else particularly to go. The Park? Albion Street? King's? His life seemed to have become a maze of dead ends.

Better to make a stand here, he decided, than run away again. She was bound to be back quite soon.

God, but it was cold! His bones were ice. He walked up and down the cramped room, ducking to avoid the heavy beams. In the hearth was white ash and a few blackened fragments of wood. He sat first in one armchair, then tried the other. Now he was facing the door. To his right was the sofa. Its covers were of frayed pink silk, its cushions hollowed and leaking feathers. The springs had gone and when you sat in it you sank almost to the floor and had to struggle to get out. He remembered that sofa and he stared at it for a long time, as a soldier might stare at a battlefield where a war had been irretrievably lost.

*

They leave the train together and walk up the footpath to the Park. To their left is a playing field, ploughed into allotments for the Dig for Victory campaign. To their right, through the perimeter fence, is the familiar huddle of low buildings. People walk briskly to ward off the cold. The December afternoon is raw and misty, the day is leaking into dusk.

She tells him she's been up to London to celebrate her birthday. How old does he think she is?

He hasn't a clue. Eighteen perhaps?

Twenty, she says triumphantly, ancient. And what was he doing in town?

He can't tell her, of course. Just business, he says. Just business.

Sorry, she says, she shouldn't have asked. She still can't get the hang of all this 'need to know'. She has been at the Park three months and hates it. Her father works at the Foreign Office and wangled her the job to keep her out of mischief. How long has he been here?

Three years, says Jericho, she shouldn't worry, it'll get better.

Ah, she says, that's easy for him to say, but surely he *does something interesting?*

Not really, he says, but then he thinks that makes him sound boring, so he adds: 'Well, quite interesting, I suppose.'

In truth he's finding it hard to keep up his end of the conversation. It's distracting enough merely to walk alongside her. They lapse into silence.

There's a noticeboard close to the main gate advertising a performance of Bach's Musikalisches Opfer *by the Bletchley Park Music Society. 'Oh, now look at that,' she says, 'I* adore *Bach', to which Jericho replies, with genuine enthusiasm, that Bach is his favourite composer. Grateful at last to have found something to talk about, he launches into a long dissertation about the* Musikalisches Opfer*'s six-part fugue, which Bach is supposed to have improvised on the spot for King Frederick the Great, a feat equivalent to playing and winning sixty games of blindfold chess simultaneously. Perhaps she knows that Bach's dedication to the King –* Regis Iussu Cantio et Reliqua Canonica Arte Resoluta *– rather interestingly yields the acrostic RICERCAR, meaning 'to seek'?*

No, oddly enough, she doesn't know that.

This increasingly desperate monologue carries them as far as the huts where they both stop and, after another awkward pause, introduce themselves. She offers him her hand – her grip is warm and firm, but her nails are a shock: painfully bitten back, almost to the quick. Her surname is Romilly. Claire Romilly. It has a pleasant ring. Claire Romilly. He wishes her a merry Christmas and turns away but she calls him back. She hopes he won't think it too fresh of her, but would he like to go with her to the concert?

He isn't sure, he doesn't know ...

She writes down the date and time just above The Times *crossword – 27 December at 8.15 – and thrusts it into his hands. She'll buy the tickets. She'll see him there.*

Please don't say no.

And before he can think of an excuse, she's gone.

He's due to be on shift on the evening of the 27th but he doesn't know where to find her to tell her he can't go. And anyway, he realises, he rather does *want to go. So he calls in a favour he's owed by Arthur de Brooke and waits outside the assembly hall, and waits, and waits. Eventually, after everyone else has gone in, and just when he's about to give up, she comes running out of the darkness, smiling her apologies.*

The concert is better than he'd hoped. The quintet all work at the Park and once played professionally. The harpsichordist is particularly fine. The women in the audience are wearing evening frocks, the men are wearing suits. Suddenly, and for the first time he can recall, the war seems a long way away. As the last notes of the third canon ('per Motum contrarium') *are dying in the air he risks a glance at Claire only to discover that she is looking at him. She touches his arm and when the fourth canon* ('per Augmentationem, contrario Motu') *begins, he is lost.*

Afterwards he has to go straight back to the hut: he's promised he'd be back before midnight. 'Poor Mr Jericho,' she says, 'just like Cinderella ...' But at her suggestion they meet again for the following week's concert – Chopin – and when that's over they walk down the hill to the station to have cocoa in the platform buffet.

'So,' she says, as he returns from the counter bearing two cups of brown froth, 'how much am I allowed to know about you?'

'Me? Oh, I'm very boring.'

'I don't think you're boring at all. In fact, I've heard a rumour you're rather brilliant.' She lights a cigarette and he notices again her distinctive way of inhaling, seeming almost to swallow the smoke, then tilting her

head back and breathing it out through her nostrils. Is this some new fashion, he wonders? 'I suppose you're married?' she says.

He almost chokes on his cocoa. 'Good God, no. I mean, I would hardly be –'

'Fiancée? Girlfriend?'

'Now you're teasing me.' He pulls out a handkerchief and dabs at his chin.

'Brothers? Sisters?'

'No, no.'

'Parents? Even you must have parents.'

'Only one still alive.'

'I'm the same,' she says. 'My mother's dead.'

'How awful for you. I'm sorry. My mother, I must say, is very much alive.'

And so it goes on, this hitherto untasted pleasure of talking about oneself. Her grey eyes never leave his face. The trains steam past in the darkness, trailing a wash of soot and hot air. Customers come and go. 'Who cares if we're without a light?' sings a crooner on the wireless in the corner, 'they can't blackout the moon ...' He finds himself telling her things he's never really spoken of before – about his father's death and his mother's remarriage, about his stepfather (a businessman, whom he dislikes), about his discovery of astronomy and then of mathematics ...

'And your work now?' she says. 'Does that make you happy?'

'Happy?' He warms his hands on his cup and considers the question. 'No. I couldn't say happy. It's too demanding – frightening, even, in a way.'

'Frightening?' The wide eyes widen further with interest. 'Frightening how?'

'What might happen ...' (You're showing off, he warns himself, stop it.) 'What might happen if you get it wrong, I suppose.'

She lights another cigarette. 'You're in Hut 8, aren't you? Hut 8's the naval section?'

This brings him up with a jolt. He looks around quickly. Another couple are holding hands at the next table, whispering. Four airmen are playing cards. A waitress in a greasy apron is polishing the counter. Nobody seems to have heard.

'Talking of which,' he says, brightly, 'I think I ought to get back.'

On the corner of Church Green Road and Wilton Avenue she kisses him, briefly, on the cheek.

The following week it is Schumann, followed by steak-and-kidney pudding and jam roly-poly at the British Restaurant in Bletchley Road ('two courses for elevenpence') and this time it's her turn to talk. Her mother died when she was six, she says, and her father trailed her from embassy to embassy. Family has been a procession of nannies and governesses. At least she's learned some languages. She'd wanted to join the Wrens, but the old man wouldn't let her.

Jericho asks what London was like in the Blitz.

'Oh, a lot of fun, actually. Loads of places to go. The Milroy, the Four Hundred. A kind of desperate gaiety. We've all had to learn to live for the moment, don't you think?'

When they say goodbye she kisses him again, her lips to one cheek, her cool hand to the other.

In retrospect, it is around this time, in the middle of January, that he should have started keeping a record of his symptoms, for it is now that he begins to lose his equilibrium. He wakes with a feeling of mild euphoria. He bounces into the hut, whistling. He goes for long walks around the lake between shifts, taking bread to feed the ducks – just for the exercise, he tells himself, but really he is scanning the crowds for her, and twice he sees her, and once she sees him and waves.

For their fourth date (the fifth, if you count their meeting on the train) she insists they do something different, so they go to the County Cinema on the High Street to see the new Noël Coward picture, In Which We Serve.

'And you really mean to tell me you've never once been here?'

They're queuing for tickets. The film's only been showing for a day and the line extends round the corner into Aylesbury Street.

'I haven't, actually, to be honest, no.'

'God, Tom, you are *a funny old darling. I think I'd* die *stuck in Bletchley without the flicks to go to.'*

They sit near the back and she laces her arm through his. The light from the projector high up behind them makes a kaleidoscope of blues and greys in the dust and cigarette smoke. The couple next to them are kissing. A woman giggles. A fanfare of trumpets announces a newsreel and there, on the screen, long columns of German prisoners, an impossible number, are shown trekking through snow, while the announcer talks excitedly about Red Army breakthroughs on the eastern front. Stalin appears, presenting medals, to loud applause. Someone shouts: 'Three cheers for Uncle Joe!' The lights come up, then dim again, and Claire squeezes his arm. The main film begins – 'This is the story of a ship' *– with Coward as an improbably suave Royal Navy captain. There's a lot of clipped excitement.* 'Vessel on fire bearing green three-oh ... Torpedo track, starboard, sir ... Carry on firing ...' *At the climax of the sea battle, Jericho looks around at the flickering of the celluloid explosions on the rapt faces, and it strikes him that he is a part of all this – a distant, vital part – and that nobody knows, nobody will ever know ... After the final credits the loudspeakers play 'God Save the King' and they all stand, many of the audience so moved by the film they begin to sing.*

They've left their bicycles near the end of an alley running beside the cinema. A few paces further on a shape rubs itself against the wall. As they come closer they can see it is a soldier with his greatcoat wrapped around a girl. Her back is to the bricks. Her white face stares at them from the shadows like an animal in its hide. The movement stops for the time it takes Claire and Jericho to collect their bicycles, then it starts again.

'What very peculiar behaviour.'

He says it without thinking. To his surprise, Claire bursts out laughing.

'What's the matter?'

'Nothing,' she says.

They stand on the pavement holding their bicycles, waiting for an Army lorry with dimmed headlights to pass, its gearbox grinding as it heads north along Watling Street. Her laughter stops.

'Do come and see my cottage, Tom.' She says it almost plaintively. 'It's not that late. I'd love to show it you.'

He can't think of an excuse, doesn't want to think of one.

She leads the way through the town and out past the Park. They don't speak for fifteen minutes and he begins to wonder how far she's taking him. At last, when they're rattling down the path that leads to the cottage, she calls over her shoulder, 'Isn't it a perfect sweetheart?'

'It's, ah, off the beaten track.'

'Now don't be horrible,' she says, pretending to be hurt.

She tells him how she found it standing derelict, how she charmed the farmer who owns it into letting her rent it. Inside, the furniture is shabby-grand, rescued from an aunt's house in Kensington that was shut up for the Blitz and never reopened.

The staircase creaks so alarmingly, Jericho wonders if their combined weight might pull it away from the wall. The place is a ruin, freezing cold. 'And this is where I sleep,' she says, and he follows her into a room of pinks and creams, crammed full of pre-war silks and furs and feathers, like a large dressing-up box. A loose floorboard goes off like a gunshot beneath his feet. There's too much detail for the eye to register, so many hat boxes, shoe boxes, bits of jewellery, cosmetic bottles ... She slips off her coat and lets it fall to the floor and flings herself flat out on the bed, then props herself up on her elbows and kicks off her shoes. She seems amused by something.

'And what's this?' Jericho, in a turmoil, has retreated to the landing and is staring at the only other door.

'Oh, that's Hester's room,' she calls.

'Hester?'

'Some bureaucratic beast found out where I was and said if I had a second bedroom I had to share. So in came Hester. She works in Hut 6. She's a sweetie, really. Got a bit of a crush on me. Take a look. She won't mind.'

He knocks, there's no reply, he opens the door. Another tiny room, but this one spartan, like a cell: a brass bedstead, a jug and bowl on a washstand, some books piled on a chair. Ableman's German Primer. *He opens it.* 'Der Rhein ist etwas langer als die Elbe,' *he reads. The Rhine is somewhat longer than the Elbe. He hears the gunshot of the floorboard behind him and Claire lifts the book from his hands.*

'Don't snoop, darling. It's rude. Come on, let's make a fire and have a drink.'

Downstairs, he kneels by the hearth and rolls a copy of The Times *into a ball. He piles on kindling and a couple of small logs, and lights the paper. The chimney draws voraciously, sucking up the smoke with a roar.*

'Look at you, you haven't even taken off your coat.'

He stands, brushing the dust away, and turns to face her. Grey skirt, navy cashmere sweater, a single loop of milk-white pearls at her creamy throat – the ubiquitous, unchanging uniform of the upper-class Englishwoman. She somehow contrives to look both very young and very mature at the same time.

'Come here. Let me do it.'

She sets down the drinks and begins to unbutton his overcoat.

'Don't tell me, Tom,' she whispers, 'don't tell me you didn't know what they were doing behind that cinema?'

Even barefoot she is as tall as he is.

'Of course I knew ...'

'In London nowadays the girls all call it a "wall job". What do you think? They say you can't get pregnant this way ...'

Instinctively, he draws his coat around her. She wraps her arms about his back.

3

Damn it, damn it, damn it.

He pitched himself forwards and out of the chair, sending the images scattering and smashing on the cold stone floor. He prowled around the tiny sitting room a couple of times, then went into the kitchen. Everything was clean and swept and put away. That would be Hester's handiwork, he guessed, not Claire's. The stove had burned down very low and was lukewarm to the touch, but he resisted the temptation to shovel in some coal. It was a quarter to one. Where was she? He wandered back into the sitting room, hesitated at the foot of the stairs, and began to climb. The plaster on the walls was damp and flaking beneath his fingers. He decided to try Hester's room first. It was exactly as it had been six weeks earlier. A pair of sensible shoes beside the bed. A cupboard full of dark clothes. The same German primer. '*An seinen Ufern sind Berge, Felsen und malerische Schlosser aus den ältesten Zeiten.*' On its shores are mountains, rocks and picturesque castles from the oldest times. He closed it and went back out on the landing.

And so, at last, to Claire's room.

He was quite clear now about what he was going to do, even though conscience told him it was wrong and logic told him it was stupid. And, in principle, he agreed. Like any good boy he had learned his Aesop, knew that 'listeners never hear good of themselves' – but since when, he thought, as he began opening drawers, since when has that pious wisdom stopped anybody? A letter, a diary, a message – anything that might tell him *why* – he had to see it, he had to, even though the chances of its yielding any comfort were nil. Where was she? Was she with another man? Was she doing what all the girls in London, darling, call a wall job?

He was suddenly in a rage and he went through her room like a housebreaker, pulling out drawers and upending them, sweeping jewellery and trinkets off the shelves, pulling her clothes down on to the floor, throwing off her sheets and blankets and wrenching up her mattress, raising clouds of dust and scent and ostrich feathers.

After ten minutes he crawled into the corner and laid his head on a pile of silks and furs.

'You're a wreck,' Skynner had said. *'You're ruined. You've lost it. Find someone more suitable than the person you were seeing.'*

Skynner knew about her, and Logie had seemed to know as well. What was it he'd called her? The 'arctic blonde'? Perhaps they all knew? Puck, Atwood, Baxter, everybody?

He had to get out, get away from the smell of her perfume and the sight of her clothes.

And it was that action that changed everything, for it was only when he stood on the landing, leaning with his back to the wall and his eyes closed, that he realised there *was* something he'd missed.

He walked back slowly and deliberately into her room. Silence. He stepped across the threshold and repeated the action. Silence again. He got down on his knees. One of auntie's Kensington rugs covered the floorboards, something oriental, stained, and tastefully threadbare. It was only about two yards square. He rolled it up and laid it on the bed. The wooden planks which had lain beneath it were bowed with age, worn smooth, fixed down by rust-coloured nails, untouched for two centuries – except in one place, where a shorter length of the old planking, perhaps eighteen inches long, was secured by four very modern, very shiny screws. He slapped the floor in triumph.

'Is there any other point to which you would wish to draw my attention, Mr Jericho?'

'To the curious incident of the creaking floorboard.'

'But the floorboard didn't creak.'

'That was the curious incident.'

In the mess of her bedroom he could see no suitable tool. He went down into the kitchen and found a knife. It had a mother-of-pearl handle with an 'R' engraved on it. Perfect. He almost skipped across the sitting room. The tip of the knife slotted into the head of the screw and the thread turned easily, it came away like a dream. So did the other three. The floorboard lifted up to reveal the horsehair and plaster of the downstairs ceiling. The cavity was about six inches deep. He took off his overcoat and his jacket and rolled up his sleeve. He lay on his side and thrust his hand into the space. To begin with he brought out nothing except handfuls of debris, mostly lumps of old plaster and small pieces of brick, but he kept on working his way around until at last he gave a cry of delight as his hand touched paper.

*

He put everything back in its place, more or less. He hung the clothes back up from the beams, piled her underclothes and her scarves back into the drawers and replaced the drawers in the mahogany chest. He heaped the trinkets of jewellery into their leather case and draped others artfully along the shelves, together with her bottles and pots and packets, most of which were empty.

He did all this mechanically, an automaton.

He remade the bed, lifting off the rug and smoothing down the eiderdown, throwing the lace cover over it where it settled like a net. Then he sat on the edge of the mattress and surveyed the room. Not bad. Of course, once she began looking for things, then she would know someone had been through it, but at a casual glance it looked the same as before – apart, that is, from the hole in the floor. He didn't know yet what to do about that. It depended on whether or not he replaced the intercepts. He pulled them out from under the bed and examined them again.

There were four, on standard-size sheets, eight inches by ten. He held one up to the light. It was cheap wartime paper, the sort Bletchley used by the ton. He could practically see a petrified forest in its coarse yellow weave – the shadows of foliage and leaf-stalks, the faint outlines of bark and fern.

In the top left-hand corner of each signal was the frequency on which it had been transmitted – 12260 kilocycles per second – and in the top right its TOI, Time of Interception. The four had been sent in rapid succession on 4 March, just nine days earlier, at roughly twenty-five-minute intervals, beginning at 9.30 p.m. and ending just before midnight. Each consisted of a call sign – ADU – and then about two hundred five-letter groups. That in itself was an important clue. It meant, whatever else they were, they weren't naval: the Kriesgmarine's signals were transmitted in groups of four letters. So they were presumably German Army or Luftwaffe.

She must have stolen them from Hut 3.

The enormity of the implications hit Jericho for a second time, winding him like a punch in the stomach. He arranged the intercepts in sequence on her pillow and tried very hard, like a defending King's Counsel, to come up with some innocent explanation. A piece of silly mischief? It was possible. She had certainly never paid much attention to security – shouting about Hut 8 in the station buffet, demanding to know what he did, trying to tell him what *she* did. A dare? Again, possible. She was capable of anything. But that hole in the floorboards, the cool deliberation of it, drew his gaze and mocked his advocacy.

A sound, a footstep downstairs, dragged him out of his reverie and made him jump to his feet.

He said, 'Hello?' in a loud voice that suggested more courage than he felt. He cleared his throat. 'Hello?' he repeated. And then he heard another noise, definitely a footstep, and definitely *outside* now, and a charge of adrenaline snapped in. He moved quickly to the bedroom door and turned the light off, so that the only illumination in the cottage came from the sitting room. Now, if anyone came up the stairs, he would be able to see their silhouette, while remaining hidden. But nothing happened. Perhaps they were trying to come round the back? He felt horribly vulnerable. He moved cautiously down the stairs, flinching at every creak. A blast of cold air struck him.

The front door was wide open.

He threw himself down the last half-dozen steps and ran outside, just in time to see the red rear light of a bicycle shoot out of the track and vanish down the lane.

He set off in pursuit but gave up after twenty paces. He didn't stand a chance of catching the cyclist.

There was a heavy frost. In every direction the ground shone a dull and luminous blue. The branches of the bare trees were raised against the sky like blood vessels. In the glittering ice, two sets of tyre-tracks were imprinted: incoming and outgoing. He followed them back to the door, where they ended in a series of sharp footprints.

Sharp, large, *male* footprints.

Jericho looked at them for half a minute, shivering in his shirtsleeves. An owl shrieked in the nearby copse and it seemed to him that its call had the rhythm of Morse: dee-dee-dee-*dah*, dee-dee-dee-*dah*.

He hurried back into the cottage.

Upstairs, he rolled the intercepts very tightly into a cylinder. He used his teeth to tear a small hole in the lining of his overcoat and pushed the signals into it. Then he quickly screwed down the floorboards and replaced the rug. He put on his jacket and coat, turned off the lights, locked the door, replaced the key.

His bicycle added a third set of impressions in the frost.

At the entrance to the lane he stopped and looked back at the darkened cottage. He had a strong sensation – foolish, he told himself – that he was being watched. He glanced around. A gust of wind stirred in the trees; in the blackthorn hedge beside him, icicles clinked and chimed.

Jericho shivered again, remounted the bike and pointed it down the hill, towards the south, towards Orion and Procyon, and to Hydra, which hung suspended in the night sky above Bletchley Park like a knife.

FOUR

KISS

KISS: the coincidence of two different cryptograms, each transmitted in a different cipher, yet each containing the same original plaintext, the solution of one thereby leading to the solution of the other.

A Lexicon of Cryptography
('Most Secret', Bletchley Park, 1943)

1

He doesn't know what wakes him – some faint sound, some movement in the air that hooks him in the depths of his dreams and hauls him to the surface.

At first his darkened room seems entirely normal – the familiar jet-black spar of the low oak beam, the smooth grey plains of wall and ceiling – but then he realises that a faint light is rising from the foot of his bed.

'Claire?' he says, propping himself up. 'Darling?'

'It's all right, darling. Go on back to sleep.'

'What on earth are you doing?'

'I'm just going through your things.'

'You're ... what?'

His hand fumbles across the bedside table and switches on the lamp. His Waralarm shows him it is half past three.

'That's better,' she says, and she turns off the blackout torch. 'Useless thing, anyway.'

And she is doing exactly what she says. She is naked except for his shirt, she is kneeling, and she is going through his wallet. She removes a couple of one-pound notes, turns the wallet inside out and shakes it.

'No photographs?' she says.

'You haven't given me one yet.'

'Tom Jericho,' she smiles, replacing the money, 'I do declare, you're becoming almost smooth.'

She checks the pockets of his jacket, his trousers, then shuffles on her knees across to his chest of drawers. He laces his hands behind his head and leans back against the iron bedstead and watches her. It is only the second time they have slept together – a week after the first – and at her insistence they have done it not in her cottage but in his room, creeping through the darkened bar of the White Hart Inn and up the creaking stair. Jericho's bedroom is well away from the rest of the household so there is no danger of them being overheard. His books are lined up on the top of the chest of drawers and she picks up each in turn, holds it upside down and flicks through the pages.

Does he see anything odd in all this? No, he does not. It merely seems amusing, flattering, even – one further intimacy, a continuation of all the rest, a part of the waking dream his life has become, governed by dream rules. Besides, he has no secrets from her – or, at least, he thinks he hasn't. She finds Turing's paper and studies it closely.

'And what are computable numbers with an application to the Entscheidungsproblem, *when they're at home?'*

Her pronunciation of the German, he registers with surprise, is immaculate.

'It's a theoretical machine, capable of an infinite number of numerical operations. It supports the assumptions of Hilbert and challenges those of Godel. Come back to bed, darling.'

'But it's only a theory?'

He sighs and pats the mattress next to him. They're sleeping in a single bed. 'Turing believes there's no inherent reason why a machine shouldn't be capable of doing everything a human brain can do. Calculate. Communicate. Write a sonnet.'

'Fall in love?'

'If love is logical.'

'Is it?'

'Come to bed.'

'This Turing, does he work at the Park?'

He makes no reply. She leafs through the paper, squinting with disgust at the mathematics, then replaces it with the books and opens one of the drawers. As she leans forwards the shirt rides higher. The lower part of her back gleams white in the shadows. He stares, mesmerised, at the soft triangle of flesh at the base of her vertebrae as she rummages among his clothes.

'Ah,' she says, 'now here is something.' She withdraws a slip of paper. 'A cheque for a hundred pounds, drawn on the Foreign Office Contingency Fund, made out to you –'

'Give me that.'

'Why?'

'Put it back.'

He is across the room and standing beside her within a couple of seconds, but she is quicker than he is. She is on her feet, on tiptoe, holding the cheque aloft, and she – absurdly – is just that half-inch taller than him. The money flutters like a pennant beyond his reach.

'I knew there would be something. Come on, darling, what's it for?'

He should have banked the damn thing weeks ago. He'd quite forgotten it. 'Claire, please ...'

'You must have done something frightfully clever in that naval hut of yours. A new code? Is that it? You broke some new important code, my clever, clever darling?'

She may be taller than he is, she may even be stronger, but he has the advantage of desperation. He seizes the firm muscle of her bicep and pulls her arm down and twists her round. They struggle for a moment and then he throws her back on the narrow bed. He prises the cheque out of her bitten-down fingers and retreats with it across the room.

'Not funny, Claire. Some things just aren't that funny.'

He stands there on the rough matting – naked, slender, panting with exertion. He folds the cheque and slips it into his wallet, puts the wallet into his jacket, and turns to hang the jacket in the wardrobe. As he does so, he is aware of a peculiar noise coming from behind him – a frightening, animal noise, something between a rasping breath and a sob. She has curled herself up tight on the bed, her knees drawn up to her stomach, her forearms pressed to her face.

My God, what has he done?

He starts to gabble his apologies. He hadn't meant to frighten her, let alone to hurt her. He goes across to the bed and sits beside her. Tentatively, he touches her shoulder. She doesn't seem to notice. He tries to pull her towards him, to roll her over on her back, but she has become as rigid as a corpse. The sobs are shaking the bed. It is like a fit, a seizure. She is somewhere beyond grief, somewhere far away, beyond him.

'It's all right,' he says. 'It's all right.'

He can't tug the bedclothes out from under her, so he fetches his overcoat and lays that across her, and then he lies beside her, shivering in the January night, stroking her hair.

They stay like that for half an hour until, at last, when she is calm again, she gets up off the bed and begins to dress. He cannot bring himself to look at her and he knows better than to speak. He can just hear her moving around the room, collecting her scattered clothes. Then the door closes quietly. The stairs creak. A minute later he hears the click of her bicycle being wheeled away from beneath his window.

And now his own nightmare begins.

First, there is guilt, that most corrosive of emotions, more torturing even than jealousy (although jealousy is added to the brew a few days later, when he happens to see her walking through Bletchley with a man he doesn't recognise: the man could be anyone, of course – cousin, friend, colleague – but naturally his imagination can't accept that). Why did he respond so dramatically to so small a provocation? The cheque could, after all, have been a reward for anything. He didn't have to tell her the truth. Now that she's gone, a hundred plausible explanations for the money come to mind. What had he done to provoke such terror in her? What awful memory had he reawakened?

He groans and draws the blankets over his head.

The next morning he takes the cheque to the bank and exchanges it for twenty large, crisp, white five-pound notes. Then he searches out the dreary little jewellery shop on Bletchley Road and asks for a ring, any ring, as long as it is worth a hundred pounds, at which the jeweller – a ferret of a man with pebble-thick glasses, who clearly can't believe his luck – produces a diamond worth less than half that amount, and Jericho buys it.

He will make it up to her. He will apologise. It will all be right.

But luck is not with Jericho. He has become the victim of his own success. A Shark decrypt discloses that a U-boat tanker – the U-459, *under Korvettenkapitän von Williamowitz-Mollendorf, with 700 tons of fuel on board – is to rendevous with, and refuel, the Italian submarine* Kalvi, *300 miles east of St Paul's Rock, in the middle of the Atlantic. And some fool at the Admiralty, forgetting that no action, however tempting, must ever be taken that will endanger the Enigma secret, orders a squadron of destroyers to intercept. The attack is made. It fails. The* U-459 *escapes. And Dönitz, that crafty fox in his Paris lair, is immediately suspicious. In the third week of January, Hut 8 decrypts a series of signals ordering the U-boat fleet to tighten its cipher security. Shark traffic dwindles. There is barely enough material to make a menu for the bombes. At Bletchley, all leave is cancelled. Eight-hour shifts drag on to twelve hours, to sixteen hours ... The daily battle to break the codes is almost as great a nightmare as it was in the depths of the Shark blackout, and Skynner's lash is felt on everybody's back.*

Jericho's world has gone from perpetual sunshine to bleak midwinter in the space of a week. His messages to Claire, of entreaty and remorse, vanish, unanswered, into a void. He can't get out of the Hut to see her. He can't work. He can't sleep. And there's no one he can talk to. To Logie, lost and vague behind his smokescreen of tobacco? To Baxter, who would regard a dalliance with a woman like Claire Romilly as a betrayal of the world proletariat? To Atwood – Atwood! – whose sexual adventures have hitherto been confined to taking the prettier male undergraduates on golfing weekends to Brancaster, where they quickly discover that all the locks have been removed from the bathroom doors? Puck would have been a possibility, but Jericho could guess at his advice – 'Take out someone else, my dear Thomas, and fuck her' – and how could he admit the truth: that he didn't want to 'fuck' anyone else, that he had never 'fucked' anyone else?

On the final day of January, collecting a copy of The Times *from Brinklow's the newsagent in Victoria Road, he spots her, at a distance, with the other man, and he shrinks into a doorway to avoid being seen. Apart from that, he never meets her: the Park has become too big, there are too many changes of shift. Eventually, he's reduced to lying in wait in the lane opposite her cottage, like a Peeping Tom. But she seems to have stopped coming home.*

And then he almost walks right into her.

It is 8 February, a Monday, at four o'clock. He's walking wearily back to the hut from the canteen; she is part of a flood of workers streaming towards the gate at the end of the afternoon shift. He has rehearsed for this moment so many times, but in the end all he manages is a whine of complaint: 'Why don't you answer my letters?'

'Hello, Tom.'

She tries to walk on, but he won't let her get away this time. He has a pile of Shark intercepts waiting for him on his desk but he doesn't care. He catches at her arm.

'I need to talk to you.'

Their bodies block the pavement. The flow of people has to pass around them, like a river round a rock.

'Mind out,' says someone.

'Tom,' she hisses, 'for God's sake, you're making a scene.'

'Good. Let's get out of here.'

He is pulling at her arm. His pressure is insistent and reluctantly she surrenders to it. The momentum of the crowd sweeps them through the gate and along the road. His only thought is to put some distance between them and the Park. He doesn't know how long they walk for – fifteen minutes, perhaps, or twenty – until, at last, the pavements are deserted and they are passing through the hinterland of the town. It is a raw, clear afternoon. On either side of them, semidetached suburban villas hide behind dirty privet hedges, their wartime gardens filled with chicken runs and the half-buried, corrugated-iron hoops of bomb shelters. She shakes her arm free.

'There's no point in this.'

'You're seeing someone else?' He hardly dares to ask the question.

'I'm always seeing someone else.'

He stops but she walks on. He lets her go for fifty yards then hurries to catch her up. By now the houses have petered out and they're in a kind of no-man's land between town and country, on Bletchley's western edge, where people dump their rubbish. A flock of seagulls cries and rises, like a swirl of waste paper caught by the wind. The road has dwindled to a track which leads under the railway to a row of abandoned Victorian brick kilns. Three red-brick chimneys, as in a crematorium, rise fifty feet against the sky. A sign says: DANGER: FLOODED CLAY PIT – VERY DEEP WATER.

Claire draws her coat around her shoulders and shivers – 'What a filthy place!' – but she still walks on ahead.

For ten minutes, the derelict brick works provide a welcome distraction. Indeed, they wander through the ruined kilns and workshops in a silence that is almost companionable. Amorous couples have scratched their formulae on the crumbling walls: AE + GS, Tony = Kath, Sal 4 Me. Lumps of masonry and brick litter the ground. Some of the buildings are open to the sky, the walls are scorched – there's clearly been a fire – and Jericho wonders if the Germans could have mistaken it for a factory, and bombed it. He turns to say as much to Claire, but she has disappeared.

He finds her outside, her back to him, staring across the flooded clay pit. It is huge, a quarter of a mile across. The surface of the water is coal-black and perfectly still, the stillness hinting at unimaginable depths.

She says: 'I ought to get back.'

'What do you want to know?' he says. 'I'll tell you everything you want to know.'

And he will, if she wants it. He doesn't care about security or the war. He'll tell her about Shark and Dolphin and Porpoise. He'll tell her about the Bay of Biscay weather crib. He'll tell her all their little tricks and secrets, and draw her a diagram of how the bombe works, if that's what she wants. But all she says is: 'I do hope you're not going to be a bore about this, Tom.'

A bore. Is that what he is? He is being a bore?

'Wait,' he calls after her, 'you might as well have this.'

He gives her the little box with the ring in it. She opens it and tilts the stone to catch the light, then snaps the lid shut and hands it back.

'Not my style.'

*

'Poor you,' he remembers her saying a minute or two later, 'I've really got under your skin, haven't I? Poor you ...'

And by the end of the week he's in the deputy director's Rover, being borne back through the snow to King's.

2

The smells and sounds of an English Sunday breakfast curled up the staircase of the Commercial Guesthouse and floated across the landing like a call to arms: the hiss of hot fat frying in the kitchen, the dirge-like strains of a church service being relayed by the BBC, the muffled crack of Mrs Armstrong's worn slippers flapping like castanets on the linoleum floor.

They were a ritual in Albion Street, these Sunday breakfasts, served up with appropriate solemnity on plain white utility crockery: one piece of bread, as thick as a hymn book, dunked in fat and fried, with two spoonfuls of powdered egg, scrambled and slopped on top, the whole mass sliding freely on a rainbow film of grease.

It was not, Jericho had to acknowledge, a great meal, nor even a particularly edible one. The bread was rust-coloured, flecked with black, and obscurely flavoured by the kippers that had been cooked in the same fat the previous Friday. The egg was pale yellow and tasted of stale biscuits. Yet such was his appetite after the excitements of the night that, despite his anxiety, he ate every scrap of it, washed it down with two cups of greyish tea, mopped up the last of the grease with a fragment of bread, and even, on his way out, complimented Mrs Armstrong on the quality of her cooking – an unprecedented gesture which caused her to poke her head around the kitchen door and search his features for a trace of irony. She found none. He also attempted a cheerful 'Good morning' to Mr Bonnyman, who was just groping his way down the banisters ('Feeling a bit rough, to be honest, old boy – something wrong with the beer in that place') and by seven forty-five he was back in his room.

If Mrs Armstrong could have seen the changes he had wrought up there, she would have been astonished. Far from preparing to evacuate it after his first night, like so many of the bedroom's previous tenants, Jericho had unpacked. His suitcases were empty. His one good suit hung in the wardrobe. His books were lined along the mantelpiece. Balanced on the top of them was his print of King's College Chapel.

He sat on the edge of the bed and stared at the picture. It was not a skilful piece of work. In fact, it was rather ugly. The twin Gothic spires were hastily drawn, the sky was an improbable blue, the blob-like figures clustered around its base could have been the work of a child. But even bad art can sometimes have its uses.

Behind its scratched glass, and behind the cheap Victorian mezzotint itself, laid flat and carefully secured, were the four undecrypted intercepts he had removed from Claire's bedroom.

He should have returned them to the Park, of course. He should have cycled straight from the cottage to the huts, should have sought out Logie or some other figure of authority, and handed them in.

Even now, he couldn't disentangle all his motives for not doing so, couldn't sort out the selfless (his wish to protect her) from the selfish (his desire to have her in his power, just once). He only knew he could not bring himself to betray her, and that he was able to rationalise this by telling himself that there was no harm in waiting till the morning, no harm in giving her a chance to explain.

And so he had cycled on, past the main gate, had tiptoed up to his room and had hidden the cryptograms behind the print, increasingly aware that he had strayed across whatever border it is that separates folly from treason, and that with every passing hour it would be harder for him to find his way back.

For the hundredth time, sitting on his bed, he ran through all the possibilities. That she was crazy. That she was being blackmailed. That her room was being used as a hiding place without her knowledge. That she was a spy.

A spy? The notion seemed fantastic to him – melodramatic, bizarre, *illogical*. For one thing, why would a spy with any sense steal cryptograms? A spy would be after decodes, surely: the answers not the riddles; the hard proof that Enigma was being broken?

He checked the door, then gently took down the picture and dismantled the frame, working the thumbtacks loose with his fingers and lifting away the hardboard backing. Now he thought about it, there *was* something distinctly odd about these cryptograms, and looking at them again he realised what it was. They should have had the thin paper strips of decode produced by the Type-X machines gummed to their backs. But not only were there no strips, there weren't even any marks to show where the strips had been torn off. So, by the look of them, these signals had never even been broken. Their secrets were intact. They were virgin.

None of it made any sense.

He stroked one of the signals between finger and thumb. The yellowish paper had a slight but perceptible odour. What was it? He held it close to his nose and inhaled. The scent of a library or an archive, perhaps? Quite a rich smell – warm, almost smoky – as evocative as perfume.

He realised suddenly that despite his fear he was actually beginning to treasure the cryptograms, as another man might treasure a favourite snapshot of a girl. Only these were better than any photographs, weren't they, for photographs were merely *likenesses*, whereas these were clues to *who she was*, and therefore wasn't he, by possessing them, in a sense, possessing her ...?

He would give her just one chance. No more.

He looked at his watch. Twenty minutes had passed since breakfast. It was time to go. He slipped the cryptograms behind the picture, reassembled the frame and replaced it on the mantelpiece, then opened the door a fraction. Mrs Armstrong's regular guests had all come in from the night-shift. He could hear their murmured voices in the dining room. He put on his overcoat and stepped out on to the landing. Such were his efforts to seem natural, Mrs Armstrong would later swear she heard him humming to himself as he descended the stairs.

'I see you smiling in the cigarette glow
Though the picture fades too soon
But I see all I want to know
They can't black out the moon ...'

*

From Albion Street to Bletchley Park was a walk of less than half a mile – left out of the door and along the street of terraced houses, left under the blackened railway bridge and sharp right across the allotments.

He strode quickly over the frozen ground, his breath steaming before him in the cold sunshine. Officially it was almost spring but someone had forgotten to pass the news on to winter. Patches of ice, not yet melted from the night before, cracked beneath the soles of his shoes. Rooks called from the tops of skeletal elms.

It was well past eight o'clock by the time he turned off the footpath into Wilton Avenue and approached the main gate. The shift change was over; the suburban road was almost deserted. The sentry – a giant young corporal, raw-faced from the cold – came stamping out of the guard post and barely glanced at his pass before waving him into the grounds.

Past the mansion he went, keeping his head down to avoid having to speak to anyone, past the lake (which was fringed with ice) and into Hut 8, where the silence emanating from the Decoding Room told him all he needed to know. The Type-X machines had worked their way through the backlog of Shark intercepts and now there was nothing for them to do until Dolphin and Porpoise came on stream, probably around mid-morning. He caught a glimpse of Logie's tall figure at the end of the corridor and darted into the Registration Room. There, to his surprise, was Puck, sitting in a corner, being watched by a pair of love-struck Wrens. His face was grey and lined, his head resting against the wall. Jericho thought he might be asleep but then he opened a piercing blue eye.

'Logie's looking for you.'

'Really?' Jericho took off his coat and scarf and hung them on the back of the door. 'He knows where to find me.'

'There's a rumour going around that you hit Skynner. For God's sake tell me it's true.'

One of the Wrens giggled.

Jericho had forgotten all about Skynner. He passed his hand through his hair. 'Do me a favour, Puck, will you?' he said. 'Pretend you haven't seen me?'

Puck regarded him closely for a moment, then shut his eyes. 'What a man of mystery you are,' he murmured, sleepily.

Back in the corridor Jericho walked straight into Logie.

'Ah, there you are, old love. I'm afraid we need to have a talk.'

'Fine, Guy. Fine.' Jericho patted Logie on the shoulder and squeezed past him. 'Just give me ten minutes.'

'No, not in ten minutes,' Logie shouted after him, 'now!'

Jericho pretended he hadn't heard. He trotted out into the fresh air, walked briskly round the corner, past Hut 6, towards the entrance to Hut 3. Only when he was within twenty paces of it did his footsteps slow, then stop.

The truth was, he knew very little about Hut 3, except that it was the place where the decoded messages of the German Army and Luftwaffe were processed. It was about twice the size of the other huts and was arranged in the shape of an L. It had gone up at the same time as the rest of the temporary buildings, in the winter of 1939 – a timber skeleton rising out of the freezing Buckinghamshire clay, clothed in a sheath of asbestos and flimsy wooden boarding – and to heat it, he remembered, they had cannibalised a big cast-iron stove from one of the Victorian greenhouses. Claire used to complain she was always cold. Cold, and that her job was 'boring'. But where exactly she worked within its warren of rooms, let alone what this 'boring' job entailed, was a mystery to him.

A door slammed somewhere behind him and he glanced over his shoulder to see Logie emerging from around the corner of the naval hut. Damn, damn. He dropped to one knee and pretended to fumble with his shoelace but Logie hadn't seen him. He was marching purposefully towards the mansion. That seemed to settle Jericho's resolve. Once Logie was out of sight, he counted himself down then launched himself across the path and through the entrance into the hut.

He did his best to look as if he had a right to be there. He pulled out a pen and set off down the central corridor, thrusting past airmen and Army officers, glancing officiously from side to side into the busy rooms. It was much more overcrowded even than Hut 8. The racket of typewriters and telephones was amplified by the membrane of wooden walls to create a bedlam of activity.

He had barely gone halfway down the passage when a colonel with a large moustache stepped smartly out of a doorway and blocked his path. Jericho nodded and tried to edge past him, but the colonel moved deftly to one side.

'Hold on, stranger. Who are you?'

On impulse Jericho stuck out his hand. 'Tom Jericho,' he said. 'Who are you?'

'Never mind who the hell I am.' The colonel had jug ears and thick black hair with a wide, straight parting that stood out like a firebreak. He ignored the proffered hand. 'What's your section?'

'Naval. Hut 8.'

'Hut 8? State your business here.'

'I'm looking for Dr Weitzman.'

An inspired lie. He knew Weitzman from the Chess Society: a German Jew, naturalised British, who always played Queen's Gambit Declined.

'Are you, by God?' said the colonel. 'Haven't you Navy people ever heard of the telephone?' He stroked his moustache and looked Jericho up and down. 'Well, you'd better come with me.'

Jericho followed the colonel's broad back along the passage and into a large room. Two groups of about a dozen men sat at tables arranged in a pair of semicircles, working their way through wire baskets stacked high with decrypts. Walter Weitzman was perched on a stool in a glass booth behind them.

'I say, Weitzman, d'you know this chap?'

Weitzman's large head was bent over a pile of German weapons manuals. He looked up, vague and distracted, but when he recognised Jericho his melancholy face brightened into a smile. 'Hello, Tom. Yes, of course I know him.'

' "*Kriegsnachrichten Für Seefahrer*," ' said Jericho, a fraction too quickly. 'You said you might have something by now.'

For a moment, Weitzman didn't react and Jericho thought he was done for, but then the old man said slowly, 'Yes. I believe I have that information for you.' He lowered himself carefully from his stool. 'You have a problem, colonel?'

The colonel thrust his chin forward. 'Yes, actually, Weitzman, I do, now you mention it. "Inter-hut communication, unless otherwise authorised, must be conducted by telephone or written memorandum." Standard procedure.' He glared at Weitzman and Weitzman stared back, with exquisite politeness. The belligerence seemed to leak out of the colonel. 'Right,' he muttered. 'Yes. Remember that in future.'

'Arsehole,' hissed Weitzman, as the colonel moved away. 'Well, well. You'd better come over here.'

He led Jericho to a rack of card-index files, selected a drawer, pulled it out and began riffling through it. Every time the translators came across a term they couldn't understand, they consulted Weitzman and his famous index-system. He'd been a philologist at Heidelberg until the Nazis forced him to emigrate. The Foreign Office, in a rare moment of inspiration, had dispatched him to Bletchley in 1940. Very few phrases defeated him.

'"*Kriegsnachrichten für Seefahrer*." "War notices for Marines."

First intercepted and catalogued, November ninth last year. As you knew perfectly well already.' He held the card within an inch of his nose and studied it through his thick spectacles. 'Tell me, is the good colonel still looking at us?'

'I don't know. I think so.' The colonel had bent down to read something one of the translators had written, but his gaze kept returning to Jericho and Weitzman. 'Is he always like that?'

'Our Colonel Coker? Yes, but worse today, for some reason.' Weitzman spoke softly, without looking at Jericho. He tugged open another drawer and pulled out a card, apparently absorbed. 'I suggest we stay here until he leaves the room. Now here's a U-boat term we picked up in January: *"Fluchttiefe."* '

' "Evasion depth," ' replied Jericho. He could play this game for hours. *Vorhalt-Rechner* was a deflection-angle computer. A cold-soldered joint was a *kalte Lötstelle*. Cracks in a U-boat's bulkheads were *Stirnwandrisse* ...

'"Evasion depth".' Weitzman nodded. 'Quite right.'

Jericho risked another look at the colonel. 'He's going out of the door ... now. It's all right. He's gone.'

Weitzman gazed at the card for a moment, then slipped it back among the rest and closed the drawer. 'So. Why are you asking me questions to which you already know the answers?' His hair was white, his small brown eyes overshadowed by a jutting forehead. Wrinkles at their edges suggested a face that had once creased readily into laughter. But Weitzman didn't laugh much any more. He was rumoured to have left most of his family behind in Germany.

'I'm looking for a woman called Claire Romilly. Do you know her?'

'Of course. The beautiful Claire. Everyone knows her.'

'Where does she work?'

'She works here.'

'I know here. Here where?'

'"Inter-hut communication, unless otherwise authorised, must be conducted by telephone or written memorandum. Standard procedure."' Weitzman clicked his heels. 'Heil Hitler!'

'Bugger standard procedure.'

One of the translators turned round, irritably. 'I say, you two, put a sock in it, will you?'

'Sorry.' Weitzman took Jericho by the arm and led him away. 'Do you know, Tom,' he whispered, 'in three years, this is the first time I have heard you swear?'

'Walter. Please. It's important.'

'And it can't wait until the end of the shift?' He gave Jericho a careful look. 'Obviously not. Well, well again. Which way did Coker go?'

'Back towards the entrance.'

'Good. Follow me.'

Weitzman led Jericho almost to the other end of the hut, past the translators, through two long, narrow rooms where scores of women were labouring over a pair of giant card indexes, around a corner and through a room lined with teleprinters. The din here was terrific. Weitzman put his hands to his ears, looked over his shoulder and grinned. The noise pursued them down a short length of passage, at the end of which was a closed door. Next to it was a sign, in a schoolgirl's best handwriting: GERMAN BOOK ROOM.

Weitzman knocked on the door, opened it and went inside. Jericho followed. His eye registered a large room. Shelves stacked with ledgers and files. Half a dozen trestle tables pushed together to form one big working area. Women, mostly with their backs to him. Six, perhaps, or seven? Two typing, very fast, the others moving back and forth arranging sheaves of papers into piles.

Before he could take in any more, a plump, harassed-looking woman in a tweed jacket and skirt advanced to meet them. Weitzman was beaming now, exuding charm, for all the world as if he were still in the tearoom of Heidelberg's Europäischer Hof. He took her hand and bowed to kiss it.

'Guten Morgen, mein liebes Fräulein Monk. Wie geht's?'

'Gut, danke, Herr Doktor. Und dir?'

'Danke, sehr gut.'

It was clearly a familiar routine between them. Her shiny complexion flushed pink with pleasure. 'And what can I do for you?'

'My colleague and I, my dear Miss Monk –' Weitzman patted her hand, then released it and gestured towards Jericho '– are looking for the delightful Miss Romilly.'

At the mention of Claire's name, Miss Monk's flirtatious smile evaporated. 'In that case you must join the queue, Dr Weitzman. Join the queue.'

'I am sorry. The queue?'

'We are all trying to find Claire Romilly. Perhaps you, or your colleague, have an idea where we might start?'

*

To say that the world stands still is a solipsism, and Jericho knew it even as it seemed to happen – knew that it isn't ever the world that slows down, but rather the individual, confronted by an unexpected danger, who receives a charge of adrenaline and speeds up. Nevertheless, for him, for an instant, everything did freeze. Weitzman's expression became a mask of bafflement, the woman's of indignation. As his brain tried to compute the implications, he could hear his own voice, far away, begin to babble: 'But I thought ... I was told – assured – yesterday – she was supposed to be on duty at eight this morning ...'

'Quite right,' Miss Monk was saying. 'It really is most thoughtless of her. And terribly inconvenient.'

Weitzman gave Jericho a peculiar look, as if to say, What have you got me into? 'Perhaps she's ill?' he suggested.

'Then surely a note would have been considerate? A message? Before I let the entire night-shift go? We can barely cope when there are eight of us. When we're down to seven ...'

She started to prattle on to Weitzman about '3A' and '3M' and all the staffing memos she'd written and how no one appreciated her difficulties. As if to prove her point, at that moment the door opened and a woman came in with a stack of files so high she had to wedge her chin on top of them to keep control. She let them fall on the table and there was a collective groan from Miss Monk's girls. A couple of signals fluttered over the edge of the table and on to the floor and Jericho, primed for action, swooped to retrieve them. He got a brief glimpse of one –

ZZZ

BATTLE HEADQUARTERS GERMAN AFRIKA KORPS LOCATED MORNING THIRTEENTH £ THIRTEENTH ONE FIVE KILOMETRES WEST OF BEN GARDANE £ BEN GARDANE

– before it was snatched out of his hands by Miss Monk. She seemed for the first time to become aware of his presence. She cradled the secrets to her plump breast and glared at him.

'I'm sorry, you are – who are you exactly?' she asked. She edged to one side to block his view of the table. 'You are – what? – a friend of Claire, I take it?'

'It's all right, Daphne,' said Weitzman, 'he's a friend of mine.'

Miss Monk flushed again. 'I beg your pardon, Walter,' she said. 'Of course, I didn't mean to imply –'

Jericho cut in: 'I wonder, could I ask you, has she done this before? Failed to turn up, I mean, without telling you?'

'Oh no. Never. I will not tolerate slacking in my section. Dr Weitzman will vouch for that.'

'Indeed,' said Weitzman, gravely. 'No slacking here.'

Miss Monk was of a type that Jericho had come to know well over the past three years: mildly hysterical at moments of crisis; jealous of her precious rank and her extra fifty pounds a year; convinced that the war would be lost if her tiny fiefdom were denied a gross of lead pencils or an extra typist. She would hate Claire, he thought: hate her for her prettiness and her confidence and her refusal to take anything seriously.

'She hasn't been behaving at all oddly?'

'We have important work to do. We've no time here for oddness.'

'When did you last see her?'

'That would be Friday.' Miss Monk obviously prided herself on her memory for detail. 'She came on duty at four, went off at midnight. Yesterday was her rest day.'

'So I don't suppose it's likely she came back into the hut, say, early on Saturday morning?'

'No. I was here. Anyway, why should she do that? Normally, she couldn't wait to get away.'

I bet she couldn't. He glanced again at the girls behind Miss Monk. What on earth were they all doing? Each had a mound of paperclips in front of her, a pot of glue, a pile of brown folders and a tangle of rubber bands. They seemed – could this be right? – to be compiling new files out of old ones. He tried to imagine Claire here, in this drab room, among these sensible drones. It was like picturing some gorgeous parakeet in a cage full of sparrows. He wasn't sure what to do. He took out his watch and flicked open the lid. Eight thirty-five. She had already been missing more than half an hour.

'What will you do now?'

'Obviously – because of the level of classification – there's a certain procedure we have to follow. I've already notified Welfare. They'll send someone round to her room to turf her out of bed.'

'And if she isn't there?'

'Then they'll contact her family to see if they know where she is.'

'And if they don't?'

'Well, then it's serious. But it never gets that far.' Miss Monk drew her jacket tight across her pigeon chest and folded her arms. 'I'm sure there's a *man* at the bottom of this somewhere.' She shuddered. 'There usually is.'

Weitzman was continuing to give Jericho imploring glances. He touched him on the arm. 'We ought to go now, Tom.'

'Do you have an address for her family? Or a telephone number?'

'Yes, I think so, but I'm not sure I should ...' She turned towards Weitzman, who hesitated fractionally, shot another look at Jericho, then forced a smile and a nod.

'I can vouch for him.'

'Well,' said Miss Monk, doubtfully, 'if you think it's permissible ...' She went over to a filing cabinet beside her desk and unlocked it.

'Coker will kill me for this,' whispered Weitzman, while her back was turned.

'He'll never find out. I promise you.'

'The curious thing is,' said Miss Monk, almost to herself, 'that she'd really become much more *attentive* of late. Anyway, this is her card.'

Next-of-kin: Edward Romilly.
Relation: Father.
Address: 27 *Stanhope Gardens, London SW.*
Telephone: Kensington 2257.

Jericho glanced at it for a second and handed it back.

'I don't think there's any need to trouble him, do you?' asked Miss Monk. 'Certainly not yet. No doubt Claire will arrive at any moment with some silly story about oversleeping –'

'I'm sure,' said Jericho.

'– in which case,' she added shrewdly, 'who shall I say was looking for her?'

'*Auf Wiedersehen, Fraulein Monk.*' Weitzman had had enough. He was already half out of the room, pulling Jericho after him with surprising force. Jericho had a last vision of Miss Monk, standing bewildered and suspicious, before the door closed on her schoolroom German.

'*Auf Wiedersehen, Herr Doktor, und Herr ...*'

*

Weitzman didn't lead Jericho back the way they had come. Instead he bundled him out of the rear exit. Now, in the cold daylight, Jericho could see why he had found it so difficult stumbling around out here the other night. They were on the edge of a building site. Trenches had been carved four feet deep into the grass. Pyramids of sand and gravel were covered in a white mould of frost. It was a miracle he hadn't broken his neck.

Weitzman shook a cigarette out of a crumpled pack of Passing Clouds and lit it. He leaned against the wall of the hut and exhaled a sigh of steam and smoke. 'Useless for me to ask, I suppose, what in God's name is going on?'

'You don't want to know, Walter. Believe me.'

'Troubles of the heart?'

'Something like that.'

Weitzman mumbled a couple of words in Yiddish that might have been a curse and continued to smoke.

About thirty yards away, a group of workmen were huddled around a brazier, finishing a tea break. They dispersed reluctantly, trailing pickaxes and spades across the hard ground, and Jericho had a sudden memory of himself as a boy, holding hands with his mother, walking along a seaside promenade, his spade clattering on the concrete road behind him. Somewhere beyond the trees, a generator kicked into life sending a scattering of rooks cawing into the sky.

'Walter, what's the German Book Room?'

'I'd better get back,' said Weitzman. He licked the ends of his thumb and forefinger and nipped off the glowing tip of his cigarette, slipping the unsmoked portion into his breast pocket. Tobacco was far too precious to waste even a few shreds.

'Please, Walter ...'

'Ach!' Weitzman made a sudden gesture of disgust with his arm, as if sweeping Jericho aside, and began making his way, unsteadily but wonderfully quickly for a man of his age, down the side of the hut towards the path. Jericho had to scramble to keep pace with him.

'You ask too much, you know –'

'I know I do.'

'I mean, my God, Coker already suspects I am a Nazi spy. Can you believe that? I may be a Jew, but for him one German is no different from another. Which, of course, is precisely *our* argument. I suppose I should be flattered.'

'I wouldn't – it's just – there's nobody else ...'

A pair of sentries with rifles rounded the corner and strolled towards them. Weitzman clamped his jaw shut and abruptly turned right off the path towards the tennis court. Jericho followed him. Weitzman opened the gate and they stepped on to the asphalt. The court had been put in – at Churchill's personal instigation, so it was said – two years earlier. It hadn't been used since the autumn. The white lines were barely visible beneath the frost. Drifts of leaves had collected against the chain-link fence. Weitzman closed the gate after them and walked towards the net post.

'It's all changed since we started, Tom. Nine-tenths of the people in the hut I don't even know any more.' He kicked moodily at the leaves and Jericho noticed for the first time how small his feet were; dancer's feet. 'I've grown old in this place. I can remember a time when we thought we were geniuses if we read fifty messages a week. Do you know what the rate is now?'

Jericho shook his head.

'Three thousand a *day*.'

'Good God.' *That's a hundred and twenty-five an hour*, thought Jericho, *that's one every thirty seconds* ...

'Is she in trouble, then, your girl?'

'I think so. I mean, yes – yes, she is.'

'I'm sorry to hear it. I like her. She laughs at my jokes. Women who laugh at my jokes must be cherished. Especially if they are young. And pretty.'

'Walter ...'

Weitzman turned towards Hut 3. He had chosen his ground well, with the instinct of a man who has been forced at some time, as a matter of personal survival, to learn how to find privacy. Nobody could come up behind them without entering the tennis court. Nobody could approach from the front without being seen. And if anyone was watching from a distance – well, what was there to see but two old colleagues, having a private chat?

'It's organised like a factory line.' He curled his fingers into the wire netting. His hands were white with cold. They clenched the steel like claws. 'The decrypts arrive by conveyor belt from Hut 6. They go first to the Watch for translation – you know that, that's my post. Two Watches per shift, one for urgent material, the other for back-breaks. Translated Luftwaffe signals are passed to 3A, Army to 3M. A for air, M for military. God in heaven, it's cold. Are you cold? I'm shaking.' He pulled out a filthy handkerchief and blew his nose. 'The duty officers decide what's important and give it a Z-priority. A single Z is low-grade – Hauptmann Fischer is to be transferred to the German Air Fleet in Italy. A weather report would be three Zs. Five Zs is pure gold – where Rommel will be tomorrow afternoon, an imminent air attack. The intelligence is summarised, then three copies are dispatched – one to SIS in Broadway, one to the appropriate service ministry in Whitehall, one to the relevant commander in the field.'

'And the German Book Room?'

'Every proper name is indexed: every officer, every piece of equipment, every base. For example, Hauptmann Fischer's transfer may at first seem quite worthless as intelligence. But then you consult the Air Index and you see his last posting was to a radar station in France. Now he is to go to Bari. So: the Germans are installing radar in Bari. Let them build it. And then, when it is almost finished, bomb it.'

'And that's the German Book?'

'No, no.' Weiztman shook his head crossly, as if Jericho were some dim student at the bottom of his class at Heidelberg. 'The German Book is the very end of the process. All this paper – the intercept, the decode, the translation, the Z-signal, the list of cross-references, all these thousands of pages – it all comes together at the end to be filed. The German Book is a verbatim transcription of all decoded messages in their original language.'

'Is that an important job?'

'In intellectual terms? No. Purely clerical.'

'But in terms of access? To classified material?'

'Ah. Different.' Weitzman shrugged. 'It would depend on the person involved, of course, whether they could be bothered to read what they were handling. Most don't.'

'But in theory?'

'In theory? On an average day? A girl like Claire would probably see more operational detail about the German armed forces than Adolf Hitler.' He glanced at Jericho's incredulous face and smiled. 'Absurd, isn't it? What is she? Nineteen? Twenty?'

'Twenty,' muttered Jericho. 'She always told me her job was boring.'

'Twenty! I swear it's the greatest joke in the history of warfare. Look at us: the hare-brained debutante, the weakling intellectual and the half-blind Jew. If only the master race could see what we're doing to them – sometimes the thought of it is all that keeps me going.' He held his watch up very close to his face. 'I must get back. Coker will have issued a warrant for my arrest. I fear I have talked too much.'

'Not at all.'

'Oh, I have, I have.'

He turned towards the gate. Jericho made a move to follow but Weitzman held up a hand to stop him. 'Why don't you wait here, Tom? Just for a moment. Let me get clear.'

He slipped out of the court. As he passed by on the other side of the fence, something seemed to occur to him. He slowed and beckoned Jericho closer to the wire netting.

'Listen,' he said softly, 'if you think I can help you again, if you need any more information – please, don't ask me. I don't want to know.'

Before Jericho could answer he had crossed the path and disappeared around the back of Hut 3.

*

Within the grounds of Bletchley Park, just beyond the mansion, in the shadow of a fir tree, stood an ordinary red telephone box. Inside it, a young man in motorcycle leathers was finishing a call. Jericho, leaning against the tree, could hear his singsong accent, muffled but audible:

'Right you are ... OK, doll ... See you.'

The dispatch rider put the receiver down with a clatter and pushed open the door.

'All yours, pal.'

The motorcyclist didn't move away at first. Jericho stood in the kiosk, pretending to fish in his pockets for change, and watched him through the glass. The man adjusted his leggings, put on his helmet, fiddled with the chin strap ...

Jericho waited until he had moved away before dialling zero.

A woman's voice said: 'Operator speaking.'

'Good morning. I'd like to make a call, please, to Kensington double-two five seven.'

She repeated the number. 'That'll be fourpence, caller.'

A sixty-mile land line connected all Bletchley Park numbers to the Whitehall exchange. As far as the operator could tell, Jericho was merely calling one London borough from another. He pressed four pennies into the slot and after a series of clicks he heard a ringing tone.

It took fifteen seconds for a man to answer.

'Ye-es?'

It was exactly the voice Jericho had always imagined for Claire's father. Languid and assured, it stretched that single short syllable into two long ones. Immediately there was a series of pips and Jericho pushed the A-button. His money tinkled into the coin-box. Already, he felt at a disadvantage – an indigent without access to a telephone of his own.

'Mr Romilly?'

'Ye-es?'

'I'm so sorry to trouble you, sir, especially on a Sunday morning, but I work with Claire ...'

There was a faint noise, and then a pause, during which he could hear Romilly breathing. A crackle of static cut across the line. 'Are you still there, sir?'

The voice, when it came again, was quiet, and it sounded hollow, as if emanating from a vast and empty room. 'How did you get this number?'

'Claire gave it me.' It was the first lie that came into Jericho's head. 'I wondered if she was with you.'

Another long pause. 'No. No, she isn't. Why should she be?'

'She's not turned up for her shift this morning. Yesterday was her day off. I wondered if she might have gone down to London.'

'Who is this speaking?'

'My name is Tom Jericho.' Silence. 'She may have spoken of me.'

'I don't believe so.' Romilly's voice was barely audible. He cleared his throat. 'I'm awfully sorry, Mr Jericho. I'm afraid I can't help you. My daughter's movements are as much a mystery to me as they seem to be to you. Goodbye.'

There was a fumbling noise and the connection was broken off.

'Hello?' said Jericho. He thought he could still hear somebody breathing on the line. 'Hello?' He held on to the heavy bakelite receiver for a couple of seconds, straining to hear, then carefully replaced it.

He leaned against the side of the telephone box and massaged his temples. Beyond the glass, the world went silently about its business. A couple of civilians with bowler hats and rolled umbrellas, fresh from the London train, were being escorted up the drive to the mansion. A trio of ducks in winter camouflage came in to land on the lake, feet splayed, ploughing furrows in the grey water.

'My daughter's movements are as much a mystery to me as they seem to be to you.'

That was not right, was it? That was not the reaction one would expect of a father on being told his only child was missing?

Jericho groped in his pocket for a handful of change. He spread the coins out on his palm and stared at them, stupidly, like a foreigner just arrived in an unfamiliar country.

He dialled zero again.

'Operator speaking.'

'Kensington double-two five seven.'

Once again, Jericho inserted four pennies into the metal slot. Once again, there was a series of short clicks, then a pause. He tightened his finger on the button. But this time there was no ringing tone, only the *blip-blip-blip* of an engaged signal, pulsing in his ear like a heartbeat.

*

Over the next ten minutes Jericho made three more attempts to get through. Each met the same response. Either Romilly had taken his telephone off the hook, or he was involved in a long conversation with someone.

Jericho would have tried the number a fourth time, but a woman from the canteen with a coat over her apron had turned up and started rapping a coin on the glass, demanding her turn.

Finally, Jericho let her in. He stood on the roadside and tried to decide what to do.

He glanced back at the huts. Their squat, grey shapes, once so boring and familiar, now seemed vaguely threatening.

Damn it. What did he have to lose?

He buttoned his jacket against the cold and turned towards the gate.

3

St Mary's Parish Church, eight solid centuries of hard white stone and Christian piety, lay at the end of an avenue of elderly yew trees, less than a hundred yards beyond Bletchley Park. As Jericho walked through the gate he saw bicycles, fifteen or twenty of them, stacked neatly around the porch, and a moment later heard the piping of the organ and the mournful lilt of a Church of England congregation in mid-hymn. The graveyard was perfectly still. He felt like a late guest approaching a house where a party was already in full swing.

'*We blossom and flourish as leaves on a tree,*
And wither, and perish, but naught changeth thee …'

Jericho stamped his feet and beat his arms. He considered slipping inside and standing at the back of the nave until the service ended, but experience had taught him there was no such thing as a quiet entry into a church. The door would bang, heads would turn, some officious sidesman would come hurrying down the aisle with a prayer sheet and a hymn book. Such attention was the last thing he wanted.

He left the path and pretended to study the tombstones. Frosted cobwebs of improbable size and delicacy shone like ectoplasm between the memorials: marble monuments for the well-to-do, slate for the farmworkers, weathered wooden crosses for the poor and infants. Ebenezer Slade, aged four years and six months, asleep in the arms of Jesus. Mary Watson, wife of Albert, taken after a long illness, rest in peace ... On a few of the graves, bunches of dead flowers, petrified by ice, testified to some continuing flicker of interest among the living. On others, yellow lichen had obscured the inscriptions. He bent and scratched away at it, hearkening to the voices of the righteous beyond the stained glass window.

'*O ye Dews and Frosts, bless ye the Lord: praise him and magnify him for ever.*

O ye Frost and Cold, bless ye the Lord: praise him and magnify him for ever ...'

Odd images chased through his mind.

He thought of his father's funeral, on just such a day as this: a freezing, ugly Victorian church in the industrial Midlands, medals on the coffin, his mother weeping, his aunts in black, everyone studying him with sad curiosity, and he all the time a million miles away, factoring the hymn numbers in his head ('Forward out of error,/Leave behind the night' – number 392 in *Ancient and Modern* – came out very prettily, he remembered, as 2 × 7 × 2 × 7 × 2 ...)

And for some reason he thought of Alan Turing, restless with excitement in the hut one winter night, describing how the death of his closest friend had made him seek a link between mathematics and the spirit, insisting that at Bletchley they were creating a new world: that the bombes might soon be modified, the clumsy electro-mechanical switches replaced by relays of pentode valves and GT1C-thyatrons to create computers, machines that might one day mimic the actions of the human brain and unlock the secrets of the soul ...

Jericho wandered among the dead. Here was a small stone cross garlanded with stone flowers, there a stern-looking angel with a face like Miss Monk. All the time he kept listening to the service. He wondered whether anyone from Hut 8 was among the congregation and, if so, who. With all else failing, might Skynner be offering up a prayer to God? He tried to imagine what fresh reserves of sycophancy Skynner would draw on to communicate with a being even higher than the First Lord of the Admiralty, and found he couldn't do it.

'*The blessing of God Almighty, the Father, the Son, and the Holy Ghost, be amongst you and remain with you always. Amen.*'

The service was over. Jericho wove quickly through the headstones, away from the church, and stationed himself behind a pair of large bushes. From here he had a clear view of the porch.

Before the war the faithful would have emerged to an uplifting peal of grandsire triples. But church bells now were to be rung only in the event of invasion, so that when the door opened and the elderly priest stationed himself to say farewell to his parishioners, the silence gave the ceremony a subdued, even melancholy air. One by one the worshippers stepped into the daylight. Jericho didn't recognise any of them. He began to think he might have come to the wrong conclusion. But then, sure enough, a small, lean young woman in a black coat appeared, still holding the prayer book from the night before.

She shook hands briefly, even curtly, with the vicar, said nothing, looped her carpetbag over the handles of her bicycle and wheeled it towards the gate. She walked quickly, with short, rapid steps, her sharp chin held high. Jericho waited until she had gone some way past him, then stepped out from his hiding place and shouted after her: 'Miss Wallace!'

She stopped and glanced back in his direction. Her weak eyesight made her frown. Her head moved vaguely from side to side. It wasn't until he was within two yards of her that her face cleared.

'Why, Mr ...'

'Jericho.'

'Of course. Mr Jericho. The stranger in the night.' The cold had reddened the sharp point of her nose and painted two neat discs of colour, the size of half-crowns, on her white cheeks. She had long, thick, black hair which she wore piled up, shot through and secured by an armoury of pins. 'What did you make of the sermon?'

'Uplifting?' he said, tentatively. It seemed easier than telling the truth.

'Did you really? I thought it the most frightful rot I've heard all year. "Suffer not a woman to teach, nor to usurp authority over the man, but to be in silence ..."' She shook her head furiously. 'Is it a heresy, do you suppose, to call St Paul an *ass*?'

She resumed her brisk progress towards the lane. Jericho fell in beside her. He had picked up a few details about Hester Wallace from Claire – that before the war she'd been a teacher at a girls' private school in Dorset, that she played the organ and was a clergyman's daughter, that she received the quarterly newsletter of the Jane Austen Society – just enough clues to suggest the sort of woman who might indeed go straight from an eight-hour night-shift to Sunday matins.

'Do you attend most Sundays?'

'Always,' she said. 'Although increasingly one wonders why. And you?'

He hesitated. 'Occasionally.'

It was a mistake and she was on to it at once.

'Whereabouts d'you sit? I don't recall ever seeing you.'

'I try to keep at the back.'

'So do I. Exactly at the back.' She gave him a second look, her wire-framed round spectacles flashing in the winter sun. 'Really, Mr Jericho, a sermon you obviously didn't hear, a pew you never occupy: one might almost suspect you of laying claim to a piety you don't rightly possess.'

'Ah ...'

'I'll bid you good day.'

They had reached the gate. She swung herself on to the saddle of her bicycle with surprising grace. This was not how Jericho had planned it. He had to reach out and hold on to the handlebars to stop her pedalling away.

'I wasn't in church. I'm sorry. I wanted to talk to you.'

'Kindly remove your hand from my machine, Mr Jericho.' A couple of elderly parishioners turned to stare at them. 'At once, if you please.' She twisted the handlebars back and forth but Jericho held on.

'I am so sorry. It really won't take a moment.'

She glared at him. For an instant he thought she might be about to reach down for one of her stout and sensible shoes and hammer his fingers loose. But there was curiosity as well as anger in her eyes, and curiosity won. She sighed and dismounted.

'Thank you. There's a bus shelter over there.' He nodded to the opposite side of Church Green Road. 'Just spare me five minutes. Please.'

'Absurd. Quite absurd.'

The wheels of her bicycle clicked like knitting needles as they crossed the road to the shelter. She refused to sit. She stood with her arms folded, looking down the hill towards the town.

He tried to think of some way of broaching the subject. 'Claire tells me you work in Hut 6. That must be interesting.'

'Claire has no business telling you where I work. Or anyone else for that matter. And, no, it is not interesting. Everything interesting seems to be done by men. Women do the rest.'

She could be pretty, he thought, if she put her mind to it. Her skin was as smooth and white as Parian. Her nose and chin, though sharp, were delicate. But she wore no make-up, and her expression was permanently cross, her lips drawn into a thin, sarcastic line. Behind her spectacles, her small, bright eyes glinted with intelligence.

'Claire and I, we were ...' He fluttered his hands and searched for the word. He was so hopeless at all this. '"Seeing one another" I suppose is the phrase. Until about a month ago. Then she refused to have anything more to do with me.' His resolution was wilted by her hostility. He felt a fool, addressing her narrow back. But he pressed on. 'To be frank, Miss Wallace, I'm worried about her.'

'How odd.'

He shrugged. 'We were an unlikely couple, I agree.'

'No.' She turned to him. 'I meant how *odd* that people always feel obliged to disguise their concern for themselves as concern for other people.'

The corners of her mouth twitched down in her version of a smile and Jericho realised he was beginning to dislike Miss Hester Wallace, not least because she had a point.

'I don't deny an element of self-interest,' he conceded, 'but the fact is, I am worried about her. I think she's disappeared.'

She sniffed. 'Nonsense.'

'She hasn't turned up for her shift this morning.'

'An hour late for work hardly constitutes a disappearance. She probably overslept.'

'I don't think she went home last night. She certainly wasn't back by two.'

'Then perhaps she overslept *somewhere else*,' said Miss Wallace, maliciously. The spectacles flashed again. 'Incidentally, might I ask *how* you know she didn't come home?'

He had learned it was better not to lie. 'Because I let myself in and waited for her.'

'So. A housebreaker as well. I can see why Claire wants nothing more to do with you.'

To hell with this, thought Jericho.

'There are other things you should know. A man came to the cottage last night while I was there. He ran away when he heard my voice. And I just called Claire's father. He claims he doesn't know where she is, but I think he's lying.'

That seemed to impress her. She chewed on the inside of her lip and looked away, down the hill. A train, an express by the sound of it, was passing through Bletchley. A curtain of brown smoke, half a mile long, rose in percussive bursts above the town.

'None of this is my concern,' she said at last.

'She didn't mention she was going away?'

'She never does. Why should she?'

'And she hasn't seemed odd to you lately? Under any sort of strain?'

'Mr Jericho, we could probably fill this bus shelter – no, we could probably fill an entire double-decker bus – with young men who are worried about their relationships with Claire Romilly. Now I'm really very tired. Much too tired and inexpert in these matters to be of any help to you. Excuse me.'

For the second time she mounted her bicycle, and this time Jericho didn't try to stop her. 'Do the letters ADU mean anything to you?'

She shook her head irritably and pushed herself away from the kerb.

'It's a call sign,' he shouted after her. 'Probably German Army or Luftwaffe.'

She applied the brakes with such force she slid off the saddle, her flat heels skittering in the gutter. She looked up and down the empty road. 'Have you gone utterly mad?'

'You'll find me in Hut 8.'

'Wait a moment. What has this to do with Claire?'

'Or, failing that, the Commercial Guesthouse in Albion Street.' He nodded politely. 'ADU, Miss Wallace. Angels Dance Upwards. I'll leave you in peace.'

'Mr Jericho ...'

But he didn't want to answer any of her questions. He crossed the road and hurried down the hill. As he turned left into Wilton Avenue towards the main gate he glanced back. She was still where he had left her, her thin legs planted either side of the pedals, staring after him in astonishment.

4

Logie was waiting for him when he got back to Hut 8. He was prowling around the confined space of the Registration Room, his bony hands clasped behind his back, the bowl of his pipe jerking around as he chomped furiously on its stem.

'This your coat?' was his only greeting. 'Better bring it with you.'

'Hello, Guy. Where are we going?' Jericho unhooked his coat from the back of the door and one of the Wrens gave him a rueful smile.

'*We're* going to have a chat, old cock. Then *you're* going home.'

Once inside his office, Logie threw himself into his chair and swung his immense feet up on to his desk. 'Close the door then, man. Let's at least *try* and keep this between ourselves.'

Jericho did as he was told. There was nowhere for him to sit so he leaned his back against it. He felt surprisingly calm. 'I don't know what Skynner's been telling you,' he began, 'but I didn't actually land a punch.'

'Oh, well, that's fine, then.' Logie raised his hands in mock relief. 'I mean to say, as long as there's no *blood*, none of your actual *broken bones* –'

'Come on, Guy. I never touched him. He can't sack me for that.'

'He can do whatever he sodding well likes.' The chair creaked as Logie reached across the desk and picked up a brown folder. He flicked it open. 'Let us see what we have here. "Gross insubordination," it says. "Attempted physical assault," it says. "Latest in a long series of incidents which suggest the individual concerned is no longer fit for active duties."' He tossed the file back on his desk. 'Not sure I disagree, as a matter of fact. Been waiting for you to show your face around here ever since yesterday afternoon. Where've you been? Admiralty? Taking a swing at the First Sea Lord?'

'You said not to work a full shift. "Just come and go as you please." Your very words.'

'Don't get smart with me, old love.'

Jericho was silent for a moment. He thought of the print of King's College Chapel with the intercepts hidden behind it. Of the German Book Room and Weitzman's frightened face. Of Edward Romilly's shaken voice: '*My daughter's movements are as much a mystery to me as they seem to be to you.*' He was aware that Logie was studying him carefully.

'When does he want me to go?'

'Well, now, you bloody idiot. "Send him back to King's and this time let the bugger walk" – I seem to recall those were my specific instructions.' He sighed and shook his head. 'You shouldn't have made him look a fool, Tom. Not in front of his clients.'

'But he *is* a fool.' Outrage and self-pity were welling in him. He tried to keep his voice steady. 'He hasn't the foggiest idea of what he's talking about. Come on, Guy. Do you honestly believe, for one minute, that we can break back into Shark within the next three days?'

'No. But there are ways of saying it and there are ways of saying it, if you follow me, especially when our dearly beloved American brethren are in the same room.'

Someone knocked and Logie shouted: 'Not now, old thing, thanks all the same!'

He waited until whoever it was had gone and then said, quietly: 'I don't think you quite appreciate how much things have changed round here.'

'That's what Skynner said.'

'Well, he's right. For once. You saw it for yourself at the conference yesterday. It's not 1940 any more, Tom. It's not plucky little Britain stands alone. We've moved on. We have to take account of what other people think. Just look at the map, man. Read the newspapers. These convoys embark from *New York*. A quarter of the ships are American. The cargo's *all* American. American troops. American crews.' Logie suddenly covered his face with his hands. 'My God, I can't believe you tried to hit Skynner. You really are pretty potty, aren't you? I'm not at all sure you're safe to walk the streets.' He lifted his feet off the desk and picked up the telephone. 'Look, I don't care what he says, I'll see if I can get the car to take you back.'

'No!' Jericho was surprised at the vehemence in his voice. In his mind he could see, perfectly replicated, the Atlantic plot – the brown landmass of North America, the Rorschach inkblots of the British Isles, the blue of the ocean, the innocent yellow discs, the shark's teeth, set and loaded like a mantrap. And Claire? Impossible to find her even now, when he had access to the Park. Shipped back to Cambridge, stripped of his security clearance, he might as well be on another planet. 'No,' he said, more calmly. 'You can't do that.'

'It's not my decision.'

'Give me a couple of days.'

'What?'

'Tell Skynner you want to give me a couple of days. Give me a couple of days to see if I can find a way back into Shark.'

Logie stared at Jericho for five seconds, then started to laugh. 'You get madder and madder as the week wears on, old son. Yesterday you're telling us Shark can't be broken in three days. Now you're saying you might be able to do it in two.'

'Please, Guy. I'm begging you.' And he was. He had his hands on Logie's desk and was leaning over it. He was pleading for his life. 'Skynner doesn't just want me out of the hut, you know. He wants me out of the Park altogether. He wants me locked up in some garret in the Admiralty doing long division.'

'There are worse places to spend the war.'

'Not for me there aren't. I'd hang myself. I belong here.'

'I have already stuck my neck out so far for you, my lad.' Logie jabbed his pipe into Jericho's chest. '"Jericho?" they said. "You can't be serious. We're in a crisis and you want *Jericho*?"' He jabbed his pipe again. 'So I said: "Yes, I know he's half bloody cracked and keeps on fainting like a maiden bloody aunt, but he's got something, got that extra two per cent. Just trust me."' Jab, jab. 'So I beg a bloody car – no joke round here, as you've gathered – and instead of getting my kip I come and drink stale tea in King's and plead with you, bloody *plead*, and the first thing you do is make us all look idiots and then you slug the head of section – all right, all right, *try* to slug him. Now, I ask you: who's going to listen to me now?'

'Skynner.'

'Come off it.'

'Skynner will have to listen, he will if you insist you need me. I know –' Jericho was inspired. 'You could threaten to tell that admiral, Trowbridge, that I've been removed – at a vital moment in the Battle of the Atlantic – just because I spoke the truth.'

'Oh, I could, could I? Thank you. Thanks very much. Then we'll both be doing long division in the Admiralty.'

'"There are worse places to spend the war."'

'Don't be cheap.'

There was another knock, much louder this time. 'For God's sake,' yelled Logie, 'piss off!' But the handle started to turn anyway. Jericho moved out of the way, the door opened and Puck appeared.

'Sorry, Guy. Good morning, Thomas.' He gave them each a grim nod. 'There's been a development, Guy.'

'Good news?'

'Frankly, no, to be entirely honest. It is probably not good news. You had better come.'

'Hell, *hell*!' muttered Logie. He gave Jericho a murderous look, grabbed his pipe and followed Puck out into the corridor.

Jericho hesitated for a second, then set off after them, down the passage and into the Registration Room. He had never seen it so full. Lieutenant Cave was there, along, it seemed, with almost every cryptanalyst in the hut – Baxter, Atwood, Pinker, Kingcome, Proudfoot, de Brooke – as well as Kramer, like a matinee idol in his American naval uniform. He gave Jericho a friendly nod.

Logie glanced around the room with surprise. 'Hail, hail, the gang's all here.' Nobody laughed. 'What's up, Puck? Holding a rally? Going on strike?'

Puck inclined his head towards the three young Wrens who made up the Registration Room's day shift.

'Ah yes,' said Logie, 'of course,' and he flashed his smoker's teeth at them in an ochre smile. 'Bit of business to attend to, girls. Hush hush. I wonder if you wouldn't mind leaving the gentlemen alone for a few minutes.'

*

'I happened to show this to Lieutenant Cave,' said Puck, when the Wrens had gone. 'Traffic analysis.' He held aloft the familiar yellow log sheet, as if he were about to perform a conjuring trick. 'Two long signals intercepted in the last twelve hours coming out of the Nazis' new transmitter near Magdeburg. One just before midnight: one hundred and eighty four-letter groups. One just after: two hundred and eleven groups. Rebroadcast twice, over both the Diana and Hubertus radio nets. Four-six-oh-one kilocycles. Twelve-nine-fifty.'

'Oh, do get on with it,' said Atwood, under his breath.

Puck affected not to hear. 'In the same period, the total number of Shark signals intercepted from the North Atlantic U-boats up to oh-nine-hundred this morning: five.'

'Five?' repeated Logie. 'Are you sure, old love?' He took the log sheet and ran his finger down the neatly inked columns of entries.

'What's the phrase?' said Puck. '"As quiet as the grave"?'

'Our listening posts,' said Baxter, reading the log sheet over Logie's shoulder. 'There must be something wrong with them. They must have fallen asleep.'

'I rang the intercept control room ten minutes ago. After I'd spoken to the lieutenant. They say there's no mistake.'

An excited murmur of conversation broke out.

'And what say you, O wise one?'

It took Jericho a couple of seconds to realise that Atwood was talking to him. He shrugged. 'It's very few. Ominously few.'

Puck said: 'Lieutenant Cave believes there's a pattern.'

'We've been interrogating captured U-boat crew about tactics.' Lieutenant Cave leaned forwards and Jericho saw Pinker flinch at the sight of his scarred face. 'When Dönitz sniffs a convoy, he draws his hearses up line abreast across the route he expects it to take. Twelve boats, say, maybe twenty miles apart. Possibly two lines, possibly three – nowadays he's got the hearses to put on a pretty big show. Our estimate, before the blackout, was forty-six operational in that sector of the North Atlantic alone.' He broke off, apologetically. 'Sorry,' he said, 'do stop me if I'm telling my grandmothers how to suck eggs.'

'Our work's rather more – ah – theoretical,' said Logie. He looked around and several of the cryptanalysts nodded in agreement.

'All right. There are basically two types of line. There's your picket line, which basically means the U-boats stay stationary on the surface waiting for the convoy to steam into them. And there's your patrol line, which involves the hearses sweeping forwards in formation to intercept it. Once the lines are established, there's one golden rule. Absolute radio silence until the convoy's sighted. My hunch is that that's what's happening now. The two long signals coming out of Magdeburg – those are most likely Berlin ordering the U-boats into line. And if the boats are now observing radio silence ...' Cave shrugged: he was sorry to have to state the obvious. 'That means they must be on battle stations.'

Nobody said anything. The intellectual abstractions of cryptanalysis had taken solid form: two thousand German U-boat men, ten thousand Allied seamen and passengers, converging to do battle in the North Atlantic winter, a thousand miles from land. Pinker looked as if he might be sick. Suddenly the oddity of their situation struck Jericho. Pinker was probably personally responsible for sending – what? – a thousand German sailors to the bottom of the ocean, yet Cave's face was the closest he had come to the brutality of the Atlantic war.

Someone asked what would happen next.

'If one of the U-boats finds the convoy? It'll shadow it. Send a contact signal every two hours – position, speed, direction. That'll be picked up by the other hearses and they'll start to converge on the same location. Same procedure, to try to draw in as many hunters as possible. Usually, they try to get right inside the convoy, in among our ships. They'll wait until nightfall. They prefer to attack in the dark. Fires from the ships that have been hit illuminate other targets. There's more panic. Also, night-time makes it harder for our destroyers to catch them.'

'Of course, the weather's appalling,' added Cave, his sharp voice cutting in to the silence, 'even for the time of year. Snow. Freezing fog. Green water breaking over the bows. That's actually in our favour.'

Kramer said: 'How long do we have?'

'Less time than we originally thought, that's for certain. The U-boat is faster than any convoy, but it's still a slow beast. On the surface it moves at the speed of a man on a bicycle, underwater it's only as fast as a man on foot. But if Dönitz knows about the convoys? Perhaps a day and a half. The bad weather will give them visibility problems. Even so – yes – I'd guess a day and a half, at the outside.'

*

Cave excused himself to go and telephone the bad news to the Admiralty. The cryptanalysts were left alone. At the far end of the hut a faint clacking noise began as the Type-X machines started their day's work.

'That'll be D-D-Dolphin,' said Pinker. 'Will you excuse me, G-G-Guy?'

Logie raised a hand in benediction and Pinker hurried out of the room.

'If only we had a four-wheel bombe,' moaned Proudfoot.

'Well, we ain't got one, old love, so don't let's waste time on that.'

Kramer had been leaning against one of the trestle tables. Now he pushed himself on to his feet. There wasn't room for him to pace, so he performed a kind of restless shuffle, smacking his fist into the palm of his left hand.

'Goddamn it, I feel so *helpless*. A day and a half. A measly, goddamn *day and a half*. Jesus! There must be *something*. I mean, you guys did break this thing once, didn't you, during the last blackout?'

Several people spoke at once.

'Oh, yes.'

'D'you remember that?'

'That was Tom.'

Jericho wasn't listening. Something was stirring in his mind, some tiny shift in the depths of his subconscious, beyond the reach of any power of analysis. What was it? A memory? A connection? The more he tried to concentrate on it, the more elusive it became.

'Tom?'

He jerked his head up in surprise.

'Lieutenant Kramer was asking you, Tom,' said Logie, with weary patience, 'about how we broke Shark during the black-out.'

'What?' He was irritated at having his thoughts interrupted. His hands fluttered. 'Oh, Dönitz was promoted to admiral. We took a guess that U-boat headquarters would be pleased as Punch.

So pleased, they'd transmit Hitler's proclamation verbatim to all boats.'

'And did they?'

'Yes. It was a good crib. We put six bombes onto it. Even then it still took us nearly three weeks to read one day's traffic.'

'With a good crib?' said Kramer. 'Six bombes. *Three weeks*?'

'That's the effect of a four-wheel Enigma.'

Kingcome said: 'It's a pity Dönitz doesn't get a promotion every day.'

This immediately brought Atwood to life. 'The way things are going, he probably will.'

Laughter momentarily lightened the gloom. Atwood looked pleased with himself.

'Very good, Frank,' said Kingcome. 'A daily promotion. Very good.'

Only Kramer refused to laugh. He folded his arms and stared down at his gleaming shoes.

They began to talk about some theory of de Brooke's which had been running on a pair of bombes for the past nine hours, but the methodology was hopelessly skewed, as Puck pointed out.

'Well, at least I've had an idea,' said de Brooke, 'which is more than you have.'

'That is because, my dear Arthur, if I have a terrible idea, I keep it to myself.'

Logie clapped his hands. 'Boys, boys. Let's keep the criticism constructive, shall we?'

The conversation dragged on but Jericho had stopped listening long ago. He was chasing the phantom in his mind again, searching back through his mental record of the past ten minutes to find the word, the phrase, that could have stirred it into life. Diana, Hubertus, Magdeburg, picket line, radio silence, contact signal ...

Contact signal.

'Guy, where d'you keep the keys to the Black Museum?'

'What, old thing? Oh, in my desk. Top right-hand drawer. Hey, where're you going? Just a minute, I haven't finished talking to you yet ...'

*

It was a relief to get out of the claustrophobic atmosphere of the hut and into the cold, fresh air. He trotted up the slope towards the mansion.

He seldom went into the big house these days but whenever he did it reminded him of a stately home in a twenties murder mystery. ('*You will recall, inspector, that the colonel was in the library when the fatal shots were fired ...*') The exterior was a nightmare, as if a giant handcart full of the discarded bits of other buildings had been tipped out in a heap. Swiss gables, Gothic battlements, Greek pillars, suburban bay windows, municipal red brick, stone lions, the entrance porch of a cathedral – the styles sulked and raged against one another, capped by a bell-shaped roof of beaten green copper. The interior was pure Gothic horror, all stone arches and stained glass windows. The polished floors rang hollow beneath Jericho's feet and the walls were decorated with dark wooden panelling of the sort that springs open in the final chapter to reveal a secret labyrinth. He was hazy about what went on here now. Commander Travis had the big office at the front looking out over the lake while upstairs in the bedrooms all sorts of mysterious things were done: he'd heard rumours they were breaking the ciphers of the German Secret Service.

He walked quickly across the hall. An Army captain loitering outside Travis's office was pretending to read that morning's *Observer*, listening to a middle-aged man in tweeds trying to chat up a young RAF woman. Nobody paid any attention to Jericho. At the foot of the elaborately carved oak staircase, a corridor led off to the right and wound around the back of the house. Midway along it was a door which opened to reveal steps down to a secondary passage. It was here, in a locked room in the cellar, that the cryptanalysts from huts 6 and 8 stored their stolen treasures.

Jericho felt along the wall for the light switch.

The larger of the two keys unlocked the door to the museum. Stacked on metal shelves along one wall were a dozen or more captured Enigma machines. The smaller key fitted one of a pair of big iron safes. Jericho knelt and opened it and began to rummage through the contents. Here they all were, their precious pinches: each one a victory in the long war against the Enigma. There was a cigar box with a label dated February 1941, containing the haul from the armed German trawler *Krebs*: two spare rotors, the Kriegsmarine grid map of the North Atlantic and the naval Enigma settings for February 1941. Behind these was a bulging envelope marked *München* – a weather ship whose capture three months after the *Krebs* had enabled them to break the meteorological code – and another labelled 'U-110'. He pulled out armfuls of papers and charts.

Finally, from the bottom shelf at the back, he withdrew a small package wrapped in brown oilcloth. This was the haul for which Fasson and Grazier had died, still in its original covering, as it had been passed out of the sinking U-boat. He never saw it without thanking God that they'd found something waterproof to wrap it in. The smallest exposure to water would have dissolved the ink. To have plucked it from a drowning submarine, at night, in a high sea ... It was enough to make even a mathematician believe in miracles. Jericho removed the oilcloth tenderly, as a scholar might unwrap the papyri of an ancient civilisation, or a priest uncover holy relics. Two little pamphlets, printed in Gothic lettering on pink blotting paper. The second edition of the U-boats' Short

Weather Cipher, now useless, thanks to the code book change. And – exactly as he had remembered – the Short Signal Book. He flicked through it. Columns of letters and numbers.

A typed notice was stuck on the back of the safe door: 'It is strictly forbidden to remove any item without my express permission. (Signed) L. F. N. Skynner, Head of Naval Section.'

Jericho took particular pleasure in slipping the Short Signal Book into his inside pocket and running with it back to the hut.

*

Jericho tossed the keys to Logie who fumbled and then just caught them.

'Contact signal.'

'What?'

'Contact signal,' repeated Jericho.

'Praise the Lord!' said Atwood, throwing up his hands like a revivalist preacher. 'The Oracle has spoken.'

'All right, Frank. Just a minute. What about it, old love?'

Jericho could see it all much faster than he could convey it. Indeed, it was quite hard to formulate it in words at all. He spoke slowly, as if translating from a foreign language, reordering it in his mind, turning it into a narrative.

'Do you remember, in November, when we got the Short Weather Cipher Book off the U-459? When we also got the Short Signal Book? Only we decided not to concentrate on the Short Signal Book at the time, because it never yielded anything long enough to make a worthwhile crib? I mean, a convoy contact signal on its own isn't worth a damn, is it? It's just five letters once in a blue moon.' Jericho withdrew the little pink pamphlet carefully from his pocket. 'One letter for the speed of the convoy, a couple for its course, a couple more for the grid reference ...'

Baxter stared at the code book as if hypnotised. 'You've removed that from the safe *without permission*?'

'But if Lieutenant Cave is correct, and whichever U-boat finds the convoy is going to send a contact signal every *two hours*, and if it's going to shadow it till nightfall, then it's possible – theoretically possible – it might send as many as four, or even five signals, depending on what time of day it makes its first sighting.' Jericho sought out the only uniform in the room. 'How long does daylight last in the North Atlantic in March?'

'About twelve hours,' said Kramer.

'Twelve hours, you see? And if a number of other U-boats attach themselves to the same convoy, on the same day, in response to the original signal, and *they* all start sending contact signals every two hours ...'

Logie, at least, could see what he was driving at. He withdrew his pipe slowly from his mouth. 'Bloody hell!'

'Then again, *theoretically*, we could have, say, twenty letters of crib off the first boat, fifteen off the second – I don't know, if it's an attack by eight boats, let's say, we could easily get to a hundred letters. It's just as good as the weather crib.' Jericho felt as proud as a father, offering the world a glimpse of his newborn child. 'It's beautiful, don't you see?' He gazed at each of the cryptanalysts in turn: Kingcome and Logie were beginning to look excited, de Brooke and Proudfoot seemed thoughtful, Baxter, Atwood and Puck appeared downright hostile. 'It was never possible till this moment, because until now the Germans have never been able to throw so many U-boats against such a mass of shipping. It's the whole story of Enigma in a nutshell. The very scale of the Germans' achievement breeds such a mass of material for us, it'll sow the seeds of their eventual defeat.'

He paused.

'Aren't there rather a lot of *ifs* there?' said Baxter drily. '*If* the

U-boat finds the convoy early enough in the day, *if* it reports every two hours, *if* the others all do the same, *if* we manage to intercept every transmission ...'

'And *if*,' said Atwood, 'the Short Signal Book we pinched in November wasn't changed last week at the same time as the Weather Cipher Book ...'

That was a possibility Jericho hadn't considered. He felt his enthusiasm crumble slightly.

Now Puck joined in the attack. 'I agree. The concept is quite brilliant, Thomas. I applaud your – inspiration, I suppose. But your strategy depends on failure, does it not? We will only break Shark, on your admission, if the U-boats find the convoy, which is exactly what we want to avoid. And suppose we do come up with that day's Shark settings – so what? Marvellous. We can read all the U-boats' signals to Berlin, boasting to Dönitz about how many Allied ships they've sunk. And twenty-four hours later, we're blacked out again.'

Several of the cryptanalysts groaned in agreement.

'No, no.' Jericho shook his head emphatically. 'Your logic is flawed, Puck. What we hope, obviously, is that the U-boats don't find the convoys. Yes – that's the whole point of the exercise. But if they do, we can at least turn it to our advantage. And it won't just be one day, not if we're lucky. If we break the Shark settings for twenty-four hours, then we'll pick up the encoded weather messages for that entire period. And, remember, we'll have our own ships in the area, able to give us the precise weather data the U-boats are encoding. We'll have the plaintext, we'll have the Shark cipher settings, so we'll be able to make a start on reconstructing the new Weather Code Book. We could get our foot back in the door again. Don't you see?'

He ran his hands through his hair and tugged at it in exasperation. Why were they all being so dim?

Kramer had been scribbling furiously in a notebook. 'He's on to something, you know.' He tossed his pencil into the air and caught it. 'Come on. It's worth a try. At least it puts us back in the fight.'

Baxter grunted. 'I still don't see it.'

'Nor do I,' said Puck.

'I suppose you don't see it, Baxter,' said Atwood, 'because it doesn't represent a triumph for the world proletariat?'

Baxter's hands curled into fists. 'One of these days, Atwood, someone's going to knock your bloody smug block off.'

'Ah. The first impulse of the totalitarian mind: violence.'

'Enough!' Logie banged his pipe like a gavel on one of the trestle tables. None of them had ever heard him shout before and the room went quiet. 'We've had quite enough of that already.' He stared hard at Jericho. 'Now, it's quite right we should be cautious. Puck, your point's taken. But we've also got to face facts. We've been blacked out four days and Tom's is the only decent idea we've got. So bloody good work, Tom.'

Jericho stared at an ink stain on the floor. *Oh God*, he thought, *here comes the housemaster's pep talk*.

'Now, there's a lot resting on us here, and I want every man to remember he's part of a team.'

'No man is an island, Guy,' said Atwood, deadpan, his chubby hands clasped piously on his wide stomach.

'Thank you, Frank. Quite right. No they're not. And if ever any of us – any of us – is tempted to forget it, just think of those convoys, and all the other convoys this war depends on. Got it? Good. Right. Enough said. Back to work.'

Baxter opened his mouth to protest, but then seemed to think better of it. He and Puck exchanged grim glances on their way out. Jericho watched them go and wondered why they were so determinedly pessimistic. Puck couldn't abide Baxter's politics and normally the two men kept their distance. But now they seemed to have made common cause. What was it? A kind of academic jealousy? Resentment that he had come in after all their hard work and made them look like fools?

Logie was shaking his head. 'I don't know, old love, what are we to do with you?' He tried to look stern, but he couldn't hide his pleasure. He put his hand on Jericho's shoulder.

'Give me my job back.'

'I'll have to talk to Skynner.' He held the door open and ushered Jericho out into the passage. The three Wrens watched them. 'My God,' said Logie, with a shudder. 'Can you imagine what he's going to say? He's going to love it, isn't he, having to tell his friends the admirals that the best chance of getting back into Shark is if the convoys are attacked? Oh, bugger, I suppose I'd better go and call him.' He went halfway into his office, then came out again. 'And you're quite sure you never actually hit him?'

'Quite sure, Guy.'

'Not a scratch?'

'Not a scratch.'

'Pity,' said Logie, half to himself. 'In a way. Pity.'

5

Hester Wallace couldn't sleep. The blackout curtains were drawn against the day. Her tiny room was a study in monochrome. A nosegay of lavender sent a soothing fragrance filtering through her pillow. But even though she lay dutifully on her back in her cotton nightgown, her legs pressed together, her hands folded on her breast, like a maiden on a marble tomb, oblivion still eluded her.

'ADU, Miss Wallace. Angels Dance Upwards ...'

The mnemonic was infuriatingly effective. She couldn't get it out of her brain, even though the arrangement of letters meant nothing to her.

'It's a call sign. Probably German Army or Luftwaffe ...'

No surprise in that. It was almost bound to be. After all, there were so many of them: thousands upon thousands. The only reliable rule was that Army and Luftwaffe call-signs never began with a D, because D always indicated a German commercial station.

ADU ... ADU ...

She couldn't place it.

She turned on her side, brought her knees up to her stomach and tried to fill her mind with soothing thoughts. But no sooner had she rid herself of the intense, pale face of Tom Jericho than her memory showed her the wizened priest of St Mary's, Bletchley, that croaking mouthpiece of St Paul's misogynies. 'It is a shame for women to speak in the church ...' (1 Corinthians 14.xxxv). 'Silly women laden with sins, led away with divers lusts ...' (2 Timothy 3.vi). From such texts he had woven a polemical sermon against the wartime employment of the female sex – women driving lorries, women in trousers, women drinking and smoking in public houses unaccompanied by their husbands, women neglecting their children and their homes. 'As a jewel of gold in a swine's mouth, so is a fair woman which is without discretion.' (Proverbs 11.xxii).

If only it were true! she thought. If only women *had* usurped authority over men! The Brylcreemed figure of Miles Mermagen, her head of section, rose greasily before her inner eye. 'My dear Hester, a transfer at the present moment is really quite out of the question.' He had been a manager at Barclays Bank before the war and liked to come up behind the girls as they worked and massage their shoulders. At the Hut 6 Christmas Party he had manoeuvred her under the mistletoe and clumsily taken off her glasses. ('Thank you, Miles,' she'd said, trying miserably to make a joke of it, 'without my spectacles you too look almost tolerably attractive ...') His lips on hers were unpleasantly moist, like the underside of a mollusc, and tasted of sweet sherry.

Claire, of course, had known immediately what to do.

'Oh, darling, poor you, and I suppose he's got a wife?'

'He says they were married too young.'

'Well, she's your answer. Tell him you think it's only fair you go and have a talk with her first. Tell him you want to be her friend.'

'But what if he says yes?'

'Oh, God! Then I suppose you'll just have to kick him in the balls.'

Hester smiled at the memory. She shifted her position in the bed again and the cotton sheet rode up and corrugated beneath her. It was quite hopeless. She reached out and switched on the little bedside lamp, fumbling around its base for her glasses.

Ich lerne deutsch, ich lernte deutsch, ich habe deutsch gelernt ...

German, she thought: German would be her salvation. A working knowledge of written German would lift her out of the grind of the Intercept Control Room, away from the clammy embrace of Miles Mermagen, and propel her into the rarefied air of the Machine Room, where the *real* work was done – where she should have been put in the first place.

She propped herself up in bed and tried to focus on *Abelman's German Primer*. Ten minutes of this was usually quite enough to send her off to sleep.

'Intransitive verbs showing a change of place or condition take the auxiliary *sein* instead of *haben* in the compound tenses ...'

She looked up. Was that a noise downstairs?

'In subordinate word order the auxiliary must stand last, directly after the past participle or the infinitive ...'

And there it was again.

She slipped her warm feet into her cold outdoor shoes, wrapped a woollen shawl about her shoulders, and went out onto the landing.

A knocking sound was coming from the kitchen.

She began to descend the stairs.

There had been two men waiting for her when she arrived back from church. One had been standing on the doorstep, the other had emerged casually from the back of the cottage. The first man was young and blond with a languid, aristocratic manner and a kind of decadent Anglo-Saxon handsomeness. His companion was older, smaller, slim and dark, with a northern accent. They both had Bletchley Park passes and said they'd come from Welfare and were looking for Miss Romilly. She hadn't turned up for work: any idea where she might be?

Hester had said she hadn't. The older man had gone upstairs and had spent a long time searching around. The blond, meanwhile – she never caught his name – had sprawled on the sofa and asked a lot of questions. There was something offensively patronising about him, for all his good manners. This is what Miles Mermagen would be like, she found herself thinking, if he'd had five thousand pounds' worth of private education. What was Claire like? Who were her friends? Who were the men in her life? Had anyone been asking after her? She mentioned Jericho's visit of the previous night and he made a note of it with a gold propelling pencil. She almost blurted out the story of Jericho's peculiar approach in the churchyard (*'ADU, Miss Wallace …'*) but by this time she had taken so strongly against the blond man's manner she bit back the words.

Knock, knock, knock from the kitchen …

Hester took the poker that stood beside the sitting-room fireplace and slowly opened the kitchen door.

It was like stepping into a refrigerator. The window was banging in the wind. It must have been open for hours.

At first she felt relieved, but that lasted only until she tried to close it. Then she discovered that the metal catch, weakened by rust, had been snapped clean off. Part of the wooden window frame around it was splintered.

She stood in the cold and considered the implications and quickly concluded there was only one plausible explanation. The dark-haired man who had appeared from behind the cottage on her return from church had obviously been in the process of breaking in.

They had told her there was nothing to worry about. But if there was nothing to worry about, why had they been prepared to force entry into the house?

She shivered and drew the shawl around her.

'Oh Claire,' she said aloud, 'oh, Claire, you silly, stupid, *stupid* girl, what *have* you done?'

She used a piece of blackout tape to try and secure the window. Then, still holding the poker, she went back upstairs and into Claire's room. A silver fox was hanging over the end of the bed, its glass-bead eyes staring, its needle teeth bared. Out of habit, she folded it neatly and placed it on the shelf where it normally lived. The room was such an expression of Claire, such an extravagance of colour and fabric and scent, that it seemed to resonate with her presence, even now, when she was away, to hum with it, like the last vibrations of a tuning fork ... Claire, holding some ridiculous dress to herself and laughing and asking her what she thought, and Hester pretending to frown with an older sister's disapproval. Claire, as moody as an adolescent, on her stomach on the bed, leafing through a pre-war *Tatler*. Claire combing Hester's hair (which, when she let it down, fell almost to her waist), running her brush through it with slow and languorous strokes that made

Hester's limbs turn weak. Claire insisting on painting Hester in her make-up, dressing her up like a doll and standing back in mock surprise: '*Why, darling, you're beautiful!*' Claire, in nothing but a pair of white silk knickers and a string of pearls, prancing about the room in search of something, long-legged as an athlete, turning and seeing that Hester was secretly watching her in the mirror, catching the look in her eyes, and standing there for a moment, hip thrust forward, arms outstretched, with a smile that was something between an invitation and a taunt, before sweeping back into motion ...

And on that cold, bright Sabbath afternoon, Hester Wallace, the clergyman's daughter, leaned against the wall and closed her eyes and pressed her hand between her legs with shame.

An instant later the noise from the kitchen started again and she thought her heart might burst with panic. She fled across the landing and into her room, pursued by the dry whine of the vicar of St Mary's – or was it really the voice of her father? – reciting from the Book of Proverbs:

'For the lips of a strange woman drop as an honeycomb, and her mouth is smoother than oil: But her end is bitter as wormwood, sharp as a two-edged sword. Her feet go down to death; her steps take hold on hell ...'

6

For the first time in more than a month, Tom Jericho found that he was busy.

He had to supervise the copying of the Short Signal Code Book, six typewritten transcripts of which were duly produced and stamped MOST SECRET. Every line had to be checked, for a single error could spell the difference between a successful break and days of failure. The intercept controllers had to be briefed. Teleprintered orders had to be sent to all the duty officers of every Hut 8 listening post – from Thurso, clinging to the cliffs on the northernmost tip of Scotland, right down to St Erth, near Land's End. Their brief was simple: concentrate everything you have on the known Atlantic U-boat frequencies, cancel all leave, bring in the lame and the sick and the blind if you have to, and pay even greater attention than usual to very short bursts of Morse preceded by E-bar – *dot dot dash dot dot* – the Germans' priority code which cleared the wavelength for convoy contact reports. Not one such signal was to be missed, understand? *Not one.*

From the Registry, Jericho withdrew three months' worth of Shark decrypts to bring himself back up to speed, and, that afternoon, sitting in his old place by the window in the Big Room, proved by slide-rule calculation what he already knew by instinct: that seventeen convoy contact reports, if harvested in the same twenty-four-hour stretch, would yield eighty-five letters of cipher encode which might – *might*, if the cryptanalysts had the requisite percentage of luck – give them a break into Shark, provided they could get at least ten bombes working in relay for a minimum of thirty-six hours ...

And all the time he thought of Claire.

There was very little, practically, he could do about her. Twice during the day he managed to get out to the telephone box to try to call her father: once as they all went off to lunch, when he was able to drop back, unnoticed by the rest, just before they reached the main gate; and the second time in the late afternoon when he pretended he needed to stretch his legs. On each occasion, the connection was made, but the phone merely rang, unanswered. He had a vague but growing feeling of dread, made worse by his powerlessness. He couldn't return to Hut 3. He didn't have the time to check out her cottage. He would have liked to go back to his room to rescue the intercepts – hidden behind a *picture* on top of the *mantelpiece*? was he *insane*? – but the round trip would have taken him the best part of twenty minutes and he couldn't get away.

In the event, it was to be well past seven before he got away. Logie was passing through the Big Room when he stopped off at Jericho's table and told him, for God's sake, to get back to his digs and get some some rest. 'There's nothing more for you to do here, old love. Except wait. I expect it'll be around this time tomorrow that we'll start to sweat.'

Jericho reached thankfully for his coat. 'Did you talk to Skynner?'

'About the plan, yes. Not about you. He didn't ask and I certainly wasn't going to bring it up.'

'Don't tell me he's forgotten?'

Logie shrugged. 'There's some other flap on that seems to have taken his mind off things.'

'What other flap?'

But Logie had moved away. 'I'll see you in the morning. You just make sure you get some kip.'

Jericho returned the stack of Shark intercepts to the Registry and went outside. The March sun, which had barely risen above the trees all day, had sunk behind the mansion, leaving a fading streak of primrose and pale orange at the rim of an indigo sky. The moon was already out and Jericho could hear the sound of bombers, far away, a lot of them, forming up for the night's attack on Germany. As he walked, he gazed around him in wonder. The lunar disc on the still lake, the fire on the horizon – it was an extraordinary conjunction of lights and symbols, almost like a portent. He was so engrossed he had almost passed the telephone box before he realised that it was empty.

One last try? He glanced at the moon. Why not?

The Kensington number still wasn't answering so he decided, on a whim, to try the Foreign Office. The operator put him through to a duty clerk and he asked for Edward Romilly.

'Which department?'

'I don't know, I'm afraid.'

The line went silent. The chances of Edward Romilly being at his desk on a Sunday night were slim. He rested his shoulder against the glass panel of the booth. A car went past slowly, then pulled up about ten yards down the road. Its brake lights glowed red in the dusk. There was a click and Jericho returned his attention to the call.

'Putting you through.'

A ringing tone, and then a cultured female voice said: 'German Desk.'

German Desk? He was momentarily disconcerted. 'Ah, Edward Romilly, please.'

'And who shall I say is calling?'

My God, he *was* there. He hesitated again.

'A friend of his daughter.'

'Wait, please.'

His fingers were clamped so tight around the receiver that they were aching. He made an effort to relax. There was no good reason why Romilly *shouldn't* work on the German Desk. Hadn't Claire told him once that her father had been a junior official at the Berlin Embassy, just as the Nazis were coming to power? She would have been about ten or eleven. That must have been where she learned her German.

'I'm afraid, sir, Mr Romilly's already left for the evening. Who shall I say called?'

'Thank you. It doesn't matter. Good night.'

He hung up quickly. He didn't like the sound of that. And he didn't like the look of this car, either. He came out of the telephone box and began to walk towards it – a low, black machine with wide running boards, edged white for the blackout. Its engine was still running. As he came closer it suddenly catapulted forwards and shot round the curving road towards the main gate. He trotted after it but by the time he reached the entrance it had gone.

*

As Jericho went down the hill, the vague outline of the town evaporated into the darkness. No generation for at least a century could have witnessed such a spectacle. Even in his great-grandfather's day there would have been some illumination – the gleam of a gaslight or a carriage lantern, the bluish glow of a night watchman's paraffin lamp – but not any more. As the light faded, so did Bletchley. It seemed to sink into a black lake. He could have been anywhere.

He was aware, now, of a certain paranoia, and the night magnified his fears. He passed an urban pub close to the railway bridge, an elaborate Victorian mausoleum with FINE WHISKYS, PORTS AND STOUTS inlaid in gold on the black masonry like an epitaph. He could hear a badly tuned piano playing 'The Londonderry Air' and for a moment he was tempted to go in, buy a drink, find someone to talk to. But then he imagined the conversation –

'So, what's your line then, pal?'

'Just government work.'

'Civil service?'

'Communications. Nothing much. Look, I say, can I get you another drink?'

'Local are you?'

'Not exactly ...'

– and he thought: no, better to keep clear of strangers; best, really, not to drink at all. As he was turning into Albion Street he heard the scrape of a footstep behind him and spun round. The pub door had opened, there was a moment of colour and music, then it closed and the road was dark again.

The guesthouse was about half way down Albion Street, on the right, and he had almost reached it when he noticed, on the left, a car. He slowed his pace. He couldn't be sure it was the same one that had behaved so oddly at the Park, although it looked quite similar. But then, when he was almost level with it, one of the occupants struck a match. As the driver leaned over to cup his hand to the light, Jericho saw on his sleeve the three white stripes of a police sergeant.

He let himself into the guesthouse and prayed he could make the stairs before Mrs Armstrong rose like a night fighter to intercept him in the hall. But he was too late. She must have been waiting for the sound of his key in the latch. She appeared from the kitchen through a cloud of steam that smelled of cabbage and offal. In the dining room, somebody made a retching noise and there was a shout of laughter.

Jericho said weakly, 'I don't think I'm very hungry, Mrs Armstrong, thanks all the same.'

She dried her hands on her apron and nodded towards a closed door. 'You've got a visitor.'

He had just planted his foot defiantly on the first stair. 'Is it the police?'

'Why, Mr Jericho, whatever would the police be doing here? It's a very nice-looking young gentleman. I've put him,' she added, with heavy significance, 'in the parlour.'

The parlour! Open nightly to any resident from eight till ten on weekdays, and from teatime onwards, Saturday and Sunday: as formal as a ducal drawing room, with its matching three-piece suite and antimacassars (made by the proprietress herself), its mahogany standard lamp with tasselled shade, its row of grinning Toby jugs, precisely lined above its freezing hearth. Who had come to see him, wondered Jericho, who warranted admission to the *parlour*?

At first he didn't recognise him. Golden hair, a pale and freckled face, pale blue eyes, a practised smile. Advancing across the room to meet him, right hand outstretched, left hand holding an Anthony Eden hat, fifty guineas' worth of Savile Row coat draped over manly shoulders. A blur of breeding, charm and menace.

'Wigram. Douglas Wigram. Foreign Office. We met yesterday but weren't introduced properly.'

He took Jericho's hand lightly and oddly, a finger crooked back into his palm, and it took Jericho a moment to realise he had just been the recipient of a masonic handshake.

'Digs all right? Super room, this. Super. Mind if we go somewhere else? Whereabouts are you based? Upstairs?'

Mrs Armstrong was still in the hall, fluffing up her hair in front of the oval mirror.

'Mr Jericho suggests we might have our little chat upstairs in his room, if that's OK with you, Mrs A?' He didn't wait for a reply. 'Let's go then, shall we?'

He held out his arm, still smiling, and Jericho found himself being ushered up the stairs. He felt as though he had been tricked or robbed but he couldn't work out how. On the landing he rallied sufficiently to turn and say, 'It's very small, you know, there's barely room to sit.'

'That's perfectly all right, my dear chap. As long as it's private. Onwards and upwards.'

Jericho switched on the dim light and stood back to let Wigram go in first. There was a faint whiff of eau de cologne and cigars as he brushed past. Jericho's eyes went straight to the picture of the chapel, which, he was relieved to note, looked undisturbed. He closed the door.

'See what you mean about the room,' said Wigram, cupping his hands to the glass to peer out of the window. 'The hell we have to go through, what? And a railway view thrown in. Bliss.' He closed the curtains and turned back to Jericho. He was cleaning his fingers on a handkerchief with almost feminine delicacy. 'We're rather worried.' His smile widened. 'We're rather worried about a girl called Claire Romilly.' He folded the blue silk square and thrust it back into his breast pocket. 'Mind if I sit down?'

He shrugged off his overcoat and laid it on the bed, then hitched up his pinstriped trousers a fraction at the knees to avoid damaging the crease. He sat on the edge of the mattress and bounced up and down experimentally. His hair was blond; so were his eyebrows, his eyelashes, the hairs on the back of his neat white hands ... Jericho felt his skin prickle with fear and disgust.

Wigram patted the eiderdown beside him. 'Let's talk.' He didn't seem the least put out when Jericho stayed where he was. He merely folded his hands contentedly in his lap.

'All right,' he said, 'we'll make a start, then, shall we? Claire Romilly. Twenty. Clerical grade staff. Officially missing for –' he looked at his watch '– twelve hours. Failed to show for her morning shift. Actually, when you start to check, not seen since midnight, Friday – dear oh dear, that's nearly two days ago now – when she left the Park after work. Alone. The girl she lives with swears she hasn't seen her since Thursday. Her father says he hasn't seen her since before Christmas. Nobody else – girls she works with, family, so forth – nobody seems to have the foggiest. Vanished.' Wigram snapped his fingers. 'Just like that.' For the first time he'd stopped smiling. 'Rather a good friend of yours, I gather?'

'I haven't seen her since the beginning of February. Is this why there are police outside?'

'But good enough? Good enough that you've *tried* to see her? Out to her cottage last night, according to our little Miss Wallace. Scurry, scurry. Questions, questions. Then, this morning, into Hut 3 – questions, questions, again. Phone call to her father – oh, yes,' he said, noticing Jericho's surprise, 'he rang us straight away to say you'd called. You've never met Ed Romilly? Lovely bloke. Never achieved his full potential, so they say. Rather lost the plot after his wife died. Tell me, Mr Jericho, why the interest?'

'I'd been away for a month. I hadn't seen her.'

'But surely you've got plenty more important things to worry about, especially just now, than renewing one acquaintance?'

His last words were almost lost in the roar of a passing express train. The room vibrated for fifteen seconds, which was the exact duration of his smile. When the noise was over, he said: 'Were you surprised to be brought back from Cambridge?'

'Yes. I suppose I was. Look, Mr Wigram, who are you, exactly?'

'Surprised when you were told *why* you were needed back?'

'Not surprised. No.' He searched for the word. 'Shocked.'

'Shocked. Ever talk to the girl about your work?'

'Of course not.'

'Of course not. Strike you as odd, though – possibly more than a coincidence, possibly even sinister – that one day the Germans black us out in the North Atlantic and two days later the girlfriend of a leading Hut 8 cryptanalyst goes missing? Actually on the same day he comes back?'

Jericho's gaze flickered involuntarily to the print of the chapel. 'I told you. I never talked to Claire about my work. I hadn't seen her for a month. And she wasn't my girlfriend.'

'No? What was she then?'

What was she then? A good question. 'I just wanted to see her,' he said lamely. 'I couldn't find her. I was concerned.'

'Got a photo of her? Something recent?'

'No. Actually, I don't have any pictures of her.'

'Really? Now here's another funny thing. Pretty girl like that. But can we find a picture? We'll just have to use the ID copy from her Welfare file.'

'Use it for what?'

'Can you fire a gun, Mr Jericho?'

'I couldn't hit a duck at a funfair.'

'Now that's what I would have thought, though one shouldn't always judge a chap by his looks. Only the Bletchley Park Home Guard had a little burglary at their armoury on Friday night. Two items missing. A Smith and Wesson .38 revolver, manufactured in Springfield, Massachusetts, issued by the War Office last year. And a box containing thirty-six rounds of ammunition.'

Jericho said nothing. Wigram looked at him for a while, as if he were making up his mind about something. 'No reason why *you* shouldn't know, I suppose. Trustworthy fellow like you. Come and sit down.' He patted the eiderdown again. 'I can't keep shouting the biggest frigging secret in the British Empire across your frigging bedroom. Come on. I won't bite, I promise.'

Reluctantly, Jericho sat down. Wigram leaned forwards. As he did so, his jacket parted slightly, and Jericho glimpsed a flash of leather and gunmetal against the white shirt.

'You want to know who I am?' he said softly. 'I'll tell you who I am. I'm the man our masters have decreed should find out just what's what down here in your little *anus mundi*.' He was speaking so quietly, Jericho was obliged to move his head in close to hear. 'Bells are going off, you see. Horrible, horrible bells. Five days ago, Hut 6 decoded a German Army signal from the Middle East. General Rommel's becoming a bit of a bad sport. Seems to think the only reason he's losing is that somehow, by some miracle, we always appear to know where exactly he's going to attack. Suddenly, the Afrika Korps want an enquiry into cipher security.

Oh dear. *Ding dong*. Twelve hours later, Admiral Dönitz, for reasons as yet unknown, suddenly decides to tighten Enigma procedure by changing the U-boat weather code. *Ding dong* again. Today, it's the Luftwaffe. Four German merchant ships loaded with goodies for the aforementioned Rommel were recently "surprised" by the RAF and sunk halfway to Tunisia. This morning, we read that the German C-in-C, Mediterranean, Field Marshal Kesselring himself, no less, is demanding to know whether the enemy could have read his codes.' Wigram patted Jericho's knee. 'Peals of alarms, Mr Jericho. A Westminster-Abbey-on-Coronation-Day peal of alarms. And in the middle of them all, your lady friend disappears, at the same time as a shiny new shooter and a box of bullets.'

*

'Exactly who or what are we dealing with here?' said Wigram. He had taken out a small black leather notebook and a gold propelling pencil. 'Claire Alexandra Romilly. Born: London, twenty-first of the twelfth, 'twenty-two. Father: Edward Arthur Macauley Romilly, diplomat. Mother: the Honourable Alexandra Romilly, *née* Harvey, deceased in motor accident, Scotland, August 'twenty-nine. The child is educated privately abroad. Father's postings: Bucharest, 'twenty-eight to 'thirty-one; Berlin, 'thirty-one to 'thirty-four; Washington, 'thirty-four to 'thirty-eight. A year in Athens, then back to London. The girl by now is at some fancy finishing school in Geneva. She returns to London on the outbreak of war, aged seventeen. Principal occupation for the next three years, as far as one can gather: having a good time.' Wigram licked his finger and turned the page. 'Some voluntary civil defence work. Nothing too arduous. July 'forty-one: translator at the Ministry of Economic Warfare. August 'forty-two: applies for clerical position, Foreign Office. Good languages. Recommended for position at Bletchley Park. See attached letter from father, blah, blah. Interviewed 10th of September. Accepted, cleared, starts work the following week.' Wigram flicked the pages back and forth. 'That's the lot. Not exactly a rigorous process of selection, is it? But then she does come from a *frightfully* good family. And Papa *does* work down at head office. And there *is* a war on. Care to add anything to the record?'

'I don't think I can.'

'How'd you meet her?'

For the next ten minutes Jericho answered Wigram's questions. He did this carefully and – mostly – truthfully. Where he lied it was only by omission. They had gone to a concert for their first date. After that they had gone out in the evenings a few times. They had seen a picture. Which one? *In Which We Serve*.

'Like it?'

'Yes.'

'I'll tell Noël.'

She had never talked about politics. She had never discussed her work. She had never mentioned other friends.

'Did you sleep with her?'

'Mind your own bloody business.'

'I'll put that down as yes.'

More questions. No, he had noticed nothing odd about her behaviour. No, she had not seemed tense or nervous, secretive, silent, aggressive, inquisitive, moody, depressed or elated – no, none of these – and at the end, they hadn't quarrelled. Really? No. So they had ... what, then?

'I don't know. Drifted apart.'

'She was seeing someone else?'

'Perhaps. I don't know.'

'Perhaps. You don't know.' Wigram shook his head in wonder. 'Tell me about last night.'

'I cycled over to her cottage.'

'What time?'

'About ten, ten-thirty. She wasn't there. I talked with Miss Wallace for a bit. Then I came home.'

'Mrs Armstrong says she didn't hear you come in until around two o'clock this morning.'

So much for tiptoeing past her door, thought Jericho.

'I must have cycled around for a while.'

'I'll say you did. In the frost. In the blackout. You must have cycled around for about three hours.'

Wigram gazed down at his notes, tapping the side of his nose. 'Not right, Mr Jericho. Can't quite put my finger on it, but definitely *not right*. Still.' He snapped the notebook shut and gave a reassuring smile. 'Time to go into all that later, what?' He put his hand on Jericho's knee and pushed himself to his feet. 'First, we must catch our rabbit. You've no idea where she might be, I suppose? No favourite haunts? No little den to run to?' He gazed down at Jericho, who was staring at the floor. 'No? No. Thought not.'

By the time Jericho felt he could trust himself to look up again, Wigram had draped his beautiful overcoat back around his shoulders and was preoccupied picking tiny pieces of lint from its collar.

'It could all be a coincidence,' said Jericho. 'You do realise that? I mean, Dönitz always seems to have been suspicious about Enigma. That's why he gave the U-boats Shark in the first place.'

'Oh absolutely,' said Wigram cheerfully. 'But let's look at it another way. Let's imagine the Germans *have* got a whisper of what we're up to here. What would they do? They couldn't exactly chuck out a hundred thousand Enigma machines overnight, could they? And then what about all those experts of theirs, who've always said Enigma is unbreakable? They're not going to change their minds without a fight. No. They'd do what they look as though they might be doing. They'd start checking every suspicious incident. And in the meantime, they'd try and find hard proof. A person, perhaps. Better still, a person with documentary evidence. God, there are enough of them about. Thousands right here, who either know all the story, or a bit of it, or enough to put two and two together. And what kind of people are they?' He withdrew a sheet of paper from his inside pocket and unfolded it. 'This is the list I asked for yesterday. Eleven people in the Naval Section knew about the importance of the Weather Code Book. Some rum names here, if you stop to think about them. Skynner we can exclude, I suppose. And Logie – he seems sound enough. But Baxter? Now Baxter's a communist, isn't he?'

'I think you'll find that communists don't have much time for Nazis. As a rule.'

'What about Pukowski?'

'Puck lost his father and his brother when Poland was invaded. He loathes the Germans.'

'The American, then. Kramer. *Kramer?* He's a second-generation German immigrant, did you know that?'

'Kramer also lost a brother to the Germans. Really, Mr Wigram, this is ridiculous ...'

'Atwood. Pinker. Kingcome. Proudfoot. de Brooke. *You* ... Who *are* you all, exactly?' Wigram looked around the tiny room with distaste: the frayed blackout curtains, the tatty wardrobe, the lumpy bed. For the first time he seemed to notice the print of the chapel above the mantelpiece. 'I mean, just because a bloke's been to King's College, Cambridge ...'

He picked up the picture and held it at an angle under the light. Jericho watched him, transfixed.

'E. M. Forster,' said Wigram thoughtfully. 'Now he's still at King's, isn't he?'

'I believe so.'

'Know him?'

'Only to nod to.'

'What was that essay of his? How did it go? The one about choosing between your friend and your country?'

'"I hate the idea of causes, and if I had to choose between betraying my country and betraying my friend, I hope I should have the guts to betray my country." But he did write that before the war.'

Wigram blew some dust off the frame and set the print carefully back on the top of Jericho's books.

'So I should hope,' he said, standing back to admire it. He turned and smiled at Jericho. 'So I should frigging well hope.'

*

After Wigram had gone, it was some minutes before Jericho felt able to move.

He lay full length on the bed, still wearing his scarf and overcoat, and listened to the sounds of the house. Some mournful string quartet which the BBC judged suitable entertainment for a Sunday night was scraping away downstairs. There were footsteps on the landing. A whispered conversation ensued which ended with a woman – Miss Jobey, was it? – having a fit of the giggles. A door slammed. The cistern above his head emptied and refilled. Then silence again.

When he did move, after about a quarter of an hour, his actions had a frantic, fumbling haste. He carried the chair over from the bedside to the door and tilted it against the flimsy panelling. He took the print and laid it face down on the threadbare carpet, pulled out the tacks, lifted off the back, rolled the intercepts into a tube, and took them over to the grate. On top of the little bucket of coal beside the hearth was a matchbox containing two matches.

The first was damp and wouldn't strike but the second did, just, and Jericho twisted it round to make sure the yellow flame caught and grew, then he applied it to the bottom of the intercepts. He held on to them as they writhed and blackened until the very last moment, until the pain obliged him to drop them in the grate, where they disintegrated into tiny flakes of ash.

FIVE

CRIB

CRIB: a piece of evidence (usually a captured code book or a length of plaintext) which provides clues for the breaking of a cryptogram; 'without question, the crib ... is the single most essential tool of any cryptanalyst' (Knox et al., op. cit., page 27).

A Lexicon of Cryptography
('Most Secret', Bletchley Park, 1943)

1

The wartime lipstick was hard and waxy – it was like trying to colour your lips with a Christmas candle. When, after several minutes of hard rubbing, Hester Wallace replaced her glasses, she peered into the mirror with distaste. Make-up had never featured much in her life, not even before the war, when there had been plenty in the shops. But now, when there was nothing to be had, the lengths one was expected to go to were quite absurd. She knew of girls in the hut who made lipstick out of beetroot and sealed it in place with Vaseline, who used shoe polish and burnt cork for mascara and margarine wrappers as a skin softener, who dusted bicarbonate of soda into their armpits to disguise their sweat ... She formed her lips into a cupid's bow, which she immediately drew back into a grimace. Really, it was quite, quite absurd.

The shortage of cosmetics seemed to have caught up at last even with Claire. Although there was a profusion of pots and bottles all over her little dressing table – Max Factor, Coty, Elizabeth Arden: each name redolent of pre-war glamour – most of them turned out on closer inspection to be empty. Nothing was left except a trace of scent. Hester sniffed at each in turn and her mind was filled with images of luxury – of satin cocktail dresses by Worth of London and gowns with daring *décolletage*, of fireworks at Versailles and the Duchess of Westminster's summer ball, and a dozen other wonderful nonsenses that Claire had prattled on about. Eventually she found a half-full pot of mascara and a glass-stoppered jar with an inch of rather lumpy face powder and set to work with those.

She had no qualms about helping herself. Hadn't Claire always told her she should? Making-up was fun, that was Claire's philosophy, it made one feel good about oneself, it turned one into someone else, and, besides, '*if this is what it takes, then, darling heart, this is simply what one does*'. Very well. Hester dabbed grimly at her pallid cheeks. If *this* was what it bloody well *took* to help persuade Miles Mermagen to approve a transfer, this was what he'd bloody well *get*.

She regarded her reflection without enthusiasm, then carefully replaced everything in its proper place and went downstairs. The sitting room was freshly swept. Daffodils above the hearth. A fire laid. The kitchen, too, was spotless. She had made a carrot flan earlier in the evening, enough for two, with ingredients she had grown herself in the little vegetable patch outside the kitchen door, and now she laid a place for Claire, and left a note telling her where to find the flan and instructions on how to heat it. She hesitated, then added at the end: 'Welcome back – from wherever you've been! – much love, H.' She hoped it didn't sound too fussy and inquisitive; she hoped she wasn't turning into her mother.

'*ADU, Miss Wallace ...*'

Of course Claire would come back. It was all a stupid panic, too absurd for words.

She sat in one of the armchairs and waited for her until a quarter to midnight, when she dared leave it no longer.

As her bicycle bounced along the track towards the lane she startled a white owl which rose silently like a ghost in the moonlight.

*

In a way it was all Miss Smallbone's fault. If Angela Smallbone hadn't pointed out in the common room after prep that the *Daily Telegraph* was holding a crossword competition, then Hester Wallace's life would have gone on undisturbed. It was not a particularly thrilling life – a placid, provincial life in a remote and eccentric girls' preparatory school near the Dorset town of Beaminster, less than ten miles from where Hester had grown up. And it was not a life much touched by war, either, save for the pale faces of the evacuee children on some of the nearby farms, the barbed wire along the beach near Lyme Regis, and the chronic shortage of teaching staff – a shortage which meant that when the Michaelmas term began in the autumn of 1942, Hester was having to take divinity (her usual subject) *and* English *and* some Latin and Greek.

Hester had a gift for crosswords and when Angela read out that night that the prize-money was twenty pounds ... well, she thought, why not? The first hurdle, an abnormally difficult puzzle printed in the next day's paper, she passed with ease. She sent off her solution and a letter arrived almost by return of post inviting her to the final, to be held in the *Telegraph*'s staff canteen, a fortnight hence, a Saturday. Angela agreed to take over hockey practice, Hester caught the train from Crewkerne up to London, joined fifty other finalists – and won. She completed the crossword in three minutes and twenty-two seconds and Lord Camrose himself presented her with the cheque. She gave five pounds to her father for his church restoration fund, she spent seven pounds on a new winter coat (second-hand, actually, but good as new), and the rest she put in her Post Office savings account.

It was on the Thursday that the second letter had arrived, this one very different. Registered post, long buff envelope. On His Majesty's Service.

Afterwards, she could never quite decide. Had the *Telegraph* held the competition at the instigation of the War Office, as a way of trawling the country for men and women with an aptitude for word puzzles? Or had some bright spark at the War Office merely seen the results of the competition and asked the *Telegraph* for a list of the finalists? Whatever the truth, five of the most suitable were summoned to be interviewed in a grim Victorian office block on the wrong side of the Thames, and three of them were ordered to report to Bletchley.

The school hadn't wanted her to go. Her mother had cried. Her father had detested the idea, just as he detested all change, and for days beforehand he was filled with foreboding ('He shall return no more to his house, neither shall his place know him any more' Job 7.x). But the law was the law. She had to go. Besides, she thought, she was twenty-eight. Was she doomed to live out the rest of her life in the same place, tucked away in this drowsy quilt of tiny fields and honey-stoned villages? Here was her chance of escape. She had picked up enough clues at the interview to guess that the work would be codes, and her fantasies were all of quiet, book-lined libraries and the pure, clear air of the intellect.

Arriving at Bletchley station in her second-hand coat on a soaking Monday morning, she was taken straight by shooting brake to the mansion and given a copy of the Official Secrets Act to sign. The Army captain who inducted them laid his pistol on the desk and said that if any of them, ever, breathed a word of what they were about to be told, he'd use it on them. Personally. Then they were assigned. The two male finalists became cryptanalysts, while she, the woman who had beaten them, was dispatched to a bedlam called Control.

'You take this form here, see, and in this first column you enter the code name of the intercept station. Chicksands, right, that's CKS, Beaumanor is BMR, Harpendon is HPN – don't worry, dear, you'll soon get used to it. Now here, see, you put the time of interception, here frequency, here call sign, here number of letter groups ...'

Her fantasies were dust. She was a glorified clerk, Control a glorified funnel between the intercept stations and the cryptanalysts, a funnel down which poured the ceaseless output of some forty thousand different radio call signs, using more than sixty separately identified Enigma keys.

'German Air Force, right, they're usually either insects or flowers. So you've got Cockroach, say, that's the Enigma key for western fighters, based in France. Dragonfly is Luftwaffe in Tunis. Locust is Luftwaffe, Sicily. You've got a dozen of those. Your flowers are the Luftgau – Foxglove: eastern front, Daffodil: western front, Narcissus: Norway. Birds are for the German Army. Chaffinch and Phoenix, they're Panzerarmee Afrika. Kestrel and Vulture – Russian front. Sixteen little birdies. Then there's Garlic, Onion, Celery – all the vegetables are weather Enigmas. They go straight to Hut 10. Got it?'

'What are Skunk and Porcupine?'

'Skunk is Fliegerkorps VIII, eastern front. Porcupine is ground-air cooperation, southern Russia.'

'Why aren't they insects as well?'

'God knows.'

The charts they had to fill in were called either 'blists' or 'hankies', the filing cabinet for miscellaneous trivia was known as Titicaca ('an Andes lake fed by many rivers,' said Mermagen portentously, 'but with no outflow'). The men gave one another silly names – 'the Unicorn-Zebra', 'the Mock Turtle' – while the girls mooned after the handsomer cryptanalysts in the Machine Room. Sitting in the freezing hut that winter, compiling her endless lists, Hester had a sense of Nazi Germany only as an endless, darkened plain, with thousands of tiny, isolated lights, flickering at one another in the blackness. Oddly enough, she thought, it was all, in its way, as remote from the war as the meadows and thatched barns of Dorset.

*

She parked her bicycle in the shed beside the canteen and was borne along by the stream of workers to be deposited near the entrance to Hut 6. Control was already in a fine state of uproar, Mermagen bustling self-importantly between the desks, knocking his head against the low-hanging lampshades, sending pools of yellow light spilling crazily in all directions. Fourth Panzer Army was reporting the successful recapture of Kharkov from the Russians and the ninnies in Hut 3 were demanding that *every* frequency in the southern sector, eastern front, be double-backed *immediately*.

'Hester, Hester, just in time. Will you talk to Chicksands, there's a good girl, and see what they can do? And while you're on, the Machine Room reckon they've got a corrupt text on the last batch of Kestrel – the operator needs to check her notes and re-send. Then the eleven o'clocks from Beaumanor all need blisting. Grab someone to help you. Oh, and the Index could do with a sorting out.'

All this before she had even taken off her coat.

It was two o'clock before there was enough of a lull for her to get away and talk to Mermagen in private. He was in his broom-cupboard office, his feet up on the desk, studying a handful of papers through half-closed eyes, in a terrific man-of-destiny pose she guessed he'd copied from some actor in the pictures.

'I wondered if I might have a word, Miles.'

Miles. She found this insistence on first-name terms a tiresome affectation, but informality was a rigid rule, an essential part of the

Bletchley ethos: *we*, the civilian amateurs shall defeat *them*, the disciplined Hun.

Mermagen continued to study his papers.

She tapped her foot. 'Miles?'

He flicked over a page. 'You have my completely divided attention.'

'My request for a transfer –'

He groaned and turned over another page. 'Not that again.'

'I've been learning German –'

'How brave.'

'You did say that *not* having German made a transfer impossible.'

'Yes, but I didn't say that *having* it made a transfer *likely*. Oh, bloody hell! Well, come in, then.'

With a sigh he put aside his papers and beckoned her over the threshold. Someone must have told him once that Brylcreem made him look racy. His oily black hair, swept back off his forehead and behind his ears, glistened like a swimmer's cap. He was trying to grow a Clark Gable moustache but it was slightly too long on the left-hand side.

'Transfers of personnel from section to section are, as I've told you before, extremely rare. We do have security to consider.'

Security to consider: this must have been how he turned down loans before the war. Suddenly he was staring at her intently and she realised he had noticed the make-up. He couldn't have looked more startled if she'd painted herself with woad. His voice seemed to drop an octave.

'Look here, Hester, the last thing I want to be is difficult. What you need is a change of scene for a day or two.' He touched his moustache lightly and gave a faint smile of recognition, as if he were surprised to find it still in place. 'Why don't you go up and take a look round one of the intercept stations, get a feel for where you fit into the chain? I know,' he added, 'I could do with a refresher myself. We could go up together.'

'Together? Yes ... Why not? And find a little pub somewhere we could stop off for lunch?'

'Excellent. Make a real break of it.'

'Possibly a pub with rooms, so we could stay overnight if it got late?'

He laughed nervously. 'I still couldn't guarantee a transfer, you know.'

'But it would help?'

'Your words.'

'Miles?'

'Mmmm?'

'I'd rather die.'

'Frigid little bitch.'

*

She filled the basin with cold water and splashed her face furiously. The icy water numbed her hands and stung her face. It trickled down inside the neck of her shirt and up the sleeves. She welcomed the shock and the discomfort. She deserved it as a punishment for her folly and delusion.

She pressed her flat stomach against the edge of the basin and stared myopically at the chalk-white face in the mirror.

Useless to complain, of course. It was her word against his. She would never be believed. And even if she was – so what? My dear, it was *simply* the way of the world. Miles could ram her up against Lake bloody Titicaca if he liked, and put his hand up her skirt, and they'd still never let her go: nobody, once they'd seen as much as she had, was ever allowed to leave.

She felt a pricking of self-pity in the corners of her eyes and immediately lowered her head back over the basin and drenched her face, scrubbing at her cheeks and mouth with a sliver of carbolic soap until the powder stained the water pink.

She wished she could talk to Claire.

'ADU, Miss Wallace ...'

Behind her in the cubicle the toilet flushed. Hurriedly, she pulled the plug out of the basin and dried her face and hands.

*

Name of intercept station, time of interception, frequency, call sign, letter groups ... Name of intercept station, time of interception, frequency, call sign, letter groups ...

Hester's hand moved mechanically across the paper.

At four o'clock the first half of the night-shift began drifting off to the canteen.

'Coming, Hetty?'

'Too much to do, unfortunately. I'll catch you up.'

'Poor you!'

'Poor you and *bloody* Miles,' said Beryl McCann, who had been to bed with Mermagen, once, and wished to God she hadn't.

Hester bent her head lower over her desk and continued to write in her careful schoolmistress copperplate. She watched the other women putting on their coats and filing out, their shoes clumping on the wooden floor. Ah, but Claire had been so *funny* about them. It was one of the things Hester loved in her the most, the way she mimicked everyone: Anthea Leigh-Delamere, the huntswoman, who liked to come on shift in jodhpurs; Binnie with the waxy skin who wanted to be a Catholic nun; the girl from Solihull who held the telephone a foot away from her mouth because her mother had told her the receiver was full of germs ... As far as Hester knew, Claire had never even *met* Miles Mermagen, yet she could impersonate him to perfection. The ghastliness of Bletchley had been their shared and private joke, their conspiracy against the bores.

The opening of the outside door let in a sudden blast of freezing air. Blists and hankies rustled and fluttered in the chill.

Bores. Boring. Claire's favourite words. The Park was boring. The war was boring. The town was *terrifically* boring. And the men were the biggest bores of all. The men – my God, what scent was it she gave off? – there were always two or three of them at least, hanging round her like tomcats on heat. And how she mocked them, on those precious evenings when she and Hester were alone together, sitting companionably by the fireside like an old married couple. She mocked their clumsy fumblings, their corny dialogue, their absurd self-importance. The only man she didn't mock, now Hester came to think of it, was the curious Mr Jericho, whom she had never even mentioned.

'ADU, Miss Wallace ...'.

Now that she had made up her mind to do it – and hadn't she always *known*, secretly, that she was going to do it? – she was astonished at how calm she felt. It would only be the briefest of glances, she told herself, and where was the harm in that? She even had the perfect excuse to slip across to the Index, for hadn't the beastly Miles, in everybody's hearing, commanded her to ensure the volumes were all arranged in proper order?

She finished the blist and slotted it into the rack. She forced herself to wait a decent interval, pretending to check the others' work, and then moved as casually as she could towards the Index Room.

2

Jericho drew back the curtains to unveil another cold, clear morning. It was only his third day in the Commercial Guesthouse but already the view had acquired a weary familiarity. First came the long and narrow garden (concrete yard with washing line, vegetable patch, bomb shelter) which petered out after seventy yards into a wilderness of weeds and a tumbledown, rotted fence. Then there was a drop he couldn't see, like a ha-ha, and then a broad expanse of railway lines, a dozen or more, which led the eye, at last, to the centrepiece: a huge Victorian engine shed with LONDON MIDLAND & SCOTTISH RAILWAY in white letters just visible beneath the grime.

What a day in prospect: the sort of day one waded through with no aim higher than to reach the other end intact. He looked at his Waralarm. It was a quarter past seven. It would be dark in the North Atlantic for at least another four hours. By his reckoning there would be nothing for him to do until – at the earliest – midnight, British time, when the first elements of the convoy would begin to enter the U-boat danger zone. Nothing to do except sit around the hut and wait and brood.

There had been three occasions during the night when Jericho had made up his mind to seek out Wigram and make a full confession, on the last of which he had actually got as far as putting on his coat. But in the end the judgement was too fine a one to call. On the one hand, yes, it was his duty to tell Wigram all he knew. On the other, no, what he knew would make little practical difference to the task of finding her, so why betray her? The equations cancelled one another out. By dawn he had surrendered, gratefully, to the old inertia, the product of always seeing both sides of every question.

And it could all still be some ghastly mistake – couldn't it, just? Some prank gone badly wrong? Eleven hours had passed since his conversation with Wigram. They might have found her by now. More likely, she would have turned up, either at the cottage or the hut – wide-eyed and wondering, darlings, what on earth the fuss was all about.

He was on the point of turning away from the window when his eye was caught by a movement at the far end of the engine shed. Was it a large animal of some sort, or a big man crawling on all fours? He squinted through the sooty glass but the thing was too far away for him to make it out exactly, so he fetched his telescope from the bottom of the wardrobe. The window sash was stuck but a few heavy blows from the heel of his hand were enough to raise it six inches. He knelt and rested the telescope on the sill. At first he couldn't find anything to focus on amid the dizzying crisscross of tracks but then, suddenly, it was filling his eye – an Alsatian dog as big as a calf, sniffing under the wheels of a goods wagon. He shifted the telescope a fraction to his left and there was a policeman dressed in a greatcoat that came down below his knees. Two policemen, in fact, and a second dog, on a leash.

He watched the little group for several minutes as they searched the empty train. Then the two teams split up, one passing further up the tracks and the other moving out of sight towards the little railway cottages opposite. He snapped the telescope shut.

Four men and two dogs for the railway yard. Say, a couple more teams to cover the station platforms. How many in the town? Twenty? And in the surrounding countryside?

'*Got a photo of her? Something recent?*'

He tapped the telescope against his cheek.

They must be watching every port and railway station in the country.

What would they do if they caught her?

Hang her?

Come on, Jericho. He could practically hear his housemaster's voice at his elbow. *Brace up, boy.*

Get through it somehow.

Wash. Shave. Dress. Make a little bundle of dirty laundry and leave it on the bed for Mrs Armstrong, more in hope than expectation. Go downstairs. Endure attempts to make polite conversation. Listen to one of Bonnyman's interminable, off-colour stories. Be introduced to two of the other guests: Miss Quince, rather pretty, a teleprincess in the naval hut, and Noakes, once an expert on Middle High German court epics, now a cryptanalyst in the weather section, vaguely known since 1940: a surly creature, then and now. Avoid all further conversation. Chew toast as stale as cardboard. Drink tea as grey and watery as a February sky. Half-listen to the wireless news: 'Moscow Radio reports the Russian Third Army under General Vatutin is making a strong defence of Kharkov in the face of the renewed German offensive ...'

At ten to eight Mrs Armstrong came in with the morning post. Nothing for Mr Bonnyman ('thank God for that,' said Bonnyman), two letters for Miss Jobey, a postcard for Miss Quince, a bill from Heffers bookshop for Mr Noakes and nothing at all for Mr Jericho – oh, except this, which she'd found when she came down and which must have been put through the door some time in the night.

He held it carefully. The envelope was poor-quality, official-issue stuff, his name printed on it in blue ink, with 'By hand, Strictly Personal' added underneath and double-underlined. The 'e' in Jericho and in 'Personal' was in the Greek form. His nocturnal correspondent was a classicist, perhaps?

He took it into the hall to open, Mrs Armstrong at his heels.

Hut 6
4.45 A.M.

Dear Mr Jericho,

As you expressed such a strong interest in medieval alabaster figurework when we met yesterday, I wondered if you might care to join me at the same place at 8 this morning to view the altar tomb of Lord Grey de Wilton (15th cent. and really *very fine*)?

Sincerely,
H. A. W.

'Bad news, Mr Jericho?' She couldn't quite suppress the note of hope in her voice.

But Jericho was already dragging on his overcoat and was halfway out of the door.

*

Even after taking the hill at a fast trot he was still five minutes late by the time he passed the granite war memorial. There was no sign of her or anyone else in the graveyard so he tried the door to the church. At first he thought it was locked. It took both hands to turn the rusty iron ring. He put his shoulder to the weathered oak and it shuddered inwards.

The church inside was cave-like, cold and dark, the shadows pierced by shafts of dusty, slate-blue light, so solid they seemed to have been propped like slabs against the windows. He hadn't been in a church for years and the chilly stink of candle wax and damp and incense brought memories of childhood crawling back. He thought he could make out the shape of a head in one of the pews nearest the altar and began to walk towards it.

'Miss Wallace?' His voice was hollow and seemed to travel a great distance. But when he came closer he saw it wasn't a head, just a priest's vestment, draped neatly over the back of the pew. He passed on up the nave to the wood-panelled altar. To the left was a stone coffin with an inscription; next to it, the smooth, white effigy of Richard, Lord Grey de Wilton, dead these past five hundred years, reclining in full armour, his head resting on his helmet, his feet on the back of a lion.

'The armour is especially interesting. But then warfare in the fifteenth century was the highest occupation for a gentleman.'

He wasn't sure where she'd come from. She was simply there when he turned round, about ten feet behind him.

'And the face, I think, is also good, if unexceptional. You weren't followed, I trust?'

'No. I don't think so, no.'

She took a few steps towards him. With her dead complexion and tapering white fingers she might have been an alabaster effigy herself, climbed down from Lord Grey's tomb.

'Perhaps you noticed the royal arms above the north door?'

'How long have you been here?'

'The arms of Queen Anne, but, intriguingly, still of the Stuart pattern. The arms of Scotland were only added as late as 1707. Now that *is* rare. About ten minutes. The police were just leaving as I arrived.' She held out her hand. 'May I have my note back, please?'

When he hesitated she presented her palm to him again, more emphatically this time.

'The *note*, please, if you'd be so good. I'd prefer to leave no trace. Thank you.' She took it and stowed it away at the bottom of her voluminous carpetbag. Her hands were shaking so much she had trouble fastening the clasp. 'There's no need to whisper, by the way. We're quite alone. Apart from God. And He's supposed to be on our side.'

He knew it would be wise for him to wait, to let her come to it in her own time, but he couldn't help himself.

'You've checked it?' he said. 'The call sign?'

She finally snapped the bag shut. 'Yes. I've checked it.'

'And is it Army or Luftwaffe?'

She held up a finger. 'Patience, Mr Jericho. Patience. First there's some information I'd like from you, if you don't mind. We might begin with what made you choose those three letters.'

'You don't want to know, Miss Wallace. Believe me.'

She raised her eyes to heaven. 'God preserve me: another one.'

'I'm sorry?'

'I seem to move in an endless round, Mr Jericho, from one patronising male to another, for ever being told what I am and am not allowed to know. Well, that ends here.' She pointed to the flagstone floor.

'Miss Wallace,' said Jericho, catching the same tone of cool formality, 'I came in answer to your note. I have no interest in alabaster figurework – medieval, Victorian or ancient Chinese, come to that. If you've nothing else to tell me, good morning to you.'

'Then good morning.'

'Good morning.'

If he'd had a hat he would have raised it.

He turned and began his progress down the aisle towards the door. You fool, said a voice at his inner ear, you bloody conceited fool. By the time he'd gone half way his pace had slowed and by the time he reached the font he stopped. His shoulders sagged.

'Checkmate, I believe, Mr Jericho,' she called cheerfully from beside the altar.

*

'ADU was the call sign on a series of four intercepts our ... mutual friend ... stole from Hut 3.' His voice was weary.

'How do you know she stole them?'

'They were hidden in her bedroom. Under the floorboards. As far as I know, we're not encouraged to take our work home.'

'Where are they now?'

'I burned them.'

They were sitting in the second row of pews, side by side, facing straight ahead. Anyone coming into the church would have thought it was a confession – she playing the priest and he the sinner.

'Do you think she's a spy?'

'I don't know. Her behaviour is suspicious, to put it charitably. Others seem to think she is.'

'Who?'

'A man from the Foreign Office called Wigram, for one.'

'Why?'

'Obviously because she's disappeared.'

'Oh, come. There must be more to it than that. All this fuss for one missed shift?'

He ran his hand nervously through his hair.

'There are ... indications – and don't, for God's sake, ask me to tell you what they are – just indications, all right, that the Germans may suspect Enigma is being broken.'

A long pause.

'But why would our mutual friend wish to help the *Germans*?'

'If I knew that, Miss Wallace, I wouldn't be sitting here with you, passing the time of day breaking the Official Secrets Act. Now, really, please, have you heard enough?'

Another pause. A reluctant nod of the head.

'Enough.'

*

She told it like a story, in a low voice, without looking at him. She used her hands a lot, he noticed. She couldn't keep them still. They fluttered like tiny white birds – now pecking at the hem of her coat, pulling it demurely across her knees, now perching on the back of the pew in front, now describing, in rapid, circling motions, how she had gone about her crime.

*

She waits until the other girls have gone off on their meal break.

She leaves the door to the Index Room open a fraction, so as not to look suspicious and to ensure a good warning of anyone's approach.

She reaches up to the dusty metal shelf and drags down the first volume.

AAA, AAB, AAC ...

She flicks through to the tenth page.

And there it is. The thirteenth entry.

ADU.

She runs her finger along the line to the row and column entries and notes their numbers on a scrap of paper.

She puts the index volume back. The row ledger is on a higher shelf and she has to fetch a stool to get it.

She stops off on her way to bob her head around the door and check the corridor.

Deserted.

Now she is nervous. Why? she asks herself. What is she doing that's so terribly wrong? She smooths her hands down over her grey skirt to dry her palms, then opens the book. She turns the pages. She finds the number. Again, she follows the line across.

She checks it once, and then a second time. There's no mistake.

ADU is the call sign of *Nachrichten-Regimenter 537* – a motorised German Army signals unit. Its transmissions are on wavelengths monitored by the Beaumanor intercept station in Leicestershire. Direction-finding has established that, since October, Unit number 537 has been based in the Smolensk military district of the Ukraine, presently occupied by Wehrmacht Army Group Centre under the command of Field Marshal Gunther von Kluge.

*

Jericho had been leaning forwards in anticipation. Now he drew back in surprise. 'A signals unit?'

He felt obscurely disappointed. What exactly had he been expecting? He wasn't sure. Just something a little more ... *exotic*, he supposed.

'537,' he said, 'is that a front-line unit?'

'The line in that sector is shifting every day. But according to the situation map in Hut 6, Smolensk is still about a hundred kilometres inside German territory.'

'Ah.'

'Yes. That was my reaction – at first, anyway. I mean, this is a standard, rear-echelon, low-priority target. This is workaday in the extreme. But there are several ... complications.' She fished in her bag for a handkerchief and blew her nose. Again, Jericho observed the slight trembling of her fingers.

*

After replacing the row volume it is the work of less than a minute to pull down the appropriate column book and make a note of the intercept serial numbers.

When she comes out of the Index Room, Miles ('that's Miles Mermagen,' she adds in parenthesis, 'Control Room duty officer: a bear of *very* little brain') Miles is on the telephone, his back to the door, oiling up to someone in authority – 'No, no, that's absolutely fine, Donald, a pleasure to be of service ...' – which suits Hester beautifully for it means he never even notices her collect her coat and leave. She clicks on her blackout torch and steps out into the night.

A gust of wind swirls down the alley between the huts and buffets her face. At the far end of Hut 8 the path forks: right will take her to the main gate and the warm bustle of the canteen, left leads into the blackness along the edge of the lake.

She turns left.

The moon is wrapped in a tissue of cloud but the pale light is just luminous enough to show her the way. Beyond the eastern perimeter fence lies a small wood which she can't see, but the sound of the wind moving through the invisible trees seems to pull her on. Past A- and B-Blocks, two hundred and fifty yards, and there it is, straight ahead, faintly outlined: the big, squat, bunkerlike building, only just completed, that now houses Bletchley's central Registry. As she comes closer her torch flashes on steel-shuttered windows, then finds the heavy door.

Thou shalt not steal, she tells herself, reaching for the handle.

No, no. Of course not.

Thou shalt not steal, thou wilt merely take a quick look, and then depart.

And, in any case, don't 'the secret things belong unto the Lord our God' (Deuteronomy 29.xxix)?

The rawness of the white neon is a shock after the gloom of the hut, and so is the calm, ruffled only by the distant clatter of the Hollerith punch-card machines. The workmen still haven't finished. Brushes and tools are stacked to one side of a reception area that is thick with the smell of building work – fresh concrete, wet paint, wood-shavings. The duty clerk, a corporal in the

Women's Auxiliary Air Force, leans across the counter in a friendly way as if she is serving in a shop.

'Cold night?'

'Rather.' Hester manages to smile and nod. 'I've got some serials to check.'

'Reference or loan?'

'Reference.'

'Section?'

'Hut 6 Control.'

'Pass?'

The woman takes the list of numbers and disappears into a back room. Through the open door Hester can see stacks of metal shelving, infinite rows of cardboard files. A man strolls past the doorway and takes down one of the boxes. He stares at her. She looks away. On the whitewashed wall is a poster, a Bateman cartoon showing a woman sneezing, accompanied by some typical, fatuous Whitehall busybodying:

THE MINISTRY OF HEALTH says:–
Coughs and sneezes spread diseases
Trap the germs by using your handkerchief
Help to keep the Nation Fighting Fit

There is nowhere to sit. Behind the counter is a large clock with 'RAF' stamped on its face – so large, in fact, that Hester can actually see the big hand moving. Four minutes pass. Five minutes. The Registry is unpleasantly hot. She can feel herself starting to sweat. The stench of paint is nauseating. Seven minutes. Eight minutes. She would like to flee, but the corporal has taken her identity card. Dear God, how could she have been so utterly stupid? What if the clerk is now on the phone to Hut 6, checking up on her? At any instant, Miles will come crashing into the

Registry: 'What the hell d'you think you're doing, woman?' Nine minutes. Ten minutes. Try to focus on something else. Coughs and sneezes spread diseases ...

She's in such a state, she actually fails to hear the clerk come up behind her.

'I'm sorry to have been so long, but I've never come across anything like this ...'

The girl, poor thing, is rather shaken.

'Why?' asked Jericho.

'The file,' said Hester. 'The file I'd asked her for? It was empty.'

*

There was a loud metallic crack behind them and then a series of short scrapes as the church door was pushed open. Hester closed her eyes and dropped to her knees on one of the cassocks, tugging Jericho down beside her. She clasped her hands and lowered her head and he did the same. Footsteps came halfway up the aisle behind them, stopped, and then resumed slowly on tiptoe. Jericho glanced surreptitiously to his left in time to see the elderly priest bending to retrieve his vestment.

'Sorry to interrupt your prayers,' whispered the vicar. He gave Hester a little wave and a nod. 'Hello there. So sorry. I'll leave you to God.'

They listened to his fussy tread fading towards the back of the church. The door was tugged shut. The latch fell with a crash. Jericho sat back on the pew and laid his hand over his heart and swore he could feel it beating through four layers of clothing. He looked at Hester – 'I'll leave you to *God?*' he repeated – and she smiled. The change it wrought in her was remarkable. Her eyes shone, the hardness in her face softened – and for the first time he briefly glimpsed the reason why she and Claire might have been friends.

*

Jericho contemplated the stained-glass window above the altar and made a steeple of his fingers. 'So what exactly are we to make of this? That Claire must have stolen the entire contents of the file? No –' he contradicted himself immediately ' – no, that can't be right, can it, because what she had in her room were the original cryptograms, not the decodes ...?'

'Precisely,' said Hester. 'There was a typewritten slip in the Registry file which the clerk showed me – words to the effect that the enclosed serial numbers had been reclassified and withdrawn, and that all enquiries should be addressed to the office of the Director-General.'

'The *Director-General*? Are you sure?'

'I *can* read, Mr Jericho,'

'What was the date on the slip?'

'March the 4th.'

Jericho massaged his forehead. It was the oddest thing he'd ever heard. 'What happened after the Registry?'

'I went back to the hut and wrote my note to you. Delivering that took the rest of my meal break. Then it was a matter of getting back into the Index Room whenever I could. We keep a daily log of all intercepts, made up from the blists. One file for each day.' Once again she rummaged in her bag and withdrew a small index-card with a list of dates and numbers. 'I wasn't sure where to start so I simply went right back to the beginning of the year and worked my way through. Nothing recorded till February the 6th. Only eleven interceptions altogether, four of which came on the final day.'

'Which was what?'

'March the 4th. The same day the file was removed from the Registry. What do you make of that?'

'Nothing. Everything. I'm still trying to imagine what a rear-echelon German signals unit could possibly say that would warrant the removal of its entire file.'

'The Director-General is who, as a matter of interest?'

'The chief of the Secret Intelligence Service. "C". I don't know his real name.' He remembered the man who had presented him with the cheque just before Christmas. A florid face and hairy country tweeds. He had looked more like a farmer than a spy master. 'Your notes,' he said, holding out his hand. 'May I?'

Reluctantly she handed him the list of interceptions. He held it towards the pale light. It certainly made a bizarre pattern. Following the initial interception, just after noon on 6 February, there had been two days of silence. Then there had been another signal at 1427 hours on the 9th. Then a gap of ten days. Then a broadcast at 1807 on the 20th, and another long gap, followed by a flurry of activity: two signals on 2 March (1639 and 1901), two on the 3rd (1118 and 1727), and finally four signals, in rapid succession, on the night of the 4th. These were the cryptograms he had taken from Claire's room. The broadcasts had begun just two days before his final conversation with Claire at the flooded clay pit. And they had ended a month later, while he was still at Cambridge, less than a week before the Shark blackout.

There was no shape to it at all.

He said: 'What Enigma key were they transmitted in? They *were* enciphered in Enigma, I take it?'

'In the Index they were catalogued as Vulture.'

'Vulture?'

'The standard Wehrmacht Enigma key for the Russian front.'

'Broken regularly?'

'Every day. As far as I know.'

'And the signals – how were they sent? They were, what, just carried on the usual military net?'

'I don't know, but I'd say almost certainly not.'

'Why?'

'There's not enough traffic, for a start. It's too irregular. And the frequency's not one I recognise. It feels to me like something rather more special – a private line, as it were. Just the two stations: a mother and a lone star. But we'd need to see the log sheets to be certain.'

'And where are they?'

'They should have been in the Registry. But when we checked we found they'd all been removed as well.'

'My, my,' murmured Jericho, 'they really have been thorough.'

'Short of tearing the sheets out of the Control Room Index, they couldn't have done much more. And *you* think *she*'s behaving suspiciously? I'll have that back now, if I may.'

She took the record of the interceptions and bent forwards to hide it in her bag.

Jericho rested his head on the back of the pew and stared up at the vaulted ceiling. Special? he thought. I'll say it was special, more than special for the Director-General himself to palm the entire bloody file, plus all the log sheets. There was no sense to it. He wished he weren't so damned tired. He needed to shut his study door for a day or two, sport his oak, find a good, fresh pile of clean notepaper and a set of sharpened pencils ...

He slowly let his gaze descend to take in the rest of the church – the saints in their windows, the marble angels, the stone memorials to the respectable dead of Bletchley parish, the ropes from the belfry looped together like a hanging spider beneath the gloomy organ loft. He closed his eyes.

Claire, Claire, what have you done? Did you see something

you weren't supposed to in that 'deadly dull' job of yours? Did you rescue a few scraps from the confidential waste when nobody was looking and spirit them home? And if you did that, why? And do they know you did it? Is that why Wigram's after you? Have you learned too much?

He saw her on her knees in the darkness at the foot of his bed, heard his own voice slurred with sleep – '*What on earth are you doing?*' – and her ingenuous reply: '*I'm just going through your things ...*'

You were always looking for something, weren't you? And when I couldn't provide it, you just went on to someone else. ('*There's always someone else,*' you said: almost the last words you ever spoke to me, remember?) What is it, then, this thing you want so badly?

So many questions. He realised he was beginning to freeze. He huddled down into his coat, burying his chin in his scarf, thrusting his hands deep into his pockets. He tried to recall the images of the four cryptograms – LCNNR KDEMS LWAZA – but the letters were blurred. He had found this before. It was impossible mentally to photograph pages of gibberish: there had to be some meaning to them, some structure, to fix them in his mind.

'*A mother and a lone star ...*'

*

The thick walls held a silence that seemed as old as the church itself – an oppressive silence, interrupted only occasionally by the rustling of a bird nesting in the rafters. For several minutes neither of them spoke.

Sitting on the hard bench, Jericho felt as though his bones had turned to ice, and this numbness, combined with the silence and the reliquaries everywhere and the sickly smell of incense, made him morbid. His father's funeral came to him for the second time in two days – the gaunt face in the coffin, his mother forcing him to kiss it goodbye, the cold skin beneath his lips giving off a sour reek of chemicals, like the school lab, and then the even worse stench at the crematorium.

'I need some air,' he said.

She gathered her bag and followed him down the aisle. Outside they pretended to study the tombs. To the north of the churchyard, screened by trees, was Bletchley Park. A motorcycle passed noisily down the lane towards the town. Jericho waited until the crack of its engine had dwindled to a drone in the distance and then said, almost to himself: 'The question I keep asking myself is why did she steal *cryptograms*. I mean, given what else she could have taken. If one was a spy –' Hester opened her mouth to protest and he held up his hand. 'All right, I'm not saying that she is, but if one was, surely one would want to steal proof that Enigma was being broken? What earthly use is an intercept?' He lowered himself to his haunches and ran his fingers over an inscription that had almost crumbled away. 'If only we knew more about them ... To whom they were sent, for instance.'

'We've been over this. They've removed every trace.'

'But someone must know something,' he mused. 'For a start, someone must have broken the traffic. And someone else must have translated it.'

'Why don't you ask one of your cryptanalyst friends? You're all terrifically good chaps together, aren't you?'

'Not especially. In any case I'm afraid we're encouraged to lead quite separate lives. There *is* a man in Hut 3 who might have seen them ...' But then he remembered Weitzman's frightened face ('*please don't ask me, I don't want to know ...*') and he shook his head. 'No. He wouldn't help.'

'Then what a pity it is,' she said, with some asperity, 'that you burned our only clues.'

'Keeping them was too much of a risk.' He was still rubbing slowly at the stone. 'For all I knew, you might have told Wigram I'd asked you about the call sign.' He looked up at her uneasily. 'You didn't, I take it?'

'Credit me with some sense, Mr Jericho. Would I be here talking to you now?' She stamped off down the row of graves and began furiously studying an epitaph.

*

She regretted her sharpness almost at once. ('He that is slow to anger is better than the mighty; and he that ruleth his spirit than he that taketh a city.' Proverbs 16.xxxii.) But then, as Jericho pointed out later, when relations between them had improved sufficiently for him to risk the observation, if she hadn't lost her temper, she might never have thought of the solution.

'Sometimes,' he said, 'we need a little tension to sharpen our wits.'

She was jealous, that was the truth of it. She had thought she knew Claire as well as anyone but it was fast becoming apparent that she knew her hardly at all, scarcely better even than he did.

She shivered. There was no warmth in this March sun. It fell on the stone tower of St Mary's as cold as light from a looking glass.

Jericho was back on his feet now, moving between the graves. She wondered whether she might have been like him if she'd been allowed to go to university. But her father wouldn't stand for it and her brother George had gone instead, as if it were God's law: men go to university, men break codes; women stay at home, women do the filing.

'Hester, Hester, just in time. Will you talk to Chicksands, there's a

good girl, and see what they can do? And while you're on, the Machine Room reckon they've got a corrupt text on the last batch of Kestrel – the operator needs to check her notes and re-send. Then the eleven o'clocks from Beaumanor ...'

She had been standing slack with defeat, gazing at a tombstone, but now she felt her body slowly coming to attention.

'The operator needs to check her notes ...'

'Mr Jericho!'

He turned at the sound of his name to see her stumbling through the graves towards him.

*

It was almost ten o'clock and Miles Mermagen was combing his hair in his office, preparatory to returning to his digs, when Hester Wallace appeared at his office door.

'No,' he said, with his back to her.

'Miles, listen, I've been thinking, you were right, I've been an utter fool.'

He squinted suspiciously at her in the mirror.

'My application for a transfer – I want you to withdraw it.'

'Fine. I never submitted it.'

He returned his attention to himself. The comb slid through the thick black hair like a rake through oil.

She forced a smile. 'I was thinking about what you said, about needing to know where one fits into the chain ...' He finished his grooming and turned his profile to the mirror, trying to look at his reflection sideways on. 'If you remember, we talked about my possibly going to an intercept station.'

'No problem.'

'I thought, well, I'm not due on shift till tomorrow afternoon – I thought I might go today.'

'Today?' He looked at his watch. 'Actually, I'm tied up, rather.'

'I *could* go on my own, Miles. And report my findings –' behind her back she dug her nails into her palm ' – one evening.'

He gave her another narrowed look and she thought, No, no, really this is too obvious, even for him, but then he shrugged. 'Why not? Better call them first.' He waved his hand grandly. 'Invoke my name.'

'Thank you, Miles.'

'Lot's wife, what?' He winked. 'Pillar of salt by day, ball of fire by night ...?'

On the way out he patted her bottom.

*

Thirty yards away, in Hut 8, Jericho was knocking on the door marked US NAVY LIAISON. A loud voice told him to 'come on in'.

Kramer didn't have a desk – the room wasn't big enough – just a card table with a telephone on it and wire baskets filled with papers stacked on the floor. There wasn't even a window. On one of the wooden partitions separating him from the rest of the hut he'd taped a recent photograph, torn out of *Life* magazine, showing Roosevelt and Churchill at the Casablanca conference, sitting side by side in a sunny garden. He noticed Jericho staring at it.

'When you fellers get me really down I look at it and think – well, hell, if they can do it, so can I.' He grinned. 'Got something to show you.' He opened his attaché case and pulled out a wad of papers marked MOST SECRET: ULTRA. 'Skynner finally got the order to give them me this morning. I'm supposed to get them off to Washington tonight.'

Jericho flicked through them. A mass of calculations that were half familiar, and some complex technical drawings of what looked like electronic circuitry.

Kramer said: 'The plans for the prototype four-wheel bombes.'

Jericho looked up in surprise. 'They're using valves?'

'Sure are. Gas-filled triode valves. GT1C thyatrons.'

'Good God.'

'They're calling it Cobra. The first three wheel-settings will be solved in the usual way on the existing bombes – that is, electromechanically. But the fourth – the *fourth* – will be solved purely electronically, using a relay rack and valves, linked to the bombe by this fat cable form, that looks like a – ' Kramer cupped his hands into a circle ' – well, that looks like a cobra, I guess. Using valves in sequence – that's a revolution. Never been done before. Your people say it should make the calculations a hundred times, maybe a thousand times, as fast.'

Jericho said, almost to himself: 'A Turing machine.'

'A what?'

'An electronic computer.'

'Well, whatever you want to call it. It works in theory, that's the good news. And from what they're saying, this may be just the start. It seems they're planning some kind of super-bombe, all electronic, called Colossus.'

Jericho had a sudden vision of Alan Turing, one winter afternoon, sitting cross-legged in his Cambridge study while the lamps came on outside, describing his dream of a universal calculating machine. How long ago had that been? Less than five years?

'And when will this happen?'

'That's the bad news. Even Cobra won't be operational till June.'

'But that's appalling.'

'Same old goddamn story. No components, no workshops, not

enough technicians. Guess how many men are working on this thing right now, as we speak.'

'Not enough, I expect.'

Kramer held up one hand and spread his fingers close to Jericho's face. 'Five. *Five!*' He stuffed the papers back into his case and snapped the lock. 'Something's got to be done about this.' He was muttering and shaking his head. 'Got to get something moving.'

'You're going to London?'

'Right now. Embassy first. Then on across Grosvenor Square to see the admiral.'

Jericho winced with disappointment. 'I suppose you're taking your car?'

'Are you kidding. With this?' He patted the case. 'Skynner's making me go with an escort. Why?'

'I was just wondering – I know this is an awful cheek, but you said if I had a favour to ask – I was wondering if I might possibly borrow it?'

'Sure.' Kramer pulled on his overcoat. 'I'll probably be gone a couple of days. I'll show you where she's parked.' He collected his cap from the back of the door and they went out into the corridor.

By the entrance to the hut they ran into Wigram. Jericho was surprised at how unkempt he looked. He had obviously been up all night. A dusting of reddish-blond stubble glinted in the sunlight.

'Ah, the gallant lieutenant and the great cryptanalyst. I heard you two were friends.' He bowed with mock formality and said to Jericho: 'I'll need to talk to you again later, old chap.'

'Now there's a guy who gives me the creeps,' said Kramer, as they walked up the path towards the mansion. 'Had him in my room for about twenty minutes this morning, asking me questions about some girl I know.'

Jericho almost trod on his own feet.

'You know Claire Romilly?'

'There she is,' said Kramer, and for an instant Jericho thought he meant Claire but actually he was pointing to his car. 'She's still warm. The tank's full and there's a can in the back.' He fished in his pocket for the key and threw it to Jericho. 'Sure I know Claire. Doesn't everybody? Hell of a girl.' He patted Jericho on the arm. 'Have a nice trip.'

3

It was another half-hour before Jericho was able to get away.

He climbed the concrete steps to the Operations Room where he found Cave sitting alone at the end of the long table, telephones on either side of him, staring up at the Atlantic Plot. Eleven Shark signals had been intercepted since midnight, he said, none of them from the anticipated battle zone, which was bad news. Convoy HX-229 was within 150 miles of the suspected U-boat lines, steaming directly due east, full tilt towards them, at a speed of 10.5 knots. SC-122 was slightly ahead of her, to the north east. HX-229A was well back, heading north up the coast of Newfoundland. 'Nearly light,' he said, 'but the weather's getting worse, poor sods.'

Jericho left him to it and went in search, first, of Logie, who dismissed him with a wave of his pipe ('Fine, old love, you rest up, curtain rises twenty hundred'), and then of Atwood, who eventually agreed to lend him his pre-war AA touring atlas of the British Isles. (' "Roll up that map," ' he quoted wistfully, as he produced it from beneath his desk, '"it will not be wanted these ten years."')

After that he was ready.

He sat in the front seat of Kramer's car and ran his hands over the unfamiliar controls and it occurred to him that he'd never quite got round to learning how to drive. He knew the basic principles, of course, but it must have been six or seven years since his last attempt, and that had been in his stepfather's huge and tanklike Humber – a vastly different proposition to this little Austin. Still, at least he wasn't doing anything illegal: in a country where one nowadays practically needed a permit to visit the lavatory, it was for some reason no longer necessary to have a driving licence.

He took several minutes trying to sort out clutch pedal from accelerator, handbrake from gear lever, then pulled out the choke and switched on the ignition. The car rocked and stalled. He put the gears into neutral and tried again and this time, miraculously, as his left foot lifted off the clutch, the car crawled forwards.

At the main gate he was waved down and managed to bring the car gliding to a halt. One of the sentries opened his door and he had to climb out while another got in to search the interior.

Half a minute later the barrier was rising and he was through.

He drove at a cyclist's pace along the narrow lanes towards Shenley Brook End, and it was this low speed that saved him. The plan he had agreed with Hester Wallace – assuming he could get Kramer's car – was that he would pick her up from the cottage, and he was just rounding the bend a quarter of a mile before the turning when something flashed dark in the field up ahead on the right. Immediately, he swerved up on to the verge and braked. He left the engine running then cautiously opened the door and clambered out on the running board to get a better view.

Policemen again. One moving stealthily around the edge of the field. Another half hidden in the hedge, apparently watching the road outside the cottage.

Jericho dropped back into the driver's seat and tapped his fingers on the steering wheel. He wasn't sure whether he had been seen but the sooner he got out of their range of vision the better. The gear change was stiff and it took both hands to jam the lever into reverse. The engine clanked and whined. First he nearly backed into the ditch, then he overcorrected and the car went weaving drunkenly across the road, mounted the opposite bank and stalled. It was not an elegant piece of parking but at least he was sufficiently far back around the curve for the policemen to be out of sight.

They had to have heard him, surely? At any moment one of them would come strolling down the lane to investigate, and he tried to think up some excuse for his lunatic behaviour, but the minutes passed and nobody appeared. He switched off the ignition and the only sound was birdsong.

No wonder Wigram looked so tired, he thought. He appeared to have taken over command of half the police force of the county – probably of the country, for all Jericho knew.

Suddenly, the scale of the odds stacked against them struck him as so overwhelming, he was seriously tempted to jack in the whole damn fool project. (*'We must go to the intercept station, Mr Jericho – go to Beaumanor and get hold of the operator's handwritten notes. They keep them for at least a month and they'll never have dreamed of removing those – I'll take a wager on it. Only we poor drones have anything to do with them.'*) Indeed, he might well have turned the car round that very minute and driven back to Bletchley if there hadn't been a loud tapping noise at the window to his left. He must have jumped a full inch in his seat.

It was Hester Wallace, although at first he didn't recognise her. She had exchanged her skirt and blouse for a heavy tweed jacket and a thick sweater. A pair of brown corduroy trousers were tucked into the tops of grey woollen socks, and her stout boots were so clogged with mud they seemed the size of a carthorse's hooves. She hefted her bulging carpetbag into the back of the Austin and sank down low in the passenger seat. She gave a long sigh of relief.

'Thank God. I thought I'd missed you.'

He leaned over and closed the door very quietly.

'How many are there?'

'Six. Two in the fields opposite. Two going from house to house in the village. Two in the cottage – one upstairs, dusting Claire's bedroom for fingerprints, and a policewoman downstairs. I told her I was going out. She tried to stop me but I said it was my one day off this week and I'd do as I pleased. I left by the back door and worked my way round to the road.'

'Did anybody see you?'

'I don't think so.' She blew warmth on her hands and rubbed them. 'I suggest we drive, Mr Jericho. And don't go back into Bletchley, whatever you do. I overheard them talking. They're stopping all cars on the main road out of town.'

She slid further down the seat so that she was invisible from outside the car unless someone came right up to the window. Jericho turned on the engine and the Austin rolled forwards. If they couldn't go back to Bletchley, he thought, then really he had no choice except to drive straight ahead.

They came round the curve and the road was clear. The turning to the cottage was on the left, deserted, but as they came level with it a policeman suddenly stepped out from the hedge opposite and held up his hand. Jericho hesitated and then pressed his foot down on the accelerator. The policeman stepped smartly out of the way and Jericho had a momentary impression of an outraged brick-red face. Then they were dropping down into the hollow and rising again and passing through the village. Another policeman was talking to a woman on the doorstep of her thatched cottage and he turned to stare at them. Jericho trod on the accelerator again and soon the village was behind them and the road was corkscrewing down into another leafy hollow. They rose into Shenley Church End, passed the White Hart Inn, where

Jericho used to live, and then a church, and almost at once they had to stop at the junction of the A5.

Jericho glanced in his mirror to check there was no one behind them. It seemed safe enough. He said to Hester: 'You can get up now.' He was in a daze. He couldn't believe what he was doing. He waited to let a couple of lorries go by, indicated, and then swung left on to the old Roman road. It ran straight and true ahead of them, northwest, for as far as they could see. Jericho changed up a gear, the Austin gathered speed, and they were clear.

*

Wartime England opened up before them – still the same but somehow subtly different: a little bit smudged, a little bit knocked about, like a prosperous estate going fast to ruin, or a genteel elderly lady fallen on hard times.

They didn't encounter any bomb damage until they reached the outskirts of Rugby, where what looked from a distance to be a ruined abbey turned out to be the roofless shell of a factory, but the depredations of war were everywhere. Fences beside the road, after three years without repairs, were sagging or collapsed. The gates and railings had gone from the fine country parks to be melted down for munitions. The houses were shabby. Nothing had been painted since 1940. Broken windows were boarded over, ironwork was rusted or coated in tar. Even the inn signs were blistered and faded. The country was degraded.

And we, too, thought Jericho, as they overtook yet another stooped figure trudging beside the road, don't we look slightly worse each year? In 1940 there had at least been the galvanising energy unleashed by the threat of invasion. And in 1941 there had been some hope when Russia and then America had entered the war. But 1942 had dragged into 1943, the U-boats had wrought murder on the convoys, the shortages had worsened and, despite the victories in Africa and on the eastern front, the war had begun to look endless – an unbroken, unheroic vista of rationing and exhaustion. The villages seemed almost lifeless – the men away, the women drafted into factories – while in Stony Stratford and in Towcester the few people who were about had mostly formed into queues outside shops with empty windows.

Beside him, Hester Wallace was silent, monitoring their progress with obsessive interest on Atwood's atlas. Good, he thought. With all the signposts and place names taken down, they would have no idea where they were if they once got lost. He didn't dare drive too quickly. The Austin was unfamiliar and (he was discovering) idiosyncratic. From time to time the cheap wartime petrol caused it to emit a loud bang. It tended to drift towards the centre of the road, and the brakes weren't too hot, either. Besides, a private car was such a rarity, he feared some officious policeman would pull them over if they went too fast and demand to see their papers.

He drove on steadily for more than an hour until, just before a market town she declared was Hinckley, she told him to turn off right on to a narrower road.

They had left Bletchley under a clear sky but the further north they had gone, the darker it had become. Grey clouds heavy with snow or rain had rolled across the sun. The tarmac pushed across a bleak, flat landscape, with not a vehicle to be seen, and for a second time Jericho experienced the curious sense that history was going backwards, that not for a quarter of a century could the roads have been this empty.

Fifteen miles further on she made him turn right again and suddenly they were climbing into much more hilly country, thickly wooded, with startling outcrops of bare rock striped white by snow.

'What place is this?'

'Charnwood Forest. We're almost there. You'd better pull over in a minute. Here, look,' she said, pointing to a deserted picnic area set just off the road. 'Here will do. I shan't be long.'

She hauled her bag from the back seat and set off towards the trees. He watched her go. She looked like a farm boy in her jacket and trousers. What was it Claire had said? '*She's got a bit of a crush on me*'? More than a bit, he thought, much more than a bit, to risk so much. It struck him that she was almost the exact physical opposite of Claire, that where Claire was tall and blonde and voluptuous, Hester was short and dark and skinny. Rather like him, in fact. She was changing her clothes behind a tree which wasn't quite wide enough and he got a sudden glimpse of her thin white shoulder. He looked away. When he looked back she was emerging from the dark woodland in an olive-green dress. The first drop of rain plopped on to the windscreen just as she got back into the car.

'Drive on then, Mr Jericho.' She found their position on the atlas again and rested her finger on it.

His hand paused on the ignition key. 'Do you think, Miss Wallace,' he said, hesitantly, 'in view of the circumstances, we might now risk first-name terms?'

She gave him a faint smile. 'Hester.'

'Tom.'

They shook hands.

*

They followed the road through the forest for about five miles and then the trees thinned and they were into high, open country. The rain and melted snow had turned the narrow lane into a mud track and for five minutes they were forced to crawl in second gear behind a pony and trap. At last the driver raised his whip in apology and turned off to the right, towards a tiny village with curls of smoke rising from half a dozen chimneys, and very soon afterwards Hester shouted: 'There!'

If they hadn't been travelling so slowly, they might have missed it: a pair of lodge gates, a private road with a red-and-white pole slung across it, a sentry box, a cryptic sign: WOYG, BEAUMANOR.

War Office 'Y' Group, Beaumanor, 'Y' being the code name for the wireless interception service.

'Here we go.'

Jericho had to admire her nerve. While he was still fumbling sweatily for his pass, she had leaned across him to proffer hers to the guard and had announced briskly that they were expected. The Army private checked her name off on a clipboard, went round to the back of the car to make a note of their registration number, returned to the window, gave Jericho's card a cursory glance, and nodded them in.

Beaumanor Hall was another of those huge, secluded country houses that had been commandeered by the military from their grateful, almost bankrupt owners, and that would never, Jericho guessed, return to private use. It was early Victorian, with an avenue of dripping elms to one side and a stable yard to the other, into which they were directed. They drove under a fine arch. Half a dozen giggling ATS girls, their coats held over their heads like tents to ward off the rain, ran out in front of them and disappeared into one of the buildings. The courtyard held a couple of small Morris commercial trucks and a row of BSA motorcycles. As Jericho parked, a uniformed man hurried over to them carrying a vast and battered umbrella.

'Heaviside,' he said, 'Major Heaviside, as in the eponymous layer. And you must be Miss Wallace and you must be ...?'

'Tom Jericho.'

'Mr Jericho. Excellent. Splendid.' He shook their hands vigorously. 'This is a treat for us, I must say. A visit from head office to the country cousins. Commander sends a thousand sorrows and says d'you mind if I do the honours? He'll try and catch us later. 'Fraid you've missed lunch, but tea? Cup of tea? *Filthy* weather ...'

Jericho had been braced for some suspicious questions, and had used the journey to rehearse some careful answers, but the major merely ushered them under his leaking umbrella and guided them into the house. He was young, tall and balding, with spectacles so smeared with debris it was a wonder he could see through them. He had sloping shoulders, like a bottle, and the collar of his tunic was blanched white with dandruff. He took them into a cold and musty drawing room and ordered tea.

By now he'd finished his potted history of the house ('designed by the same bloke who built Nelson's Column, so they tell me') and was well embarked on a detailed history of the wireless interception service ('started out in Chatham till the bombing got too bad ...'). Hester was nodding politely. A woman Army private brought them tea as thick and brown as shoe polish and Jericho sipped it and glanced impatiently around the empty walls. There were holes in the plaster where the picture hooks had been pulled out, and grimy shadows traced the outlines of large frames, now removed. An ancestral seat without ancestors, a house without a soul. The windows looking out on to the garden were crossed with strips of sticky tape.

He pointedly took out his watch and opened it. Almost three o'clock. They would need to be moving soon.

Hester noticed he was fidgeting. 'Perhaps,' she said, leaping into a brief lull in the major's monologue, 'we might take a look around?'

Heaviside looked startled and clattered his teacup into his saucer. 'Oh, crumbs, sorry. Right. If you're fit, then, we'll make a start.'

The rain was mixed with snow now, and the wind was blowing it hard, in waves, from the north. It lashed their faces as they came around the side of the big house and as they picked their way through the mud of a flattened rose garden they had to raise their arms against it, like boxers warding off blows. There was an odd keening, howling noise, like nothing Jericho had ever heard before, coming from beyond a wall.

'What the devil's that?'

'The aerial farm,' said Heaviside.

Jericho had only visited an intercept station once before, and that had been years ago, when the science was still in its infancy: a shack full of shivering Wrens perched on top of the cliffs near Scarborough. This was of a different order. They went through a gate in the wall and there it was – dozens of radio masts laid out in odd patterns, like the stone circles of the Druids, across several acres of fields. The metal pylons were bound together by thousands of yards of cable. Some of the taut steel hummed in the wind, some screamed.

'Rhombic and Beveridge configurations,' shouted the major above the racket. 'Dipoles and quadra-headrons ... Look!' He tried to point and his umbrella was abruptly snapped inside out. He smiled hopelessly and waved it in the direction of the masts. 'We're about three hundred feet up here, hence this bloody wind. The farm's got two main harvests, can you see? One's pointing due south. That picks up France, the Med, Libya. The other's targeted east to Germany and the Russian front. The signals go by coaxial cables to the intercept huts.' He spread his arms wide and bellowed, 'Beautiful, isn't it? We can pick up everything for the best part of a thousand miles.' He laughed and waved his hands as if he were conducting an imaginary choir. 'Sing to me, you buggers.'

The wind slashed sleet in their faces and Jericho cupped his hands to his ears. It felt as though they were interfering with nature, tapping into some rushing elemental force they had no business dabbling in, like Frankenstein summoning down lightning into his laboratory. Another gust of wind knocked them backwards and Hester clutched at his arm for support.

'Let's get out of here,' yelled Heaviside. He gestured for them to follow him. Once they were on the other side of the wall they had some shelter from the wind. An asphalt road girdled what looked, at a distance, to be an estate village nestling in the grounds of the big house: cottages, farm sheds, a greenhouse, even a cricket pavilion with a clock tower. All dummy frontages, explained Heaviside, cheerfully, designed to fool German air reconnaissance. This was where the work of interception was done. Was there anything they were especially interested in?

'How about the eastern front?' said Hester.

'Eastern front?' said Heaviside. 'Fine.'

He bounded ahead of them through the puddles, still trying to shake out his broken umbrella. The rain worsened and their fast walk turned into a run as they sprinted for the hut. The door banged shut behind them.

'We rely on the feminine element, as you can see,' said Heaviside, taking off his spectacles and drying them on the corner of his tunic. 'Army girls and civilian women.' He replaced his glasses and blinked around the hut. 'Good afternoon,' he said to a stout woman with sergeant's stripes. 'The supervisor,' he explained, then added in a whisper: 'Bit of a dragon.'

Jericho counted twenty-four wireless receivers, arranged in pairs, on either side of a long aisle, each with a woman hunched over it wearing headphones. The room was quiet apart from the hum of the machines and the occasional rustle of intercept forms.

'We've three types of sets,' Heaviside went on quietly. 'HROs, Hallicrafter 28 Skyriders and American AR-88s. Each girl has her own frequencies to patrol, though we'll double back if things get busy.'

'How many people d'you have working here?' asked Hester.

'Couple of thousand.'

'And you intercept everything?'

'Absolutely. Unless you tell us not to.'

'Which we never do.'

'Right, right.' Heaviside's bald head was glistening with rainwater. He bent forwards and shook himself vigorously, like a dog. 'Except that time the other week, of course.'

*

Afterwards, what Jericho would remember most was how coolly she handled it. She didn't even blink. Instead she actually changed the subject and asked Heaviside how fast the girls had to be ('we insist on a speed of ninety Morse characters a minute, that's the absolute minimum') and then the three of them began to stroll down the central aisle.

'These are sets tuned to the eastern front,' said Heaviside, when they were about halfway down. He stopped and pointed to the elaborate pictures of vultures stuck on the side of several of the receivers. 'Vulture's not the only German Army key in Russia, of course. There's Kite and Kestrel, Smelt for the Ukraine –'

'Are the nets particularly active at the moment?' Jericho felt it was time he should say something.

'Very much so, since Stalingrad. Retreats and counterattacks all along the front. Alarms and excursions. You've got to hand it to these Reds, you know – they can't half fight.'

Hester said casually: 'It would have been a Vulture station you were told not to intercept?'

'That's right.'

'And this would have been around the 4th of March?'

'Bang on. About midnight. I remember because we'd just sent four long signals and were feeling fairly well chuffed when your chap Mermagen comes on the blower in a frightful panic and says: "No more of *that*, thanks very much, not now, not tomorrow, not for ever more."'

'Any reason?'

'No reason. Just stop. Thought he was going to have a heart attack. Oddest damned thing I ever heard.'

'Perhaps,' suggested Jericho, 'knowing you were busy, they wanted to knock out low-priority traffic?'

'Balls,' said Heaviside, 'pardon me, but really!' His professional pride was wounded. 'You can tell your Mr Mermagen from me that it was nothing we couldn't handle, was it, Kay?' He patted the shoulder of a strikingly pretty ATS operator, who took off her headphones and pushed back her chair. 'No, no, don't get up, didn't mean to interrupt. We were just discussing our mystery station.' He rolled his eyes. 'The one we're not supposed to hear.'

'Hear?' Jericho looked at Hester sharply. 'You mean it's still broadcasting?'

'Kay?'

'Yes, sir.' She had a rather melodious Welsh accent. 'Not so often now, sir, but he was awful busy last week.' She hesitated. 'I don't, like, try to listen, on purpose, sir, but he does have the most beautiful fist. Real old school. Not like some of the *kids* –' she spat out the word ' – they're using nowadays. Nearly as bad as the Italians, they are.'

'A man's style of Morse,' said Heaviside pompously, 'is as distinctive as his signature.'

'And what is his style?'

'Very fast but very clear,' said Kay. 'Rippling, I'd say. Fist like a concert pianist, he has.'

'Think she rather fancies this chap, don't you, Mr Jericho?'

Heaviside laughed and gave her shoulder another pat. 'All right, Kay. Good work. Back to it.'

They moved on. 'One of my best,' he confided. 'Can be pretty ghastly, you know, eight hours listening at a stretch, just taking down gibberish. Specially at night, in the winter. Bloody freezing out here. We have to issue 'em with blankets. Ah, now, here, look: here's one coming in.'

They stood at a discreet distance behind an operator who was frantically copying down a message. With her left hand she kept fractionally adjusting the dial on the wireless set, with her right she was fumbling together message forms and carbon paper. The speed with which she then started to take down the message was astonishing. 'GLPES,' read Jericho over her shoulder, 'KEMPG NXWPD ...'

'Two forms,' said Heaviside. 'Log sheet, on which she records the whispers: that's tuning messages, Q-code and so forth. And then the red form which is the actual signal.'

'What happens next?' whispered Hester.

'There are two copies of each form. Top copy goes to the Teleprinter Hut for immediate transmission to your people. That's the hut we passed that looks like the cricket pavilion. The other copies we keep here, in case there's a garble or something goes missing.'

'How long do you keep them?'

'Couple of months.'

'Can we see?'

Heaviside scratched his head. 'If you want. Not much to it, though.'

He led them to the far end of the hut, opened a door, turned on the light and stood back to show them the interior. A walk-in cupboard. A bank of about a dozen dark green filing cabinets. No window. Light switch on the left.

'How are they arranged?' asked Jericho.

'Chronologically.' He closed the door.

Not locked, noted Jericho, continuing his inventory. And the entrance not really visible, either, except to the four operators nearest to it. He could feel his heart beginning to thump.

'Major Heaviside, sir!'

They turned to find Kay standing, beckoning to them, one of her headphones pressed to her ear.

'My mystery piano player, sir. He's just started doing his scales again, sir, if you're interested.'

Heaviside took the headset first. He listened with a judicious expression, his eyes focused on the middle distance, like an eminent doctor with a stethoscope being asked to give a second opinion. He shook his head and shrugged and passed the headphones to Hester.

'Ours not to reason why, old chap,' he said to Jericho.

When it was Jericho's turn, he removed his scarf and placed it carefully on the floor next to the cable form that connected the wireless set to the aerials and the power supply. Putting on the headphones was rather like putting his head under water. There was a strange rush of sounds. A howl that reminded him of the wind in the aerial farm. A gunfire crackle of static. Two or three different and very faint Morse transmissions braided together. And suddenly, and most bizarrely, a German diva singing an operatic aria he vaguely recognised as being from the second act of *Tannhäuser*.

'I can't hear anything.'

'Must have drifted off frequency,' said Heaviside.

Kay turned the dial minutely anticlockwise, the sound wowed up and down an octave, the diva evaporated, more gunfire, and then, like stepping into an open space, a rapid, staccato *dab-dab-*

dee-dah-dah of Morse, pulsing clearly and urgently, more than a thousand miles distant, somewhere in German-occupied Ukraine.

*

They were halfway to the Teleprinter Hut when Jericho raised his hand to his throat and said, 'My scarf.'

They stopped in the rain.

'I'll get one of the girls to bring it over.'

'No, no, I'll fetch it, I'll catch you up.'

Hester took her cue. 'And how many machines did you say you have?' She began to walk on.

Heaviside hesitated between the two of them, then hurried after Hester. Jericho could have kissed her. He never heard the major's answer. It was whipped away by the wind.

You are calm, he told himself, you are confident, you are doing nothing wrong.

He went back into the hut. The woman sergeant had her fat back to him, leaning over one of the interceptors. She never saw him. He walked swiftly down the central aisle, looking straight ahead, and let himself into the storeroom. He closed the door behind him and turned on the light.

How long did he have? Not long.

He tugged at the first drawer of the first filing cabinet. Locked. Damn it. He tried it again. Wait. No, it *wasn't* locked. The cabinet was fitted with one of these irritating anti-tilt mechanisms, which prevented two drawers being opened at once. He looked down and saw that the bottom drawer was protruding slightly. He closed it gently with his foot and to his relief the top drawer slid open.

Brown cardboard folders. Bundles of smudged carbons, held together by metal paperclips. Log sheets and W/T red forms. Day, Month and Year in the top right-hand corner. Meaningless jumbles of handwritten letters. This folder for 15 January 1943.

He stepped back and counted quickly. Fifteen four-drawer cabinets. Sixty drawers. Two months. Roughly a drawer a day. Could that be right?

He strode over to the sixth cabinet and opened the third drawer down.

February the 6th.

Bingo.

He held the image of Hester Wallace's neat notation steady in his mind. 6.2./1215. 9.2./1427. 20.2./1807. 2.3./1639, 1901 ...

It would have helped if his fingers hadn't swollen to the size of sausages, if they weren't shaking and slippery with sweat, if he could somehow catch his breath.

Someone must come in. Someone must hear him, surely, opening and closing the metal drawers like organ stops, pulling out two, three, four cryptograms and the log sheets, too (Hester had said they'd be useful), stuffing them into his inside coat pocket, five, six – dropped it, damn – seven cryptograms. He almost gave up at that – 'Quit while you're ahead, old love' – but he needed the final four, the four Claire had hidden in her room.

He opened the top drawer of the thirteenth filing cabinet, and there they were, towards the back, virtually in sequence, thank you, God.

A footstep outside the storeroom. He grabbed the logs and red forms and had just about got them into his pocket and the drawer shut when the door opened to silhouette the trim figure of Kay the intercept girl.

'I thought I saw you come in,' she said, 'only you left your scarf, see?' She held it up and closed the door behind her, then slowly advanced down the narrow room towards him. Jericho stood paralysed with an idiot grin on his face.

'I don't mean to bother you, sir, but it is important, isn't it?' Her dark eyes were wide. He dimly registered again that she was very pretty, even in her Army uniform. The tunic was belted tight at her waist. Something about her reminded him of Claire.

'I'm sorry?'

'I know I shouldn't ask, sir – we're never meant to ask, are we? – but, well, *is it*? Only no one ever tells us, see? Rubbish, that's all it is to us, just rubbish, rubbish, all day long. And all night, too. You try to go to sleep and you can still hear it – beep-beep-bloody-beep. Drives you barmy after a bit. I joined up, see, volunteered, but it's not what I expected, this place. Can't even tell my mum and dad.' She had come up very close to him. 'You *are* making sense of it? It *is* important? I won't tell,' she added, solemnly, 'honest.'

'Yes,' said Jericho. 'We are making sense of it, and it is important. I promise you.'

She nodded to herself, smiled, looped his scarf around his neck and tied it, then walked slowly out of the storeroom, leaving the door open. He gave it twenty seconds, then followed her. Nobody stopped him as he went out through the hut and into the rain.

4

Heaviside didn't want them to leave. Jericho tried feebly to protest – the light was bad, he said, they had a long journey ahead, they had to beat the blackout – but Heaviside was horrified. He insisted, *insisted* they at least take a look at the direction finders and the high-speed Morse receivers. He was so enthusiastic, he looked as though he might burst into tears if they said no. And so they trailed meekly after him across the slick wet concrete, first to a row of wooden huts dressed up to look like a stable block and then to another fake cottage.

The chorus of the aerial farm sang weirdly in the background,

Heaviside became increasingly excited describing abstruse technicalities of wavelength and frequency, Hester pretended heroically to be interested and carefully avoided meeting Jericho's eye, and all the time Jericho walked around unhearing, in a cocoon of anxiety, nerved for the distant sounds of discovery and alarm. Never had he been more desperate to get away from anywhere. From time to time his hand stole into his inside coat pocket, and once he left it there, reassured to feel the roughness of the intercepts safely between his fingers, until he realised he was doing a passable impersonation of Napoleon, whereupon he promptly snatched it out again.

As for Heaviside, such was his pride in Beaumanor's work, he clearly would have kept them there for another week if he could. But when, an interminable half-hour later, he suggested a visit to the motor pool and the auxiliary generators, it was Hester, so cool until then, who finally snapped and said, rather too firmly in retrospect, that no, thank you, but really they did have to get going.

'Honestly? It's a heck of a long way to have come for just a couple of hours.' Heaviside looked mystified. 'The commander will be disappointed to miss you.'

'Alas,' said Jericho. 'Some other time.'

'Up to you, old boy,' said Heaviside huffily. 'Don't want to press ourselves on you.' And Jericho cursed himself for hurting his feelings.

He walked them round to their car, halting on the way to point out an antique ship's figurehead of an admiral, perched on top of an ornamental horse trough. Some wit had draped a pair of Army knickers over the admiral's sword and they hung limply in the raw damp. 'Cornwallis,' said Heaviside. 'Found him in the grounds. Our lucky charm.'

When they said goodbye he shook hands with them each in turn, Hester first, then Jericho, and saluted as they got into the

Austin. He turned as if to go, then froze, and suddenly ducked down to the window.

'What was it you said you did again, Mr Jericho?'

'Actually, I didn't.' Jericho smiled and turned the engine on. 'Cryptanalytic work.'

'Which section?'

'Can't say, I'm afraid.'

He jammed the gear stick into reverse and executed a clumsy three-point turn. As they pulled away he could see Heaviside in the rear-view mirror, standing in the rain, his hand protecting his eyes, watching them. The curve of the drive took them off to the left and the image vanished.

'Pound to a penny,' muttered Jericho, 'he's on his way to the nearest telephone.'

'You got them?'

He nodded. 'Let's wait till we get clear of here.'

Out through the gates, along the lane, past the village, towards the forest. The rain was blowing across the dark slope of woodland in ghostly white columns, like the banners of a phantom army. A large and lonely bird was flying through the cloudburst, very high and far away. The windscreen wipers scudded back and forth. The trees closed in around them.

'You were very good,' said Jericho.

'Until the end. By the end it was unendurable, not knowing if you'd managed it.'

He started to tell her about the storeroom, but then he noticed a track coming up, leading off from the side of the road into the privacy of the wood.

The perfect spot.

They bounced along the rough trail for about a hundred yards, plunging into puddles that turned out to be potholes a foot deep. Water fountained out on either side of them, tearing against the underside of the chassis. It spouted through a hole at Hester's feet and drenched her shoes. When at last the headlights showed a patch of bog too wide to negotiate, Jericho turned off the engine.

There was no sound except for the pattering of the rain on the thin metal roof. Overhanging branches blotted out the sky. It was almost too dark to read. He turned on the interior light.

*

'VVVADU QSA? K,' said Jericho, reading off the whispers on the first log sheet. 'Which, if I remember my days in traffic analysis, roughly translates as: This is station call sign ADU requesting reading of my signal strength, over.' He ran his finger down the carbon copy. Q-code was an international language, the Esperanto of wireless operators; he knew it off by heart. 'And then we get VVVCPQ BT QSA4 QSA? K. This is station call-sign CPQ, break, your signal strength is fine, what is my signal strength? Over.'

'CPQ,' said Hester, nodding. 'I recognise that call sign. That has something to do with Army High Command in Berlin.'

'Good. One mystery solved, then.' He returned his attention to the log sheet. 'VVVADU QSA3 QTC1 K: Smolensk to Berlin, your signal strength is reasonable, I have one message for you, over. QRV, says Berlin: I am ready. QXH K: broadcast your traffic, over. Smolensk then says QXA109: my message consists of 109 cipher groups.'

Hester fluttered the first cryptogram triumphantly. 'Here it is. One hundred and nine exactly.'

'OK. Fine. So that goes through – straight away, presumably, because Berlin replies: VVVCPQ R QRU HH VA. Message received and understood, I have nothing for you, Heil Hitler and good night. All very smooth and methodical. Right out of the manual.'

'That girl in the Intercept Hut said he was precise.'

'What we don't have, unfortunately, is Berlin's replies.' He riffled through the log sheets. 'Easy contact on the 9th as well, and again on the 20th. Ah,' he said, 'now on the 2nd of March it looks to have been more tricky.' The form was indeed a mass of terse dialogue. He held it up to the light. Smolensk to Berlin: QZE, QRJ, QRO. (Your frequency is too high, your signals are too weak, increase your power.) And Berlin snapping back: QWP, QRX10 (observe regulations, wait ten minutes) and finally an exasperated QRX (shut up). 'Now this is interesting. No wonder they suddenly start to sound like strangers.' Jericho squinted at the carbon copy. 'The call sign in Berlin has changed.'

'Changed? Absurd. Changed to what?'

'TGD.'

'*What*? Let me see that.' She snatched the form out of his hand. 'That's not possible. No, no. TGD simply isn't a Wehrmacht call sign.'

'How can you be sure?'

'Because I know it. There's a whole Enigma key named after TGD. It's never been broken. It's famous.' She had started to wind a lock of hair nervously around her right index finger. 'Notorious might be a better word.'

'What is it?'

'It's the call sign of Gestapo headquarters in Berlin.'

'Gestapo?' Jericho fumbled through the remaining log sheets. 'But all the messages from March the 2nd onwards,' he said, 'that's eight out of the eleven, all the long ones, including the four in Claire's room – they're all addressed to that call sign.' He gave the forms to her so she could check for herself and sat back in his seat.

A gust of wind stirred the branches above them, sending a shower of rainwater rattling like a volley across the windscreen.

*

'Let's try and construct a thesis,' said Jericho after a minute or two, as much to hear a human voice as anything. The random pattering of the downpour and the crepuscular gloom of the forest were beginning to affect his nerves. Hester had pulled her feet up from the sodden floor and was huddled up very small on the front seat, staring out at the forest, hugging her legs, occasionally massaging her toes through her damp stockings.

'March the 4th is the key day,' he went on. (*Where was I on 4 March? In another world: reading Sherlock Holmes in front of a Cambridge gas fire, avoiding Mr Kite and learning to walk again.*) 'Up to that day, everything is proceeding normally. A signals unit hibernating in the Ukraine, dormant all winter, has come to life in the warmer weather. First, a few signals to Army HQ in Berlin, and then a burst of longer traffic to the Gestapo –'

'That's not normal,' said Hester scathingly. 'An Army unit transmitting reports in a Russian-front Enigma key to the headquarters of the secret police? Normal? I'd call that unprecedented.'

'Quite.' He didn't mind being interrupted. He was glad of a sign she was listening. 'In fact, it's so unprecedented, someone at Bletchley wakes up to what's happening and starts to panic. All previous signals are removed from the Registry. And just before midnight on that same day your Mr Mermagen telephones Beaumanor and tells them to stop interception. Ever happen before?'

'Never.' She paused, then moved her shoulder slightly in concession. 'Well, all right, *maybe*, when traffic's very heavy, a low-priority target *might* be neglected for a day or so. But you saw the size of Beaumanor. And that's not as big as the RAF's station at Chicksands. And there must be a dozen smaller places, maybe more. We're always being told by people like you that the whole point of the exercise is to monitor *everything*.'

He nodded. This was true. It had been their philosophy from

the beginning: be inclusive, miss nothing. It isn't the big boys who give you the cribs – they're too good. It's the little fellows – the long-forgotten incompetents stuck in out-of-the-way places, who always begin their messages 'situation normal, nothing to report' and then use the same nulls in the same places, or who habitually encipher their own call-signs, or who set the rotors every morning with their girlfriend's initials ...

Jericho said: 'So he wouldn't have told them to stop on his own authority?'

'Miles? God, no.'

'Who gives him his orders?'

'That depends. Hut 6 Machine Room, usually. Sometimes the Hut 3 Watch. They decide priorities.'

'Could he have made a mistake?'

'In what sense?'

'Well, Heaviside said Miles called Beaumanor just before midnight on the 4th in a panic. I was wondering: what if Miles had been told earlier in the day that this unit was no longer to be intercepted, but forgot to pass on the message.'

'Eminently possible. Likely, in fact, knowing Miles. Yes, yes, *of course*.' Hester turned round to face him. 'I see what you're driving at. In the time between Miles being told to pull the plug and the order reaching Beaumanor, four more messages had been intercepted.'

'Exactly. Which came into Hut 6 late on the night of the 4th. But by then the order had already been issued that they weren't to be decoded.'

'So they just got caught up in the bureaucracy and were passed along the line.'

'Until they ended up in the German Book Room.'

'In front of Claire.'

'Undecrypted.'

Jericho nodded slowly. Undecrypted. That was the crucial point. That explained why the signals in Claire's bedroom had showed no signs of damage. There had never been any strips of Type-X decode gummed to their backs. They had never been broken.

He peered into the wood but he didn't see trees, he saw the German Book Room on the morning after the night of 4 March, when the cryptograms would have arrived to be filed and indexed.

Would Miss Monk herself have rung the Hut 6 duty officer, or would she have delegated the task to one of her girls? 'We've got four orphan intercepts here, without the solutions. What, pray, are we supposed to do with them?' And the reply would have been – what? Oh, Christ! File them? Forget them? Dump them in the bin marked CONFIDENTIAL WASTE?

Only none of those things had happened.

Claire had stolen them instead.

'*In theory*?' Weitzman had said. '*On an average day? A girl like Claire would probably see more operational detail about the German armed forces than Adolf Hitler. Absurd, isn't it?*'

Ah, but they weren't supposed to *read* it, Walter, that was the point. Well-bred young ladies wouldn't dream of reading someone else's mail, unless they were told to do so for King and country. They certainly wouldn't read it for themselves. That was the reason why Bletchley employed them.

But what was it Miss Monk had said of Claire? '*She'd really become much more attentive of late* ...' Naturally she had. *She* had begun to read what was passing through her hands. And at the end of February or the beginning of March she had seen something that had changed her life. Something to do with a German rear-echelon signals unit whose wireless operator played Morse code to the Gestapo as if it were a Mozart sonata. Something so utterly 'un-boring, darling', that when Bletchley had decided they couldn't bear to read the traffic any more, she had felt compelled to steal the last four intercepts herself.

And why had she stolen them?

He didn't even need to pose the question. Hester had reached the answer ahead of him, although her voice was faint and disbelieving and almost drowned out by the rain.

'She stole them to read them.'

*

She stole them to read them. The answer slid beneath the random pattern of events and fitted it like a crib.

She stole the cryptograms to read them.

'But is it really feasible?' asked Hester. She seemed bewildered by the destination to which her logic had led her. 'I mean, could she really have done it?'

'Yes. It's possible. Hard to imagine. Possible.'

Oh, the nerve of it, thought Jericho. Oh, the sheer breathtaking bloody *nerve* of it, the cool deliberation with which she must have plotted it. Claire, my darling, you really are a wonder.

'But she couldn't have managed it on her own,' he said, 'not locked away at the back of Hut 3. She'd have needed help.'

'Who?'

He raised his hands from the steering wheel in a hopeless gesture. It was hard to know where to begin. 'Someone with access to Hut 6 for a start. Someone who could look up the Enigma settings for German Army key Vulture on March the 4th.'

'Settings?'

He glanced at her in surprise, then realised that the actual workings of an Enigma was not the sort of information she would have needed to know. And in Bletchley, what you didn't need to know you were never told.

'*Walzenlage*,' he said. '*Ringstellung*. *Steckerverbindungen*. Wheel order, ring setting and cross-plugging. If Vulture was being read every day, they'd already have had those in Hut 6.'

'Then what would you have had to do?'

'Get access to a Type-X machine. Set it up in exactly the right way. Type in the cryptograms and tear off the plaintext.'

'Could Claire have done that?'

'Almost certainly not. She'd never have been allowed anywhere near the decoding room. And anyway she wasn't trained.'

'So her accomplice would have needed some skill?'

'Skill, yes. And nerve. And time, come to that. Four messages. A thousand cipher groups. Five thousand individual characters. Even an expert operator would need the best part of half an hour to decode that much. It *could* have been done. But she would have needed a superman.'

'Or woman.'

'No.' He was remembering the events of Saturday night: the sound downstairs in the cottage, the big male footprints in the frost, the cycle tracks and the red rear light of the bicycle shooting away from him into the darkness. 'No. It's a man.'

If only I'd been thirty seconds quicker, he thought, I'd have seen his face.

And then he thought: Yes, and maybe got a bullet in my own for my trouble: a bullet from a stolen Smith and Wesson .38, manufactured in Springfield, Massachusetts.

He felt a sudden prickle of ice-cold moisture on the back of his wrist and glanced up. He followed its trajectory to a spot in the roof, just before the windscreen. As he watched, another dark bubble of rainwater slowly swelled, ripened to a rich rust colour, and dropped.

Shark.

He realised guiltily he had nearly forgotten it.

'What's the time?'

'Almost five.'

'We should be getting back.'

He rubbed at his hand and reached for the ignition.

*

The car wouldn't start. Jericho twisted the key back and forth and pumped away frantically at the accelerator but all he managed to coax from the engine was a dull turning noise.

'Oh, hell!'

He turned up his collar, got out and went round to the boot. As he opened the lid a brace of pigeons took off behind him, wings snapping like firecrackers. There was a starting handle under the spare can of petrol and he inserted that into the hole in the front bumper. *'You do this the wrong way, lad,'* his stepfather had told him, *'and you can break your wrist.'* But which was the right way? Clockwise or anticlockwise? He gave the handle a hopeful tug. It was horribly stiff.

'Pull out the choke,' he shouted to Hester, 'and press your foot down on the third pedal if she starts to fire.'

The little car rocked as she slid across into the driver's seat.

He bent to his task again. The forest floor was only a couple of feet from his face, a pungent brown carpet of decaying leaves and fir cones. He heaved a couple more times until his shoulder ached. He was beginning to sweat now, perspiration mingling with the rainwater, dripping off the end of his nose, trickling down his neck. The insanity of their whole undertaking seemed encapsulated in this moment. The greatest convoy battle of the war was about to start, and where was he? In some primeval bloody forest in the middle of bloody nowhere poring over stolen Gestapo cryptograms with a woman he barely knew. What in the name of reason did they think they were doing? They must be – he tightened his grip – *crazy* ... He jerked viciously on the starting handle and suddenly the engine caught, spluttered, nearly died, then Hester revved it loudly. The sweetest sound he'd ever heard, it split the forest. He slung the handle into the boot and slammed the lid.

The gearbox whined as he reversed along the track towards the road.

*

The overhanging branches made a tunnel of the soaking lane. Their headlights glinted on a film of running water. Jericho drove slowly around and around the same course, trying to find some landmark in the gloom, trying not to panic. He must have taken a wrong turning coming out of the clearing. The steering wheel beneath his hands felt as wet and slippery as the road. Eventually they came to a crossroads beside a vast and decaying oak. Hester bent her head again to the map. A lock of long black hair fell across her eyes. She used both hands to pile it up. She clenched a pin between her teeth and muttered through it: 'Left or right?'

'You're the navigator.'

'And you're the one who decided to drive us off the main road.' She skewered her hair savagely back in place. 'Go left.'

He would have chosen the other way but thank God he didn't because she was right. Soon the road ahead began to brighten. They could see patches of weeping sky. He pressed his foot down and the speedometer touched forty as they passed out of the forest and into the open. When, after a mile or so, they came to a village, she told him to pull up outside the tiny post office.

'Why?'

'I need to find out where we are.'

'You'd better be quick.'

'I've really no intention of sight-seeing.'

She slammed the door behind her and ran through the rain,

sidestepping the puddles with a gym mistress's agility. A bell tinkled inside the shop as she opened the door.

Jericho glanced ahead, then checked in his mirror. The village appeared to consist of nothing more than this one street. No parked vehicles that he could see. No one about. He guessed that a private car, especially one driven by a stranger, would be a rarity, a talking-point. In the little red-brick cottages and the half-timbered houses he could already imagine the curtains being twitched back. He turned off the windscreen wipers and sank lower in his seat. For the twentieth time his hand went to the bulge of cryptograms in his inside pocket.

Two Englands, he thought. One England – this one – familiar, safe, obvious. But now another, secret England, secluded in the grounds of stately houses – Beaumanor, Gayhurst, Woburn, Adstock, Bletchley – an England of aerial farms and direction finders, clattering bombes and, soon, the glowing green and orange valves of Turing machines (*'it should make the calculations a hundred times, maybe a thousand times as fast'*). A new age beginning to be born in the parklands of the old. What was it that Hardy had written in his *Apology*? 'Real mathematics has no effects on war. No one has yet discovered any warlike purpose to be served by the theory of numbers.' The old boy couldn't guess the half of it.

The bell tinkled again and Hester emerged from the post office holding a newspaper over her head like an umbrella. She opened the car door, shook the paper and threw it, not very gently, into his lap.

'What's this for?' It was the *Leicester Mercury*, the local rag: that afternoon's edition.

'They print appeals for help, don't they? From the police? When someone is missing?'

It was a good idea. He had to concede it. But although they

checked the paper carefully – twice, in fact – they could find no photograph of Claire and no mention of the hunt for her.

*

Dropping southwards, heading for home. A different route for the return journey, more easterly – this was Hester's plan. To keep their spirits up, she occasionally recited the names of the villages and checked them in the gazetteer as they rattled down their empty high streets. Oadby, she said, ('note the early English to Perpendicular church'), Kibworth Harcourt, Little Bowden, and on across the border out of Leicestershire and into Northamptonshire. The sky over the distant pale hills brightened from black to grey and finally to a kind of glossy, neutral white. The rain slowed, then stopped. Oxendon, Kelmarsh, Maidwell ... Square Norman towers with arrow-slits, thatched pubs, tiny Victorian railway stations nesting in a bosky countryside of high hedges and dense copses. It was enough to make you want to burst into a chorus of 'There'll Always Be an England' except that neither of them felt like singing.

Why had she run? That was what Hester said she couldn't understand. Everything else seemed logical enough: how she would have got hold of the cryptograms in the first place, why she might have wanted to read them, why she would have needed an accomplice. But why then commit the one act guaranteed to draw attention to yourself? Why fail to turn up for your morning shift?

'You,' she said to Jericho, after she had thought it over for a few more miles. There was a hint of accusation in her voice. 'I think it must be you.'

Like a prosecuting counsel she took him back over the events of Saturday night. He had gone to the cottage, yes? He had discovered the intercepts, yes? A man had arrived downstairs, yes?

'Yes.'

'Did he see you?'

'No.'

'Did you *say* anything?'

'I may have shouted "Who's there?" or something of the sort.'

'So he could have recognised your voice?'

'It's possible.'

But that would mean I knew him, he thought. Or at least that he knew me.

'What time did you leave?'

'I don't know exactly. About half past one.'

'There you are,' she said. 'It *is* you. Claire returns to the cottage after you've gone. She discovers the intercepts are missing. She realises that you must have them because this mysterious man has told her you were there. She believes you'll take them straight to the authorities. She panics. She runs ...'

'But that's madness.' He took his eyes off the road to stare at her. 'I'd never have betrayed her.'

'So *you* say. But did *she* know that?'

Did she know that? No, he realised, returning his attention to the wheel, no, she did not know that. Indeed, on the basis of his behaviour on the night she found the cheque, she had good reason to assume he was a fanatic about security – a pretty ironic conclusion, given he now had eleven stolen cryptograms stuffed inside his overcoat pocket.

A twenty-year-old bus with an outside staircase to its upper deck, like something out of a transport museum, pulled over to the grass verge to let them overtake. The schoolchildren on board waved frantically as they passed.

'Who were her boyfriends? Who was she seeing apart from me?'

'You don't want to know. *Believe me*.' There was relish in the way she threw back at him the words he had used to her in church. He couldn't blame her for it.

'Come on, Hester.' He gripped the steering wheel grimly and glanced into the mirror. The bus was receding from view. A car was emerging from behind it. 'Don't spare my blushes. Let's keep it simple. Just confine it to men from the Park.'

Well, they were impressions, she said, rather than names. Claire had never mentioned names.

Give me the impressions, then.

And she did.

The first one she'd encountered had been young, with reddish hair, clean-shaven. She'd met him on the stairs with his shoes in his hand one morning in early November.

Reddish hair, clean-shaven, repeated Jericho. It didn't sound familiar.

A week later she'd cycled past a colonel parked in the lane in an Army staff car with the headlights dowsed. And then there was an Air Force man called Ivo Something, with a weird vocabulary of 'prangs' and 'crates' and 'shows' that Claire used to mimic fondly. Was he Hut 6 or 3? She was fairly sure Hut 3. There was an Honourable Evelyn double-barrelled someone-or-other – 'thoroughly *dis*honourable, darling' – whom Claire had met in London during the Blitz and who now worked in the mansion. There was an older man who Hester thought had something to do with the Navy. And there was an American: he was definitely Navy.

'That would be Kramer,' said Jericho.

'You know him?'

'He's the man who lent me the car. How recent was that?'

'About a month ago. But I got the impression he was just a friend. A source of Camels and nylons, nothing special.'

'And before Kramer there was me.'

'She never talked about you.'

'I'm flattered.'

'Given the way she used to talk about the others, you should be.'

'Anyone else?'

She hesitated. 'There may have been someone new in the last month. She was certainly away a good deal. And once, about two weeks ago, I had a migraine and came home early off shift and I *thought* there was a man's voice coming from her room. But if there was they stopped talking when they heard me on the stairs.'

'That's eight then, by my count. Including me. And leaving out any others you've forgotten or don't know about.'

'I'm sorry, Tom.'

'It's quite all right.' He managed to arrange his face into a parody of a smile. 'If anything it's rather fewer than I'd thought.' He was lying, of course, and he guessed she knew it. 'Why is it, I wonder, that I don't hate her for it?'

'Because that's the way she is,' said Hester, with unexpected ferocity. 'Well, she never made much secret of it, did she? And if one hates her for what she is – then, really, one can't have loved her very much in the first place, can one?' Her neck had blushed a deep pink. 'If all one wants is a reflection of oneself – well, honestly, there's always the mirror.'

She sat back, apparently as surprised by this speech as he was.

He checked the road behind them. Still empty apart from the same, solitary car. How long since he'd first noticed it? About ten minutes? But now he came to think of it, it had probably been there a good while longer, certainly since before they overtook the school bus. It was lying about a hundred yards back, low and wide and dark, its belly close to the ground, like a cockroach. He squeezed his foot harder on the accelerator and was relieved to see the gap between them widen until at last the road dipped and turned and the big car disappeared.

A minute later it was back again, maintaining exactly the same distance.

The narrow lane ran between high, dark hedges flecked with buds. Through them, as through a magic lantern, Jericho caught odd glimpses of tiny fields, a ruined barn, a bare, black elm, petrified by lightning. They came to a longish stretch of flat road.

There was no sun. He calculated there must be about half an hour of daylight left.

'How far is it to Bletchley?'

'Stony Stratford coming up, then about six miles. Why?'

He looked again in the mirror and had just begun to say, 'I fear –' when a bell started to clamour behind them. The big car had finally tired of following and was flashing its headlights, ordering them to pull over.

Until this moment, Jericho's encounters with the police had been rare, brief and invariably marked by those exaggerated displays of mutual respect customary between the guardians of the law and the lawful middle classes. But this one would be different, he saw that at once. An unauthorised journey between secret locations, without proof of ownership of the car, without petrol coupons, at a time when the country was being scoured for a missing woman: what would that earn them? A trip to the local police station, for sure. A lot of questions. A telephone call to Bletchley. A body search.

It didn't bear contemplating.

And so, to his astonishment, he found himself measuring the road ahead, like a long-jumper at the start of his run. The red roofs and the grey church spire of Stony Stratford had begun to poke above the distant line of trees.

Hester grabbed the edges of her seat. He jammed his foot down hard to the floor.

*

The Austin gathered speed slowly, as in a nightmare, and the police car, responding to the challenge, began to gain on them. The speedometer climbed past forty, to fifty, to fifty-five, to nearly sixty. The countryside seemed to be racing directly at them, only swerving at the last second to flash by narrowly on either side. A main road appeared ahead. They had to stop. And if Jericho had been an experienced driver that is what he would have done, police or no police. But he hesitated until there was nothing he could do but brake as hard as he dared, change down into second gear and yank the steering wheel hard left. The engine screamed. They spun and cornered on two tyres, he and Hester pitched sideways by the force. The clanging bell was drowned by the roar of an engine and suddenly the radiator grille of a tank transporter was rushing to fill the rear-view mirror. Its bumper touched them. An outraged blast from its hooter, as loud as a foghorn, seemed to blow them forwards. They shot across the bridge over the Grand Union Canal and a swan turned lazily to watch them and then they were doglegging through the market town – right, left, right, shuddering over cobbled alleys, the wheel shaking in Jericho's hands – anything to get off this wretched Roman road. Abruptly the houses receded and they were out in open country again, running alongside the canal. A narrowboat was being towed by a weary carthorse. The bargeman, lying stretched out beside the tiller, raised his hat to them.

'Left here,' said Hester, and they swung away from the canal into a lane that was not much better than the forest track: just two strips of potholed, tarmaced road, extending ahead like tyre tracks, separated by a mound of grass that scraped the bottom of the car. Hester turned and knelt on her seat, staring out of the back window for any sign of the police, but the countryside had closed behind them like a jungle. Jericho drove on slowly for two miles. They passed through a tiny hamlet. A mile the other side of it a space had been dug out to allow cars – or, more likely, carts – to pass one another. He drove up into it and switched off the engine.

*

They did not have much time.

Jericho kept watch on the lane while she changed in the back seat of the Austin. According to the map, they were only about a mile due west of Shenley Brook End and she was insistent she could make it back to the cottage on foot across open country before dark. He marvelled at her nerve. To him, after the encounter with the police, everything had taken on a sinister aspect: the trees gesticulating at one another in the wind, the patches of dense shadow now gathering at the edges of the fields, the rooks that had erupted, cawing, from their nests and were now circling high above them.

'Can't we read them?' Hester had asked, after they had parked. He had taken the cryptograms from his pocket so that they could decide what to do with them. 'Come on, Tom. We can't just burn them. If she thought she could read them, why can't we?'

Oh, a dozen reasons, Hester. A hundred. But here were three to be going on with. First, they would need the Vulture settings that were in use on the days the signals were sent.

'I can try to get those,' she had said. 'They must be in Hut 6 somewhere.'

Very well, maybe she could. But even if she managed it, they would still need several *hours* to themselves on a Type-X machine – and not one of the Type-Xs in Hut 8, either, because naval Enigmas were wired differently from Army ones.

She had made no answer to that.

And, third, they would need to find a place to hide the cryptograms, because otherwise, if they were caught with them, they'd both be on trial *in camera* at the Old Bailey.

No answer to that, either.

There was a movement in the hedge about thirty yards ahead of him. A fox came nosing out of the undergrowth and stepped into the lane. Halfway across it stopped and stared directly at him. It held itself perfectly still and sniffed the air, then slouched off into the opposite hedgerow. Jericho let out his breath.

And yet, and yet ... Even as he had ticked off all the obvious objections, he had known that she was right. They couldn't simply destroy the cryptograms now, not after all they had gone through to get them. And once that was conceded then the only logical reason for keeping them was to try to break them. Hester would have to steal the settings somehow while he looked for a way of gaining access to a Type-X machine. But it was dangerous – he prayed that she could see that. Claire was the last person to steal the cryptograms and there was no telling what had happened to her. And somewhere – maybe looking for them now, for all they knew – was a man who left large footprints in the frost; a man apparently armed with a stolen pistol; a man who knew that Jericho had been in Claire's room and had taken away the signals.

I am no hero, he thought. He was scared half to death.

The car door opened and Hester emerged, dressed again in trousers, sweater, jacket and boots. He took her bag and stowed it in the Austin's boot.

'Are you sure you don't want me to drive you?'

'We've been over this. It's safer if we split up.'

'For God's sake then be careful.'

'You should worry about yourself.' The air was milky with the approaching dusk – damp and cold. Her face was beginning to blur. She said: 'I'll see you tomorrow.'

She swung herself easily over the gate and set off directly across the field. He thought she might turn and wave but she never looked back. He watched her for about two minutes, until she had safely reached the far side. She searched briefly for a gap in the hedge, then vanished like the fox.

5

The lane led him up over the Chase, past the big wireless masts of the Bletchley Park out-station at Whaddon Hall, and down to the Buckingham Road. He peered along it, cautiously.

According to the map, only five roads, including this one, connected Bletchley with the outside world, and if the police were still watching the traffic they would stop him, he was certain. Short of flying a swastika the Austin could hardly have looked more suspicious. Mud was spattered over the bodywork to the height of the windows. Grass was wrapped tightly around the axles. The back bumper was buckled where the tank transporter had struck it. And the engine, after Stony Stratford, had acquired a kind of urgent death rattle. He wondered what on earth he would say to Kramer.

The road was quiet in both directions. He passed a couple of farmhouses and within five minutes he was entering the outskirts of the town. He drove on past the suburban villas with their white pebble-dashed frontages and their fake Tudor beams, then left up the hill towards Bletchley Park. He turned into Wilton Avenue and immediately braked. Parked at the end of the street beside the guard post was a police car. An officer in a greatcoat and cap was talking earnestly to the sentry.

Once again, Jericho had to use both hands to jam the gear lever into reverse, then he backed out very slowly into Church Green Road.

He had moved beyond panic now and was in some calm place at the centre of the storm. 'Act as normally as possible', that had been his advice to Hester when they had decided to keep the cryptograms. 'You're not on duty until four tomorrow afternoon? Fine, then don't go in before that time.' The injunction must apply to him as well. Normality. Routine. He was expected in Hut 8 for the night's attack on Shark? He would be there.

He drove on up the hill and parked the car in a street of private houses about three hundred yards from St Mary's Church. Where to hide the cryptograms? The Austin? Too risky. Albion Street? Too likely to be searched. A process of elimination brought him to the answer. Where better to hide a tree than in a forest? Where better to conceal a cryptogram than in a code-breaking centre? He would take them into the Park.

He transferred the wad of paper from the inside pocket of his overcoat to the hiding place he had made in the lining and locked the car. Then he remembered Atwood's atlas and unlocked it again. Bending to retrieve the book he casually checked the road. A woman in the house opposite was standing on her doorstep, in an oblong of yellow light, calling her children in from play. A young couple strolled past, arm in arm. A dog loped miserably along the gutter and stopped to cock its leg against the Austin's front tyre. An ordinary, English provincial street at twilight. *The world for which we fight*. He closed the door quietly. Head down, hands in pockets, he set off at a brisk walk for the Park.

*

It was a matter of pride with Hester Wallace that, when it came to walking, she had the stamina of any man. But what had looked on the map to be a straight and easy mile had turned into a crooked ramble three times as long, across tiny fields enclosed by tangled hedges and by ditches swollen wide as moats with brown meltwater, so that it was almost dark by the time she reached the lane.

She thought she might be lost but after a minute or two the narrow road began to seem familiar to her – a pair of elms grown too close together, as if from the same root; a mossy and broken stile – and soon she could smell the fires in the village. They were burning green wood and the smoke was white and acrid.

She kept a look out for policemen, but saw none – not in the field opposite the cottage, nor in the cottage itself, which had been left unlocked. She bolted the front door behind her, stood at the bottom of the stairs and called out a greeting.

Silence.

Slowly she climbed the stairs.

Claire's room was in chaos. *Desecrated* was the word that came to mind. The personality it had once reflected was disarranged, destroyed. Her clothes had all been strewn about, the sheets stripped off her bed, her jewellery scattered, her cosmetics opened up and spilled by clumsy male hands. At first she thought the surfaces were coated in talcum, but the fine white dust had no smell, and she realised it must be fingerprint powder.

She made a start at clearing it up, but soon abandoned it and sat on the edge of the naked mattress with her head in her hands until a great wave of self-disgust made her leap to her feet. She blew her nose angrily and went downstairs.

She lit a fire in the sitting room and set a kettle full of water on the hearth. In the kitchen she riddled the stove and managed to coax a glow from the pale ash, piled on some coal and set a saucepan to boil. She carried in the tin bath from the outhouse, bolting and locking the back door behind her.

She would stifle her terrors with routine. She would bathe. She would eat the remains of last night's carrot flan. She would retire early and hope for sleep.

Because tomorrow – *tomorrow* – would be a frightening day.

*

Inside Hut 8 there was a crowded, nervous atmosphere, like the green room of a theatre on opening night.

Jericho found his usual place next to the window. To his left: Atwood, leafing through Dilly Knox's edition of the mimes of Herodas. Pinker opposite, dressed as if for Covent Garden, his black velvet jacket slightly too long in the sleeve, so that his stubby fingers protruded like mole's paws. Kingcome and Proudfoot were playing with a pocket chess-set. Baxter was rolling a series of spindly cigarettes with a little tin contraption that didn't work properly. Puck had his feet up on the desk. The Type-Xs clacked sporadically in the background. Jericho nodded a general good evening, gave Atwood back his atlas – 'Thank you, dear boy. Good trip?' – and draped his overcoat over the back of his slatted chair. He was just in time.

'Gentlemen!' Logie appeared in the doorway and clapped twice to draw their attention, then stepped aside to allow Skynner to precede him into the room.

There was a general clatter and scraping of chair legs as they all clambered to their feet. Someone stuck their head round the door of the Decoding Room and the racket of the Type-Xs ceased.

'Easy, everybody,' said Skynner and waved them back into their seats. Jericho found that by tucking his feet under his chair he could rest his ankle against the stolen cryptograms. 'Just stopped by to wish you luck.' Skynner's heavy body was swathed like a Chicago gangster's in half an acre of pre-war, double-breasted pin-stripe. 'I'm sure you're all aware of what's at stake here as well as I am.'

'Shut up, then,' whispered Atwood.

But Skynner didn't hear him. This was what he loved. He stood with his feet planted firmly apart, his hands clasped behind his back. He was Nelson before Trafalgar. He was Churchill in the Blitz. 'I don't think I'm exaggerating when I say this could be one of the most decisive nights of the war.' His gaze sought out each of them in turn, coming last of all to Jericho and sliding away with a flicker of distaste. 'A mighty battle – probably the greatest convoy battle of the war – is about to start. Lieutenant Cave?'

'According to the Admiralty,' said Cave, 'at nineteen hundred hours this evening, convoys HX-229 and SC-122 were both warned they had entered the presumed operational area of the U-boats.'

'There we are, then. "Out of this nettle, danger, may we pluck this flower, safety."' Skynner nodded abruptly. 'Go to it.'

'Haven't I heard that before somewhere?' said Baxter.

'*Henry IV* Part One.' Atwood yawned. 'Chamberlain quoted it before he went off to meet Herr Hitler.'

After Skynner had gone, Logie went round the room handing out copies of the convoy contact section of the Short Signal Code Book. To Jericho, as a mark of recognition, he gave the precious original.

'We're after convoy contact reports, gentlemen: as many of them as possible in the twenty-four hours between midnight tonight and midnight tomorrow – in other words, the maximum amount of crib covering one day's Enigma settings.'

The instant an E-bar signal was heard, the duty officer of the receiving station would telephone to alert them. When the contact report arrived by teleprinter a minute later, ten copies would be made and distributed. No fewer than twelve bombes – Logie had the personal guarantee of the Hut 6 bombe controller – would be placed at their disposal the moment they had a worthwhile menu to run.

As he finished his speech, the blackout shutters began to be fixed to the windows and the hut battened down for the night.

*

'So, Tom,' said Puck pleasantly. 'How many contact reports do you think we will need for this scheme of yours to succeed?'

Jericho was leafing through the Short Signal Code Book. He glanced up. 'I tried to work it out yesterday. I'd say about thirty.'

'Thirty?' repeated Pinker, his voice rising in horror. 'But that would m-m-mean a mmm-mmm-mmm –'

'Massacre?'

'Massacre. Yes.'

'How many U-boats would be needed to produce thirty signals?' asked Puck.

Jericho said: 'I don't know. That would depend on the time between the initial sighting and the start of the attack. Eight. Perhaps nine.'

'Nine,' muttered Kingcome. 'Christ! Your move, Jack.'

'Will someone tell me, then, please,' said Puck, 'for what I am supposed to be hoping? Am I hoping that the U-boats find these convoys or not?'

'Not,' said Pinker, looking round the table for support. 'Obviously. We w-w-want the convoys to escape the U-boats. That's what this is all about.'

Kingcome and Proudfoot nodded but Baxter shook his head violently. His cigarette disintegrated, sprinkling shreds of tobacco down the front of his cardigan. 'Damn it,' he said.

'You'd really s-s-sacrifice a c-c-convoy?' asked Pinker.

'Of course.' Baxter carefully brushed the loose tobacco into his palm. 'For the greater good. How many men has Stalin had to sacrifice so far? Five million? Ten million? The only reason we're still in the war is the butcher's bill on the eastern front. What's a convoy in comparison, if it gets us back into Shark?'

'What do you say, Tom?'

'I don't have an answer. I'm a mathematician, not a moral philosopher.'

'Bloody typical,' said Baxter.

'No, no, in terms of moral logic, Tom's is actually the only rational reply,' said Atwood. He had laid aside his Greek. This was the sort of discussion he liked. 'Consider. A madman seizes both your children at knife-point and says to you: "One must die, make your choice." Towards whom do you direct your reproaches? Towards yourself, for having to make a decision? No. Towards the madman, surely?'

Jericho said, staring at Puck: 'But that analogy doesn't answer Puck's point about what one should *hope* for.'

'Oh, but I would argue that that is *precisely* what it does answer, in that it rejects the premise of his question: the presumption that the onus is on us to make a moral choice. *Quod erat demonstrandum*.'

'Nobody can split a hair f-finer than F-Frank,' said Pinker, admiringly.

'"The *presumption* that the onus is on us to make a moral choice,"' repeated Puck. He smiled across the table at Jericho. 'How very Cambridge. Excuse me. I think I must visit the lavatory.'

He made his way towards the back of the hut. Kingcome and Proudfoot returned to their chess game. Atwood picked up Herodas. Baxter fiddled with his cigarette-rolling machine. Pinker closed his eyes. Jericho leafed through the Short Signal Code Book and thought of Claire.

*

Midnight came and went without a sound from the North Atlantic and the tension which had been building all evening began to slacken.

The 2 a.m. offering from the cooks of the Bletchley Park canteen was enough to make even Mrs Armstrong blanch – boiled potatoes in cheese sauce with barracuda, followed by a pudding made from two slices of bread stuck together with jam and then deep-fried in batter – and by four, the digestive effects of this, combined with the dim light in Hut 8 and the fumes from the paraffin heater, were casting a soporific pall over the naval cryptanalysts.

Atwood was the first to succumb. His mouth dropped open and the top plate of his dentures came loose so that he made a curious clicking sound as he breathed. Pinker wrinkled his nose in disgust and went off to make a nest for himself in the corner, and soon afterwards Puck, too, fell asleep, his body bent forwards, his left cheek resting on his forearms on the table. Even Jericho, despite his determination to stand guard over the cryptograms, found himself slipping over the edge into unconsciousness. He pulled himself back a couple of times, aware of Baxter watching him, but finally he couldn't fight it any longer and he slid into a turbulent dream of drowning men whose cries sounded in his ears like the wind in the aerial farm.

SIX

STRIP

STRIP: to remove one layer of encipherment from a cryptogram which has been subjected to the process of super-encipherment (US, qv), i.e., a message which has been enciphered once, and then re-enciphered to provide double security.

A Lexicon of Cryptography
('Most Secret', Bletchley Park, 1943)

1

Later, it would transpire that Bletchley Park knew almost everything there was to know about *U-653*.

They knew she was a Type VIIc – 220 feet long, 20 feet wide, with a submerged displacement of 871 tons and a surface range of 6,500 miles – and that she had been manufactured by the Howaldts Werke of Hamburg, with engines by Blohm und Voss. They knew she was eighteen months old, because they had broken the signals describing her sea-trials in the autumn of 1941. They knew she was under the command of Kapitänleutnant Gerhard Feiler. And they knew that on the night of 28 January 1943 – the final night, as it happened, that Tom Jericho had spent with Claire Romilly – *U-653* had slipped her moorings at the French naval port of Saint-Nazaire and had moved out under a dark and moonless sky into the Bay of Biscay to begin her sixth operational tour.

After she had been at sea for a week, the cryptanalysts in Hut 8 broke a signal from U-boat headquarters – then still in their grand apartment building off the Bois de Boulogne in Paris – ordering *U-653* to proceed on the surface to naval grid square KD 63 'AT MAXIMUM MAINTAINABLE SPEED WITHOUT REGARD TO THE THREAT FROM THE AIR'.

On 11 February she joined ten other U-boats in a new mid-Atlantic patrol line code-named Ritter.

Weather conditions in the North Atlantic were particularly

foul in the winter of 1942–3. There were a hundred days when the U-boats reported winds topping force 7 on the Beaufort scale. Sometimes the gales reached over 100 miles per hour, whipping up waves more than 50 feet high. Snow, sleet, hail and frozen spray lashed submarines and convoys alike. One Allied ship rolled over and sank in minutes simply from the weight of ice on her superstructure.

On 13th February, Feiler broke radio silence to report that his watch officer, one Leutnant Laudon, had been washed overboard – a blatant disregard of operational procedure on Feiler's part which brought not condolences but a terse rebuke from his controllers, broadcast to the entire submarine fleet:

FEILER'S MESSAGE ABOUT LOSS OF WATCH OFFICER SHOULD NOT HAVE BEEN SENT UNTIL W/T SILENCE WAS BROKEN BY GENERAL CONTACT WITH ENEMY.

It was only on the 23rd, after nearly four weeks at sea, that Feiler redeemed himself by at last making contact with a convoy. At 6 p.m. he dived to avoid an escorting destroyer, and then, when night came, rose to attack. He had at his disposal twelve torpedoes, each 23 feet long with its own electric motor, capable of running through a convoy, turning in a half circle and running back, turning again and so on, and on, until either its power ran out or a ship was sunk. The sensing mechanism was crude; it was not unknown for a U-boat to find itself being pursued by its own armaments. They were called FATs: *Flachenabsuchendertorpedos*, or 'shallow searching torpedoes'. Feiler fired four of them.

FROM: FEILER

IN NAVAL GRID SQUARE BC 6956 AT 0116. FOUR-FAN AT A CONVOY PROCEEDING ON A SOUTHERLY COURSE AT 7 KNOTS.

ONE STEAMSHIP OF 6,000 GROSS REGISTERED TONS: LARGE EXPLOSION AND A CLOUD OF SMOKE, THEN NOTHING MORE SEEN. ONE STEAMSHIP OF 5,500 GRT LEFT BURNING. 2 FURTHER HITS HEARD, NO OBSERVATIONS.

On the 25th, Feiler radioed his position.

On the 26th, his luck turned bad again.

FROM: U-653

AM IN NAVAL GRID SQUARE BC 8747. HIGH PRESSURE GROUP 2 AND STARBOARD NEGATIVE BUOYANCY TANK UNSERVICEABLE. BALLAST TANK 5 NOT TIGHT. IS MAKING ODD NOISES. DIESEL PRODUCING DENSE WHITE SMOKE.

Headquarters took all night to consult its engineers and replied at ten the following morning:

TO: FEILER

THE CONDITION OF BALLAST TANK NO 5 IS THE ONLY THING WHICH MAY ENFORCE RETURN PASSAGE. DECIDE FOR YOURSELF AND REPORT.

By midnight, Feiler had made his decision:

FROM: U-653

AM NOT RETURNING.

On 3 March, in mountainous seas, *U-653* came alongside a U-boat tanker and took on board 65 cubic metres of fuel and provisions sufficient for another fourteen days at sea.

On the 6th, Feiler was ordered into station in a new patrol line, code-named *Raubgraf* (Robber Baron).

And that was all.

On 9 March the U-boats abruptly changed their Weather Code Book, Shark was blacked out, and *U-653*, along with one hundred and thirteen other German submarines then known to be operating in the Atlantic, vanished from Bletchley's view.

*

At 5 a.m. GMT on Tuesday 16 March, some nine hours after Jericho had parked the Austin and walked into Hut 8, *U-653* was heading due east on the surface, returning to France. In the North Atlantic it was 3 a.m.

After ten days on station in the *Raubgraf* line, with no sign of any convoy, Feiler had finally decided to head for home. He had lost, along with Leutnant Laudon, four other ratings washed overboard. One of his petty officers was ill. The starboard diesel was still giving trouble. His one remaining torpedo was defective. The boat, which had no heating, was cold and damp, and everything – lockers, food, uniforms – was covered in a greenish-white mould. Feiler lay on his wet bunk, curled up against the cold, wincing at the irregular beat of the engine, and tried to sleep.

Up on the bridge, four men made up the night watch: one for each point of the compass. Cowled like monks in dripping black oilskins, lashed to the rail by metal belts, each had a pair of goggles and a pair of Zeiss binoculars clamped firmly to his eyes and was staring blindly into his own sector of darkness.

The cloud cover was ten-tenths. The wind was a steel attack. The hull of the U-boat thrashed beneath their feet with a violence that sent them skidding over the wet deck plates and knocking into one another.

Facing directly ahead, towards the invisible prow, was a young Obersteurmann, Heinz Theen. He was peering into such an infinity of blackness that it was possible to imagine they might have fallen off the edge of the world, when suddenly he saw a light. It flared out of nowhere, several hundred yards in front of him, winked for two seconds, then disappeared. If he hadn't had his binoculars trained precisely upon it, he would never have seen it.

Astonishing though it seemed, he realised he had just witnessed someone lighting a cigarette.

An Allied seaman lighting a cigarette in the middle of the North Atlantic.

He called down the conning tower for the captain.

By the time Feiler had scrambled up the slippery metal ladder to the bridge thirty seconds later the cloud had shifted slightly in the high wind and shapes were moving all around them. Feiler swivelled through 360 degrees and counted the outlines of nearly twenty ships, the nearest no more than 500 yards away on the port side.

A whispered cry, as much of panic as command: 'Alarrrmmm!'

*

The *U-653* came out of her emergency dive and hung motionless in the calmer water beneath the waves.

Thirty-nine men crouched silently in the semidarkness, listening to the sounds of the convoy passing overhead: the fast revs of the modern diesels, the ponderous churning of the steamers, the curious singing noises of the turbines in the warship escorts.

Feiler let them all go by. He waited two hours, then surfaced.

The convoy was already so far ahead as to be barely visible in the faint dawn light – just the masts of the ships and a few smudges of smoke on the horizon, and then, occasionally, when a high wave lifted the U-boat, the ironwork of bridges and funnels.

Feiler's task under standing orders was not to attack – impossible in any case, given his lack of torpedoes – but to keep his quarry in sight while drawing in every other U-boat within a radius of 100 miles.

'Convoy steering 070 degrees,' said Feiler. 'Naval grid square BD 1491.'

The first officer made a scrawled note in pencil then dropped down the conning tower to collect the Short Signal Code Book. In his cubbyhole next to the captain's berth the radioman pressed his switches. The Enigma came on with a hum.

2

At 7 a.m., Logie had sent Pinker, Proudfoot and Kingcome back to their digs to get some decent rest. 'Sod's law will now proceed to operate,' he predicted, as he watched them go, and sod's law duly did. Twenty-five minutes later, he was back in the Big Room with the queasy expression of guilty excitement which would characterise the whole of that day.

'It looks like it may have started.'

St Erith, Scarborough and Flowerdown had all reported an E-bar signal followed by eight Morse letters, and within a minute one of the Wrens from the Registration Room was bringing in the first copies. Jericho placed his carefully in the centre of his trestle table.

RGHC DMIG. His heart began to accelerate.

'Hubertus net,' said Logie. '4601 kilocycles.'

Cave was listening to someone on the telephone. He put his hand over the mouthpiece. 'Direction finders have a fix.' He clicked his fingers. 'Pencil. Quick.' Baxter threw him one. '49.4 degrees north,' he repeated. '38.8 degrees west. Got it. Well done.' He hung up.

Cave had spent all night plotting the convoys' courses on two large charts of the North Atlantic – one issued by the Admiralty, the other a captured German naval grid, on which the ocean was divided into thousands of tiny squares. The cryptanalysts gathered round him. Cave's finger came down on a spot almost exactly midway between Newfoundland and the British Isles. 'There she is. She's shadowing HX-229.' He made a cross on the map and wrote 0725 beside it.

Jericho said: 'What grid square is that?'

'BD 1491.'

'And the convoy course?'

'070.'

Jericho went back to his desk and in less than two minutes, using the Short Signal Code Book and the current Kriegsmarine address book for encoding naval grid squares ('Alfred Krause, Blucherplatz 15': Hut 8 had broken that just before the blackout) he had a five-letter crib to slide under the contact report.

R G H C D M I G

D D F G R X ? ?

The first four letters announced that a convoy had been located steering 070 degrees, the next two gave the grid square, the final two represented the code name of the U-boat, which he didn't have. He circled R-D and D-R. A four-letter loop on the first signal.

'I get D-R/R-D,' said Puck a few seconds later.

'So do I.'

'Me too,' said Baxter.

Jericho nodded and doodled his initials on the pad. 'A good omen.'

*

After that, the pace of events began to quicken.

At 8.25, two long signals were intercepted emanating from Magdeburg, which Cave at once surmised would be U-boat headquarters ordering every submarine in the North Atlantic into the attack zone. At 9.20, he put down the telephone to announce that the Admiralty had just signalled the convoy commander with a warning that he was probably being shadowed. Seven minutes later, the telephone rang again. Flowerdown intercept station. A second E-bar flash from almost the same location as the first. The Wrens hurried in with it: KLYS QNLP.

'The same hearse,' said Cave. 'Following standard operating procedure. Reporting every two hours, or near as damn it.'

'Grid square?'

'The same.'

'Convoy course?'

'Also the same. For now.'

Jericho went back to his desk and manipulated the original crib under the new cryptogram.

K L Y S Q N L P
D D F G R X ? ?

Again, there were no letter clashes. The golden rule of Enigma, its single, fatal weakness: *nothing is ever itself – A can never be A, B can never be B* ... It was working. His feet performed a little tap dance of delight beneath the table. He glanced up to find Baxter staring at him and he realised, to his horror, that he was smiling.

'Pleased?'

'Of course not.'

But such was his shame that when, an hour later, Logie came

through to say that a second U-boat had just sent a contact signal, he felt himself personally responsible.

SOUY YTRQ.

At 11.40, a third U-boat began to shadow the convoy, at 12.20, a fourth, and suddenly Jericho had seven signals on his desk. He was conscious of people coming up and looking over his shoulder – Logie with his burning hayrick of a pipe and the meaty smell and heavy breathing of Skynner. He didn't look round. He didn't talk. The outside world had melted for him. Even Claire was just a phantom now. There were only the loops of letters, forming and stretching out towards him from the grey Atlantic, multiplying on his sheets of paper, turning into thin chains of possibility in his mind.

*

They didn't stop for breakfast, nor for lunch. Minute by minute, throughout the afternoon, the cryptanalysts followed, at third hand, the progress of the chase two thousand miles away. The commander of the convoy was signalling to the Admiralty, the Admiralty had an open line to Cave, and Cave would shout each time a fresh development looked like affecting the hunt for cribs.

Two signals came at 13.40 – one a short contact report, the other longer, almost certainly originating from the U-boat that had started the hunt. Both were for the first time close enough to be fixed by direction finders on board the convoy's own escorts. Cave listened gravely for a minute, then announced that HMS *Mansfield*, a destroyer, was being dispatched from the main body of merchantmen to attack the U-boats.

'The convoy's just made an emergency turn to the southeast. She's going to try to shake off the hearses while *Mansfield* forces them under.'

Jericho looked up. 'What course is she steering?'

'What course is she steering?' repeated Cave into the telephone. 'I *said*,' he yelled, 'what fucking *course* is she steering?' He winced at Jericho. The receiver was jammed tight to his scarred ear. 'All right. Yes. Thank you. Convoy steering 118 degrees.' Jericho reached for the Short Signal Code Book.

'Will they manage to get away?' asked Baxter.

Cave bent over his chart with a ruler and protractor. 'Maybe. It's what I'd do in their place.'

A quarter of an hour passed and nothing happened.

'Perhaps they have done it,' said Puck. 'Then what do we do?'

Cave said: 'How much more material do you need?'

Jericho counted through the signals. 'We've got nine. We need another twenty. Another twenty-five would be better.'

'Jesus!' Cave regarded them with disgust. 'It's like sitting with a flock of carrion.'

Somewhere behind them a telephone managed half a ring before it was snatched out of its cradle. Logie came in a moment later, still writing.

'That was St Erith reporting an E-bar signal at 49.4 degrees north, 38.1 degrees west.'

'New location,' said Cave, studying his charts. He made a cross, then threw his pencil down and leaned back in his chair, rubbing his face. 'All she's managed to do is run straight from one hearse into another. Which is what? The fifth? Christ, the sea must be teeming with them.'

'She isn't going to get away,' said Puck, 'is she?'

'Not a chance. Not if they're coming in from all around her.'

A Wren moved among the cryptanalysts, doling out the latest cryptogram: BKEL UUXS.

Ten signals. Five U-boats in contact.

'Grid square?' said Jericho.

*

Hester Wallace, was not a poker player, which was a mistake on her part as she had been blessed with a poker face that could have made her a fortune. Nobody watching her wheel her bicycle into the shed beside the canteen that afternoon, or seeing her flick her pass at the sentry, or squeezing up against the corridor wall in Hut 6 to let her march by, or sitting opposite her in Intercept Control – nobody would have guessed the turmoil in her mind.

Her complexion was, as ever, pale, her forehead slightly creased by a frown that discouraged conversation. She wore her long, dark hair like a headache, savagely twisted up and speared. Her costume was the usual uniform of the West Country schoolmistress: flat shoes, grey woollen stockings, plain grey skirt, white shirt and an elderly but well-cut tweed jacket which she would shortly take off and hang over the back of her chair, for the afternoon was warm. Her fingers moved across the blist in a short, staccato pecking motion. She had hardly slept all night.

Name of intercept station, time of interception, frequency, call sign, letter groups ...

Where was the record of settings kept? That was the first matter to determine. Not in Control, obviously. Not in the Index Room. Not in the Registry. And not next door in the Registration Room, either: she had already made a quick inspection there. The Decoding Room was a possibility, but the Type-X girls were always complaining they were cramped for space, and sixty separate Enigma keys, their settings changed daily – in the case of the Luftwaffe, sometimes twice a day – well, that was a minimum of five hundred pieces of information every week, 25,000 in a year, and this was the war's fourth year. That would suggest a sizeable catalogue; a small library, in fact.

The only conclusion was that they had to be kept where the cryptanalysts worked, in the Machine Room, or else close by.

She finished blisting Chicksands, noon till three, and moved towards the door.

Her first pass through the Machine Room was spoiled by nerves: straight through it to the other end of the hut without even glancing from side to side. She stood outside the Decoding Room, cursing her fears, pretending to study the noticeboard. With a shaking hand she made a note about a performance of *Die Fledermaus* by the Bletchley Park Music Society which she had no intention of ever attending.

The second run was better.

There was no machinery in the Machine Room – the origin of its name was lost in the glorious mists of 1940 – just desks, cryptanalysts, wire baskets filled with signals and, on the wall to the right, shelf after shelf of files. She stopped and looked around distractedly, as if searching for a familiar face. The problem was, she knew nobody. But then her gaze fell upon a bald head with a few long, ginger hairs combed pathetically across a freckled crown, and she realised that wasn't entirely true.

She knew Cordingley.

Dear old, dull old Donald Cordingley, the winner – in a crowded field – of the Dullest Man in Bletchley contest. Ineligible for military service due to a funnel chest. By profession: actuary. Ten years' service with the Scottish Widows Assurance Society in the City of London, until a lucky third place in the *Daily Telegraph* crossword competition won him a seat in the Hut 6 Machine Room.

Her seat.

She watched him for a few more seconds, then moved away.

When she got back to Control Miles Mermagen was standing by her desk.

'How was Beaumanor?'

'Engrossing.'

She had left her jacket over her chair and he ran his hand over the collar, feeling the material between his thumb and forefinger, as if checking it for quality.

'How'd you get there?'

'A friend gave me a lift.'

'A male friend, I gather.' Mermagen's smile was wide and unfriendly.

'How do you know that?'

'I have my spies,' he said.

*

The ocean was alive with signals. They were landing on Jericho's desk at the rate of one every twenty minutes.

At 16.00 a sixth U-boat fastened on to the convoy and soon afterwards Cave announced that HX-229 was making another turn, to 028 degrees, in her latest and (in his opinion) hopeless attempt to escape her pursuers.

By 18.00 Jericho had a pile of nineteen contact signals, out of which he had conjured three four-letter loops and a mass of half-sketched bombe menus that looked like the plans for some complex game of hopscotch. His neck and shoulders were so knotted with tension he could barely straighten up.

The room by now was crowded. Pinker, Kingcome and Proudfoot had come back on shift. The other British naval lieutenant, Villiers, was standing next to Cave, who was explaining something on one of his charts. A Wren with a tray offered Jericho a curling Spam sandwich and an enamel mug of tea and he took them gratefully.

Logie came up behind him and tousled his hair.

'How are you feeling, old love?'

'Wrecked, frankly.'

'Want to knock off?'

'Very funny.'

'Come into my office and I'll give you something. Bring your tea.'

The 'something' turned out to be a large, yellow Benzedrine tablet, of which Logie had half a dozen in an hexagonal pillbox.

Jericho hesitated. 'I'm not sure I should. These helped send me funny last time.'

'They'll get you through the night, though, won't they? Come on, old thing. The commandos swear by them.' He rattled the box under Jericho's nose. 'So you'll crash out at breakfast? So what? By then we'll either have this bugger beaten. Or not. In which case it won't matter, will it?' He took one of the pills and pressed it into Jericho's palm. 'Go on. I won't tell Nurse.' He closed Jericho's fingers around it and said quietly: 'Because I can't let you go, you know, old love. Not tonight. Not you. Some of the others, maybe, but not you.'

'Oh, Christ. Well, since you put it so nicely.'

Jericho swallowed the pill with a mouthful of tea. It left a foul taste and he drained his mug to try and swill it away. Logie regarded him fondly.

'That's my boy.' He put the box back in his desk drawer and locked it. 'I've been protecting your bloody back again, incidentally. I had to tell him you were much too important to be disturbed.'

'Tell who? Skynner?'

'No. Not Skynner. Wigram.'

'What does he want?'

'You, old cock. I'd say he wants you. Skinned, stuffed and mounted on a pole somewhere. Really, I don't know, for such a quiet bloke, you don't half make some enemies. I told him to come back at midnight. All right by you?'

Before Jericho could reply the telephone rang and Logie grabbed it.

'Yes? Speaking.' He grunted and stretched across his desk for a pencil. 'Time of origin 19.02, 52.1 degrees north, 37.2 degrees west. Thanks, Bill. Keep the faith.'

He replaced the receiver.

'And then there were seven ...'

*

It was dark again and the lights were on in the Big Room. The sentries outside were banging the blackout shutters into place, like prison warders locking up their charges for the night.

Jericho hadn't set foot out of the hut for twenty-four hours, hadn't even looked out of the window. As he slipped back into his seat and checked his coat to make sure the cryptograms were still there, he wondered vaguely what kind of day it had been and what Hester was doing.

Don't think about that now.

Already, he could feel the Benzedrine beginning to take effect. The muscles of his heart seemed feathery, his body charged. When he glanced across his notes, what had seemed inert and impenetrable a half-hour ago was suddenly fluid and full of possibility.

The new cryptogram was already on his desk: YALB DKYF.

'Naval grid square BD 2742,' called Cave. 'Course 055 degrees. Convoy speed nine and a half knots.'

Logie said: 'A message from Mr Skynner. A bottle of Scotch for the first man with a menu for the bombes.'

Twenty-three signals received. Seven U-boats in contact. Two hours to go till nightfall in the North Atlantic.

*

20.00: nine U-boats in contact.

20.46: ten.

*

The Control Room girls took a table near the serving hatch for their evening meal. Celia Davenport showed them all some pictures of her fiancé, who was fighting in the desert, while Anthea Leigh-Delamere brayed endlessly about a meet of the Bicester Hunt. Hester passed on the photographs without looking at them. Her eyes were fixed on Donald Cordingley, queuing to collect his lump of coelacanth, or whatever other obscure example of God's aquatic creatures they were now required to eat.

She was cleverer than he, and he knew it.

She intimidated him.

Hello, Donald, she thought. *Hello, Donald ... Oh, nothing much, just this new back-break section, coming along with bucket and shovel after the Lord Mayor's parade ... Now, listen, Donald, there's this funny little wireless net, Konotop–Pribiki–Poltava, in the southern Ukraine. Nothing vital, but we've never quite broken it and Archie – you must know Archie? – Archie has a theory it may be a variant on Vulture ... Traffic runs through February and the first few days of March ... That's right ...*

She watched him as he sat alone and picked at his lonely supper. She watched him, indeed, as if she *were* a vulture. And when, after fifteen minutes, he rose and scraped the leftovers from his plate into the swill bins, she rose as well, and followed him.

She was vaguely aware of the other girls staring after her in astonishment. She ignored them.

She tracked him all the way back to Hut 6, gave him five minutes to settle down, then went in after him.

The Machine Room was shaded and somnolent, like a library at dusk. She tapped him lightly on the shoulder.

'Hello, Donald.'

He turned round and blinked up at her in surprise. 'Oh, hello.' The effort of memory was heroic. 'Hello, Hester.'

*

'It's almost dark out there,' said Cave, looking at his watch. 'Not long now. How many have you had?'

'Twenty-nine,' said Baxter.

'I believe you said that would be enough, Mr Jericho?'

'Weather,' said Jericho, without looking up. 'We need a weather report from the convoy. Barometric pressure, cloud cover, cloud type, wind speed, temperature. Before it gets too dark.'

'They've got ten U-boats on their backs and you want them to tell you the *weather?*'

'Yes, please. Fast as they can.'

The weather report arrived at 21.31.

There were no more contact signals after 21.40.

*

Thus convoy HX-229 at 22.00:

Thirty-seven merchant vessels, ranging in size from the 12,000-ton British tanker *Southern Princess* to the 3,500-ton American freighter *Margaret Lykes*, making slow progress through heavy seas, steering a course of 055 degrees, direct to England, lit up like a regatta by a full moon to a range of ten miles visibility – the first such night in the North Atlantic for weeks. Escort vessels: five, including two slow corvettes and two clapped out, elderly ex-American destroyers donated to Britain in 1940 in exchange for bases, one of which – HMS *Mansfield* – had lost touch with the convoy after charging down the U-boats because the convoy commander (on his first operational command) had forgotten to signal her with his second change of course. No rescue ship available. No air cover. No reinforcements within a thousand miles.

'All in all,' said Cave, lighting a cigarette and contemplating his charts, 'what you might fairly call a bit of a cock-up.'

The first torpedo hit at 22.01.

At 22.32, Tom Jericho was heard to say, very quietly, 'Yes.'

3

It was chucking-out time at the Eight Bells Inn on the Buckingham Road and Miss Jobey and Mr Bonnyman had virtually exhausted the main topic of their evening's conversation: what Bonnyman dramatically termed the 'police raid' on Mr Jericho's room.

They had heard the details at supper from Mrs Armstrong, her face still flushed with outrage at the memory of this violation of her territory. A uniformed officer had stood guard all afternoon on the doorstep ('in full view of the entire street, mind you'), while two plain-clothes men carrying a box of tools and waving a warrant had spent the best part of three hours searching the upstairs back bedroom, before leaving at teatime with a pile of books. They had dismantled the bed and the wardrobe, taken up the carpet and the floorboards, and brought down a heap of soot from the chimney. 'That young man is out,' declared Mrs Armstrong, folding her hamlike arms, 'and all rent forfeit.'

'"*All rent forfeit,*"' repeated Bonnyman into his beer, for the sixth or seventh time. 'I love it.'

'And such a quiet man,' said Miss Jobey.

A handbell rang behind the bar and the lights flickered.

'Time, gentlemen! Time, please!'

Bonnyman finished his watery bitter, Miss Jobey her port and lemon, and he escorted her unsteadily, past the dartboard and the hunting prints, towards the door.

The day that Jericho had missed had given the town its first real taste of spring. Out on the pavement the night air was still mild. Darkness touched the dreary street with romance. As the departing drinkers stumbled away into the blackout, Bonnyman playfully pulled Miss Jobey towards him. They fell back slightly into a doorway. Her mouth opened on his, she pressed herself up against him, and Bonnyman squeezed her waist in return. Whatever she might have lacked in beauty – and in the blackout, who could tell? – she more than made up for in ardour. Her strong and agile tongue, sweet with port, squirmed against his teeth.

Bonnyman, by profession a Post Office engineer, had been drafted into Bletchley, as Jericho had guessed, to service the bombes. Miss Jobey worked in the upstairs back bedroom of the mansion, filing Abwehr hand-ciphers. Neither, in accordance with regulations, had told the other what they did, a discretion which Bonnyman had extended somewhat to cover in addition the existence of a wife and two children at home in Dorking.

His hands slipped down her narrow thighs and began to hoist her skirt.

'Not here,' she said into his mouth, and brushed his fingers away.

*

Well (as Bonnyman would afterwards confide with a wink to the unsmiling police inspector who took his statement), the things a grown man has to do in wartime, and all for a simple you-know-what.

First, a cycle ride, which took them along a track and under a railway bridge. Then, by the thin beam of a torch, over a padlocked gate and through mud and brambles towards the hulk of a broken building. A great expanse of water somewhere close by. You couldn't see it, but you could hear the lapping in the breeze and the occasional cry of a waterfowl, and you could sense a deeper darkness, like a great black pit.

Complaints from Miss Jobey as she snagged her precious stockings and wrenched her ankle: loud and bitter imprecations against Mr Bonnyman and all his works which did not augur well for the purpose he had in mind. She started whining: 'Come on, Bonny, I'm frightened, let's go back.'

But Bonnyman had no intention of turning back. Even on a normal evening, Mrs Armstrong monitored every peep and squeak in the ether of the Commercial Guesthouse like a one-woman intercept station; tonight, she'd be on even higher alert than usual. Besides, he always found this place exciting. The light flashed on bare brick and on evidence of earlier liaisons – *AE + GS, Tony = Kath*. The spot held an odd erotic charge. So much had clearly happened here, so many whispered fumblings ... They were a part of a great flux of yearning that went back long before them and would go on long after them – illicit, irrepressible, eternal. This was *life*. Such, at any rate, were Bonnyman's thoughts, although naturally he didn't express them at the time, nor afterwards to the police.

'And what happened next, sir? Precisely.'

He won't admit to this either, thank you very much, precisely or imprecisely.

But what did happen next was that Bonnyman wedged the torch in a gap in the brickwork where something had been torn from the wall, and threw his arms around Miss Jobey. He encountered a little light resistance at first – some token twisting and turning and 'stop it', 'not here' – which quickly became less convincing, until suddenly her tongue was up to its tricks again and they were back where they'd left off outside the Eight Bells Inn. Once again his hands began to ride up her skirt and once again she pushed him away, but this time for a different reason. Frowning slightly, she ducked and pulled down her knickers. One step, two steps, and they had vanished into her pocket. Bonnyman watched, enraptured.

'What happened next, inspector, *precisely*, is that Miss Jobey and myself noticed some hessian sacking in the corner.'

She with her skirt up above her knees, he with his trousers down around his ankles, shuffling forwards like a man in leg-irons, dropping heavily to his knees, a cloud of dust from the sacks rising and blossoming in the torch-beam, then much squirming and complaining on her part that something was digging into her back.

They stood and pulled away the sacks to make a better bed.

'And that was when you found it?'

'That was when we found it.'

The police inspector suddenly brought his fist down hard on the rough wooden table and shouted for his sergeant.

'Any sign of Mr Wigram yet?'

'We're still looking, sir.'

'Well, bloody well find him, man. Find him.'

4

The bombe was heavy – Jericho guessed it must weigh more than half a ton – and even though it was mounted on castors it still took all his strength, combined with the engineer's, to drag it away from the wall. Jericho pulled while the engineer went behind it and put his shoulder to the frame to heave. It came away at last with a screech and the Wrens moved in to strip it.

The decryptor was a monster, like something out of an H. G. Wells fantasy of the future: a black metal cabinet, eight feet wide and six feet tall, with scores of five-inch-diameter drum wheels set into the front. The back was hinged and opened up to show a bulging mass of coloured cables and the dull gleam of metal drums. In the place where it had stood on the concrete floor there was a large puddle of oil.

Jericho wiped his hands on a rag and retreated to watch from a corner. Elsewhere in the hut a score of other bombes were churning away on other Enigma keys and the noise and the heat were how he imagined a ship's engine room might be. One Wren went round to the back of the cabinet and began disconnecting and replugging the cables. The other moved along the front, pulling out each drum in turn and checking it. Whenever she found a fault in the wiring she would hand the drum to the engineer who would stroke the tiny brush wires back into place with a pair of tweezers. The contact brushes were always fraying, just as the belt which connected the mechanism to the big electric motor had a tendency to stretch and slip whenever there was a heavy load. And the engineers had never quite got the earthing right, so that the cabinets had a tendency to give off powerful electric shocks.

Jericho thought it was the worst job of all. A pig of a job. Eight hours a day, six days a week, cooped up in this windowless, deafening cell. He turned away to look at his watch. He didn't want them to see his impatience. It was nearly half past eleven.

His menu was at that moment being rushed into bombe bays all across the Bletchley area. Eight miles north of the Park, in a hut in a clearing in the forested estate of Gayhurst Manor, a clutch of tired Wrens near the end of their shift were being ordered to halt the three bombes running on Nuthatch (Berlin-Vienna-Belgrade

Army administration), strip them and prepare them for Shark. In the stable block of Adstock Manor, ten miles to the west, the girls were actually sprawled with their feet up beside their silent machines, drinking Ovaltine and listening to Tommy Dorsey on the BBC Light Programme, when the supervisor came storming through with a sheaf of menus and told them to stir themselves, fast. And at Wavendon Manor, three miles northeast, a similar story: four bombes in a dank and windowless bunker were abruptly pulled off Osprey (the low-priority Enigma key of the Organisation Todt) and their operators told to stand by for a rush job.

Those, plus the two machines in Bletchley's Hut 11, made up the promised dozen bombes.

The mechanical check completed, the Wren went back to the first row of drums and began adjusting them to the combination listed on the menu. She called out the letters to the other girl, who checked them.

'Freddy, Butter, Quagga ...'

'Yes.'

'Apple, X-ray, Edward ...'

'Yes.'

The drums slipped on to their spindles and were fixed into place with a loud metallic click. Each was wired to mimic the action of a single Enigma rotor: 108 in all, equivalent to thirty-six Enigma machines running in parallel. When all the drums had been set, the bombe was trundled back into place and the motor started.

The drums began to turn, all except one in the top row which had jammed. The engineer gave it a whack with his spanner and it, too, began to revolve. The bombe would now run continuously on this menu – certainly for one day; possibly, according to Jericho's calculations, for two or three – stopping occasionally when the drums were so aligned they completed a circuit. Then the readings on the drums would be checked and tested, the machine restarted, and so it would go on until the precise combination of settings had been found, at which point the cryptanalysts would be able to read that day's Shark traffic. Such, at any rate, was the theory.

The engineer began dragging out the other bombe and Jericho moved forward to help, but was stopped by a tugging on his arm.

'Come on, old love,' shouted Logie above the din. 'There's nothing more we can do here.' He pulled at his sleeve again.

Reluctantly, Jericho turned and followed him out of the hut.

*

He felt no sense of elation. Maybe tomorrow evening or maybe on Thursday, the bombes would give them the Enigma settings for the day now ending. Then the real work would begin – the laborious business of trying to reconstruct the new Short Weather Code Book – taking the meteorological data from the convoy, matching it to the weather signals already received from the surrounding U-boats, making some guesses, testing them, constructing a fresh set of cribs ... It never ended, this battle against Enigma. It was a chess tournament of a thousand rounds against a player of prodigious defensive strength, and each day the pieces went back to their original positions and the game began afresh.

Logie, too, seemed rather flat as they walked along the asphalt path towards Hut 8.

'I've sent the others home to their digs for some kip,' he was saying, 'which is where I'm going. And where you ought to go, too, if you're not too high to sleep.'

'I'll just clear up here for a bit, if that's all right. Take the code book back to the safe.'

'Do that. Thanks.'

'And then I suppose I'd better face Wigram.'

'Ah yes. Wigram.'

They went into the hut. In his office, Logie tossed Jericho the keys to the Black Museum. 'And your prize,' he said, holding up a half-bottle of scotch. 'Don't let's forget that.'

Jericho smiled. 'I thought you said Skynner was offering a full bottle.'

'Ah, well, yes, I did, but you know Skynner.'

'Give it to the others.'

'Oh, don't be so bloody pious.' From the same drawer Logie produced a couple of enamel mugs. He blew away some dust and wiped their insides with his forefinger. 'What shall we drink to? You don't mind if I join you?'

'The end of Shark? The future?'

Logie splashed a large measure of whisky into each mug. 'How about,' he said, shrewdly, offering one to Jericho, 'how about *your* future?'

They clinked mugs.

'*My* future.'

They sat in their overcoats, in silence, drinking.

'I'm defeated,' said Logie at last, using the desk to pull himself to his feet. 'I couldn't tell you the year, old love, never mind the day.' He had three pipes in a rack and he blew noisily through each of them, making a harsh, cracking sound, then slipped them into his pocket. 'Now don't forget your scotch.'

'I don't want the bloody scotch.'

'Take it. Please. For my sake.'

In the corridor, he shook Jericho's hand, and Jericho feared Logie was going to say something embarrassing. But whatever it was he had in mind, he thought better of it. Instead, he merely gave a rueful salute and lurched along the passage, banging the door behind him.

*

The Big Room, in anticipation of the midnight shift, was almost empty. A little desultory work was being done on Dolphin and Porpoise at the far end. Two young women in overalls were on their knees around Jericho's desk, gathering every scrap of waste paper into a couple of sacks, ready for incineration. Only Cave was still there, bent over his charts. He looked up as Jericho came in.

'Well? How's it going for you?'

'Too early to tell,' said Jericho. He found the code book and slipped it into his pocket. 'And you?'

'Three hit so far. A Norwegian freighter and a Dutch cargo ship. They just went straight to the bottom. The third's on fire and going round and round in circles. Half the crew lost, the other half trying to save her.'

'What is she?'

'American Liberty ship. The *James Oglethorpe*. Seven thousand tons, carrying steel and cotton.'

'American,' repeated Jericho. He thought of Kramer.

'*My brother died, one of the first ...*'

'It's a slaughter,' said Cave, 'an absolute bloody slaughter. And shall I tell you the worst of it? It's not going to finish tonight. It's going to go on and on like this for days. They're going to be chased and harried and torpedoed right the way across the bloody North Atlantic. Can you imagine what that feels like? Watching the ship next to you blow up? Not being allowed to stop and search for survivors? Waiting for your turn?' He touched his scar, then seemed to realise what he was doing and let his hand fall. There was a terrible resignation in the gesture. 'And now, apparently, they're picking up U-boat signals swarming all around SC-122.'

His telephone began to ring and he swung away to answer it. While his back was turned, Jericho quietly placed the half-empty half-bottle of scotch on his desk, then made his way out into the night.

*

His mind, on a fuel of Benzedrine and scotch, seemed to be wheeling away on a course of its own, churning like the bombes in Hut 11, making bizarre and random connections – Claire and Hester and Skynner, and Wigram with his shoulder holster, and the tyre tracks in the frost outside the cottage, and the blazing Liberty ship going round and round over the bodies of half her crew.

He stopped by the lake to breathe some fresh air and thought of all the other occasions when he had stood here in the darkness, gazing at the faint silhouette of the mansion against the stars. He half-closed his eyes and saw it as it might have been before the war. A midsummer evening. The sounds of an orchestra and a bubble of voices drifting across the lawn. A line of Chinese lanterns, pink and mauve and lemon, stirring in the arboretum. Chandeliers in the ballroom. White crystal fracturing on the smooth surface of the lake.

The vision was so strong that he found he was sweating in his overcoat against the imagined heat, and as he climbed the slope towards the big house he fancied he saw a line of silver Rolls-Royces, their chauffeurs leaning against the long bonnets. But as he drew closer he saw that the cars were merely buses, come to drop off the next shift, pick up the last, and that the music in the mansion was only the percussion of telephone bells and the tapping of hurrying footsteps on the stone floor.

In the labyrinth of the house he nodded cautiously to the few people he passed – an elderly man in a dark grey suit, an Army captain, a WAAF. They appeared seedy in the dingy light and he guessed, by their expressions, he must look pretty odd himself.

Benzedrine could do funny things to the pupils of your eyes, he seemed to remember, and he hadn't shaved or changed his clothes for more than forty hours. But nobody in Bletchley was ever thrown out for simply looking strange, or the place would have been empty from the start. There was old Dilly Knox, who used to come to work in his dressing gown, and Turing who cycled in wearing a gas mask to try to cure his hay fever, and the cryptanalyst from the Japanese section who had bathed naked in the lake one lunchtime. By comparison, Jericho was as conventional as an accountant.

He opened the door to the cellar passage. The bulb must have blown since his last visit and he found himself peering into a darkness as chill and black as a catacomb. Something gleamed very faintly at the foot of the stairs and he groped his way down the steps towards it. It was the keyhole to the Black Museum, traced in luminous paint: a trick they had learned in the Blitz.

Inside the room the light switch worked. He unlocked the safe and replaced the code book and for a moment he was seized by the crazy notion of hiding the stolen cryptograms inside it as well. Folded into an envelope they might pass unnoticed for months. But when, after tonight, was he likely to pass this way again? And one day they would be discovered. And then all it would take would be a telephone call to Beaumanor and everything would be unravelled – his involvement, Hester's ...

No, no.

He closed the steel door.

But still he couldn't quite bring himself to leave. So much of his life was here. He touched the safe and then the rough, dry walls. He drew his finger through the dust on the table. He contemplated the row of Enigmas on the metal shelf. They were all encased in light wood, mostly in their original German boxes, and even in repose they seemed to exude a compelling, almost menacing power. These were far more than mere machines, he thought. These were the synapses of the enemy's brain – mysterious, complex, *animate*.

He stared at them for a couple of minutes, then began to turn away.

He stopped himself.

'Tom Jericho,' he whispered. 'You bloody fool.'

The first two Enigmas he lifted down and inspected turned out to be badly damaged and unusable. The third had a luggage label attached to its handle by a bit of string: 'Sidi Bou Zid 14/2/43'. An Afrika Korps Enigma, captured by the Eighth Army during their attack on Rommel last month. He laid it carefully on the table and unfastened the metal clasps. The lid opened easily.

This one was in perfect condition: a beauty. The letters on the keys were unworn, the black metal casing unscratched, the glass bulbs clear and gleaming. The three rotors – stopped, he saw, at ZDE – glinted silver beneath the naked light. He stroked it tenderly. It must only just have left its makers. 'Chiffreirmaschine Gesellschaft,' read their label. 'Heimsoeth und Rinke, Berlin-Wilmersdorf, Uhlandstrasse 138.'

He pushed a key. It was stiffer than on a normal typewriter. When he had depressed it far enough, the machine emitted a clunk and the right-hand rotor moved on a notch. At the same time, one of the bulbs lit up.

Hallelujah!

The battery was charged. The Enigma was live.

He checked the mechanism. He stooped and typed C. The letter J lit up. He typed L and got a U. A, I, R and E yielded, successively, X, P, Q and Q again.

He lifted the Enigma's inner lid and detached the spindle, set the rotors back at ZDE and locked them into place. He typed the cryptogram JUXPQQ and C-L-A-I-R-E was spelled out letter by letter on the bulbs in little bursts of light.

He fumbled through his pockets for his watch. Two minutes to twelve.

He folded the lid back into place and hoisted the Enigma up on its shelf. He made sure to lock the door behind him.

To the people whom he ran past in the mansion's corridors, who was he? Nothing. Nobody. Just another peculiar cryptanalyst in a flap.

*

Hester Wallace, as agreed, was in the telephone box at midnight, the receiver in her hand, feeling more foolish than afraid as she pretended to make a call. Beyond the glass, two currents of pale sparks were flowing quietly in the dark, as one shift streamed in from the main gate and the other ebbed towards it. In her pocket was a sheet of Bletchley's wood-flecked, brownish notepaper on which were jotted six entries.

Cordingley had swallowed her story whole – indeed, he had been, if anything, a little *too* eager to help. Unable at first to locate the relevant file, he had called in aid a pimply, jug-eared youth with wispy yellow hair. Could this child, she had wondered, this foetus-face, really be a cryptanalyst? But Donald had whispered yes, he was one of the best: now the professions and the universities had all been picked over, they were turning to boys straight out of school. Unformed. Unquestioning. The new elite.

The file had been procured, a space cleared in a corner, and never had Miss Wallace made a pencil move more quickly. The worst part had been at the end: keeping her nerve and not fleeing when she'd finished, but checking the figures, returning the file to the Foetus, and observing the normal social code with Donald –

'*We really must have a drink one of these evenings.*'

'Yes really we must.'

'I'll be in touch, then.'

'Absolutely. So shall I.'

– neither, of course, having the slightest intention of ever doing so.

Come on, Tom Jericho.

Midnight passed. The first of the buses lumbered by – invisible, almost, except for its exhaust fumes, which made a puff of pink cloud in its red rear lights.

And then, just as she was beginning to give up hope, a blur of white. A hand tapped softly on the glass. She dropped the telephone and shone her torch on to the face of a lunatic pressed close to the pane. Dark wild eyes and a convict mask of shadowed beard. 'There's really no need to scare me half to death,' she muttered, but that was in the privacy of the phone booth. As she came out, all she said was: 'I've left your numbers on the telephone.'

She held the door open for him. His hand rested on hers. A brief moment of pressure signalled his thanks – too brief for her to tell whose fingers were the coldest.

'Meet me here at five.'

*

Exhilaration gave fresh energy to her tired legs as she pedalled up the hill away from Bletchley.

He needed to see her at five. How else could one interpret that, except as meaning he had found a way? A victory! A victory against the Mermagens and the Cordingleys!

The gradient steepened. She rose to tread the pedals. The bicycle waved from side to side like a metronome. The light danced on the road.

Afterwards, she was to reproach herself severely for this premature jubilation, but the truth was she would probably never have seen them anyway. They had positioned themselves quite carefully, drawn up parallel with the track and hidden by the hawthorn hedge – a professional job – so that when she came round the corner and began to bounce over the potholes towards the cottage she passed them in the shadows without a glance.

She was six feet from the door when the headlights came on – slitted blackout headlights, but dazzling enough to splash her shadow against the whitewashed wall. She heard the engine cough and turned, shielding her eyes, to see the big car coming at her – calm, unhurried, implacable, nodding over the bumpy ground.

5

Jericho told himself to take his time. There's no hurry. You've given yourself five hours. Use them.

He locked himself into the cellar room, leaving the key half turned in the keyhole, so that anyone trying to insert *their* key from the other side would find it blocked. He knew he'd have to open up eventually – otherwise, what was he? Just a rat in a trap. But at least he would now have thirty seconds' warning, and to give himself a cover story, he reopened the Naval Section safe and spread a handful of maps and code books across the narrow table. To these he added the stolen cryptograms and key settings, and his watch, which he placed before him with its lid open. Like preparing for an examination, he thought. '*Candidates must write on one side of the paper only; this margin to be left blank for the use of the examiner.*'

Then he lifted down the Enigma and removed the cover.

He listened. Nothing. A dripping pipe somewhere, that was all. The walls bulged with the pressure of the cold earth; he could smell the soil, taste the spores of damp lime plaster. He breathed on his fingers and flexed them.

He would work backwards, he decided, deciphering the last cryptogram first, on the theory that whatever had caused Claire's disappearance was contained somewhere in those final messages.

He ran his fingers down the columns of notation to find the Vulture settings for 4 March – panic day in the Bletchley Registry.

III V IV GAH CX AZ DV KT HU LW GP EY MR FQ

The Roman numerals told him which three out of the machine's five rotors were to be used that day, and what order they were to be placed in. GAH gave him the rotor starting positions. The next ten letter pairs represented the cross-pluggings he needed to make on the plugboard at the back of the Enigma. Six letters were left unconnected which, by some mysterious and glorious fold in the laws of statistics, actually increased the number of potential different cross-pluggings from almost 8 million million (25 × 23 × 21 × 19 × 17 × 15 × 13 × 11 × 9 × 7 × 5 × 3) to more than 150 million million.

He did the plugging first. Short lengths of corded, chocolate-coloured flex, tipped at either end by brass plugs sheathed in bakelite that sank with satisfying precision into the lettered sockets: C to X, A to Z ...

Next he lifted the Enigma's inner lid, unlocked the spindle, and slid off the three rotors that were already loaded. From a separate compartment he withdrew the two spares.

Each rotor was the size and thickness of an ice-hockey puck, but heavier: a code wheel with twenty-six terminals – pin-shaped and spring-loaded on one side, flat and circular on the other – with the letters of the alphabet engraved around the edge. As the rotors turned against one another, so the shape of the electrical circuit they completed varied. The right-hand rotor always moved on a letter each time a key was struck. Once every twenty-six letters, a notch in its alphabet ring caused the middle rotor also to move on a place. And when, eventually, the middle rotor reached its turnover position, the third rotor would move. Two rotors moving together was known at Bletchley as a crab; three was a lobster.

He sorted the rotors into the order of the day – III, V and IV – and slipped them on to the spindle. He twirled III and set it at the letter G, V at A and IV at H, and closed the lid.

The machine was now primed just as its twin had been in Smolensk on the evening of 4 March.

He touched the keys.

He was ready.

*

The Enigma worked on a simple principle. If, when the machine was set in a particular way, pressing key A completed a circuit that illuminated bulb X, then it followed – because electric current is reciprocal – that, in the same position, pressing key X would illuminate bulb A. Decoding was designed to be as easy as encoding.

Jericho realised quite quickly that something was going wrong. He would type a letter of the cryptogram with his left index finger and with his right hand make a note of the character illuminated on the display panel. T gave him H, R gave him Y, X gave him C ... This was no German he recognised. Still, he went on in the increasingly desperate hope it would start to come right. Only after forty-seven letters did he give up.

```
HYCYKWPIOROKDZENAJEWICZJPTAKJHRUTBPYSJMOTYLPCIE
```

He ran his hands through his hair.

Sometimes an Enigma operator would insert meaningless padding around proper words to disguise the sense of his message, but never this much, surely? There *were* no proper words that he could discern hidden anywhere in this gibberish.

He groaned, leaned back in his chair and stared at the flaking plaster ceiling.

Two possibilities, each equally unpleasant.

One: the message had been super-enciphered, its plaintext scrambled once, and then again to make its meaning doubly obscure. A time-consuming technique, usually reserved for only the most secret communications.

Two: Hester had made a mistake in transcription – had got, perhaps, just one letter wrong – in which case he could sit here, literally for the rest of his life, and still he would never make the cryptogram disgorge its secrets.

Of the two explanations, the latter was the more likely.

He paced around his cell for a while, trying to get some circulation back into his legs and arms. Then he set the rotors back at GAH and made an attempt to decipher the second message from 4 March. The same result:

SZULCJK UKAH ...

He didn't even bother with the third and fourth but instead played around with the rotor settings – GEH, GAN, CAH – in the hope she might simply have got one letter wrong, but all the Enigma winked at him was more gobbledygook.

*

Four in the car. Hester in the back seat next to Wigram. Two men in the front. The doors all locked, the heater on, a stench of cigarette smoke and sweat so strong that Wigram had his paisley scarf pressed delicately to his nose. He kept his face half-turned from her all journey and didn't say a word until they reached the main road. Then they pulled across the white lines to overtake another car and their driver switched on a police bell.

'Oh, for Christ's sake, Leveret, cut it out.'

The noise stopped. The car swerved left, then right. They jolted down a rutted track and Hester's fingers sank deeper into the leather upholstery as she strained to avoid toppling into Wigram. She hadn't spoken, either – it was her single, token gesture of defiance, this silence. She was damned if she was going to show her nerves by babbling like a girl.

After a couple of minutes they stopped somewhere and Wigram sat motionless, a statesman, while his men in the front seats scrambled out. One of them opened his door. Torches flashed in the darkness. Shadows appeared. A welcoming committee.

'Got those lights up yet, inspector?' asked Wigram.

'Yes, sir.' A deep male voice; a Midlands accent. 'A lot of complaints from the air raid people, though.'

'Well, they can frig off for a start. Jerry wants to bomb this place, he's welcome. Got the plans?'

'Yes, sir.'

'Good-oh.' Wigram grabbed the roof and hoisted himself out on the running board. He waited a second or two and when Hester didn't move he ducked back inside and flexed his fingers irritably. 'Come on, come on. D'you expect me to carry you?'

She slid across the seat.

Two other cars – no, *three* other cars with their headlights on, showing the cut-out patterns of men moving, plus a small Army truck and an ambulance. It was the ambulance that shook her. Its doors were open and, as Wigram guided her past it, his hand lightly on her elbow, she caught the smell of disinfectant, saw the dun-coloured oxygen cylinders, the stretchers with their coarse brown blankets, their leather straps, their innocent white sheets. Two men sat on the rear bumper, legs outstretched, smoking. They stared at her without interest.

'Been here before?' said Wigram.

'Where are we?'

'Lovers' lane. Not your scene, I fancy.'

He was holding a flashlight and as he stood aside to usher her through a gate she saw a sign: DANGER: FLOODED CLAY PIT – VERY DEEP WATER. She could hear a guttural engine somewhere ahead, and the cry of sea-birds. She started to shake.

'*The hand of the Lord was upon me, and carried me out in the spirit of the Lord, and set me down in the midst of the valley which was full of bones.*'

'D'you say something?' asked Wigram.

'I don't believe so.'

Oh, Claire, Claire, Claire ...

The engine noise was louder now, and seemed to be coming from inside a brick building to her left. A faint white light shone up through the gaps in its roof to reveal a tall, square chimney, its lower part engulfed by ivy. She was vaguely aware that they were at the head of a procession. Behind them came the driver, Leveret, and then the second man from the car wearing a belted gaberdine, and then the police inspector.

'Mind yourself here,' warned Wigram, and he tried to take her arm again but she shook him off. She picked her own way between the clumps of brick and the towering weeds, heard voices, turned a corner, and was confronted by a dazzling line of arc lights illuminating a broad path. Six policemen were working their way along it, in parallel, on their hands and knees among a glitter of broken glass and rubble. Behind them, one soldier tended a shuddering generator; another unreeled a drum of cable; a third was rigging more lights.

Wigram grinned and winked at her, as if to say: See what I can command. He was pulling on a pair of light brown, calfskin gloves. 'Got something to show you.'

In a corner of the building, a police sergeant stood beside a rumpled heap of sacks. Hester had to will her legs to move forwards. *Please, Lord, don't let it be her.*

'Get your notebook out,' said Wigram to the sergeant. He hoisted the tails of his overcoat and squatted on his haunches. 'I am showing the witness, first, one ladies' coat, ankle-length by the look of it, colour grey, trimmed with black velvet.' He drew it completely out of the sack and turned it over. 'Grey satin lining. Quite badly stained. Probably blood. Need to check it. Collar label: "Hunters, Burlington Arcade". And the witness responded?' He held it up, without looking round.

Remember, I said, 'That's too beautiful to put on every day,' and you said, 'Silly old Hester, that's the only reason there is to wear it'?

'And the witness *responded?*'

'It's hers.'

' "It's hers." Got that? Good. OK. Next. One ladies' shoe. Left foot. Black. High heel. Heel snapped off. Hers, d'you think?'

'How can I tell? One shoe –'

'Largish. Say, size seven. Eight. What size did she take?'

A pause, then Hester, quietly: 'Seven.'

'We've found the other one outside, sir,' said the inspector. 'Near the water's edge.'

'And a pair of knickers. White. Silk. Badly blood-stained.' He held them out at arm's length between finger and thumb. 'Recognise these, Miss Wallace?' He let them drop and rummaged in the bottom of the sack. 'Final item. One brick.' He shone his flashlight onto it; something glinted. 'Also bloodstained. Blonde hairs attached.'

*

'Eleven main buildings,' said the inspector. 'Eight of them with kilns, four with chimneys still standing. Rail spur here with sidings, linking into the main line, and a branch going off here, right through the site.'

They were outside now, at the spot where the second shoe had been found, and the map was spread over a rusting water tank. Hester stood away from them, Leveret watching her, his hands hanging loosely by his sides. There were more men moving down by the water's edge, torches stabbing the night.

'Local fishing club use a shed here, near the jetty. Three rowing boats usually stored.'

'Usually?'

'Door's been kicked in, sir. Season's over. That's why nobody discovered it. A boat's missing.'

'Since?'

'Well, there was some fishing on Sunday. Deep ledgering for carp. That was the last day of the season. Everything was all right then. So any time from Sunday night onwards.'

'Sunday. And we're now into Wednesday.' Wigram sighed and shook his head.

The inspector spread his hands. 'With respect, sir, I have three men stationed in Bletchley. Bedford lent us six, Buckingham nine. We're two miles from the centre of town. There is a limit. Sir.'

Wigram didn't seem to hear him. 'And how big's the lake?'

'About a quarter of a mile across.'

'Deep?'

'Yes, sir.'

'What – twenty, thirty feet?'

'At the edges. Shelving to sixty. Could be seventy. It's an old working. They built the town with what they dug out here.'

'Did they really?' Wigram flashed his light across the lake. 'Makes sense, I suppose. Making one hole out of another.' Mist was rising, swirling in the breeze like steam above a cauldron. He swung the beam round and pointed it back at the building. 'So what happened here?' he said softly. 'Our man lures her out for a shag on Sunday night. Kills her, probably with that brick. Drags her down here ...' The beam traced the path from the kilns to the water. 'Strong man – must have been, she was a big girl. Then what? Gets a boat. Stuffs the body in a sack maybe. Weights it with bricks. That's obvious. Rows it out. Dumps it. A muffled splash at midnight, just like in the pictures ... He probably meant to come back for the clothes as well, but something put him off. Perhaps the next pair of lovebirds had already arrived.' He played the light over the mist again. 'Seventy feet deep. Frigging hell! We'll need to put a submarine down there to find her.'

'May I go now?' said Hester. She had kept herself very quiet and composed so far, but now the tears had started and she was drawing in great gulps of air.

Wigram aimed the beam at her wet face. 'No,' he said sadly. 'I'm rather afraid you can't.'

*

Jericho was replugging the cipher machine as quickly as his numb fingers would permit him.

Enigma settings for German Army key Vulture, 6 February 1943:

IVIII DMR EY JL AK NV FZ CT HP MX BQ GS

The final four cryptograms were hopeless, a disaster, mere

chaos out of chaos. He had wasted too much time on them already. He would begin again, this time with the first signal. E to Y, J to L. And if this didn't work? Don't even think it. A to K, N to V ... He lifted the lid, unfastened the spindle, slid off the rotors. Above his head, the great house was silent. He was too deeply entombed to hear a footstep. He wondered what they were doing up there. Looking for him? Probably. And if they woke up Logie it wouldn't take them long to find him. He slid the rotors into place – first, fifth, third – and clicked them round to DMR.

Almost at once he began to sense success. First C and X, which were nulls, and then A, N, O, K, H.

An OKH ...

To OKH. *Oberkommando des Heeres.* The High Command of the Army.

A miracle.

His finger hammered away at the key. The lights flashed.

An OKH/BEFEHL. To the office of the Commander-in-Chief.

Dringend.

Urgent.

Melde Auffindung zahlreicher menschlicher Überreste zwölf Km westlich Smolensk ...

Discovered yesterday twelve kilometres west Smolensk human remains ...

*

Hester was locked in the car with Wigram, Leveret standing guard outside.

Jericho. He was asking her about Jericho. Where was he? What was he doing? When did she last see him?

'He's left the hut. He's not at his digs. He's not at the cottage. I ask you: Where the hell else is there to go in this frigging town?'

She said nothing.

He tried shouting at her, pounding his fist on the seat in front, and then, when that didn't work, he gave her his handkerchief and tried sympathy, but the scent of cologne on the silk and the memory of the blonde hair gilding the brick made her want to be sick and he had to wind his window down and get Leveret to come round and open her door.

'They've found the boat, sir,' said Leveret. 'Blood in the bottom.'

*

Just before three o'clock, Jericho had the first message deciphered:

TO THE OFFICE OF THE COMMANDER IN CHIEF. URGENT. DISCOVERED TWELVE KILOMETRES WEST SMOLENSK EVIDENCE HUMAN REMAINS. BELIEVED EXTENSIVE, POSSIBLY THOUSANDS. HOW AM I TO PROCEED? LACHMAN, OBERST, FIELD POLICE.

Jericho sat back and contemplated this marvel. Well, yes, Herr Oberst, how are you to proceed? I die to know.

Once again he began the tedious procedure of replugging and re-rotoring the Enigma. The next signal had been sent from Smolensk three days later, on 9 February. A, N, O, K, H, B, E, F, E, H, L ... The exquisite formality of the German armed forces unfolded before him. And then a null, and then G, E, S, T, E, R, N, U, N, D, H, E, U, T, E.

Gestern und heute. Yesterday and today.

And so on, letter by letter, inescapably, remorselessly – press, *clunk*, light, note – stopping occasionally to massage his fingers and straighten his back, the whole ghastly story made worse by the slowness with which he had to read it, his eyeballs pressed to the crime. Some of the words gave him difficulty. What was *mumifiziert*? Could it be 'mummified'? And *Sagemehl geknebelt*? 'Gagged with sawdust'?

PRELIMINARY EXCAVATION UNDERTAKEN IN FOREST NORTH DNIEPER CASTLE YESTERDAY AND TODAY. SITE APPROXIMATELY TWO HUNDRED SQUARE METRES. TOPSOIL COVERING TO DEPTH OF ONE POINT FIVE METRES PLANTED PINE SAPLINGS. FIVE LAYERS CORPSES. UPPER MUMMIFIED LOWER LIQUID. TWENTY BODIES RECOVERED. DEATH CAUSED BY SINGLE SHOT HEAD. HANDS BOUND WIRE. MOUTHS GAGGED CLOTH AND SAWDUST. MILITARY UNIFORMS, HIGH BOOTS AND MEDALS INDICATE VICTIMS POLISH OFFICERS. SEVERE FROST AND HEAVY SNOWFALL OBLIGE US SUSPEND OPERATIONS PENDING THAW. I SHALL CONTINUE MY INVESTIGATIONS. LACHMAN, OBERST, FIELD POLICE.

Jericho took a tour around his little cell, flapping his arms and stamping his feet. It seemed to him to be peopled with ghosts, grinning at him with toothless mouths blasted into the backs of their heads. He was walking in the forest himself. The cold sliced his flesh. And when he stopped and listened he could hear the sound of trees being uprooted, of spades and pickaxes ringing on frozen earth.

Polish officers?

Puck?

The third signal, after a gap of eleven days had been sent on 20th February. *Nach Eintreten Tauwetter Exhumierungen im Wald bei Katyn fortgesetzt ...*

FOLLOWING THAW KATYN FOREST EXCAVATIONS RESUMED EIGHT

HUNDRED YESTERDAY. FIFTY-TWO CORPSES EXAMINED. QUANTITIES OF PERSONAL LETTERS, MEDALS, POLISH CURRENCY RECOVERED. ALSO SPENT PISTOL CARTRIDGE CASES SEVEN POINT SIX FIVE MILLIMETRE STAMPED QUOTE GECO D UNQUOTE. INTERROGATION LOCAL POPULATION ESTABLISHES ONE EXECUTIONS CONDUCTED NKVD DURING SOVIET OCCUPATION MARCH AND APRIL NINETEEN HUNDRED AND FORTY. TWO VICTIMS BELIEVED BROUGHT FROM KOZIELSK DETENTION CAMP BY RAIL TO GNIEZDOVO STATION TAKEN INTO FOREST AT NIGHT IN GROUPS ONE HUNDRED SHOTS HEARD. THREE TOTAL NUMBER VICTIMS ESTIMATED TEN THOUSAND REPEAT TEN THOUSAND. ASSISTANCE URGENTLY REQUIRED IF FURTHER EXCAVATION DESIRED.

Jericho sat motionless for fifteen minutes, gazing at the Enigma, trying to comprehend the scale of the implications. This was a secret it was dangerous to know, he thought. This was a secret big enough to swallow a person whole. Ten thousand Poles – our gallant Allies, survivors of an army that had charged the Wehrmacht's Panzers on horseback, waving swords – *ten thousand* of them trussed, gagged and shot by our other, more recent, gallant Allies, the heroic Soviet Union? No wonder the Registry had been cleared.

An idea occurred to him and he went back to the first cryptogram. For if one looked at it thus:

HYCYKWPIOROKDZENAJEWICZJPTAKJHRUTBPYSJMOTYLPCIE

it was meaningless, but if one rearranged it thus:

HYCYK, W., PIORO, K., DZENAJEWICZ, J., PTAK, J., HRUT, B., PYS, J., MOTYL, P., –

then out of the chaos was conjured order. Names.

He had enough now. He could have stopped. But he went on anyway, for he was never a man to leave a mystery partially solved, a mathematical proof only half worked-out. One had to sketch in the route to the answer, even if one had guessed at the destination long before the journey's end.

Enigma settings for German Army key Vulture, 2 March 1943:

III IV II   LUK   JP DY QS HL AE NW CU IK FX BR

An Ostubaf Dorfmann. Ostubaf for *Obersturmbannführer*. A Gestapo rank.

TO OBERSTURMBANNFUHRER DORFMANN RHSA
ON ORDERS OFFICE COMMANDER IN CHIEF NAMES OF POLISH
OFFICERS IDENTIFIED TO DATE IN KATYN FOREST AS FOLLOWS

He didn't bother to write them down. He knew what he was looking for and he found it after an hour, buried in a babble of other names. It wasn't sent to the Gestapo on the 2nd, but on the 3rd:

PUKOWSKI, T.

6

A few minutes after 5 a.m., Tom Jericho surfaced, molelike, from his subterranean hole, and stood in the passage of the mansion, listening. The Enigma had been returned to its shelf, the safe locked, the door to the Black Museum locked as well. The cryptograms and the settings were in his pocket. He had left no trace. He could hear footsteps and male voices coming towards him and he drew back against the wall, but whoever they were they didn't come his way. The wooden staircase creaked as they passed on, out of sight, up to the offices in the bedrooms.

He moved cautiously, keeping close to the wall. If Wigram had gone looking for him in the hut at midnight and failed to find him, what would he have done? He would have gone to Albion Street. And seeing Jericho hadn't turned up there, he might by now have roused a considerable search party. And Jericho didn't want to be found, not yet. There were too many questions he had to ask, and only one man had the answers.

He passed the foot of the staircase and opened the double doors that led to the lobby.

You became her lover, didn't you, Puck? The next after me in the great revolving door of Claire Romilly's men. And somehow – how? – you knew that something terrible was going on in that ghastly forest. Wasn't that why you sought her out? Because she had access to information you couldn't get to? And she must have agreed to help, must have started copying out anything that looked of interest. (*'She'd really been much more attentive of late...'*) And then there came the nightmare day when you realised – who? your father? your brother? – was buried in that hideous place. And then, the next day, all she could bring you was cryptograms, because the British – the British: your trusty Allies, your loyal protectors, to whom the Poles had entrusted the secret of Enigma – the British had decided that in the higher interest they simply didn't want to know any more.

Puck, Puck, what have you done?

What have you done with her?

There was a sentry in the Gothic entry hall, a couple of cryptanalysts talking quietly on a bench, a WAAF with a stack of box files struggling to find the doorhandle with her elbow. Jericho opened it for her and she smiled her thanks and made a rolling motion with her eyes, as if to say: *What a place to find ourselves at five o'clock on a spring morning*, and Jericho smiled and nodded back, a fellow sufferer: *Yes, indeed, what a place* ...

The WAAF went one way and he went the other, towards the morning star and the main gate. The sky was black, the telephone box almost invisible in the shadows of the arboretum. It was empty. He walked straight past it and pushed his way into the vegetation. Sir Herbert Leon, the last Victorian master of the Park, had been a dedicated arborist, planting his realm with three hundred different species of tree. Forty years of re-seeding, followed by four years without pruning, had turned the arboretum into a labyrinth of secret chambers, and here Jericho squatted on the dry earth and waited for Hester Wallace.

By five fifteen it was clear to him she wasn't coming, which suggested she had been detained. In which case, they were almost certainly looking for him.

He had to get out of the Park, and he couldn't risk the main gate.

At five twenty, when his eyes were thoroughly used to the dark, he began to move northwards through the arboretum, back towards the house, his bundle of secrets heavy in his pocket. He could still feel the effects of the Benzedrine – a lightness in his muscles, an acuteness in his mind, especially to danger – and he offered a prayer of thanks to Logie for making him take it, because otherwise by now he'd be half-dead.

Puck, Puck, what have you done?

What have you done with her?

He came out cautiously from between two sycamores and

stepped on to the lawn at the side of the mansion. Ahead of him was the long, low outline of the old Hut 4, with the mass of the big house behind it. He skirted it and went around the back, past some rubbish bins and into the courtyard. Here were the stables where he'd started work in 1939, and beyond those the cottage where Dilly Knox had first pried into the mysteries of the Enigma. Drawn up in a semicircle on the cobbles he could just make out the gleaming cylinders and exhausts of half a dozen motorcycles. A door opened and in the brief glow he saw a dispatch rider, padded, helmeted and gauntleted, like a medieval knight. Jericho pressed himself against the brickwork and waited while the motorcyclist adjusted his pillion, then kicked the machine into life and revved it. Its red light dwindled and disappeared through the rear gate.

He considered, briefly, trying to get out using the same exit, but reason told him that if the main entrance was probably being watched, then so was this. He stumbled on past the cottage, past the back of the tennis courts, and finally past the bombe hut, throbbing like an engine shed in the darkness.

By now a faint blue stain had begun to seep up from the rim of the sky. Night – his friend and ally, his only cover – was preparing to desert him. Ahead, he could begin to make out the contours of a building site. Pyramids of earth and sand. Squat rectangles of bricks and sweet-smelling timber.

Jericho had never before paid much notice to Bletchley's perimeter fence, which turned out, on inspection, to be a formidable stockade of seven-foot-high iron stakes, tapering at their tips into triple spears, bent outwards to deter incursion. It was as he was running his hands over the galvanised metal that he heard a swish of movement in the undergrowth just beyond it, to his left. He took a few steps backwards and retreated behind a stack of steel girders. A moment later, a sentry ambled past, in no great state of alertness, to judge by his slouched silhouette and the shuffle of his step.

Jericho crouched lower, listening as the sounds faded. The perimeter was perhaps a mile long. Say, fifteen minutes for a sentry to complete a circuit. Say, two sentries patrolling. Possibly three.

If there were three, he had five minutes.

He looked around to see what he could use.

A two-hundred-gallon drum proved too heavy for him to shift, but there were planks, and some thick sections of concrete drainage pipe, both of which he found he was able to drag over to the fence. He started to sweat again. Whatever they were building here, it was going to be vast – vast and bombproof. In the gloom the excavations were fathomless. 'FIVE LAYERS CORPSES. UPPER MUMMIFIED LOWER LIQUID ...'

He upended the pipes and stood them about five feet apart. He laid a plank on top. Then he hefted a second set of pipes on to the first, picked up another length of timber and staggered over with it balanced on his shoulder. He set it down carefully, making a platform with two steps – about the first practical thing he had made since boyhood. He climbed on to the rickety structure and seized the iron spears. His feet scrabbled for a purchase on the rails. But the fence was designed to keep people out, not in. Fuelled by chemicals and desperation, Jericho was just able to pull himself astride it, twist, and lower himself down the other side. He dropped the last three feet and stayed there, squatting in the long grass, recovering his breath, listening.

His final act was to put his foot through the railings and kick away the planks.

He didn't wait to see if the noise had attracted attention. He set off across the field, walking at first, then trotting and finally running, sliding and skidding over the dewy grass. There was a big military camp to his right, concealed by a line of trees only just now materialising. Behind him, he could sense the dawn on his shoulders, brightening by the minute. He looked back only when he reached the road, and that was his last impression of Bletchley Park: a thin line of low, black buildings – mere dots and dashes along the horizon – and above them in the eastern sky an immense arc of cold blue light.

*

He had been to Puck's digs once before, on a Sunday afternoon a year ago, for a game of chess. He had a vague memory of an elderly landlady who doted on Puck pouring them tea in a cramped front room, while her invalid husband wheezed and coughed and retched upstairs. He could remember the game quite clearly, it had a curious shape to it – Jericho very strong in the opening, Puck in the middle, and Jericho again at the end. A draw agreed.

Alma Terrace. That was it. Alma Terrace. Number nine.

He was moving quickly – long strides and an occasional, loping run – keeping to the side of the pavement, down the hill and into the sleeping town. Outside the pub lingered a soapy smell of last night's beer. The Methodist chapel a few doors down was dark and bolted, its blistered sign unchanged since the outbreak of war: 'Repent ye: for the Kingdom of Heaven is at hand.' He went under the railway bridge. On the opposite side of the road was Albion Street, and a little further along the Bletchley Working Men's Club ('The Co-Operative Society Presents a Talk by Councillor A. E. Braithwaite: The Soviet Economy, Its Lessons for Us'). After another twenty yards he turned left into Alma Terrace.

It was a street like so many others: a double row of tiny red-brick houses running parallel with the railway. Number nine was a clone of all the rest: two little windows upstairs and one downstairs, all three swathed in blackout curtains as though in mourning, a spade's length of front yard with a dustbin in it, and a wooden gate to the road. The gate was broken, the timber splintered grey and smooth like driftwood, and Jericho had to hoist it open. He tried the door – locked – and hammered on it with his fist.

A loud coughing – as loud and immediate as a woken guard dog. He stepped back a pace and after a couple of seconds one of the upstairs curtains flickered open. He shouted: 'Puck, I need to talk to you.'

A steady clop-clop of hooves. He glanced up the road to see a coal dray turning into the street. It passed by slowly and the driver took a good, long look at him, then flicked the reins and the big horse responded, the tempo of its hooves increasing. Behind him Jericho heard a bolt being worked and drawn back. The door opened a crack. An old woman peered out.

'I'm so sorry,' said Jericho, 'but it's an emergency, I need to speak to Mr Pukowski.'

She hesitated, then let him in. She was less than five feet tall, a wraith, with a pale blue, quilted housecoat clutched across her nightdress. She spoke with her hand held in front of her mouth and he realised she was embarrassed because she didn't have her teeth in.

'He's in his room.'

'Could you show me?'

She shuffled down the passage and he followed. The coughing from upstairs had intensified. It seemed to shake the ceiling, to swing the grimy lampshade.

'Mr Puck?' She tapped on the door. 'Mr Puck?' She said to Jericho: 'He must be still asleep. I heard him come in late.'

'Let me. May I?'

The little room was empty. Jericho was across it in three strides, pulling back the curtains. Grey light lit the kingdom of the exile: a single bed, a washstand, a wardrobe, a wooden chair, a small mirror of thick, pink, crystalled glass with birds carved into it, suspended above the mantelpiece by a metal chain. The bed had been lain on rather than slept in, and a saucer by the bedhead was filled with cigarette stubs.

He turned back to the window. The inevitable vegetable patch and hooped bomb shelter. A wall.

'What's over there?'

'But the door was bolted –'

'On the other side of the wall? What's over there?'

With her hand in front of her mouth she looked aghast. 'The station.'

He tried the window. It was jammed shut.

'Is there a back door?'

She led him through a kitchen that couldn't have altered much since Victorian days. A mangle. A hand pump for raising water to the sink ...

The back door was unlocked.

'He's all right isn't he?' She'd stopped worrying about her teeth. Her mouth was trembling, the skin around it furrowed, sunken, brown.

'I'm sure. You go back to your husband.'

He was following Puck's trail now. Footprints – large footprints – led across the vegetable patch. A tea chest stood against the wall. It bowed and splintered as Jericho mounted it, but he was just able to fold himself over the top of the sooty brickwork. For a moment he almost tumbled head first on to the concrete path, but then he managed to brace himself and brought his legs up.

In the distance: the whistle of a train.

*

He hadn't run like this for fifteen years, not since he was a schoolboy being screamed at on a five-mile steeplechase. But here they were again, as grim as ever, the familiar instruments of torture – the knife in his side, the acid in his lungs, the taste of rust in his mouth.

He tore through the back entrance into Bletchley Station and flailed around the corner on to the platform, through a cloud of leaden-coloured pigeons that flapped and rose heavily and settled again. His feet rang on the ironwork of the footbridge. He took the stairs two at a time and ran across the gantry. A fountain of white smoke spurted up to his left, his right, and filtered through the floorboards, as the locomotive passed slowly underneath.

The hour was early, the waiting crowd was small, and Jericho was halfway down the steps to the northbound platform when he spotted Puck about fifty yards away, standing close to the tracks, holding a small suitcase, his head turning to follow the slow parade of compartments. Jericho stopped and clutched the hand rail, bent forwards, struggling for air. The Benzedrine, he realised, was wearing off. When the train at last jolted to a stop, Puck looked around, walked casually towards the front, opened a door and disappeared.

Using the rail to support himself, Jericho picked his way down the last few steps and almost toppled into an empty compartment.

He must have blacked out, and for several minutes, because he never heard the door slam behind him or the whistle blow. The next thing he was conscious of was a rocking motion. The banquette was warm and dusty to his cheek and through it he could feel the soothing rhythm of the wheels – *dah-dah-dee-dee, dee-dee-dah-dah, dah-dah-dee-dee* ... He opened his eyes. Smudges of bluish cloud edged in pink slipped slowly across a square of white sky. It was all very beautiful, like a nursery, and he could have fallen asleep again, but for a vague recollection that there was something dark and threatening he was supposed to be afraid of, and then he remembered.

Levering himself up, he ministered to his aching head – shook it, rotated it in a figure of eight, then pushed down the window and thrust it into the cold draught of rushing air. No sign of any town. Just flat, hedged countryside, interspersed with barns and ponds that glinted in the morning light. The track was curving slightly and ahead he could see the locomotive flying its long pennant of smoke above a black wall of carriages. They were heading north on the main west-coast line, which meant – he tried to recall – Northampton next, then Coventry, Birmingham, Manchester (probably), Liverpool ...

Liverpool?

Liverpool. And the ferry across the Irish Sea.

Jesus.

He was stunned by the unreality of it all, yet at the same time by its simplicity, its obviousness. There was a communication cord above the opposite row of seats ('Penalty for improper use: £20') and his immediate reaction was to pull it. But then what? *Think*. He would be left, unshaven, ticketless, drug-eyed, trying to convince some sceptical guard there was a traitor on board, while Puck – what would Puck do? He would climb down from the train and disappear. Jericho suddenly saw the full absurdity of his own situation. He didn't even have enough money to buy a ticket. All he had was a pocketful of cryptograms.

Get rid of them.

He pulled them from his pocket and tore them into fragments, then hung his head back out of the window and released them into the slipstream. They were whipped away, borne up and over the top of the carriage and out of sight. Craning his head the other way, he tried to guess how far up the train Puck was. The force of the wind stifled him. Three carriages? Four? He pulled back in and closed the window, then crossed the swaying compartment and slid open the door to the corridor.

He peered out, carefully.

The rolling stock was standard, pre-war, dark and filthy. The corridor, lit for the blackout by faint blue bulbs, was the colour of a poison bottle. Four compartments off to one side. A connecting door at the front and rear led into the adjacent carriages.

Jericho lurched towards the head of the train. He glanced into each compartment as he passed. Here were a pair of sailors playing cards, there a young couple asleep in one another's arms, there again a family – mother, father, boy and girl – sharing sandwiches and a flask of tea. The mother had a baby at her breast and turned away, embarrassed, when she saw him looking.

He opened the door leading to the next carriage and stepped into no man's land. The floor shifted and pitched beneath his feet like a catwalk at a funfair. He stumbled and banged his knee. Through a three-inch gap he could see the couplings clanking and, beneath them, the rushing ground. He let himself into the other carriage in time to see the big, unsmiling face of the guard emerging from a compartment. Jericho slipped smartly into the lavatory and locked himself in. For a moment he thought he was sharing it with some tramp or derelict but then he realised that this was *him* – the yellowish face, the dwindled and feverish eyes, the windblown hair, the two days' growth of blue-black beard – this was *his* reflection. The toilet was blocked and stinking. A trail of sodden, soiled paper curled from its bowl and wrapped around his feet like an unravelled bandage.

'Ticket please.' The guard rapped loudly. 'Slide your ticket under the door, please.'

'It's in my compartment.'

'Oh, is it then?' The handle rattled. 'You'd better come and show me.'

'I'm not feeling awfully well.' (Which was true.) 'I've left it out for you.' He pressed his burning forehead to the cool mirror. 'Just give me five minutes.'

The guard grunted. 'I'll be back.' Jericho heard the rush of wheels as the connecting door opened, then the slam of it closing. He waited a few seconds then flipped open the lock.

There was no sign of Puck in this carriage, or in the next, and by the time he'd leaped the gyrating iron plates into the third he could sense the train beginning to slow. He moved on down the corridor.

Two compartments filled with soldiers, six in each, sullen-looking, their rifles stacked at their feet.

Then one empty compartment.

Then Puck.

*

He was sitting with his back to the engine, leaning forwards – the same old Puck, handsome, intense, his elbows on his knees, engrossed in conversation with someone just out of Jericho's line of sight.

It was Claire, thought Jericho. It had to be Claire. It would be Claire. He was taking her with him.

He turned his back on the compartment and moved discreetly crabwise, pretending to look out of the dirty window. His eyes registered an approaching town – scrubland, goods wagons, warehouses – and then an anonymous platform with a clock frozen at ten to twelve, and faded posters with jolly, buxom girls advertising long-dead holidays in Bournemouth and Clacton-on-Sea.

The train crawled along for a few more yards, then stopped abruptly opposite the station buffet.

'Northampton!' shouted a man's voice. 'Northampton Station!'

And if it was Claire, what would he do?

But it wasn't her. He looked and saw a *man*, a young man – neat, dark, tanned, aquiline: in every essence, *foreign* – saw him only briefly because the man was already up on his feet and releasing Puck's hand from a double clasp. The young man smiled (he had very white teeth) and nodded – some transaction had been completed – and then he was stepping out of the compartment and was moving quickly across the platform, sharp shoulders slicing through the crowd. Puck watched him for a moment, then pulled the door shut and sank back into his seat, out of sight.

Whatever his escape plans, they did not appear to include Claire Romilly.

Jericho jerked his gaze away.

Suddenly he saw what must have happened. Puck cycling over to the cottage on Saturday night to retrieve the cryptograms – and instead finding Jericho. Puck returning later to discover the cryptograms were missing. And Puck assuming, naturally, that Jericho had them and was about to do what any loyal servant of the state would do: run straight to the authorities and turn Claire in.

He glanced back at the compartment. Puck must have lit a cigarette. Films of smoke were settling into wide, steel-blue strata.

But you couldn't allow that, could you, because she was the only link between you and the stolen papers? And you needed time to plan this escape with your foreign friend.

So what have you done with her?

A whistle. A frantic working-up of steam. The platform shuddered and began to slide away. Jericho barely noticed, unconscious of everything except the inescapable sum of his calculations.

*

What happened next happened very quickly and if there was never to be a single, coherent explanation of events, that was due to a combination of factors: the amnesia induced by violence, the deaths of two of the participants, the bureaucratic fog-machine of the Official Secrets Act.

But it went something like this.

About two miles north of Northampton Station, close to the village of Kingsthorpe, a set of points connected the west-coast main line with the branch line to Rugby. With five minutes notice, the train was diverted off its scheduled course, westwards down the branch line, and very shortly afterwards a red signal warned the driver of an obstruction on the tracks ahead.

The train was therefore already slowing, although he didn't recognise it, when Jericho slid open the door to Puck's compartment. It moved very easily, at a finger's pressure. The layers of smoke rippled and erupted.

Puck was just extinguishing the cigarette (his ashtray was subsequently found to contain five stubs) and he was pushing down the window – presumably because he had noticed the loss of speed, and maybe the diversion, and was suspicious and wanted to see what was happening. He heard the door behind him and turned, and his face, in that instant, became a skull. His flesh was shrunken, tautened, masklike. He was already a dead man, and he knew it. Only his eyes were still alive, glittering beneath his high forehead. They flickered from Jericho to the corridor to the window and back to Jericho. A frantic effort was going on behind them, you could see, a mad and hopeless attempt to compute odds, angles, trajectories.

Jericho said: 'What have you done with her?'

Puck had the stolen Smith and Wesson in his hand, safety catch off. He brought it up. His eyes went through the same routine: Jericho, corridor, window, then Jericho again and finally the window. He tilted his head back, keeping the gun held out at arm's length, and tried to see up the track.

'Why are we stopping?'

'What have you done with her?'

Puck waved him back with the gun, but Jericho didn't care what happened now. He took a step closer.

Puck began to say something like 'Please don't make me' and then – farce, as the door slid open and the guard came in for Jericho's ticket.

For a long moment they stood there, this curious trio – the guard with his large, bland face, creasing with surprise; the traitor with his wavering pistol; the cryptanalyst between them – and then several things happened more or less at once. The guard said 'Give me that' and made a lunge at Puck. The gun went off. The noise of it was like a physical blow. The guard said 'Ooof?' in a puzzled way, and looked down at his stomach as if he had a bad twinge of indigestion. The wheels of the train locked and screamed and suddenly they were all on the floor together.

It may have been that Jericho was the first to crawl free. Certainly he had a memory of actually helping Puck to his feet, of pulling him out from beneath the guard, who was making a ghastly keening sound and leaking blood everywhere – from his mouth and his nose, from the front of his tunic, even from the bottom of his trouser legs.

Jericho knelt over him and said, rather fatuously, because he'd never seen anyone injured before: 'He needs a doctor.' There was a commotion in the corridor. He turned to find that Puck had the outside door open and the Smith and Wesson pointed at him. He was clasping the wrist of his gun hand and wincing as if he'd sprained it. Jericho closed his eyes for the bullet and Puck said – and this

Jericho was sure of, because he spoke the words very deliberately, in his precise English: 'I killed her, Thomas. I am so terribly sorry.'

Then he vanished.

*

The time by now was just after a quarter past seven – 7.17, according to the official report – and the day was coming up nicely. Jericho stood on the threshold of the carriage and he could hear blackbirds singing in the nearby copse, and a skylark above the field. All along the train, doors were banging open in the sunshine and people were jumping out. The locomotive was leaking steam and beyond it a group of soldiers were scrambling down the slight embankment, led – Jericho was surprised to see – by Wigram. More soldiers were deploying from the train itself, to Jericho's right. Puck was only about twenty yards away. Jericho jumped down to the grey stones of the track and set off after him.

Someone shouted, very loudly, almost directly behind him: 'Get out of the fucking way, you fucking idiot!' – wise advice, which Jericho ignored.

It couldn't end here, he thought, not with so much still to know.

He was all in. His legs were heavy. But Puck wasn't making much progress either. He was hobbling across a meadow, trailing a left ankle which autopsy analysis would later show had a hairline fracture – whether from his fall in the compartment or his leap from the train, no one would ever know, but every step must have been agony for him. A small herd of Jersey cattle watched him, chewing, like spectators at a running track.

The grass smelled sweet, the hedges were in bud, and Jericho was very close to him when Puck turned and fired his pistol. He couldn't have been aiming at Jericho – the shot went wide of anything. It was just a parting gesture. His eyes were dead now.

Sightless, blank. There was an answering crackle from the train. Bees buzzed past them in the spring morning.

Five bullets hit Puck and two hit Jericho. Again, the order is obscure. Jericho felt as though he had been struck from behind by a car – not painfully, but terrifically hard. It winded him and pitched him forward. He somehow kept on going, his legs cartwheeling, and saw tufts flying out of Puck's back, one, two, three, and then Puck's head exploded in a red blur, just as a second blow – irresistible this time – spun Jericho from his right shoulder round in a graceful arc. The sky was wet with spray and his final thought was what a pity it was, what a *pity* it was, ***what a pity it was*** that rain should spoil so fine a morning.

SEVEN

PLAINTEXT

PLAINTEXT: The original, intelligible text, as it was before encipherment, revealed after successful decoding or cryptanalysis.

A Lexicon of Cryptography
('Most Secret', Bletchley Park, 1943)

1

The apple trees wept blossom in the wind. It drifted across the graveyard and piled like snow against the slate and marble tombs.

Hester Wallace leaned her bicycle beside the low brick wall and surveyed the scene. Well, this was life, she thought, and no mistake about it; this was nature going on regardless. From inside the church rolled the booming notes of the organ. 'O God, Our Help in Ages Past …' She hummed to herself as she tugged on her gloves, tucked a few stray hairs under the band of her hat, straightened her shoulders and strode on up the flagstone path towards the porch.

The truth was, if it hadn't been for her, there would never have been a memorial service. It was she who persuaded the vicar to open the doors of St Mary's, Bletchley, even though she had to concede that 'the deceased', as the vicar primly put it, was not a believer. It was she who booked the organist and told him what to play (Bach's Prelude and Fugue in E flat major to see them all in, the Sanctus from Fauré's *Requiem* to get them all out). It was she who chose the hymns and the readings and had the service cards printed, she who decorated the nave with spring flowers, she who wrote out the notices and posted them around the Park ('a short service of remembrance will be held on Friday 16 April at 10 o'clock …'), she who lay awake the night before, worrying in case nobody bothered to come.

But they came all right.

Lieutenant Kramer came in his American naval uniform, and old Dr Weitzman came from the Hut 3 Watch, and Miss Monk and the girls from the German Book Room, and the heads of the Air Index and the Army Index, and various rather sheepish-looking young men in black ties, and many others whose names Hester never knew but whose lives had clearly been touched by the six-month presence at Bletchley Park of Claire Alexandra Romilly, born 21.12.22 and died (according to the police's best estimate) 14.3.43: Rest in Peace.

Hester sat in the front pew with her Bible marked at the passage she intended to read (I Corinthians 15.li-lv: 'Behold, I show you a mystery ...') and every time someone new came in she turned to see if it was *him*, only to glance away in disappointment.

'We really ought to begin,' said the vicar, fussing with his watch. 'I've a christening due at half past.'

'Another minute, vicar, if you'd be so good. Patience is a Christian virtue.'

The scent of the Easter lilies rose above the nave – virgin-white lilies with green, fleshy stems, white tulips, blue anemones ...

It was a long time since she had seen Tom Jericho. He might be dead for all she knew. She had only Wigram's word that he was still alive, and Wigram wouldn't even tell her which hospital he was in, let alone allow her to visit. He had, though, agreed to pass on an invitation to the service, and the following day he announced that the answer was yes, Jericho would love to come. 'But the poor chap's still quite sick, so don't count on it is my advice.' Soon Jericho would be going away, said Wigram, going away for a good long rest. Hester hadn't cared for the way he had said this, as if Jericho had somehow become the property of the state.

By five past ten the organist had run out of music to play and there was an awkward hiatus of shuffling and coughing. One of the

German Book Room girls began to giggle until Miss Monk told her loudly to hush.

'Hymn number 477,' said the vicar, with a glare at Hester. '"The Day Thou gavest, Lord, is ended."'

The congregation stood. The organist hit a shaky D. They started to sing. From somewhere near the back she could hear Weitzman's rather beautiful tenor. It was only as they reached the fifth verse ('So be it, Lord; thy throne shall never,/Like earth's proud empires, pass away') that Hester heard the door scrape open behind them. She turned, and so did half the others, and there, beneath the grey stone arch – thin and frail and supported by the arm of Wigram, but alive, thank God: indisputably alive – was Jericho.

*

Standing at the back of the church, in his overcoat with its bullet holes freshly darned, Jericho wished several things at once. He wished, for a start, that Wigram would take his bloody hands off him, because the man made his flesh crawl. He wished they weren't playing this particular hymn because it always reminded him of the last day of term at school. And he wished it hadn't been necessary to come. But it was. He couldn't have avoided it.

He detached himself politely from Wigram's arm and walked, unaided, to the nearest pew. He nodded to Weitzman and to Kramer. The hymn was ending. His shoulder ached from the journey. 'Thy Kingdom stands and grows for ever,' sang the congregation, 'Till all Thy creatures own Thy sway.' Jericho closed his eyes and inhaled the rich aroma of the lilies.

*

The first bullet, the one that had hit him like a blow from a car, had struck him in the lower left-hand quadrant of his back, had passed through four layers of muscle, nicked his eleventh rib and had exited through his side. The second, the one that had spun him round, had buried itself deep in his right shoulder, shredding part of the deltoid muscle, and that was the bullet they had to cut out surgically. He lost a lot of blood. There was an infection.

He lay in isolation, under guard, in some kind of military hospital just outside Northampton – isolated, presumably, in case, in his delirium, he babbled about Enigma; guarded in case he tried to get away: a ludicrous notion, as he didn't even know where he was.

His dream – it seemed to him to go on for days, but perhaps that was just a part of the dream: he could never tell – his dream was of lying at the bottom of a sea, on soft white sand, in a warm and rocking current. Occasionally he would float up and it would be light, in a high-ceilinged room, with a glimpse of trees through tall, barred windows. At other times, he would rise to find it dark, with a round and yellow moon, and someone bending overhead.

The first morning he woke up he asked to see a doctor. He wanted to know what had happened.

The doctor came and told him he had been involved in a shooting accident. Apparently, he had wandered too close to an Army firing range ('you bloody silly fool') and he was lucky he hadn't been killed.

No, no, protested Jericho. It wasn't like that at all. He tried to struggle up but the pain in his back made him cry out loud.

They gave him an injection and he went back to the bottom of the sea.

Gradually, as he started to recover, the equilibrium of his pain began to shift. In the beginning, it was nine-tenths physical to one-tenth mental; then eight-tenths to two-tenths; then seven to three, and so on, until the original proportions were reversed and he almost looked forward to the daily agony of the changing of his dressings, as an opportunity to burn away the memory of what had happened.

He had part of the picture, not all of it. But any attempt to ask questions, any demand to see someone in authority – any behaviour, in short, that might be construed as 'difficult' – and out would come the needle with its little cargo of oblivion.

He learned to play along.

He passed the time by reading mystery stories, Agatha Christie mostly, which they brought him from the hospital library – little red-bound volumes, warped with use, with mysterious stains on their pages which he preferred not to study too closely. *Lord Edgeware Dies*, *Parker Pyne Investigates*, *The Seven Dials Mystery*, *Murder at the Vicarage*. He got through two, sometimes three a day. They also had some Sherlock Holmes and one afternoon he lost himself for a blissful couple of hours by trying to solve the Abe Slaney cipher in *The Adventure of the Dancing Men* (a simplified Playfair grid system, he concluded, using inverted and mirror images) but he couldn't check his findings as they wouldn't let him have pencil and paper.

By the end of the first week, he was strong enough to take a few steps down the corridor and visit the lavatory unaided.

In all this time, he had only two visitors: Logie and Wigram.

Logie must have come to see him some time at the beginning of April. It was early evening, but still quite light, with shadows dividing the little room – the bed of tubular metal, painted white and scratched; the trolley with its jug of water and metal basin; the chair. Jericho was dressed in blue-striped pyjamas, very faded; his wrists on the counterpane were frail. After the nurse had gone, Logie perched uneasily on the edge of the bed and told him that everyone sent their best.

'Even Baxter?'

'Even Baxter.'

'Even Skynner?'

'Well, no, maybe not Skynner. But then I haven't seen much of Skynner to be honest. He's got other things on his mind.'

Logie talked for a bit about what everyone was doing, then started telling him about the convoy battle, which had gone on for most of the week, just as Cave had predicted. Twenty-two merchantmen sunk by the time the convoys reached air-cover and the U-boats could be driven off. 150,000 tons of Allied shipping destroyed and 160,000 tons of cargo lost – including the two weeks' supply of powdered milk that Skynner had made that disastrous joke about, remember? Apparently, when the ship went down, the sea had turned white. '*Die grösste Geleitzugschlacht aller Zeiten,*' German radio had called it, and for once the buggers weren't lying. The greatest convoy battle of all time.

'How many dead?'

'About four hundred. Mostly Americans.'

Jericho groaned. 'Any U-boats sunk?'

'Only one. We think.'

'And Shark?'

'Hanging in there, old love.' He patted Jericho's knee through the bedclothes. 'You see, it *was* worth it in the end, thanks to you.'

It had taken the bombes forty hours to solve the settings, from midnight on Tuesday until late on the Thursday afternoon. But by the weekend the Crib Room had made a partial recovery of the Weather Code Book – or enough of it to give them a toehold – and now they were breaking Shark six days out of seven, although sometimes the breaks came in quite late. But it would do. It would do until they got the first of the Cobra bombes in June.

A plane passed low overhead – a Spitfire, to judge by the crack of its engine.

After a while, Logie said quietly: 'Skynner's had to hand over the plans for the four-wheel bombes to the Americans.'

'Ah.'

'Well, *of course*,' said Logie, folding his arms, 'it's all *dressed up* as cooperation. But nobody's fooled. Leastways, *I'm* not. From now on, we're to teleprinter a copy of all Atlantic U-boat traffic to Washington the moment we receive it, then it's two teams working in friendly consultation. Blah, blah, blah. What bloody have you. But it'll come down to brute force in the end. It always does. And when they've got ten times the bombes we have – which won't take very long, I reckon, six months at the outside – what chance do we stand? We'll just do the interception and they'll do all the breaking.'

'We can hardly complain.'

'No, no. I know we can't. It's just ... Well, we've seen the best days, you and I.' He sighed and stretched out his legs, contemplating his vast feet. 'Still, there is one bright side, I suppose.'

'What's that?' Jericho looked at him, then saw what he meant, and they both said 'Skynner!' simultaneously, and laughed.

'He is *bloody* upset,' said Logie contentedly. 'Sorry about your girl, by the way.'

'Well ...' Jericho made a feeble gesture with his hand and winced.

There was a difficult silence, mercifully ended by the nurse coming in and telling Logie his time was up. He got to his feet with relief and shook Jericho's hand. 'Now you get well, old love, d'you hear what I'm saying, and I'll come and see you again soon.'

'Do that, Guy. Thank you.'

But that was the last time he saw him.

*

Miss Monk approached the pulpit to give the first reading: 'Say Not the Struggle Naught Availeth' by Arthur Hugh Clough, a poem she declaimed with great determination, glaring at the congregation from time to time, as if defying them to contradict her. It was a good choice, thought Jericho. Defiantly optimistic. Claire would have enjoyed it:

'And not by eastern windows only,
When daylight comes, comes in the light,
In front the sun climbs slow, how slowly,
But westward, look, the land is bright.'

'Let us pray,' said the vicar.

Jericho lowered himself carefully to his knees. He covered his eyes and moved his lips like all the others, but he had no faith in any of it. Faith in mathematics, yes; faith in logic, of course; faith in the trajectory of the stars, yes, perhaps. But faith in a God, Christian or otherwise?

Beside him, Wigram uttered a loud 'Amen'.

*

Wigram's visits had been frequent and solicitous. He would shake Jericho's hand with the same peculiar and tenuous grip. He would plump his pillows, pour his water, fuss with his sheets. 'They treating you well? You want for nothing?' And Jericho would say yes, thank you, he was being well looked after, and Wigram would always smile and say *super*, how *super* everything was – how *super* he was looking, what a *super* help he had been, even, once, how *super* the view was from the sickroom window, as if Jericho had somehow created it. Oh yes, Wigram was charming. Wigram dispensed charm like soup to the poor.

In the beginning it was Jericho who did most of the talking, answering Wigram's questions. Why hadn't he reported the cryptograms in Claire's room to the authorities? Why had he gone to Beaumanor? What had he taken? How? How had he broken the intercepts? What had Puck said to him as he leaped from the train?

Wigram would then go away, and the next day, or the day after, come back and ask him some more. Jericho tried to mix in some questions of his own, but Wigram always brushed them away. Later, he would say. Later. All in good time.

And then one afternoon he came in beaming even more broadly than usual to announce that he had completed his enquiries. A little web of wrinkles appeared at the edges of his blue eyes as he smiled down at Jericho. His lashes were thick and sandy, like a cow's.

'So, my dear chap, if you're not too exhausted, I suppose I should tell you the story.'

*

Once upon a time, said Wigram, settling himself at the bottom of the bed, there was a man called Adam Pukowski, whose mother was English and whose father was Polish, who lived in London until he was ten, and who, when his parents divorced, went away with his father to live in Cracow. The father was a professor of mathematics, the son showed a similar aptitude, and in due course found his way into the Polish Cipher Bureau at Pyry, south of Warsaw. War came. The father was called up with the rank of major to rejoin the Polish Army. Defeat came. Half the country was occupied by the Germans, the other half by the Soviet Union. The father disappeared. The son escaped to France to become one of the fifteen Polish cryptanalysts employed at the French cipher centre at Gretz-Armainvillers. Defeat came again. The son escaped via Vichy France to neutral Portugal, where he made the acquaintance of one Rogerio Raposo, a junior member of the Portuguese diplomatic service and an extremely dodgy character.

'The man on the train,' murmured Jericho.

'Indeed.' Wigram sounded irritated at being interrupted: this was his moment of glory, after all. 'The man on the train.'

From Portugal, Pukowski made his way to England.

Nineteen-forty passed with no news of Pukowski's father or, indeed, of any of the other ten thousand missing Polish officers. In 1941, after Germany invaded Russia, Stalin unexpectedly became our ally. Representations were duly made about the vanished Poles. Assurances were duly given: there were no such prisoners in Soviet hands; any there might have been had been released long ago.

'Anyway,' said Wigram, 'to cut a long story a whole lot shorter, it appears that at the end of last year, rumours began to circulate among the Poles in exile in London that these officers had been shot and then buried in a forest near Smolensk. I say, is it hot in here or is it me?' He got up and tried to open the window, failed, and returned to his perch on the bed. He smiled. 'Tell me, was it you who introduced Pukowski to Claire?'

Jericho shook his head.

'Ah, well,' sighed Wigram, 'I don't suppose it matters. A lot of the story is lost to us. Inevitably. We don't know how they met, or when, or why she agreed to help him. Or even what she showed him exactly. But I think we can guess what must have happened. She'd make a copy of these signals from Smolensk, and sneak them out in her knickers or whatever. Hide them under her floorboards. Lover-boy would collect them. This may have gone on for a week or two. Until the day came when Pukowski saw that one of the dead men was his own father. And then the next day Claire had nothing to bring him but the undecoded intercepts, because *someone* –' Wigram shook his head in wonder ' – someone very, very senior *indeed*, I have since discovered, had decided they just didn't want to know.'

He suddenly reached over and picked up one of Jericho's discarded mystery stories, flicked through it, smiled, replaced it.

'You know, Tom,' he said thoughtfully, 'there's never been anything like Bletchley Park in the history of the world. There's never been a time when one side knew so much about its enemy. In fact, sometimes, I think, it's possible to know too much. When Coventry was bombed, remember? Our beloved Prime Minister discovered from Enigma what was going to happen about four hours in advance. Know what he did?'

Again Jericho shook his head.

'Told his staff that London was about to be attacked and that they should go down to the shelters, but that he was going upstairs to watch. Then he went out on to the Air Ministry roof and spent an hour waiting in the freezing cold for a raid he *knew* was going to happen somewhere else. Doing his bit, d'you see? To protect the Enigma secret. Or, another example: take the U-boat tankers. Thanks to Shark, we know where they're going to be, and when, and if we knocked them out we might save hundreds of Allied lives – in the short term. But we'd jeopardise Enigma, because if we did that, Dönitz would know we must be reading his codes. You see what I'm driving at? So Stalin has killed ten thousand Poles? I mean, *please*, Uncle Joe's a national hero. He's winning the frigging war for us. Third most popular man in the country, after Churchill and the King. What's that Hebrew proverb? "My enemy's enemy is my friend"? Well, Stalin's the biggest enemy Hitler's got, so as far as we're concerned, for present purposes, he's a bloody good friend of ours. Katyn massacre? Katyn frigging *massacre*? Thanks awfully, but, really, do shut up.'

'I don't suppose Puck would have seen it quite like that.'

'No, old chap, I don't suppose he would. Shall I tell you something? I think he rather hated us. After all, if it hadn't been for the Poles, we might not even have broken Enigma in the first place. But the people he really hated were the Russians. And he was prepared to do anything to get revenge. Even if it meant helping the Germans.'

'"My enemy's enemy is my friend,"' murmured Jericho, but Wigram wasn't listening.

'And how could he help the Germans? By warning them Enigma wasn't safe. And how could he do *that*?' Wigram smiled and spread his hands. 'Why, with the assistance of his old friend from 1940, Rogerio Raposo, recently transferred from Lisbon and now employed as a courier at the Portuguese legation in London. How about some tea?'

*

For the dear ones parted from us
We would raise our hymns of prayer;
By the tender love which watcheth
Round thy children everywhere ...

*

Senhor Raposo, said Wigram, sipping his tea after the nurse had gone, Senhor Raposo, presently a resident of His Majesty's Prison, Wandsworth, had confessed to everything.

On 6 March, Pukowski had gone to see Raposo in London, handed him a thin, sealed envelope and told him he could make a great deal of money if he delivered it to the right people.

The following day, Raposo flew on the scheduled British Imperial Airways flight to Lisbon carrying said envelope, which he passed to a contact of his on the staff of the German naval attaché.

Two days after that, the U-boat service changed its Short Weather Code Book, and a general review of cipher security began – Luftwaffe, Afrika Korps ... Oh, the Germans were interested, of course they were. But they weren't about to abandon what their experts still insisted was the most secure enciphering system ever devised. Not on the basis of one letter. They suspected a trick.

They wanted proof. They wanted this mysterious informant in Berlin, in person.

'That's our best guess, anyway.'

On 14 March, two days before the start of the convoy battle, Raposo made his next weekly trip to Lisbon and returned with specific instructions for Pukowski. A U-boat would be waiting to pick him up off the coast of northwest Ireland on the night of the 18th.

'And that was what they were discussing on the train,' said Jericho.

'And that was what they were discussing on the train. Quite right. Our man Puck was collecting his ticket, so to speak. And shall I tell you the really frightening thing?' Wigram took another sip of tea, his little finger delicately crooked, and looked at Jericho over the rim of his cup. 'If it hadn't been for you, he might just have got away with it.'

'But Claire would never have gone along with this,' protested Jericho. 'Passed on a few intercepts – yes. For a lark. For love, even. But she wasn't a *traitor*.'

'Lord, no.' Wigram sounded shocked. 'No, I'm sure Pukowski never even told her for *one minute* what he was planning to do. Consider it from his point of view. She was the weak link. She could have given him away at any moment. So imagine how he must have felt when he saw *you* walk back through the door from Cambridge on that Friday night.'

Jericho remembered the look of horror on Puck's face, that desperate attempt to force a smile. He had already seen what must have happened: Puck leaving a message at the cottage that he needed to talk to her, Claire hurrying back into the Park at four in the morning – *click click click* on her high heels in the darkness. He said quietly, almost to himself: 'I was her death warrant.'

'I suppose you were. He must've known you'd try and get in

touch with her. And then, the next night, when he went round to the cottage to get rid of the evidence, the stolen cryptograms, and found you there ... Well ...'

Jericho lay back and stared at the ceiling as Wigram rattled through the rest of the story. How, on the night the convoy battle had started, just before midnight, he'd been called by the police and told that a sack full of women's clothing had been found. How he'd tried to find Jericho, but Jericho had disappeared, so he'd grabbed Hester Wallace instead and taken her down to the lakeside. How it had been obvious at once what had happened, that Claire had been bludgeoned, or maybe bludgeoned and strangled, and her body rowed out into the lake and dumped.

'Mind if I smoke?' He lit up without waiting for a reply, using his saucer as an ashtray. He examined the tip of his cigarette for a moment. 'Where was I exactly?'

Jericho didn't look at him. 'The night of the convoy battle.'

Ah, yes. Well, Hester had refused to talk at first, but there's nothing like shock to loosen the tongue and eventually she'd told him everything, at which point Wigram had realised that Jericho wasn't a traitor; realised, in fact, that if Jericho had broken the cryptograms he was probably closer to discovering the traitor than *he* was.

So he had deployed his men. And watched.

This would have been about five in the morning.

First, Jericho was seen hurrying down Church Green Road into the town. Then he was observed going into the house in Alma Terrace. Then he was identified boarding the train.

Wigram had men on the train.

'After that, the three of you were just flies in a jam jar, frankly.'

All passengers disembarking at Northampton were stopped and questioned, and that took care of Raposo. By then, Wigram had arranged for the train to be diverted into a branch line where he was waiting to search it at leisure.

His men had orders not to shoot unless they were shot at first. But no chances were going to be taken. Not with so much at stake.

And Pukowski had used his pistol. And fire had been returned.

'You got in the way. I'm sorry about that.' Still, as he was sure Jericho would agree, preserving the Enigma secret had been the most important objective. And that had been accomplished. The U-boat that had been sent to pick up Puck had been intercepted and sunk off the coast of Donegal, which was a double bonus, as the Germans probably now thought that the whole business had been a set-up all along, designed to trap one of their submarines. At any rate, they hadn't abandoned Enigma.

'And Claire?' Jericho was still staring at the ceiling. 'Have you found her yet?'

'Give us time, my dear fellow. She lies under at least sixty feet of water, somewhere in the middle of a lake a quarter of a mile across. That may take us a while.'

'And Raposo?'

'The Foreign Secretary spoke to the Portuguese ambassador that morning. Under the circumstances, he agreed to waive diplomatic immunity. By noon we'd taken Raposo's flat apart. Dreary place at the wrong end of Gloucester Road. Poor little sod. He really was only in it for the money. We found two thousand dollars the Germans had given him, stuffed in a shoe box on top of his wardrobe. Two grand! Pathetic.'

'What will happen to him?'

'He'll hang,' said Wigram pleasantly. 'But never mind about him. He's history. The question is, what are we going to do with *you*?'

After Wigram had gone, Jericho lay awake for a long time, trying to decide which parts of his story had been true.

*

'Behold, I show you a mystery,' said Hester.

'We shall not all sleep, but we shall all be changed,

'In a moment, in the twinkling of an eye, at the last trump: for the trumpet shall sound, and the dead shall be raised incorruptible, and we shall be changed.

'For this corruptible must put on incorruption, and this mortal must put on immortality.

'So when this corruptible shall have put on incorruption, and this mortal shall have put on immortality, then shall be brought to pass the saying that is written, Death is swallowed up in victory.

'O death, where is thy sting? O grave, where is thy victory?'

She closed her Bible slowly and regarded the congregation with a dry and level eye. In the end pew she could just make out Jericho, white-faced, staring straight ahead.

'Thanks be to God.'

*

She found him waiting for her outside the church, the white blossom raining down on him like confetti. The other mourners had gone. He had his face raised to the sun and she guessed from the way he seemed to be drinking in the warmth that he hadn't seen it for a long while. As he heard her approach, he turned and smiled and she hoped her own smile hid her shock. His cheeks were concave, his skin as waxy as one of the candles in church. The collar of his shirt hung loosely from his gaunt neck.

'Hello, Hester.'

'Hello, Tom.' She hesitated, then held out her gloved hand.

'Super service,' said Wigram. 'Absolutely super. Everybody's said so, haven't they Tom?'

'Everybody. Yes.' Jericho closed his eyes for a second and she understood immediately what he was signalling: that he was sorry Wigram was there, but that he couldn't do anything about it. He released her hand. 'I didn't want to leave,' he said, 'without seeing how you were.'

'Oh, well,' she said, with a jollity she didn't feel, 'bearing up, you know.'

'Back at work?'

'Yes, yes. Still blisting away.'

'And still in the cottage?'

'For now. But I think I'll move out, as soon as I can find myself another billet.'

'Too many ghosts?'

'Something like that.'

She suddenly found herself loathing the banality of the conversation but she couldn't think of anything better to say.

'Leveret's waiting,' said Wigram. 'With the car. To run us to the station.' Through the gate Hester could see the long black bonnet. The driver was leaning against it, watching them, smoking a cigarette.

'You're catching a train, Mr Wigram?' asked Hester.

'*I'm* not,' he said, as if the notion was offensive. 'Tom is. Aren't you, Tom?'

'I'm going back to Cambridge,' explained Jericho. 'For a few months' rest.'

'In fact we really ought to push off,' continued Wigram, looking at his watch. 'You never know – there's always a *chance* it may be on time.'

Jericho said, irritably: 'Will you excuse us for just one minute, Mr Wigram?' Without waiting for a reply, he guided Hester away from Wigram, back towards the church. 'This bloody man won't leave me alone for a second,' he whispered. 'Listen, if you can bear it, will you give me a kiss?'

'What?' She wasn't sure she could have heard him correctly.

'A kiss. Quickly. Please.'

'Very well. It's no great hardship.'

She took off her hat, reached over and brushed his thin cheek with her lips. He held her shoulders and said softly in her ear: 'Did you invite Claire's father to the service?'

'Yes.' He had gone mad, she thought. The shock had affected his mind. 'Of course I did.'

'What happened?'

'He didn't reply.'

'I knew it,' he whispered. She felt his grip tighten.

'Knew what?'

'She isn't dead ...'

'How touching,' said Wigram loudly, coming up behind them, 'and I hate to break things up, but you're going to miss your train, Tom Jericho.'

Jericho released her and took a step back. 'Look after yourself,' he said.

For a moment she couldn't speak. 'And you.'

'I'll write.'

'Yes. Please. Be sure you do.'

Wigram tugged at his arm. Jericho gave her a final smile and a shrug, then allowed himself to be led away.

She watched him walk painfully up the path and through the gate. Leveret opened the car door and as he did so, Jericho turned and waved. She raised her hand in return, saw him manoeuvre himself stiffly into the back seat, then the door slammed shut. She let her hand drop.

She stayed there for several minutes, long after the big car had pulled away, then she replaced her hat and went back into the church.

2

'I almost forgot,' said Wigram, as the car turned down the hill. 'I bought you a paper. For the journey.'

He unlocked his briefcase and took out a copy of *The Times*, opened it to the third page and handed it to Jericho. The story consisted of just five paragraphs, flanked by an illustration of a London bus and an appeal for the Poor Clergy Relief Corporation:

MISSING POLISH

OFFICERS

GERMAN ALLEGATIONS

> The Polish Minister of National Defence, Lieutenant-General Marjan Kukiel, has issued a statement concerning some 8,000 missing Polish officers who were released from Soviet prison camps in the spring of 1940. In view of German allegations that the bodies of many thousands of Polish officers had been found near Smolensk and that they had been murdered by the Russians, the Polish Government has decided to ask the International Red Cross to investigate the matter ...

'I particularly like that line,' said Wigram, 'don't you: "released from Soviet prison camps"?'

'That's one way of putting it, I suppose.' Jericho tried to give him back the paper, but Wigram waved it away.

'Keep it. A souvenir.'

'Thanks.' Jericho folded the paper and slipped it into his pocket, then stared firmly out of the window to forestall any further conversation. He'd had enough of Wigram and his lies. As they passed under the blackened railway bridge for the final time he surreptitiously touched his cheek and he suddenly wished he could have brought Hester with him for this last act.

At the station, Wigram insisted on seeing him on to the train, even though Jericho's luggage had been sent on ahead at the beginning of the week and there was nothing for him to carry. And Jericho consented in return to have Wigram's hand for support as they crossed the footbridge and strolled along the length of the Cambridge train in search of an empty seat. Jericho was careful to make sure that he, rather than Wigram, chose the compartment.

'Well, then, my dear Tom,' said Wigram, with mock sadness, 'I'll bid you goodbye.' That peculiar handshake again, the little finger somehow tucked up into the palm. Final things: did Jericho have his travel warrant? Yes. And he knew that Kite would be meeting him at Cambridge to escort him by taxi to King's? Yes. And he'd remembered that a nurse would be coming in from Addenbrooke's Hospital every morning to change the dressing on his shoulder? Yes, yes, yes.

'Goodbye, Mr Wigram.'

He settled his aching back into a seat facing away from the engine. Wigram closed the door. There were three other passengers in the compartment: a fat man in a dirty fawn raincoat, an elderly woman in a silver fox, and a dreamy-looking girl reading a copy of *Horizon*. They all looked innocent enough, but how could one tell? Wigram tapped on the window and Jericho struggled to his feet to lower it. By the time he had it open, the whistle had blown and the train was beginning to pull away. Wigram trotted alongside.

'We'll be in touch when you're fit again, all right? You know where to get hold of me if anything comes up.'

'I certainly do,' said Jericho, and slid the window up with a bang. But still Wigram kept pace with the compartment – smiling, waving, running. It had become a challenge for him, a terrific joke. He didn't stop until he reached the end of the platform, and that was Jericho's final impression of Bletchley: of Wigram leaning forwards, his hands on his knees, shaking his head and laughing.

*

Thirty-five minutes after boarding the train at Bletchley, Jericho disembarked at Bedford, bought a one-way ticket to London, then waited in the sunshine at the end of the platform, filling in *The Times* crossword. It was hot, the tracks shimmered; there was a strong smell of baking coal dust and warm steel. When he'd finished the final clue he stuffed the newspaper, unread, into a rubbish bin and walked slowly up and down the platform, getting used to the feel of his legs. A crowd of passengers was beginning to build up around him and he scanned each face automatically, even though logic told him it was unlikely he was being followed: if Wigram had feared he might abscond, he surely would have arranged for Leveret to drive him all the way to Cambridge.

The tracks began to whine. The passengers surged forwards. A military train passed slowly southwards, with armed soldiers on the engine footplate. From the carriages peered a line of gaunt, exhausted faces, and a murmur went through the crowd. German prisoners! German prisoners under guard! Jericho briefly met the eyes of one of the captives – owlish, bespectacled, unmilitary: more clerk than warrior – and something passed between them, some flash of recognition across the gulf of war. A second later the white face blurred and disappeared, and soon afterwards the London express pulled in, packed and filthy. 'Worse than the bloody Jerries' train,' complained a man.

Jericho couldn't find a seat, so he stood, leaning against the door to the corridor, until his chalk complexion and the sheen of perspiration on his forehead prompted a young Army officer to give up his place. Jericho sat down gratefully, dozed, and dreamed of the German prisoner with his sad owl's face, and then of Claire on that first journey, just before Christmas, their bodies touching.

By 2.30 he was in London, at St Pancras Station, moving awkwardly through the mass of people towards the entrance to the Underground. The lift was out of action so he had to take the stairs, stopping on every landing to recover his strength. His back was throbbing and something wet was trickling down his spine, but whether it was sweat or blood he couldn't tell.

On the eastbound Circle Line platform, a rat scurried through the rubbish beneath the rails towards the tunnel mouth.

*

When Jericho failed to emerge from the Bletchley train, Kite was irritated but unconcerned. The next train was due in within a couple of hours, there was a good pub just around the corner from the station, and that was where the college porter chose to do his waiting, in the amiable company of two halves of Guinness and a pork pie.

But when the second train terminated at Cambridge, and still there was no sign of Jericho, Kite went into a sulk that lasted him throughout the half hour it took him to trudge back to King's.

He informed the domestic bursar of Jericho's non-appearance, and the domestic bursar told the Provost, and the Provost dithered over whether or not to call the Foreign Office.

'No consideration,' complained Kite to Dorothy Saxmundham in the Porter's Lodge. 'Just no bloody consideration at all.'

*

With the solution in his pocket, Tom Jericho left Somerset House and made his slow way westwards, along the Embankment, towards the heart of the city. The south bank of the Thames was a garden of ruins. Above the London docks, silver-coloured barrage balloons turned and glinted and nodded in the late afternoon sun.

Just beyond Waterloo Bridge, outside the entrance to the Savoy, he managed at last to find a taxi for hire and directed the driver to Stanhope Gardens in South Kensington. The streets were empty. They reached it quickly.

The house was big enough to be an embassy, wide and stucco-fronted, with a pillared entrance. It must have been impressive once, but now the plasterwork was grey and flaking and in places great chunks of it had been blasted away by shrapnel. The windows of the top two storeys were curtained, blind. The house next door was bombed out, with weeds growing in the basement. Jericho climbed the steps and pressed the bell. It seemed to ring a long way off, deep within the bowels of the dead house, and left a heavy silence. He tried again, even though he knew it was useless, then retreated across the road to wait, sitting on the steps of the opposite house.

Fifteen minutes passed, and then, from the direction of Cromwell Place, a tall, bald man appeared, startlingly thin – a skeleton in a suit – and Jericho knew at once it must be him. Black jacket, grey-striped trousers, a grey silk tie: all that was needed to complete the cliché was a bowler hat and a rolled umbrella. Instead, incongruously, he carried, as well as his briefcase, a string bag full of groceries. He approached his vast front door wearily, unlocked it and vanished inside.

Jericho stood, brushed himself down and followed.

The door bell tolled again; again, nothing happened. He tried a second time, and a third, and then, with difficulty, got down on his knees and opened the letter flap.

Edward Romilly was standing at the end of a gloomy passage with his back to the door, perfectly still.

'Mr Romilly?' Jericho had to shout through the flap. 'I need to speak to you. Please.'

The tall man didn't move. 'Who are you?'

'Tom Jericho. We spoke once on the telephone. Bletchley Park.'

Romilly's shoulders sagged. 'For God's sake, will you people just *leave me alone*!'

'I've been to Somerset House, Mr Romilly,' said Jericho, 'to the Registry of Births, Marriages and Deaths. I have her death certificate here.' He pulled it out of his pocket. 'Claire Alexandra Romilly. Your daughter. Died on 14 June 1929. At St Mary's Hospital, Paddington. Of spinal meningitis. At the age of six.' He propelled it through the letter flap and watched it slither across the black and white tiles towards Romilly's feet. 'I'm going to have to stay here, sir, I'm afraid, for as long as it takes.'

He let the flap snap shut. Weary with self-disgust, he turned away and leaned his good shoulder against one of the pillars. He looked across the street to the little communal gardens. From beyond the houses opposite came the pleasant hum of the early-evening traffic on Cromwell Road. He grimaced. The pain had begun to move out from his back now, establishing lines of communication into his legs, his arms, his neck; everywhere.

He wasn't sure how long he knelt there, looking at the budding trees, listening to the cars, until at last behind him Romilly unlocked the door.

*

He was fifty or thereabouts, with an ascetic, almost monkish face, and as Jericho followed him up the wide staircase, he found himself thinking, as he often did on meeting men of that generation, that this would be roughly the age of his father now, if he had lived. Romilly led Jericho through a doorway into darkness and tugged open a pair of heavy curtains. Light spilled into a drawing room full of furniture draped in white sheets. Only a sofa was uncovered, and a table, pushed up close to a marble fireplace. On the table was some dirty crockery; on the mantelpiece, a large pair of matching silver photograph frames.

'One lives alone,' said Romilly apologetically, fanning away the dust. 'One never entertains.' He hesitated, then walked over to the fireplace and picked up one of the photographs. 'This is Claire,' he said, quietly. 'Taken a week before she died.'

A tall, thin girl with dark ringlets smiled up at Jericho.

'And this is my wife. She died two months after Claire.'

The mother had the same colouring and bone-structure as the daughter. Neither looked remotely like the woman Jericho knew as Claire.

'She was driving alone in a motorcar,' went on Romilly, 'when it ran off an empty road and struck a tree. The coroner was kind enough to record it as an accident.' His Adam's apple bobbed as he swallowed. 'Does anyone know you're here?'

'No, sir.'

'Wigram?'

'No.'

'I see.' Romilly took the pictures from him and replaced them on the mantelpiece, realigning them precisely as they had been. He stared from mother to daughter and back again.

'This will sound absurd to you,' he said eventually, without looking at Jericho, 'it sounds absurd to *me*, now – but it seemed to be a way of *bringing her back*. Can you understand that? I mean, the idea that another girl of exactly her age would be going around, using her name, doing what she might have done ... Living her life ... I thought it might make sense of what had happened, d'you see?

Give her death a purpose, after all these years. Foolish, but ...' He raised a hand to his eyes. It was a minute before he could speak. 'What exactly do you want from me, Mr Jericho?'

Romilly lifted a dustsheet and found a bottle of whisky and a pair of tumblers. They sat on the sofa together staring at the empty fire.

'What exactly do you want from me?'

The truth, at last, perhaps? Confirmation? Peace of mind? An ending ...

And Romilly seemed to want to give it, as if he recognised in Jericho a fellow sufferer.

It had been Wigram's bright idea, he said, to put an agent into Bletchley Park. A woman. Someone who could keep an eye on this peculiar collection of characters, so essential to the defeat of Germany, yet so alien to the tradition of intelligence; who had, indeed, destroyed that tradition, turning what had been an art – a game, if you like, for gentlemen – into a science of mass production.

'Who *were* you all? *What* were you? Could *all* of you be trusted?'

No one at Bletchley was to know she was an agent, that was important, not even the commander. And she had to come from the right kind of background, that was absolutely vital, otherwise she might have been dumped at some wretched out-station somewhere, and Wigram needed her *there*, at the heart of the place.

Romilly poured himself another drink and offered to top up Jericho's, but Jericho covered his glass.

Well, he said, sighing, putting the bottle at his feet, it was harder than one might think to manufacture such a person: to conjure her into life complete with identity card and ration books and all the other paraphernalia of wartime life, to give her the right background ('the right *legend*,' as Wigram had termed it), without at the very least dragging in the Home Office and half a dozen government agencies who knew nothing of the Enigma secret.

But then Wigram had remembered Edward Romilly.

Poor old Edward Romilly. The widower. Barely known outside the Office, abroad these past ten years, with all the right connections, initiated into Enigma – and, more importantly, with the birth certificate of a girl of exactly the right age. All that was required of him, apart from the use of his daughter's name, was a letter of introduction to Bletchley Park. In fact, not even that, since Wigram would write the letter: a signature would suffice. And then Romilly could continue with his solitary existence, content to know he had done his patriotic duty. And given his daughter a kind of life.

Jericho said: 'You never met her, I suppose? The girl who took your daughter's name?'

'Good God, no. In fact, Wigram assured me I'd never hear another word about it. I made that a condition. And I didn't hear anything, for six months. Until you called one Sunday morning and told me my daughter had disappeared.'

'And you got straight on the telephone to Wigram to report what I'd said?'

'Of course. I was horrified.'

'And naturally you demanded to know what was happening. And he told you.'

Romilly drained his scotch and frowned at the empty tumbler. 'The memorial service was today, I think?'

Jericho nodded.

'May I ask how it went?'

'"For the trumpet shall sound,"' said Jericho, '"and the dead shall be raised incorruptible, and we shall be changed ..."' He looked away from the photograph of the little girl above the fireplace. 'Except that Claire – my Claire – isn't dead, is she?'

*

The room darkened, the light was the colour of the whisky, and now Jericho was doing most of the talking.

Afterwards, he realised he never actually told Romilly how he had worked it all out: that host of tiny inconsistencies that had made a nonsense of the official version, even though he recognised that much of what Wigram had told him must have been the truth.

The oddity of her behaviour, for a start; and the failure of her supposed father to react to her disappearance, or to show up at her memorial service; the puzzle of why her clothes had been so conveniently discovered when her body had not; the suspicious speed with which Wigram had been able to halt the train ... All these had clicked and turned and rearranged themselves into a pattern of perfect logic.

Once one accepted she was an informer, everything else followed. The material which Claire – he still called her Claire – had passed to Pukowski had been leaked with Wigram's approval, hadn't it?

'Because really – in the beginning, anyway – it was nothing, just chickenfeed, compared with what Puck already knew about naval Enigma. Where was the harm? And Wigram let her go on handing it over because he wanted to see what Puck would do with it. See if anyone else was involved. It was bait, if you like. Am I right?'

Romilly said nothing.

It was only later that Wigram had realised he'd made the most almighty miscalculation – that Katyn, and more especially the decision to stop monitoring it, had tipped Puck over the edge into treason, and that somehow he'd managed to tell the Germans about Enigma.

'I assume it wasn't Wigram's decision to stop the monitoring?'

Romilly gave a barely perceptible shake of his head. 'Higher.'

How high?

He wouldn't say.

Jericho shrugged. 'It doesn't matter. From that point on, Puck must have been under twenty-four-hour watch, to find out who his contact was and to catch them both red-handed.

'Now, a man under round-the-clock surveillance is not in a position to murder anyone, least of all an agent of the people doing the watching. Not unless they are spectacularly incompetent. No. When Puck discovered I had the cryptograms he knew Claire would have to disappear, otherwise she'd be questioned. She had to vanish for at least a week, so he could get away. And preferably for longer. So between them they *staged* her murder – stolen boat, bloodstained clothes beside the lake. He guessed that would be enough to make the police call off their hunt. And he was right: they have stopped looking for her. He never suspected she was betraying *him* all the time.'

Jericho took a sip of whisky. 'Do you know, I really think he may have loved her – that's the joke of it. So much so that his last words, literally, were a lie – "*I killed her, Thomas, I'm so very sorry*" – a deliberate lie, a gesture from the edge of the grave, to give her a chance to get away.

'And that, of course, was the cue for Wigram, because from his point of view, that confession neatly tied up everything. Puck was dead. Raposo would soon be dead. Why not leave "Claire" to rest at the bottom of the lake as well? All that he needed to do to round the story off was to pretend that it was *me* who led him to the traitor.

'So to say that she's still alive is not an act of faith, but merely logical. She *is* alive, isn't she?'

A long pause. Somewhere a trapped fly barged against a window pane.

Yes, said Romilly, hopelessly. Yes, he understood that to be the case.

*

What was it Hardy had written? That a mathematical proof, like a chess problem, to be aesthetically satisfying, must possess three qualities: inevitability, unexpectedness and economy; that it should 'resemble a simple and clear-cut constellation, not a scattered cluster in the Milky Way'.

Well, Claire, thought Jericho, here is my proof.

Here is my clear-cut constellation.

*

Poor Romilly, he didn't want Jericho to leave. He had bought some food, he said, on his way home from the office. They could have supper together. Jericho could stay the night – God knew, he had enough room ...

But Jericho, looking around at the furniture dressed as ghosts, the dirty plates, the empty whisky bottle, the photographs, was suddenly desperate to get away.

'Thank you, but I'm late.' He managed to push himself to his feet. 'I was due back in Cambridge hours ago.'

Disappointment settled like a shadow across Romilly's long face. 'If you're sure I can't persuade you ...' His words were slightly slurred. He was drunk. On the landing he bumped against a table and switched on a tasselled lamp, then conducted Jericho, unsteadily, down the stairs to the hall.

'Will you try and find her?'

'I don't know,' said Jericho. 'Perhaps.'

The death certificate was still lying on the letter-stand in the hall. 'Then you'll need this,' said Romilly, picking it up. 'You must show it to Wigram. If you like, you can tell him you've seen me. In case he tries to deny everything. I'm sure he'll have to let you see her then. If you insist.'

'Won't that get you into trouble?'

'Trouble?' Romilly gave a laugh. He gestured behind him, at his mausoleum of a house. 'D'you think I care about *trouble*? Come on, Mr Jericho. Take it.'

Jericho hesitated, and in that moment he had a vision of himself – a few years older, another Romilly, struggling vainly to breathe life into a ghost. 'No,' he said at last. 'You are very kind. But I think I ought to leave it here.'

*

He left the silent street with relief and walked towards the sound of traffic. On Cromwell Road he hailed a cab.

The spring evening had brought out the crowds. Along the wide pavements of Knightsbridge and in Hyde Park it was almost like a festival: a profusion of uniforms, American and British, Commonwealth and exile – dark blue, khaki, grey – with everywhere the splashes of colour from the summer dresses.

She was probably here, he thought, tonight, somewhere in the city. Or perhaps that would have been considered too risky, and she had been sent abroad by now, to lie low until the whole business had been forgotten. It occurred to him that a lot of what she had told him might actually be true, that she could well be a diplomat's daughter.

On Regent Street, a blonde-haired woman on the arm of an American major came out of the Café Royal.

He made a conscious effort to look away.

ALLIED SUCCESS IN NORTH ATLANTIC read a newspaper placard on the opposite side of the street. NAZI U-BOATS SUNK.

He pulled down the window and felt the warm night air on his face.

And here was something very odd. Staring out at the teeming streets he began to experience a definite sense of – well, he could not call it *happiness*, exactly. *Release*, perhaps, would be a better word.

He remembered their last night together. Lying beside her as she wept. What had that been? Remorse, was it? In which case, perhaps she *had* felt something for him.

'*She never talked about you,*' Hester had said.

'*I'm flattered.*'

'*Given the way she used to talk about the others, you should be …*'

And then there had been that birthday card: 'Dearest Tom … always see you as a friend … perhaps in the future … Sorry to hear about … in haste … Much love …'

It was a solution, of a sort. As good a solution, at any rate, as he was likely to get.

At King's Cross Station he bought a postcard and a book of stamps and sent a message to Hester asking her to visit him in Cambridge as soon as she could.

On the train he found an empty compartment and stared at his reflection in the glass, an image which gradually became clearer as the dusk gathered and the flat countryside disappeared, until he fell asleep.

*

The main gate to the college was closed. Only the little doorway cut into it was unlocked and it must have been ten o'clock when Kite, dozing beside the coke stove, was woken by the sound of it opening and closing. He lifted the corner of the blackout curtain in time to see Jericho walking into the great court.

Kite quietly let himself out of the Porter's Lodge to get a better view.

It was unexpectedly bright – there were a lot of stars – and he thought for a moment that Jericho must have heard him, for the young man was standing at the edge of the lawn and seemed to be listening. But then he realised that Jericho was actually looking up at the sky. The way Kite told it afterwards, Jericho must have stood that way for at least five minutes, turning first towards the chapel, then the meadow, and then the hall, before moving off purposefully towards his staircase, passing out of sight.

Acknowledgments

I owe a debt of gratitude to all those former employees of Bletchley Park who spoke to me about their wartime experiences. In particular, I would like to thank Sir Harry Hinsley (Naval Section, Hut 4), Margaret Macintyre and Jane Parkinson (Hut 6 Decoding Room), the late Sir Stuart Milner-Barry (former head of Hut 6), Joan Murray (Hut 8) and Alan Stripp (Japanese ciphers).

Roger Bristow, Tony Sale and their colleagues at the Bletchley Park Trust answered my questions with great patience and allowed me to wander about the site at will.

None of these kind people bears any responsibility for the contents of this book, which is a work of the imagination, not of reference.

For those readers who would like the facts on which this novel is based, I strongly recommend *Top Secret Ultra* by Peter Calvocoressi (London, 1980), *Codebreakers* edited by F. H. Hinsley and Alan Stripp (Oxford, 1993), *Seizing the Enigma* by David Kahn (Boston, USA, 1991), *The Enigma Symposium* by Hugh Skillen (Middlesex, two volumes, 1992 and 1994), *The Hut 6 Story* by Gordon Welchman (New York, 1982) and *GCHQ* by Nigel West (London, 1986).

Details of the action in the North Atlantic are drawn from the original, decoded signals of the U-boats, held at the Public Record Office in London, and also from *Convoy* by Martin Middlebrook (London, 1976) and *The Critical Convoy Battles of March 1943* by

Jürgen Rohwer (English translation, London, 1977).

Finally, I would like to record my special thanks to Sue Freestone and David Rosenthal, neither of whom ever lost faith in *Enigma*, even on those occasions when it was a mystery to its author.

Robert Harris
June 1995

About the author

Robert Harris, 41, was a reporter on the BBC's *Panorama* and *Newsnight* programmes before becoming Political Editor of the *Observer* in 1987, and then a columnist on the *Sunday Times.* His five non-fiction books include *Selling Hitler* (1986), an account of the forging of Hitler's diaries.

Fatherland (1992) was short-listed for the Whitbread First Novel prize, and was followed by *Enigma* (1995). They have sold six million copies worldwide and have been translated into 30 languages. His latest bestselling novel, *Archangel,* is now available in Hutchinson.

He lives in Berkshire with his wife, Gill Hornby, and their three young children.